'This is a rarity in the handbook form, a work of novelty and inspiration addressing law in the Anthropocene. Ambitious, argute, and cutting edge, these essays engage in a material, affective and supra-disciplinary manner with the fluid presences and synaesthetically apprehended atmospherics of legality.'

Peter Goodrich, Professor of Law and Director of the Program in Law and Humanities, Cardozo School of Law, New York.

'This major new collection challenges received notions of what legal theory and scholarship entail. Working from the field's "edges", its orientation to connection, and new intellectual conversations, foreground the rich, embodied, hopeful and disturbing practices of our existence, inviting legal and non-legal scholars to rethink what they know and feel about law.'

Davina Cooper, Research Professor, Dickson Poon School of Law, King's College London.

Routledge Handbook of Law and Theory

This handbook sets out an innovative approach to the theory of law, reconceptualising it in a material, embodied, socially contextualised and politically radical way. The book consists of original contributions authored by prominent academics, all of whom provide a valuable overview of legal theory as a discipline.

The book contains five sections:

- Spatiotemporal
- Sense
- Body
- Text
- Matter

Through this structure, the handbook brings the law into active discussion with other disciplines, as well as supra-disciplinary debates on the areas of spatiality, temporality, materiality, corporeality and sensorial studies, capturing the most exciting developments in current legal theory, and anticipating future research in the area.

The handbook is essential reading for scholars and students of jurisprudence, sociology of law, critical legal studies, socio-legal theory and interdisciplinary legal studies, as well as those people from other disciplines interested in the way the law converses with interdisciplinarity.

Andreas Philippopoulos-Mihalopoulos is Professor of Law and Theory and Director of the Westminster Law and Theory Lab at the University of Westminster, UK.

Routledge Handbook of Law and Theory

Edited by Andreas Philippopoulos-Mihalopoulos

Routledge
Taylor & Francis Group
LONDON AND NEW YORK

First published 2019
by Routledge
2 Park Square, Milton Park, Abingdon, Oxon OX14 4RN

and by Routledge
605 Third Avenue, New York, NY 10017

First issued in paperback 2021

Routledge is an imprint of the Taylor & Francis Group, an informa business

Publisher's Note
The publisher has gone to great lengths to ensure the quality of this reprint but points out that some imperfections in the original copies may be apparent.

British Library Cataloguing-in-Publication Data
A catalogue record for this book is available from the British Library

Library of Congress Cataloging-in-Publication Data
Names: Philippopoulos-Mihalopoulos, Andreas, author.
Title: Routledge handbook of law and theory / Andreas Philippopoulos-Mihalopoulos.
Description: Abingdon, Oxon [UK] ; New York, NY : Routledge, [2018] | Includes bibliographical references and index.
Identifiers: LCCN 2018001605 | ISBN 9781138956469 (hbk) | ISBN 9781317353003 (web pdf) | ISBN 9781317352990 (epub) | ISBN 9781317352983 (kindle)
Subjects: LCSH: Law—Philosophy.
Classification: LCC K237 .P45 2018 | DDC 340/.1—dc23
LC record available at https://lccn.loc.gov/2018001605

ISBN 13: 978-1-03-209495-3 (pbk)
ISBN 13: 978-1-138-95646-9 (hbk)

Typeset in Bembo
by Apex CoVantage, LLC

Contents

Figures and Table

Figures

Table

Contributors

Maria Aristodemou is Reader in Law, Literature and Psychoanalysis and Head of Department at the School of Law, Birkbeck College, University of London. Her current research explores the intersections between legal and psychoanalytic theory and practice, particularly in its Lacanian manifestations. She is the author of, among others, *Law & Literature: Journeys From Her to Eternity* (Oxford: Oxford University Press 2000) and *Law, Psychoanalysis, Society: Taking the Unconscious Seriously* (Oxford: Routledge 2014), and is a contributor and co-editor of *Crime, Fiction and the Law* (Oxford: Routledge, 2016).

Olivia Barr is Senior Lecturer at Melbourne Law School, University of Melbourne. Olivia writes in jurisprudence, and her cross-disciplinary work engages with geography, anthropology, philosophy and contemporary public art practices. She recently published *A Jurisprudence of Movement: Common Law, Walking, Unsettling Place* (Routledge 2016).

Anne Bottomley (Kent Law School) and **Nathan Moore** (Birkbeck Law School) have presented and written together frequently, often in presentations and papers drawing on film, music, architecture and art to explore the potential for a Deleuzean perspective in legal scholarship. Nathan Moore's *The Decision: Artisans in an Age of Control* (Fordham University Press) is forthcoming.

Chris Butler is Lecturer at the Griffith Law School, Australia. He researches the political, spatial and aesthetic forms of resistance to legal and institutional modes of ordering, and his work has appeared in *Social and Legal Studies, Law and Critique, Griffith Law Review* and *Law, Text, Culture.* Chris has written widely on the implications of Henri Lefebvre's social theory for critical legal scholarship, and his book *Henri Lefebvre: Spatial Politics, Everyday Life and the Right to the City* (2012) is published by Routledge. More recently, Chris collaborated with Edward Mussawir in editing a collection of essays entitled *Spaces of Justice: Peripheries, Passages, Appropriations* (Routledge 2017).

Emilie Cloatre is Reader in Law at Kent Law School. Her research focuses on the relationship between law and medicine, and is located at the intersection of socio-legal studies and science and technology studies. She is the author of *Pills for the Poorest: An Exploration of TRIPS and Access to Medication in Sub-Saharan Africa* (Palgrave MacMillan) and co-editor of *Knowledge, Technology and Law* (Routledge). She directed the AHRC Network Technoscience, Law and Society from 2013 to 2015 (with Martyn Pickersgill) and currently holds a Wellcome Investigator Award for a project entitled 'Law, Knowledges and the Making of Modern Healthcare' (2017–2022).

Dave Cowan is Professor of Law and Policy at the University of Bristol Law School. He researches housing issues generally from a socio-legal perspective, on which he has written widely. His most recent work has focused on shared ownership, its history and construction. He is the editor of the award-winning Palgrave Socio-Legal Series.

Luis Eslava is Senior Lecturer in International Law and Co-Director of the Centre for Critical International Law at Kent Law School. He is also a Senior Fellow at Melbourne Law School, an International Professor at Universidad Externado de Colombia, and a core faculty member of the Institute for Global Law and Policy, Harvard Law School. Bringing together insights from anthropology, history and legal and social theory, his work focuses on the multiple ways in which international norms, aspirations and institutional practices, both old and new, come to shape and become part of our everyday life. He is the author of *Local Space, Global Life: The Everyday Operation of International Law and Development* (Cambridge University Press, 2015) and co-editor of *Imperialismo y Derecho Internacional* (Siglo del Hombre, 2016) with Liliana Obregón and René Urueña, and *Bandung, Global History, and International Law: Critical Pasts and Pending Futures* (Cambridge University Press, 2017) with Michael Fakhri and Vasuki Nesiah.

Lucy Finchett-Maddock is Lecturer in Law at the University of Sussex. Her work predominantly focuses on the intersection of property within law and resistance, interrogating the spatio-temporality and aesthetics of formal and informal laws, property (squatting and housing), commons and protest. She is the author of the monograph *Protest, Property and the Commons: Performances of Law and Resistance* (Routledge, 2016). Her work also looks to broader questions around the intersection of art and law, resistance, legal and illegal understandings of art, property, aesthetics and politics. She is currently developing an 'Art/Law Network', where artists, activists and agitators come together to collaborate for social change.

Emily Grabham is Professor of Law at the University of Kent. Her research interests include labour law, law and time, and feminist legal theory. She pursues an interdisciplinary approach to legal research, drawing on methods and perspectives from feminist legal theory, social anthropology, sociology, and science and technology studies. Her publications include a monograph *Brewing Legal Times: Things, Form and the Enactment of Law* (2016, University of Toronto Press), a forthcoming edited collection (*Making Law's Times: Critical Perspectives on Law, Regulation, and Temporality* with Siân

Beynon-Jones) and articles in a wide range of peer reviewed journals including *Economy & Society*, *Australian Feminist Studies*, *Body & Society*, *Social & Legal Studies*, *Oxford Journal of Legal Studies*, and *Canadian Journal of Law & Society*.

Anna Grear is Professor of Law and Theory at Cardiff Law School, in the School of Law and Politics, Cardiff University, UK, and Founder and Editor in Chief of the *Journal of Human Rights and the Environment*. Anna's research has always grappled, in one way or another, with the issues central to how law constructs and mediates the world, how law populates the world with persons, systems, strategies and mechanisms and the patterns related to law's injustice. Her work calls on insights from a range of disciplines despite being firmly located within a combination of critical legal theory and jurisprudence.

Hyo Yoon Kang is Senior Lecturer at Kent Law School, University of Kent. She has worked and published at the intersection of intellectual property, science and technology studies and history of sciences. Her research interests are in knowledge production, legal techniques, digital technologies and media theories. She read law at the London School of Economics and the European University Institute and conducted postdoctoral research at the Max Planck Institute for the History of Science. She currently co-organises the AHRC Research Network Grant on 'Legal Materiality' with Sara Kendall and conducts an ERC-sponsored project examining how scientists read legal texts, such as patent documents.

Sarah Keenan is Senior Lecturer at Birkbeck Law School, London. Her research engages with property from critical race and feminist perspectives, focusing on the conceptual and material overlap between ownership and membership. She has previously worked as a solicitor in the community sector in Australia and is involved in anti-racist activism based in London. She is currently a Leverhulme Fellow working on the project 'Making Land Liquid: The Temporality of Title Registration'. Her book *Subversive Property: Law and the Production of Spaces of Belonging* was published by Routledge in 2015.

Elena Loizidou is Reader in Law and Political Theory at the University of London, Birkbeck College, School of Law. She is the author of *Judith Butler: Ethics, Law, Politics* (London: Routledge-Glasshouse, 2007) and the editor of *Disobedience Theory and Practice* (London: Routledge, 2013) and has authored numerous articles and chapters on feminism, anarchism and the law.

James R. Martel teaches Political Theory in the Department of Political Science at San Francisco State University. Most recently, he is the author of *The Misinterpellated Subject* (Duke University Press, 2017). He is currently working on a book, currently under review with Amherst College Press, entitled *Unburied Bodies: Subversive Corpses and the Authority of the Dead*. He works on issues of legal philosophy, political theory, post-colonial studies, comparative literature and anarchist studies.

Nicola Masciandaro is Professor of English at Brooklyn College, CUNY, and a specialist in medieval literature. He is the editor of the journal *Glossator* (Open Humanities Press) and co-author of *The Voice of the Hammer* (Notre Dame, 2007), *Dark Nights of the Universe* (NAME Publications, 2013), *Sufficient Unto the Day* (Schism, 2014), *Floating Tomb* (Mimesis, 2015), and *SACER* (Schism, 2017).

Renisa Mawani is Professor of Sociology and recurring Chair of the Law and Society Program at the University of British Columbia. She works in the fields of critical theory and colonial legal history and has published widely on law, colonialism and legal geography. In 2015–2016, she received the Killam Prize for Graduate Instruction, received a Dean of Arts Faculty Research Award and was a Wall Scholar at the Peter Wall Institute for Advanced Studies.

Dragan Milovanovic received his PhD from SUNY at Albany. He is Brommel Distinguished Research Professor at Northeastern Illinois University. He has published extensively in postmodern criminology, law and transformative justice. His current work advocates a paradigm change in the social sciences toward a quantum holography ontology.

Yoriko Otomo (PhD, LLB/BA (Hons) University of Melbourne) is a writer, critic and artist. The author of *Unconditional Life: The Postwar International Law Settlement* (Oxford University Press, 2016), Yoriko has co-edited key publications in human–animal studies (*Making Milk: The Past, Present and Future of Our Primary Food*, Bloomsbury 2017; *Law and the Question of the Animal: A Critical Jurisprudence*, Routledge 2012) and is a Board Member of Minding Animals International. She was previously a tenured senior lecturer at SOAS Law School (University of London) where she is currently a research associate.

Andrea Pavoni is a post-doctoral fellow at DINAMIA'CET, Centre for Socio-economic and Territorial Studies, at the University Institute of Lisbon, Portugal. He completed his PhD at the University of Westminster, London, in 2013. He is a fellow at the Westminster Law and Theory Lab, co-editor of the 'Law and the Senses' series (University of Westminster Press), and associate editor at the journal *Lo Squaderno, Explorations in Space and Society*.

Andreas Philippopoulos-Mihalopoulos is Professor of Law & Theory at the University of Westminster, and founder and Director of the Westminster Law & Theory Lab. Andreas also pursues an art practice under the name of *picpoet* and has published one artist's book and one fiction book. Edited volumes include *Law and the City* (2007), *Law and Ecology* (2012), and with Victoria Brooks *Research Methods in Environmental Law: A Handbook* (2017). He has also published the monographs *Absent Environments* (2007), *Niklas Luhmann: Law, Justice, Society* (2010), and *Spatial Justice: Body, Lawscape, Atmosphere* (2014).

Alain Pottage is Professor of Law at the London School of Economics.

Honni van Rijswijk is Senior Lecturer at UTS Law School, Sydney. Honni has published on law in the writings of Alexis Wright, suffering in Virginia Woolf and feminist aesthetics in Sarah Kane and is working on a monograph that focuses on the figure of the girl.

Laurent de Sutter is Professor of Legal Theory at Vrije Universiteit Brussel. He is the author of a dozen books dedicated to the relationship between law, images and transgression, translated into various languages. They include, recently, *Théorie du kamikaze* (Paris: Puf, 2016), *'Quand l'inspecteur s'emmêle' de Blake Edwards* (Crisnée: Yellow Now, 2016), *Poétique de la police* (Aix-en-Provence, Rouge Profond, 2017) and *Narcocapitalism* (Cambridge: Polity, 2017). He is the editor of the 'Perspectives Critiques' series at Presses Universitaires de France and the 'Theory Redux' series at Polity Press, and is one of the general editors of *Law & Literature.*

Christopher Tomlins is Elizabeth Josselyn Boalt Professor of Law at the University of California, Berkeley. His most recent book is *Searching for Contemporary Legal Thought* (Cambridge and New York: Cambridge University Press, 2017), co-edited with Justin Desautels-Stein.

Illan rua Wall is a political and legal theorist who works on questions of crowds, protest, riots, disorder and revolt. He is an Associate Professor at the University of Warwick, School of Law, holding a PhD from Birkbeck College, University of London. His first monograph, *Human Rights and Constituent Power* (Routledge), was published in 2012. He is on the editorial board of the journal *Law and Critique*, a founding editor of the blog criticallegalthinking.com and the new open access publisher *Counterpress*. He will launch a new podcast series entitled *Orders in Decay* in 2018.

Introduction

The *and* of law and theory

*Andreas Philippopoulos-Mihalopoulos**

Why this volume

The *Routledge Handbook of Law and Theory* attempts to reconceptualise legal theory in a material, socially contextualised, affectively engaged and politically radical way. Its main purpose is to offer a new collective approach to the theory of law, unbound by the grand legal abstractions of pure textuality, strict normativity, universalised judgement, abstract political thinking, theoretically poor doctrinal or empirical work, and decontextualised philosophical inquiry. This volume distinguishes itself from positivist legal theory, most strands of traditional philosophy of law (e.g., Coyle, 2017; Golding and Edmundson, 2004), but also from most forms of by now more or less normalised sociolegal or critical legal theory. This is because the volume represents an attempt to escape the often superficial veneer of interdisciplinarity in legal theory, and seriously situate legal thinking in the open plane of other disciplines as well as non-disciplines (namely, boundaries between disciplines, conceptual advancements that belong to many disciplines at the same time and ethical calls for not settling in a discipline), determined by such new parameters as the post/nonhuman, the anthropocenic, the material, the ontological, the ecological and so on. To this effect, the volume engages with supradisciplinary debates on the areas of spatiality, temporality, materiality, corporeality and sensorial studies, anticipating and perhaps even shaping in this way future developments of current legal theory.

This collection does not emerge in a vacuum. There is a plethora of accounts of law that engage seriously with the above considerations. These accounts have been variously originating in gender studies (e.g., Cooper, 2013; Drakopoulou, 2009; Motha, 2007), law and space (e.g., Blomley, 2003; Delaney, 2010; Mulcahy, 2010; Dahlberg, 2012), law and time (Douglas, 2011; Lefebvre, 2008; Valverde, 2014), law and the (racialised/queer/marginalised/controlled) body (Hirvonen, 2012; Manderson, 2015; Cooper et al., 2008; Bhandar, 2012; Hanafin, 2007; Bainham et al., 2002), law and the senses (Bently and Flynn, 1996; Mandic et al., 2013), animal studies (Braverman, 2012; Otomo and Mussawir, 2013), art and law (Goodrich, 2014; Ben-Dor, 2011; Bruncevic, 2017; Hirvonen, 2012; Young, 2013; Leiboff, 2007), law and the postcolonial (Haldar, 2007; Bhandar, 2014; Fitzpatrick, 2008), governmentality and issues of limits of resistance (Lindahl, 2013; Douzinas, 2012; Guardiola-Rivera, 2008; Zartaloudis, 2015; Leung, 2013), and law and broadly critical economics and development (Alessandrini, 2013; Macmillan, 2009; Bedford, 2010). There has also been an increased engagement with authors such as Deleuze, Foucault, Butler, Braidotti, Latour, Luhmann, Bennett, Malabou and several others who, although not originating in law, have managed to find their way in contemporary legal thinking. Of interest is the fact that a considerable amount of these studies successfully balance rigorous theoretical engagement and grounded, contextualised work. This is not always easy when serious interdisciplinary work is undertaken. The demands are high on both law and whatever other discipline(s) is involved; and while it is understood that one returns to the law and its discipline when one undertakes interdisciplinary *legal* research, the texts produced might be too demanding, theoretical and abstract, or too concrete and technical for the more settled legal readership. It is not uncommon for theoretically inclined legal research to move too deep into terminological and conceptual abstraction of, say, anthropology, art or literary studies; or for empirically inclined legal research to delve too wholeheartedly into the technicalities of, say, the pharmaceutical industry, principles of architecture, or neurology. For the above reasons, a guiding criterion for the kind of pieces commissioned for this volume is the balance of the theoretical and the broadly understood applied.

Another equally important guiding criterion, intimately connected to the exigencies of balanced interdisciplinary work, is that the work included here precipitates a collapse of the long-accepted distinction between critical legal studies on the one hand and sociolegal studies on the other.[1] It is the position of this volume (and its editor) that the above distinction (and others along the lines of 'high theory' versus grounded thought, concreteness versus abstraction, utopia versus pragmatism and so on) has outlived its usefulness and even relevance. Sadly, these distinctions are still weaponised in order to perpetuate obscurely motivated scholarly classifications and turf-preservations. One of the unfortunate consequences of this polarisation is the marginalisation (or at best the begrudging acceptance) of a burgeoning number of scholars in the last decade or so, who have resisted such hardlines and who have produced work that theorises practice and applies theory, if not in equal measure, at least without falling into an old-fashioned binary.[2]

There is little doubt that several theoretical research publications pay scant attention to how theory is translated into practice, and how, more broadly, theory can make a difference; likewise, a considerable amount of applied research is barely interested in the benefits that more extensive theorisation brings in terms of diagonal, creative and unhinged thinking. A return, however, to the distinction between critical and sociolegal would not be useful. Likewise, it is perhaps time to understand that the pertinent categorisation can no longer be 'high' (and therefore, what? unconnected? theological? immaterial?) and 'low' (dirty? *too* applied? too low-brow?) theory. There is good legal thinking that is aware of its potential effect on reality and works on this in order to give direction to its theoretical development. And then, there is not so good legal thinking that remains unconnected to reality and deliberately ignores its own transformative potential. Unless broadly understood as contextualisation, affective engagement and personal involvement, neither empirical studies nor mere theoretical work have a monopoly on reality.

One of the main purposes of this volume is to leave these distinctions behind, and offer instead a new bridging mode of legal theoretical thinking: what the title of the book refers to as 'law and theory'.

Turning points

The context in which this volume emerges is a broader sense of urgency for a new legal theoretical approach. This is testified by the recent abundance of publications that aim to do precisely that (see, e.g., Stone et al., 2012; Banakar and Travers, 2013; Del Mar and Goodrich, 2014; Christodoulidis et al., forthcoming) and attest to a turning point in legal theory, a point of fumbling amongst various novel developments both in law and in the wider spectrum of knowledge. Even the more conservative attempts to restore, retain and reinforce the traditional boundaries of the discipline, with the usual recourse to definitions (e.g., what is law/regulation/normativity) and categorisations (e.g., doctrinal/sociolegal/theoretical research), are no longer impervious to at least some of the forays made by more adventurous theoretical enquiries. Thus, feminist legal studies, deconstruction and systems theory, to mention just a few examples, even if not yet part of the canon, tend to put an appearance in most legal theory books that aim to offer a survey (often for educational reasons) of the currents of legal thought. Needless to say, they are usually squeezed into the final chapter of the book, often for completion's sake than for their perceived actual relevance.

Such books would probably fail to recognise some of the chapters in this volume as belonging to the area of 'philosophy of law' or even the broader term 'legal theory'. It is a compliment of sorts, then, to think of this volume as a collection of 'last chapters', lines that trail off an otherwise solid structure, threads that have been left unstitched. It shows that the contributors to the volume keep up with the times that demand alternative, minoritarian thinking (a process of theorising that Bottomley and Moore in this volume find that is "working always in-between the materiality of becoming"); they are in contact with what really matters in law and beyond law; and they act in full awareness of their limited possibility to suggest supposedly solid solutions. In that sense, the contributions here, despite the frequent political utopianism, supradisciplinary material, methodological adventurousness and free-thinking legalities, are much more realistic and in touch with the world at large than are most accounts of traditional philosophy of law and quite a few of the more standard sociolegal and critical theoretical endeavours.

This is because this volume is traversed by a perhaps uncomfortable understanding: to pretend that, at this stage of planetary turning, the law and its theory can offer anything different, more solid or definitive than a space of openness and receptivity of thought, is delusional at best and dishonest at worst. At risk of sounding apocalyptic, I would enumerate the following three factors that contribute to this planetary turning: the epoch of the Anthropocene; the renewed attention on nonhuman agents and the consequent reimagining of the human; and the current global politics of intense material instability. We are in trouble if any legal scholar is still asking 'what's this got to do with law?' – a seemingly innocent yet haunting question that has clipped many a daring wing that might have been trying to think of other laws and other societies. It is time, therefore, to acknowledge what the world has to do with the law, and the law with the world. The geological epoch of the Anthropocene, which recognises human presence and anthropogenic change as geologically measurable, can be defined legally as enhanced human responsibility towards the earth (Kotzé, 2017; Philippopoulos-Mihalopoulos, 2017). This has obviously more than just an ecological dimension: it is, properly speaking, a geophilosophical opening that understands legal responsibility (and human responsibility for that matter, denuded from human suprematism and metaphysical privilege) as part of an intricate continuum between human and nonhuman, organic and inorganic, personal and political. This requires of the law a reconceptualisation, not only of the nonhuman (including the inorganic) agent and its capacity for legal action, but also a reconceptualisation of the human in ways previously unthinkable for the legal science of consciousness and legal capacity. Rather than considering these emergent agencies as merely exacerbating the current and ongoing global political, financial, religious, social and environmental instability (an instability that has become too stable to talk about crisis anymore), legal theory is now called to think imaginatively on how to include them as tools against the instability. In other words, how to use strategically such abstractions (or at least things that were so far considered abstractions for law, such as objects, animals, insects, senses, atmospheres, quanta and so on) in order to resist the ongoing instability and its potential lethal planetary results.

In this sense, this volume pushes the boundaries of legal theoretical thinking towards an even more intimate connection between the law and the world at large, and tries to conceive of the legal in its interfolding, not only with the political as it has been happening overwhelmingly in most of the more radical legal theoretical collections, but also with the corporeal, the spatiotemporal, the material and immaterial, and the ontological.

Law and theory

The decision to call this volume *Law and Theory*, and not Legal Theory, Theory of Law, Philosophy of Law, Jurisprudence, Law and Humanities, and so on, has been determined by three factors. The first is the humble realisation that we are not there yet: we, as legal scholars, have not managed to link successfully law and other disciplines in a way that would allow not only law to be guided by the findings of other disciplines (this is more or less achieved), but significantly, to also allow law and its theory to spread outside its disciplinary boundaries and be read, thought and actively used by other disciplines. The non-legal academics who read and actively engage with legal theory are certainly a growing number, largely because of the indefatigable efforts of such publishers as Routledge's Glasshouse. Yet, they are still not on par with say, non-geographers who read geography, non-philosophers who read philosophy or even non-economists who read economics. Without serious elaboration, law is regularly substituted in the non-legal literature by a generic idea of rights, democracy or behavioural patterns – but even they come under the explicit umbrella of politics rather than law. This of course occurs for good reasons: political theory has traditionally been a natural bedfellow for legal theory. But this blurring is no longer productive. Non-legal theory misses out on a vast amount of nuances, ways of thinking and avenues of acting, if law is constantly supplanted by politics. Issues such as democracy, human rights, popular resistance or revolution, while as important today as earlier, need to be combined with a material, emplaced and embodied, yet equally theorised, understanding of the law, if we want law to be making the difference that it is capable of, especially with regards to other disciplines.

In short, law has not yet carved a suitably open supradisciplinary space for itself in which to move freely and become the object of debate by other disciplines. For this realisation, *Law and Theory* invites other disciplines by opening up to them. Thus, the second reason for the choice of title is that the theory used here is not legal theory. It might become legal theory, and in some cases has been well integrated in existing legal theory; yet so far it retains a freshness, an angularity and perhaps even certain estranging traits that still have the capacity of throwing us out of kilter. Rather than enclosing the theory within law, *Law and Theory* retains the parallelism between law on the one hand, and (legal/non-legal) theory on the other, encouraging in this way productive friction and creative mispairings.

Finally, the third reason is this astonishingly simple word *and*, and the vast openings that offers. Derrida's writing on this is instructive: "and at the beginning, there is the *and*" (Derrida, 2004: 21, my translation). This beginning (that never properly begins) tells us that the starting *and* augurs the end of origin: there has never been an origin to the word, to the law, to this very sentence. Nothing is 'the' origin since there is always something that precedes the initial *and*. We might as well be done with our (peculiarly legal) obsession for origin. Allowing the *and* to begin and further to connect makes no promises other than an attempt to put together two or more things that might not fit together. Derrida refers to *and* as both association and dissociation, conjunction and collection. When talking of Foucault's *and* that appears on the title of the latter's book *Les Mots et les Choses*,[3] Derrida plays with us by saying that

> between the words *and* the things, there cannot be a conjunction or a homogenous collection, no enumeration or simple addition etc. The words and the things neither add up nor follow each other in the same series. . . . Except . . . if we consider, which is not altogether illegitimate, that the words are and the words and the things.
>
> (2004: 22, my translation)

Or, in the case of this volume, that the law is and the law and the theory.

To this, I feel the need to add something that comes from a seemingly very different source: Deleuze's stuttering, full of glottal stops and tremolos, allows the language itself to stutter:

> the disjunctions become included or inclusive, and the connections, reflexive.... Every word is divided, but into itself; and every word is combined, but with itself. It is as if the entire language started to roll from right to left, and to pitch backward and forward: the two stutterings.
>
> (Deleuze, 1997: 110)

This is clearly not the place for an analysis of the connection between Deleuzian stuttering and Derridean *and*, but I would like to keep one thing from all this: that the *and* of this volume's title encourages us to think at the same time of a parallelism and a continuum between law and theory. Parallelism in the sense that the two are not the same, and that space is needed for both to develop their ambit away from the other; and continuum because just as the law is and the law and the theory, in the same way the theory is and the law and the theory. And since the *and* at the beginning disrobes us of any illusion of origin, we need to start at the only place we can: "Creative stuttering is what makes language grow from the middle, like grass" (Deleuze, 1997: 111). Let's grow from the middle then, right in the middle of law and theory, at the locus of this little *and* word.

There is little point in denying that this volume is also a personal project – and not just because of the choice of title, but that too: when some years ago I had to choose my own professorial title (which was accepted, after some institutional haggling mainly attributed to uncertainty – "are you sure you do not mean professor of legal theory?"), I felt attracted to this stuttering of the *and*, and the difficulty that caused to some people (academics or not) to remember it. But it often generated questions, which I was only too happy to think along with the people who were asking, trying to understand, even I, what this choice of title meant. In a way, the same wondering mood also permeates this volume. The fact that it has been personally commissioned by Routledge has given me somewhat shameless license to experiment with the contributions, the topics and even the arrangement of the parts. My editorial touch has been mostly light, since the ideas proffered by the authors were so strong that my role was reduced to that of a feverishly enthusiastic reader. It is my conviction that the contributors in this collection have produced work that holds a radiant promise for the future of law and theory.

Parts and chapters

The division of the volume in parts is largely arbitrary, since most of the chapters deal with most or indeed all the areas. It would be absurd to expect that the spatiotemporal, the body, sense, text and matter will not be intimately connected and cross-pollinated when it comes to a new material, emplaced, embodied understanding of law and theory. What I tried to do, however, with this division and order is to tease different connections between, say, legal materiality and textuality, more-than-human legal bodies, or sense-thinking from the usual phenomenological, human-subject bound topic, to an ontological opening.

The first part of the volume is dedicated to the *spatiotemporal*. Spatiality is the most common manifestation of new material legalities, whether connected to sociolegal understandings of locality, international legal spatialisations of jurisdiction, capitalist productions of space such as shopping malls and gated communities, and so on. Legal spatiality has recently been discovering issues of movement and pause, as well as the legal side of spatial justice. Time, on the other hand, has been the traditional province of classic philosophical analyses, often seen through phenomenological or historical perspectives in law. The relevance of time for the law has never waned but is now different. Time is now considered to be the element returning after space, therefore an ingredient of a spatiotemporal and material understanding of the law. We begin with Luis Eslava's 'Dense Struggle: On Ghosts, Law and the Global Order', in which Eslava combines his ethnographic journey alongside a group of internally displaced people in Bogotá with a theoretical exploration of the nature of law and of the clashes between our assumedly modern global world and the spectral other-worldly. We move on to Chris Butler's 'Spatial Abstraction, Legal Violence and the Promise of Appropriation', a Lefebvrian investigation of capitalist spatial abstractions, placing particular emphasis on the right to the city and spatial justice, with the aim to construct a relational theory of legal spatiotemporalities. Sarah Keenan's 'A Prison Around Your Ankle and a Border in Every Street: Theorising Law, Space and the Subject', through a critical race and disability study of electronic surveillance tagging, finds that subjects are spatially constituted and indeed 'take space with' them. Emily Grabham's '"Praxiographies" of Time: Law, Temporalities, and Material Worlds' brings together legal temporalities discourses with new materialism, and watches objects and other nonhuman agents coming into being through a praxiographic approach (Mol, 2003), namely an approach based on enactment rather than knowledge. Lucy Finchett-Maddock's 'Continua of (In)Justice' explores the spatiotemporal continua of justice and injustice in relation to current theories and her work on squatters' rights, dwelling on issues of entropy and processual definitions of justice. Finally, in 'Movement: An Homage to Legal Drips, Wobbles and Perpetual Motion', Olivia Barr looks at the ontology of movement in law. Through her ethnographic work on walking, largely influenced by Australian Aboriginal practices, movement is revealed to be law's mode of existence.

The second part moves on to *sense*, both sensorial and directional. The area of law and the senses has been around for a while in terms of legal theory but never fully developed. Yet, it would seem to be one of the most obvious ways of addressing the ways in which the legal enters life, whether it is through biopolitics or affective politics. While the visual has been addressed in the past, other senses have taken a back seat. In the chapters, distinct senses are being represented in their relation to the law, but an attempt is also made to address the multisensorial (through the synaesthetic and the atmospheric), as well as the sensorial as nonhuman, non-phenomenological and institutionalised. Andrea Pavoni begins with 'Disenchanting Senses: Law and the Taste of the Real', an overview of law and senses through aesthetic and speculative theories, and then a close reading of issues of taste and law, related in particular to wine. Nicola Masciandario's 'Synaesthesia: The Mystical Sense of Law' continues with an overview of the sensorial, but this time from the point of view of the sense of law and the law of sense. Through Rimbaud's poetry, the chapter fuses the textual and the sensorial of the law. In Dragan Milovanovic's 'Touching You, Touching Me in Law and Justice: Toward a Quantum Holographic Process-Informational Understanding', the textuality of the quantum hologram sides with the physicality of intimacy and closeness of a collective legal agent and attempts to flesh out positive legal affects, connected to the waves emitted by the human heart. The part closes with Illan rua Wall's 'Turbulent Legality: Sovereignty, Security and the Police', where the sensorial becomes atmospheric, at the same time diffused and accentuated, and the sense of public order and its supposedly peaceful context is argued to be there essentially as management of bodies and their movements.

The third part is dedicated to the *body*. Corporeality has recently entered the theory of law in terms of its spatial and material extensions, as well as the repercussions of a newly imagined corporeality for the law. Depending on the theoretical perspective, the term 'body' includes inanimate objects, or the term 'object' includes animate bodies. In all cases, the challenge is to think of the body in terms of law's given textuality, as well as in the context of nonhuman bodies. Elena Loizidou's 'Sequences on Law and the Body' offers us an overview of corporeality in law, divided into the two fields (or as she calls them *sequences*) of discursive and material accounts. The body of the law is folded with the body in law, and we are slowly prepared for the eventual phasing out of law from legal theory. Or the law being so immanently embodied that it becomes ontological resistance, as Laurent de Sutter shows in 'On Resisting Bodies', while employing the Femen activists and their juridical battle as an example of how the body, rather than being manacled to the law, is the law's greatest hurdle. A slightly different but no less important body is dealt with in Renisa Mawani's 'Insect Wars: Bees, Bedbugs, and Biopolitics', where animality is seen in its biopolitical, anticolonial dimension, and specifically insects are being drafted as juridical figures and military weapons, precipitating thus the interrelationality between human/nonhuman life and death. Anna Grear's 'Anthropocene "Time"? A reflection on temporalities in the "New Age of the Human"' takes the planet as a juridical body and studies its temporality in relation to Donna Haraway's Capitalocene and Chthulucene concepts, with a reference to broadly understood environmental law and governance as an example of planetary law. Finally, Yoriko Otomo's 'Making Lawful Animals' offers a meditation on animality and food, through the double medium of a traditional but purposefully brief academic text and a poem that opens up the ethical challenge of anthropophagy.

The fourth part focuses on the *textual*, revisited now that the lessons from the linguistic turn have been digested in law. The new legal textuality relies on deconstruction, while taking into consideration other theoretical currents, such as the psychoanalytical, the historical or the visual. What is more, this is a new textuality, material and spread onto the world. Honni van Rijswijk in 'Feminist genres of violence and law's aggressive realism' reads the film *Dogville* as a locus for law's abstractions and the violence they exert on women. Through an analysis of the film's law, the textual and material dimension of the law emerges, that employs its 'aggressive realism' to assert its exclusivity of judgment. Maria Aristodemou's empirical focus is the 2015 Greek referendum where democracy is practiced in an innocuous, decaffeinated way. 'From Decaffeinated Democracy to Democracy in the Real in Ten (Lacanian) Sessions' charts the fate of current democracies through the psychoanalytic tools of the discredited Big Other and the desire of self-legislation of the Real. Christopher Tomlins's 'Why Law's Objects Do Not Disappear: On History as Remainder' offers a legal-historical repost to object-oriented ontology by combining the textuality of naming and the elusiveness of soul traces, and culminates with an alchemic dance, with the law as its central black additive. James R. Martel's 'Must the Law Be a Liar? Walter Benjamin on the Possibility of an Anarchist Form of Law' enters the penumbra of Benjamin's truth and lies in relation to law, and fleshes out the possibility of an anarchist, nonviolent, local law that is not espoused to legal truth. Alain Pottage's 'Literary Materiality' bridges naturally this and the next part of the volume, with its analysis of the materiality of books, that most embodied manifestation of the textual, and the repercussions for copyright law of the passage from the Kantian transcendental to the intangible.

Finally, the fifth part goes deeper into the *material* in law. Materiality has been touched mostly superficially by current legal analyses whether in the metaphorical 'material considerations' for the law, or the concrete architectural qualities of courts, or criminological and anthropological studies of legal objects. We are now catching up with the rise of new materialism, object-oriented ontologies and speculative realism that have put in a solid appearance in other areas of humanities and social sciences. Emilie Cloatre and Dave Cowan's 'Legalities and Materialities' opens the part with an overview of law and materiality, with a particular focus on the posthuman as methodology in law. Their attention then shifts to anthropological approaches to law and the posthuman materiality in order to assert the need for empirical attentiveness to the micro-details of the law. Hyo Yoon Kang's 'Law's Materiality: Between Concrete Matters and Abstract Forms, or How Matter Becomes Material' carries on with the overview but this time by focussing on the distinction between matter and materiality in law, the need for concrete attention to legal materialities, and the law as matter which involves the various textual, spatial and ritual orderings of the law. Andreas Philippopoulos-Mihalopoulos's 'To Have to Do With the Law: An Essay' is an experimental text with three voices, part jury ethnography, part lawscape theory and part essay writing theory, performing the materiality of the law while at the same time critiquing it through the implicit dialogue amongst the voices. Finally, Anne Bottomley and Nathan Moore's 'On New Model Jurisprudence: The Scholar/Critic as (Cosmic) Artisan' begins with a critical overview of law/theory combinations, and after focussing on the English educational legal system and its repercussions for legal theoretical thinking, they bring in the figure of the artisan as the one who critically practices theory.

Notes

* I am indebted to Routledge for the trust, to the multiple reviewers for their invaluable comments during the long process of editing of this work, to the handbook advisors Davina Cooper, Margaret Davies and Peter Goodrich, and to Maria Javed for her precious editorial and administrative assistance.

1 In that sense, this volume tries to move more in the direction of law and humanities, while retaining both a strong continental theoretical tradition and a materially oriented attitude to law.

2 As examples, the work of authors such as Perry-Kessaris, 2017; Grabham, 2016; Bottomley and Wong, 2009, and so on, has been instrumental in moving beyond such distinctions.

3 Which, in its English translation of Foucault (1970) 2002, lost this little abyss between its words and its things, and had it replaced it with a grand 'order', which apparently was the original wish of the author.

Bibliography

Alessandrini, Donatella, 'A Social Provisioning Employer of Last Resort: Post-Keynesianism Meets Feminist Economics', *World Review of Political Economy*, 4, 230–254, 2013.

Bainham, Andrew, Sclater, Shelley Day and Richards, Martin (eds), *Body Lore and Laws Essays on Law and the Human Body*, Oxford: Hart, 2002.

Banakar, Reza and Travers, Max (eds), *Law and Social Theory*, Oxford: Hart, 2013.

Bedford, Kate, 'Doing Business with the Ladies: Gender, Legal Reform, and Entrepreneurship in the International Finance Corporation', *Labor, Capital and Society*, 42, 2010.

Ben-Dor, Oren (ed.), *Law and Art: Justice, Ethics and Aesthetics*, London: Routledge, 2011.

Bently, Lionel and Flynn, Leo (eds), *Law and the Senses: Sensational Jurisprudence*, London: Pluto Press, 1996.

Bhandar, Brenna, 'Dis-assembling Legal Form: Ownership and the Racial Body', in M. Stone, I. Wall and C. Douzinas (eds), *New Critical Legal Thinking: Law and the Political*, London: Routledge, 2012.

Bhandar, Brenna, 'Property, Law, and Race: Modes of Abstraction', *UC Irvine Law Review*, 1(4), 203–218, 2014.

Blomley, Nicholas, *Unsettling the City: Urban Land and the Politics of Property*, London: Routledge, 2003.

Bottomley, Anne and Wong, Simone (eds), *Changing Contours of Domestic Life, Family and Law: Caring and Sharing*, Oxford: Hart Publishing, 2009.

Braverman, Irus, *Zooland: The Institution of Captivity*, Stanford: Stanford University Press, 2012.

Bruncevic, Merima, *Law, Art and the Commons*, London: Routledge, 2017.

Christodoulidis, Emilios, Dukes, Ruth and Goldoni, Marco (eds), *Research Handbook on Critical Legal Theory*, Cheltenham, UK: Edward Elgar, forthcoming 2019.

Cooper, Davina, Grabham, Emily and Krishnadas, Jane (eds), *Law, Power and the Politics of Subjectivity: Intersectionality and Beyond*, London: Routledge, 2008.

Cooper, Davina, *Everyday Utopias: The Conceptual Life of Promising Spaces*, Durham: Duke, 2013.

Coyle, Sean, *Modern Jurisprudence: A Philosophical Guide*, Oxford: Hart, 2017.

Dahlberg, Leif, *Spacing Law and Politics: The Constitution and Representation of the Juridical*, London: Routledge, 2012.

Delaney, David, *The Spatial, the Legal and the Pragmatics of World-Making: Nomospheric Investigations*, London: Routledge, 2010.

Deleuze, Gilles, *Essays Critical and Clinical*, trans. Daniel W. Smith and Michael A. Greco, Minneapolis: University of Minnesota Press, 1997.

Del Mar, Maksymilian and Goodrich, Peter (eds), *Legal Theory and the Humanities*, Aldershot: Ashgate, 2014.

Derrida, Jacques, 'Et cetera. . . (and so on, und so weiter, and so forth, et ainsi de suite, und so überall, etc.)', in Marie-Louise Mallet and Ginette Michaud (eds), *Derrida, L'Herne*, Paris: Editions de L'Herne, 2004.

Douglas, Stacy, 'Between Mo(nu)ments: Memorialising Past, Present and Future at the District Six Museum and Constitution Hill', *Law and Critique*, 22(2), 177–187, 2011.

Douzinas, Costas, 'Stasis Syntagma: The Names and Types of Resistance', in M. Stone, I. Wall and C. Douzinas (eds), *New Critical Legal Thinking: Law and the Political*, London: Routledge, 2012.

Drakopoulou, Maria, 'The Ethic of Care, Female Subjectivity and Feminist Legal Scholarship' in Joanne Conaghan (ed.), *Feminist Legal Studies*, London: Routledge, 2009.

Fitzpatrick, Peter, *Law as Resistance: Modernism, Imperialism, Legalism*, Aldershot: Ashgate, 2008.

Foucault, Michel, *The Order of Things: An Archaeology of the Human Sciences*, unknown trans., London: Routledge, 2002.

Golding, Martin and Edmundson, William (eds), *The Blackwell Guide to the Philosophy of Law and Legal Theory*, Hoboken, NJ: Wiley-Blackwell, 2004.

Goodrich, Peter, *Legal Emblems and the Art of Law: Obiter Depicta as the Vision of Governance*, Cambridge: Cambridge University Press, 2014.

Grabham, Emily, *Brewing Legal Times: Things, Form and the Enactment of Law*, Toronto: University of Toronto Press, 2016.

Guardiola-Rivera, Oscar, *Being Against the World: Rebellion and Constitution*, London: Routledge, 2008.

Haldar, Piyel, *Law, Orientalism and Postcolonialism: The Jurisdiction of the Lotus-Eaters*, London: Routledge, 2007.

Hanafin, Patrick, *Conceiving Life: Reproductive Politics and the Law in Contemporary Italy*, Aldershot: Ashgate, 2007.

Hirvonen, Ari, 'Body Politics: Normative Gaze, Carnal Intimacy and Touching Pain in Vanessa Beecroft's Art', in Leif Dahlberg (ed.), *Visualizing Law and Authority: Essays on Legal Aesthetics*, Berlin & Boston: de Gruyter, Vol 23, 141–163, 2012.

Kotzé, Louis (ed.), Environmental Law and Governance for the Anthropocene, Oxford: Hart, 2017.

Leiboff, Marett, *Creative Practice and the Law*, Rozelle NSW: Thompson, 2007.

Lefebvre, Alexander, *The Image of Law: Deleuze, Bergson, Spinoza*, Stanford: Stanford University Press, 2008.

Leung, Gilbert, 'Breach of the Peace or Violence and/of Silence', in Elena Loizidou (ed.), *Disobedience*, London: Routledge, 2013.

Lindahl, Hans, *Fault Lines of Globalization: Legal Order and the Politics of A-Legality*, Oxford: Oxford University Press, 2013.

Macmillan, Fiona, 'Development, Cultural Self-Determination, and the World Trade Organization', in Amanda Perry-Kessaris (ed.), *Law in Pursuit of Development: Principles into Practice?* London: Routledge, 2009.

Manderson, Desmond, 'Bodies in the Water: On Reading Images More Sensibly', *Law and Literature*, 27(2), 279–293, 2015.

Mandic, Danilo, Nirta, Caterina, Pavoni, Andrea and Philippopoulos-Mihalopoulos, Andreas (eds), *Law and the Senses Series*, www.westminster.ac.uk/westminster-law-and-theory-lab/publications/the-westminster-law-and-the-senses-series, 2013-present.

Mol, Annemarie, *The Body Multiple: Ontology in Medical Practice*, Durham: Duke University Press, 2003.

Moran, Les, 'Lesbian and Gay Bodies of Law', in D. Richardson and V. Seidman (eds), *Handbook of Lesbian and Gay Studies*, London: Sage, 2002.

Motha, Stewart, 'Veiled Women and the Affect of Religion in Democracy', *Journal of Law and Society*, 34(1), 139–162, 2007.

Mulcahy, Linda, *Legal Architecture: Justice, Due Process and the Place of Law*, London: Routledge, 2010.
Otomo, Yoriko and Mussawir, Edward (eds), *Law and the Question of the Animal*, London: Routledge, 2013.
Perry-Kessaris, Amanda, 'The Pop-up Museum of Legal Objects Project: An Experiment in "sociolegal design"', *Northern Ireland Legal Quarterly*, ISSN 0029–3105, 2017.
Philippopoulos-Mihalopoulos, Andreas, 'Critical Environmental Law as Method in the Anthropocene' in A. Philippopoulos-Mihalopoulos and V. Brooks (eds), *Research Methods in Environmental Law: A Handbook*, Cheltenham: Edward Elgar, 2017.
Stone, Matthew, Wall, Illan and Douzinas, Costas (eds), *New Critical Legal Thinking: Law and the Political*, London: Routledge, 2012.
Valverde, Mariana, *Chronotopes of Law: Jurisdiction, Scale and Governance*, London: Routledge, 2014.
Young, Alison, *Street Art, Public City: Law, Crime and the Urban Imagination*, London: Routledge, 2013.
Zartaloudis, Thanos, 'Violence Without Law? On Pure Violence as a Destituent Power', in B. Moran and C. Salzani (eds), *Towards the Critique of Violence – Walter Benjamin and Giorgio Agamben*, London: Bloomsbury, 2015.

Part I
Spatiotemporal

1

Dense struggle

On ghosts, law and the global order

*Luis Eslava**

Introduction

What follows is an invitation to think the world and its laws otherwise, together with its dramas and occult forces, in five steps. The first section lays the ground for the analysis. The second takes the reader to a protest of internally displaced people (IDPs) in Bogotá, Colombia. The third section reminds us of the ongoing presence of the uncanny in our present, legally constructed world. In the fourth, a ghost appears. Finally, a call for moving beyond disenchantment is enacted. This will be a long journey, one that, I hope, will also be worthwhile.

The global emplotment

Today's global order is characterised by a constellation of ever more closely imbricated relationships among different laws, levels of government, managerial techniques, economic, political and social forces and deeply engrained antagonisms. A sense of confusion, claustrophobia, constant surveillance and insidious but ever-elusive command have come to define these, our times. In this chapter, I try to rethink the global order we inhabit as a site of dense struggle. In order to do this, I stay with the global order, as closely as I can, not just to (re)confirm how intricate and dense that order is, but also to show precisely what results from it, and in particular what it produces on its margins – home to the apparently anti-modern, the popular, the otherworldly.

Three suggestions emerge from this exercise. As the reader will see, in paying attention to the products of today's global order, it is possible to question anew – to theorise again – what law does and how it is experienced in our global times. At the same time, this exercise helps us recalibrate what our response should be once we remember that our assumedly uniform late modern, globalised, capitalist and disenchanted present is healthily plagued by frictions and clashes. These are contradictions that result from the encounter between tectonic social and political visions. Through these clashes, other worlds speak. Finally, this exercise invites us to consider the value of getting down and dirty with law, of approaching it ethnographically in a moment that continually forces us to transcend the usual divisions between (among other supposed binaries) the international and the local, the 'rational' and the 'barbaric', the legal and the violent.

Let me explain what lies behind these ideas before we move into the story that forms the core of this chapter in the next section. Regardless of how much concepts and areas of study like 'globalisation', 'globalisation and the law', 'global governance' and 'global law' have come to be discussed and debated in recent decades, there is still a persistent tendency to discuss 'the global' in a way that reduces it to exceptional moments, norms and events. Episodic, supra-national, 'international' (in a narrow sense), foreign, external, extraordinary and non-quotidian – these are the features that continue to define, and become attached to, 'global' moments and sites, and the order they are a part of. As Eve Darian-Smith has argued, socio-legal and theory-informed approaches to the relation between law and the global order often stay within, in order to depart from, the traditional dichotomies between international and domestic legal and between social and economic orders, and in doing so they naturalise those dichotomies (Darian-Smith, 2013: 1–20). As a result, approaches to 'the global' tend to be confined to particular instantiations when something external – i.e., non-native – pierces the national veil, or when an 'international' event is able to capture 'local' imaginations across disparate geographies. However, this neat analytical arrangement I have just described is constantly surpassed by the intense dynamism of our present moment, and most importantly, perhaps, by the structural forces that have come to underpin most aspects of our everyday existence. Capitalism and its legal dimensions, as we will see in this chapter, are key organising vectors of this new but long-in-the-making reality. They have become important underlying aspects of our global order, forcing us to redefine what were once believed to be the natural limits of the international, the separation between global structural forces and pure ideas of agency and, above all, pristine readings of the local (see, e.g., Eslava, 2014, 2015, 2017). Rather than neatness, what we witness today, therefore, are overlapping ground-level processes of mutual reconstruction and recolonisation involving both sides of these dichotomies. These processes are reconstituting both places and subjects that until recently were considered to be guarded by either the nation-state, typically post-colonial states in the case of the Global South, or more generally by the power of human resilience or localism.

Perhaps one of the best known (and still one of the most useful) terms employed to define this enmeshing of the global and the local is Zygmunt Bauman's concept of 'glocalization' (Bauman, 1998). First emerging as a business concept in the 1980s, but then famously theorised and brought into the social sciences by Bauman in the heyday of globalisation studies in the 1990s, the term glocalization tries to capture the way in which localities all over the world have been turned into 'local laboratories' in which countless global forces and issues, like population flows, neoliberal adjustments and environmental degradation, are experienced and dealt with (Bauman, 2013: 2). In such localities, both global phenomena and localised responses to them are 'put into test and either rejected or incorporated in daily practice' (ibid.). According to Bauman, 'this is what has stripped to-day "localities", and big cities more drastically than any other among them, of a considerable part of their past autonomy and their earlier capacity of composing and running their own agenda' (ibid.). Simultaneously, however, this process has invested localities 'with an unprecedented importance through assigning to them a crucial role in the job of sustaining the present-day global order' (ibid.). For Bauman, glocalization should therefore be understood as a creator of 'local workshops' where global problems are felt, recycled and perhaps repaired (ibid.).

Bauman's analysis continues to have traction because of his invitation to approach globalisation as a widespread and dynamic process, one that is not simply restricted to economic variables but in which social, historical and material concerns are equally left, right and centre. His analysis also invites us to pay attention to the way in which what results from the encounter between the global and the local are rarely neat syntheses, carefully delineated third entities, or simply the global or local, but the 'glocal'. If there are processes of 'glocalization', we need to accept that they take place in messy and uneven social, political, cultural and economic terrains and that they produce messy outcomes.

This point about the out-of-syncness – the out-of-whackness – that is usually involved in the global-local encounter is particularly important because what we can witness at the ground level, as I began to suggest above, are re-arrangements and clashes that take place on landscapes that are neither uniform nor evenly 'modern' or fully capitalist. In other words, tectonic confrontations rather than mere processes of synthesis seem to be the norm in the meeting of the global and the local. The implications of this point are especially poignant if we pay attention to the disorderly margins of the global order, as Jean and John Comaroff have called them (Comaroff and Comaroff, 2006: 1–56). In the post-colony which often inhabits these margins, we witness more than just the clash between hegemonic and alternative socio-political forces. Here, in the South – the South in the South or the South in the North, which is home to a far more explicit set of 'laboratories' than the centre, the North in the South or the North in the North – there is also a whole armoury of alternative cosmologies and popular imaginaries that refuse, and have always refused, to be fully enrolled in the project of modernity. In communication with, but resistant to being totally subsumed in, the tide of modernity, the guardians of such cosmologies counterpoise, negotiate and re-render 'the global' through their own categories, forms and images. Again, the end result is not a series of neat products, pure defeats or victories. These outcomes are dense, the products of dense struggles, in a dense global world.

In his now-classic study, *The Modernity of Witchcraft*, first published in French in 1995, Peter Geschiere demonstrated how this line of thinking about globalisation can help us make sense of the proliferation in the use of magic, witchcraft and mediums in recent decades, particularly in the South (Geschiere, 1997). For Geschiere, '[i]t is true that modern techniques . . . now penetrate the remotest corners of the globe', and that 'one cannot deny that peripheral groups are now increasingly involved in the world market not only as producers but also as consumers: new fashions and the latest gadgets turn up everywhere' – a process that has only accelerated since the publication of his study (ibid.: 8). However, he continues, and this is crucial, 'the paradox is that these processes do not lead to increasing cultural uniformity – the global victory of Coca-Cola, so much feared by anthropologists like Lévi-Strauss' (ibid.). On the contrary,

> the modern world . . . is marked by increasingly cultural heterogeneity. Idiosyncratic cultural traits are grafted upon new means of communication and processes of commodification: "traditional" more often "pseudotraditional," traits are reproduced in new forms and on a wider scale.
>
> (ibid.)

Behind the ease with which the world of the 'traditional' as well as the supernatural have come to incorporate and respond to the new power relations of the money economy, however, lie 'sharp feelings of impotence' (ibid.: 9). These feelings reflect a desire to find meaning in the drastic politico-economic changes of the neoliberal age together with ways of 'gain[ing] control over them' (ibid.: 3). In this context, the appearance of ghosts – the figures in which I am most interested in this chapter – should not, any more than magic, mediums and witchcraft, be understood as expressions of savage animism. They are instead the 'dark side' of kinship in the domestic sphere, and of the state and the global order in the public sphere. They are responses to the need to 'have a grip on power' (ibid.: 8–9). They are 'dark' – and here I am paraphrasing Geschiere – because they express the frightening realisation that there is jealousy and therefore aggression within the family, the state and the world, where there should be trust and solidarity (ibid.: 11).

Just as E.E. Evans-Pritchard noted in regards to the use of oracles and magic by the Azande in the transient terrain of southern Sudan under British colonial rule; or as David Lan argued in his study of spirit mediums in the context of the guerrilla anti-colonial liberation movement in Zimbabwe; or as Michael Taussig pointed out in his ethnography of shamanic practices in post-colonial Colombia, what we will see in the story I am about to tell, therefore, is 'the non-modern', 'the otherworldly', entering into 'co-operation' with marginal communities facing a world that is in convulsion (Evans-Pritchard, 1976; Lan, 1985; Taussig, 1987). Appealing once again to the analysis of the Comarroffs, when ghosts appear – like witches or spirits – they represent 'a finely calibrated gauge of the impact of global cultural and economic forces on local relations' (Comaroff and Comaroff, 1993: xxviii–xxix). They are 'modernity's prototypical malcontents' (ibid.). And, as such, they must be understood as the consolidated legacy of these immaterial forces – a legacy so intense that it grows a body of its own every now and then. These ghosts are the palpable manifestations of a dense struggle, in an equally dense global world.

Tellingly, this continuous and increasing presence of the otherworldly has been accompanied by a sort of a 'metamorphosis' in the reading of ghosts and the ghostly in recent years. Once understood, and understandable, only as fakes, mistakes or, at best, anachronistic plot devices which could be discarded or not depending on one's level of 'mysticism' or 'primitivism', today ghosts have become 'influential conceptual metaphors permeating global popular culture and academia alike' (del Pilar Blanco and Peeren, 2013: 1–5). Ghosts and other subterranean forces are now read in terms of 'spectres' and the questions unleashed by 'spectrality' (del Pilar Blanco and Peeren, 2010: x). In this re-reading, what has been gained is an appreciation of the importance of paying attention to the permanent disjunctures – 'the complex and often contradictory processes of globalisation, (trans)nationalism, and localisation' – that lie at the very core of the project of modernity (ibid.: xiv). Following Derrida, it can be argued that ghosts and spectres should be read, in this context, as figurations that, in signalling about what is being lost and what is in danger, force us to accept a '*politics* of memory, of inheritance, and of generations' (Derrida, 1993, as cited in del Pilar Blanco and Peeren, 2013: 7, emphasis in original). Always hesitantly and always in unruly patterns, according to María del Pilar Blanco and Esther Peeren, ghosts draw our attention to 'the insufficiency of the present moment, as well as the disconsolations and erasures of the past, and a tentative hopefulness for future resolutions' (del Pilar Blanco and Peeren, 2013: 16).

In this 'spectral turn' that has accompanied the arrival of the twenty-first century, ghosts express the moment 'when your bearings in the world lose direction' (Gordon, 2008: xvi). Key here is the insight that ghosts reveal themselves to people in 'complex' situations; to people for whom 'life is complicated' (ibid.: 1). In this moment, as Avery Gordon has put it, people tell stories about 'themselves, about their troubles, about their social worlds, and about their society's problems'. These stories weave between and become entangled with 'what is immediately available as a story and what [people's] imaginations are reaching toward' (ibid.: 4). The actuality of ghosts, according to this take, must not necessarily lie at the centre of the analysis. What is crucial, instead, is the fact that they actually surface in the social realm, and that in so doing they speak about a world of troubles and in trouble.

Ghosts must, in other words, be understood as 'a constituent element of modern social life' (ibid.: 7). However, they do seem to surface, more often than not, in spaces and before people that are located in precarious positions within the global order and its dominant rationalities. This is where the law comes in. 'It is through law that persons, variously figured, gain or lose definition', according to Colin Dayan, and it is through law that persons 'become victims of prejudice or inheritors of privilege' (Dayan, 2011: xi). Once discriminated against or stripped of personhood, those at the losing end 'become inconsequential' (ibid.). 'The unloved, unwanted, and abandoned are not always', however, 'left alone' (ibid.: 35). Sometimes, even worse, they acquire this condition by being managed, manipulated, even 'made ready for predation' (ibid.: 35). Dayan has for this reason associated the proliferation of ghost-talk and spectral visions with the long history of Western law from the Enlightenment onwards, and the associated consolidation of capitalism from that time to the present. Our law, which presents itself as disenchanted and therefore as rational and neutral, is, according to this reading, the scaffolding that underpins a structure within which ongoing dispossession can take place (ibid.: xii). This process is particularly sinister because of law's endemic but covert role in the malfunctioning of our global world (ibid.: 9). In its capacity to redefine persons and normalise differences usually occluded from view, law creates people and spaces where the presence of death, fear and panic is never far away. Again, in people's efforts to get a grip on this situation, ghosts and spectres manifest as an entanglement of 'what is immediately available' and what the imagination is 'reaching toward' (Gordon, 2008: 4). They often act in 'co-operation' with those who witness them. As Christiane Wilke has described in her work on haunted courts and judgments, ghosts often speak about justice: 'they are reminders of a need for justice and can point to the impossibility of justice within the constraints of the law or a courtroom' (Wilke, 2010: 77).

The commitment of the ethnographic gaze to making sense of life in its fullest, towards a different way of knowing and writing about our world, makes it a particularly suitable vantage point from which to grasp the connection between ghosts, law and the global order. Adopting this gaze can, I suggest, help us understand the role of international and domestic norms and institutions, as well as the political economy they hold in place, in the constitution of local everyday realities, with all their violence and phantasmagoria. It can also help us to grasp the struggles that are experienced in the midst of this configuration, and the languages and images that emerge from them. People's dreams, their most intimate visions, are informed by and themselves speak about the global order and its permutations on the ground. Turning an ethnographic gaze on this excess can enable us, in turn, to build a politics of solidarity in the course of our engagement with 'most of the world' (Chatterjee, 2004). This solidarity accepts the challenge of fostering new legal and political forms of support for popular struggles, but defines itself against the demonisation of popular imaginations. It advances what Gordon, thinking with Taussig, identifies as 'a sympathetic magic': a magic that is 'necessary because in the world and between us as analysts and the worlds we encounter to translate into world-making words are hauntings, ghosts and gaps, seething absences, and muted presences' – all of them social realities that we should not go on forgetting (Gordon, 2008: 21; see also Taussig, 1993).

Violence and the otherworldly

Some questions to restate the issue that concerns us here in a slightly different way: How can we make sense of popular struggles in this period of late capitalist modernity? What do the experiences, voices and visions of groups involved in such struggles tell us about the actual functioning of our world – a world mined with growing inequalities and ever more intrusive levels of bureaucratic managerial techniques, all of this held together by the increasing ubiquity of law? What does the silencing of the marginalised groups which engage in such struggles – and their refusal to be silenced – teach us about political action in our supposedly disenchanted times? And, more specifically, what can we learn from the arrival of otherworldly forces – a ghost, for example – in their midst?

In what follows, I explore these questions by returning to a body of visual and ethnographic material that I gathered over a period of six months in 2009, when I accompanied a group of IDPs in the city of Bogotá. The group was formed by around sixty families, most of them displaced from rural and semirural areas in the central part of Colombia. Like many of the other 7.7 million Colombians who have become victims of internal displacement since the mid-1980s (UNHRC, 2017; IDMC, 2017), these families had been displaced from their lands as the Colombian civil war between official armed forces, paramilitary groups and guerrilla groups intensified under the two consecutive governments of Álvaro Uribe (2002–06 and 2006–10) and as the infamous 'War on Drugs' began a more virulent chapter in the country's history, thanks to US military aid and its 'Plan Colombia'.[1]

Over the course of the six months I spent with them, this group engaged in a long and unsuccessful protest for the recognition of their rights as IDPs[2] – rights confirmed in international treaties, in national legislation and by the Colombian Constitutional Court (see, e.g., Ibáñez and Velásquez, 2008; Universidad de los Andes-The Brookings Institution and Acción Social, 2009). Their protest was directed against the local administration of Bogotá, the national government and various international institutions, especially the United Nations High Commissioner for Refugees (UNHCR).[3] During these six months, they squatted in the central and most important plaza of Bogotá and Colombia: the *Plaza de Bolívar*; after that, they occupied a large park that had recently been inaugurated on the edges of the city centre, the *Parque Tercer Milenio*, along with other displaced families; and finally, they ended up living for several weeks in a 'temporary housing solution'. This temporary accommodation (which I will refer to as 'the refuge') was provided by the local administration in exchange for their decision to accept its request that they leave *Parque Tercer Milenio* and stop occupying other public spaces (Figures 1.1–1.3).

The protest of this group of families was widely covered in Colombia's print media and television news, and their occupation of public spaces became a topic of heated debate and conversation among local elites and politicians at all levels of government. News media during this time carried sensationalist headlines and expressed excessive concerns about the pressure put by this group and other families of IDPs on the city's services and infrastructure (see, e.g., El Tiempo.com, 2009).

After six months of fighting for the fulfilment of their rights, the group abandoned their protest on the basis of an agreement that they signed with national and local authorities, with the oversight of international officials. The authorities promised in that agreement to provide each of the families with a stable housing solution, regular humanitarian help and resources with which to establish a productive project. Time has proven, however, that the group's deep suspicions about the authorities' willingness to honour the agreement were correct. As I am writing this, almost a decade after the families ended their protest, the promises made in the agreement have still not quite been fulfilled, just as the families had feared.[4]

In spite of their doubts, the families signed the agreement because, by that stage, they were physically, emotionally and mentally exhausted. Their protest, especially during its final weeks, was marked by internal divisions, domestic violence among group members, confrontations with the police and long, restless nights. They arrived at this unhappy state thanks to a combination of many different factors – including the length of their protest, the refusal of different levels of government to take

Figure 1.1 Group of IDPs in *Plaza de Bolívar.*

responsibility for their situation, their own memories of war and displacement, the chronic poverty suffered by members of the group, and the claustrophobia generated by living crammed together in the refuge for many months.

As I will describe in more detail below, the refuge was an enormous, hollow, enclosed industrial shed, located in a derelict part of the city centre. It was guarded by police officers, and routinely visited by national officials and waves of social workers from the local administration. Occasionally, international delegations and religious groups also visited the shed. These actors ran questionnaires on the members of the group, collected information from them and asked them, again and again, for proof of their identity as displaced persons. Rarely, however, did any of these actors arrive at

Figure 1.2 IDPs' occupation of *Parque Tercer Milenio*.

Figure 1.3 Refuge for IDPs offered by the local administration.

the shed with essential goods or clothing, or with the offer of any long-lasting solutions to their problems (Figures 1.4–1.5).

In combination, all of these factors led the group to realise that neither the local administration, nor the national government, nor any of the international institutions involved were prepared to pay real attention to their claims or to be moved by their protest. After six months of mobilisation, many of the group reached the conclusion that they had no choice but to endure their situation, pack up their stuff and move on with their lives.[5]

What I would like to discuss here is perhaps the most puzzling part of those six months. It is only with time that I started to make sense and realise the importance of thinking through what this group of IDPs shared with me about a ghost that came to interrupt their nights in the refuge, halfway through the time they were housed there. It took me a long time to realise that this ghost – a white woman, with long hair, seen quietly strolling around the refuge at nighttime – was an embodiment of the group's frustrations with the global order at that particular point in their protest. It was at this point that it became all too clear to them that this global order had placed them at the centre of a tight arrangement of institutions, jurisdictions, legal norms and economic interests, while remaining largely unresponsive to their claims.

As I began to suggest in the previous section, in inviting the reader to revisit this episode with me, I wish to think about our current global order as a site of dense struggle. This idea refers, in the particular case of the group of IDPs I followed, to the innate complexity of global patterns of accumulation, wealth distribution,

Figure 1.4 Inner rooms of the refuge.

Figure 1.5 Main entrance of the refuge.

jurisdictional realms, administrative procedures and laws that closely follow current localised injustices. These patterns comprise the very infrastructure of the current global order in our time of late capitalist modernity.[6]

The idea of dense struggle points, at the same time, and again in the case of this group of IDPs, to the excess of violence *and* otherworldly forces, emotions and phantasmic embodiments that accompanies today's global order no less than the patterns just described. This excess is indeed part, as Georges Bataille would put it, of the 'general economy' of our world (see especially Bataille, 1991). As the events that I discuss in the next sections show only too clearly, this excess of violence and otherworldly forces – of desires, dreams, fears and spectra – is systematically ignored, hidden away, managed and regularised by the official managerial practices and discourses enacted by local, national and international institutions and echoed by private actors and the vast majority of citizens. Each of these actors are frequently, if not permanently, engaged in a struggle to conceal this violence and regularise this otherworldliness, recoding it either as the seemingly inevitable surpluses of today's order or as folk reactions to the tide of late modernity. The aim of this recoding, I suggest, is deactivation. Its objective is to present the material and spectral dark sides of today as irrational upshots that should not interrupt the business of everyday life and the motions of the global economy.

As Susan Marks has argued, our failure to pay attention to this violence and human drama is not the result of ignorance. Far from it. Not paying attention, turning our gaze away is an effective ideological mechanism that keeps us functioning in the face

Figure 1.6 IDPs at *Parque Tercer Milenio.*

of a world ridden by systemic (environmental, economic, political and social) issues and by our complicity in their production (Marks, 2009: 49). Regardless of our constructed ignorance, however, the excess of violence and otherworldliness that I have been talking about here finds itself re-surfacing, densifying, in different shapes in the vernaculars of popular politics (see especially Chatterjee, 2004). In doing so, this excess ends up accompanying the days, and especially the nights, of subjects who, like the IDPs that I followed in Bogotá, are critical 'for' and 'of' today's processes of global ordering (Tuitt and Fitzpatrick, 2003: xi) (Figure 1.6).

Oh yes, that, our world

In the preamble of *The Communist Manifesto*, originally published in 1848, Karl Marx and Friedrich Engels made the dictum:

> A spectre is haunting Europe – the spectre of communism. All the powers of old Europe have entered into a holy alliance to exorcise this spectre: Pope and Tsar, Metternich and Guizot, French Radicals and German police-spies.
>
> (Marx and Engels, 2012: 73)

History has proven Marx and Engels correct. Communism was not the only force in the rising. Counter-revolutionary forces were also getting ready to squash it. And this still seems to be the case. The dissatisfaction felt throughout Europe at the time at which *The Communist Manifesto* was being written, and that has grown, spread and mutated into different forms across the world since then, has been vanquished, time and again, by capitalism's resurgence in varied guises – from yesterday's (neo) colonial ventures to today's (post)neoliberal (re)structurings. That today the 'world's eight richest billionaires control the same wealth between them as the poorest half of the globe's population' is just one telling fact that confirms this sad state of affairs (Elliot, 2017).

To affirm that law lies behind this situation would not be a surprise. But just to attest the obvious, one need only remember that there is not a single legal avenue available to significantly reverse the spiralling imbalances that today mark the global distribution of wealth and its accompanying processes of environmental decay, socio-spatial segregation, forced displacement and jobless growth, not to mention the urbanisation of poverty, the delegitimation of public action on the part of the state, and the rise of private security forces, paramilitarism and vigilantism across the planet (see, e.g., Davis, 2006; Harvey, 2006: 9–68; Abrahamsen and Williams, 2010; Li, 2013; Moore, 2015). After all, these ills are legally constructed phenomena one and all, making it impossible for law to challenge them in any structural sense. Law has been, for all these reasons, instrumental in the constitution of our lopsided present. And even when used to counter such trends, law seems able to do little more than create partial individual victories, or liminal islands of hope, with limited resources and bureaucratic arbitrariness at all times being the common denominator (see, e.g., Gupta, 2012; Morss, 2013). As I began to suggest in the first section, law makes and unmakes persons, and it is through law that they become 'victims of prejudice or inheritors of privilege' (Dayan, 2011: xi).

It is in this way that the triumph of capitalist modernity has generated a particular kind of world. This is a world which reifies itself before our eyes, and which trickles down from the sites of high international and transnational manoeuvres to national machinations, to local arrangements – to those minute practices and legal relations that form the day-to-day of our current sociality.

For these reasons, an enabling blindness, coupled with enduring legal fictions, jurisdictional constructions and a particular kind of zombie-like economics, as Ben Fine has put it, have come to play a key function in the maintenance of our everyday existence (Fine, 2009). These are the outer expressions of that 'spirit', of that ethos or disposition of capitalism and modernity so famously described by Max Weber (Weber, 2009 [1920]).[7] I will return to that 'spirit' shortly. For now, however, it is important to consider how these phenomena enable us to walk on our streets, feeling secure in the assumption that there is still something that resembles a collective project and a moral and political horizon within our political communities. But as soon as one starts questioning that blindness, scratches the surface of those legal fictions or cross-examines the zombie and the 'modernity' that it feeds on, a hard reality emerges from the shadows – asking, demanding, from one, you, everyone: 'The people without housing are asking for their rights' (Figure 1.7).

In the scenario I have just set up, in which the violence generated by the current order is constantly covered up, expressions of dissatisfaction and claims for redress

Figure 1.7 Placard used during a march organised during the IDPs' protest: 'The people without housing are asking for their rights.'

coming from those who have been obliterated must be properly justified. Yet this is not all. As the group of IDPs that I followed in Bogotá found out, those who decide today to contest the status quo must also be ready to engage in endless Kafkaesque exercises if they are to be able to locate some of those multiple authorities and elusive forces that govern their lives, for these authorities and forces play continuous tricks of mimesis and vanishings on them. These tricks are backed up again by law and are consequential to a particular kind of economic rationality – one that has at its heart an 'economy of sacrifice' (Orford, 2005). As the group of IDPs learnt, they were not simply a collection of expendable lives. They were, instead, a group of important subjects of management and regularisation. Theirs was a condition which did not imply a solution to their problems, but rather the administration – really, the didactical curtailing – of their desires and aspirations, while the world continued to race around them. This left them asking local, national and global officials, 'Leaders, face the displaced population. Stop hiding away' (Figure 1.8).

Confronting this systematic management and regularisation of the violence that they experience and their aspirations for a better life, people who, like this group of IDPs, today decide to go to the streets to fight must also prove that they are not criminals, that they are not against the law. And here we should understand not being criminal, not being *facinorosus*, on the basis of the Latin origins of the concept: that of being in a state of wickedness, sinfulness or, better, having departed the realm of proper judgment. The possibility of asking the system to respond to its own collateral

Figure 1.8 Placard used during a march organised during the IDPs' protest: 'Leaders, face the displaced population. Stop hiding away.'

effects has become not just difficult for the 'criminal' in this sense but *de facto*, if not *de jure*, illegal and in addition, an act of madness. Facing this criminalisation of dissent, and without many resources, the group of IDPs could only claim, on a fragile placard: 'We are displaced people. We are not criminals' (Figure 1.9).

Membership in official political communities – particularly for those in precarious positions in the Global South, as well as in the Global North – requires today, for these reasons, a readiness to accept that the prevalent order is neither in favour of marginalised communities nor in a position to exclude them fully. Here lie the roots of a particular model of political membership, very distant from the romantic liberal promise of citizenship through political assertion. Realising this should make us aware that a larger 'pedagogy of disenchantment', as I would call it, runs beneath current practices of managing and regularising the violence endured, and the aspirations felt, by people at the margins of the global order (see Eslava, 2012).

Citizens placed in precarious positions need to learn to conduct themselves in a strategic way: not aspiring too much, always conscious of their place within the grand scheme of things. Their citizenship is one attained and secured through carefully managed disillusionment. Theirs should be a 'citizenship by disenchantment'. The violence, frustrations and fears that ignite, frame and underpin their claims must, therefore, be inhibited and kept under control. And in this sense, their struggles and personal experiences of the world are dense, but this density must not be fully articulated. This form of dense struggle is the contemporary version of that 'spectre' to

Figure 1.9 Placard used during a march organised during the IDPs' protest: 'We are displaced [people]. We are not criminals.'

which Marx and Engels referred in *The Communist Manifesto*, although now it is a spectre suppressed (or, rather, highly disarticulated) by tighter biopolitical mechanisms and a more omnipresent form of global economy.

This management and regularisation of violence and suppression of subaltern aspirations is terribly present in today's rapidly globalising cities in the Global South. These cities have become ideal spaces for the reproduction of global capital, as well as living spaces for a new global elite. In these cities, the pressure to show developmental results while remaining competitive and financially proficient has produced an explosive cocktail of new biopolitical technologies and material and extra-material forces that are resulting in successive waves of class clashes and social agitation.[8] Like any other kind of spectre, the suppressed aspirations and violence, as endured now by urban peripheral subjects, are only waiting to surface, either in the form of new political upheavals, or as something else (see Figure 1.10).

History has presented us, thus, with another lesson to learn from Marx and Engels's opening dictum in *The Communist Manifesto*. The past couple of centuries have revealed that, besides the question of capitalist expansion at the material level, a battle has been underway at the level of metaphor, emotional forces and, for that matter, also spirits, spectres, ghosts, phantoms and even monsters (McNally, 2011).

Marx and Engels were clear about this. For them, the 'spectre of communism' was haunting Europe in the middle of the nineteenth century. But insofar as there was a spectre of communism around, there was also the 'spirit of capitalism'. As frames

Figure 1.10 IDPs protesting in Bogotá's *Plaza de Bolivar.*

of mind and ideological representations of the world, as *weltanschauung*, communism and capitalism were both subjectively loaded from the start. They were powerful circumscriptions of emotions and desires from their moment of conceptualisation – so much so that the same Marx and Engels claimed, immediately after their famous opening dictum, that it was necessary to give a distinctive political party formation to the 'spectre of communism'. The abstract spirit, the abstract body of thoughts and dreams for a future of subaltern rule, had in their view to be embodied, incarnated as it were, into formal politics and effective material forms if already-embodied forms of capitalist rule were to be confronted effectively.

Being aware of this immaterial, subjective, even uncanny, all-too-human side of capitalism and communism reminds us how the battles of our present still involve

Figure 1.11 March of IDPs on the streets of Bogotá.

both forces and vernacular expressions that exceed economic technicalities, secular politics and secular law. When these forces and vernaculars turn into spectres, what surfaces is what Tarik Kochi describes as a messianic conception of justice – one that may not be achievable within the confines of the present but which still calls for a different world and a different law (Kochi, 2002) (Figure 1.11).

The modern uncanny

Our present is marked by the emergence of new forms of re-enchantment and by the rise of new occult economies and allegations of witchcraft. Spectres and ghosts, in this context, have come to populate those same spaces created in, and by, our current global order: from 'new developmental states', to rural areas in transition, to the rapidly globalising cities of the South, to gated communities, to new Christian churches, to humanitarian projects, to 'native' jurisdictions and 'ethnic' villages (see, e.g., Comaroff and Comaroff, 1999; Dolan, 2002; Robbins, 2004; Tomlinson, 2009; O'Neil, 2010; James, 2012; Johnson, 2013).

This uncanny side of our present is the outcome of the contradictory effects of the current political and economic order and its culture. At a moment in which consumption has come to occupy a central place in social reproduction, political dissent is readily managed, and when very few are legitimately enriched while many others are impoverished, or brought *just above* the poverty line, social sacrifice on behalf of economic proficiency is seen as a public good, and state action is reduced to the task of coordinating political discourses without sufficient means to respond to social needs or actually to curb private power. In this scenario, the occult has come to play a crucial role in public and private life. And the occult has returned, as it has always done, in order to incarnate the very unspeakable violence, aspirations and fears lying beneath what first appears as prosaic, everyday life (Figure 1.12).

The effects of this configuration of forces became clear to me when members of the group of IDPs I followed in Bogotá began to tell me that a ghost had begun to appear during nighttime in the refuge in which they had been housed by the local administration when they agreed to leave *Parque Tercer Milenio*. The entrance of the uncanny into their protest at this point was, as I learnt, a response to the way in which the refuge suddenly came to symbolise the inability of the current order to respond to the needs of the group and to their experience of violence and displacement.

Soon after the group of IDPs arrived at the refuge, they became aware that they had moved from a moment of open confrontation with the administration to a stage of early regularisation and incorporation into the dynamics of the state. They had, of course, already long been a part of the state and the official order. For instance, they had already committed to presenting themselves according to the official concept of IDPs. The difference was, however, that before arriving at the refuge, this self-understanding – this visualisation of themselves as IDPs – was still open-ended. It was an unfulfilled claim and, for this reason, it was somehow full of potential.

The claim of this group to be a group of IDPs and their fight to obtain the rights promised by this category had ignited their protest and had given them a purpose for

Figure 1.12 IDPs at *Parque Tercer Milenio*.

which to keep demonstrating on the streets of the city. For this reason, on the day the administration offered them the refuge, they were thrilled. I was with them at that moment, taking down their tents, packing up their belongings and then travelling in the bus to their new, as yet unknown home. The atmosphere was tense but also, above all, it was a time to celebrate. It was an occasion to take photographs, to feel proud of their efforts, to leave behind, at least in part, the marginal position they had been occupying up to that point. They were happy to be recognised by the state as subjects of special attention (Figure 1.13). But as soon as they arrived at the refuge their feelings started to change (Figure 1.14). Hemmed in by a crowd of police officers, social workers from the local administration and journalists ready to capture their anxious faces, they had to form a long queue in front of the refuge and allow the authorities to scrutinise their pasts, once again, before they were allowed in. As the hours passed and anxieties about the mis-recording of personal details and the splitting up of families turned into panic, a feeling of frustration began to emerge. Dreams were quickly being put into check. Big expectations slammed immediately.

As days passed in the refuge, the group realised that they had lost the public visibility that they had enjoyed in the *Plaza de Bolivar* and *Parque Tercer Milenio*, where their protest was on full display to pedestrians, car drivers, business owners and the media. At the same time, they also began to experience the uneasiness that anyone might feel living and sleeping in a big, enclosed and empty industrial shed. Entry and exit controlled, with high walls, bare ceiling, large spaces, collective toilets, and organised almost like a labyrinth, the architecture of the shed was formally soulless

Figure 1.13 Leaving *Parque Tercer Milenio.*

Figure 1.14 Arriving for the first time at the refuge.

but emotionally charged. It transmitted to the group the manner in which the state, and more generally the current global order, was prepared to deal with them: through formal, bureaucratic procedures and as second-class subjects only (Figure 1.15).

These feelings seemed to be confirmed by two additional facts. The refuge was located at the edge of the city centre, in a dilapidated and rough area, occupied by automobile and motorcycle repair shops and brothels and controlled by petty drug dealers. Second, the facility had been used in the past by the local administration as a shelter for homeless people and stray dogs. For the group of IDPs the new feeling of isolation and the architecture, location and institutional memory of the refuge were devastating.

In addition to these features, the general organisation and daily running of the refuge was disconcerting. The refuge was divided into two large zones, each of them of equal size: a South Zone and a North Zone – the latter being the one in which the group was housed. Each of the zones had its own entrance on opposite sides of the large block in which the refuge was located. A thick wall divided the two zones, and only two small metal doors connected the South Zone and the North Zone. These doors were permanently locked and were only used by the officials in charge of the refuge (Figures 1.16–1.17).

When the group first arrived, the whole facility was empty. However, only a few days later, the local administration started to house other groups of IDPs in the South Zone of the building. These were mostly IDPs with an Afro-Colombian background, who also had been protesting in *Parque Tercer Milenio*.

Figure 1.15 Main entrance to refuge (North Zone).

The group I was following and the group of newly arrived IDPs were advised by officials to avoid contact with each other. According to the officials, the administration was negotiating the demands of each group separately, and mingling with each other would only cause trouble and confusion.

I was impressed that both groups stuck to this order. But the fear of ruining what little rapport that they had established with the authorities, as well as tensions between the groups based on assumptions about race, and a general suspicion on the part of each about the other, in a situation of competition for scarce resources, was enough to keep them separated. The problem was, however, that they were all living under the same roof, and their daily lives were separated only by a wall. This made IDPs

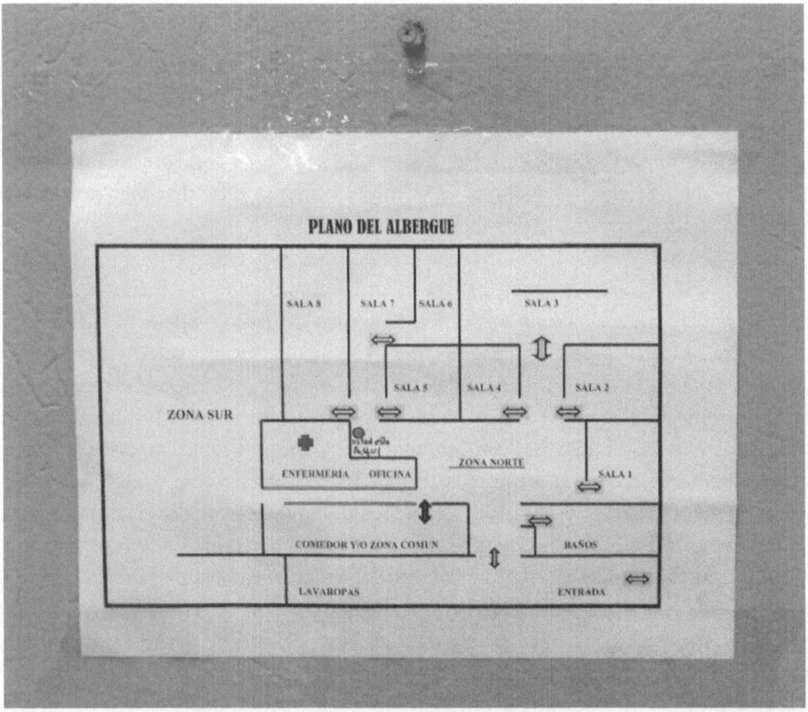

Figure 1.16 Organisation of the North Zone section of the refuge, according to one of the maps put up by the administration on different walls of the facility.

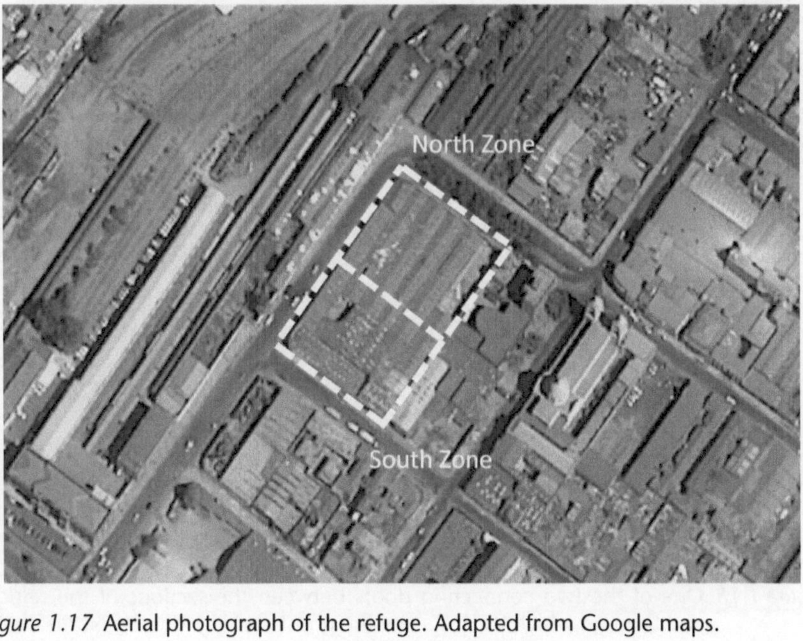

Figure 1.17 Aerial photograph of the refuge. Adapted from Google maps.

on both sides anxious about the possibility that the other group might be receiving preferential treatment from authorities, and hence about how the other group was handling their negotiations. Common noises and the occasional scream from people arguing on the other side of the refuge were the only response that they got to these anxieties and the many questions they generated.

The daily experience of living in the refuge became, as a result of this, more and more oppressive, certainly for the group of IDPs that I followed, and no doubt for the other group as well. It was characterised by endless, circular discussions about their future. On some occasions during these discussions, members of the group would fantasise about what they could do if the authorities decided to fulfil their rights – fantasies that ranged from returning immediately to their places of origin to throwing a big party to commemorate the occasion. Yet in other moments, the common topic of conversation was the authorities' disinterest and the idea that their relocation to the refuge had been a strategy to silence their dissatisfactions and hence to erase the violence that underpinned their personal stories of displacement. Anxiety, fear and a profound sense of shame about having placed their hopes of fighting the official order in the hands of that order itself began to surface at these moments. These feelings were only aggravated by the poverty that coloured every aspect of their day-to-day existence, and by the fight among local, national and international authorities about which was responsible for the group's fate.

It was in this context of strong obfuscation that the group began to tell me that the ghost had started to appear in the refuge at nighttime. According to them, the eerie

Figure 1.18 One of the two connecting doors between the sections of the refuge and through which the IDPs saw the ghost coming into the North Zone.

figure of a tall, white woman with long hair had been sighted by several members of the group coming into the North Zone through one of the small metal doors that connected the two sections of the refuge. The ghost had been seen walking near the collective toilets and occasionally entering into the areas of the refuge that were used as dormitories. Several of those who had reportedly seen this ghost claimed that it resembled other IDPs who had been at some point part of their protest, or who were still part of the group but who were not sleeping in the refuge on that particular night. The ghost, this all seemed to suggest, appeared in the form of a creole figure in distress – one occupying a transient position, very much like the IDPs themselves. During this time, children in the refuge began suddenly to cry at night, and adults were having intense nightmares (Figures 1.18–1.19).

Figure 1.19 Section of the collective toilets.

The ghost became a regular feature of life in the refuge for some weeks. Even police officers stationed at the refuge began to share their own version of these events, confirming that they, too, had seen the ghost. Interestingly, the arrival of the uncanny at this point in the protest became something that everyone in the group agreed upon and related to the difficult situation that they were experiencing. This seemed to be of particular significance, given that the group was already going through intense internal debates about whether they had lost track of their efforts to resist their marginalisation by agreeing to move to the refuge, and whether local, national and international agencies were ever going to be willing to recognise their rights.

The ghost became for them, in this way, a collective confirmation that their situation had reached a new low, and that being in the refuge had exacerbated their powerlessness in relation to the authorities. Even though I never saw it myself, the ghost acted for me, too, as an entry point, allowing me to understand, to a much more intense degree, the group's deep frustrations with a system that, rather than responding to their demands, was instead asphyxiating their aspirations and silencing their experience of violence.

Ghostly real

As we just saw in the last section, one of the most perplexing circumstances that surrounded the appearance of the ghost in the refuge was that it occurred at the precise moment at which the group of IDPs formally entered into the realm of the official. It could just as plausibly have occurred earlier, when they were protesting in perhaps more difficult conditions, at *Plaza de Bolívar* or *Parque Tercer Milenio*. But instead, the ghost waited for the group to get closer to the official order – to get within the official as such, as symbolised by the refuge – before revealing herself.

In many significant ways, therefore, the emergence of the ghost during the protest at this point ran against the notion of the official – with its different practices, logics, spaces and levels of government – as the site of secular political practices, economic circulation and social reproduction. It ran against the view of the official as the archetypal, already-disenchanted realm of capitalist modernity, the official as an 'iron cage' (Weber, 2004 [1919]). Instead, when the group came face-to-face with the official, what they found was a site inundated with murky practices, inbuilt biases, administrative uncertainties – above all, a place in which they were forced to learn the lesson that their situation was *their own* problem, regardless of what the law seemed to say.

This was, of course, a hard lesson to learn. The official, as embedded in the state, remained the main, the hegemonic, space for ensuring their political existence in this world, and perhaps the only agent capable of helping them engage with the economic system on a less unequal footing (Figure 1.20).

But as the days in the refuge dragged on, it was confirmed to the group that the state, and the political and economic order in which the state was entrenched, was not prepared to respond to their claims. And with this, the group came to understand that the current order, instead of being an already-disenchanted place, was in fact still a site plagued with erratic, mysterious behaviours.

Figure 1.20 IDPs marching in the streets of Bogotá and calling the state to fulfill its obligations towards its displaced population according to National Law 387/1997: 'The displaced population is part of Colombia. Fulfill Law 387.'

So instead of disenchantment as such, it struck me as I sat with them day after day, that what the group had begun to experience as it got closer to the official order was, once again, a 'pedagogy of disenchantment': a process designed to teach them not to aspire to too much, and to remain conscious of their (marginal) place within the grand scheme of things. They had to learn to restrain their aspirations and endure the violence that they had experienced and were continuing to experience. In particular, their close(r) encounter with the official taught them not to look too closely at the shadowy side of their times – of our current times.

The emergence of the ghost was compatible with this obscurity. And in being so, this inexplicable figure responded – paradoxically – to the need of the group to make sense of their situation, to have again some 'grip on power' (Geschiere, 1997: 8–9). Its appearance was not the return of pre-modern imaginaries within secular times. It was, instead, a contemporary form of phantasmagoria, a popular alter-modernity perhaps, attuned to the mysterious operations of the current global order, its laws and its economic forces. As Freud might have put it, human sites shot through with phantasmagoria like nightmares, dreams and ghostly appearances, stem not from the bizarre and the unexpected but rather from the conditions of 'normal' life (Freud, 1964 [1933]: 16). Ghosts appear when that very 'normal' life has 'become so intolerably distressing that the threatened ego throws itself into the arms of the unconscious instinctual forces in a desperate revolt' (ibid.) (Figure 1.21).

Figure 1.21 The IDPs' refuge.

Yet, and in spite of all this, the ghost had a positive side. Although very frightening when she appeared at night, she served as a common reference point for conversation during the day. This was incredibly important for the group given the harsh situation that they were experiencing, and the long, monotonous days, with little food, spent waiting for news from the authorities. The very incommensurability of the ghost also seems to have been a kind of sublime response to the way in which the official order (occasionally) addressed their needs. At a point at which the group realised that the state was only ready to interact with them as second-class citizens and through limited bureaucratic means (for example, through the temporary housing solution or through occasional distribution of vouchers to buy a narrow array of staples, as it is possible to see in Figure 1.22), the ghost appeared to somehow symbolise and hence to legitimate the deepness of the group's vulnerability and their struggle.

Of course, the legitimation offered by the ghost operated beyond a state-centric logic. Although also seen, as I mentioned above, by some of the police officers stationed at the refuge, it was largely incomprehensible to the authorities and their institutions. Even worse, it was read as an affirmation of the rural background and low formal education level of the group. Perhaps because of this ineffectiveness, or counter-effectiveness, the ghost ceased her nighttime visits to the refuge at a certain point. In fact, the more the frustration of the IDPs grew, the less she appeared. By the time the group had decided, as they eventually did after almost four months in the refuge, to sign an agreement with the local administration and stop their protest, she was long gone. Her presence – the excess that she had represented and the affective

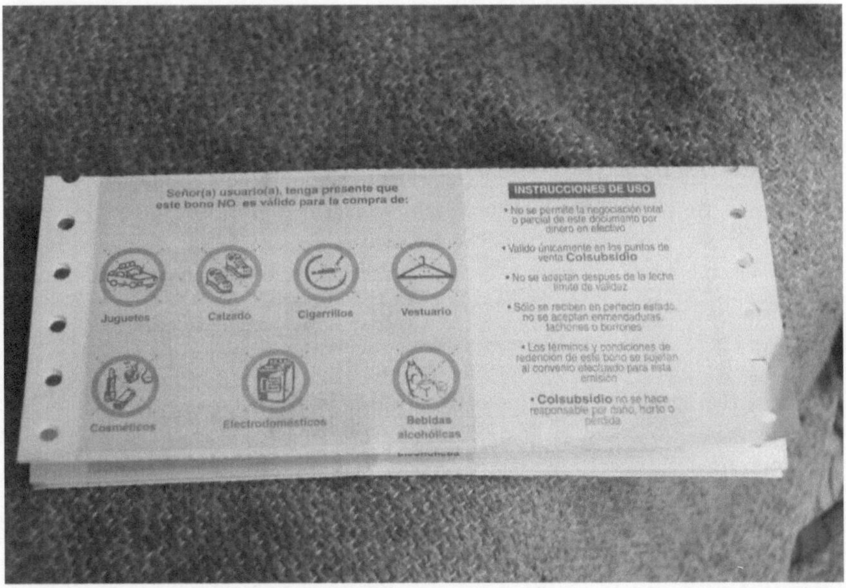

Figure 1.22 Vouchers given to IDPs to buy basic staples.

chains that she had dragged around with her – had been 'mopped up' by the official order, as Andreas Philippopoulos-Mihalopoulos would put it (Philippopoulos-Mihalopoulos, 2015: 107–150).

In one conversation, which took place not long after the agreement with the local administration was signed, one of the members of the group told me that the authorities had used an old, very well-known strategy with them that had been employed by hunters in the forests of Colombia for many generations. In order to capture monkeys, hunters used to drive the animals to their cave. Once there, the hunters would simply wait for the monkeys at the entrance to the cave, until, thanks to lack of food or drink, the monkeys would eventually try to escape. Drained of energy, the monkeys, like the IDPs, re-entered the world only to hand themselves over to their hunters. Still, after all the years that have passed since they eventually left the refuge, the mixture of the dispassionate technique of the stake-out and the violence of the hunt that is enclosed in this analogy remains the best illustration that I can think of to describe what the group of IDPs experienced during their protest. When they signed the agreement and in doing so gave up their struggle, they were physically and politically devastated, well on the road of disenchantment. But at the same time, the IDPs remained only too aware of all the otherworldly forces that underpinned their fate no less than they underpinned the global order that decided it.

What to do, then, with the appearance of a ghost in the midst of a popular struggle? I think we can see the start of an answer to this question in an article by the socio-legal scholar Oishik Sircar, published in 2012. Commenting on the limits of law in contemporary India – a country, like many others, that is saturated with rule of law and human rights talk – Sircar unveils some of the ways in which the present moment uses the legalisation of social dissatisfactions as a way to manage collective aspirations and political horizons. In this context, the law functions for those in need, as well as for their spectators, as *pharmakon*: as both cure and poison at the same time.[9]

To overcome this paradox – one that seems more prevalent in but by no means exclusive to the postcolonial Global South – Sircar invites us to explore alternative registers already present in social struggles such as the one I have examined in this chapter. His invitation is for us to advance a 'radical reimagination of emancipation', one 'that is not trapped in the [current order], but rather is embedded in and embodied by the everyday and ordinary struggles (Sircar, 2012: 527).' For Sircar, these alternative registers are useful, if not essential detours. They allow us to 'traverse uncharted paths to arrive at our favoured destinations' (ibid.: 569).

My aim in this chapter, a detour of its own, has been to locate the struggles of the group of IDPs that I followed in Bogotá in 2009 as both an element in and a consequence of the current global order. In doing so, I have situated the ghostly appearances that occurred in the refuge offered to them by the administration of Bogotá as the outcome of, and as a testament to, the way in which their claims for justice went unheard. In my attention to the interconnection between the situation of this group and the uncanny, I have sought to reveal the dense layering of forces that shape the daily life of many people who, like the IDPs, are engaged in processes of popular resistance.

In order to respond to the density of forces existing in such popular struggles, one should start by questioning then not only the limits of official administrative responses and their laws but also their apparently already-disenchanted quality. Official and legal responses operate in an enchanted milieu, while still pushing a pedagogy of disenchantment.

Departing from this understanding, it might be more possible to see how what appear, on the surface, to be no more than mundane practices of administration and legal management of social affairs are often, in fact, exercises aimed at obscuring the violence that is endured, every day, by 'most of the world' (Chatterjee, 2004). At the same time, remaining in the realm of enchantment enables us to see how the current global order, with its particular form of political economy, does not function as an indeterminate system in which suffering occurs simply thanks to mismanagement or the absence of law (Roy, 2014). Instead, we can remain aware of how the current global order works, as Marx and Engels put it in *The Communist Manifesto*, as 'a society that has conjured up such gigantic means of production and of exchange, [that] it is like the sorcerer who is no longer able to control the powers of the nether world [which] he has called up by his spells' (Marx and Engels, 2012: 78–79).

Notes

* I must thank Eric Loefflad for his research assistance, Anne Hughes, Julieta Lemaitre, Sally Engle Merry, Shaun McVeigh, Sundhya Pahuja and Juan Manuel Viatela for invaluable conversations and bibliographical suggestions that helped me to have a better grasp of the ideas and

visual material that I explore here, and especially to Andreas Philippopoulos-Mihalopoulos for his insightful editorial suggestions and to Rose Parfitt for countless discussions about this project. I am equally grateful for *Critical Legal Thinking*, in which a preliminary version of this article was published. All the photos as well as all the limitations in this chapter are mine.

1 On the long war on drugs in Colombia and 'Plan Colombia', see Franz, 2016.

2 I have also discussed their protest in Eslava, 2012.

3 On similar protests by IDPs and refugees in other parts of the world, see Amisi and Ballard, 2006; Shindo, 2009; Lecandet, 2016; Olatunji, 2016.

4 On issues associated with the fulfilment of IDPs' rights in Colombia, see Højen, 2015; Lemaitre and Bergtora Sandvik, 2015; Bradley, 2016; Barrera Ramirez and Dario Franco, 2016; Oslender, 2016; Lemaitre and Bergtora Sandvik, 2017.

5 Although remarkable for their decision to openly challenge authorities with their occupation of public spaces for such a long time, the story of this group is far from being foreign to many other groups of IDPs in Colombia. See, e.g., Volckhausen, 2013; Grajales, 2015.

6 On the broad political economic features of this late modernity, see Harvey, 1989: 141–172. On the socio-anthropological, institutional, legal and political aspects of this time, particularly from the perspective of the Global South, see, e.g., Comaroff and Comaroff, 2006: 22; Comaroff and Comaroff, 2009: 31.

7 For an examination of Weber's analysis of capitalism as a form of spirit, ethos and disposition, see especially Appadurai, 2011.

8 See, in the case of Bogotá, Eslava, 2015; Austin Zeiderman, 2013a; Zeiderman, 2013b; Pérez, 2013; Wall and Olarte, 2012. In the case of Rio de Janeiro and Istanbul, see Dias and Eslava, 2013; Eslava, 2014.

9 Sircar borrows here from Derrida's reading of *Pharmakon*: Derrida, 1981.

Bibliography

Abrahamsen, Rita and Williams, Michael C., *Security Beyond the State: Private Security in International Politics*, Cambridge: Cambridge University Press, 2010.

Amisi, Baruti and Ballard, Richard, 'In the Absence of Citizenship: Congolese Refugee Struggle and Organization in South Africa', in Richard Ballard, Adam Habib and Imraan Valodia (eds), *Globalisation, Voices of Protest: Social Movements in Post-apartheid South Africa*, Scottsville: University of KwaZulu-Natal Press, 2006.

Appadurai, Arjun, 'The Ghost in the Financial Machine', *Public Culture,* 23(3), 517–539, 2011.

Barrera Ramirez, Juliana Andrea and Dario Franco, Hernan, 'The Effect of Conflict and Displacement on the Health of Internally Displaced People: The Colombian Crisis', *University of Ottawa Journal of Medicine,* 6(2), 26–29, 2016.

Bataille, Georges, *The Accursed Share: An Essay on General Economy, Vol. 1: Consumption*, Cambridge, MA: Zone Books, 1991.

Bauman, Zygmunt, 'On Glocalization: or Globalization for Some, Localization for Some Others', *Thesis Eleven*, 54(1), 37–49, 1998.

Bauman, Zygmunt, 'Glocalization and Hybridity', *Glocalism: Journal of Culture, Politics and Innovation*, 1(1), 1–5, 2013.

Bradley, Miriam, 'UNHCR Accountability for IDP Protection in Colombia', in Kristin Bergtora Sandvik and Katja Lindskov Jacobsen (eds), *UNHCR and the Struggle for Accountability: Technology, Law and Results-Based Management*, London: Routledge, 2016.

Chatterjee, Partha, *The Politics of the Governed: Reflections on Popular Politics in Most of the World*, New York: Columbia University Press, 2004.

Comaroff, Jean and Comaroff, John, *Modernity and Its Malcontents: Ritual and Power in Postcolonial Africa*, Chicago: University Chicago Press, 1993.

Comaroff, Jean and Comaroff, John L., 'Occult Economies and the Violence of Abstraction: Notes from the South African Postcolony', *American Ethnologist*, 26(2), 279–303, 1999.

Comaroff, John L. and Comaroff, Jean, 'Law and Disorder in the Postcolony: An Introduction', in Jean Comaroff and John L. Comaroff (eds), *Law and Disorder in the Postcolony*, Chicago: Chicago University Press, 2006.
Comaroff, John L. and Comaroff, Jean, 'Reflections on the Anthropology of Law, Governance and Sovereignty', in Franz von Benda-Beckmann, Keebet von Benda-Beckmann and Julia Eckert (eds), *Rules of Law and Laws of Ruling: On the Governance of Law*, Farnham: Ashgate Publishing, 2009.
Darian-Smith, Eve, *Laws and Societies in Global Contexts*, Cambridge: Cambridge University Press, 2013.
Davis, Mike, *Planet of Slums*, London: Verso, 2006.
Dayan, Colin, *The Law is a White Dog: How Legal Rituals Make and Unmake Persons*, Princeton: Princeton University Press, 2011.
del Pilar Blanco, María and Peeren, Esther, 'Introduction: Conceptualizing Spectralities', in María del Pilar Blanco and Esther Peeren (eds), *The Spectralities Reader: Ghosts and Haunting in Contemporary Cultural Theory*, London: Bloomsbury, 2013.
del Pilar Blanco, María and Peeren, Esther (eds), *The Haunted Spaces of Everyday Culture, Popular Ghosts*, London: Continuum, 2010.
Derrida, Jacques, *Dissemination*, trans. Barbara Johnson, Chicago: University of Chicago Press, 1981.
Derrida, Jacques, *Specters of Marx: The State of the Debt, the Work of Mourning, & the New International*, trans. Peggy Kamuf, London: Routledge, 1993.
Dias, Maria Clara and Eslava, Luis, 'Horizons of Inclusion: Life Between Laws and Developments in Rio de Janeiro', *University of Miami Inter-American Law Review*, 44(2), 177–218, 2013.
Dolan, Catherine S., 'Gender and Witchcraft in Agrarian Transition: The Case of Kenyan Horticulture', *Development and Change*, 33(4), 659–681, 2002.
Elliot, Larry, 'World's Eight Richest People Have Same Wealth as Poorest 50%,' *The Guardian*, 2017. www.theguardian.com/global-development/2017/jan/16/worlds-eight-richest-people-have-same-wealth-as-poorest-50.
El Tiempo.com, 'Alcaldes pagan tiquete a desplazados para que viajen a Bogotá, denuncia Secretaría de Gobierno,' 2009. www.eltiempo.com/archivo/documento/CMS-5748508.
Eslava, Luis, 'El Derecho Urbano en un Mundo Globalizado', in Mauricio Rengifo and Juan Felipe Pinilla (eds), *La Ciudad y el Derecho: Una Introducción al Derecho Urbano Contemporáneo*, Bogota: Temis & Universidad los Andes, 2012.
Eslava, Luis, 'Istanbul Vignettes: Observing the Everyday Operation of International Law', *London Review of International Law*, 2(1), 3–47, 2014.
Eslava, Luis, *Local Space, Global Life: The Everyday Operation of International Law and Development*, Cambridge: Cambridge University Press, 2015.
Eslava, Luis, 'The Materiality of International Law: Violence, History and Joe Sacco's The Great War', *London Review of International Law*, 5(1), 49–86, 2017.
Evans-Pritchard, E.E., *Witchcraft and Magic among the Azande*, Oxford: Clarendon Press, 1976.
Fine, Ben, 'Development as Zombieconomics in the Age of Neoliberalism', *Third World Quarterly*, 30(5), 885–904, 2009.
Franz, Tobias, 'Plan Colombia: Illegal Drugs, Economic Development and Counterinsurgency – A Political Economy Analysis of Colombia's Failed War', *Development Policy Review*, 34(4), 563–591, 2016.
Freud, Sigmund, *New Introductory Lectures in Psycho-Analysis*, trans. James Strachey, first published 1933, London: Hogarth Press and the Institute of Psycho-analysis, 1964.
Geschiere, Peter, *The Modernity of Witchcraft: The Politics and the Occult in Postcolonial Africa*, Charlottesville: University Press of Virginia, 1997.
Gordon, Avery F., *Ghostly Matters: Haunting and the Sociological Imagination*, New ed., Minneapolis: University of Minnesota Press, 2008.
Grajales, Jacobo, 'Land Grabbing, Legal Contention and Institutional Change in Colombia', *Journal of Peasant Studies*, 42(3–4), 541–560, 2015.

Gupta, Akhil, *Red Tape: Bureaucracy, Structural Violence, and Poverty in India*, Durham: Duke University Press, 2012.

Harvey, David, *The Condition of Postmodernity: An Inquiry into the Conditions of Cultural Change*, Oxford: Blackwell Publishers, 1989.

Harvey, David, *Spaces for Global Capitalism: Towards a Theory of Uneven Geographical Development*, London: Verso, 2006.

Højen, Louise, 'Colombia's "Invisible Crisis": Internally Displaced Persons', *Council on Hemispheric Affairs*, 2015. www.coha.org/colombias-invisible-crisis-internally-displaced-persons/.

Ibáñez, Ana María and Velásquez, Andrea, Report: Public Policies to Assist Internally Displaced Persons: The Role of Municipal Authorities, *Brookings Institution*, 2008. www.brookings.edu/research/public-policies-to-assist-internally-displaced-persons-the-role-of-municipal-authorities/.

Internal Displacement Monitoring Centre (IDMC), 'Colombia', 2017. www.internal-displacement.org/countries/colombia.

James, Erica Caple, 'Witchcraft, Bureaucraft, and the Social Life of (US)Aid in Haiti', *Cultural Anthropology*, 27(1), 50–75, 2012.

Johnson, Andrew Alan, 'Progress and its Ruins: Ghosts, Migrants, and the Uncanny in Thailand', *Cultural Anthropology*, 28(2), 299–319, 2013.

Kochi, Tarik, 'Anticipation, Critique and the Problem of Intervention: Understanding the Messianic: Derrida through Erns Bloch', *Law and Critique*, 13(1), 29–50, 2002.

Lan, David, *Guns & Rain: Guerrillas & Spirit Mediums in Zimbabwe*, Berkeley, Los Angeles: University of California Press, 1985.

Lecandet, Clara, 'Refugee Politics: Self-Organized "Government" and Protests in the Agamé Refugee Camp' (2005–13)', *Journal of Refugee Studies*, 29(2), 187–207, 2016.

Lemaitre, Julieta and Bergtora Sandvik, Kristin, 'Shifting Frames, Vanishing Resources, and Dangerous Political Opportunities: Legal Mobilization Among Displaced Women in Colombia', *Law and Society Review*, 49(1), 5–38, 2015.

Lemaitre, Julieta and Bergtora Sandvik, Kristin, 'Finding the Roads to Justice: Examining Trajectories of Transition for Internally Displaced Women in Colombia', *Stability: International Journal of Security & Development*, 6(1), 1-18, 2017.

Li, Tania Muray, 'Jobless Growth and Relative Surplus Populations', *Anthropology Today*, 29(3), 1–2, 2013.

Marks, Susan, 'Human Rights and the Bottom Billion', *European Human Rights Law Review*, 1, 37–49, 2009.

Marx, Karl and Friedrich Engels, *The Communist Manifesto*. Edited by Jeffrey C. Isaac, first published 1848, New Haven, London: Yale University Press, 2012.

McNally, David, *Monsters of the Market: Zombies, Vampires and Global Capitalism*, Leiden: Brill, 2011.

Moore, Jason, *Capitalism in the Web of Life: Ecology and the Accumulation of Capital*, London: Verso, 2015.

Morss, John, *International Law as the Law of Collectives*, Farnham: Ashgate Publishing, 2013.

Olatunji, Omirin, 'Nigeria: More IDPs Protest in Maiduguri,' *All Africa*, 2016. http://allafrica.com/stories/201609070425.html.

O'Neill, Kevin Lewis, 'I Want More of You: The Politics of Christian Eroticism in Postwar Guatemala', *Comparative Studies in Society and History*, 52(1), 131–156, 2010.

Orford, Anne, 'Beyond Harmonization: Trade, Human Rights and the Economy of Sacrifice', *Leiden Journal of International Law*, 18(2), 179–213, 2005.

Oslender, Ulrich, 'The Banality of Displacement: Discourse and Thoughtlessness in the Internal Refugee Crisis in Colombia', *Political Geography*, 50(1), 10–19, 2016.

Federico Pérez, 'Peopling Space: Contemporary Redevelopment in Bogotá,' *Open Democracy*, 2013. www.opendemocracy.net/opensecurity/federico-p%C3%A9rez/peopling-space-contemporary-redevelopment-in-bogot%C3%A1.

Philippopoulos-Mihalopoulos, Andreas, *Spatial Justice: Body, Lawscape, Atmosphere,* London: Routledge, 2015.

Robbins, Joel, *Becoming Sinners: Christianity and Moral Torment in a Papua New Guinea Society*, Berkeley, Los Angeles: University of California Press, 2004.

Roy, Arundhati, *Capitalism: A Ghost Story*, Chicago: Haymarket Books, 2014.

Shindo, Reiko, 'Struggle for Citizenship: Interaction Between Political and Civil Society at a Kurd Refugee Protest in Tokyo', *Citizenship Studies*, 13(3), 219–237, 2009.

Sircar, Oishik, 'Spectacles of Emancipation: Reading Rights Differently in India's Legal Discourse', *Osgoode Hall Law Journal*, 49(3), 527–573, 2012. Taussig, Michael, *Mimesis and Alterity: A Particular History of the Senses*, London: Routledge, 1993.

Taussig, Michael, *Shamanism, Colonialism and the Wild Man: A Study of Terror and Healing*, Chicago: University of Chicago Press, 1987.

Tomlinson, Matt, *In God's Image: The Metaculture of Fijian Christianity*, Berkeley, Los Angeles: University of California Press, 2009.

Tuitt, Patricia and Fitzpatrick, Peter, 'Introduction', in Peter Fitzpatrick and Patricia Tuitt (eds), *Critical Beings: Law, Nation, and the Global Subject*, Farnham: Ashgate Publishing, 2003.

UNHCR, 'Global Trends: Forced Displacement in 2016,' 2017. www.unhcr.org/uk/statistics/unhcrstats/5943e8a34/global-trends-forced-displacement-2016.html?query=colombia.

Universidad de los Andes-The Brookings Institution and Acción Social, 'Protecting the Displaced in Colombia: The Role of Municipal Authorities – Summary Report,' 2009. www.unhcr.org/4b0d30c49.html.

Volckhausen, Taran, 'Displaced Colombians Protest in Front of the European Union to Demand Social Justice,' *Colombia Reports*, 2013. https://colombiareports.com/displaced-colombians-protest-front-european-union-demand-social-justice/.

Wall, Illan rua and Olarte, Carolina, 'Displacement and the City: The Occupation of Public Space in Bogota', *Social and Legal Studies*, 21(3), 321–339, 2012.

Weber, Max, 'Politics as Vocation', in David Owen and Tracy B. Strong (eds), *The Vocation Lectures*, trans. Rodney Livingstone, first published 1919, Indianapolis: Hackett Publishing Company, 2004.

Weber, Max, *The Protestant Ethic and the Spirit of Capitalism*, trans. Stephen Kalberg, 4th ed., first published in 1920, Oxford: Oxford University Press, 2009.

Wilke, Christiane, 'Enter Ghost: Haunted Courts and Haunting Judgments in Transitional Justice', *Law and Critique*, 21(1), 73–92, 2010.

Zeiderman, Austin, 'Living Dangerously: Biopolitics and Urban Citizenship in Bogota', *American Ethnologist*, 40(1), 71–87, 2013a.

Zeiderman, Austin, 'Securing Bogotá,' *Open Democracy*, 2013b, www.opendemocracy.net/opensecurity/austin-zeiderman/securing-bogot%c3%a1.

2

Spatial abstraction, legal violence and the promise of appropriation

Chris Butler

Explorations of the social, embodied and imaginary dimensions of space have been a consistent feature of the successive waves of theoretical innovation within the humanities and social sciences during recent decades. Certain strands of critical legal theory and the development of the interdisciplinary field of law and geography studies reflect this emergence of new orientations towards questions of space, relationality and the material. An important background influence for much of this work is Henri Lefebvre's *The Production of Space*, which retains its currency, more than 40 years since it was written (Lefebvre, 1991). Of particular significance is Lefebvre's depiction of the abstract constellation of spatial tendencies that characterises contemporary capitalism and his concept of the 'right to the city', which is often invoked as a means for opening up a range of conceptual and political possibilities for the reappropriation of space. Lefebvre's exposition of these ideas was crucial to the emergence of the field of critical geography during the 1970s, and his work has consistently been a starting point for the progressive waves of theoretical innovation and radical activist scholarship within geography, planning and urban sociology which have explored the cultural, political and corporeal aspects of spatial form and socio-spatial relations.

In recent years, Lefebvre's work has been adapted for various uses by a growing community of scholars who have contributed to the 'spatial turn' within socio-legal and critical legal studies. Within these fields, there is now a general acknowledgement of the importance of Lefebvre's famous assertion of the produced nature of space (Blomley, 2003; Butler, 2009; Delaney, 2004, 2010; de Villiers, 2016; Keenan, 2015; Finchett-Maddock, 2016; Martin et al., 2010; Philippopoulos-Mihalopoulos, 2010, 2011, 2015; Valverde, 2011) – alongside the recognition of his foundational contribution to the study of everyday life (Sarat and Kearns, 1993; van Marle and de Villiers, 2013) and a developing interest in his concept of the right to the city (Butler, 2012; Fernandes, 2007; Layard, 2010). While there is a growing theoretical sophistication within much of this scholarship, it is also the case that the philosophical underpinnings of Lefebvre's writings on spatial questions have rarely been explored in depth.[1] In this chapter, one of my aims is to return to Lefebvre's theory of the production of space, and in particular his depiction of 'abstract space', in order to explore the inherently political character of spatial production. In doing so, I reflect on the role that law plays in reproducing forms of spatial abstraction and their associated modes of violence and domination. But I am also interested in how struggles such as the right to the city, which resist law's abstract violence, do not solely operate at the level of political contestation but are also constituted as aesthetic demands for the appropriation of space by inhabiting bodies. Finally, I consider the implications of Lefebvre's account for an understanding of the concept of 'spatial justice' as a rupture of the imaginary boundary between the possible and the impossible, which challenges us to juridically reassemble the relationships between bodies which inhabit and appropriate their own spaces.

I begin by sketching out one of the central theoretical propositions which drives Lefebvre's account of the production of space – his embrace of a relational theory of space, drawn primarily from the philosophy of Leibniz, which rejects Newtonian notions of 'absolute space'. While it is certainly the case that in recent years the invocation of one or another relational version of space has become something of an orthodoxy within contemporary geography and urban studies, here I outline the distinctive characteristics of Lefebvre's theoretical contribution to this broader literature (Jones, 2009; Murdoch, 2006). In particular, I draw attention to his assertion of the necessity for space to be inhabited by bodies and the implications this poses for the politics of space. It is through charting juridico-political conflicts over divergent uses and forms of bodily occupation of space that the long and complex history of spatial modes of production can be understood.

This task provides the main thread of Lefebvre's narrative in *The Production of Space* as he charts the historical emergence of what he terms 'abstract space'. Central to his argument is a recognition of the role played by spatialised modes of abstraction, such as law and the interventions of state power in fragmenting, homogenising and hierarchically ordering abstract space, and thereby generating its characteristic forms of violence and domination. There are clear resonances here with a range of critiques of legal abstraction, but one distinctive aspect of Lefebvre's account which is of great importance is his concept of 'concrete abstraction', which he derives from Marx's account of abstract labour in the *Grundrisse* (Marx, 1973). This concept allows us to understand law as an abstraction which becomes spatially grounded through its ordering and control of material bodies, their practices and the relations between them. A crucial aspect of Lefebvre's account is that the inherent tendencies of abstract space never entirely extinguish alternative spatial forms, and it is through an understanding of the body's political and aesthetic appropriation of space that he identifies the potential emergence of emancipatory possibilities. This brings us to Lefebvre's emphasis on the relationship between the right to the city and appropriation, which has been invoked in numerous interpretations of his work, as a means of recuperating the social dimensions of inhabitance in the face of the destructive pressures imposed by the coercive powers of both capital and the neoliberal state.

In this context, I argue that although the right to the city is a radical demand which arises out of a politics of inhabitance, it is oriented towards the political and aesthetic appropriation of space, and therefore involves a rejection of both the violent abstractions of juridification and the moralistic repudiation of abstraction *per se*. It is only through understanding the right to the city in this way that it might be possible to deploy this concept as a ground for resistance to dominant forms of spatial production. Thinking of the right to the city as both a strategic and utopian element in the pursuit of a politics of inhabitance also allows us to reimagine the concept of spatial justice, not as the closure of redemptive resolution, but as a moment of rupture, through which challenges to the dominance of law's 'rule by abstraction' may be expressed.

Space and relationality

A defining characteristic of Lefebvre's *The Production of Space* is a commitment to a relational theory of space which he explicitly counterposes to theories of 'absolute space' associated with Newtonian physics and Kantian transcendental idealism, which depend upon the idea that space is a container or framework, with an independent existence to objects or relations. An important influence on Lefebvre's thinking in this respect is Leibniz's understanding of space as a set of relations that is dependent on the objects and processes through which it is constituted (Ballard, 1960; Barbour, 1982; Cassirer, 1943; Sklar, 1974). Lefebvre argues for the need to theoretically engage the physical, mental and social dimensions of space in order to comprehend its character as a social product. Rather than following the assumptions of a 'common sense' philosophy of space as an ontologically empty vessel and an epistemologically *a priori* category, Lefebvre argues that the multiple aspects of space can only be drawn together by understanding their place within processes of social and cultural production (Lefebvre, 1991: 297). This account presupposes that any spatial ordering is the product of a given set of social arrangements, and hence its stability is always contingent and provisional. In other words, the production of space is an inherently political process (Lefebvre, 1991: 31).

Of course Lefebvre is not alone in proposing a relational theory of space, and the last four decades have seen the extension and proliferation of such conceptualisations within critical strains of geography, planning and urban studies. As Martin Jones explains, what each of these relational accounts have in common is a recognition that

> Space does not exist as an entity in and of itself, over and above material objects and their spatiotemporal relations and extensions. In short, objects *are* space, space *is* objects, and moreover objects can be understood *only* in relation to other objects – with all this being a perpetual becoming of heterogeneous networks and events that connect internal spatiotemporal relations.
>
> (Jones, 2009: 491, emphasis in original)

An influential early proponent of a relational approach to space within the emerging critical geography scholarship in the 1970s was David Harvey, who, like Lefebvre, draws on Leibniz (in association with Whitehead) in asserting the importance of a philosophy of 'internal relations' for both dialectical forms of explanation, and as a crucial theoretical component in the development of 'historical-geographical materialism' (Harvey, 1996: 69–76, 249–255; 2006: 121–126). For Harvey, such a perspective allows us to understand how space and time are 'ordering systems inherent within social practices and activities' and accordingly, any semi-permanent 'spatial assemblage' is continually subject to 'processes that create, sustain and dissolve them' (Harvey, 1996: 253, 261; Murdoch, 2006: 19).

One of the most powerful extensions to this relational mode of theorising within geography and allied disciplines has been Doreen Massey's long-term project to use a relational understanding of space to confront the assumptions that lie behind various forms of philosophical devaluation of the spatial (Massey, 2005: 9, 1992, 1999). For Massey, this denigration of space is not solely driven by the historicism of the traditional humanities, but extends its influence across the breadth of critical thought. In developing her argument, Massey pursues a confrontation with thinkers such as Henri Bergson, Ernesto Laclau and Michel de Certeau – each of whom she charges with negatively associating space with forms of representation and stasis (Massey, 2005). This is not a new claim in the case of Bergson, who has often been held responsible as one of the central architects of the modernist subordination of space to time and duration (Soja, 1989). In a now classic essay, Foucault inquires:

> Did it begin with Bergson, or before? Space was treated as the dead, the fixed, the undialectical, immobile. Time, on the contrary, was richness, fecundity, life, dialectic.
>
> (Foucault, 1980: 70)

While it needs to be acknowledged that there are a range of more sympathetic interpretations of Bergson's renowned rejection of the 'spatialisation of time' (Fraser, 2008; Seigworth, 2000), Massey is clear in her assertion that it is not simply Bergson's prioritisation of time over space that is problematic, but his entire 'mode of conceptualisation' of the relationship between space and time (Massey, 2005: 21). While making an argument about the errors of attempting to derive 'history from a succession of slices through time', Bergson characterises such static, instantaneous time-slices in spatial terms. He then complicates his position by associating space with 'representation' (or the fixing of meaning), which effectively deprives space of dynamism and 'radically counterpose[s] it to time' (Massey, 2005: 21; Bergson, 1910). This move allows Bergson to juxtapose the heterogeneous difference of duration to the 'spatialised time of metrication with its quantitative segments and instants' (Boundas, 1996: 92).

In extending her critique to the work of Laclau, Massey draws attention to the ways in which he uncritically associates space with representation and hegemonic closure. For Laclau, space is defined as 'any repetition that is governed by a structural law of successions' and therefore spatialisation necessarily involves the hegemonic production of ideological representations of the world as coherent (Laclau, 1990: 41). This leads him to understand all attempts to represent forms of dislocation as the construction of 'a moment in permanent structural relation with other moments', through which 'the pure temporality of the 'event' is eliminated'. Accordingly, Laclau argues that this process of closing off the dynamic disruption of temporality constitutes the 'spatial domesticization of time' . . . (Laclau, 1990: 72) As Massey points out, this means that 'any postulated causal structure which is complete and self-determining is labelled as 'spatial' (Massey, 1992: 68). The difficulty that Massey has with both these positions is that they conflate the activity of 'spatialisation' with space as a dimension:

> Representation is seen to take on aspects of spatial*isation* in the latter's action of setting things down side by side; of laying them out as a discrete simultaneity. But representation is also in this argument understood as fixing things, taking the time out of them. The equation of spatialisation with the production of 'space' thus lends to space not only the character of a discrete multiplicity but also the characteristic of stasis.
>
> (Massey, 2005: 23, emphasis in original)

Massey's response to this denigration of the spatial is to argue that space is simultaneously 'the product of interrelations', 'the sphere of coexisting heterogeneity', and an open process of becoming (Massey, 2005: 9). On this view, space is better understood as 'the simultaneous coexistence of social relations that cannot be conceptualized as other than dynamic' (Massey, 1992: 81).[2]

In the wake of these formative influences, the last decade has seen an explosion of conceptual innovation in the development of a relational spatial paradigm within the social sciences and humanities. This includes work such as Sarah Whatmore's articulation of the hybrid ethical relations between human and non-human actors (Whatmore, 2002); Nigel Thrift's non-representational geography (Thrift, 2008); the advocacy of a 'flat ontology' of space as a substitution for scalar hierarchies of scale by Sallie Marston and her colleagues (Marston et al., 2005); Marcus Doel's Deleuzian-inspired escape from the illusions of 'pointillism' (Doel, 1999); a range of theoretical contributions to the development of 'new materialisms' (Coole and Frost, 2010); and at least some uses of assemblage thinking in recent geographical theorising (Anderson et al., 2012; McFarlane, 2011a, 2011b). The theoretical emergence of a relational conception of space has also made its way into the field of critical legal geography, as recognised in the introductory overview to the recent collection *The Expanding Spaces of Law*, and is also acknowledged by Andreas Philippopoulos-Mihalopoulos in an early formulation of his retheorisation of the concept of spatial justice (Braverman et al., 2014: 17–18; Philippopoulos-Mihalopoulos, 2011: 199).

While there is a remarkable fertility to much of this scholarship, it is also true that an attachment to one or another relational approach to space has now become something of an orthodoxy within geography and related disciplines (Graham and Healey, 1999; Murdoch, 2006; Sheppard, 2008: 2608–2609 and Jones, 2009, 2010). For some commentators, this has generated a proliferation of dramatic 'rhetorical and imaginative frameworks' which collapse space into a 'swirl of flows, networks, and trajectories', but it has done little to establish conceptual clarity about space and spatiality (Malpas, 2012: 228). In other respects, this widespread adoption of the terminology of relationality within the spatial disciplines has tended to obscure significant ontological differences between each of these strands of thinking. In particular, it is clear that the adoption of an immanent or flat ontology by a number of these writers clearly conflicts with the depth-theoretical orientations of Massey, Harvey and Lefebvre. As Massey emphasises,

> Seeing space as a moment in the intersection of configured social relations (rather than as an absolute dimension) means that it cannot be seen as static. There is no choice between flow (time) and a flat surface of instantaneous relations (space). Space is not a 'flat surface' in that sense because the social relations which create it are themselves dynamic by their very nature. . . . [A]s a result of the fact that it is conceptualized as created out of social relations, space is by its very nature full of power and symbolism, a complex web of relations of domination and subordination, of solidarity and cooperation.
>
> (Massey, 1992: 81)

In his most recent work on spatial justice, Philippopoulos-Mihalopoulos has moved beyond what he identifies as the limitations of a relational conceptualisation of space as 'process', which fails to account for both the disruptive and radically unpredictable character of space, and the 'materiality of law' (Philippopoulos-Mihalopoulos, 2015: 26–27). As an alternative, Philippopoulos-Mihalopoulos argues for an understanding of space which can account for the ontological withdrawal of singular, material bodies from the spatial assemblages of which they form part (Philippopoulos-Mihalopoulos, 2015: 49–50). In his words:

> Space is encountered in its ruptured immanence as *a* space: a space of specific assemblage. . . . Each body is an assemblage, and each body can be organised in assemblages with other bodies. Bodies are and produce space. . . . But these bodies differentiate themselves from other bodies. . . . Each body is a singularity, forever withdrawing, yet forever claiming its material agency, its singularity in space. . .
>
> (Philippopoulos-Mihalopoulos, 2015: 51–52, 59, emphasis in original)

In this regard Philippopoulos-Mihalopoulos's thinking parallels the rejection by object-oriented philosophers such as Graham Harman and Timothy Morton of the idea that objects (and bodies) can be defined by their relations (Harman, 2012: 187; Morton, 2011: 184–185). This position is neatly summarised by Harman in the eminently reasonable assertion that 'relations do not exhaust a thing – instead they *rely* on the thing' (Harman, 2009: 132). But, as Jane Bennett has recently argued, this does not necessarily mean that we must make a brutal choice between relationality and the ontological integrity of objects and bodies. Given that our everyday experience 'routinely identifies some effects as coming from individual objects and some from larger systems', it is a valid theoretical project to have regard to 'objects' and 'relations', even if it is not possible to 'give equal attention to both at once' (Bennett, 2015: 228). Throughout the discussion that follows, I implicitly endorse these sentiments in presupposing that Lefebvre's relational account of space is capable of accommodating both the materiality of objects and entities and the relations through which they connected. Using this approach, space can be understood as produced by a multitude of relationally bonded bodies and processes, and the apparent permanence of any given spatial entity or form of spatial ordering is a provisional stabilisation of the relations that constitute it. Accordingly, space is always subject to the inherently contested and political character of its production (Anderson, 2008: 231; Harvey, 1996: 261–262).

Spatial abstraction and legal violence

One of the ways in which Lefebvre's emphasis on the inevitably political character of space is revealed most clearly is in his insistence on the necessity of space to be '*occupied*' by the body (Lefebvre, 1991: 169, emphasis in original). Unlike the separation between spatial form and material content which characterises an absolute conception of space, Lefebvre's endorsement of a Leibnizian position leads him to presuppose 'an immediate relationship between the body and its space, between the body's deployment in space and its occupation of space' (Lefebvre, 1991: 169–170; de Villiers, 2016: 3–4).[3] Lefebvre explains the inextricable relationship between bodily inhabitance and the production of space in the following terms:

> Before producing effects in the material realm (tools and objects), before producing itself by drawing nourishment from that realm, and before reproducing itself by generating other bodies, each living body is space and has its space: it produces itself in space and it also produces that space.
>
> (Lefebvre, 1991: 170)

It is through political struggles over the inhabitance of space that the history of spatial modes of production are written, and in *The Production of Space* Lefebvre charts the historical emergence of what he terms 'abstract space' – a form of space which is emblematic of contemporary capitalism. In this account, the shift from the 'metaphysical closure' of the Greek civil order to the forms of secular difference and relativity that characterised the Roman city-state was accompanied by new manifestations of authority, including the legal codification of private land ownership and the rise of patriarchal social relations which subjected space 'to the unifying but abstract principle of property' (Lefebvre, 1991: 239, 252). While the organisation of space in Rome opened up greater possibilities for diversity, it also provided a crucial juridico-political framework for the development and consolidation of an abstract mode of spatial production from the late Middle Ages through to the turn of the twentieth century. Contemporary capitalist society represents the apogee of abstract space for Lefebvre, with its simultaneous tendencies towards the fragmentation, homogenisation and hierarchical ordering of space (Lefebvre, 2003a: 210; Butler, 2012: 48–51; Butler, 2009: 323–325; Dimendberg, 1998; Wilson, 2013). Lefebvre argues that it is through these tendencies that capitalist social relations have been able to entrench and reproduce themselves within everyday life (Lefebvre, 1976: 21).

In general terms, Lefebvre's critique of abstract space is compatible with a broad category of writing within the humanities and social sciences which is suspicious of the intellectual limitations and pernicious political consequences of abstraction. Some of the theoretical orientations which share this distrust include varieties of empiricist sociology, western Marxism, and the turn to what Peter Osborne refers to as forms of 'historicist particularism' in the quest to capture the vibrancy of experiences which are repressed by the dominance of abstraction (Osborne, 2004: 22). The most distinctive aspect of Lefebvre's discussion of abstract space is his attempt to model it on Marx's account of abstract labour in the *Grundrisse*. In this work, Marx argues that labour can only be considered as a general, 'abstract' category with the emergence of a social formation in which individuals are no longer 'organically linked' to their 'concrete' skills and practices, which have been rendered quantifiable and exchangeable (Marx, 1973: 104). In this way, the abstraction of labour becomes 'true in practice' and is but one example of how capitalist social relations establish a mode of social domination based on the 'rule by abstractions' (Marx, 1973: 105, 164; Postone, 1993: 126; Loftus, 2015: 369).

Lefebvre adopts this methodological frame as the basis for his own theorisation of how the development of an abstract mode of spatial production has accompanied the historical rise of abstraction in thought and practice under capitalism (Stanek, 2011: 133–164). It is obvious that economic processes of exchange, commodification and accumulation have played a crucial role here, but Lefebvre is highly critical of the one-sided and obsessive focus on economic determination within orthodox Marxism (Lefebvre, 1991: 246). Instead he extrapolates from Marx's reference to the 'rule by abstractions' by emphasising how the production of abstract space has been profoundly shaped by juridico-political conflicts and the exercise of state power (Lefebvre, 2009a: 214; Wilson, 2013: 369–370). Indeed, the introduction of the juridical relations of private property over the entirety of physical space and the law's imposition of the contractual form over customary relationships were essential elements in the historical emergence of abstract space (Lefebvre, 1991: 263; Cunningham, 2008: 455–456). One consequence of this is the necessity to recognise the destructive capacities that spatial abstraction carries in its wake. While the self-presentation of liberal capitalist society embodies normative attachments to civil order and political consensus and a social compact based on a notional commitment to non-violence, the production of abstract space depends on juridico-political processes which are inherently coercive. This is particularly so in relation to the forms of control which are inflicted on the body and are characteristic of what Lefebvre, in a more polemical register, depicts as a 'violence intrinsic to abstraction'.

> Abstraction passes for an 'absence' – as distinct from the concrete 'presence' of objects, of things. Nothing could be more false. For abstraction's *modus operandi* is devastation, destruction (even if such destruction may sometimes herald creation).... The violence of abstraction unfolds in parallel with what we call 'history'.
>
> (Lefebvre, 1991: 289, emphasis in original)

This identification of the destructive potential of abstraction has obvious resonances with a vast scholarship on the violence of law's particular forms of abstraction. At one level, law's tendencies towards formalism and reductionism are manifestations of a 'conceptual one-sidedness' which dramatically misrecognises the relational totality of the social (Osborne, 2004: 25; Hegel, 1966: 116; Cunningham, 2008: 464–466). This misrecognition leads the law to engage in a metaphorical separation of social relations and to break down individual bodies into manageable and regulated locations, which are the subject of isolated conflicts and potential rights claims (Douzinas, 2000: 230). But we may equally consider other examples of the destructive potential of legal abstractions, including the originary violence of law's self-definition (Benjamin, 1985; Derrida, 1990; Hirvonen, 2011; Sarat and Kearns, 1992); assertions of sovereign power by state institutions (Mieville, 2005; Motha, 2002); the construction of individualist and masculinist images of legal subjectivity (Drakopoulou, 2006; Hunter, 2006); systems of interpretation and administration underlying criminal justice and regimes of punishment (Cover, 1986); and the imposition of the juridical form of private property (Blomley, 2003).

Through these instances of abstract violence, law is deeply involved in entrenching and reproducing the three tendencies of spatial abstraction that Lefebvre identifies in *The Production of Space*: fragmentation, homogenisation and hierarchical ordering. Through its commitment to the generality of legal rules and the equality of legal subjects, law both reproduces spatial hierarchies and operates as a force for the homogenisation of socio-spatial relations.[4] In addition, the real and discursive violence of law plays an essential role in processes of spatial fragmentation such as systems of land-use planning, through which legislation and regulatory instruments cleave through space, prohibiting or permitting particular spatial uses and enforcing such divisions in practice (Lefebvre, 1991: 317; Butler, 2005: 21; Butler, 2008). At the level of the nation-state, a more extreme example can be seen in the spatial divisions imposed between citizens and aliens in the Australian government's implementation of a militarised system of immigration control entitled 'Operation Sovereign Borders', which relies on the redrawing of national boundaries, the maritime interdiction of vessels carrying asylum seekers and the indefinite offshore detention of their passengers (Chambers, 2015; Hodge, 2015; Basaran, 2008; Salter, 2008). This complex of regulatory and military strategies has been repeatedly criticised as breaching Australia's international legal obligations (Klein, 2014; Schloenhardt and Craig, 2015), and the ways in which its operation has become normalised as a centrepiece of Australia's immigration system provides a stark reminder of the crucial role that juridico-political power plays in the reproduction of abstract space (Brenner and Elden, 2009).

These examples reflect the ways in which law's abstractions are clearly not confined to the level of epistemology or methodology, but are spatially grounded in the material practices of individual bodies and the relations between them. Recalling Lefebvre's reading of the *Grundrisse*, law can be classified as a 'concrete abstraction' – an abstraction which takes on a real existence and effectively becomes spatialised through its ordering and control of material bodies and their practices (Lefebvre, 1991: 100, 341–342; Cunningham, 2005: 18–19; Stanek, 2011: 143–145, 149–158; Loftus, 2015: 371, 376). Lefebvre's interpretation of the concept of concrete abstraction has strong parallels with Alfred Sohn-Rethel's relatively neglected account of 'real abstraction', which he takes from Marx's analysis of the commodity or value form (Sohn-Rethel, 1978; Toscano, 2008a, 2008b). Noting an 'irreconcilable contradiction' between traditional forms of philosophical abstraction and Marx's identification of the abstraction of the commodity form, Sohn-Rethel claims that the latter

> [i]s purely social in character, arising in the spatio-temporal sphere of human interrelations. It is not people who originate these abstractions but their actions. . . . In order to do justice to Marx's *Critique of Political Economy* the commodity or value abstraction revealed in his analysis must be viewed as a *real abstraction* resulting from spatio-temporal activity.
>
> (Sohn-Rethel, 1978: 20, emphasis in original)

Alberto Toscano argues that Sohn-Rethel's thesis of how real abstractions are not confined to the realm of thought but 'originate' in social practice, reveals the futility of attempts to address their dominating and oppressive tendencies through the intellectual 'cultivation of new, more tolerant, more inclusive abstractions', without also addressing the ways in which the abstract is 'woven into the fabric of our social relations' (Toscano, 2008a: 72). An analogy can be drawn here with the use of Lefebvre's conceptualisation of concrete abstraction in analysing law's complicity in the reproduction of abstract space. While struggles to confront and resist law's violence must necessarily expose its ideological mystifications and the forms of misrecognition that flow from its abstract character, they also require more than this. Challenges to the specifically juridical forms of concrete abstraction that underpin processes of oppression and domination require the reframing of their modes of expression, the practices which reinforce them and the spatial relations that such forms of ordering produce. It is to the political possibilities beyond abstract space that I now turn.

The right to the city and the appropriation of space

While much of the narrative in *The Production of Space* is focused on the coercive and often destructive tendencies that are inherent to abstract space, Lefebvre also makes clear that this is a mode of spatial production which is never fully accomplished – never entirely capable of establishing a totalising hold over spatial relations. Indeed, it is constantly confronted by contradictions which suggest alternative and potentially emancipatory spatial possibilities. A crucial example can be seen in the contradiction between abstract space's domination of nature and the 'appropriation of space', which he argues was not adequately recognised by Marx, and all too often has contributed to the harnessing of the latter's ideas in the pursuit of plans for the productivist mastery over the natural world (Lefebvre, 1991: 165; Brenner, 2008). While dominated and appropriated spaces have not always mutually excluded each other, the rise of capital accumulation and the expansion of state power has progressively accentuated their separation and mutual opposition. In this context, Lefebvre identifies the potential of a postcapitalist mode of spatial production, which is directed towards a restoration of the integrity of the body's relationship to space through appropriation. Characterising this spatial form as 'differential space', Lefebvre argues that it encompasses physical, mental and social uses which nurture differences and particularities, while resisting the ways in which the 'functions, elements and moments of social practice' are fractured by abstract space (Lefebvre, 1991: 52).

The vehicle through which Lefebvre envisages that the appropriation of differential space may be best pursued is the political demand for the 'right to the city' – or what he describes in subsequent work as the 'right to space' (Lefebvre, 1996, 2009b: 193–194). This is a concept which was first introduced in the midst of the revolutionary events of May 1968, and he incorporates it into a broader reimagining of social citizenship in his late collaborative work with the Group de Navarrenx (Lefebvre, 1990). While appropriated space is always subject to challenge from the violence, destruction and domination of abstract space, Lefebvre identifies the seeds of the right to the city in struggles against the incessant pressures to produce space in the manner of a manufactured commodity (Lefebvre, 1991: 166–167). It is thus an assertion of the entitlement of all inhabitants to collaborate in collective, creative struggles to prioritise the appropriation of space and its use values, over its domination by the logic of exchange and strategic interventions by a positivist state technocracy (Lefebvre, 1996).

In political terms, the right to the city is radically opposed to the violence of abstract space and it inevitably depends on expanded forms of democratic participation by inhabitants in urban decision-making processes. This draws out Lefebvre's longstanding concerns with the dependence of emancipatory political movements on forms of self-management or *autogestion* (Lefebvre, 2009c; Rose, 1978). Rather than relying on the institutions and legal processes of the liberal capitalist state to act as a guardian of the public interest, autogestion is a direct confrontation with the state's role in the planning and policing of space (Lefebvre, 1991: 383; Brenner, 2008: 239–241; Purcell, 2013: 316–318). As he states in an essay written in the mid-1960s, prior to his mature writings on the production of space:

> The principal contradiction that *autogestion* introduces and stimulates is its own contradiction with the State. In essence, *autogestion* calls the State into question as a constraining force erected above society as a whole, capturing and demanding the rationality that is inherent to social relations (to social practice) . . . [It] cannot escape this brutal obligation: to constitute itself as a power which is not that of the State.
>
> (Lefebvre, 2009c: 147, emphasis in original)

This characterisation of the right to the city as a central component of a radical politics of spatial autogestion is complicated by the ways in which it has been adopted by a wide range of scholarly disciplines, activist movements and proposals for the reform of urban decision-making and improved municipal infrastructure (Brown and Kristiansen, 2009; Cities Alliance, 2010; Coggin and Pieterse, 2012; Fernandes, 2007; HABITAT III, 2016; Harvey, 2008; Marcuse, 2009; Mitchell, 2003; Purcell, 2002,

2013, 2014; de Souza, 2010; UNESCO, 2006; UN-HABITAT, 2010). At one level, this explosion of interest in the right to the city could be interpreted as an encouraging openness to Lefebvre's ideas, but it also raises a number of theoretical and political questions about how a single concept can be applied in such varied contexts. As Kafui Attoh explains, many writers have not adequately considered 'what kind of right' the right to the city is, and quite often the forms in which it is presented are incommensurable (Attoh, 2011). Although limited by his own reliance on the normative positivism of Jeremy Waldron, Attoh is correct to acknowledge the necessity of the compromises that follow from the institutionalisation and juridification of the right to the city.

It is of course unwise to unreflectively dismiss attempts to codify material social improvements and procedural protections which are implemented under the banner of the right to the city. However, the reduction of this concept to the status of a positivist juridical right in order to position it within a broadly social liberal, distributive rights agenda (as proposed in a number of state-based initiatives and proposals developed by some non-government organisations), runs the inherent danger of constricting the capacity of this right to meaningfully resist the forces of spatial abstraction (Coggin and Pieterse, 2012; Fernandes, 2007; UNESCO, 2006; Brown and Kristiansen, 2009). Often it is more accurate to understand this discursive embrace of the right to the city as part of a widespread trivialisation and deradicalisation of the original formulation of the concept, which in political terms, fails to pose a challenge to the institutions and social forces which generate abstract space (Belda-Miquel et al., 2016; de Souza, 2010: 319; Purcell, 2013: 316).

Alongside his portrayal of the right to the city as a political demand for the self-management of space, Lefebvre also explores the aesthetic dimensions of struggles for the right to the city, understood as spatial projects of the collective imaginary and examples of creative work rather than utilitarian production. This orientation derives from Lefebvre's previously mentioned understanding of the 'immediate relationship' between the occupying body and its production of space (Lefebvre, 1991: 170). He regards the inhabitance of the total body as opening up possibilities for the recovery of the full range of sensory faculties, in the face of an increasingly dominant 'logic of visualisation' which is instrumental to the reproduction of abstract space (Lefebvre, 1991: 98–99, 139, 286). But as generators of rhythms, as 'deployments of energy' and as gestural systems, bodies also have the capacity to transform their surrounding spaces and reappropriate them for uses and forms of enjoyment which may conflict with externally imposed spatial regimes (Lefebvre, 1991: 171). An example of such a transformation, is sketched out in Lefebvre's preface to Philippe Boudon's study of the practices of the residents of Le Corbusier's Quartiers Modernes Frugès housing project at Pessac, in remoulding the spaces of their standardised residential apartments (Lefebvre, 1972).

Similar principles guide Lefebvre's thinking about the reappropriation of space at the municipal scale, and he states that 'the *urban* is more or less the *oeuvre* of its citizens instead of imposing itself upon them as a system, as an already closed book' (Lefebvre, 1996: 117, emphasis in original). Accordingly, the right to the city opens up possibilities for the appropriation of space to become a creative and fulfilling aesthetic experience, prioritising the usage of space by its inhabitants over its exchange value. However, one important consequence of this attention to the aesthetic character of the right to the city is that it assists in breaking down the crude binary distinction between abstraction and appropriation that is often attributed to Lefebvre in some of the more simplistic interpretations of his work. In particular, it is often assumed that his critique of abstract space operates in a solely polemical mode and is implacably opposed to all forms of abstract concept formation, rationality or representation (Dimendberg, 1998: 37). As David Cunningham notes, it would be highly naïve to imagine the prospect of establishing a differential space through practices of appropriation, which in some way remain untainted by any forms of abstraction (Cunningham, 2005: 23). Indeed, having regard to the creative dimensions of political struggles over the production of space allows us to incorporate the aesthetic potential of abstractions – in art, architecture and forms of creative practice – into the construction of new forms of inhabitance.

A more nuanced reading of Lefebvre's account of the production of space allows us to acknowledge the degree to which he recognises not only the ubiquity of abstractions within modernity but also the necessity of generating alternative forms of abstraction which can be politically and aesthetically concretised within the practices of everyday life. This is a point which coincides with the reflections of Antonio Negri on the melancholy task of visual artists of the post-1968 era, who attempted to engage with the contradictions of contemporary capitalism:

> artistic development transforms the abstraction of the social relations in which we are immersed into corporeal figures, releasing the vitality of the flesh into images that move and inflect themselves, in a process of continuous transformation.
> (Negri, 2008: 22)

Following this line of thought, we can conceptualise the right to the city not as an absolute absence of abstraction but as a demand for the political and aesthetic transformation of the relations between abstraction and appropriation. In doing so, it implies a rejection of both the violent abstraction of positivist juridical rights and the moralistic repudiation of all forms of institutional order.

The 'impossible possibility' of spatial justice

This understanding of the collective, creative production of space as a mediation between the domains of appropriation and abstraction flows directly from Lefebvre's relational approach to spatiality and his reliance on the inherent association between the body and its occupation of space. It also brings us to the relevance of Lefebvre's theorisation of space for an understanding of the allied concept of spatial justice, which has enjoyed an enthusiastic revival in recent years. Emerging from its neglected and marginal status within geography, spatial justice is now invoked in a wide variety of disciplinary contexts, including explorations of the idea of the just city (Fainstein,

2010; Marcuse et al., 2009; Fincher and Iveson, 2012), the rediscovery of earlier scholarship on the just allocation of urban resources and services (Harvey, 1973; Pirie, 1983; Soja, 2010), and as a rallying slogan for a reinvigorated urban politics (Harvey, 1996; Dikeç, 2001; Iveson, 2011).

However, in much of this literature, conceptualisations of spatial justice have tended to draw heavily on orthodox political theory sources such as John Rawls's *A Theory of Justice* or versions of Iris Marion Young's pluralist politics of difference (Rawls, 1999; Young, 1990). As a consequence, the idea of spatial justice has often been conflated with the weakly defined, policy-oriented and institutionally acceptable formulations of the right to the city which I identified previously. Even in the late work of the prominent political geographer Edward Soja, where he attempts to develop a specifically 'spatial theory of justice', the two terms are constantly used interchangeably (Soja, 2010: 95–101). While Soja explicitly acknowledges the ways in which the right to the city is regularly reduced to little more than a liberal version of municipal rights, it is far from clear how his formulation of spatial justice assists in countering such interpretations, or in clarifying the meaning of the former concept (Soja, 2010: 107; cf. Cunningham, 2010).

For Andreas Philippopoulos-Mihalopoulos, the limitations of much of this literature on spatial justice derives from its failure to adequately theorise the inextricable relation – indeed the 'ontological tautology' – between space and law (Philippopoulos-Mihalopoulos, 2010, 2011, 2015: 4). One clear problem he identifies is the reliance on an idealised association between space and its presumed role as a saviour in the resolution of injustice. Such accounts depend on a form of spatial fetishism which 'marginalises the disorder, fragmentation and unpredictability that comes with space', in favour of a moralising depiction of its inherent solutions for manifestations of deprivation and dispossession (Philippopoulos-Mihalopoulos, 2015: 27, 183). Philippopoulos-Mihalopoulos argues that if spatial justice is to be a meaningful concept, it must both address the intimate relation between the abstractions of law and space and heed the corporeality and materiality of this relation. It cannot 'remain the lukewarm hybrid of socially "just" spectres, distributive justice wish lists, neoliberal articulations of participation, parochial territorialism and geopolitical analyses' (Philippopoulos-Mihalopoulos, 2015: 175). In countering the absences and limitations in much of this literature, Philippopoulos-Mihalopoulos proposes a reconceptualisation of spatial justice as the

> ultimate expression of one's spatial and legal claim to a unique corporeal position which by necessity excludes all others: . . . *spatial justice is the struggle between bodies to be in a specific space at a specific time.*
>
> (Philippopoulos-Mihalopoulos, 2015: 176, emphasis in original)

This physical impossibility of more than one body simultaneously occupying the same space highlights the violent tendencies that are inherent to space. It also provides the encouragement for Philippopoulos-Mihalopoulos to define the unfolding and emergence of spatial justice in terms of the body's ontological withdrawal from engineered atmospheres and conflicts with other bodily assemblages, vying for their own 'emplacement'. An indispensable aspect of this argument is a formulation of 'withdrawal' which is far from passive. Indeed, Philippopoulos-Mihalopoulos declares that '[w]ithdrawal is not yielding to the other body, just as spatial justice is not a retreat' (Philippopoulos-Mihalopoulos, 2015: 198) – rather it is a 'rupture of the atmosphere' which binds bodies together (Philippopoulos-Mihalopoulos, 2015: 192). This perspective on spatial justice is a radical challenge to the paradigms associated with both liberal formulations of 'social justice in space' and the strains of legal geography which resist fully engaging with the ontological realities of law and space. It is a remarkable intervention which forces us to seriously consider the spatiality and materiality of bodies and the assemblages which they constitute.

I agree with Philippopoulos-Mihalopoulos on the need to base our understanding of spatial justice on much more rigorous theoretical foundations, and it is entirely reasonable for us to be impatient with the limitations of vague constructions of sociological relationality and the geographical orthodoxies that have developed around relational space. As has been acknowledged previously, a stated adherence to a relational theory of space does not necessarily avoid the problems of spatial fetishism or the positioning of spatial justice within the narrow parameters of distributional politics (de Villiers, 2016: 5–6). However, these intellectual dead-ends should not be attributed to relational modes of thinking *per se*, but are the product of unimaginative forms of conceptualisation, which underplay the full political and ontological implications which follow from an adequate theorisation of processes of spatial production. In this context, I think there is a greater role that Lefebvre's relational approach to space can play in the rethinking of spatial justice than has often been recognised.

As mentioned above, the right to the city is simultaneously a strategic and utopian demand, generated through a relational politics of bodily inhabitance, which is aimed at reworking the relationships between practices of appropriation and forms of spatial abstraction. Spatial justice also has an inherently political dimension, but it extends beyond this field and provides a glimpse of the potential reassembly of the spatial relations between inhabiting and producing bodies. Lefebvre's methodological reflections on the critique of everyday life provide a useful vocabulary in this context for thinking of spatial justice as a 'moment' which erupts from within the bodily rhythms and relations of the everyday. As fleeting, sensate interruptions of the routines of everyday life, moments are attempts 'to achieve the total realisation of a possibility' (Lefebvre, 2002: 348). In this formulation, spatial justice can be understood as a rupture of the 'artificial divide between the possible and the impossible' – a moment which crystallises and starkly reveals the utopian promises and dystopian horrors that are potentially embedded within the body's inhabitance of space (Butler, 2017: 122; Tomba, 2009: 130).

But crucially, each moment is caught up in its tragic relation with the everyday and is always 'destined to fail' in its initial self-projection as an absolute. It is in this sense that Lefebvre characterises the moment as an 'impossible possibility' (Lefebvre, 2002: 347, 2003b; 39–40; Pinder, 2015; Coleman, 2013). This implies that the moment of spatial justice cannot be conceptualised as a form of pure or 'abstract' utopia of appropriated space. Such an interpretation would rely on a simplistic form of spatial fetishism which fantasises the appropriation of space as a miraculous salve for the violence of abstraction. Just as this is an entirely implausible basis on which to think through the politics of the right to the city, so too spatial justice does not lie beyond this world but is necessarily embedded in the concrete practices of material and spatially related bodies. As James Martel notes in a recent study of the work of Walter Benjamin, justice cannot be primarily understood as a question of waiting or deferral, but is better understood as simultaneously 'in the world', while remaining unknowable and beyond our senses (Martel, 2012: 78–79).

Accordingly, spatial justice is neither a pacific resolution of difference and discord nor a transcendence of the world we inhabit. It is an emergence from within the constellation of spatial relations which ground everyday life, while simultaneously challenging the boundaries between possibility and impossibility. The recognition that there is no 'outside' realm in which spatial justice dwells resonates with Philippopoulos-Mihalopoulos's assertion that '[s]patial justice is not about another world. It is about reorienting the current world in order to allow a different lawscape to emerge' (Philippopoulos-Mihalopoulos, 2015: 197–198). This also guides us back to the association between spatial justice and legal relations. On the interpretation offered here, spatial justice can be understood as a momentary explosion and exposé of the spatial and material possibilities that are generated through struggles to reconfigure the relationships between abstraction and appropriation. But despite its capacity to suggest the potential of challenges to existing relations of inhabitance, we cannot rely on spatial justice to provide readymade ethical or normative 'solutions' for specific legal and political conflicts (Philippopoulos-Mihalopoulos, 2015: 177–178).

The resolution of such conflicts necessarily involves an entanglement with the legal abstractions which frame and order spatial production through ideological, coercive and aesthetic configurations of modes of practice. Drawing on Lefebvre's concept of concrete abstraction enables us to understand how law is spatialised and materially carried by bodies as they engage in the practices of everyday life. While law is violent, manipulative and constraining and harbours inherent tendencies towards inertia, it is also subject to constant pressures – not just through institutional limits – but also through the resistance of bodies, which contest its assertions of authority. The right to the city is an example of such a demand for the political and aesthetic production of space as an *oeuvre*. Similarly, spatial justice reveals fleeting moments in which new configurations of spatial relations between bodies can be glimpsed and felt –through either accommodation or conflict. On this view, spatial justice is the impossible possibility of the juridical reassembly of spatial relationships amongst bodies inhabiting and appropriating their own spaces. Lefebvre's relational theory of space allows us to conceptualise not just the spatial dimensions of abstraction or the inevitably political aspects of law's abstract character, but also the ways in which the rule by specific, concrete abstractions may be confronted by political and aesthetic struggles for the appropriation of space. In this sense it provides a methodological lens through which we may imagine how what is currently legally and politically impossible may become a possibility.

Notes

1 Two important exceptions in this regard are Philippopoulos-Mihalopoulos (2015) and de Villiers (2016), who have both devoted considerable attention to the philosophical influences on Lefebvre's writings on space.
2 In particular, Massey takes issue with Laclau's identification of space as 'any repetition that is governed by a structural law of successions': Laclau (1990) *New Reflections on the Revolution of Our Time*, Verso, London: 41.
3 In addressing the influence of Leibniz on Lefebvre's thinking, de Villiers has recently cautioned against the ways in which the former's philosophy of space can easily be co-opted by positivist interpretations of law's spatial turn and undermine the radical potential of the concept of spatial justice (de Villiers, 2016: 5–6).
4 Within public law scholarship in common law jurisdictions, the work of A.V. Dicey is often taken as the classic statement of the importance of the generality of legal rules and formal equality (Dicey 1959: 183–195).

Bibliography

Anderson, Ben, '*For Space* (2005): Doreen Massey', in P. Hubbard et al. (eds), *Key Texts in Human Geography*, London: Sage, 227–235, 2008.

Anderson, Ben et al., 'On Assemblages and Geography', *Dialogues in Human Geography*, 2(2), 171–189, 2012.

Attoh, Kafui A., 'What Kind of Right is the Right to the City?' *Progress in Human Geography*, 35(5), 669–685, 2011.

Ballard, Kaith, 'Leibniz's Theory of Space and Time', *Journal of the History of Ideas*, 21(1), 49–65, 1960.

Barbour, Julian, 'Relational Concepts of Space and Time', *The British Journal for the Philosophy of Science*, 33(3), 251–274, 1982.

Basaran, Tugba, 'Security, Law, Borders: Spaces of Exclusion', *International Political Sociology*, 2(4), 339–354, 2008.

Belda-Miquel, Sergio et al., 'Institutionalization and Depoliticization of the Right to the City: Changing Scenarios for Radical Social Movements', *International Journal of Urban and Regional Research*, 40(2), 321–339, 2016.

Bennett, Jane, 'Systems and Things: On Vital Materialism and Object-oriented Philosophy', in R. Grusin (ed.), *The Nonhuman Turn*, Minneapolis: University of Minnesota Press, 223–239, 2015.

Benjamin, Walter, 'Critique of Violence', in *One-Way Street and Other Writings*, London: Verso, 132–54, 1985.

Bergson, Henri, *Time and Free Will: An Essay on the Immediate Data of Consciousness*, trans. F.L. Pogson, London: G. Allen & Unwin, 1910.

Blomley, Nicholas, 'Law, Property, and the Geography of Violence: The Frontier, the Survey, and the Grid', *Annals of the Association of American Geographers*, 93(1), 121–141, 2003.

Boundas, Constantin, 'Deleuze-Bergson' On the Ontology of the Virtual', in P. Patton (ed.), *Deleuze: A Critical Reader*, Oxford: Blackwell, 1996.

Braverman, Irus et al. 'Expanding the Spaces of Law', in I. Braverman et al. (eds), *The Expanding Spaces of Law: A Timely Legal Geography*, Stanford: Stanford University Press, 1–29, 2014.

Brenner, Neil, 'Henri Lefebvre's Critique of State Productivism', in Kanishka Goonewardena et al. (eds), *Space, Difference, Everyday Life: Reading Henri Lefebvre*, New York: Routledge, 231–49, 2008.

Brenner, Neil and Elden, Stuart, 'Henri Lefebvre on State, Space, Territory', *International Political Sociology*, 3, 353–377, 2009.

Brown, Alison and Kristiansen, Annali, *Urban Policies and the Right to the City: Rights, Responsibilities and Citizenship*, Paris: UNESCO, 2009.

Butler, Chris, 'Reading the Production of Suburbia in Post-war Australia', *Law Text Culture,* 9, 11–33, 2005.

Butler, Chris, 'Slicing through Space: Mobility, Rhythm and the Abstraction of Modernist Transport Planning', *Griffith Law Review*, 17(2), 470–488, 2008.

Butler, Chris, 'Critical Legal Studies and the Politics of Space', *Social and Legal Studies*, 18(3), 313–332, 2009.

Butler, Chris, *Henri Lefebvre: Spatial Politics, Everyday Life and the Right to the City,* Abingdon: Routledge, 2012.

Butler, Chris, 'Space, Politics, Justice', in C. Butler and E. Mussawir (eds), *Spaces of Justice: Peripheries, Passages, Appropriations*, Abingdon: Routledge, 113–131, 2017.

Cassirer, Ernst, 'Newton and Leibniz', *The Philosophical Review,* 52(4), 366–391, 1943.

Chambers, Peter, 'The Embrace of Border Security: Maritime Jurisdiction, National Sovereignty, and the Geopolitics of Operation Sovereign Borders', *Geopolitics*, 20(2), 404–437, 2015.

Cities Alliance, *The City Statute of Brazil: A Commentary*, São Paulo: Cities Alliance and Ministry of Cities, Brazil, 2010.

Coggin, Thomas and Pieterse, Marius, 'Rights and the City: An Exploration of the Interaction Between Socio-economic Rights and the City', *Urban Forum*, 23(3), 257–278, 2012.

Coleman, Nathaniel, 'Utopian Prospect of Henri Lefebvre', *Space and Culture*, 16(3), 349–363, 2013.

Coole, Diana and Frost, Samantha, *New Materialisms: Ontology, Agency and Politics*, Durham, NC: Duke University Press.

Cover, Robert, 'Violence and the Word', *Yale Law Journal*, 95, 1601–1629, 1986.

Cunningham, David, 'The Concept of Metropolis: Philosophy and Urban Form', *Radical Philosophy*, 133, 13–25, 2005.

Cunningham, David, 'Spacing Abstraction: Capitalism, Law and the Metropolis', *Griffith Law Review*, 17(2), 454–469, 2008.

Cunningham, David, 'Rights, Politics and Strategy: A Response to *Seeking Spatial Justice*', *City*, 14(6), 604–606, 2010.

de Souza, Marcelo L., 'Which Right to Which City? In Defence of Political-strategic Clarity', *Interface*, 2(1), 315–333, 2010.

de Villiers, Isolde, 'Leibniz, Lefebvre and the Spatial Turn in Law', *Hervormde Teologiese Studies*, 72(1), 1–6, 2016.

Delaney, David, 'Tracing Displacements: Or Evictions in the Nomosphere', *Environment and Planning D: Society and Space,* 22(6), 847–860, 2004.

Delaney, David, *The Spatial, the Legal and the Pragmatics of World-Making: Nomospheric Investigations*, Abingdon: Routledge, 2010.

Derrida, Jacques, 'Force of Law: The "Mystical Foundation of Authority"', *Cardozo Law Review*, 11, 919–1045, 1990.

Dicey, A.V., *Introduction to the Study of the Law of the Constitution*, 10th ed., London: Macmillan, 1959.

Dikeç, M., 'Justice and the Spatial Imagination', *Environment and Planning A*, 33(10), 1785–1805, 2001.

Dimendberg, Edward, 'Henri Lefebvre on Abstract Space', in A. Light and J. Smith (eds), *Philosophy and Geography II: The Production of Public Space*, Lanham: Rowman & Littlefield, 17–47, 1998.

Doel, Marcus, *Poststructuralist Geographies: The Diabolical Art of Spatial Science*, Lanham: Rowman & Littlefield, 1999.

Douzinas, Costas, 'Human Rights and Postmodern Utopia', *Law and Critique,* 11(2): 219–240, 2000.

Drakopoulou, Maria, 'Of the Founding of Law's Jurisdiction and the Politics of Sexual Difference: The Case of Roman Law', in S. McVeigh (ed.), *Jurisprudence of Jurisdiction*, London: University College London Press, 33–60, 2006.

Fainstein, Susan, *The Just City*, Ithaca: Cornell University Press, 2010.

Fernandes, Edesio, 'Constructing the "Right to the City" in Brazil', *Social and Legal Studies*, 16(2), 210–219, 2007.

Fincher, Ruth and Iveson, Kurt, 'Justice and Injustice in the City', *Geographical Research*, 50(3), 231–241, 2012.

Finchett-Maddock, Lucy, *Protest, Property and the Commons: Performances of Law and Resistance*, Abingdon: Routledge, 2016.

Fraser, Benjamin, 'Toward a Philosophy of the Urban: Henri Lefebvre's Uncomfortable Application of Bergsonism', *Environment and Planning D: Society and Space*, 26(2), 338–358, 2008.

Foucault, Michel, 'Questions on Geography' in C. Gordon (ed.), *Power/Knowledge: Selected Interviews and Other Writings 1972–77*, New York: Pantheon Books, 1980.

Graham, Stephen and Healey, Patsy, 'Relational Concepts of Space and Place: Issues for Planning Theory and Practice', *European Planning Studies*, 7(5), 623–646, 1999.

HABITAT III, 'Quito Declaration on Sustainable Cities and Human Settlements For all', 2016. https://habitat3.org/the-new-urban-agenda (accessed 20 September 2017).

Harman, Graham, *Prince of Networks: Bruno Latour and Metaphysics*, Melbourne: re.press, 2009.

Harman, Graham, 'The Well-wrought Broken Hammer: Object-oriented Literary Criticism', *New Literary History*, 43(2), 183–203, 2012.

Harvey, David, *Social Justice and the City*, Baltimore: Johns Hopkins University Press, 1973.

Harvey, David, *Justice, Nature and the Geography of Difference*. Oxford: Blackwell, 1996.

Harvey, David, 'Space as a Keyword', in *Spaces of Global Capitalism: Towards a Theory of Uneven Geographical Development*, London: Verso, 2006.

Harvey, David, 'The Right to the City', *New Left Review*, 53, 23–40, 2008.

Hegel, Georg, 'Who Thinks Abstractly?', in W. Kaufmann (ed.), *Hegel: Texts and Commentary*, Garden City, NY: Doubleday & Co., 113–118, 1966.

Hirvonen, Ari, 'The Politics of Revolt: On Benjamin and Critique of Law', *Law and Critique*, 22, 101–18, 2011.

Hodge, Paul, 'A Grievable Life? The Criminalisation and Securing of Asylum Seeker Bodies in the "violent frames" of Australia's Operation Sovereign Borders', *Geoforum*, 58, 122–131, 2015.

Hunter, Rosemary, 'Law's (masculine) Violence: Reshaping Jurisprudence', *Law and Critique*, 17(1), 27–46, 2006.

Iveson, Kurt, 'Social or Spatial Justice? Marcuse and Soja on the Right to the City', *City*, 15(2), 250–259, 2011.

Jones, Martin, 'Phase Space: Geography, Relational Thinking, and Beyond', *Progress in Human Geography*, 33(4), 487–506, 2009.

Jones, Martin, 'Limits to "Thinking Space Relationally"', *International Journal of Law in Context*, 6(3), 243–255, 2010.

Keenan, Sarah, *Subversive Property: Law and the Production of Spaces of Belonging*, Abingdon: Routledge, 2015.

Klein, Natalie, 'Assessing Australia's Push Back the Boats Policy under International Law: Legality and Accountability for Maritime Interceptions of Irregular Migrants', *Melbourne Journal of International Law*, 15(2), 414–443, 2014.

Laclau, Ernesto, *New Reflections on the Revolution of Our Time*, London: Verso, 1990.

Layard, Antonia, 'Shopping in the Public Realm: A Law of Place', *Journal of Law and Society*, 37(3), 387–544, 2010.

Lefebvre, Henri, 'Preface', in P. Boudon (ed.), *Lived-In Architecture: Le Corbusier's Pessac Revisited*, trans. G. Onn, Cambridge, MA: MIT Press, 1972.

Lefebvre, Henri, *The Survival of Capitalism: Reproduction of the Relations of Production*, London: Allison & Busby, 1976.

Lefebvre, Henri, 'Du pacte social au contrat de citoyennete', in Group de Navarrenx (eds), *Du Contrat de Citoyenneté,* Paris: Editions Syllepse et Editions Periscope: 15–37, 1990.
Lefebvre, Henri, *The Production of Space,* Oxford: Blackwell, 1991.
Lefebvre, Henri, 'Right to the City', in E. Kofman and E. Lebas (eds), *Writings on Cities,* Oxford: Blackwell, 1996.
Lefebvre, Henri, *Critique of Everyday Life II: Foundations For a Sociology of the Everyday,* London: Verso, 2002.
Lefebvre, Henri, 'Preface to the New Edition: The Production of Space', in S. Elden, E. Lebas, and E. Kofman (eds), *Key Writings,* London: Continuum: 206–213, 2003a.
Lefebvre, Henri, *The Urban Revolution,* Minneapolis: University of Minnesota Press, 2003b.
Lefebvre, Henri, 'Space and Mode of Production', in N. Brenner and S. Elden (eds), *State, Space, World: Selected Essays,* Minneapolis: University of Minnesota Press, 210–222, 2009a.
Lefebvre, Henri, 'Space: Social Product and Use Value', in N. Brenner and S. Elden (eds), *State, Space, World: Selected Essays,* Minneapolis: University of Minnesota Press, 185–195, 2009b.
Lefebvre, Henri, 'Theoretical Problems of Autogestion', in N. Brenner, and S. Elden (eds), *State, Space, World: Selected Essays,* Minneapolis: University of Minnesota Press: 138–152, 2009c.
Loftus, Alex, 'Violent Geographical Abstractions', *Environment and Planning D: Society and Space,* 33(2), 366–381, 2015.
McFarlane, Colin, 'Assemblage and Critical Urbanism', *City,* 15(2), 204–224, 2011a.
McFarlane, Colin, 'The City as Assemblage: Dwelling and Urban Space', *Environment and Planning D: Society and Space,* 29(4), 649–671, 2011b.
Malpas, Jeff, 'Putting Space in Place: Philosophical Topography and Relational Geography', *Environment and Planning D: Society and Space,* 30(2), 226–242, 2012.
Marcuse, Peter, 'From Critical Urban Theory to the Right to the City', *City* 13(2–3), 185–197, 2009.
Marcuse, Peter et al. (eds), *Searching for the Just City: Debates in Urban Theory and Practice,* New York: Routledge, 2009.
Marston, Sallie et al., 'Human Geography Without Scale', *Transactions of the Institute of British Geographers NS* 30(4), 416–432, 2005.
Martel, James, *Divine Violence: Walter Benjamin and the Eschatology of Sovereignty.* Abingdon: Routledge, 2012.
Martin, Deborah et al., 'Making Law, Making Place: Lawyers and the Production of Space', *Progress in Human Geography* 34(2), 175–192, 2010.
Marx, Karl, *Grundrisse: Foundations of the Critique of Political Economy (Rough Draft),* Harmondsworth: Penguin, 1973.
Massey, Doreen, 'Philosophy and Politics of Spatiality: Some Considerations. The Hettner-Lecture in Human Geography', *Geographische Zeitschrift,* 87(1), 1–12, 1999.
Massey, Doreen, 'Politics and Space/time', *New Left Review,* I/196, 65–84, 1992.
Massey, Doreen, *For Space,* London: Sage, 2005.
Miéville, China, *Between Equal Rights: A Marxist Theory of International Law,* Leiden: Brill, 2005.
Mitchell, Don, *The Right to the City: Social Justice and the Fight for Public Space,* New York: Guilford Press, 2003.
Morton, Timothy, 'Here Comes Everything: The Promise of Object-oriented Ontology', *Qui Parle* 19(2), 163–190, 2011.
Motha, Stewart, 'The Sovereign Event in a Nation's Law', *Law and Critique,* 13(3), 311–338, 2002.
Murdoch, Jonathan, *Post-Structuralist Geography: A Guide to Relational Space.* London: Sage, 2006.
Negri, Antonio, 'Metamorphoses', *Radical Philosophy,* 149, 21–25, 2008.
Osborne, Peter, 'The Reproach of Abstraction', *Radical Philosophy,* 127, 21–28, 2004.
Pinder, David, 'Reconstituting the Possible: Lefebvre, Utopia and the Urban Question', *International Journal of Urban and Regional Research* 39(1), 28–45, 2015.

Postone, Moishe, *Time, Labor, and Social Domination: A Reinterpretation of Marx's Critical Theory*, Cambridge: Cambridge University Press, 1993.
Philippopoulos-Mihalopoulos, Andreas, 'Spatial Justice: Law and the Geography of Withdrawal', *International Journal of Law in Context*, 6(3), 201–216, 2010.
Philippopoulos-Mihalopoulos, Andreas, 'Law's Spatial Turn: Geography, Justice and a Certain Fear of Space', *Law, Culture and the Humanities*, 7(2), 187–202, 2011.
Philippopoulos-Mihalopoulos, Andreas, *Spatial Justice: Body, Lawscape, Atmosphere*, Abingdon: Routledge, 2015.
Pirie, Gordon. 'On Spatial Justice', *Environment and Planning A*, 15, 465–73, 1983.
Purcell, Mark, 'Excavating Lefebvre: The Right to the City and its Urban Politics of the Inhabitant', *GeoJournal*, 58, 99–108, 2002.
Purcell, Mark, 'The Right to the City: The Struggle for Democracy in the Urban Public Realm', *Policy & Politics,* 43(3), 311–27, 2013.
Purcell, Mark, 'Possible Worlds: Henri Lefebvre and the Right to the City', *Journal of Urban Affairs*, 36(1), 141–154, 2014.
Rawls, John, *A Theory of Justice*, Cambridge, MA: Belknap Press of Harvard University Press, 1999.
Rose, Ed, 'Generalized Self-management: The Position of Henri Lefebvre', *Human Relations*, 31(7), 617–630, 1978.
Salter, Mark, 'When the Exception becomes the Rule: Borders, Sovereignty, and Citizenship', *Citizenship Studies*, 12(4), 365–380, 2008.
Sarat, Austin and Kearns, Thomas (eds), *Law's Violence*, Ann Arbor, MI: University of Michigan Press, 1992.
Sarat, Austin and Kearns, Thomas, 'Editorial Introduction' in Austin Sarat and Thomas Kearns (eds), *Law in Everyday Life*, Ann Arbor, MI: University of Michigan Press, 1993.
Schloenhardt, Andreas and Craig Colin, '"Turning Back the Boats": Australia's Interdiction of Irregular Migrants at Sea', *International Journal of Refugee Law*, 27(4), 536–572, 2015.
Seigworth, Gregory, 'Banality For Cultural Studies', *Cultural Studies*, 14(2), 227–268, 2000.
Sheppard, Eric 'Geographic Dialectics?', *Environment and Planning A*, 40(11), 2603–2612, 2008.
Sohn-Rethel, Alfred, *Intellectual and Manual Labour: A Critique of Epistemology*, New Jersey: Humanities Press, 1978.
Soja, Edward, *Postmodern Geographies: The Reassertion of Space in Critical Social Theory*, London: Verso, 1989.
Soja, Edward, *Seeking Spatial Justice*, Minnesota: University of Minnesota Press, 2010.
Sklar, Lawrence, *Space, Time, and Spacetime*, Berkeley, CA: University of California Press, 1974.
Stanek, Łukasz, *Henri Lefebvre on Space: Architecture, Urban Research, and the Production of Theory*, Minneapolis: University of Minnesota Press, 2011.
Thrift, Nigel, *Non-Representational Theory: Space/Politics/Affect*, Abingdon: Routledge, 2008.
Toscano, Alberto, 'The Culture of Abstraction', *Theory, Culture and Society*, 25(4), 57–75, 2008a.
Toscano, Alberto, 'The Open Secret of Real Abstraction', *Rethinking Marxism*, 20(2), 273–287, 2008b.
Tomba, Massimiliano, 'Another Kind of *Gewalt*: Beyond Law, Re-reading Walter Benjamin', *Historical Materialism*, 17, 126–144, 2009.
UNESCO, *Urban Policies and the Right to the City: International Public Debates*, Paris: UNESCO, 2006.
UN-HABITAT, *The Right to the City: Bridging the Urban Divide*, Rio de Janeiro: World Urban Forum, United Nations, 2010.
Valverde, Mariana, 'Seeing Like a City: The Dialectic of Modern and Premodern Ways of Seeing in Urban Governance', *Law & Society Review*, 45(2), 277–312, 2011.
van Marle, Karin and de Villiers, Isolde, 'Law and Resistance in the City of Pretoria: Space, History and the Everyday', *Australian Feminist Law Journal*, 38(1), 129–145, 2013.

Whatmore, Sarah, *Hybrid Geographies: Natures Cultures Spaces*, London: Sage, 2002.
Wilson, Japhy, '"The Devastating Conquest of the Lived by the Conceived": The Concept of Abstract Space in the Work of Henri Lefebvre', *Space and Culture*, 16(3), 364–380, 2013.
Young, Iris M., *Justice and the Politics of Difference*, Princeton, NJ: Princeton University Press, 1990.

3

A prison around your ankle and a border in every street

Theorising law, space and the subject

Sarah Keenan

On 19 June 2015, Britain's High Court ordered that the electronic monitoring tag worn by 'DD', a 'terrorism-related activity' suspect, be removed due to the disproportionate effect the tag was having on DD's mental health and on the everyday life of his family.[1] DD is a refugee who suffers from post-traumatic stress disorder from the extreme violence he lived through in Somalia. While 'wearing' the unremovable tag around his ankle, DD was restricted in his movement and activities. He was forbidden from being in the same room as a wide range of common devices such as mobile phones unless they were switched off, and he required Home Office permission to meet with friends. Unable to engage in normal social interaction, DD's children felt humiliated and distressed and fell behind at school. DD was required to keep the tag charged, which meant sitting himself with his tag connected to a mains socket for extended periods every day. Suffering from a psychotic illness, DD believed that the tag contained a bomb that could be detonated by MI5 at any moment. During the three years he 'wore' the ankle tag, DD developed severe insomnia and suicidal feelings, banging his head against the wall or floor and hearing voices in his head, ultimately leading to the High Court decision that the tag be removed on human rights grounds. Although he was ostensibly living at home with his family, able to leave his house to go to work and other 'normal' activities, there was no escape for DD. He had a prison around his ankle.

Just a few weeks after the High Court's *DD* decision, the British government announced that it would pass laws introducing possible prison sentences for landlords who fail to check their tenants' visas and making it easier for landlords to evict tenants without the so-called 'right to rent' (Bate and Ota, 2016: 3). As part of her efforts to convince poor African migrants that 'our streets are not paved with gold' (Dathan, 2015), then Home Secretary Theresa May made the announcement as an intensification of the 'hostile environment' for irregular migrants which she had already begun creating. The Immigration Act 2014 had introduced a host of measures to restrict access to essential services for irregular migrants living in Britain (Bate and Ota, 2016). The Immigration Act 2016 (which is now in force) bolstered this hostile environment by creating the new offence of leasing premises to a migrant without a valid visa.[2] Landlords who commit the offence are liable for a fine and/or up to five years in prison.[3] The new provision passed despite the Residential Landlord Association, migrant rights groups and various charities opposing it. As the Church of England put it, the new Act creates "a border in every street" (Robinson, 2014).

Like the 'prison walls' that surrounded DD, the 'borders' produced by the right-to-rent requirement are both invisible and real, intermittent and permanent; these 'walls' and 'borders' attach to individual subjects wherever they go and are internal to the community/nation space that the subject has already entered. In this piece, I explore how space, the subject and the connection between them can be theorised in the context of landscapes such as these – prisons around ankles and borders on every street. Discussing the case studies of *DD* and the right to rent, I seek to make explicit the spatiality of law's production of subjects, in turn showing the varied and ever-evolving ways through which law produces material boundaries. Bringing together and building on legal geography, critical race theory and critical disability studies, I put forward the concept of 'taking space with you' as a way to understand landscapes such as those produced by electronic tags and internal borders. What emerges is a picture of both space and the subject that is far more dynamic, blurred and contingent than law would have us believe.

Theorising law, space and the subject

The liberal democratic state, and the law it creates, are underpinned and legitimised by notions of universality and neutrality – theoretically, state law delivers justice to all subjects on an equal basis, free of any political agenda. Critical race and feminist theorists have long noted the flaws in this theorisation, demonstrating ways in which law operates unevenly depending on who you are (Bell, 2000; MacKinnon, 1983). More recently, legal geography has also demonstrated ways in which law operates unevenly depending on *where* you are (Blomley, 1994). Coming from a variety of perspectives and with subject matter ranging from clear geopolitical conflicts, such as the Israeli planning laws used to destroy Palestinian homes in Jerusalem (Braverman, 2007), to seemingly mundane issues, such as the hidden politics of English hedgerow maintenance (Holder, 1999), legal geography explores the effects of law on physical space and the effects which physical space in turn has on the subjects who live and move through it. By exploring the materiality of particular places, legal geography exposes some of the differential material effects of law; the uneven ways in which law shapes landscapes. As I have discussed elsewhere, legal geography tends to use case studies to show how physical space – whether an area, a city or a border – has social meaning and effects, some of which are violent (Keenan, 2015). Waldron's discussion of the prohibition of sleeping in public, for example, explains how this law, though framed as universal, in practice affects homeless people disproportionally and makes the city a hostile and dangerous place for them (see Waldron, 1997). Legal geography, consistent with other bodies of critical legal theory, shows law's uneven effects on different categories of subjects.

In an attempt to move beyond the law/space binary which legal geography tends to take as its analytical starting point, some theorists have used neologisms to demonstrate the inextricable connection between the two. David Delaney's 'nomosphere' (2010), Nicole Graham's 'lawscape' (2011) and Andreas Philippopoulos-Mihalopoulos's 'lawscape' and 'atmosphere' (2007, 2015) each achieve new ways of theorising law, space and the subject, each from distinct perspectives. As Bennett and Layard point out, there is also a long history of scholarship preceding what is now known as legal geography that shows how legal rules, practices and governance produce landscapes and places (e.g., Harvey, 1981, Lefebvre, 1991, McAuslan, 1980) (Bennett and Layard, 2015: 408). Work by scholars who may not define themselves as 'legal geographers' also continues to be relevant to understanding the connection between law, space and the subject. For example, critical migration law scholars (see Dembour, 2015, El-Enany, 2015) demonstrate the disjuncture between the way in which law constructs the relationship between space and the subject, and the actual lived relationship that people have with the places they reside.

Some of the most insightful and reflexive work on law, space and the subject has come from critical race scholars. Sherene Razack's analysis of the murder trial of Aboriginal sex worker Pamela George suggests that in the Canadian context, law attaches spaces of violence to Aboriginal subjects wherever they move (2002). George was killed in 1995 by two white male college students on an end-of-term drinking spree. The men enticed George into their car and then drove her to an isolated area outside the city where they beat her and left her to die. Analysing the police investigation and the trial transcript, Razack demonstrates how George was seen 'to belong to a space of prostitution and Aboriginality, in which violence routinely occurs' while the men who killed her were seen as belonging to a space of white middle-class respectability (ibid.: 124). Even posthumously, George remained conceptually and practically attached to a space in which violence is normalised.

In her book on inquests and inquiries into Aboriginal deaths in custody, Razack deepens her analysis of the spatiality which law constructs for racialised bodies (Razack, 2015). Razack discusses the inquiry into the death of Frank Paul, an Aboriginal man who died of hyperthermia due to acute alcohol toxication after police left him in a Vancouver alleyway in December 1998. Engaging with Samira Kawash, Razack describes how Paul came to embody a specific Aboriginal homelessness and placelessness which meant that he needed to be constantly removed from public spaces of the settler state (ibid.: 43–45). Razack argues that Paul was constructed by police as belonging to an 'alien' world which needed to be expunged from the Canadian state (ibid.: 44). Analysing the inquest into the death in custody of Paul Alphonse, who was stomped on so hard that a boot print was left on his chest, Razack argues that police and other settlers view the Indigenous body as 'the frontier, the site on which a savage war is fought . . . considered as bestial, close to nature, and a threat, the Indigenous body must be violated if the border between wilderness and civilisation is to be maintained' (ibid.: 84). Razack argues that the racial/proprietal line between Indigenous and settler is marked out spatially: 'it is not only that Indigenous peoples must be confined to reserves, but their own necessary incursions into settler spaces . . . must also be policed and constrained' (ibid.: 167). In each of these cases, Razack demonstrates that within the broader space of a settler colonial state, the Indigenous subject takes a space of racialised violence with him or her – whether it is to alleyways, city outskirts, police vans or rural areas. This space of racialised violence, Razack argues, is in turn constitutive of white settler space. Discussing the spatiality of settler colonialism in Australia, Suvendrini and Pugliese similarly argue that foundational and ongoing white violence against Indigenous bodies – violence minimised and justified by Australian law – constructs national space today (2011).

Feminist scholarship emphasising the importance of the public/private spatial divide also productively complicates the relationship between law, space and the subject. Carol Sanger explains how the introduction of the motor car in the United States in the early 1900s failed in its promise to increase the free and safe movement of women through public space (2001). Although cars increased women's mobility in the physical sense of enabling women with cars to go further and faster in a vehicle that insulated them from direct contact with the outside, the car also increased women's domestic duties because they became responsible for the delivery of children, husbands and goods (ibid.: 36). The layout of modern cities and the gendered division of labour that it supports – with women being responsible for domestic life in the suburbs and men performing paid work in the city – is dependent on the existence of the car (ibid.: 35).[4] The car also became a site where rape and other violence against women was an increased danger (ibid.: 37). So while the car offered women a new-found mobility that could take them greater physical distances, in a shorter period of time and with a kind of new safety and social acceptance, it also worsened both the gendered division of labour and the gendered vulnerability to violence in an enclosed space with male acquaintances. Women could move further and faster, but their space of gendered violence and oppression went with them. And the gendered, mobile space of the car in turn contributed to the construction of the city space, including its various spaces of sexual violence. Indeed, the murder of Pamela George discussed above is demonstrative of the mobile space of sexual violence against women facilitated by cars.

In the cases discussed by Razack and Sanger, law was productive of subjects who were mobile, but always spatialised in a particular way despite their physical location. So the woman in the car could move from place to place but would take her gendered space with her, including her vulnerability to being sexually assaulted; and the Indigenous subject could move out of reserves and out of racialised parts of the city, but a space of violence always went with him or her. The movement of this conceptual and social space attached to the subject has physical effects.

Understanding dynamic space: 'We don't cross borders, borders cross us'

Legal geography, critical race and feminist engagements with law and space suggest an understanding of space as consisting of multiple, dynamic realities, which affect different subjects in different ways. Geographer Doreen Massey's work on space and place offers a theorisation which accounts for these differences. Instead of thinking of places as bounded areas, Massey imagines them as 'articulated moments in networks of social relations and understandings', where most of those relations and understandings are constructed on a scale that extends much further than what for that moment is defined as the place itself (Massey, 1993: 66). This is place as a collision or intersection within multiple networked systems rather than as a discrete and permanent site – it is a *moment* because it is temporary rather than permanent, and it is *articulated* because it is only when that moment is named as place that it acquires meaning as place. Because the same moment will be experienced and articulated differently by different subjects, this understanding of place also accounts for the same place having mismatched and even contrasting meanings. The place that is 'the British Border' at Heathrow Terminal 4 airport on any given day, for example, is a familiar workplace for UK Border Agency officers, a congested but still fast-moving queue for EU-passport holders, and a very physical barrier – a place of life and death – for a refugee who has just landed with the hope of being granted asylum. The meaning attached to place is always temporary and subjective.

Place, for Massey, is thus a point or moment within the much larger and ever-evolving dimension of space. As Massey argues, space is not 'already there', but is constituted through interactions on an ongoing basis (Massey, 2006: 9). As it is the product of interactions, space is necessarily multiplicitous rather than unitary, and as interactions are themselves processes rather than conclusions, space is always under construction, it is never finished or closed (ibid.). As Massey puts it, space is 'a simultaneity of stories so far' (ibid.). On this understanding, space and place are intimately connected to the subjects who move in and through them and to modes of regulation and norms of behaviour, such as those articulated and enacted through law. Space is constantly produced and reproduced in part by the subjects who move through it.

This understanding of space and place allows for spatial entities such as nation-states and prisons to be understood beyond their bounded physical landmass. Nation-state borders, as Etienne Balibar has argued, are not simple lines of demarcation, but complex institutions (2002: 84–85). Bridget Anderson, Nandita Sharma and Cynthia Wright argue that borders are the mark of a relationship based on deep divisions and inequalities between people (2009: 6). Borders, they argue, 'follow people and surround them as they try to access paid labour, welfare benefits, health, labour protections, education, civil associations, and justice' (ibid.). Or as Sydney activist group Cross Border Collective put it, 'we don't cross borders, borders cross us'.[5] Border control regimes today operate upon particular individuals in physical locations far from the physical perimeters of nation-states. This idea of the border as an institution rather than a line calls for a complication of any idea of the nation-state as a bounded physical entity. Inderpal Grewal has powerfully argued for an understanding of 21st-century 'America' as a nationalist discourse, one that produces different kinds of agency and diverse subjects, both inside and outside the territorial bounds of the United States (2005: 2). Although this discourse of America is a nationalist one, it is produced through and productive of cultural, political and economic practices that are transnational, evolving through networks which reach well beyond the boundaries of the nation-state (ibid.: 198). Grewal argues that the meaning of being an American is not defined through legal citizenship but rather through participation in consumer citizenship – cultural inclusion through consumptive participation in the free market capitalist economy (ibid.: 8–10). As well as complicating the idea of the place that is America today, Grewal's analysis demonstrates that the realities of both identity production and space-subject connection are far more complicated than is assumed in laws relating to citizenship and migration.

Thinking through the related production of subjectivities through space and law goes some way to understanding the landscape of electronic tags and borders on every street. The surveillance and visa-checking measures imposed by law not only shape the space in and through which legal subjects live, they also produce new categories of subjects: subjects who experience prison boundaries and nation-state borders no matter their physical location. Massey's understanding of place as articulated moment – a moment which will be experienced differently by different subjects – helps explain how what is to most people a relatively inconspicuous plastic ankle tag is to DD a mobile prison, and what is to most people a house for rent is to an irregular migrant in England today a national border. This spatialisation of subjects can make those subjects vulnerable to particular kinds of violence (e.g., physical incarceration, deportation, police brutality). Balibar's and Anderson et al.'s theorisations of borders as complex institutions and Grewal's theorisation of transnational America help in understanding the ongoing production of space and subjectivities through political and legal processes. But if subjectivities are produced through space and law, how can we understand the boundaries of the subject? Where does the subject end and space begin?

The space you take with you

In addressing the question of where the subject ends and space begins, I have previously argued that it is useful to examine property as a particularly intimate relation between space and the subject, a relation in which the separation between space and subject can become blurred. Specifically, I have argued that property can be understood as a spatially contingent relation of belonging which is constitutive of the subject (Keenan, 2015). As well as property ownership, belonging can signify membership of a community, a relationship to place, and/or a behaviour or identity that 'fits' (Cooper, 1998). Nira Yuval-Davis et al. describe belonging as being about emotional attachment, about feeling safe and/or 'at home' (Nira Yuval-Davis et al.,

2006). Belonging connotes a sense of emotional, social and spatial propriety. Davina Cooper considers belonging in two ways: firstly the relationship whereby an object, space, or rights over it belong to a subject ('subject-object'), and secondly the constitutive relationship of part to whole whereby attributes, qualities or characteristics belong to a thing or a subject ('part-whole') (2007: 629). Both types of belonging implicate social relations and networks that extend beyond the immediate subject and object of property; property is instead understood as 'a set of networked relations in which the subject is embedded' (ibid.: 636). In order to constitute property, I argue that the set of networked relations to which Cooper refers must not only include one of belonging, but also be structured in such a way that the relation of belonging is conceptually, socially and physically supported or 'held up' by space (Keenan, 2015). Whether the relation of belonging is one of ownership (subject-object belonging) or of membership (part-whole belonging), space must hold up the relation in order for it to constitute property. Indeed, I argue that ownership and membership overlap. Drawing on Margaret Davies (1999) and Cheryl Harris (1993), I argue that 'having' and 'being' are intimately related and overlapping issues.

While Cheryl Harris argues that whiteness is property in an ownership sense (whiteness as an object that the white subject owns), it can also be understood as property in the membership sense: whiteness as a social category of which the white subject is a part. Whiteness is a relation of belonging; white people can enjoy the privileges of whiteness because they *belong to* the various social relations and networks that constitute whiteness. As sociologists such as Ruth Frankenberg have shown, those relations and networks are complex and far-reaching. Whiteness, like all identity categories, is socially constructed through historically specific fusions of political, economic and other forces (1993). And whiteness in turn 'constructs daily practices and worldviews in complex relations with material life' (Frankenberg, 1993: 228). That is, whiteness is productive of subjectivities. Understanding property as belonging helps to illuminate how a subject's location within and relationship to physical and social space can affect who that subject is. Belonging is a material relation that connects and can even blur space and the subject such that it can be difficult to determine where one ends and the other begins.

In her work on phenomenology, Sara Ahmed explores the way particular bodies come to be orientated in space, and how space takes shape through having bodies 'extended into it' in particular ways (2007: 11). Looking specifically at race and sexuality, Ahmed argues that these characteristics, which are generally described as bodily properties, are better understood as spatial orientations. For Ahmed, spaces become contoured by being repetitively oriented around some bodies more than others:

> What is repeated is a very style of embodiment, a way of inhabiting space, which claims space by the accumulation of gestures of 'sinking' into that space. If whiteness allows bodies to move with comfort through space, and to inhabit the world as if it were home, then those bodies take up more space.
>
> (Ahmed, 2007: 159)

The subject is thus produced as 'white' through the shaping of space. Ahmed argues that 'we do not acquire our orientations just because we find things here or there. Rather certain objects are available to us because of lines that we have already taken' (2007: 21). So although subjects such as the Aboriginal subjects discussed by Razack seem to 'take space with them', they do not do this in the sense that they pick up an original or essential space and carry it with them from one location to another. Rather, subjects exist in and are constituted by space – combining with space such that they cannot be easily separated from it, conceptually or materially. Who subjects are, what is materially within their reach and their vulnerability to violence is therefore constantly (re)determined by where they have been and what has happened around them.

If we conceptualise the ongoing (re)constitution of the space-subject connection which Razack and Ahmed describe as 'taking space with you', the questions that then arise are, firstly, what constitutes 'the space you take with you' and secondly, how does this 'taking' happen? Merleau-Ponty's *Phenomenology of Perception* offers answers to both questions in his description of the body in motion as inseparable from its previous position in time and space (2010: 162). The body here-now is in a live relation with the body there-then; they cannot be disconnected. Merleau-Ponty writes of the body rather than the subject, but his writing offers a useful way to understand the subject as an embodied and spatial being. For Merleau-Ponty, the body is both the essential mechanism for perceiving space and time, and itself a part of space and time: 'I am not in space and time, nor do I conceive space and time; I belong to them, my body combines with them and includes them' (ibid.). The body thus takes space with it because it is itself part of space (Keenan, 2015: 160). The body *belongs to*, *combines with* and *includes* time and space. The body thus necessarily takes space with it, and is necessarily more than a closed, complete physical entity. For Merleau-Ponty, the space the body takes with it is constituted by where and when the body has come from. The taking of space happens not as a matter of agency but as a matter of spatial structure.

Critical disability scholar Margrit Shildrick argues that Merleau-Ponty's account of embodiment is 'effectively coincident with the emergence of the subject' (Shildrick, 2015: 14). That is, the body appears in Merleau-Ponty's writing as and with the body. This account, Shildrick continues, 'relies on a sense of both the intercorporeality of our everyday engagements with others . . . and of the environment itself shaping intentional action' (ibid.). As subjects, we are shaped by our physical interactions with other subjects and with the broader spaces in which we live. Through those physical interactions, we in turn shape those spaces, making them more likely to accommodate us and others materially similar to us. The shaping of space is a political issue, as the kind of space each subject takes with her helps determine not only her access to resources but also her vulnerability to violence. Engaging with Donna Haraway's provocation 'why should our bodies end at the skin?' from her classic 'Cyborg Manifesto' (Haraway, 1991), Shildrick points out both the impossibility of limiting 'the human/machine interface' of conventional prostheses (such as medically produced prosthetic limbs used by people with disabilities) to their intended function, and the contingent and relational process of assemblage in the Deleuzian sense (Shildrick, 2015: 21). The embodied subject extends past the bounds of the skin, making, unmaking and varying herself as she moves through life as a hybrid of organic and non-organic components. This reality debunks liberal conceptualisations of subjects as fully bounded bodies, separate and distinct from each other and from their environments.

While Shildrick's analysis is concerned with the normative standards used to judge particular bodies and subjects as less whole or complete than others because of disability, her analysis is also useful in understanding the inseparability of subjects and spaces more broadly. Critical disability scholars such as Shildrick show that embodied subjects are hybrids – combining with, separating from and being both enabled and obstructed by biomedical prosthetics and physical environments (Pothier and Devlin, 2006; Goodley, 2007). This hybridity is not only true for subjects whose bodies are 'disabled' – anyone who has taken medication, had a tooth cavity filled or ascended via an elevator is, to some extent, a cyborg: embodied subjects who combine with technology in such ways are each 'unnatural' to some extent. There is no purely organic, bounded embodied subject who lives in isolation from others and from the space in which it exists.

Nor is the hybridity of the embodied subject limited to issues of ability. Race, gender and other markers of belonging are also materialised, on an individual level, through intimate interactions between the body and that beyond it. Living in a particular place, wearing particular kinds of clothing or consuming particular kinds of food can operate as signifiers of racial difference, even though they are not part of the body (Lentin, 2008). Structures of oppression such as able-ism, racism and sexism operate spatially. As Sara Ahmed argues, racism can operate as an obstructive 'brick wall' built up by history, a wall that can appear in different places and times, but only in front of particular subjects (2012). The interaction between the subject and the 'brick wall' – the process of coming up against the 'brick wall' racialises (or in other contexts, disables or genders) the subject. The 'brick wall' of racism is a space that many subjects take with them as they move, whether the journey is across the world or across the road. While race is a social construct originating in European colonial thought (Augstein, 1996), it is also a structure of oppression that is reproduced on an everyday level by laws and norms that restrict the physical spaces that particular subjects can safely occupy. The category of race and the racist environments that maintain it are produced through the repeated operation of 'brick walls' which hinder the paths of particular subjects and let them know they do not belong. Embodiment, or *the kind of space you take with you*, is produced through the subject's interactions with the material and social world. Taking space with you can thus best be understood as the process that every embodied subject goes through as she moves through life, combining and connecting with, enabled, obstructed, and to an extent defined by the heterogeneous multiplicity beyond the skin.

Below, I explore the process of taking space with you in the context of electronic tags and the 'right to rent' requirement set out in the Immigration Acts of 2014 and 2016.

DD v. Secretary of State for the Home Department

A new kind of penal subject

The electronic tag is a technology which encapsulates the material way in which law can combine space and the subject, producing bespoke landscapes of regulation for tagged subjects wherever they may travel, and in turn constructing the hybrid subject. While prosthetic limbs combine with bodies to enable those bodies to do what they otherwise could not, electronic tags combine with bodies to prevent them from doing what they otherwise could. Electronic monitoring technology such as tags is defined by Nellis and Rossell as 'a form of remote surveillance control, a means of flexibly regulating the spatial and temporal schedules of an offender's life' (2011, cited in Nellis et al., 2013: 4–5). Originating in the US in the 1980s, electronic monitoring is now used in over 30 countries worldwide (ibid.: 1). First introduced in Britain in 1988, electronic tagging was seen as a way to reduce prison numbers while still punishing the offender and to cut public costs involved in the criminal justice system by introducing a scheme that would be maintained by private providers (Mair and Nellis, 2013: 65). According to criminologists Nellis, Beyens and Kaminsky, the intended effect of monitoring is to remind the offender that he is being watched,

> and that his compliance with the spatial and temporal regulations that the court or prison has imposed on him will be relayed to a judicial or penal authority, with the possibility that he may be 'breached' and subject to a more severe penalty.
>
> (2013: 5)

While the ankle tag is the physical element that attaches to the subject, the electronic monitoring process involves a range of different technologies and apparatuses including charge points and central monitoring centres. The subject is made aware that the tag and related technology will be used to monitor his location at all times, so positioning relative to any zones that he is either confined to or prohibited from entering can be enforced upon him without putting up any physical barriers or changing the space for other subjects.

Because those who are subject to electronic monitoring experience a level of punitive surveillance that is distinct from both probation and community service, Nellis, Beyens and Kaminsky argue that electronic monitoring 'has created a new category of penal subject' (2013: 1). The electronically tagged subject is not a prisoner in the traditional sense because he is not physically incarcerated in an institutional building dedicated to the confinement of those who have been convicted or charged with a crime. Indeed, the physical tag itself is fairly innocuous as an object. In DD's case, the tag was

> slightly larger than a sports watch . . . mounted on a single band of soft material which can allow a sock to be worn beneath it but is small enough so that it cannot slip off the foot . . . it is waterproof.
>
> (*DD* at [26])

But the physical tag attached to the subject's ankle, in combination with the subject's knowledge of the physical areas to which he is confined at particular times *and* of the constant monitoring of his location through the tag means that the subject is spatially confined and subjectively disciplined and punished. In these ways, the tagged subject is spatialised as a prisoner despite his location outside of prison. He becomes a hybrid of his organic body and the networked inorganic material which is attached to him, his body extending past the skin and his consequent position and capabilities in the world defining his subjectivity.

To continue the Supreme Court's description in *DD*, the tag

> transmits a signal which can be picked up by a monitoring box which should be kept on an immovable item in the appellant's residence. Outside the residence the tag records its location. At all times the information is relayed to the monitoring company. Thus it can indicate, for example, if the appellant were to enter any area which he was prohibited from entering. In order to comply with the obligation to keep the tag charged, the appellant must attach it to a charging unit which is connected to a mains socket.
>
> (at [26]–[27])

The set of networked relations in which the tagged subject is embedded burdens him with a disabling property – the tag and its wider technology dictate where the subject belongs and the suspect/offender group to which he belongs. The body of the subject combines with the tag, becoming a hybrid, his existence as a tagged subject an assemblage of actions (both his own and others'), rules, systems, negotiations, tests, technicians, beliefs and expectations. Similar to Shildrik's description of the Paralympic athlete's body as a relational artefact, the body of the tagged subject neither ends at the skin, nor expresses solely his incorporation of the tag – his tagged body can only be understood in terms of its permeability and of the ongoing process involved with producing it (Shildrick, 2015: 20). Echoing Balibar's and Anderson et al.'s understanding of the border, the 'walls' that confine the tagged subject are not simple lines of territorial demarcation, but complex institutions. Those institutions are productive of both a space of confinement and regulation, and a surveilled and punished subjectivity. Like Ahmed's 'brick walls' which block the path of racialised subjects (while white subjects walking the same path continue smoothly on), these walls are not made of actual bricks. Nonetheless, the walls that confine the tagged subject prevent that subject from going to particular places and from being and thinking in particular ways. These walls are produced through that subject's own embodied subjectivity.

The 'new kind of penal subject' produced by tags is one which invokes, to a notable degree, the subject's own mentality in his spatial confinement. The tagged subject exists in and is constituted by the space of the tag and its network – what is around his ankle and in his head determines what is materially within his reach, his vulnerability to actual imprisonment, deportation or other state sanction and, to a significant extent, who he is. While he wears the tag, no matter his physical location, he is always in a particular place in Massey's sense – in an articulated moment, an intersection within multiple networked systems rather than a discrete and permanent site. For DD, the tag and its associated Terrorism Prevention and Investigation Measures ('TPIM') requirements of regularly charging at a mains point and having very limited access to electronic communication devices in his home contributed to his growing psychosis and acute paranoia. He and his family became socially isolated because of the limitations on DD's movement, all communication from their home, and their feelings of humiliation and sadness at the TPIM. DD was obsessively worried about not properly charging the tag and about inadvertently damaging it. While DD's severe insomnia, self-harm and suicidal feelings were extreme, his belief that the tag was there to punish him, that it contained a camera and a bomb and that voices and noises emanated from it are an extension to a psychotic level of the compliant mentality which the tag is designed to create. Indeed, without the subject's own knowledge that he is constantly being monitored and will be punished if he breaches his spatial boundaries, the tags would not work. Whereas walls constrain the incarcerated prisoner and the panopticon invokes the incarcerated prisoner's own mentality in controlling what he does, the tagged subject's mind and body constrain his behaviour and location.

The use of electronic tags for the monitoring of terrorist suspects in Britain was introduced in 2005 pursuant to the Prevention of Terrorism Act (ibid.: 73). Under the 2005 Act, the Secretary of State could make an individual subject to a Control Order if he had 'reasonable grounds for suspecting' that that individual is or had been involved in terrorism-related activity (s2(1)(a)). Control Orders were thus grantable upon a standard of proof lower than both the criminal 'beyond reasonable doubt' and the civil 'balance of probabilities' and allowed restrictions to be placed upon the movement, activities, social relations and life choices of the controlled person, who could be required to wear an electronic tag at all times (Zedner, 2007).[6] Control Orders were criticised for damaging the basic presumptions of criminal procedure and for imposing considerable psychological burdens on those subject to them (ibid.). Lucia Zedner noted that many individuals subject to Control Orders had poor mental health histories, and that

> Control Orders leave their subjects unable to know the evidence against them; subject to extensive and indefinite restrictions upon their liberty and their quality of life; and powerless to challenge the grounds for their imposition. Coupled to these burdens is the knowledge that, in some cases at least, attempts are being made to return them to countries where they may face prosecution or risk human rights violations, including torture or even death.
>
> (2007: 181)

Control Orders were replaced by TPIMs in 2011. While TPIMs were intended to address some of the civil liberties concerns raised in relation to Control Orders, their restrictive measures and low standard of proof remain (Walker and Horne, 2012). Significantly, TPIMs can still require subjects to wear an electronic tag at all times and can still restrict the possession and/or use of electronic devices such as mobile phones. It was pursuant to the 2011 Act that, in October 2012, DD was placed on a TPIM.

Weighed down by history

How did DD arrive in his position of suffering psychosis and paranoia from a TPIM tag around his ankle? Born in Somalia in 1976, DD came to Britain in 2003 and was granted refugee status. As set out by the Supreme Court, DD 'had when 14 or 15 experienced the murder of his uncle, aunt and two cousins and their bodies had been left to rot in his family home since the warlords responsible for their murder would not permit them to be buried' (at [42]). He left Somalia and returned in 2003, after which 'His father, older brother and brother in law were murdered in front of him and he was kidnapped and held for ransom by the militia men who had been responsible for some two weeks' (at [42]). Upon his release, he came to Britain. 'Following the deaths of his brother and mother in 2007', the court continues, 'his mood lowered and he began to hear noises and voices associated with his experiences' (at [42]). In 2008 DD was arrested and charged with two offences under the Terrorism Act 2006, one relating to the dissemination of terrorist publications and one relating to receiving money knowing or having reasonable grounds to suspect it would be used to support terrorism (at [13]). He was acquitted in 2009 (at [18]), but was put on a TPIM in 2012 (at [1]) because the Security Service assessed that despite his acquittal, DD was

> a supporter of the Somali based terrorist organisation Al-Shabaab and had . . . been involved in sending funds and equipment to support its activities and radicalising, recruiting, assisting and funding individuals to travel to Somalia for terrorist related activity. He had contributed to, indeed had been involved in setting up, extremist websites. He raised money for Al-Shabaab and intended to travel to Somalia for terrorist related activity purposes.
>
> (at [8])

Al-Shabaab, which had become a proscribed terrorist organisation in Britain in 2010, emerged in 2006 out of the latest wave of violence and unrest that has plagued Somalia since Italian and British colonialism (Gartenstein-Ross, 2009). It was earlier formations of violence and unrest that forced DD to leave Somalia in 2003, and which remain with him today in what has been diagnosed as PTSD. Ahmed writes that our spatial orientations and what is materially within our reach do not happen by chance, but as a result of 'lines we have already taken' (2007: 21). In DD's case, those lines include the complex post-colonial conflicts in Somalia, where he encountered extreme and enduring violence at close proximity and on multiple occasions, and from which he attempted to flee. Though not convicted of any offence, DD's historical trajectories and encounters with law have positioned him as belonging to a space of violence, constant suspicion and pre-crime, embodying a threat that must be pre-emptively stopped and punished. Through the tag, law has produced a landscape in which the subject is physically, psychically and juridically inseparable from his surrounding space. Combining with the tag, DD's body is literally weighed down by his history. Until the Supreme Court decision ordering it be removed, the tag and its associated processes combined with DD's body to form a hybrid which took a space of imprisonment – complete with 'walls', state violence and surveillance – with him wherever he went.

The Immigration Acts 2014 and 2016

A new kind of bordered landscape

While electronic tags create a landscape in which 'brick walls' exist for particular subjects by physically attaching a networked device to the bodies of those subjects, the Immigration Act 2016 (building on the Immigration Act 2014) creates a landscape in which 'brick walls' exist for particular subjects by creating administrative barriers. As part of the government's plan to create a 'hostile environment' for irregular migrants in Britain, the Immigration Acts of 2014 and 2016 introduce a scheme of regulation which creates a landscape in which a subject's immigration status acts as a physical barrier to safe housing and other basic needs. To use Andreas Philippopoulos-Mihalopoulos's terms, 'the lawscape emanates from every body . . . human, natural, artificial bodies come together in determining and being determined by the law' (2015: 69). The particular 'lawscape' of the Immigration Act's brick walls emanates only from particular racialised bodies: they take the space of the border (or for Ahmed, the 'brick wall' of racism) with them wherever they move. While a subject's visa status has traditionally been checked at the border, the Acts introduce a range of 'in-country' immigration status checks, meaning that those who provide not only housing but also banking services, drivers' licences and marriage will be required to check the immigration status of applicants before providing them with the relevant service/access. Should landlords and other providers fail to check applicants' visa statuses or should they provide housing to a subject without a valid visa, they will be liable for a civil penalty (Immigration Act 2016 s39).

Human rights group Liberty describes the new immigration checks as 'gateway requirements' for access to basic services (Robinson, 2014), the Asylum Support Appeals Project described them as 'hurdles' (2017), and the Church of England predicted they would create 'a border in every street' (Schatzberger, 2015: 399). The in-country 'gateways', hurdles' and 'borders' that these groups refer to are, like Sara Ahmed's 'brick walls', not simply metaphorical. For subjects who have had their claims for asylum rejected, who have overstayed their visas or who for other reasons do not have either EU citizenship or a valid British passport or visa, these regulations constitute material barriers to physical spaces. These barriers exist only for particular subjects, so like electronic tags, the Act produces landscapes of bespoke regulation not by building physical walls but by ensuring that particular subjects are out of place and vulnerable to potential deportation no matter their physical location.

Many predicted that landlords will simply opt to rent to tenants with 'British-sounding names' so as to avoid the risk of contravention and the need to perform extra paperwork, and a 2017 report into the effect of the Act confirms this to be the case (Patel and Peel, 2017). As well as creating a 'hostile environment' for irregular migrants, the combining of private property and border controls reproduces a national space in which all non-white subjects seeking rental accommodation are liable to be spatialised as aliens, taking a space of exclusion and vulnerability with them wherever they go. In a direct application of Ahmed (2007) above, 'whiteness allows bodies to move with comfort through space, and to inhabit the world as if it were home' and British space in turn becomes contoured around white bodies. Those who come up against the 'brick wall' of right to rent cannot move with comfort through space; instead they are delayed and halted in their attempts to inhabit the world as home. This interaction embodies the delayed/halted subject as racially other. Every halting interaction a subject has with the internal British border produced by the Immigration Acts positions the subject as outside the (white) British space of belonging. The space that the irregular migrant – and those who resemble her – takes with her as she travels within Britain is a process of constant negotiation with borders. This process not only determines the subject's identity but also literally restricts the physical spaces in which she can safely exist. Her body does not end at the skin because a border appears before her, in every street. As Jon Burnett argues, the aim of the Immigration Act is to make life intolerable for undocumented migrants so as to force them to leave – their destitution is used as a government tool of deportation (2016: 8). Like electronic tags, the embodied subjectivity produced by the right to rent requirements becomes a key component in the subject's spatial confinement.

Weighed down by history II

Race is, as Stuart Hall argued, a floating signifier: it is not a biological truth but rather a discursive system of human classification, a system in which meanings can change over time (1997). Understanding how particular subjects have come to be embodied as white or non-white requires an understanding of the historical production of Britain as a spatial entity. This is a particularly complex history because, as Kojo Koram has argued, Britain 'has never really existed as a nation, it has only really functioned as an empire' (Koram, 2016); an empire which sought to extend its borders to encompass as much of the world as possible. As Nadine El-Enany sets out, British immigration law has long coincided with the crumbling of empire, operating as a 'brick wall' for particular subjects, and producing categories of race in the process (El-Enany, forthcoming). In an attempt to keep the empire together, the British Nationality Act 1948 was passed, granting British citizenship to all nationals of Commonwealth countries and British colonies – meaning that there were some 600 million British citizens (ibid.). As El-Enany explains, when dark-skinned British citizens began arriving in Britain throughout the 1950s and 60s, increasingly restrictive immigration legislation was passed to limit their presence. The Immigration Act 1971 restricted the right to enter and remain in Britain to those whose parents or grandparents were born in Britain (ibid.). While not framed in explicitly racist language, the law had racist motives. It effectively made it more difficult for non-white British subjects to come to Britain, and this was its intended effect: coming on the heels of white supremacist Enoch Powell's 1968 'rivers of blood' speech, and growing racist and xenophobic sentiment among white British voters (ibid., see also Gilroy, 1987). Unless they had the requisite bloodline to Britain stretching back to a time when the motherland was overwhelmingly Anglo-Celtic, citizens of Britain's remaining colonies and those of Commonwealth countries had to apply for permission to be cleared to enter Britain.

The 1971 Act thus constructed an initial 'brick wall' for some British subjects, creating them as a racial category in the process. This wall operated at or before the point of entry into the actual British landmass. As Gina Clayton argues, the entry clearance system is part of the government's plan to create a bureaucratic 'security ring' around Britain (Clayton, 2012: 211). Entry clearance requirements impose an administrative border on subjects born in particular places, a border that extends all the way into their home states and areas they might pass through on the journey to Britain. The extension of the border well outside territorial boundaries of the nation-state has been referred to as the 'external border' (Van Houtum, 2010). The operation of the British external border in Calais under the Sangette Protocol[7] for example enables British border officers to prevent people from coming to Britain well before they reach British territory. The external borders of Britain and other EU countries are policed by FRONTEX, which effectively enforces EU borders in locations across the world but most notably in the Mediterranean and along the northern and western African coast, where boats might attempt to enter EU territorial waters. Tens of thousands of people have died trying to cross the EU's external borders (ibid.: 968).

While the 1971 Act and provisions such as the Sangette Protocol produce an 'external border' for Britain, the new Immigration Acts produce 'internal borders', but they follow the same logic of ensuring the British islands remain dominated by those with Anglo-Celtic roots. Subjects whose parents and grandparents faced the 'brick wall' of entry clearance requirements must now also expect to come up against brick walls when trying to rent a home or access other services within Britain. Echoing Balibar's and Anderson et al.'s understanding of the border, borders are complex institutions that follow particular subjects. The subject *belongs to, combines with* and *includes* time and space – in this instance, the time of colonial history and the spatial reality of the border, which travel with her as she looks for a home, along every British street.

Conclusion

In this chapter, I have developed the idea of 'taking space with you' in the contexts of electronic surveillance tags and the Immigration Acts of 2014 and 2016. I have argued that there is a complex and intimate relationship between law, space and the subject, a relationship that cannot be understood on the law's own terms or through liberal frameworks of individual subjects whose bodies end at the skin. To begin to understand the landscape of electronic tagging and the 'right to rent' rules requires thinking through the historically produced networks and hybridity which define and limit subjects and spaces. Legal geography demonstrates connections between law and space, while critical race theory and critical disability studies provide theoretical frameworks to understand the intimate, constitutive relationship between space and the subject. In particular, Margaret Shildrik's discussion of embodied subjects as hybrids and Sara Ahmed's description of 'brick walls' which block the paths of racialised subjects help to illuminate the complex ways in which law constructs subjects today, subjects who take space with them as their bodies combine and connect with that beyond the skin in multiple ways.

The space that DD – a Somalian refugee suspected of involvement with terrorism – took with him while the TPIM demanded that he wear an electronic tag confined him to a particular physical and social space, one that was inescapable and drove him to psychosis. 'Brick walls' appeared before him – and to an extent, before his family – while the rest of the world went on around him. Electronic tags create a landscape in which 'brick walls' exist for particular subjects by physically attaching a networked device to the bodies of those subjects. While the barriers put in place by the 2014 and 2016 Immigration Acts do not operate directly upon the body in the way that electronic tags do, they produce a similarly spatialised subject, one who encounters a border in every street. As technology and bureaucracy continue to grow, theorists grappling with law must take seriously the complex materiality of 'identity' and belonging, the ongoing weight of history and the spatiality of the subject. For while these landscapes are oppressive and dangerous, the dynamic multiplicity of space means that it is possible to reshape 'Britain' such that the subjects of empire and their children might finally leave the resilient and sticky space of colonially built brick walls behind.

Notes

1 *DD v. Secretary of State for the Home Department* [2015] EWHC 1681 (Admin).

2 Section 39 of the Immigration Act 2016 amends the Immigration Act 2014, inserting s33A which creates the offence. Note that at the time of writing, this provision is in force for England.

3 Immigration Act 2014 s33C.

4 This argument is consistent with feminist geographers who have pointed out the spatial construction of masculine city and feminine domestic home (see Massey, 1994, McDowell, 2013).

5 Cross Border Collective, Sydney (www.crossbordersydney.org, accessed 16 March 2017). The notion of 'We didn't cross the border, the border crossed us' has long been present in Chicana feminist historiography, including Gloria Anzaldua's *Borderlands/La Frontera: The New Mestiza* (1987): Roberto D Hernandez, 'Sonic Geographies and Anti-Border Musics: "We Didn't Cross the Border, The Border Crossed Us"' in *Performing the US Latina and Latino Borderlands* edited by Arturo J. Aldama, Chela Sandoval, Peter J. García, Indiana University Press 2012: 245.

6 This discussion relates to non-derogating Control Orders. Under the 2005 Act the Secretary of State could also make derogating Control Orders, which required the civil standard of proof and effected a deprivation of liberty on the controlled subject: see Zedner, 2007.
7 The Sangette Protocol was agreed in 1991 between Britain and France.

Bibliography

Ahmed, Sara, *Queer Phenomenology: Orientations, Objects, Others*, Durham and London: Duke University Press, 2007.

Ahmed, Sara, *On Being Included: Racism and Diversity in Institutional Life*, Durham: Duke University Press, 2012.

Anderson, Bridget, Sharma, Nandita and Wright, Cynthia, 'Editorial: Why No Borders?' *Refuge*, 26(2), 5–18, 2009.

Anzaldua, Gloria, *Borderlands/La Frontera: The New Mestiza*, San Francisco: Aunt Lute Books, 1987.

Asylum Support Appeals Project, 'Briefing Note: The Right to Rent Scheme and Asylum Support,' June 2017. www.asaproject.org/uploads/June_2017_-_Briefing_note_-_The_right_to_rent.pdf, (accessed 19 June 2017).

Augstein, Hannah Franziska, *Race: The Origins of An Idea, 1760–1850*, Bristol: Thoemmes Press, 1996.

Balibar, Etienne, *Politics and the Other Scene*, London: Verso, 2002.

Bate, Alex and Ota, Shiro, 'Right to Rent: Private Landlords' Duty to Carry Out Immigration Status Checks', *House of Commons Library*, February 12, 2016.

Bell, Derrick, *Race, Racism, and American Law* (4th edition), New York: Aspen Publishers, 2000.

Bennett, Luke and Layard, Antonia, 'Legal Geography: Becoming Spatial Detectives,' *Geography Compass*, 9(7), 406–422, 2015.

Blomley, Nick, *Law, Space and the Geographies of Power*. New York, London: The Guildford Press, 1994.

Braverman, Irus, 'Powers of Illegality: House Demolitions and Resistance in East Jerusalem,' *Law & Social Inquiry*, 32, 333–368, 2007.

Burnett, Jon, *Entitlement and Belonging: Social Restructuring and Multicultural Britain*, London: Institute of Race Relations, 2016.

Clayton, Gina, *Textbook on Immigration and Asylum Law*, Oxford: Oxford University Press, 2012.

Cooper, Davina, *Governing Out of Order: Space, Law and the Politics of Belonging*, London: Rivers Oram Press, 1998.

Cooper, Davina, 'Opening Up Ownership: Community Belonging, Belongings, and the Productive Life of Property,' *Law & Social Inquiry*, 32(3), 625–664, 2007.

Dathan, Matt, 'Calais Migrant Crisis: UK Streets Are "Not Paved with Gold" – Theresa May signs £7m Deal to Stop Migrants Entering Britain,' *The Independent*, 20 August 2015. www.independent.co.uk/news/uk/politics/calais-migrant-crisis-uk-streets-are-not-paved-with-gold-theresa-may-signs-7m-deal-to-stop-migrants-10463896.html (accessed 19 June 2017).

Davies, Margaret, 'Queer Property, Queer Persons: Self-Ownership and Beyond,' *Social and Legal Studies*, 8(3), 327–352, 1999.

Delaney, David, *The Spatial, the Legal and the Pragmatics of World-Making: Nomospheric Investigations*, Abingdon: Routledge, 2010.

Dembour, Marie-Bénédicte, *When Humans Become Migrants: Study of the European Court of Human Rights with an Inter-American Counterpoint*, Oxford: Oxford University Press, 2015.

El-Enany, Nadine, 'On Pragmatism and Legal Idolatry: Fortress Europe and the Desertion of the Refugee,' *International Journal on Minority and Group Rights*, 22(1), 7–38, 2015.

El-Enany, Nadine, *(B)ordering Britain: The Migrant, The Refugee and The State*, London: Hart forthcoming, 2018.

Frankenberg, Ruth, *The Social Construction of Whiteness: White Women, Race Matters*, London: Routledge, 1993.

Gartenstein-Ross, Daveed, 'The Strategic Challenge of Somalia's Al-Shabaab: Dimensions of Jihad,' *Middle East Quarterly*, (Fall) 25–36, 2009.

Gilroy, Paul, *There Ain't No Black in the Union Jack*, Oxford: Routledge, 1987/2013.

Goodley, Dan, 'Towards Socially Just Pedagogies: Deleuzoguattarian Critical Disability Studies,' *International Journal of Inclusive Education*, 11(3), 317–334, 2007.

Graham, Nicole, *Lawscape: Property, Environment, Law*, Abingdon: Routledge, 2011.

Grewal, Inderpal, *Transnational America: Feminisms, Diasporas, Neoliberalisms*, Durham and London: Duke University Press, 2005.

Hall, Stuart, *Race: The Floating Signifier*, Northampton: Media Education Foundation, 1997.

Haraway, Donna, 'A Cyborg Manifesto: Science, Technology, and Socialist-feminism in the Late Twentieth Century,' *Simians, Cyborgs and Women: The Reinvention of Nature*, 149–181, 1991.

Harris, Cheryl I., 'Whiteness as Property,' *Harvard Law Review*, 106(8), 1707–1791, 1993.

Harvey, David, The Spatial Fix – Hegel, Von Thunen and Marx,' *Antipode*, 13(3), 1–13. 1981.

Hernandez, Roberto D., 'Sonic Geographies and Anti-Border Musics: "We Didn't Cross the Border, The Border Crossed Us",' in Arturo J. Aldama, Chela Sandoval and Peter J. García (eds), *Performing the US Latina and Latino Borderlands*, Bloomington: Indiana University Press, 235–257, 2012.

Holder, Jane, 'Hedgerows, Laws and Cultural Landscape', in Jane Holder and David McGillivray (eds), *Locality and Identity: Environmental Issues in Law and Society*. Aldershot: Ashgate, 1999.

Keenan, Sarah, *Subversive Property: Law and the Production of Spaces of Belonging*, Oxford: Routledge, 2015.

Koram, Kojo, '"I'm Not Looking For a New England": On the Limitations of Radical Nationalism,' *Novara Media*, 9, October 2016. http://novaramedia.com/2016/10/09/im-not-looking-for-a-new-england-on-the-limitations-of-a-radical-nationalism/ (accessed 19 June 2017).

Lefebvre, Henri, *The Production of Space*, trans. Donald Nicholson-Smith. Oxford: Blackwell, 1991.

Lentin, Alana, *Racism: A Beginner's Guide*, London: Oneworld Publications, 2008.

Nellis, Mike, Beyens, Kristel and Kaminski, Dan (eds), *Electronically Monitored Punishment: International and Critical Perspectives*, New York: Routledge, 2013.

MacKinnon, Catharine A., 'Feminism, Marxism, Method, and the State: Toward Feminist Jurisprudence,' *Signs: Journal of Women in Culture and Society* 8(4), 635–658, 1983.

Mair, George and Nellis, Mike, '"Parallel tracks": Probation and Electronic Monitoring in England and Wales, and Scotland,' in Mike Nellis, Kristel Beyens and Dan Kaminski (eds), *Electronically Monitored Punishment: International and Critical Perspectives*. New York: Routledge, 63–81, 2013.

Massey, Doreen, 'Politics and Space/Time,' in Michael Keith and Steve Pile (eds), *Place and the Politics of Identity*, London: Routledge, 141–160, 1993.

Massey, Doreen, *Space, Place and Gender*, London: Polity Press, 1994.

Massey, Doreen, *For Space*, London: Sage, 2006.

McAuslan, Patrick, *The Ideologies of Planning Law*, Oxford: Pergamon Press, 1980.

McDowell, Linda, *Gender, Identity and Place: Understanding Feminist Geographies*, Cambridge: Polity Press, 2013.

Merleau-Ponty, Maurice, *Phenomenology of Perception*, Abingdon: Routledge, 2010.

Patel, Chai and Peel, Charlotte, *Passport Please: The Impact of the Right to Rent Checks on Migrants and Ethnic Minorities in England*, London: Joint Council for the Welfare of Immigrants, February 2017.

Perera, Suvendrini and Pugliese, Joseph, 'Death in a Dry River: Black Life, White Property, Parched Justice,' *Somatechnics*, 1(1), 65–86, 2011.

Philippopoulos-Mihalopoulos, Andreas, 'In the Lawscape,' in Andreas Philippopoulos-Mihalopoulos (ed.), *Law and the City*, Abingdon: Routledge-Cavendish, 2007.
Philippopoulos-Mihalopoulos, Andreas, *Spatial Justice: Body, Lawscape, Atmosphere*, Oxford: Routledge, 2015.
Pothier, Dianne and Devlin, Richard, *Critical Disability Theory: Essays in Philosophy, Politics, Policy, and Law*, Vancouver: UBC Press, 2006.
Razack, Sherene, *Dying From Improvement: Inquests and Inquiries Into Indigenous Deaths in Custody*, Toronto: University of Toronto Press, 2015.
Razack, Sherene H., 'Gendered Racial Violence and Spatialized Justice: The Murder of Pamela George,' in Sherene H. Razack (ed.), *Race, Space and the Law: Unmapping a White Settler Society*, Toronto: Between the Lines, 122–156, 2002.
Robinson, Rachel, 'A Border in Every Street,' *Liberty*, 3, April 2014. www.liberty-human-rights.org.uk/news/blog/border-every-street (accessed 19 June 2017).
Sanger, Carol, 'Girls and the Getaway: Cars, Culture, and the Predicament of Gendered Space,' in David Delaney and Richard T. Ford, Nicholas Blomley (eds), *The Legal Geographies Reader: Law, Power and Space*, Oxford: Blackwell, 31–41, 2001.
Schatzberger, Eliot, 'The Immigration Act 2014: "Not on the List You're Not Coming In; Landlords Forced to Discriminate",' *Conveyancer*, 5, 395–407, 2015.
Shildrick, Margrit, 'Why Should Our Bodies End at the Skin?: Embodiment, Boundaries, and Somatechnics,' *Hypatia*, 30(1), 13–29, 2015.
Travis, Alan, 'Immigration Bill: Theresa May Defends Plans to Create "Hostile Environment",' *The Guardian*, 10 October 2013. www.theguardian.com/politics/2013/oct/10/immigration-bill-theresa-may-hostile-environment (accessed 19 June 2017).
Van Houtum, Henk, 'Human Blacklisting: The Global Apartheid of the EU's External Border Regime,' *Environment and Planning D: Society and Space*, 28(6), 957–976, 2010.
Waldron, Jeremy, 'Homelessness and the Issue of Freedom,' in Robert E. Goodin and Philip Pettit (eds), *Contemporary Political Philosophy: An Anthology*. Oxford: Blackwell, 1997.
Walker, Clive and Horne, Alexander, 'The Terrorism Prevention and Investigation Measures Act 2011: One Thing but Not Much the Other?' *Criminal Law Review*, 421–438, 2012.
Yuval-Davis, Nira, Kannabiran, Kalpana and Vieten, Ulrike M., 'Introduction,' in Nira Yuval-Davis, Kalpana Kannabiran and Ulrike M. Vieten (eds), *The Situated Politics of Belonging*. London: Sage, 2006.
Zedner, Lucia, 'Preventive Justice or Pre-punishment? The Case of Control Orders,' *Current Legal Problems*, 60(1), 174, 2007.

4

'Praxiographies' of time

Law, temporalities, and material worlds

Emily Grabham

Introduction

In the early 2000s, I worked for a legal collective in London, England, providing advice and representation to queers on employment issues. My position title, 'lesbian caseworker', dated from an earlier era, but I kept it because it neatly, if ambiguously, juxtaposed identity and function. Bikes and stacks of papers littered our open plan office. Alongside a large bank of filing cabinets stood our 'homophobic' photocopier, so named because it would jam during marathon copying sessions on the evenings before important tribunal dates. Our pink-headed notepaper, alternately a source of embarrassment and pride when corresponding with city law firms, became progressively more out of date; we kept it because we couldn't afford to replace it. We didn't have time, either, to clear out the ten years' worth of voluntary sector leaflets homed in our meeting room.

In the midst of all this, the piles of paper on the desk of the 'gay men's caseworker' were steadily out-growing the usual bounds of polite messiness. Not an untidy man by nature, he often found himself inundated with medical reports, disease manuals, and correspondence with clinicians. As a result of advising numerous people living with HIV, my colleague had developed a practice expertise in disability discrimination law. He spent hours writing instructions to medical experts, drafting and arguing over medical reports, and attending tribunal hearings, all so that his clients could make the preliminary legal point that their HIV met the definition of 'disability' for the purposes of the discrimination laws in force at the time. This was before these people had even arrived at the real substance of their work problems: the fudged 'risk assessments' excluding them from jobs, the shunning, employers' mistaken assumptions around HIV transmission and life expectancy, all with real and apparent material effects. The relevant legal test was whether their condition was 'more likely than not' to be an impairment in the future. In this context, the irony of having to provide evidence of a poor prognosis to an employment tribunal just at the point at which anti-retrovirals were transforming many people's experiences of HIV was not lost on any of us.

Sometime later, having left legal practice for an academic job, I tried to make sense of these experiences. Engaged in research on law and time, it became apparent that what my colleague was doing in the early 2000s was no less significant to the creation of a specifically *legal* temporality – 'likelihood' – than anything else would be. This is not to say that he was some kind of magician, conjuring time from nowhere, but rather that in the process of his everyday work, he contributed to the emergence and stability of 'likelihood' in mundane ways, even as he was critical of it. Far from being abstract and metaphysical, likelihood was constituted in tangible ways, through interactions between people, technologies, things, and laws. In this case, likelihood was dependent for its survival on medical reports, the retrovirus itself, and the means through which clinicians were able to measure its existence, prevalence, and effects (e.g., through viral load tests and T-cell counts).

I began a research project on the temporal concepts underpinning early legal approaches to HIV discrimination in Canada and the United Kingdom. Operating in a climate of persistent fear and generalized misunderstanding about the potential transmission risks of HIV, many people living with HIV in the 1980s and 1990s faced work-based discrimination and dismissal. Activists pursued legal innovation either to secure the continued employment of these people or to obtain much-needed financial compensation where possible. My research involved documentary analysis, doctrinal research, and interviews of lawyers, policy-makers, and activists on their experiences of HIV-related discrimination activism and legal claims. This research underpinned my understanding of the legal regulation of disability as broadly a bio-political endeavour, and legal definitions of disease and disability as what Elizabeth Freeman would term 'chrono-normative', remobilizing exclusionary norms of health and the life course through powerful concepts of time (Freeman, 2011).

Yet the legal temporalities that emerged through the interview and documentary research processes were not what I had expected. They included 'prognosis,' 'likelihood,' 'progression,' and 'uncertainty,' and when they appeared in informants' accounts or in legal and policy documents, first-person written accounts, legislation, and cases, they were more often than not accompanied by 'things' and apparently 'non-legal' technologies: T-cell counts, viral load measurements, medical reports, questionnaires. Encountering these things over and over again, I was confronted by a particularly intractable analytic problem that threatened to drag the project into a kind of generalized obviousness and irrelevance: the 'thing-ness' of legal time. These temporalities and their material accomplices did not seem much like the experiences or interpretations of time I had expected to find. They were too specific and mundane. In comparison to concepts of past, present, and future, for example, or 'preemption' (Anderson, 2010) or memorialization (Douglas, 2011), these temporalities in this context appeared slightly askew, overly technical, and not 'wholly' legal (often being, for example, medico-legal). Even worse, legal time appeared to be just as much about the objects as about human experience, even though the temporalities had immense significance for many people. My understanding of temporal mechanisms, despite having been influenced by approaches to power and social action drawn from governmentality, critical legal studies, and legal geography, could not at that point accommodate processes of creating legal times that seemed to involve nonhuman as well as human actors.

How can a form or an antibody test assist in creating legal time? Isn't it the people who have experiences of time and the objects that are enrolled in these political and legal actions? Carol Greenhouse registers a similar conundrum in her landmark anthropological reflection on the relationship between social time and legal ordering – *A Moment's Notice*:

> The bureaucrat with the hourglass did not just keep the time; he *started* it and *stopped* it. He literally created time and ended it with each intervention of the advocate.
>
> (Greenhouse, 1996: 22)

Approaching legal-temporal mechanisms as biopolitical or even chrono-normative projects helped to conceptualize 'likelihood,' for example, as the temporal feature of a set of disciplinary mechanisms that constructed HIV as a disability in law. But it did not, in itself, assist with the question of how to understand the interlinking of law, time, and things (tests, medical reports) as it arose through creating 'likelihood' as a concern. The valences, constructions, and shades of time percolating through the research seemed ungeneralizable to the extent that they were attached to very specific things and, moreover, that these things were of different types, were variously 'legal' or 'medical,' and could not articulate themselves in my framework of analysis, despite having clear effects.

To give one example: in the late 1980s in Canadian provincial human rights law, the legal test for covering HIV as a disability was from the relatively 'early' point in HIV infection – 'manifesting antibodies' (*Biggs v. Hudson* (1988)). Yet this legal test could not have existed, and could not now work, without the clinical innovation of the HIV antibody test, which provided clinicians with a means of visualizing the virus and its biological effects. Furthermore, the 'manifesting antibodies' legal test could not have wider significance without government clinical guidelines posing a standardized temporal schema – 'progression' – for understanding and treating HIV-related illnesses. Only with both the antibody test and the clinical guidelines – and, indeed, the antibodies, but that is another question altogether – did the newly legally significant legal-temporal concept of HIV progression make any sense.

I found myself thinking and writing about tests and clinical guidelines and not, I thought, about time. If anything, despite my having been influenced by theories of temporalization, time remained the ether in which the tests floated. My focus on things often felt as though it actively precluded an in-depth analysis of temporalization: the temptation was to understand the analytic endeavour as either metaphysical or about the things and objects emerging through the research, with time disappearing from view on either account. At best, it might have been possible to conclude that the antibody test created a new legal *interpretation* or *disciplinary production* of time, which was fundamentally a matter of human subjectivity or governance: the human creation of law *in or through* time. Yet this did not do justice to the production of material and environmental contexts through law.

In this chapter, I argue that it is at least partly our relationship with 'things' that creates legal time. As Michel Serres has put it: '(t)ime doesn't flow; it percolates' (Serres and Latour, 1995: 58). Human action does not exist *within* time, but instead generates temporalities, including legal temporalities, in assemblages of human and nonhuman actors. The things we might follow in such an analysis include objects in the legal field such as case reports, medical reports, medical tests, drugs, files, and classification systems. We might also focus on ways of *doing law* with these things: adjudicating, litigating, documenting and certifying, as well as many other actions that would not, on the face of it, seem 'legal' (in good law and society tradition). In following this enquiry, I ask what our understanding of law and time might look like if we follow things as well as people, if we allow objects open access to new worlds, and if we pay attention to the agentic potential of matter, metals, or particles, for example, and not merely conscious human behaviour. This approach departs from existing scholarship on law and time by emphasizing the specificities of law's material forms. It extends existing literatures on time by encouraging us to confront the multiple, mundane ways in which time is enacted through legal assemblages. And it challenges scholarship on the materialities of time to consider what emerges when we consider specifically legal modes, raising issues that are not present elsewhere (such as dilemmas over the status of legal form).

We already have at our disposal many rich accounts of the close interconnections between inventions, institutions, and new understandings of time that can inform our understanding of time's relationship with objects and matter. A wide range of work has accounted for the significance of objects and material artefacts in culture (Henare et al., 2007; Pottage and Mundy, 2004; Candlin and Guins, 2009). Actor network theory and object-related anthropology have helped to uncover the many ways in which things exert effects (or can be understood to 'speak') in networks or assemblages of human and nonhuman actors (e.g., Holbraad, 2011; Latour, 2005). Research in political theory is increasingly focused on the participation of nonhumans in political events and the significance of the temporal paradigm of the 'Anthropocene' for thinking about human action (Bennett, 2010). Technologies such as clocks, schedules, calendars, railroads, and 'standard time' have helped to create particular temporal paradigms, which are culturally specific (Zerubavel, 1985; O'Malley, 1996). As the anthropologist Kevin Birth puts it: 'The artifactual determination of time does not represent a coherent, consistent cultural system . . . but represents instead the sedimentation of generations of solutions to different problems' (Birth, 2012: 2).

Similarly, however, scholarship on time is diverse and growing (see, e.g., Bastian, 2014). Within studies of labour, an influential literature now focuses on qualities of time and temporal orientations found in the so-called 'new economy' (Adkins, 2008; Waldby and Cooper, 2010; Amoore, 2004). Feminist and queer scholarship has critiqued the heteronormative underpinnings of familial and reproductive time, its cultural formations and political effects (Freeman, 2005, 2011; Dinshaw et al., 2007; Halberstam, 2005), as well as its implications for queer inter-generationality, utopia, and hope (Munoz, 2009; Edelman, 2004). Critical re-readings of postcolonial temporalities provide new perspectives on the politics of revolution and tragedy (e.g., Scott, 2014). For its part, scholarship and artistic practice on 'black quantum futurism' adopts quantum physics and social memory to re-shape the futures and possibilities of African-descended peoples (Phillips, 2015). Recent theorizations of time in social and political theory help us to understand how changing temporal orientations – new forms of emergency and urgency, apparently uncertain worlds and futures, new configurations of labour time, and fresh horizons of speculation – authorize multiple shades and tactics of intervention (Adkins, 2012; Amoore, 2013; de Goede, 2012; de Goede and Amoore, 2008).

Understanding the relationship between time and things in a *legal* context is the aim of the present chapter, however. A vibrant body of work already exists on law and time (for example, Cooper, 2013; Douglas, 2011; Engel, 1987; Keenan, 2013; Mawani, 2014; Richland, 2013), which has the conceptual openness to think through the questions of materiality outlined above. Similarly, growing scholarship theorizing the material in law (Lynch and McNally, 2003; Pickersgill, 2011; Pottage, 2012), while friendly to this kind of approach, is only beginning to take it up in relation to the study of time.[1] By outlining in the present chapter an approach to legal temporalities that describes the role of nonhumans and objects, I hope to provide a conceptual account for the material, apparent, and often close-at-hand characteristics of the temporalities that came up in my fieldwork.

The chapter proceeds with an explanation of what a 'praxiographic' approach to time might mean, before drawing on the work of Bruno Latour, Michel Serres, and Carol Greenhouse to propose a critical non-modern attitude that might allow us to perceive the 'sorting' of (legal) times. Subsequent sections illuminate and contextualize Latour's writings, first, on how time is folded in interactions between humans and nonhumans, and second, his view that the 'folding' concept is of less use when analyzing legal temporalities. Inspired by recent scholarship on law, materiality, and nonhuman agencies, this chapter concludes by arguing that legal objects can be seen to fold time, or create new material ontologies of time, in assemblages of human and nonhuman actors.

Praxiographies of time

In the introduction to her ethnography of atherosclerosis, Annemarie Mol proposes an approach to research that focuses on enactment rather than knowledge, multiplying our potential objects of analysis (Mol, 2003, p. vii). Mol terms this kind of research a 'story about practices' or a 'praxiography' (Mol, 2003: 31), which foregrounds practices, watching for objects to come into being instead of being viewed from different perspectives. 'The body, the patient, the disease, the doctor, the technician, the technology: all of these are more than one,' she states, referring to the incommensurability of world-making practices in the medical diagnosis and treatment of vascular disease (Mol, 2003: 5).

Inspired by Mol, my current research is oriented at the 'more than one-ness' of time, and in particular, legal temporalities. Adopting an approach that is friendly to multiple ontologies of time, I attempt to follow time-making practices that are connected with law. Such a move involves diagnosing time, watching it, and working out where it might have come from. When agency is the domain purely of humans, then time is about history: it's about the forward or circular movement of events or themes; it's about epochs and narratives. As hardly bears repeating, Bruno Latour's task in *We Have Never Been Modern*, for example, has been to provide an account of the condition of modernity and to reconstruct the separation between humans and nonhumans in order to arrive at what he terms the 'full constitution' (Latour, 1993: 14). Part of this task requires taking on what Latour calls the 'temporal framework of the moderns' (Latour, 1993: 67), a paradigm characterized by the 'arrow of time', definitive temporal breaks, and, most importantly, the passing of time. Moderns, as Latour puts it, understand time passing as if it abolishes all that is left behind; yet they also want to keep, date, save, and display the past. This idea of time passing irreversibly is, as such, a *technique* of modernity, a 'classificatory device' for evacuating the work that goes into keeping the natural and the social separate (Latour, 1993: 73).

Latour's account has the temporal framework of the moderns arising as a result of the expulsion from the field of agency, politics, and action, of objects and other types of nonhuman actor (what Latour would term 'quasi-objects') (Latour, 1993: 73). Purification allows the moderns to hold in place two fields of time: one ahistorical field populated by universal and necessary things or forces of nature; the other, much more contingent field of human history, detached from things. In challenging 'natural' time and the temporal framework of the moderns, Latour's perspective is not unique. Carol Greenhouse proposes that 'all formal temporal representations, not just linear time, involve modernist assertions' (Greenhouse, 1996: 219). Greenhouse's account emphasizes the role of power, law, authority, and culture in the construction of modernity as an epoch and 'period' of time. According to Greenhouse, therefore, time is created and naturalized in the West through specific legal modes. As we have already seen, Greenhouse writes of the bureaucratic appropriation of time from God. Yet Greenhouse's bureaucrat raises a conundrum: how is it possible to start and stop time with an hourglass? This, I argue, requires an approach to temporalization that allows nonhuman actors to exert shades of agency. Reading Latour and Greenhouse alongside each other, we might say that the way we normally talk about time, as a container or a given, posits natural time as existing separately from human time, and grants nonhuman actors or materialities (including 'things') little or no agentic capacity. But if for whatever reason we leave the concept of linear, container time to one side, or at least view it as only one of a number of temporal modes which are no less real for being achieved, then we have a distinct problem: how to think about the creation of time by humans in connection with nonhumans (such as Greenhouse's hourglass) and various forms of matter. This, in turn, requires understanding the relationship between time, agency, causation, and materiality in new ways.

Latour refers to a process of 'sorting' through which temporalities are created out of elements belonging to different times. He proposes that identifying 'sorting' processes can lead us to a fuller account of the role of nonhumans, not only in political life but also in sustaining particular understandings of time:

> We have never moved either forward or backward. We have always actively sorted out elements belonging to different times. We can still sort. *It is the sorting that makes the times, not the times that make the sorting*. Modernism – like its anti- and post-modern corollaries – was only the provisional result of a selection made by a small number of agents in the name of all. If there are more of us who regain the capacity to do our own sorting of the elements that belong to our time, we will rediscover the freedom of movement that modernism denied us – a freedom that, in fact, we have never really lost.
>
> (Latour, 1993: 76, emphasis in original)

Latour has clearly been influenced by Michel Serres in these temporal propositions. In a well-known set of interviews Latour conducted with Serres in 1991, Serres elucidated his proposition that 'all authors are our contemporaries' – even authors such as Pythagoras or Lucretius. This is held because of his disaggregated definition of time and, hence, the 'contemporary':

> What things are contemporary? Consider a late-model car. It is a disparate aggregate of scientific and technical solutions dating from different periods. One can date it component by component: this part was invented at the turn of the century, another, ten years ago, and Carnot's cycle is almost two hundred years old. Not to mention that the wheel dates back to neolithic times.
>
> (Serres and Latour, 1995: 45)

Serres's proposition means, furthermore, that the past is not frozen, or out of date, and that we are not at the cutting edge of time. The Enlightenment, in categorizing non-scientific truths as outside of reason, did so through the temporal mechanism of consigning such truths to archaism, stating not that they were false but that they were 'out of date'. In this way, a temporal rupture, as Serres puts it, acts as a 'dogmatic expulsion' (Serres and Latour, 1995: 49–50). Much more, Serres argues, can be gained by thinking about time through frames of disorder and proximity that we see, for example, in chaos theory:

> Time does not always flow according to a line . . . not according to a plan but, rather, according to an extraordinarily complex mixture, as though it reflected stopping points, ruptures, deep wells, chimneys of thunderous acceleration, rendings, gaps – all sown at random, at least in a visible disorder . . . Once you understand this, it's not hard to accept the fact that time doesn't always develop according to a line and thus things that are very close can exist in culture, but the line makes them appear very distant from one another.
>
> (Serres and Latour, 1995: 57)

Through the Serres-inspired metaphor of 'sorting', then, Latour introduces a project of following the temporalities occasioned by the meetings, connections, juxtapositions of a wide range of elements and agencies, human and nonhuman. The 'extraordinarily complex mixture' that we may wish to trace in analyzing law and time, instead of acting as a backdrop to human action, is constantly percolating, folding in on itself. Time does not push forward these percolations. Instead, out of teeming knotted clusters of human and nonhuman connections, new temporalities emerge and act and have effects.

Temporal 'hinges', legal effects

The approach that I propose therefore rests on three broad conceptual moves. First, displacing an ontological split between nature and society unmoors the idea of one overarching time and the necessity of time's *passing*, as such. If we increase the range and types of actors beyond merely following humans and our interpretations of time, it is easier to hold the idea of universal, natural time, *as distinct from* social time in productive critique. Time, as such, need not be an overarching principle or universal ontological ground, on the one hand, or merely an experience on the other. Instead, time is the identifiable result of a provisional hooking together of elements into something that, in modern terms, looks cohesive.

Second, the linear passage of time as a classificatory device or technique, which accompanies the moderns' purification of nature and society (after Latour), and which results from law and specific modes of social ordering (after Greenhouse), is both real and constructed; as previously argued, it is no less real for being achieved. In other words, it is not necessary to state that there is no ontological grounding for time just because time is not natural as such: the ontological status of new classificatory devices of time should point us in the direction of multiple ontologies of time. As Mol puts it, 'if reality is done, if it is historically, culturally and materially located, then it is also multiple' (1999: 75). Third, as the final section argues, temporalities are the result of human and nonhuman relationships, so that, if these relationships shift, new temporalities emerge.

Yet we have seen that Greenhouse reaches a limit of explanation when she states that the bureaucrat with the hourglass started and stopped time. One way of responding to this is to think about linear bureaucratic time as merely an arrangement like any other, generated through diverse relationships between humans and nonhumans. Objects such as the hourglass participate with humans in such an arrangement of temporal possibilities; we could imagine the hourglass helping to enunciate linear time through its design, which is to perform the act of measuring (via the passing of sand through a glass vessel) a time that moves forward to emptiness (at the top of the hourglass) and plenitude (at the bottom of the hourglass). Here the specific temporality of sand-measuring-time or hourglass-time is a legal temporality which is real *and* achieved. Hourglass-time could be traced through what Mol terms a 'story about practices' (Mol, 2003: 31), which would have to include innovations, technologies and practices including the making of the glass, the design and manufacture of the hourglass, and the role and symbolism of the movement of the sand, as much as it would need to account for the messy lives of bureaucratic action. Hence, hourglass time is linear, real, symbolic, *and* constructed.

In some strands of ANT – actor network theory – the juncture at which human actor meets object or form has been described as a kind of 'folding', through which legal time is created as an effect. In a piece entitled *Where Are the Missing Masses?* Latour (1992) addresses the phenomenon of delegation. A door is persistently left open at his place of work. A technological device – the hinge – initially performed the work of allowing the door to be opened and closed. However, the hinged door, when left open, also allows cold into the building. Briefly put, the door-closing issue could be solved by delegating the work to a human groom or porter, who would be relatively expensive and require some discipline to do their work consistently. In the midst of this discussion, Latour raises the different temporal dimensions of delegations to nonhumans (hinges, for example) and to humans (porters):

> The first one evokes the past perfect ("once hinges had been installed . . ."), the second the present tense ("when the groom is at his post . . ."). There is a built-in inertia in the first that is largely lacking in the second . . . A profound temporal shift takes place when nonhumans are appealed to; time is *folded*.
>
> (Latour, 2009: 234)

Latour refers, then, to a 'profound temporal shift', or alternation of tenses, occasioned by the innovation or use of the hinge. He does not provide any further explanation of the folding metaphor in this piece but it is likely that it comes, again, from his productive engagements with Serres. As Serres puts it, time 'can be schematized by a kind of crumpling, a multiple, foldable diversity' (Serres and Latour, 1995: 59). What Latour does with the door metaphor is to bring this theory of multiple, crumpling times into his flat ontological field populated by human and nonhuman actors. Latour's assertion about time being folded in the appeal to nonhumans is not merely a statement about the human *experience* of interacting with objects and vital matter, but rather, in the context of his wider understanding of temporalities, it is a specific assertion about relationships and connections, or about how time occurs within human–nonhuman assemblages. Folding is just as much down to the hinge as it is to the people going through the door. It is in this way that a new temporality, or temporal mode, becomes alive, matters, is materialized through the hinge.

In what might appear to be a counter-intuitive move, this chapter takes up the question of 'folding' to analyze the materialization of *legal* temporalities. We are back to objects, technologies, and other 'things': the hourglass or, to take up the example from the introduction, objects such a legal documents or technologies such as the HIV antibody test. At this point, we arrive at an engagement with topological concepts of time in analyzing law and legality; what might otherwise be termed the 'folding' of time in and through *legal* assemblages. Latour's subsequent writings on law seem to discourage such a move. He does not view law in itself as having the same capacities to fold relations and time as would the hinge in his own example above. In his ethnography of the Conseil d'État, Latour specifically distinguishes law from other techniques, arguing that it cannot have the same effects in relation to human action as a range of other nonhuman artefacts. As he puts it,

> law . . . never manages to *fold* space-time, to replace its injunctions by another matter. The humblest technique – this lamp, this ashtray, this paper-clip – mixes periods, places, and totally heterogeneous materials; it folds them into the same black box, causing those who use them to act, by diverting the course of their action. Law is incapable of that. . . (L)aw, unlike other techniques, is neither folded nor delegated. It has meaning only if it is unfolded, deployed, spread out.
> (Latour, 2010: 272–273, emphasis in original)

There are very good reasons for Latour's attention to law's specific style of recursivity, its apparent inability to imagine a world outside of itself (Pottage, 2014). Yet there are also good reasons why we might contextualize Latour's argument and assert that in certain circumstances law can and *does* 'fold space-time'. In the remainder of this chapter, I sketch two reasons for opening up to the possibility that legal temporalities can be enunciated or 'folded' through human-legal-nonhuman assemblages. The first is an argument about law and materiality. The distinction between law and matter, or in Latour's example above, between law and paperclip, is often very difficult to work out. If, as recent law and society scholarship would have us think, law and paperclip are potentially indivisible, or if the law is in the paperclip (or *is* the paperclip) and vice versa, then it is not obvious that law is incapable of folding time or delegating actions. Folding can happen through an object or material actant that has already been materialized as legal. Second is an argument, or set of observations, about materiality and time. ANT and much current law and society scholarship has a variety of agentic or semi-agentic roles for nonhumans, 'things'. More specifically for this argument, thinkers such as Elizabeth Grosz and Jane Bennett have accounted for the *temporal* implications of a wide variety of nonhuman agencies and vital materiality through concepts of becoming and what Bennett would term 'conatus'. If we allow these concepts to have implications for how we imagine the domain of law – in other words, if the material worlds of law extend into vital materiality – then these are temporalizing worlds. I set out both arguments in a little more detail below, and finish with some concluding remarks on what this means for how we think about legal temporalities.

Law and materiality

According to some, there has been a tendency within law and society scholarship to approach material forms through legal categories instead of allowing their specific physical and cultural properties to come through (Levi, 2009). Yet a wide range of current scholarship encourages analytically productive ambivalence about whether, when, and how law is material. As such, the approach I am using in this account of legal temporalities tries not to presume, in advance, what is law and what is non-law, aiming to displace such a distinction wherever possible. As Alain Pottage puts it, we should, by contrast: 'begin with materiality rather than "law"; and, in so doing, we should recognize that the vicissitudes of "materiality" dissolve the instances – in this case "law" – that they are supposed to constitute' (Pottage, 2012: 183). The implication here is that it might be much more difficult than hitherto imagined to work out the difference between the law and the paperclip, in Latour's example, with the effect that this distinction need not stand in the way of law having effects in folding time.

Within recent work in legal geography, and in law and science and technology studies ('law and STS'), law is often not immediately visible. Here, there is often an attempt not to define an artefact or process in advance as being 'legal' or 'social' without following these relationships in more detail (Rooke et al., 2012: 43). Following 'legal things' might entail using a concept like 'socio-materiality' to describe the interaction of human and nonhuman actors within performative legal and scientific networks, describing the processes through which theories and material worlds, and a range of actors, are co-ordinated and co-constituted as 'socio-technical agencement', a type of performative material agency (Faulkner et al., 2012: 10). Or it might involve, for example, analyzing the materializing practice of 'pedestrianism' (the legal structuring of sidewalks as finite public resources, under threat from specific actors) without recourse, in the first instance, to legal categories such as public and private (Blomley, 2011). In these kinds of account, regulation in/through assemblages might or might not enact 'law', and 'legal effects' might be enacted in a wide variety of ways.

Tracing the 'things' involved in these examples shows the huge amount of work needed to create and extend what later become recognized as legal assemblages. Through complex interactions, innovative 'things' – such as nicotine gum – sometimes fail to circulate when put into contact with regulatory processes (Rooke et al., 2012). 'Law' and 'regulation' play an ambivalent role in these constellations, sometimes themselves failing to circulate, sometimes requiring other human or nonhuman actors in order to survive (in the case of pharmaceutical patents in Djibouti, for example, drug packaging (Cloatre, 2013)). These sorts of enquiries can aid an object-friendly account of law and time that does not preclude law from having timely effects.

Taking a slightly different approach, Amiria Henare, Martin Holbraad, and Sari Wastell have explored a methodology in which things themselves might 'dictate a *plurality* of ontologies' (Henare et al., 2007: 7). Their key proposition is that objects need not merely point beyond themselves to concepts or epistemological frameworks, but instead might open up new worlds. Such an analysis works at the far 'posthumanist extreme' of approaches challenging the human/thing distinction (Holbraad, 2011: 11). Drawing on the work of Marilyn Strathern and others, their analysis involves troubling the very distinction between objects and concepts and undermining the idea that objects are distinct from their meanings:

> Rather than accepting that meanings are fundamentally separate from their material manifestations (signifier v. signified, word v. referent, etc.), the aim is to explore the consequences of an apparently counter-intuitive possibility: that *things might be treated as* sui generis *meanings*.
>
> (Henare et al., 2007: 3, emphasis in original)

Instead of providing the focus for theoretical reflections, things are permitted to 'dictate the terms of their own analysis' (Henare et al., 2007: 4), hence the adoption of a stance that recognizes the radical implications of different 'worlds' or ontologies:

> If we are to take others seriously, instead of reducing their articulations to mere 'cultural perspectives' or 'beliefs' (i.e. 'worldviews'), we can conceive them as enunciations of different 'worlds' or 'natures', without having to concede that this is just shorthand for 'worldviews'.
>
> (Henare et al., 2007: 10)

Henare, Wastell, and Holbraad argue that if anthropology has been the study of diverse epistemologies, then within humanist approaches, matter and things have been viewed as coterminous with one 'reality', juxtaposed with a plurality of *interpretations* of that same matter. On this account, if someone were to tell an anthropologist that powder is power, an inquiry would still be needed into the content, context, and meaning of that interpretation of matter. Yet what is required by the ontological turn is to accept, first, that powder is power, and second, that the anthropologist really does not know what her interlocutor is talking about (Henare et al., 2007: 12).

In such an account, things are concepts and they open up new worlds instead of new interpretations of one world:

> We start with the ordinary (representationist/epistemological) assumption that concepts are the site of difference. Then we argue that in order for difference to be taken seriously (as 'alterity'), the assumption that concepts are ontologically distinct from the things to which they are ordinarily said to 'refer' must be discarded. From this it follows that alterity can quite properly be thought of as a property of things – things, that is, which *are concepts* as much as they appear to us as 'material' or 'physical' entities. Hence the first answer to the incredulous question of *where* 'different worlds' might be, is *here*, in front of us, in the things themselves.
>
> (Henare et al., 2007: 13, emphasis in original)

The act of understanding objects, therefore, does not merely require interpretation of a 'new' epistemology, but the work of 'conceiving' the distinct world of the object-concept. This is the only way, according to Henare and colleagues, that anthropological and other scholarly methods can fully respond to alterity.

Taking these theories into account, we might hope to conduct any analysis of legal temporalities without necessarily determining in advance first what is 'legal' in any given assemblage and second how it becomes legal. This is obviously easier said than done. We might also be open to the possibility, following Henare and colleagues, that understanding things and materialities is an act of conceiving new worlds instead of merely interpreting legal objects. As such, when we encounter a (legal) object, we might be alive to the possibility that 'different worlds' reside within the objects themselves; that the objects we encounter are in fact object-concepts. On this account, there is little reason why the object-concepts we encounter should not bring with them, into our analysis, their own temporalities or temporal worlds. There is little reason why they should not 'fold' time.

Materialities, agencies, and temporalities

Within legal assemblages, the question, then, is not only how to *interpret* legal things, but what worlds (including what legal worlds) material actors help conjure or invite us to access. This requires moving past distinctions between matter and meaning in thinking about temporalization (Tutton, 2017). As Andreas Philippopoulos-Mihalopoulos puts it:

> material agency emerges through assemblages (agencements) of matter (which include space, bodies, objects, networks, and law) that form, at a given time, a material legal presence.
>
> (Philippopoulos-Mihalopoulos, 2014: 412)

Drawing on Philippopoulos-Mihalopoulos's account of material agency, a more specific question for the purposes of this chapter would be how to conceive of the *temporalizing* effects that legal objects (or object-concepts) have through their actions. This admittedly assumes some degree of agency on the part of nonhuman actors if and when assemblages become understood to be legal. At this point, enquiries into becoming (following Elizabeth Grosz) or conatus (following Jane Bennett) can illuminate the lively, temporalizing effects of hitherto excluded actants in ways that can help us to perceive the potential 'folding' actions of legal objects and materialities.

In Elizabeth Grosz's work, we find an analogous refusal of the temporo-ontological project of the moderns to that found in the work of Latour and Serres, but one with a distinct philosophical outlook. As Grosz indicates, thinkers such as Darwin, Nietzsche, Bergson, and Deleuze each reject common sense understandings of time as progress and lineage, and, crucially for the present inquiry, each refuses the 'neutral immersion of things in a temporal medium' (Grosz, 1999: 4). Time, as a 'materializing if not material' force, thus links the world, consisting of human and nonhuman actors, with the generation of specific temporal modes, in diffuse and diverse ways. Against the logic of causality, time 'unfolds . . . with its own enigmas and impetus' (Grosz, 1999: 4).

This is another post-human ontology of time, in which the time of the cosmos or the natural world framing human consciousness and experience (different epistemologies of time within an overarching framework) is juxtaposed with the unpredictable generation of new temporal modes through and against new material forms. As Grosz puts it:

> time is dynamized, seen as a virtual force and as that which builds, binds, contains, and transforms all relations, whether natural, cultural or personal while also ensuring their dispersal, their development beyond current forms and parameters.
>
> (Grosz, 1999: 5)

The attention to *becoming and generation* that Grosz pursues in her critical engagement with Deleuze and Darwin in particular requires scepticism of any clear distinction between life and non-life, the organic and the inorganic. Such scepticism results in deliberations over the ontological status, for example, of viruses: Grosz asks whether we should define them as self-reproducing organisms or biochemical programmes (Grosz, 1999: 23):

> How can any clear line be drawn in any case, such that material objects are characterised by inertia and by temporal self-containment (i.e., by being) that the organic world enlivens (through becoming)?
>
> (Grosz, 1999: 23)

The temporal significance of this kind of question resides in the extent to which we perceive material phenomena, such as viruses, to be lively or inert. Many foundational definitions that order the modern world are, in this way, achieved through temporal distinctions that have significant political and ethical consequences. What is seen to be capable of agentic or semi-agentic movement or action – the growth of a plant, for example, or a geological shift, compared to the movement of an animal or human being – depends upon a perception of concerted action in time or actions upon a wider environment.

Bennett, for her part, has turned her attention to nonhuman matter – stem cells, electricity, metals, and trash – and its lively effects (Bennett, 2010). She questions what politics would look like if the vitality of nonhuman entities were taken into account. Specifically, in proposing an account of 'thing-power', Bennett draws on Spinoza's concept of *conatus*: a tendency to persist, shared by all bodies, human and nonhuman. Vibrant matter, in this account, is an 'active, earthy, not-quite-human capaciousness', and matter, far from being automative or mechanical, is vital, possessing what she terms a *conative* force (Bennett, 2010: 2). She retains a similar concept of distributive agency as that found in much ANT work, through which agency is conceived as a 'human-nonhuman working group' (Bennett, 2010, p. xvii). Her work purposefully flattens distinctions between humans and matter, adopting alternative accounts of agentic action (for example, the electrical power grid as 'agentic assemblage'; the concept of conatus) and, crucially, its temporal relations. She draws on Manuel de Landa's attempt at a materialist non-linear history, for example, to think about the emergence of bones through mineralization, and Vernadsky to think about humans' role as two-legged forms that redistribute oxygen (Bennett, 2010: 11, in conversation with de Landa, 2000). By shifting the temporal frame, Bennett argues, the aliveness of matter can sometimes be better perceived. For example, by adopting the 'long view' of evolutionary rather than biological time, it is possible to perceive a 'mineral efficacy', through which mineral materials are active, and human beings (our bones, for example) are understood as effects (Bennett, 2010: 11). In other words, the ability to shift between temporal registers is key to understanding, perceiving, and accounting for vital materialities: the time of minerals, the time of metals and chemical reactions, for example.[2]

This is a different account in which time, again, is not (or not only) aligned with intention, agency, subjectivity, and history, but instead can be seen to be mobilized through the interactions of agents of different types, and at different scales, within tangled assemblages (humans, metals, bones, for example). Once again, we see the avoidance of a containing type of linear time in favour of a flat ontological field in which matter can become alive or, despite being perceptibly inert, can operate in ways that elide distinctions between the human, the mineral, and the biological, for example. Bennett's attention to matter has much to tell us about time, including that there is nothing more special or distinctive about human temporalities and there is nothing less interesting about the temporalities of rocks, seasons, plants, or cells. In this 'active, earthy, not quite human capaciousness' (Bennett, 2010: 2), the inauguration of legal temporal schemas need not be attached to a thinking mind, intentional relationships, or to any form of agency we have come to recognize so far. Furthermore, to the extent that such capaciousness becomes active through legal assemblages, it is the temporalities of assemblages themselves or mesh-works (De Landa, 2000), and not only single, disaggregated actors, that could be the focus of analytic attention.

Concluding remarks

Through my fieldwork on HIV legal activism, I have come to understand how temporalities of likelihood and progression were conjured at least partly through the things people used when they 'did law' – antibody tests, for example, and medical reports. As such, these temporalities were not either 'natural' or 'social' but always both, brewed through changing relationships of humans and material forms. Far from being merely aspects of human conscious experience or social practice, likelihood and progression were instantiated, picked over, contested, in relationship with technicalities, things, humans, and legal form.

It is therefore possible to understand legal objects and legal relations as having something similar to what Latour would term 'folding' effects in relation to time. But this only works if we draw on a wide range of intellectual resources, for example Bennett's approach to vital materiality, Grosz's work on becoming, socio-material approaches in law and STS, and new approaches to objects in anthropology. If assemblages are viewed dynamically, it is not always necessary to name some relations as legal and also for that very reason unable to fold time. Similarly, if we work with a broad account of vital materiality, then the types of temporal action available and in view for legal analysis might include what Bennett would term conatus, or a 'not-quite-human capaciousness' through which the lively temporalizing effects of material actants can be discerned to have similar effects as Latour's 'folding'. The crucial point is that no legal-temporal register exists outside of what is materialized in diverse ways through confederations of human and nonhuman actors, and, furthermore, that what is created through these processes is a cluster of very material times.

As a result of these deliberations, I have reached for an approach to law and temporalization that is attentive to the world-making capacities of 'things' and other nonhumans: a 'praxiographic' approach (Mol, 2003), in other words. Thinking about 'things' in the context of law and time, it might be that actors engaged in the process of percolating legal temporalities do not merely cause new or alternative shades of interpretation, but fresh questions of ontology. Legal temporalities, in this theorization, are created through the connections between actors in a network or between nodal points across an assemblage. Human action is important, but not central, and indeed the 'human' can be understood just as much as a question of 'vital materiality' (cells, viruses, bones, electrical currents, following Jane Bennett (Bennett, 2010)) as conscious embodied subjectivity. For their part, legal temporalities are not only produced by human actions and subjective experiences of time, but inaugurated by vital matter in various forms, modes, and relationships: assemblages of objects, humans, animals, minerals, for example. In this account, 'time' and the 'legal' exceed the domain of the human and are material as much as symbolic. Seeking to understand the conative force of objects and other nonhumans, we can access not merely new interpretations of the 'world' (as provided by previous anthropological stances), but 'new worlds' themselves.

Notes

1 Questions of legality and temporality have emerged within influential law and society or legal anthropology research – the work, for example, of Annelise Riles, Alain Pottage, and Javier Lezaun – and it has provided a means of accessing new approaches to law, time, legal technicalities, and material worlds. Yet this scholarship has not yet been explicitly considered as 'law and time' research, despite its enormous insights (see further Grabham, 2016). Given constraints of space, it is not possible to cover this point in more detail in the current piece.

2 However, importantly, we only need this shift when adjusting the status of human actants to vital materiality, and human power to thing-power (Bennett, 2010: 10). In other words, the reason for re-framing human temporalities is not to extend the project of humanism or to put human time better into the context of an overarching 'natural' time, but instead to conceive of the electricity of our neurons, for example, as 'lively and self-organizing, rather than as passive or mechanical means under the direction of something nonmaterial, that is, an active soul or mind' (Bennett, 2010: 10).

Bibliography

Adkins, Lisa, 'From Retroactivation to Futurity: The End of the Sexual Contract?' *NORA – Nordic Journal of Feminist and Gender Research*, 16, 182–201, 2008.

Adkins, Lisa, 'Out of Work or Out of Time? Rethinking Labor after the Financial Crisis,' *The South Atlantic Quarterly*, 111, 621–641, 2012. doi:10.1215/00382876-1724111

Amoore, Louise, 'Risk, Reward and Discipline at Work,' *Economics Society*, 33, 174–196, 2004. doi:10.1080/03085140410001677111

Amoore, Louise, *The Politics of Possibility: Risk and Security Beyond Probability*, Durham: Duke University Press, 2013.

Anderson, Ben, 'Preemption, Precaution, Preparedness: Anticipatory Action and Future Geographies,' *Progress in Human Geography*, 34(6), 777–798, 2010.

Bastian, Michelle, 'Time and Community: A Scoping Study', *Time & Society*, 23, 137–166, 2014.

Bennett, Jane, *Vibrant Matter: A Political Ecology of Things*, Durham: Duke University Press, 2010.

Birth, Kevin K., *Objects of Time: How Things Shape Temporality*, New York: Palgrave Macmillan, 2012.

Blomley, Nicholas, *Rights of Passage: Sidewalks and the Regulation of Public Flow, Social Justice*, London: Routledge, 2011.
Candlin, Fiona and Guins, Raiford, *The Object Reader*, London: Routledge, 2009.
Cloatre, Emilie, *Pills for the Poorest: An Exploration of TRIPS and Access to Medication in Sub-Saharan Africa*, New York: Palgrave Macmillan, 2013.
Cooper, Davina, 'Time Against Time: Normative Temporalities and the Failure of Community Labour in Local Exchange Trading Schemes,' *Time & Society*, 22(1): 31–54, 2013.
de Goede, Marieke, *Speculative Security: The Politics of Pursuing Terrorist Monies*, Minneapolis: University of Minnesota Press, 2012.
de Goede, Marieke and Amoore, Louise, 'Transactions after 9/11: The Banal Face of the Preemptive Strike,' *Transactions – Institute of British Geographers*, 33, 173–185, 2008.
De Landa, Manuel, *A Thousand Years of Nonlinear History*, New York: Zone Books, 2000.
Dinshaw, Carolyn, Edelman, Lee, Ferguson, A. Roderick, Freccero, Carla, Freeman, Elizabeth, Halberstam, Judith, Jagose, Annamarie, Nealon, Christopher and Hoang, Nguyen Tan, 'Theorizing Queer Temporalities', *GLQ: A Journal of Lesbian and Gay Studies*, 13, 177–195, 2007.
Douglas, Stacy, 'Between Constitutional Mo(nu)ments: Memorialising Past, Present and Future at the District Six Museum and Constitutional Hill,' *Law & Critique*, 22, 171–187, 2011.
Edelman, Lee, *No Future: Queer Theory and the Death Drive*, Durham: Duke University Press, 2004.
Engel, David M., Litigation across Space and Time: Courts, Conflict, and Social Change. Law Soc. Rev. 24, 333, 1990.
Faulkner, Alex, Lange, Bettina and Lawless, Christopher, 'Introduction: Material Worlds: Intersections of Law, Science, Technology, and Society', *Journal of Law and Society*, 39, 1–19, 2012. doi:10.1111/j.1467-6478.2012.00567.x
Freeman, Elizabeth, 'Time Binds, or Erotohistoriography', *Social Text*, 23, 57–68, 2005.
Freeman, Elizabeth, *Time Binds: Queer Temporalities, Queer Histories*, Durham: Duke University Press, 2011.
Grabham, Emily, *Brewing Legal Times: Things, Form and the Enactment of Law*, Toronto: University of Toronto Press, 2016.
Greenhouse, J. Carol, *A Moment's Notice: Time Politics across Cultures*, Ithaca, NY: Cornell University Press, 1996.
Grosz, Elisabeth, *Becomings: Explorations in Time, Memory, and Futures*, Ithaca, NY: Cornell University Press, 1999.
Halberstam, Jack, *In a Queer Time and Place: Transgender Bodies, Subcultural Lives/, Sexual Cultures*. New York: New York University Press, 2005.
Henare, Amiria, Holbraad, Martin and Wastell, Sari (eds), *Thinking Through Things: Theorising Artefacts Ethnographically*, London: Routledge, 2007.
Holbraad, Martin, 'Can the Thing Speak?' *OAC Press Working Paper Series* 7. http://openanthcoop.net/press/http://openanthcoop.net/press/wp-content/uploads/2011/01/HolbraadCan-the-Thing-Speak2.pdf. 2011.
Keenan, Sarah, Subversive Property: Law and the Production of Spaces of Belonging, Social Justice. Routledge, London, 2014
Latour, Bruno, 'Where Are the Missing Masses? The Sociology of a Few Mundane Artifacts', in Wiebe E. Bijker and John Law (eds), *Shaping Technology/Building Society: Studies in Sociotechnical Change* (pp. 225–258), Cambridge, MA: MIT Press, 1992.
Latour, Bruno, *We Have Never Been Modern*, Cambridge, MA: Harvard University Press, 1993.
Latour, Bruno, *Reassembling the Social: An Introduction to Actor-Network-Theory*, Oxford: Oxford University Press, 2005.
Latour, Bruno, 'Where Are the Missing Masses? The Sociology of a Few Mundane Artifacts', in F. Candlin and R. Guins (eds), *The Object Reader* (pp. 229–254), London: Routledge, 2009.
Latour, Bruno, *The Making of Law: An Ethnography of the Cônseil d'État*, trans. Marina Brilman and Alain Pottage, Cambridge, UK: Polity Press, 2010.

Levi, Ron, 'Gated Communities in Law's Gaze: Material Forms and the Production of a Social Body in Legal Adjudication,' *Law and Social Inquiry*, 34, 635–669, 2009.
Lynch, Michael and McNally, Ruth, '"Science,""common sense," and DNA evidence: a legal controversy about the public understanding of science' Public Understanding of Science Vol 12(1) 83–103, 2003.
Mawani, Renisa, Law as Temporality: Colonial Politics and Indian Settlers. Irvine Law Rev. 4, 65–96, 2014.
Mol, Annemarie, *The Body Multiple: Ontology in Medical Practice*, Durham: Duke University Press, 2003.
Munoz, Jose, *Cruising Utopia: The Then and There of Queer Utopia*, New York: New York University Press, 2009.
O'Malley, Michael, *Keeping Watch – A History of American Time*, Washington: Smithsonian, 1996.
Pickersgill, Martyn, 'Connecting neuroscience and law: anticipatory discourse and the role of sociotechnical imaginaries,' *New Genetics & Society,* 30(1): 27–40, 2011.
Philippopoulos-Mihalopoulos, Andreas, 'Critical Autopoiesis and the Materiality of Law', *International Journal for the Semiotics of Law*, 27(2), 389–418, 2014.
Pottage, Alain and Mundy, Martha, *Law, Anthropology, and the Constitution of the Social: Making Persons and Things*, Cambridge: Cambridge University Press, 2004.
Pottage, Alain, 'The Materiality of What?' *Journal of Law and Society*, 39, 167–183, 2012. doi:10.1111/j.1467–6478.2012.00576.x
Pottage, Alain, 'Law After Anthropology: Object and Technique in Roman Law', *Theory, Culture & Society*, 31(2–3), 147–166, 2014.
Richland, Justin, 'Jurisdiction: Law's Grounding in Language,' *Annual Review of Anthropology,* 42: 209–26, 2013.
Rooke, Catriona, Cloatre, Emilie and Dingwall, Robert, 'The Regulation of Nicotine in the United Kingdom: How Nicotine Gum Came to Be a Medicine, but Not a Drug', *Journal of Law and Society*, 39, 39–57, 2012. doi:10.1111/j.1467–6478.2012.00569.x
Scott, David, *Omens of Adversity: Tragedy, Time, Memory, Justice*, Durham: Duke University Press, 2014.
Serres, Michel and Latour, Bruno, *Conversations on Science, Culture, and Time*, Ann Arbor: University of Michigan Press, 1995.
Tutton, Richard, 'Wicked Futures: Meaning, Matter and the Sociology of the Future,' *Sociological Review*, 65, 478–492, 2017. doi:10.1111/1467–954X.12443
Waldby, Catherine and Cooper, Melinda, 'From Reproductive Work to Regenerative Labour The Female Body and the Stem Cell Industries', *Feminist Theory,* 11, 3–22, 2010. doi:10.1177/1464700109355210
Zerubavel, Eviatar, *Hidden Rhythms: Schedules and Calendars in Social Life,* Berkeley: University of California Press, 1985.

Cases

Biggs v. Hudson (1988) 9 CHRR D/5391; 1988 CLB 12733.

5

Continua of (in)justice

*Lucy Finchett-Maddock**

Introduction

Since the writing of this chapter, there has been a tumultuous alteration in the political landscape, leading to speculation about the very reasoning and appropriateness of writing intricate theory on the metaphysics of law, space and time, in the form of spatial justice. Questions around the role of the academic and the usefulness of relatively opaque philosophical engagement beyond the academy in understanding the contemporary milieu are counterposed with a realisation of the need for expertise in aiding how we might dissect what is real, or at least not non-truth, as a monotony of violent racial, post-truth and austerity-starved ideological divisions cut through mind and paper.

But where are we if we do not respond to the events unfolding, whether as fodder emanating from visceral reaction, or carefully prepared impasses, theoretical or otherwise, that reflect on the reverberations happening to and interrupting material bodies, or just following on-screen simulacra? Is it not now more than ever that we need a theoretically informed political movement to inspire and inform our political ends? Feminist, critical race theorists have responded in an upsurge of intersectional and decolonial thinking quarterised by the shifting right-wing political agendas, critiquing the grand Western totalitarian narratives that perpetuate in our legal, political and educational institutions, and society in general. On the other hand, history may be even telling us that those forms of ideology theoretically engaged with post-modernism and post-structuralism, aware of their construction, are exploited by those with the most political and financial leverage. Those in power realise the full potential of media propaganda where alternative facts are conjured through the deliberate self-reflective performance of 'truth' and the electorate give up on any validation as they struggle to breathe in the crossfire of information.

What Harvey has described as the 'spatial fix' of capital (2001), as it seeks to resolve its inner crisis through proprietorial geographical expansion and categorisation and institutionalisation, has no concern for which vessel it uses, whether it be the left or the right of the political spectrum as they bicker over their share or decisions put in the hands of the disempowered who feel a similar need to escape – the desire to control has overtaken any desire to balance. As we will learn, in order for there to be life itself there must be available that which feeds it (*negative entropy*) – contingency and necessity, space and time – but that the very content of this negative entropy makes a big difference to the direction and traversing of any system, whether it be world geopolitics expressing what we'll learn to be a continua of (in)justice.

This piece seeks to explicate these very processes of entropy and the congenital role of uncertainty that this infers within spatial justice and the origins of law and legal innovation, by arguing a genealogical account of spatial justice expressed through entropy movements, as most useful in understanding the machinations of justice and injustice today.

It draws a comparison between Philippopoulos-Mihalopoulos's work on *lawscaping* and its continuum (2015), Santos's *continuum of formalism* (1977) and my understanding of this in relation to the production of an '*a-legal vacuum*' (Finchett-Maddock, 2016). The differences between these alternate understandings of continua are highlighted through the work of speculative thinkers Meillassoux (2008) and Hägglund (2011) in distinguishing *processual* and *originary* conceptions of justice, spatially and temporally construed, taking into consideration the forces of *uncertainty* (or what shall be described as the processes of *negative and positive entropy*) within the instituting of spatial justice.

First shall be considered the literature on spatio-temporal understandings of justice, followed by a discussion of the conceptions of continua discussed by Philippopoulos-Mihalopoulos, Santos and myself. Following this discussion shall be outlined what this means to the two different understandings of legal innovation in processual and originary understandings of justice, specifically in discussing the lawscape, in contrast with a-legal vacuums. The role of entropy (in both negative and positive forms) and uncertainty will be highlighted as key in understanding motions of justice and injustice, described through a summary of two approaches to material innovation in the work of speculative realists Meillassoux and Hägglund. This understanding of justice and legal innovation concludes in the hope of contributing towards a useful framework in understanding a turbulent political backdrop, with the resultant effects of injustice felt spatially and temporally as a result.

Spatio-temporal understandings of justice

Philippopoulos-Mihalopoulos explains how a there has been a redirecting in conceptions of law and justice, to incorporate the spatial nature of law and the world around us, with 'spatial justice' being the most "radical offspring of law's spatial turn" (2015: 174). What does spatial justice mean? For the now well-known 'spatial turn' in law (Philippopoulos-Mihalopoulos, 2011a, 2011b; de Villiers, 2016), space and spatiality has increasingly become the currency interrogating the world around us and our place in it. It is seen as the product and producer of social life – not just something acting as a container but giving reality and force to our material (and immaterial) world, whether that be architecture, infrastructure, property, justice or aesthetics. Everything and anything exists within and as a space, and it was this concern for not just language describing the world, but also the coordinates within which we inhabit the world, that informed the beginnings of a spatially construed justice.

Henri Lefebvre's *The Production of Space* (1991), described the contents of space as made up of social (spatial) practices (1991: 18), where "(Social) space is a (social) product" (1991: 26). Space is something that is constructed by those (bodies) in its milieu, and is not just a physical and architectural trait. Doreen Massey (*For Space*, 2005) also located space as the coming together of product and practice, as transgressive and the home of power: "Space is by its very nature, full of power and symbolism, a complex web of relations of domination and subordination, of solidarity and cooperation" (Massey, 1992). Edward Soja linked spatial justice with a more territorially bounded conception of justice, the spatiality of (in)justice (Soja, 2010: 5) and the production of unjust geographies (Soja, 2010: 31). Soja is also known for his continuation of the Lefebvrian 'trialectics' and Foucaultian 'heterotopias' (1958, 1991) and a development of 'third space' (1996), which we will discuss later in relation to the 'vacuum'. This was later followed by David Harvey's adaptation, again of Lefebvre's ideas, in the concern for the 'right to the city', denoting urban space with rights and the rights to access space (1973, 2008).

The work of legal geographers (Blomley, 1994; Delaney, 1986, 2011) and lawyers, working with emplaced spatial concepts (Philippopoulos-Mihalopoulos, 2011a, 2011b, 2015; Cooper, 1998; Graham, 2011; Keenan, 2014; Blandy, 2010; Layard, 2016), have contributed to a body of law and space work, where relations of rights, violence, identity and property are identified in maps, boundaries, fences, housing, squats and common land, highlighting the corporeal and geographically bounded nature of law and justice. Cooper and Keenan specifically speak of property in terms of part/whole relations, construing identity and belonging in spatial and temporal terms (Cooper, 1998; Keenan, 2014). The work on squatters' rights relating to the argument in this piece specifically argues the finite nature of space, the role of squatting as a practice and reality in highlighting this, and the underlying role of land and materiality within law and space (Finchett-Maddock, 2016).

Patchett and Keenan's timely edited collection on spatial justice and the diaspora brings together conversations on space and race (2017), those that have been left wanting in law and space literature thus far, illustrating the spatial and justice-laden relations of race and diaspora and its encounter with law: "As diasporic communities are often scattered because geopolitical forces have rendered their homeland a difficult or impossible place to live, diaspora is also a concept that tends to be close to questions of justice" (2017: 2). The collection seeks to bring together the work of post-colonial thinkers such as that of Avtar Brah (1996) and Stuart Hall (2012), amongst other scholars engaging in spatio-diasporic thinking.

Given the turn to spatiality within law and juridical concepts, some of the literature has been questioned for its satisfactoriness in describing space itself (Philippopoulos-Mihalopoulos, 2015: 180). Both Harvey's and Soja's forms of spatial justice are argued as not professing to a conceptualisation of spatial justice but to a spatial perspective on social justice, and they describe versions of spatial justice that are geographically informed, such as in the work of legal geography, resulting in the substitution and subordination of the central import of space itself (Philippopoulos-Mihalopoulos, 2011b: 1–6). Philippopoulos-Mihalopoulos asserts, "If spatial justice is to be claimed by the law, it can no longer remain the lukewarm hybrid of socially 'just' spectres, distributive justice wish lists, neoliberal articulations of participation, parochial territorialism and geopolitical analyses" (2015: 175) or an 'add space and stir' conception of spatial justice where no consideration has been given to what space really is.

In his 2015 work on the lawscape, Philippopoulos-Mihalopoulos seeks to offer an unbounded spatial justice described as the moment when one body withdraws to make way for another. This is a complex theoretical encounter of the central emplacement of what I would call 'corporeal justice' (in the sense that justice relates to the space in which bodies are encountered and not wholly the more traditional conception in which a punishment is exacted on the body, although this is still relevant) within spatial justice. Spatial justice relies upon the supposition that no two bodies can be in the same place at the same time, and thus in order for a situation to be annulled, one of the bodies has to withdraw from the space (or *lawscape*, as he terms it). Within this, there is an "acknowledgement of the impossibility of common space, and a resolute withdrawal before the priority of the space of the other" (2015: 216).

On first sight, the reliance of corporal emplacement would automatically take us back to *where* we are from one moment to the next, denoting a connection of justice with place and resource. So to what point have we come in the development of spatial justice as an actual *thing* – is it purely space we are talking about, or are there other elements involved? Keenan has previously highlighted the conceptual, social and cultural relations of space that proffer us 'spaces of belonging', highlighting space that is not landed but moveable, bringing together the critical role space plays in constructions of race, property, the injustice and violence this construes as a result (2014). It is arguable that through further considering the multi-dimensional nature of spatial justice as occurring in perturbations of space *and* time, and the co-terminous relation of the two, that we may see the value of considering a genealogical or processual approach, or both, incorporating a *temporal* or *spatio-temporal* justice.

Some of the literature on temporal justice really does just repeat the social justice formula, common within the spatial justice writings of Goodin (2010), Ackerman (1997) and Eriksson (1994), as a list of distributive justice claims and aspirations. In Robert Goodin's 'Temporal Justice' (2010) he speaks more of the concern for 'work-life balance' in terms of the unjust distribution of 'discretionary time', the time spent out of work by one social group to another (2010: 1):

> Control over one's time, the capacity to spend it as one wishes, is another important resource; and its distribution raises another important aspect of justice. The

> magnitude of the gap between the discretionary time enjoyed by the best and worst is a measure of temporal injustice.

Feminist thinking around the public/private divide, or that of the Marxist tradition, has a rich history in critiquing the division of time as subservient to the alienating means of capital and surplus value, exemplified in the writings of Rancière on the means of production's temporal division of art and life, which is not overtly related to in these literatures.[1]

If one is to consider spatial justice, the temporal nature of its movement is almost a given and has been discussed as so (Massey, 1992, 2005; Keenan, 2014; Philippopoulos-Mihalopoulos, 2011a, 2011b, 2015). It is interesting to consider how alternate considerations of continua may inform the spatio-temporal nature of justice, injustice, legal origin and innovation.

Continua

How does space, time and justice relate to *continua*, as expressed in the works of Philippopoulos-Mihalopoulos, Boaventura de Sousa Santos and myself? I would suggest that all three formulations depict a *movement* and a *processual* understanding of justice and allow a literal 'walking with the law', as Bottomley and Lim would concur (2009), as well as all ultimately hinting to the question of origin. To follow is an exposition of what we mean by continua or continuum in relation to spatial justice, and why the distinctions are important to highlight in relation to the origin of law.

Lawscaping

What characterises the continuum in Philippopoulos-Mihalopoulos's work? As described already, the understanding of spatial justice refers to where one body cannot be in the same place at the same time, therefore requiring one of the bodies to *withdraw* back into the lawscape in order for there to be a rebalancing of spatial occupation. He explains in his introduction to his lawscaping text (2015: 3):

> there is a continuum that contains everything, including its own ruptures, conflicts, invisibilisations, dissimulations. The continuum is not some anything-goes well-wishing culturally relative flat ontology but a tilted, power-structured surface, on which bodies move and rest and position themselves, thus effecting the tilt while being affected by it. It is all about how bodies positions themselves.

So, bodies position themselves along this continuum of the lawscape, whereby at any given juncture there may be the possibility of conflict, or where the law becomes 'brittle', as he terms it (2015: 73–79), and it is here where the continuum subsumes and recapitulates the potential intersections of each 'rupture'. Philippopoulos-Mihalopoulos delimits the lawscape continua as one of many "continuum, which is used in plural forms, multiplying as lawscape or atmosphere, both bringing us back from the illusions of rupture and enabling ruptures to take place" (2015: 2). The meaning of rupture in this context is whereby out of a situation of violence and injustice, there formulates something which is new, something that may appear as though it comes from outside the lawscape, but actually is just invisible until the point it becomes visible, in a process of *dissimulation*. Centrally, there is nothing external to the lawscape; it is an assemblage (2015: 8) where each and everything is a part of everyone else, as if an atomical shifting, and that this is autopoietic, self-creating. The assemblant nature of the lawscape refers to a Spinozan philosophical backbone (2001), repeating the horizontal war machine and plane of immanence of Deleuze and Guattari (2004), the actor network connections of Latour (2007) and the non-linear self-organisation of de Landa (2000) and Johnson (2001). He claims that "all bodies are part of the continuum, which I understand as a surface of assemblages that, significantly, has no outside" (2015: 8). Negating the outside is congenital to his thesis, as this is how bodies and objects within the continuum are positioned in relation to one another and connected through the flow of movement whereby a rupture purely reveals parts that are never fully present, that are withdrawn, whether to make way for the Other or not (2015: 3).[2]

This most prescient and contrasting conception of lawscape to that of an Arendtian extra-legal conception of legal innovation, where the denoting of rupture or change in the movement of the lawscape is not coming from an external source but moving in an autopoietic fashion, reveals some systems theory influences. The lawscape is also ahistorical, we know of its *processes* but we do not know where it comes from *originally*. We will look to Santos's continuum of formalism next before moving to a re-reading of it in terms of *nonlinear informalities*.

Continuum of formalism

How does the burgeoning continua of the lawscape compare to that of Boaventura de Sousa Santos's 'continuum of formalism'? It first appeared in his article 'The Law of the Oppressed: The Construction and Reproduction of Legality in Pasargada' (1977), taken from his 1974 thesis 'Law Against Law: Legal Reasoning in Pasargada Law'. The piece focused on the formation of legalities from a Southern setting informing the understanding of institutionalisation processes of extra-state justice. This extra-state justice he equated to popular justice, sometimes in conflict, and sometimes in parallel with, the law of the state (1977: 5). Pasargada was a fictitious suburb of Rio de Janeiro, hence the name 'Pasargada Law' (1977: 1–9), a form of bottom-up dispute prevention and dispute settlement of the 'Pasargada Residents Association'. As a result of selectively borrowing from the practices and customs of the official legal system, at the same time as asserting their own form of bottom-up law, Santos argued that the law created, existed and correspondingly occupied a position along a 'continuum of formalism' (1977: 90). Law is thus created out of necessity, where the state system does not accommodate for the said community and other methods of cohesion have had to be developed in order to assert justice in one form or another. Here "the strategy of legality tends to transform itself in the legality of the strategy" (1977: 104).

The term continuum of formalism is one that helps to explicate a movement from that which is not law, to law, demonstrative of the process of institutionalisation itself as integral and affective within the formation of state law specifically. The continuum, in this sense, is a form of institutionalisation, initiating processes through which state law is formed. The law is formulated from that which is not law (that which is outside) from the practices and actions of the Pasargada settlers, forming a linear trajectory of movement from non-institutionalised and informal law, on to formal institutionalised legality.

A good example of a continuum of formalism can be found within the organisation of social centres, or political squats, that tend to be organised in horizontal anti-authoritarian hierarchies, free of concerns of the system of capital, until over time, they either are evicted or, if they wish to last longer, become rented, eventually owned or co-owned in some form. This replicates a continuum of formalism from informal to formal, in a linear trajectory of *institutionalisation* (Finchett-Maddock: 2016).

Speaking of institutionalisation not only reminds us of Santos's continuum of formalism, but also of the work of the 'philosopher of autonomy', Cornelius Castoriadis and his descriptions of the 'imaginary institution of society'. He begins with the thesis that every society 'institutes itself' through the creation of 'social imaginary significations' (Castoriadis, 1975). This process of institutionalisation takes on recognisable forms of authority that occupy time and space in ways with which we become familiar, such as the seat of government, the courts and the architectures of legal and political authority that surround us and convince us of their infallibility.

Santos's continuum of formalism works if you believe there is such a thing as an *outside* of law, which reminds us of the kind of questions the lawscape and the spatial justices described previously have just raised. Santos's look to the processes gives freedom to focus on the creation of forms of law and forms of justice and can assist us in understanding the institutionalising nature of continua, as well as the possible divergence between a law that becomes instituted and a law that does not, or a form of justice that is instituted and that which is not. It also may well connect us with a notion of where law comes from, its origin, illustrating informal laws emanating from resistance to state law and how these laws then might become formalised, spatially and temporally coordinated.

Nonlinear informality

The continuum of formalism in the context of Santos's work describes a process of institutionalisation, and this is repeated through my own work on the example of social centres, with additional concern for the continua reflecting what is outside of state formalisation as well, thus giving way to forms of 'nonlinear informality'. This nonlinear informality is a form of noninstitutionalised institutionalisation, making way for what Castoriadis would terms as 'self-institution' (1975: 31). What this self-institution of course reveals is that all law, whether of a plural nature or otherwise, is the product of "a society that self-institutes itself explicitly, not once and for all, but continuously" (1975: 31).

Philippopoulos-Mihalopoulos's lawscape, and the continua in which it unfolds and unravels, is not a legal pluralist supposition, but a legal omnipotence where law is everywhere at any given time. The laws of which Santos speaks are those that are bottom-up, contingent on the practices and actions of groups that have not been formally recognised by state law, their dispute resolution mechanisms not as yet entirely incorporated into the state, but certainly on their way in the processes of the continua of formalism that he describes. For myself, there is a divergence between law and resistance, perhaps the moment where the lawscape becomes brittle, to use Philippopoulos-Mihalopoulos's language, where in an assemblant fashion, each are contingent of one another. There is a break between the linear trajectory of processes of legal institutionalisation and that of resistant forms, which results in both informal and formal law, and equally contingent as the spatial justice of the lawscape.

The question is, what differentiates between laws that supposedly happen prior to institutionalisation and continue in a formal manner, and those that remain operating in a nonlinear fashion, continuously evading constitution? Law and resistance being within one another assumes that there is a juncture or moment in time and space that performs and enacts a process and product of either a law of the state or a law of resistance, where one becomes more constituent of law than of resistance. I talk about this shortly as a third space or *a-legal vacuum*, a concept which does not exist within the lawscape. The moment of alteration in the lawscape is the interruption of the continua, the folding of law and space where at given coordinates, law becomes 'visible' (2015: 73–79), law is of an ethereal and invisible constitution the remainder of the time, implying there is no innovation of law that is outside of law.

For myself, and referring to Rousseau's market forces interjecting between state and citizen (1998 [1762]), to the Arendtian extra-legal (1970), this juncture must be interrupted by an external presence influencing the direction of one over the other, which is where the work of legal pluralism and Philippopoulos-Mihalopoulos departs. This moment deciphers the difference between law that will become state law and law that might become a '*law of resistance*'. It is at this point that I argue all non-institutionalised law resulting from presence (i.e., from the direct decision-making of a collective) is fed by an external force of law, and not one that comes from an internal fold of the lawscape. For institutionalised (representative law) that informs a constitutional context, this outside law is a law of resistance. There are, however, two suppositions here that this point relies on which have been reasserted as problematic in an era of post-truth politics – the first being that the ultimate kind of institutional law we are talking of gives preference to, and relies upon, that of a democratic constitution; the second being that one cannot assume that the will of the majority is in the best interests of all, as we have seen in the culpable role of the franchise in increasingly divisive British and American politics. Arguably, the entire schema of politics has been tainted by the interests of capital and neoliberalism, it therefore making it difficult to see any representative form of institutionalised politics as posing objective arguments upon which the collective of a democratic state can make an informed decision. This reinforces the institutionalised nature of state law, the usefulness of seeing the origins of law and how these beginnings are warped through the interjection of individual property rights as the dominating force of legal social organisation, at least in the Common Law context that has spread across the globe and informs the cross-sovereign regime of market-fused law of neoliberalism. Considering any crisis of representation, within *presence* and not *re*-presence, there is no need for institutions and the process of institutionalisation to hold legitimacy, as it is constituent power itself, in the Negrian sense (1999). At the same time, both the law of the state and this proposed informal law of resistance come from this external presence; it is through the divergent manipulation of enforcement, representation and hierarchies of power that the two normative frameworks become expressed, radically and differently.

It is the introduction of individual property rights into law and resistance that determines whether to direct a continuum of formalism as expressed by the creation of state law or to remain in a '*nonlinear informality*' as manifested by examples of laws of resistance (and presence), such as those of the social centre phenomena, that I discuss in my work on the performances of social centre law (2016). Laws of resistance that remain nonlinear and informal are thus always collective by nature, allowing for the performative and practicing temperament of laws of resistance. This is also true of state law, but the practice of state law becomes fetishised with the process and product of the institution of individual property rights (as expressed through the monopoly of force, representation and hierarchy), as it forgets its collective origin and insists on the import of moving in a linear trajectory, in order to legitimate itself.

In my work I argue that state law, to enact itself as state law, thus aspires to move in a *linear* progression in a continuum of formalism as described by Santos, in order for it to institute and constitute itself. It has to *think* it is moving in a linear progression, although, in agreement with Philippopoulos-Mihalopoulos and any other assemblant and complex-adaptive thinker, everything moves in a nonlinear fashion, based on the laws of uncertainty and *entropy* that we will discuss in relation to space, time and the speculative thought of Meillassoux and Hägglund shortly. What this discussion of the different continua has revealed is that each of them describe the processes and the origin of spatio-temporal justice, even if in the lawscape at least, there is not the intention to refer to the latter but this occurs by inferring an ahistory. It is to this space-time of the origin, and vacuum, that we come to via an understanding of the movement of entropy and uncertainty.

Lawscape and vacuum

Philippopoulos-Mihalopoulos would argue that there is nothing outside the lawscape, the law only withdrawing in order to make way for spatial justice. I premise my work on there being an '*a-legal vacuum*' within continua of formalisms or nonlinear informalisms in order for there to make way for contingency and uncertainty, in which justice can be spatially and temporally performed.

When you look at the three differing conceptions of continua, it is fair to say that there is a spatial and temporal concern that describes the processes of temporal and spatial *law*, evident in each of the examples. Lawscape does not seek to refer to the violent reasons why these assemblant ruminations are occurring, but more *how*.

In a similar fashion, Santos is concerned with the processes of formalisation of law, as well as nonlinear informality, whereby the practices and performances of law and resistance are described as the processes of informal and formal law set in spatial and temporal terms. Lawscape does not question the origin; for Santos's continuum, however, there is an underlying question that propels all legal pluralism: where does law come from? This description of processes, such as put forward by Santos, automatically infers the next step would indeed be to locate the origin.

Discussing the question of origins and processes of law specifically in relation to property, Zartaloudis places emphasis on investigating the change and *process* that occurs in the formation of state law, as opposed to continuously seeking to question its foundation. He states in his 'The Trust: The Invention of the Uses and the Franciscan Influence in England' (2012):

> (a) It is crucial to avoid this obsessive origin for practical reasons as well as for the fact that the method of the origin presupposes an approach that hinders study. Instead, we can think of the quest for sources in the sense of an 'amalgam' (though one that does not fuse its elements into a unity), or even better in the sense of an 'assemblage' (whereby different sources, concepts and situational contingencies intersect without a central unifying reason); (b) it is important to avoid the characterisation and understanding of the designated 'pre-juridical' (concept, practice, custom, etc.) in juridical terms, since this always hinders the appreciation of how assemblages, in fact, form.

Zartaloudis's acceptance of the assemblant nature of law would fall into the processual formulation of justice, moving beyond questioning its origins and to looking explicitly at the manner in which state law comes to be formed, echoing the object-oriented lawscape of Philippopoulos-Mihalopoulos. However, both arguments within processorial and ahistorical spatial justice merely reassert the import of origin, even in understanding pure process and an ontology of spatial justice. By asserting that there is nothing outside the lawscape, automatically there is a metaphysical statement about the atomical and assemblant nature of the spatial justice being described. Within lawscape, there is a lack in genealogy and recognition of preceding violent legacies that led the lawscape to its positioning and placement in precedence.[3] This might be of course altered from the kind of justice that we see exacted within courts, where in any case there is a shrewd application of law to facts; however, a spatial justice must give dividends to reparation and restoration, a purposive and progressive reading of law given its temporal transgression. A form of genealogy can also account for the integral role of uncertainty within spatial justice and legal innovation, the guiding force for where law has come from and where law might go.

What is the difference between the vacuum of alegality and the lawscape, and what does this mean for the spatio-temporal continua of justice? Is this just seeking to describe the formation of law, and are we automatically inferring justice when we speak of law, or the lawscape? As we know, the lawscape continua does not take anything from outside of itself, it just *is*, thus ontologically and epistemologically separate from the notion of anything existing outside of the bricolage of law – there can be no such thing as a-legality.

Contrastedly, a continua of nonlinear informality has tried to incorporate the question of origin through deciphering the moment at which resistances become law and vice versa, whereby through locating the moment at which it occurs, the catalyst of space-time of justice (and injustice) might be found, within an a-legal vacuum.

The vacuum, just like the Burroughsian Interzone (1998; 2009), is similar to Soja's Third Space, the space in which all that is expelled from both legality and illegality finds its home, and Lefebvre's trialectics, three modes of being in presence, absence and another. This is the production of the vacuum, the interstitial moment, 'The Aleph' in Borges-esque sense; a chink in the world machine that means nothing and everything all at once. This zone relies on its generating a boundary in order to exist; it relies on the line, the law, in order for it to happen at all. According to Lindahl, the a-legal refers to a series of founding acts which are neither legal nor illegal in nature, a-legal because they "presuppose a legal order as the condition for their intelligibility" (Lindahl, 2008: 125). These foundational acts are of an a-legal form because they "institute the distinction itself between legality and illegality. Only retrospectively, if they catch on, can they come to manifest themselves, albeit precariously and incompletely, as legal acts" (2008: 125).

The a-legal vacuum is the space of the threshold, the amplitude within the line as the no-man's land of a law of resistance that Lambert would term as the 'thickness of the line' (2013). Yet even the vacuum is contingent of primordial law and resistance, in reference to not just the process but also the *origin* of law. An *ex nihilo* of a-legality is argued as the meeting created by movements of both continua of formalism and informal nonlinearity. It is a stopgap in the flow of institutionalisation whereby a law of resistance which precedes state law can exist even if for a moment; in a similar vein to the work of Meillassoux (2008), reminiscent of some of the scientifically informed work of Barad on the role of the 'void'. According to Barad, indeterminacy is not the state of a thing, but an unending dynamism (2012: 8), and even in a zero state, there is such a thing as zero matter (2012: 9) whereby the nothingness is pregnant with more nothingness – she describes a vacuum as a womb.

This liminal juncture of measurement and measured, the threshold as well as the space bounded by the threshold, paradoxically is described by Barad as being openness itself. Even the boundary is porous, which reflects the construct of lawscape similarly; therefore, law is always in a state of animation, emergence, becoming and openness. If we see all law as open to change and unfixed, which each of the formulations of continua concur, then this reflects exactly the way in which all systems occur as a result of movements of *entropy* and uncertainty, from an open systems complexity perspective as opposed to a closed systems theory approach, which I will explain now. This is similarly reflected in the work of object-oriented philosophy and speculative realist accounts of materiality such as is exemplified now by the work of Graham Harman (2010; 2018), Meillassoux (2008) amongst others, that seeks to describe both the processes and origins of space and time. By accounting for uncertainty, the spatio-temporal crystallisation of law is explained, as uncertainty *is* space and time, giving way to justice and injustice by formal and informal continua that internalise and catalyse uncertainty to create the space-time continua of (in)justice as a result.

Entropy, uncertainty and speculative continua

The role of uncertainty is key in the nonlinear informality and the continua of nonlinear informality, as well as the continua of lawscape and formalism in Philippopoulos-Mihalopoulos and Santos respectively. Uncertainty materialises and pinpoints junctures of time and space, which brings us back to the spatio-temporal concern of these continua of justice and injustice. It also shapes the direction of the continua, in both the lawscape and nonlinear informality.

Uncertainty refers back to complex ecological systems and their lack of predictability, meaning that human-ecological results can be hard to foresee. Accounting for the uncertain nature of systems is complexity or *emergence*, determined as bottom-up behaviour (in a very similar fashion to which Santos refers), "when the actions of multiple agents interacting dynamically and following local rules rather than top-down commands result in some kind of visible macro-behaviour or structure" (Escobar, 2003: 351). This self-organisation reminds us of the way in which lawscapes and nonlinear informality express these assemblant, leaderless principles of self-organisation very clearly. This is emergence from the grassroots – disordered, spontaneous, bottom-up constituent power, as opposed to the top-down vertical force inherent within the institution of state law, that seeks to deny its nonlinear nature and assert totalities as opposed to openings.

Uncertainty, or what Meillassoux would term as *hyperchaos*, within nonlinear space and time, plays a similar role. The spontaneity of lawscapes and nonlinear continua account for their unpredictability, whereas linear time (reminiscent of the continuum of formalism and institutionalisation of law through the interjection of private property) relies on the scientific explanation of the arrow of time and the gathering of *entropy* as the measurement of disorder within a system, also explained within theories of complexity. Entropy in fact supports the possibilities of *both* linear and nonlinear time.

Entropy is the measurement of disorder in a system – it occurs within and as a result of systems and can only ever be supplemented and not reduced, thus giving scientists good reason to confirm that time can only ever go in one direction. There is the *slightest* of possibilities, however, that as a result of the emergent movement and interfacing of each new part of a burgeoning system, that time could be reversed, thus allowing for the chaotic movement of entropy production – *uncertainty*, the processes of *nonlinear* time resulting in new trajectories in space and time, of which we can at the moment only speculate.

What makes there a past and a present in systems, space and time in material actuality is this nod to randomness and uncertainty, which is more accurately described as 'negative entropy'. If entropy is the amount of energy a system has used, then negative entropy is the amount of energy or 'orderliness' that a system 'sucks' from its environment to ensure a balance between order and disorder and that the system does not tip into total chaos, annihilating itself. Negative or 'negentropy', as termed by Léon

Brillouin, is described by scientist Schrödinger where "the essential thing in metabolism is that the organism succeeds in freeing itself from all the entropy it cannot help producing while alive" (Schrödinger, 1944: 67–75). Thus negative entropy is "itself a measure of order" (1944: 67–75). The character of negative entropy alters dependent on whether it is a closed or open system, arguably there being infinite possibilities of alteration because of the uncertainty of environmental conditions occurring in an open system. This question of what is an open or a closed system is central to an understanding of both emergence and materialism, both schools of thought seeing dynamic processes within not just open, animate or 'alive' objects but those so too that are supposedly closed and inert (such as a table or a building, for instance).

This issue of uncertainty plays a pivotal role within the work of speculative realists, and it is where a speculative understanding of entropy can animate the spatio-temporal formation of justice described by continua of linear, nonlinear and lawscape forms.

The congenital link of uncertainty and chaos between entropy processes and speculative thought, particularly that of Meillassoux, brings together the two intertwined epistemologies to explain the integral nature of uncertainty in time and space, indeed uncertainty as time and space itself. Meillassoux derives the necessity of contingency as *hyperchaos*: the result being that anything is possible from one moment to the next. This gives us an indication of the kind of reality with which we are dealing when referring to the thought of Meillassoux, whereby according to Hallward it is a realism that "does not involve the way things are so much as the possibility that they might always be otherwise" (2011: 131).

For Meillassoux, the task of speculative thinking is to remove ourselves from the shackles of Kantian performativity and think in terms of the possibility that there exist relations which are external to our understanding of them. This view of the world would be supportive of the equal import of not only non-Western metaphysics, the kind of configuring of spatial justice and diaspora that Patchett and Keenan have promoted, and forms of law and spatial justice altered to that which we have never dreamt of knowing. Meillassoux claims that '*correlationism*' consists in disqualifying the claim that it is possible to consider the realms of subjectivity and objectivity independently of one another (2008: 13), and so the job of speculative thought is to acknowledge this correlative thinking as a reality in itself, and that there are further phenomenon outside of this parallelist supposition. This of course may seem a familiar retake of Cartesian dualism, but it is radical to the extent that it reveals our own blind spots to reality because of our own perception, the supposed institutions of epistemology that we have adhered to in Western and non-Western thought, revealing a totalitarian impossibility. Controversially, Meillassoux does seek to highlight the existence of something absolute beyond our consciousness through the *de facto* existence of 'arché-fossils', or events which happened prior to the arrival of human consciousness, such as the beginnings of life itself, or even to the origins of law, and he sees the Achilles heel of correlationism as its inability to cope with what he refers to as 'ancestral' statements (Hallward, 2011: 136).

Meillassoux's hyperchaos is reflected in entropy processes, assuming that there are movements between metabolisms whereby one system bifurcates into another drawing negentropy to expel the positive used vitality, allowing the possibility that there are spatial and temporal dynamics of becoming and uncertainty at play, upon which and through which law and justice are conceived, that are outside of the scope of human malleability. Similarly to Meillassoux, complexity theorists relay the existence of formations that are neither predictable nor unpredictable, the only thing that can be confirmed is that random fluctuations *will* occur, which is, according to Cilliers (2005), an acceptance of an almost Habermasian 'performative contradiction'[4] in complexity and entropy.[5]

What I find so important for spatial justice, continua and legal innovation, to this exploration into the surrealisms of speculative reason, is the fact that not only can it account for a de-centring of human action, as well as white Western epistemologies from a dominating genealogy of the world, but it reasserts the congenital power of spatio-temporality to organise life around us and the possibilities that this holds for the aspirations for justice. Not only does a speculative approach to entropy attest to one form of time, but it may account for many (Finchett-Maddock, 2017), describing the central import of uncertainty to spatio-temporal processes and origins of justice at once, as well as proposing the import of genealogy, whether nonlinear or linear.

It is a debate between thinkers on the malleability if time itself between Meillassoux and Hägglund that highlights the two frameworks of lawscape and the a-legal vacuum, highlighting the import of understanding uncertainty's role in spatial justice and legal innovation overall.

Meillassoux's philosophy of time is based upon his acknowledgement of there being an external reality, a realism which has happened prior to human explanation and thus is governed beyond us.[6] This beyond, or absolute as Meillassoux sees it, is the power of time itself which has the capability to destroy as much as it does to create (2008: 62): "it is absolutely necessary that every entity might not exist . . . the absolute is the absolute impossibility of a necessary being". He returns us to the very enquiry of not just legal philosophy, the search for the origin, but to thought and epistemology as a whole, whereby he states that "time without development *[devenir]*" has the "potential to generate life *ex nihilo*, to draw spirit from matter or creativity from stasis – or even to resurrect an immortal mind from a lifeless body" (Hallward, 2011: 133).[7] Meillassoux thus gives us an account of the a-legal vacuum, the life *ex nihilo*, where contingency and necessity come as one, where nothing is pregnant with more of the Baradian nothing, and uncertainty itself giving way to space, time and justice continua.[8]

Is law negentropy or is time itself justice? This absence of law as the creator of all laws is reminiscent of the entropic performative contradiction, whereby in order to proclaim the world is valueless, one makes a value-laden statement to ground the same. By asserting that at any given moment of order there can be disorder, is to assert the 'virtual power of contingency', a deviation of negentropy reverting itself and becoming entropy *per se*. Meillassoux even attests the possibility of God, not in the sense that he may currently exist but that thought the swerve of clinamen, it is not impossible that she or he can come into matter in some form or another in the future at the same time.

If one were to equate the lawscape's ahistorical processual consideration of spatial justice, deconstructionist Hägglund would agree with the assemblant nature of law, disagreeing with Meillassoux, stating there can be no "contingency without the succession of time, which entails irreversible destruction and rules out the possibility of resurrection *a priori*" (2011: 116). This relies upon the creation of positive entropy, the purported arrow of time, which is one and the same as Meillassoux's reliance on a temporal absolute once again. From Hägglund's point of view, there is no 'flow' of time outside of spatialisation, a process which he refers to as '*arché-materiality*', Kantian succession, "since time has to be spatialised in order to flow in the first place. Thus, everything we say about time (that it is 'passing', 'flowing', 'in motion' and so on is a spatial metaphor" (2011: 119). For Hägglund, time is irreversible (2011: 116) and must entail negative entropy in order for it to iterate itself; it is nothing but the negativity that is intrinsic to succession (2011: 121). He argues that if matter intrinsically houses negentropy then time itself can never move from one moment to the next, eliminating the possibility of succession where every moment must entirely negate itself or there would "be no time, only a presence forever remaining the same" (2011: 118).

Hägglund's assertion is a sensible one and refers us back to the assemblant nature of continua, the lawscape. It describes the assemblant movement of spatial and temporal justice, and yet again, does nothing to tell us as to the origins, and even would go so far as to purport that searches for origins are violent in their impossibilities, just as with Meillassoux and an a-legal vacuum, to leave the genealogy out is an equally violent move.

Continua of (in)justice

To accept the now is to move with the flow of space and time, justice itself being the flow of space and time; it is similarly fair to remember what was external to law, where it came from, what is occurring from one coordinate to the next.

Any sense of justice in a nonlinear continua traverses the inculcation of order over disorder, a pinpointing of the moment before something becomes valuable, exploitable and fixed, where forces of destruction are actually those dressed up as progress, marching in a linear formation, and yet towards their own heat death. Arguably, one can assimilate a resemblance of Meillassoux's theory of radical contingency with the uncertain movement of continua, whether informal, lawscaping or formal. It speaks of the processes of one stage of space and time to the next and its spontaneous character, and also seeks to tell us where the laws of physics and space-time break down.

Arguably, uncertainty is what creates space and time, the lead character, in the play of law and spatio-temporality. By delving into the work of two metaphysically opposing thinkers, speculative realist Quentin Meillassoux and material deconstructionist Martin Hägglund, in relation to lawscape and the a-legal vacuum, we can see the role that uncertainty plays in creating both the spatio-temporal processes of lawscaping *and* the origins of justice within the a-legal vacuum.

Uncertainty has very clearly created space and time in the political tectonics of a late capitalist world, the void through which kernels of nihilism have made themselves known, in the internet sphere, the atmospheres, before our eyes. As the link between partisan nationalist/racist bias of media and the outcome of the EU Referendum vote demonstrates, "It was the machine-like feedback loop that repeated 'difference' and 'separate-ness' until the hate began to bloom" (Verso Editors, 2016).[9]

Negative alterations in geopolitics are a reminder of the Nietzschean 'eternal return' highlighting the positive and negative forces at play in continua of justice (positive and negative entropy), the singular and plural agency of self-destruction as contrary to any balancing of the continua, from creation to annihilation. As Nietzsche stated, humankind is still in a process of becoming, "and should thus not be regarded as a fixed magnitude from which one might draw a conclusion as to the originator" (1997: 16). This becoming, alternating nature of us, in space and time, needs to be remembered so that we coordinate ourselves in the continua of positive and negative entropy, aware of our effects and affects on others, on time and space around us, on our relation with uncertainty, justice and injustice.

Ultimately, in a similarly incalculable Derrideanness, spatial justice is argued as equating to uncertainty, the ever-indiscriminate guard of external forces, a denial of completeness, and an embracement of becoming. This piece, as in any other piece, is an opportunity to try and link up the external with the internal, the now with the past, and the future, to apprehend and understand what creates and destroys forms of justice, and injustice – to respond, alter and change through theoretical insight, a questioning of who we are and where we come from "[where] we are all situated in a continuum of indistinction our responsibility heightened because of our indistinction" (Philippopoulos-Mihalopoulos, 2015: 61). It is hoped it has contributed to this task and placing law and theory as central.

Notes

* I would like to give my dearest thanks to Andreas Philippopoulos-Mihalopoulos for his kind offer of my work being included in this collection. Thank you to Sabrina Gilani and Kenny Veitch for their time in giving me comments on this piece. Thanks once again to Charlie Blake for inspiring my interest in speculative realism and to Swastee Ranjan for the privilege of working with her on her understanding of the lawscape and aesthetics, the influence of which no doubt feeds back into this work.

1 Dietrich Henckel and Susanne Thomaier (2013) do speak of the role of temporal justice in the rhythms of cities, in a nod to the congenital role of space in time, and vice versa, but using the same language of efficiency and distribution that are hinged to a liberal vision of categorisation. Tim Hayward and Yukinori Iwaki (2016) relay a concern for global inequalities' manifestation of injustice with respect to space and time, relaying an argument similar to those of justice and sustainability.

2 Philippopoulos-Mihalopoulos relays four main points in relation to the continuum, the first being that there are many and not just one, such as the lawscape continuum formed by space and law, but other multivariant scales of continua that can be localised or elsewhere (2015: 9). The second contention that despite the assemblant nature of all, each body retains its singularity despite its assemblage position, so each body retains its borders despite being part of a greater structure. A third relates to rupture, whereby the rupture ontologically is part of the continuum and does not offer a portal to an outside, but allows the continuum to gain momentum to carry on spreading spatially and temporally (2015: 9). The fourth

point refers to the continuum as tilted, leaning to one side (2015: 11), to reassert the spatiality of the lawscape and the direction of its shifting.

3 Thanks to PhD student Swastee Ranjan and colleague Sabrina Gilani for our discussion on the lawscape and history that reminded me of the violence of ahistoricity.

4 This is whereby entropy looks like an absolute statement regarding the nature of systems, and yet within that statement it is propounding that there can never be a totalising law, it will always annihilate itself.

5 Similarly, what both speculative reason and complexity face are counterjections of biological reductionism, whereby entropy denotes systems which should be confined to the natural world, to biology and not psychological or social worlds, and absolutism can obviously lead to totalitarianism.

6 Like other forms of speculative thinking, this is radically altered from a Cartesian conception of mind/body duality, accepting that we are limited to our own perception of the world, that we affect the world, but perhaps that the world may also affect us back.

7 This conception of absolute time could be questionable – by referring back to a Newtonian temporal absolute is merely to claim time as a separate entity, it can only exist in one form, and thus supporting the power to create totalitarian forms of knowledge around time. Despite this, the radical contingency of time absolute of which Meillassoux speaks negates this categorisation and straight-jacketing of time.

8 This is radical thought and one that is bound to attract opposition but at the same time is refreshing to the extent that it acknowledges time can move in an infinite number of mysterious ways. The role of entropy here is fundamental and questions where negative entropy, at the very start of life, must have come from. Can it be that all life already invests within itself the *poiesis* available to it to become other than to itself? In a sense is there ever a moment whereby there is no negentropy and life begins *ex nihilo*? Meillassoux believes that this is so, and the reason for this is contingency itself – there is no necessity for its creation (2008: 53): "There is no reason for anything to be or to remain thus and so rather than otherwise. . . . Everything could actually collapse: from trees to stars, from stars to laws, from physical laws to logical laws; and this not by virtue of some superior law whereby everything is destined to perish, but by virtue of the absence of any superior law capable of preserving anything, no matter what, from perishing".

9 As in the case of Brexit and the phenomenon of Trump, it was capital's destructive desire to control and categorise, manifested in the self-interest of institutionalised, representative law, that lit this tinderbox of artificial lines of division and violence between peoples who then have their own addiction to the capital to feed, in order to support its own habit. Capital is literally sucking the life force, the negative entropy, uncertainty and the space-time continua of justice itself, as it seeks to control, totalise, cope with its impending death, where William Davies has argued that destructive self-harm of Brexit (2016: 12).

Bibliography

Ackerman, Bruce, 'Temporal Horizons of Justice', Faculty Scholarship Series 128, 1997, http://digitalcommons.law.yale.edu/fss_papers/128.

Arendt, Hannah, *Crises of the Republic*, London: Harcourt, 1970.

Barad, Karen, *What is the Measure of Nothingness? Infinity, Virtuality, Justice*, 100 Notes, Museum Fridericianum Verantsaltungs-GmBH, Ostfildern: Hatje-Cantz Verlag, 2012.

Blandy, Sarah and Sibley, David, 'Law, Boundaries and the Production of Space', *Social and Legal Studies*, 19(3), 275–284, 2010.

Blomley, Nicholas, *Law, Space and the Geographies of Power*, New York: Guilford Press, 1994.

Bottomley, Anne and Lim, Hilary (eds), *Feminist Perspectives on Land Law, Feminist Perspectives*, London: Cavendish/Routledge, 2009.

Brah, Avtar, *Cartographies of Diaspora*, London, New York: Routledge, 1996.

Burroughs, William, 'International Zone', in J. Grauerholz and I. Silverberg (eds), *Word Virus: The William Burroughs Reader*, London: Fourth Estate, 1998.
Burroughs, William, *Interzone*, London: Penguin, 2009.
Castoriadis, Cornelius, *The Imaginary Institution of Society*, Cambridge: MIT Press, 1975.
Cilliers, Paul, 'Complexity, Deconstruction and Relativism', *Theory, Culture & Society*, 22(5), 255–267, 2005.
Cooper, Davina, *Governing out of Order: Space, Law and the Politics of Belonging*, London: Rivers Oram, 1998.
Davies, William, 'Thoughts on the Sociology of Brexit', in *The Brexit Crisis,* London: Verso, 2016.
De Landa, Manuel, *A Thousand Years of Nonlinear History*, New York: Swerve Editions, 2000.
Delaney, David, *Place Race and the Law*, Austin, TX: University of Texas Press, 1986.
Delaney, David, *The Spatial, the Legal and the Pragmatics of World-Making: Nomospheric Investigations*, London: Routledge, 2011.
Deleuze, Gilles and Guattari, Felix, *A Thousand Plateaus: Capitalism and Schizophrenia*, London: Continuum, 2004.
De Villiers, Isolde, I., 'Leibniz, Lefebvre and the Spatial Turn in Law', *HTS Teologiese Studies/ Theological Studies,* 72(1), 2016.
Eriksson, Elsevier, 'On Discount, Temporal Justice, Sustainability and Limited Foresight', *Ricerche Economiche*, 48, 341–355, 1994.
Escobar Artur, 'Actors, Networks, and New Knowledge Producers: Social Movements and the Paradigmatic Transition in the Sciences', in Boaventura de Sousa Santos (ed.), *Conhecimento Prudente para una Vida decente: 'Um Discurso sobre as Ciêncas' Revisitad*, Porto: Afrontamento, 2003.
Finchett-Maddock, Lucy, *Protest, Property and the Commons: Performances of Law and Resistance*, London: Routledge, 2016.
Finchett-Maddock, Lucy, 'Speculative Entropy: "Dynamism, Hyperchaos and the Fourth Dimension in Environmental Law Practice"', in Andreas Philippopoulos-Mihalopoulos and Victoria Brooke (eds), *Handbook of Research Methods in Environmental Law (Research Methods in Law Series)* London: Edward Elgar, 2017.
Graham, Nicole, *Lawscape: Property, Environment, Law*, Abingdon and New York: Routledge, 2011.
Goodin, Robert E., 'Temporal Justice', *Journal of Social Policy*, 39, 1–16, 2010.
Hägglund, Martin, 'Radical Atheist Materialism: A Critique of Meillassoux,' in Levi Bryant, Nick Srnicek and Graham Harman (eds), *The Speculative Turn: Continental Materialism and Realism*, Melbourne: Re-Press, 2011.
Hallward, Peter, 'Anything is Possible: A Reading of Quentin Meillassoux's After Finitude,' in Levi Bryant, Nick Srnicek and Graham Harman (eds), *The Speculative Turn: Continental Materialism and Realism*, Melbourne: Re-Press, 2011.
Hall, Stuart, 'Avtar Brah's Cartographies: Moment, Method, Meaning', *Feminist Review*, 100, 27–38, 2012.
Harman, Graham, *Towards Speculative Realism*, London: Zero, 2010.
Harman, Graham, *Object-Oriented Ontology: A New Theory of Everything*, London: Zero, 2018.
Harvey, David, *Social Justice and the City,* London: Edward Arnold, 1973.
Harvey, David, 'Globalisation and the Spatial Fix', *Geograpische Review*, 23–30, 2001.
Harvey, David, 'The Right to the City', *New Left Review,* 53, 23–40, 2008.
Hayward, Tim and Iwaki, Yukinori, 'Had We but World Enough, and Time: Integrating the Dimensions of Global Justice', *Critical Review of International Social and Political Philosophy,* 19(4), 383–399, 2016.
Henckel, Dietrich and Thomaier, Susanne, 'Efficiency, Temporal Justice, and the Rhythm of Cities in Space – Time Design of the Public City', *Urban and Landscape Perspectives*, 15, 99–117, 2013.
Johnson, Stephen, *Emergence*, New York: Scribner, 2001.

Keenan, Sarah, *Subversive Property: Law and the Production of Spaces of Belonging*, London: Routledge, 2014.
Lambert, Leopold, *Weaponised Architecture: The Impossibility of Innocence*, Barcelona: DPR, 2013.
Latour, Bruno, *Reassembling the Social: An Introduction to Actor-Network-Theory*, London: Clarendon, 2007.
Layard, Antonia, 'Public Space: Property, Lines, Interruptions', *Journal of Law, Property and Society*, 2, 1–47, 2016.
Lefebvre, Henri, *Critique of Everyday Life: Volume I: Introduction*, London: Verso [1958].
Lefebvre, Henri, *The Production of Space*, Cambridge, MA: Blackwell, 1991.
Lindahl, Hans, 'Border Crossings by Immigrants: Legality, Illegality and A-legality', *Res Publica*, 14, 117–135, 2008.
Massey, Doreen, *For Space*, London: Sage, 2005.
Massey, Doreen, 'Politics and Space/Time', *New Left Review*, 1, 196, 1992, http://newleftreview.org/I/196/doreen-massey-politics-and-space-time.
Meillassoux, Quentin, *After Finitude: An Essay on the Necessity of Contingency*, London: Continuum, 2008.
Negri, Antonio, *Insurgencies: Constituent Power and the Modern State*, Minneapolis: University of Minnesota Press, 1999.
Nietzsche, Friedrich, *Thus Spake Tharathustra*, London: Wordsworth Editions, 1997.
Patchett, Emma and Keenan, Sarah (eds), *Spatial Justice and Diaspora*, Oxford: Counterpress, 2017.
Philippopoulos-Mihalopoulos, Andreas, 'Law, Space, Bodies: The Emergence of Spatial Justice', in Laurent De Sutter (ed.), *Deleuze and Law*, Edinburgh: Edinburgh University Press, 2011a.
Philippopoulos-Mihalopoulos, Andreas, 'Law's Spatial Turn: Geography, Justice and a Certain Fear of Space', *Law Culture and the Humanities*, 20(5), 1–6, 2011b.
Philippopoulos-Mihalopoulos, Andreas, *Spatial Justice: Body, Lawscape, Atmosphere, Space Materiality and the Normative Series*, London: Routledge, 2015.
Rousseau, Jean-Jacques, *The Social Contract or Principles of Political Right*, London: Wordsworth Editions, 1998 [1762].
Santos, Boaventura de Sousa, 'The Law of the Oppressed: The Construction and Reproduction of Legality in Pasargada', *Law and Society Review*, 1, 5–126, 1977.
Schrödinger, Erwin, *What is Life?*, Cambridge: Cambridge University Press, 1944.
Soja, Edward, *Third Space: Journeys to Los Angeles and Other Real-and-Imagined Places*, Cambridge: Blackwell, 1996.
Soja, Edward, *Seeking Spatial Justice*, Minneapolis: University of Minnesota Press, 2010.
Spinoza, Benedict, *Ethics*, Hertfordshire: Wordsworth Classics, 2001.
Verso Editors, *The Brexit Crisis*, London: Verso, 2016.
Zartaloudis, Thanos, 'The Trust: The Invention of the Uses and the Franciscan Influence in England', *Divus Thomas*, 115(2), 167–228, 2012.

6

Movement

An homage to legal drips, wobbles and perpetual motion

Olivia Barr

Introduction

Law moves, whether we notice it or not. In this chapter, I explore some of the ways law moves, and why this matters. Theoretically, movement is too often overlooked in our thinking about law or, if not, placed as simply a consequence. Yet, as this chapter shows, movement is far from a consequence of law, but rather, it is how law is: a mode of existence. However, the difficulty is one of perception: of noticing movement. Despite often-repeated images, discourses and conceits of legal stability, such as those captured in concepts of sovereignty and territory, and concomitant perceptions of solidity, certainty and stability, law moves amorphously in both space and time, and does so in material forms. This chapter explores how we might begin to see these movements.

There are many ways the story of movement and its relation to law can be told. One option is to survey the relevant intellectual terrain. Surveys, whether academic, geographic or otherwise, aim to view, examine or inspect in detail a topic, site or location for a specific purpose. As a method, surveys involve the act of looking from a commanding position with the aim of taking a general or comprehensive view of the topic by providing insight through an omnipotent condensation of details. This chapter does not attempt such a task.

> But counting the blades is futile: you would never learn their number. A lawn does not have precise boundaries.
>
> (Calvino, 1999: 28).

Like trying to count every blade of grass to understand a lawn, an attempt to account comprehensively for law's movements is futile. More than just futile, it is a political task that masks hidden assumptions too often aligned with positivism and its ongoing projections of apolitical, gender-biased objectivity. However, as feminists have long observed from less commanding positions, the pretense of objectivity masks much.

A survey, of course, is only one way to share knowledge. Instead of conducting a survey, I take heed of feminist critiques of research methods, methodologies and epistemologies (Code, 1981, Harding, 1987, Haraway, 1991) and in this instance take as my motivation what Lorraine Code calls to 'create exemplary kinds of knowing' (1993: 39).

In this chapter, I explore the jurisprudential importance of movement via a series of examples, and a little bit of story-telling. The story-telling method is mainly drawn from the descriptive and perceptive intensity of Italo Calvino's novel *Mr Palomar* (1999), where the titular character provides some unexpected guidance for legal theory, while the examples dance between literature, science, architecture and law. Weaving throughout the chapter is walking, which I use as an illustration of how law moves in material ways. Throughout the chapter, I argue that taking movement seriously, whether through walking or other material forms, deepens our understanding of the space, time and place of law. In thinking movement with law, and law with movement, a world of conceptual and practical possibilities opens that is radical, different and future. This is the critical potential of movement, and the critical potential of writing and thinking a jurisprudence of movement. Before radical change can occur, a first and major challenge, however, is noticing movement.

The challenge of perception

Popular not only in Italy but also across the world, Italo Calvino was one of the most-translated Italian writers at the time of his death in 1985. He is best known for his disorienting short stories, especially his trilogy *Our Ancestors* (1998), although in legal theory, Calvino is probably best known for his novel *Invisible Cities* (1997). Yet it is his final novella, *Mr Palomar* (1999), that offers a quirky but highly perceptive guide into the deceptively complex world of movement.

> Nobody looks at the moon in the afternoon, and this is the moment when it would most require our attention, since its existence is still in doubt.
>
> (Calvino, 1999: 31)

Like most of Calvino's writings, *Mr Palomar* is hard to describe, especially in terms of its 'beautiful, nimble, solitary feats of imagination' (Heaney, 1985: A1) and its intensely realist whimsical pleasure. A very short book, *Mr Palomar* is a series of succinct meditations on different subjects by a character called Mr Palomar who 'bears the same name as a famous observatory' (Calvino, 1999: 34) and seems to be Calvino himself. Throughout the different scenes, from an Italian beach to a Parisian cheese shop to a Japanese garden, Mr Palomar shares with the reader a conglomerate gasp of observations. As American author Gore Vidal wrote about these observations:

> He looks; he describes; he has a scientist's respect for data . . . He wants us to see not only what he sees but what we may have missed by not looking with sufficient attention.
>
> (Vidal, 1985: 3)

As Vidal notes, the character Mr Palomar wields an urgency of attention towards his physical surrounds and shares with the reader a complex exercise in perception, interspersed with his worries about myriad calamities that may occur if, as individuals or societies, we continue to fail to see. This method of looking with sufficient attention, as a mode of perception, is the inspiration for this chapter.

Calvino's *Mr Palomar* has not gone unnoticed by legal thinkers, most notably the European Court of Justice ('ECJ'). In *Federal Republic of Germany and Kingdom of Denmark v. Commission of the European Communities* C-465/02 and C-466/02 [2005] ECR 9115, the ECJ considered whether to include the name 'feta' in the European Community register of Geographical Indications and Designations of Origin. Interestingly, the Opinion of Mr Ruiz-Jarabo drew on Mr Palomar's method of heightened observation and his ability to see beyond what the eye can see in the following passage of his judgment:

> The sheep and goats of Thrace and Thessaly are very similar to one another but are strikingly different from Scottish, French and Spanish sheep and goats. The same applies to the food they eat, the mountains or meadows where they live, the climate they experience, and all the other conditions which have a bearing on how the cheese comes into being. In that connection, I should like to quote again from *Palomar* by Italo Calvino, in which the experiences of the hero in a shop in Paris is recounted in a masterly fashion: 'behind each cheese there is a different grass under a different sky: fields encrusted with salt deposited every day by the tides of Normandy; fields perfumed with aromas of sun and wind from Provence; there are different cattle with their cowsheds and seasonal moves to new pastures; there are secrets of production handed down over the centuries. This shop is a museum: when visiting it Mr Palomar feels, behind every object displayed, the presence of the civilization which gave it shape, as if he were in the Louvre.'[1]

It is not only the ECJ that has found legal inspiration in the method of Mr Palomar. English legal theorist William Twining has subjected Calvino's *Mr Palomar* to a jurisprudential gaze in the context of comparative law (1999), legal pluralism (2010) and globalisation (1999, 2010). Twining appears drawn to the melancholic but delightfully earnest character of Mr Palomar for his strikingly familiar habit – at least to lawyers – of giving intensely detailed descriptions of a variety of phenomena, but descriptions (as seen in the cheese shop) that go beyond a physical line of sight. Placing Mr Palomar's method in the context of law, the desire to notice and describe as a route to mastering legal phenomena, coupled with the slippery elusiveness of comprehensive understanding, becomes frighteningly familiar to lawyers, jurists, law students and jurisprudents alike. As Twining writes:

> As a jurist, I often feel like Mr Palomar. One's efforts to master even a single legal phenomenon – to obtain a comprehensive understanding of it – seem futile. Even a single rule or concept can be as elusive as a wave or a tuft of grass.
> (1999: 218)[2]

Whether it is the ECJ, Twining, an experienced legal practitioner or an incoming law student, one reason this sense of futility arises in the common law method of intense description is, I suspect, a gross underestimation of movement.

Take the moon, for example. As introduced in the quote earlier in this section on the challenge of perception (Calvino, 1999: 31), Mr Palomar notices the moon in the afternoon, precisely in the moment when it is, he suggests, too often overlooked. In the chapter 'Moon in the Afternoon', from which this quote is taken, Mr Palomar watches the moon as it comes into visibility. He meticulously describes micro-changes in the moon ('a transparent wager, or a half-dissolved pastelle' (1999: 31)) and the blue of the sky ('veered successively towards periwinkle, towards violet . . . then towards ashen and beige' (1999: 32)), as well as the shifting but always imprecise borders between the two ('the whiteness of the moon has received an impulse to emerge more firmly' (1999: 32)). Despite these descriptive efforts of relentless observation, their imprecise nature means Mr Palomar is unable to attain his desired state of absolute comprehension:

> What remains uncertain, rather, is whether this gain in evidence and (we might as well say it) splendor is due to the slow retreat of the sky, which, as it moves away, sinks deeper and deeper into darkness, or whether, on the contrary, it is the moon that is coming forward, collecting the previously scattered light and depriving the sky of it, concentrating it all in the round mouth of its funnel.
>
> (1999: 32)

What moves when we watch the moon rise? Is it the moon or the sky or both? An odd question in some ways, especially if we remain wed to internalised rationalised perceptions of what moves, because if we do not look, the answer surely is the moon. It is the moon, isn't it, that rises, shifting into increasing sight as its light shines? But if we look more closely and see beyond what we usually see, as Mr Palomar does, could it be the sky that retreats, moving into the depths of darkness? To understand multiple movements of the sky, moon and their complex and changing relation, we need to look carefully and take up the challenge of perception as Mr Palomar does:

> The moon is the most changeable body in the visible universe, and the most regular in its complicated habits: it never fails to show up for an appointment and you can always wait for it at the appointed spot; but if you leave it in one place you always find it next in another, and if you recall its face turned in a certain way, you see it has already changed its pose, a little or a lot. In any case, following it steadily, *you do not realise it is imperceptibly eluding you*. Only the clouds intervene to create the illusion of a rapid dash and rapid metamorphoses, or rather, to underline vividly what would otherwise escape the eye.
>
> (1999: 32–33, emphasis added)

Whether it is the moon, the location of feta in a shop still charmed by its prior life in the lowlands or highlands of Thrace or Thessalia, or the feeling of futility Twining experiences when attempting to capture a legal rule, Mr Palomar is correct: 'you do not realise it is imperceptibly eluding you' (ibid.). But what is the reason for this imperceptible elusiveness? One reason is the failure to notice movement, its repetitions and irregularities, and as we shall shortly see, a failure to look beyond the eye. The first step in remedying this failure involves noticing movement that is not simply a destination or conclusion (i.e., the moon rises, the moon sets), but rather movement as relentless activity (i.e., the sky changes colour). This is the challenge Mr Palomar took on when he tried to perceive the moon in the afternoon and understand and describe its shifting relations as shadows, light and colours weave in patterns beyond description.

While we can leave the challenge of perceiving the afternoon moon with Mr Palomar, the same challenge awaits legal theorists in the context of law. This is because the place of movement in law, if noticed at all, is not only hard to see with our eyes, but is often rendered as a destination or conclusion. Like many legal theorists, such a 'destination' is present in Twining's all-too-familiar attempt to arrive at an ontological destination of full comprehension by mastering a legal phenomenon or rule. Yet Twining's recognition of a sense of futility – as he says 'a single rule or concept can be as elusive as a wave or a tuft of grass' (ibid.) – reveals possibilities for noticing more complex sites of movement within law and legal thought. Poignantly, in their 'imperceptible elusiveness' (ibid.), the material movements of an afternoon, moon and grass blades are more complex than simply destinations. So too are the movements in law and legal thought, material and otherwise.

What happens, then, if we place Italo Calvino's Mr Palomar in the midst of Michel de Certeau's philosophical *Practice of Everyday Life* (1984) in an effort to deepen perceptions of this complex of movements? Despite the possibility that de Certeau's highly extolled chapter 'Walking the City' (1984) might be a 'critically exhausted text whose bones have been picked over one too many times' (Morris, 2004: 676), I hold out hope it remains an important text in legal theory and jurisprudence. For legal thinking, de Certeau's work continues to offer jurisprudential insight into relations between perception, scale and judgment, and I suggest movement. Leaving aside de Certeau's conceptual distinction between strategies and tactics, let's place Mr Palomar in the well-rehearsed opening scene:

> Seeing Manhattan from the 110th floor of the World Trade Centre. . . . A wave of verticals. Its agitation is momentarily arrested by vision. The gigantic mass is immobilized before the eyes. . . . A city composed of paroxysmal places in monumental reliefs. The spectator can read in it a universe that is constantly exploding.
> (De Certeau, 1984: 91)

While Italo Calvino's Mr Palomar never climbed the World Trade Centre in New York, at least not in the book, let's imagine he did. Standing in the 100th-floor window, high up above the city, what would Mr Palomar perceive? Like the moon appearing in the afternoon, the challenge becomes one of perceiving the immobilisation before his eyes, adjusting between scales and noticing movement. How might

Mr Palomar describe the constantly exploding universe? With his habits of categorical noticing, he might see details upon details, pigeons, people, clouds, depths reflecting light, and kaleidoscopic patterns might all emerge: a site rich for description and meditation. Not just people moving in various transport devices or the just-visible shifts of colours in the sky, he might also contemplate the stratospheric pull of gravity we can never see or the microcosmic detail of concrete pavings slowly sinking into the unsettled earth while immigrant weeds rise before our eyes so incapable of perceiving invisible micro-movements.

This is the challenge of perception, which is a challenge heightened in the context of movement. In an occularcentric world, so characteristic of modernity where many cultures give primacy to the sense of sight; the reliance on the eye to help us see becomes the biomechanical highway to perception. Yet there are minor roads. Attending to the sensorial in all its capacities requires decentering the eye and its visionary bias in both a perceptual and epistemological sense (e.g., Bentley and Flynn (eds) 1996). For Mr Palomar on the 110th floor, this requires a shift from looking out with his eyes to a more complex sensorial attention to his body: What can he hear, taste, feel and smell? Can he feel the air drifting across his body; rays of sunlight on his skin; debris of dust tickling his nose? Can he smell the remnants of industrial cleaning products or hear the sound of his own heart pumping blood around his body?

If we shift beyond Aristotle's classical model of the five senses of sight, hearing, touch, smell and taste (350BC, Book II, DA II.7–11), then Mr Palomar's vestibular system might also perceive his balance in relation to gravity, such as the feeling of vertigo if he looks directly down from the 110th floor. He might also employ his kinaesthetic sense of proprioception and experience the stillness within his body or a sense of movement as he shuffles foot to foot. Even further, his thermoception might notice changes in temperature, while his sense of nociception might register physiological pain, such as a cramp in one leg preceding his shuffling from foot to foot. Shifting from Mr Palomar's 'self-correcting' lens (Heaney, 1985: A1) that operates in relation to his external senses, consider his internal senses of common wit, imagination, fantasy, instinct and memory, which are also known as 'the wits' (Shakespeare, 1609). Looking out, the clouds might lead him into flights of imagination, or the 'bricked memories' (Barr, 2017) of a street mural, window frame or street corner might trigger Mr Palomar into a flow of memory where another time and place are re-experienced on the 110th floor. Whether externally or internally, with the use of sight or other senses, it is not only visually Mr Palomar can perceive relentless movement.

The challenge of perception, therefore, is both material and sensorial. It is one that demands a wide-ranging practice to move into a state of awareness and potential understanding. One of the constant inhibitors roadblocking our abilities to perceive is an overlooking of movement, or rather, a constant attempt to 'pin movement' down in order to notice it. This is a desire to 'freeze-frame' the world, or 'immobilize' it in de Certeau's words, which is a desire I imagine Mr Palomar experienced staring out the 110th-floor window. Like the methodological limitations of a survey, as Brian Massumi observed in a 2002 interview with Mary Zournazi, this is a challenge of critique more generally: 'because in order to critique something in any kind of definitive way you have to pin it down' (Zournazi, 2002). Movement, however, cannot be pinned down.

The challenge of perception, then, becomes not only a challenge to perceive movement through multiple senses, but also a challenge to develop a critical practice that allows us to perceive movement without pinning it down: stilling, stifling, erasing. While this might be a potentially insurmountable challenge, as we quickly learn from an attention to movement, the process and practice count more than the destination. With Mr Palomar in de Certeau's window as our guide, and taking up his method as our own, let's attempt to perceive movement without squishing it under our thumb to hold it still. This requires thinking a little more carefully about movement in general, across different disciplinary landscapes, before contemplating its relations to law.

What is movement?

Movement is more than its metaphor. For Aristotle, this means movement is 'the actuality (*entelechia*) of a potentiality as such' or 'the actuality of a potentiality, qua potential' (2006: 201). For the *Oxford English Dictionary*, movement is a noun:

> movement, n.
> I. A change of place or position; a progress, change, development, etc.
> II. Other uses.

Whether it is through Aristotelian metaphysics, dictionaries or etymology, it is clear movement is many things, so much so a definition of movement is often circular. Yet in a sense, movement is surprisingly simple. At least it is materially, and to some extent aesthetically, but once movement is placed within the vicinity of law, it has the potential to reconfigure worlds and offer radical possibilities, at least that is the hope. If this is the case, then what is movement? Where is it? How might we define it? Deny it? Think through it? With it? And mostly, what might change if we move with movement in our thoughts, our walks, our wanderings and wonderings, and most importantly, our laws? To this end, I offer a few comments on some of the material, conceptual and aesthetic dimensions of movement.

First, and materially, as something already placed in the world, movement often triggers images of transportation, such as a car, bicycle, train or walking on foot. It also often connotes certain organisations, such as a social movement or union. Movement might refer to a trend or a tendency, a course or series of actions towards a shared goal, such as a crowd or mass movement of people in political movements of protest, or movements of people against their will ushered into transportation across borders, or it might even evoke a military manoeuvre. Materially and bodily, a movement is often linked with the human bowels: a motion of faeces. Second, conceptually and often aesthetically, movement might refer to a dance or to a part of a musical composition, or on a more minor scale, the transition between notes or passages and changes in speed or tempo within music. This recalls ideas of movement in art, painting or sculpture, as well as architecture, where a fluid composition and harmony of design are often described as conveying an impression of movement or its companion-sibling 'motion'. In literature, movement might refer to the quality of a text in its ability to convey certain sensory perceptions, such as a narrative movement in literature or to be moved by poetic impulses. Less artistically, but central to finance, movements on the stock market indicate a change in price or value, or a stock or share, or the market as a whole. Likewise, in the business world, to have found 'movement' in a problem or a project is to express a development or progress towards a solution. In philosophy, movement might reference the course of thought in reasoning. Not so much a movement of the bowels, but on this occasion, a movement in thought.

As can be seen from these examples, movement is more than its metaphor, and folds in understandings of movement as a material activity and one with conceptual and aesthetic detail. To better understand how these different aspects of movement can at times coagulate, take for example, the walker. Obviously walking is a physical activity, and one that moves us from place to place, whether home to work, tram stop to shops, public park to private space. It is also clear we walk with different rhythms; wandering eyes or introspective gazes; smooth sways, ungainly staggers and all sorts of bellicose swaggers. We move differently, which is part of the delight of humanity. At different times, our gaits might shift rhythm from walking (one foot in contact with the ground) to skipping (which is the equivalent of a horse's canter) to more accelerated gaits of jogging, running or sprinting. Yet even when walking, material movement is different and not entirely straightforward, or even straight-forward. For instance, when barefoot (or wearing oxymoronic barefoot shoes) the strike of the foot shifts from heel or mid-foot when walking to forefoot when running (McDougall, 2009). Once wrapped in iridescent big-brand sneakers that buffer the foot from the ground and shift the angles of contact, gaits change. Whether leading with the heel or not, the geometry of impact and micro-details of contact will differ.

Yet it is not just the biomechanics of walking that illustrate diverse rhythms of material movements. There is also diversity in the aesthetics of walking, its various affects and the way in which we understand its meanings. Whether roaming city streets as a *flâneur* (Baudelaire, 1964; Benjamin, 1999, 2006) or *flâneuse* (Elkin, 2016), or strolling the countryside as a writer (Rousseau, 1979), poet (Wordsworth, 1793) or artist (Long, 2002), there are both material and aesthetic movements to the various forms and practices of walking. Walking away from a traumatic experience or holding your breath as you remove yourself from a sense of danger involves different physical movements: pace, breath, footstep, head-turn (or not). It also evokes, like the *flâneuse* or a walking artist or a person literally strolling down memory lane, a different affective experience, and is understood by someone observing differently again.

What, then, links the walker with these other examples of movement, from faeces to cars to musical scores? As captured in the earlier *Oxford English Dictionary* quote, the main definitional sense of movement is one of a change in place or position, whether this is a change in physical location or a more visceral change in emotional stance or intellectual positioning. Change is dynamic, alive and everywhere. Change, therefore, is a crucial aspect of movement. All the examples provided so far contain blatant changes. But what about changes we cannot see? Changes Mr Palomar cannot see? What about movements beyond any of our senses? Decentre the human of the Anthropocene, and consider the molecular: red blood cells coursing in a body, photosynthesis in plants where bacteria convert sunlight into energy and geological breakdowns of our stratospheres as earthquakes crash into our senses or more mundanely, soil settles. While I'm not Mr Palomar, I know where I live, and I live on a clay belt where a long drought recently ended. Without seeing its geological depths, I know when the clay changes as it soaks and dries, visible in the shifting cracks in old and new homes and as bluestone cobble laneways reshape.

If this much changes when we walk – our actions, our bodies, the spaces we create, the land beneath our feet etc. – then is there anything that doesn't move, and doesn't change place or position? The scientific answer is 'no' or, more precisely, 'not that we know of'. Dark matter moves, galaxies pass through each other, and anything that has energy is affected by gravitational pulls. Let's go galactic. While people rarely do, a building such as the World Trade Center, holding Mr Palomar, stands still, surely? Except in earthquakes, of course, but is this still-still? According to scientists, whichever frame you use, the building is moving. Consider a few of these movements.

First, the building is on a globe – Earth – which is spinning around an axis, orbiting the sun, moving in relation to planets etc., so the building is always moving. Add in an expanding universe and the layers of movement become overwhelming. Not surprisingly, this has led to complex and ongoing debates from Zeno's paradoxes onwards about absolute and relational accounts of movement (e.g., Huggett and Hoefer, 2017). For our purposes, perceiving a building moving on a spinning globe raises Einstein's theory of relativity, as well as the work of Newton and Galileo, which is not just that all things are relative, but more importantly that motion or movements are relational. What this means is that nothing is ever truly at rest relative to everything, but only and always at rest relative to themselves. In other words, everything moves. Everything.

Second, less galactically and returning to the building, there are other forms of movement at play. If it is a tall building, like the World Trade Center, the windows might shudder in high winds or even sway a little, causing minor motion sickness in those susceptible to inner-ear imbalances. On a micro-scale, in addition to the buffering of the wind, the glass itself is moving. Yet when most people look at a window, they don't see this, but instead see solid panes of glass. Physicists however have long been examining the mysteries of window glass. Is glass a solid or an extremely slow moving liquid? This is a topic in condensed matter physics. Recent research by physicist Eric Weeks and his team at Emory University on what is called 'colloidal glass transition' has observed the motion of colloidal particles, finding: 'This motion is slower in confinement, thus producing glass behaviour in a sample which is a liquid in an unconfined geometry' (Nugent et al., 2007: 025702–1). For non-scientists, like me, the press release from Emory University is helpful in explaining this scientific finding in simpler terms: 'unlike liquids, glasses aren't comfortable in confined spaces' (Emory University, 2007: 1). This 'discomfort' is because glass is amorphous, which means it is a solid but without a crystalline structure, and therefore it still has a fluidity: it moves. If glass moves, does this mean glass drips, as urban myth suggests? Perhaps, but scientists argue the reason why some old windows are thicker at the bottom is not because glass is a liquid (even though it is) but rather a matter of craft and a 'failure' to make perfectly flat panes of glass. I'm less sure of this conclusion because cultural norms change over time, and it might just be that glass windows were made in a time before the dominance of post-Enlightenment's preference for still surfaces and relentlessly flat lines. Irrespective of critiques of centuries-past craftsmanship, the molecular structure of glass can be understood as a material mixture of space and time which moves, dripping in its material form while appearing solid, still, translucent, understandable.

Therefore, we can notice two important features of movement. The first is that while movement involves change, whether galactic or microscopic, it is clearly not limited to human sensory perception. If we allow ourselves to recognise that movement is not confined to human-centric perception, what opens is the possibility of an ontology of movement that requires navigating not only human perception, but also posthuman and even cosmic perceptions, experiences and understandings of movement. Linking these, what we might start to notice is what Andreas Philippopoulos-Mihalopoulos describes as movement's 'institutional affect' (2015: ch 3). The second is that movement is not limited to straight lines. In addition to limiting perception of movement to physical sight, another major risk of flattening movement into change is limiting movement to a light linearity of process: from problem to solution, from protest to revolution, or between different parts of a musical score. Movement as change often translates into movement as destination, which is only one developmental aspect to movement, and one often rendered linear in both time and space, always heading towards a goal or destination. While this is an aspect of movement and ought not be ignored, it is not all of movement. Galaxies spin, glass drips and neither moves in straight lines. For the purposes of this chapter, the over-investment of movement as simply change or destination is a layering of movement that needs to be held at bay if movement is going to serve any critical potential in the context of law. To take movement seriously, we need to look beyond our eyes and beyond the destination.

Having considered a variety of aspects and examples, it is apparent that movement is everywhere: there is nothing scientists know of that does not move. We have also noticed that to move is to change, yet that is not all there is to movement. To move is not necessarily limited to a single direction across a map, in the world, between notes or paint-strokes or thoughts. Rather, movement is fabulously non-linear and wonderfully without destination. As photosynthesis circulates, glass panels drip, the world spins, gravity pulls, hearts beat blood and lungs expand with breath, what we start to realise is that there is no horizontal or vertical grid along which the material world operates. Rather, there are simply categories of understanding that help us organise and order this dynamic chaos of movement for the purpose of navigating our elusive comprehension. Like the survey discussed earlier, Yfat Hachamovitch (2000) showed how the grid is a technique, and one which links with law through its categorisation, classification and control of the earth as it is transformed into manageable property. Unsettling the grid and its conceptual grip on an ever-moving material world, and therefore unsettling the straight lines of territory and legal thought, is precisely what needs to occur, and precisely the possibility of movement. The question then becomes, if movement is everywhere, and its everywhere is dynamic and non-linear, then why aren't law and movement more readily linked? In other words, how is movement masked in law and legal thought?

How to perceive law as movement?

If scientists are correct, and everything in the world is in constant and perpetual motion, then why isn't law also moving? Is law the exception? Or is it, perhaps, the norm, but a norm where perpetual motion is relentlessly overlooked because we are not in the habit of thinking or perceiving law in motion? And if it is a case of oversight, then what habits do we have when it comes to seeing, noticing or thinking law and its relation (or non-relation) to movement? How might we learn to perceive movement in or as law? As Mr Palomar realises in a chapter called 'On Becoming Angry with the Young':

> The fact is that he would like not so much to affirm a truth of his own as to ask questions, and he realizes that no one wants to abandon the train of his own discourse to answer questions that, coming from another discourse, would necessitate rethinking the same things with other words, perhaps ending up on strange ground, far from safe paths.
>
> (Calvino, 1999: 95)

We are invested in the questions we ask and answer. Because of this investment, while not impossible, it is often difficult to move beyond a more familiar set of questions offered by particular discourses or disciplines we inhabit, let alone communicate across boundaries. But contemporary jurisprudence and legal theory with its cross-disciplinary curiosities is precisely the site for such explorations beyond the safety net of familiar grounds. If we do take the risk to rethink 'the same things with other words', in this case rethink law with movement, then rather than being fearful of straying far from 'safe paths', my hope is the opposite (Calvino: ibid.). I hope we do end up 'on strange ground' (ibid.), where we do not yet know what is possible.

This chapter opened with the provocation that 'law moves, whether we notice it or not' (Barr, 2016). The task now is to notice. Having introduced the challenges of perception and the complexity of movement, it is now possible to approach this opening provocation and see whether it is possible to notice. Navigating some of the more persistent images and concepts of legal stability, it is important to notice how these legal images are often linked with a solid, certain and stable material world, which of course is a world we now know not to be stable. Like perceiving the amorphous crystalline structure of glass that moves before our non-seeing eyes, this section explores how we might be able to see through some of the common projections of law and its stability to perceive legal movements. Continuing to embrace the descriptive method of Mr Palomar, this section offers three observations on the topics of drips, wobbles and perpetual motion.

Drips

Recall the structure of glass, seeming so materially and visually steady while it drips amorphously in its crystalline structure as Mr Palomar stares through its transparency, looking down on the city of New York from the 110th floor. Likewise, this section contemplates how often, out of our sight, law drips too. Consider some of the key ideas that provide the conceptual ground for the location or place of law: ideas that seem as solid and stable and transparent as glass, habitually hiding their conceptually crystalline structure from sight. More specifically, think of sovereignty, territory and the nation-state. What image do they evoke about the place of law? Is it stable? Is it moving? Is it neither? One common image projected by sovereignty, territory and the state is an image of a certain physical place of law: a steady place that a state-based law calls home; a legal home supported by a landscape named 'territory'. Now of course we now know the land and physical ground holding the concept of territory in place is moving, whether it's a slow-moving rift in the tectonic plates in Iceland, a 10-metre annual circumnavigational shift in the ice at the South Pole or the claypit drying beneath the receding foundations of my Melbourne home. The question then becomes, does sovereignty and territory move too? The answer, of course, is yes they do, and do so in at least two ways.

The first and boldest move is the one of inaugural proclamation. 'Raising the flag' is a well-recognised activity performed in international law to draw attention to claims of sovereignty. As with all flags raised to salute Empire, proclaim allegiance or claim new lands, often fluttering in imaginary light winds, a flag does not just flutter without support. Flags are attached to flagpoles that dig themselves into the soil in order to be raised. It is important also to recognise that flagpoles need to be planted somewhere, and that each somewhere interrupts the ground, whether by moving soil or cutting through stone. In Australia, where I write, there are several of these 'somewheres', the most recognisable being 31A Loftus Street, Sydney: the site of the 'first flag'.[3]

Within this inaugural proclamation, there are two further movements occurring simultaneously. The first is the actual raising of the flag, which is a movement upwards to mark foundations symbolically, ceremonially and legally. The second movement runs counter by physically marking foundations by digging into earth. This second activity moves not just the dirt beneath the flagpole, but magics a law from its home origins (i.e., the English metropole) and sends it swiftly out across the earthly landscape of what is now Australia until it runs into the liminal spaces of white sand, tidal mudflats or sandstone cliffs, preventing the legal concept of sovereignty and territory from taking hold in deep oceanic spaces beyond the stretch of the domestic maritime legal imagination. This image of swift movement to inviolable permanent stability was not only repeated but legally reinforced in Australia's key case of *Mabo v. Queensland (No 2)* (1993) 175 CLR 1, where Justice Brennan wrote:

> The hypothesis being that there was no local law in existence in the territory, the law of England *became* the law of the territory (and not merely the personal law of the colonists).
>
> (*Mabo* at 36, emphasis added)

Justice Brennan's leading judgment in Australia's leading case of *Mabo* captures the hyper-velocity of this inaugural move of an instantaneous legal inhalation of a continental landmass: a landmass inhaling English law. This is one version of a fairly common image of sovereign territory, which is one that after the initial move of becoming is forgotten seems impenetrably stable, erasing the click-of-the-fingers movement as if it never were. This erasure is the work of the mythology of sovereignty, and one that explicitly ignores the technical activity of jurisdiction as can be seen, for instance, through Justice Brennan's erasure of 'personal law' and its distinct rhythms of legal movement.

The second move is a little slower. More doctrinally, and operating with less galactic velocity that risks causing conceptual indigestion, this can be understood as the distinction between discovery and occupation under the doctrine of discovery (Grotius, 1609; Miller et al., 2010). While the flag is the ceremonial planting of discovery (a claim that 'I' am here), it is not sufficient in and of itself to project any version of an incoming law beyond the confines of the flagpole itself (or perhaps the few human-feet surrounding). It is simply step one in a two-step dance. In other words, captured in the singular past tense of Justice Brennan's 'became', the ceremonial flag of discovery is over-emphasised (i.e., step 1), while the slow work of 'occupation' sidelined (i.e., step 2). In addition to the flag, it is an uncontroversial requirement of the international doctrine that for sovereignty to 'move in' a second activity of occupation needs to occur: a slow-moving domination of human occupation of another's land. Unlike the instantaneous click of the fingers a flag performs, sending law into new spaces bounded by geographical features such as coastlines and river heads (Benton, 2010), this second move drips-in-horizontal-drops as occupation stretches across landscapes until a slow saturation has occurred, masking the ongoing legal movements and activities of continued occupation.

Unlike the image of sovereign territory dispersed in the flutter of the flag or embedded within the snap-of-the-fingers 'became' of Justice Brennan's judgment in *Mabo*, this slower movement of occupation relies on techniques of jurisdiction. As Dorsett and McVeigh write:

> Jurisdiction is, however, more than simply pronouncing existing law. In some formulations jurisdiction inaugurates law itself. Thus, to exercise jurisdiction is to bring law into existence . . . in a certain way and by certain means.
>
> (2012: 4–5)

Building on Dorsett and McVeigh's recovery of the jurisprudential work of jurisdiction, I have previously made the argument that jurisdiction is *how* law moves (Barr, 2016). For now, however, it is sufficient to notice jurisdiction as a device that might assist in cutting through some of these persistent images of legal stability – such as those of sovereign territory – and notice slow, perpetual and ongoing movements in law: the unending process of legal occupation.

While it is sometimes hard to take jurisdiction seriously and imagine anything other than a sovereign and hyper-territorial state, such as Australia, controlling the continent with its Westminster structures of government, take for example the ongoing claims of Aboriginal sovereignty in Australia and temporarily engage with them as questions of jurisdiction. To be clear, this is not an exercise in 'demotion' from sovereignty to jurisdiction as the politics and legality of the 's-word' are intensely crucial (Behrendt, 2000). However, such a move requires taking seriously the jurisdictional claims of the Aboriginal sovereignty movement. This is turn requires taking seriously the jurisdictional challenges inherent in recent state government treaty-talks in Victoria and South Australia.[4] It also requires taking seriously the jurisdictional geography (Barr, 2016) of the Aboriginal Tent Embassy (Foley et al., 2014).[5] The Tent Embassy is one of Australian's longest running protests and has been located since 1972 on the lawns of Federal Parliament. With a controversial new 2.6-metre prefabricated 'protective' fence being erected around Federal Parliament (McIlroy, 2017), interrupting the architectural 'transparency' of the legislature, this new fence keeps out spatially not just the 'we' of 'we the people' but geographically excludes from the circumference of sovereign power the jurisdictional claims of Aboriginal sovereignty and Aboriginal forms of law as materially uttered through the ceremonial flag and fire of the Tent Embassy. Noticing jurisdiction and the ways in which it links and relates different types of law – in this case Australian common laws and Aboriginal and Torres Strait Islander laws – offers a radically different image of the multiple places of different laws and their changing relations.

In other words, taking jurisdiction seriously assists in perceiving some movements of some laws. If you do look carefully, what becomes apparent is not only that law drips within the still glass image of the sovereign place of the state in its territorial authority, but that these drips continue today, and they do so through jurisdiction (Barr, 2016). Not just then, but now. Not just there, but here. The act of dripping in a non-gravitational pull *towards and across* the ground is a result of a continuous yet slow introduction of a legal fluid into the landscape: a dynamic and active passage through space and time. This is law wetting the landscape, drowning our sight, asking us to fall (again) for the impossibility solid image of a state's legal stability. Yet this 'solid' image is one that is made again and again through ongoing legal practices of occupation. As wild animals instinctively know, lack of movement and utter stillness is a trap, a snare, and one we need to notice and navigate carefully.

Wobbles

Having peered through one glass version of law contained in the conceit of sovereign territory and seen the possibility of slower more detailed movements, consider a second and different relation between law and movement as one of consequence. It helps to consider movement within particular legal systems. In the two major legal families of common law and civil law, which both feature legislation and cases as major sources of law, case law remains a key distinguishing feature (van Caenegem, 1987). For the common law and common lawyer, the doctrine of *stare decisis* binds legal principles to determining points in litigation according to the ghosts of prior precedent. A decision or judgment within a case alters legal principles for future like cases. In other words, the consequence of each case is a change or movement in legal principle in the sense of a new destination. This is one way of understanding the relation between law and movement, where any movements within law are gravitationally drawn towards a stable new destination or outcome understood in terms of a change in rule.

Likewise, movement as destination also operates in legislation. On the one hand, a change in legislative text alters legal rules, norms, rights and obligations governing a particular society. When legislatures change legislation, there are discernible movements in law and its detailed rules, processes and efficacy. Again, like the destination of a case, this is movement or change in legislation as a consequence of a legal process. This is movement as a destination *for* law. Yet, while techniques of statutory interpretation differ somewhat between civil and common law legal traditions, it is fair to say that in whichever language and legal culture they appear, words are often fickle and at times raise competing interpretations, depending on their context, and hence demanding the task of legal interpretation. This is because meanings move: they shift with time, within sentences and between interpretive locations. This is not so much movement as destination but rather an acknowledgement of the relentless and rather 'wobbly' activity of movement within law and its legal meanings, as meanings shift, sometimes subtly, sometimes drastically.

In case law, the task of deciphering meaning also moves unsteadily. As incoming common law students (as well as lawyers transferring from a civil law tradition) quickly learn, in a common law jurisdiction, the task of reading and deciphering a lengthy and often verbose case to identify a *ratio* or *rationes decidendi* as the legal rule or rules capturing the crux of the reason or rationale for the decision is quite a bizarre and imprecise task. What becomes apparent is that unlike legislation, the legal rule emanating from a case is not fixed in words, although there are more acceptable modes of expression at differing levels of abstraction. My expression of a *ratio* is not necessarily the same as yours. A little like the children's game of 'Chinese Whispers', over time, and subjected to multiple iterations, a *ratio* can change as it is interpreted and reinterpreted.

This is more than a change in destination, but a more complex and dynamic movement that shifts meaning back and forth, and every which way. All of this is to say that when it comes to legal rules in legislation and cases: they move. There is no stability. Never. Yet somehow there is still a sense of stability – a projection of calm – that masks this well-known movement of legal principles. This is a more complex sense of movement than mere destination or new consequences, but rather a feeling that there are unsteady foundations below a superficially calm legal surface.

It is not just judgments that mask unsteady movements. Consider the place of movement within evidence in a trial. Recently I attended a performance of

'Please, Continue (Hamlet)' (Bernat and Duyvendak, 2017). This is a theatre production that subjects Hamlet to a criminal trial performed by a rotating door of local 'real-world' judges, lawyers and QCs from the relevant local jurisdiction. Accused of murdering Polonius, each night an actor playing Hamlet is subjected to a 'real' legal drama where lawyers are provided with a brief and argue the case for prosecution or defence before a judge, using the local rules of evidence and modified procedures. The jury is drawn from the public, which in this case is the audience. After 150-odd performances around the world in both common and civil law jurisdictions, the verdict varied 50/50: roughly half the juries convict and the other half acquit. At the Melbourne performance I attended, Hamlet was found not guilty.

Leaving aside the intriguingly wild variety of sentences across the world, which is the judgment (i.e., the focus of most doctrinal and theoretical analysis), what was most striking in this mock trial for theatre was what occurred before the judgment in the evidentiary movements hyper-present in the performance. The dynamic activity of evidence as it was stuttered, cried and whispered in a theatre-turned-courtroom made it blindly apparent that the processes of common law are never fixed, not just in judgment but in evidence too. No trial is the same, no set of questioning equal, so why are we surprised when outcomes or destinations vary? The differing questions, modes of speech, shiver of a cloak; these all radiate through the façade of a stable outcome: a truth of guilty or not. Words move, evidence shifts, yet there is no stillness here: neither in the *ratio* of a judgment, the text of an Act or the evidence of a trial: all there is are small unsteady movements, light rocking motions of hesitation, vacillation, uncertainty or instability that occasionally distil into what looks like a stable consequence but might in fact be perpetual motion.

Perpetual motion

Finally, how might we notice perpetual motion in law? If law is in perpetual motion in all these various registers – materially, conceptually, doctrinally – how do we live with that? A final example builds on the earlier discussion of the doctrine of discovery and pushes back against the past-tense 'became' of Justice Brennan in *Mabo* by considering an example of the dripping occupation of legal footprints. This final example also returns to the earlier discussion of walking, noticing that while it is an activity that individually is rarely perpetual (except perhaps for sleepwalkers) collectively and across the globe, it is. Adding to the earlier discussion of walking, consider Sir William Blackstone's legal observation of the English subject:

> For as the law is the birthright of every subject, so wherever they go they carry their laws with them.
>
> (Blackstone, 1765: 106)

If we carry laws wherever we go, then how might we walk with law? Remaining with the method, if we walk with law, what, then, are our legal footprints?

Moving with the feet of the British Empire, and moving with the feet of today's global citizens, 'wherever' we go, we 'carry' our laws with us (Barr, 2017). Each step, each dance, each movement on earth – we move; law moves – perpetual material and legal motion. It is like a global performance of Hans Christian Andersen's *The Red Shoes* (1983), except that instead of one girl doomed to dance continually in her red velvet shoes, it is a global population that walks – not with red shoes, but with law etched onto the soles of their feet. Constantly in motion – if not me, then perhaps you – the kaleidoscopic patterns of legal movement could be mapped with tracking devices into GPS artworks, although the detail will quickly blur into a dark map of motion, imperceptively eluding, like Mr Palomar's afternoon moon.

My basic proposition is that walking is a legal practice (Barr, 2013). As legal subjects, despite our political dislikes, we are inescapably attached to law. For the common law subject, this attachment heightens as common law attaches through the body, and more specifically, the feet (Barr, 2017). If we want to notice the perpetual motion of law's movements, then, one place to pay attention is our footprints. Unlike Justice Brennan's 'became', the shifting nature of legal footprints means the work of occupation under the doctrine of discovery is never complete. More insidiously, by masking the significance of our legal footprints under grand narratives of sovereignty, and the word-breath of a singular past tense 'became', the dynamic activity of law's perpetual motion is rendered invisible: amorphous glass rendered solid.

This is not new, at least not for common law. As Peter Goodrich writes:

> The history of the common law has always been a history of movement, of a wandering *nomos*, a narrative of itinerant justice and itinerant justices. Its movement has been both literal and metaphysical, a question of a peripatetic court and also of laws of transmission of legal knowledge: moveable bodies become moveable signs.
>
> (Goodrich, 1990: 297)

As Goodrich notes, both literally and metaphysically, law – at least common law – has always moved. As I have suggested here, and illustrated in more detail elsewhere, it also continues to move (Barr, 2016), whether through footsteps or courthouses. For it is not only the movement of walking but perpetual motion too that can be seen in the contemporary practice of the historical habit of 'circuit courts'; for instance, where courts continue to relocate across landscapes to hear matters, despite the ease with which people can travel or technology can replace the need.

Therefore, whether it is walking, courts, monuments, flags or evidence in a theatrical Hamlet, across different modes of drips, wobbles and perpetual motion, the relationship between law and movement has shifted from no relationship, to an unseen and hidden one, to one of destinations, and finally to one of relentless and constant activity. As we continue to grapple with the consequences of this observation, and the reasons for which noticing perpetual motion in law matters, Henri Lefebvre's work on space and rhythm has great relevance here, as the task becomes to rethink law and shake off its static-stillness. As Lefebvre (1991) showed in his shift from abstract to productive space – a space that is also always in motion – and Chris Butler (2013) has offered more generally in his wide-ranging examination of Lefebvre's work in the context of law, by noticing the intertwined nature of law and movement, it opens up new lines of flight in relation to questions of law, space and place. For if law is ever moving, constantly in motion, then where is it now? What about . . . now? Wherever the when, and whenever the where, the importance of perceiving movement is the radical possibility that law is not everywhere, at least not always. Territory is not truth, maps are freeze-frames, footsteps matter. Having ended up on 'strange ground, far from safe paths' (Calvino: ibid.), where law is not as everywhere as it might seem, then conceptually, politically and doctrinally we are faced with a whole set of new but unanswered questions about the space, place and movement of law.

Conclusion

This chapter is concerned with the importance of movement in contemporary legal thought. It has paid homage to movement in two senses. The first is a sense of public acknowledgement or allegiance in the intertwined relationship between law and movement. The second is a sense that in doing so, this chapter incorporates elements of style and content characteristic of other works beyond jurisprudence, such as works of literature and foundational principles of physics. In the words of Mr Palomar, this homage matters because

> 'It is only after you have come to know the surface of things,' he concludes, 'that you venture to seek what is underneath. But the surface is inexhaustible.'
>
> (Calvino 1999: 51)

If law is ever going to be – or ever was – more than its legal texts, institutions and discourses and take part in its material life that turns so rapidly in the Anthropocene, then it is crucial we take time to think about movement and about the complex relations between law and movement. Taking the central point to its logical extremes and stating the juridical importance of movement most boldly, it can be posited that without movement, there is no law. Strange grounds, indeed.

Following this path, without movement, law becomes rendered into stagnant institutions, mundane rules and ethereal authorities that author from above from stratospheric heights without ever touching the ground. Law becomes life-less, existing only in a static and pallid state, and it becomes increasingly difficult to imagine alternate legal futures. This is because without movement, law is life-less, dried up, freeze-framed, anaemic and stale. Yet if we want colour in our worlds, if we want to notice the life in our pulsing blood, it is important to pay legal attention to the ever-motion of law's movements. In turn, a turn of course that is never still and always moves in non-linear cycles, and with the aid of movement, it becomes possible to rethink law, and rethink contemporary legal thought. This is the promise of movement. This is the promise of law.

Notes

1 *Federal Republic of Germany and Kingdom of Denmark v. Commission of the European Communities* C-465/02 and C-466/02 [2005] ECR 9115 at 9175 (para 198), Opinion of Mr Ruiz-Jarabo (citing page 85 of *Mr Palomar* in the 1983 edition edited by Giulio Einaudi, Turin).

2 As captured in the quote earlier in this section, this is a reference to the chapter 'The Infinite Lawn' (Calvino, 1999: 28) where Mr Palomar contemplates, attempts to count and muses on the complex composition and indefinite boundaries of a lawn.

3 Prior to the establishment of the Colony of New South Wales, the Union flag was first raised by the British in ceremonies of possession at Botany Bay on 29 April 1770 and then on what was named 'Possession Island' on 22 August 1770 (Barr, 2016: 110–116). The one that is remembered, however, is the flag waving upon colonial 'settlement' several years later. Just behind Circular Quay and the iconic sites of the Opera House and the Sydney Harbour Bridge, there is an underwhelming memorial outside Customs House. Unlike the soil parted for a flagpole on 26 January 1788, on a concrete footpath outside a loading site, an engraved concrete stack supports an ungalvanised dark metal flagpole raising a drooped British flag. The engraving reads:

> This flag was erected to commemorate the location at which the first ceremony of saluting the flag by Captain Arthur Philip R.N. and is company took place to mark the foundation of Australia on 26 January 1788.

4 One challenge is whether state governments in Australia have the jurisdictional ability to make treaties with Aboriginal nations, or whether only the federal government does? On the one hand, state governments retain the original plenary powers of British colonies, but on the other hand, in the act of federation, each state 'gifted' certain powers to the federal government. As a result, the federal government – not state governments – has explicit treaty-making powers in the external affairs power of section 51(xxix) of the *Commonwealth Constitution.*

5 The Aboriginal Tent Embassy is one of the longest running protests in Australia. Established on 26 January 1972 by four Aboriginal men (Michael Anderson, Billy Craigie, Tony Coorey and Bertie Williams), the Tent Embassy is a protest site consisting of a tent, a fire and a series of protest signs continuously occupied by activists, situated directly in front of – and in the architectural sight lines of – Australia's federal parliament. It works as a visual reminder of the non-recognition of Aboriginal sovereignty, and is not considered an official embassy by the Australian government. There are a number of other Tent Embassies throughout Australia, but this is the original and remains standing today.

Bibliography

Books, chapters and articles

Andersen, Hans Christian, *The Red Shoes*, trans. A. Bell, illustrations C. Iwasaki, London: Neugebauer, 1983.

Aristotle, 'On the Soul,' in Aristotle, *On the Soul: Parval Naturalia; On Breath*, first published 350BC, trans. W.S. Hett, Loeb Classical Library 299, Cambridge: Harvard University Press, 1957.

Aristotle, *Physics*, trans. R. Waterfield, Oxford: Oxford University Press, 2006.

Barr, Olivia, 'Walking with Empire,' *Australian Feminist Law Journal*, 38(1), 59, 2013.

Barr, Olivia, *A Jurisprudence of Movement: Common Law, Walking, Unsettling Place*, Abingdon: Routledge, 2016.
Barr, Olivia, 'Legal Footprints,' *Law Text Culture*, 21, 214–251, 2017.
Baudelaire, Charles, *The Painter of Modern Life and Other Essays*, trans. J. Mayne. New York: Phaidon, 1964.
Behrendt, Larissa, 'Slicing the Circle: Treaty, Native Title, Aboriginal Sovereignty and the Compartmentalizing of Indigenous Rights in Australia,' Paper presented to the Indigenous Bar Association Conference in Ottawa, 2000, 4.
Benjamin, Walter, *The Arcades Project*, trans. H. Eiland and K. McLaughlin. Cambridge, MA: Belknap Press, 1999.
Benjamin, Walter, *The Writer of Modern Life: Essays on Charles Baudelaire*, trans. H. Eiland. Cambridge, MA: Belknap Press, 2006.
Bently, Lionel and Flynn, Leo, *Law of the Senses: Sensational Jurisprudence*, London: Pluto Press, 1996.
Benton, Lauren, *A Search for Sovereignty: Law and Geography in European Empire 1400–1900*, Cambridge: Cambridge University Press, 2010.
Blackstone, William, *Commentaries on the Laws of England*, Oxford: Clarendon Press, 1765.
Blomley, Nicholas, *Rights of Passage: Sidewalks and the Regulation of Public Flow*, Abingdon: Routledge, 2011.
Butler, Chris, *Henri Lefebvre: Spatial Politics, Everyday Life and the Right to the City*, Abingdon: Routledge, 2013.
Calvino, Italo, *Invisible Cities*, trans. W. Weaver, London: Vintage, 1997.
Calvino, Italo, *If on a Winter's Night a Traveller*, trans. W. Weaver, London: Vintage, 1998.
Calvino, Italo, *Mr Palomar*, trans. W. Weaver, London: Vintage, 1999.
Calvino, Italo, *Our Ancestors: Three Novels: The Cloven Viscount; Baron in the Trees; The Non-Existent Knight*, trans. A. Colquhoun, London: Vintage, 1998.
de Certeau, Michel, *The Practice of Everyday Life*, trans. S. Rendell, Berkeley: University of California Press, 1984.
Code, Lorraine, 'Is the Sex of the Knower Epistemologically Significant?' *Metaphilosophy* 12, 267–276, 1981.
Code, Lorraine, 'Taking Subjectivity into Account,' in L. Alcoff, and E. Potter (eds), *Feminist Epistemologies*, New York: Routledge, 1993.
Code, Lorraine, 'How do We Know? Questions of Method in Feminist Practice,' in S.D. Burt and L. Code (eds), *Changing Methods: Feminists Transforming Practice*, Peterborough: Broadview Press, 14–44, 1995.
Dorsett, Shaunnagh and McVeigh, Shaun, *Jurisdiction*, Abingdon: Routledge, 2012.
Elkin, Lauren, *Flâneuse: Women Walk the City in Paris, New York, Tokyo, Venice and London*, New York: Random House, 2016.
Foley, Gary, Schapp, Andrew and Howell, Edwina (eds), *The Aboriginal Tent Embassy: Sovereignty, Black Power, Land Rights and the State*, Abingdon: Routledge, 2014.
Florence, Ronald, *The Perfect Machine: Building the Palomar Telescope*, New York: HarperCollins, 1994.
Goodrich, Peter, *Languages of Law: From Logics of Memory to Nomadic Masks*, London: Weidenfeld & Nicolson, 1990.
Grotius, Hugo, *The Freedom of the Seas or the Right which Belongs to the Dutch to Take Part in the East Indian Trade*, trans. R. van Damen Magoffin, Oxford: Oxford University Press, 1916 (first published 1609).
Hachamovitch, Yfat, 'Ploughing the Delirium,' in V. Foti (ed.), *Merleau-Ponty: Difference, Materiality, Painting*, Atlantic Highlands, NJ: Humanity Books, 2000.
Haraway, Donna, *Simians, Cyborgs and Women: The Reinvention of Nature*, New York: Routledge, 1991.

Harding, Sandra (ed.), *Feminism and Methodology*, Bloomington: Indiana University Press, 1987.
Lefebvre, Henri, *The Production of Space*, trans. D. Nicholson-Smith, Oxford: Blackwell Publishing, 1991.
Lefebvre, Henri, *Rhythmanalysis: Space, Time and Everyday Life*, trans. S. Elden and G. Moore, London: Continuum, 2004.
Long, Richard, *Walking the Line*, London: Thames & Hudson, 2002.
McDougall, Christopher, *Born to Run: A Hidden Tribe, Superathletes, and the Greatest Race the World has ever Seen*, New York: Alfred A. Knopf, 2009.
McFarlane, Robert, *The Old Ways: A Journey on Foot*, New York: Hamish Hamilton, 2012.
Miller, Robert J., Ruru, Jacinta, Behrendt, Larissa and Lindberg, Tracey, *Discovering Indigenous Lands: The Doctrine of Discovery in the English Colonies*, Oxford: Oxford University Press, 2010.
Morris, Brian, 'What We Talk About When We Talk About "Walking in the City,"' *Culture Studies*, 18(5), 675–697, 2004.
Nugent, Carolyn R., Edmond, Kazem V., Patel, Hetal N. and Weeks, Eric R, 'Colloidal Glass Transition Observed in Confinement,' *Physical Review Letters*, 99, 025702, 2007.
Philippopoulos-Mihalopoulos, Andreas, *Spatial Justice: Body, Lawscape, Atmosphere*, Abingdon: Routledge, 2015.
Rousseau, Jean-Jacques, *Reveries of the Solitary Walker*, trans. P. France, Harmondsworth, UK: Penguin Books, 1979.
Shakespeare, William, 'Sonnet 121,' in W. Shakespeare (ed.), *The Sonnets*, first published 1609, Project Gutenberg, London: Thomas Thorpe, 1997.
Solnit, Rebecca, *Wanderlust: A History of Walking*, London: Verso, 2001.
Twining, William, 'Globalization and Comparative Law', *Maastricht Journal of European and Comparative Law*, 6(3), 217–245, 1999.
Twining, William, 'Normative and Legal Pluralism: A Global Perspective', *Duke Journal of Comparative and International Law*, 20, 473–518, 2010.
van Caenegem, Raoul, 'The Common Law is Different: Ten Illustrations,' in *Justices, Legislators and Professors: Chapters in European Legal History*, Cambridge: Cambridge University Press, 1987.
Wordsworth, William, *Descriptive Sketches: Taken During a Pedestrian Tour in the Italian, Grison, Swiss and Savoyard Alps*, Joseph Johnson: St Pauls Church-Yard, 1793.
Zournazi, Mary, 'Navigating Movements: A Conversation with Brian Massumi,' in M. Zournazi (ed.), *Hope: New Philosophies for Change*, Abingdon: Routledge, 2002, ch 10.

Cases

Federal Republic of Germany and Kingdom of Denmark v. Commission of the European Communities C-465/02 and C-466/02 [2005] ECR 9115.
Mabo v. Queensland (No 2) (1993) 175 CLR 1

Other

Bernat, Roger and Duyvendak, Yan, 'Please, Continue (Hamlet): An Australian Exclusive', *Melbourne Festival*, Arts Centre Melbourne, 5 October 2017.
Emory University, 'Physicist Opens New Window on Glass Puzzle' *PhysOrg*. 9 August 2007. https://phys.org/news/2007-08-physicist-window-glass-puzzle.html.
Heaney, Seamus, 'The Sensual Philosopher,' in 'Book Reviews', in *The New York Times* A1. 29 September 1985. www.nytimes.com/books/98/12/20/specials/heaney-calvino.html.

Huggett, Nick and Hoefer, Carl, 'Absolute and Relational Theories of Space and Motion', in Edward N. Zalta (ed.), *The Stanford Encyclopedia of Philosophy*, https://plato.stanford.edu/archives/spr2017/entries/spacetime-theories/. (Spring 2017 edition).

McIlroy, Tom, '"Appalling": Security Fence Erected at Parliament House', *The Guardian (Australia),* 13 September 2017. www.theguardian.com.au/story/4918831/appalling-security-fence-erected-at-parliament-house/?cs=7.

Onions, Charles Talbut (ed.), *The Oxford English Dictionary of English Etymology*, Oxford: Clarendon Press, 1966.

Vidal, Gore, 'On Italo Calvino,' *The New York Review of Books,* 32(18), 1, 1985. www.nybooks.com/articles/1985/11/21/on-italo-calvino/ (accessed 21 November 1985).

Part II
Sense

7

Disenchanting senses

Law and the taste of the real

Andrea Pavoni

I

Non è troppo importante il gusto, è importante la verità.[1]

Plato told us that beauty is a pleasure that cannot be known, while truth is a knowledge that cannot be seen. What is more visible (the beautiful, what is 'more apparent') is excluded from the domain of knowledge, the invisible realm of the ideas. The sensible and the intelligible thus lie on each side of an unsurpassable 'fracture between science, which knows the truth but is unable to enjoy it, and taste, which enjoys beauty but is unable to provide a reason for that' (Agamben, 2015: 12, my translation).

The starry sky is beautiful, Plato observes in *The Republic*, and yet truth is to be found *beyond* such beauty, "to be apprehended by reason and intelligence, but not by sight" (1920 [4th C. BCE]: 529). This is the task of Plato's episteme, according to Simplicio: to find the invisible laws that would account for the regularity of their movements, so as to 'save the appearances of the erring stars'.[2] Yet, really *saving* the appearances cannot do without the sensible. This would mean losing them altogether. Instead, as Giorgio Agamben explains, that requires bridging the gap between sensible and intelligible, towards the knowledge of appearances as such, a science of the visible beauty, able to know the beautiful and to sense the truth (2015: 18).

Thus overcome would be the 'wrenching duality' of aesthetics, split between the theory of the sensible, which deals with the form of the possible experience, and the theory of art, "which deals with the reality of the real insofar as it is thought" (Deleuze, 1994 [1968]: 68; 2004 [1969]: 260). According to Gilles Deleuze, whose philosophical project may be distilled exactly as the attempt to develop such a 'science of the sensible', "everything changes once we determine the conditions of real experience, which are not larger than the conditioned and which differ in kind from the categories": hence "the two senses of the aesthetic become one", and appearances are truly saved (1994 [1968]: 68).

§

In legal theory, this fracture takes the form of a rift opposing the realm of the senses from the anaesthetic domain of the law. The late 'sensory turn' in legal thinking, notably anticipated by Bently and Flynn (1996), has been for the most part unable to overcome this opposition, mainly assuming senses as what escapes the law, that has been in turn depicted as dealing with the senses only in the negative mode, that is, by seeking to minimise, moderate, and moralise them (but see Hamilton et al., 2017). This resulted in accounts that are normally polarised between "the ways in which law and its legal techniques seek to control and discipline the human experience of the senses, and the complicated ways that the sensorial leaks out of those efforts or dances around them altogether" (ibid.: 2). Two long-standing presuppositions cement this opposition. On the one hand, law is assumed as separated from the sensorial. On the other, the sensorial is romanticised as immediate, 'natural' and belonging to the dimensions of the phenomenological, the subjective, the human. Focusing on the sense of taste, in this chapter I set up to confront these two assumptions, exhuming the constitutive sensoriality of law hidden beneath its anaesthetic pretence and disenchanting senses from their romantic humanism, by unfolding their post-phenomenological and inhuman dimension. This is done through four steps, each occupying two sections of the text.

First, I engage with the notion of human-world *correlation* (Meillassoux, 2009) and the possibility to break it, via Deleuze's aesthetics, and thus unlock the access to the *real*, without jettisoning the domain of the sensible in the process, as it is instead done in most of recent attempts within the field of *Speculative Realism*. Second, I engage with the sense of taste, the anti-metaphysical sense *par excellence*, arguing that beneath its judgemental propensity, taste holds the keys to disintegrate both the unity of the subject and the integrity of the body, releasing us simultaneously to the posthuman ecology of being-together and the indigestible inhumanity of the real. Third, I turn to law by assuming tasting, outside of metaphor, as the way in which law deals with the world, and speculating on how this understanding may be mobilised to break the 'legal correlation' (i.e., law's mechanism of exception) so as to force law, paraphrasing Steven Shaviro (2007: 13), "to feel the intolerable intensity of the actual", and reorient itself accordingly. Fourth, I distil the discussion by diving into the field where law and taste perhaps most explicitly converge, wine. Particularly looking at the newly emerged Natural Wine Movement, I explain how, whether opportunely reoriented, law may be constructively *used* as a sort of sensing machine, an inhuman apparatus to sense, indeed taste, the real.

II

> But there is a last enterprise that might be undertaken. It would be to seek experience at its source, or rather above that decisive turn where, taking a bias in the

> direction [*s'infléchissant dans le sens*] of our utility, it becomes properly human experience.
>
> (Bergson, 1988 [1896]: 184)

It is perhaps in the thought of Immanuel Kant, that aesthetics' 'wrenching duality' is most forcefully reasserted and yet, at the same time, surreptitiously compromised. Kant notably reoriented philosophy from the *transcendent*, the metaphysical domain of essences, to the *transcendental*, the conditions of possibility of experience. The archetypal phenomenologist, Kant refused to understand phenomena as mere *appearances* of superior ideas, and assumed them as manifestations (*apparitions*), in relation to the conditions of possibility of appearing itself.

Kant never questioned the priority of cognition and reason, deemed different like 'day and night' from sensibility, which he referred to as the "appearance of something, and the way we are affected by that something" (1996 [1781]: 96). Yet, in the *Third Critique*, the sensible resurfaces as a seismic ground threatening his rationalising edifice. As Shaviro explains, by positing a spatio-temporal reality of objects that "*affect* us, prior to any knowledge of them on our part", Kant implicitly maintains that "feeling, or being-affected, rather than active cognition, is the basis of experience" (2007: 10–11, emphasis in original). Whether it depends on sensible intuition, however, experience is radically singularised and thus, evidently, no longer amenable to Kant's universalising project.

To deal with this conundrum, the German philosopher excogitated a typically juridical solution, seeking to *legislate* over the sensible by establishing generalisable conditions of experience, by means of tracing them back to the unifying principle of the transcendental subject. The transcendental, in other words, was locked within the centripetal structure of the I-subject, which Kant presented as the *de jure* centre of will, the proprietor of thought, and the source of consciousness.

It is in such a Kantian way that law normally deals with the senses, recognising their unruly potential and thus seeking to entrap them within its categories: to juridify and pacify the senses, that is, and generalise them accordingly, into common sense. Yet, there remains a dimension of the sensorial that cannot be reduced into categories, a dimension that can be only singularly *felt*. This is not a dimension law cannot control because it is excessive *to* law itself but, more precisely, because law belongs to it. Although, *de jure*, law is a *project* aimed at manipulating, governing and channelling senses into precise categories, boundaries and definitions; *de facto*, it is a material *process* emerging out of the sensorial intermingling of human and non-human, tangible and intangible bodies, as such inseparable from this continuum.

This is the contradiction the young Jean-Paul Sartre saw within the structure of the transcendental subject, whose *de jure* presupposition "affirms nothing about the de facto existence of the 'I think'" (1957: 2). This subject is far too cumbersome, its structural conditions far too generic to grasp the concrete singularity of aesthetic experience, i.e., the *real* conditions of experience. What if, Sartre speculated, beneath the subject's self-constitution via the reflexive act of consciousness there be an irreflexive substratum, a radical anteriority that would expose the fragility of this presupposed catafalque? Thus the transcendental subject would disintegrate, releasing a transcendental *field*, not 'belonging' to any I-subject since being the latter's processual, material and immanent 'condition of possibility', the *event* of its surfacing (ibid.: 106). If on the one hand this assumption, i.e., the condition of "being consigned to a passivity that cannot be assumed", would lead existentialism to an impasse (Agamben, 1999: 100), on the other it will open the path towards emancipating thought and experience from the individual, the subjective, the phenomenological and indeed the human: that is, towards unfolding the transcendental field, or plane of immanence, as the realm of the pure appearing (taking place) of beings, of their event.

III

> *L'événement n'est pas ce qui arrive (accident), il est dans ce qui arrive le pur exprimé qui nous fait signe et nous attend.*
>
> (Deleuze, 1969: 175)[3]

Something happens, something takes place, an actual state of affair emerges, yet 'the event is not what occurs (occurrence), is within what occurs', an empty, mobile, differential frontier that insists on the situation without coinciding with it. In every occurrence, every taking-part, every entering in relation, there is an event, the *taking place* of these relations, that always differs with the mere presence (phenomenology) since being difference in itself, immanently beyond 'actual' relations, although never 'ontologically' separated from them: the empty time of an event which insists on the present without coinciding with it. The event, Deleuze observes, is "never present but always yet to come and already passed . . . being neutral in relation to all its temporal actualizations" (2004 [1969]: 100).[4]

From Kant onwards, Quentin Meillassoux (2009) argues, *correlation* substituted *substance* as the basic category (and entrapment) of Western thought.[5] The human-world correlation, as Claire Colebrook observes in a sweeping and inspiring generalisation, could be seen as the hidden presupposition ultimately preventing the various groundbreaking philosophies of last century to actually break any ground. The *experience* of phenomenology, the *da-sein* of Heidegger, the *pre-conscious* and *non-representational* involvement in the world of neuro-cognitive studies, the *networks* of ANT (actor network theory), the *life* of vitalism: different ways, she maintains, to equally posit "some ground from which all relations emerge" and thus, ultimately, to reduce the world to a world *for us* (2014: 25). This is most evident, and notwithstanding its claim to perform a radical decentring of the anthropological premises of contemporary philosophical thought, in "those varieties of post-humanism – Ray Brassier argues – whose levelling of the difference between the human and the nonhuman is predicated on dissolving the distinction between sapience and sentience end up promoting an unbridled anthropomorphism" (2015: 222) or, as Colebrook quips, a veritable ultra-humanism (2014: 34).

How to truly break open the correlation and reorient us towards a world independent from human existence, cognition, imagination: a world *not* for us? Contemporary speculative philosophy attempts to do so by reasserting an insurmountable separation between knowing and sensing, and championing "sapience as the gateway onto nonhuman reality" (Brassier, 2015: 222). This approach, however, by affirming one side of the wrenching dualism whilst rejecting the other, ultimately leaves the fracture unquestioned.

Deleuze offers another way out, towards an excess that is not opposed to sensible experience, but is rather understood as the 'concrete' condition of the possibility of experience: "the necessary *excess* of experience: that which overfills any sense of immediacy" and without which experience "would be so self-contained that change or becoming would not be possible" (McCormack, 2012: 721).[6] Not an excess *to* something (e.g., human, body, subject, consciousness, representation, structure, etc.), which would simply re-introduce a more original relation, but an excess in itself, as the very *event* of the relation: if 'the constituted is the correlation I-world, the subject-object nexus[, t]he constituent is the *event* of that correlation, which has no other place than in the correlation, yet cannot be said as correlation' (Ronchi, 2011: 11, my translation).

Such event expresses the virtual, inhuman viewpoint of a world *not for us*, utterly indifferent to our inescapable involvement with it, to which we are open nonetheless, *here-and-now*. Not simply non-presentational then: the event's viewpoint is not even 'presented', it "concerns an emerging situation's 'making-available' a multiplicity of viewpoints (potentially) to the bodies (humans, bits of matter, animality, languages and so on) that compose it" (Woodward, 2010: 331). This is the deep sense of Spinoza's maxim: *we do not know what a body can do*. Not an epistemological and 'correlational' limit (i.e., our incapacity to know), but an ontological statement (i.e., independently from *us*, a body is never exhausted by its relations): we do not know what a body can do because "only the event can know what a body can do" (ibid.).

Contrary to frequent trivialisation, Deleuze's philosophy does not aim at post-human dissolution but at inhuman absolution: absolving (i.e., untying) thought from the human condition, and thus the all-too-human necessity to make sense, envelop and digest the world.[7] Crucially, however, this move is performed by remaining *within* the sensible and gesturing towards another sense: "the creation from experience of something like a pure predicate released from subject-object relations, opening the idea of the appearance as such, in itself" (Colebrook, 2014: 73). Before affecting us, the 'originally affective quality of the real' has to do with the singular taking place of *what* occurs (Ronchi, 2015: 63, my translation).

Deleuze is interested in finding ways to grasp, to be sensible to, and thus worthy of, this affective quality. This is the anti-juridical core of Deleuze's thought. Whilst Kant is informed by a juridical attitude aimed "to distinguish legitimate from illegitimate uses of reason", Deleuze is a convinced constructivist, "concerned with pushing forces to the limits of what they can do, rather than with evaluating their legitimacy" (Shaviro, 2007: 3). Neither relying on the hyper-rationality of normative knowledge nor on the irrationality of a supposedly anomic sensing, he intends to do so through the speculative construction of an inhuman apparatus for sensing the real.[8] This is the potential he finds in cinema, and its capacity – via montage – to create an 'artificial eye' that would oppose the 'natural perception' championed by phenomenology, unlocking a vision *without* human eye.

Accessing the real, by definition, requires going beyond the organic limits of the human eye. Dismissive of existentialist technophobia, Deleuze believes in the potential of operationalizing technology into the aesthetic task to build a third artificial eye to see the real:

> if from the point of view of the human eye montage is undoubtedly a construction, from the point of view of another eye, it ceases to be one; it is the pure vision of a non-human eye, of an eye which would be in things.
>
> (2013[1983]: 81)

Hence his admiration for Russian pioneer Dziga Vertov and his capacity, through montage, to manufacture a "non-human eye, the cine-eye [which] is not the eye of a fly or of an eagle . . . it is the eye of matter, the eye in matter", the viewpoint of the event (ibid.).

What if we follow this reflection by focusing on tasting, rather than seeing? What if we use law, rather than cinema, to think this paradoxical strategy? The rest of the chapter is dedicated to the unfolding of these two questions, mobilising law as a technology to build an inhuman apparatus to sense – an artificial tongue to taste – the real. It is first to taste that we should thus move.

IV

> *Solus ergo gustus proprie et principaliter ad rerum naturas investigandas pre ceteris sensibus est destinatus.*[9]

In a recently republished short essay titled *Gusto* [*Taste*], Agamben develops an insightful argument on the potential for taste to reconcile the fracture of modern aesthetic between a science that knows the truth without pleasure, and a sensibility that enjoys the beautiful without being able to rationally explain why. Taste, the anti-metaphysical sense, has no place in the metaphysical partition of sensible and intelligible, and 'allows for what is by definition impossible: the knowledge of the sensible appearance . . . as true and the perception of the truth as appearance and pleasure' (2015: 28, my translation).

On the one hand, taste is quintessentially tied to knowledge. To taste is always to discriminate over what is good and what is not: to emit judgements. In this sense, taste is also more specifically tied to the domain of the normative, although a normativity that rests over a highly unstable ground, since lacking any higher truth to fund it: *de gustibus non disputandum est*. This apparent groundlessness of aesthetic judgements Kant found 'puzzling': "though these judgments do not by themselves contribute anything whatever to our cognition of things, they still belong to the cognitive power alone and prove a direct relation of this power to the feeling of pleasure or displeasure" (1987 [1790]: 6–7). Indeed, these judgements seem to point to 'another knowledge', one that is unable to provide a reason for knowing, and yet is able to enjoy it (*ne gode*, Agamben, 2015: 11).

In fact, on the other hand, taste is the hedonistic sense of pleasure *par excellence*, unique among the senses to require a dedicated capital vice. It is a sense that must controlled, disciplined and moderated, not to turn into gluttony. For this reason, in the history of philosophy it has been posited as inferior with respect to the aural and the visual – i.e., the senses of intellect and reason – since it was deemed much too close to the animal, the elemental, the corporeal. Yet, what is peculiar to taste and its mode of knowing is exactly the fact that it has fundamentally to do with the material act of ingesting, and as such with the incontrollable fact of letting other bodies physically enter one's own. Taste always means testing, trying and guessing, i.e., wandering into an uncertain zone of synesthetic immersion where the boundary-making machine of the subject begins to tilt. In this sense, taste poses an immunitary threat to 'somatic integrity', invading and dismantling the physical and conceptual unity of the subject (Guha, 2011), destabilising any stable, isolated and unitary understanding of our-selves, and making explicit the ontological reality of being-in-the-world as an always tentative immersion in a co-constituted materiality: being as *tasting-the-world*.

This (literally) unspoken side of taste was already evident in Kant's description of the *disgusting* object, which "is presented as if it insisted, as it were, on our enjoying it even though that is just what we are forcefully resisting" (1987 [1790]: 180). Kant's attempt to ground aesthetic on the elimination of disgust, and the body, was bound to clash with the stubborn resistance of the real, as the constitutive excess to the correlative ingestion of subsumption. "'I' do not assimilate it", utters Julia Kristeva, describing the nauseating experience of the lips touching the surface of the milk. Disgust, as the taste of a radical otherness that I try to expel but ultimately cannot since, whether vomiting, it is *myself* that I would spit out (1982: 3).

No surprise that it is exactly in food loathing, she continues, that the most elementary form of *abjection* can be found, that is, the experience of facing something beyond recognition, utterly unfamiliar, an 'abominable limit' that throws me into 'a place where meaning collapses' (ibid.). Disgust, most evidently when physically expressed via nausea and vomit, makes explicit taste's three-step disintegration of the transcendental subject's distance, immunity and unity.[10] First, the violation of one's bodily integrity which any act of ingestion entails. Second, the awareness of being consigned to a passivity that cannot be assumed. Third, the sense of an inassimilable (indigestible) reality to which we are nonetheless released, of which we are part: each ingestion *is* indigestion.

We are reminded of Sartre's *Nausea* in which the protagonist Roquentin finds himself 'wordless' and 'defenceless' before the senseless materiality of things, that insist upon touching, penetrating and ultimately dissolving him (2000 [1938]). It is in these very terms that Roger Caillois described the experience of the schizophrenic, for whom space appears as a 'devouring force', by which is pursued, devoured and digested 'in a gigantic phagocytosis', to the point that 'he feels himself becoming space' (1984 [1935]: 30). Any dialectic circle tilts before a concept-less exteriority that cannot be subsumed, i.e., ingested, within an historical, meaningful narration, and by which, in turn, we are devoured (Brassier, 2007).

We should interpret seriously Italo Calvino's claim that the realm of gustative experience is the only real alternative to vision, insofar as it is a directly lived 'physical introjection' of the world that makes us aware of being part of the 'universal cannibalism' of being (1986). It is by tasting that we become aware of being matter, a body among other bodies, entering a continuum of material transformations of decomposition and regeneration whose immanence radically denies any transcendent God, Law or thought (Thacker, 2011).

Unsurprisingly, taste has historically been 'defined' through the notion of *je ne sais quoi*, as a way to make sense of (or, more likely, resign oneself to) this seemingly unsolvable conundrum. Yet, what if tasting was to be reconfigured so that such *je ne sais quoi*, from a human limit (knowing without feeling, feeling without knowing), be turned into an inhuman pleasure that knows, and inhuman knowledge that senses? Thus, tasting would be appropriate to an empiricism that "truly becomes transcendental", as it occurs "only when we apprehend directly in the sensible that which can only be sensed, the very being of the sensible" (Deleuze, 1994 [1968]: 56–57).

V

> We were too quick to forget that *homo sapiens* refers to those who react to sapidity, appreciate it and seek it out, those for whom the sense of taste matters – savouring animals – before referring to judgement, intelligence or wisdom, before referring to talking man . . . Sensation, it used to be said, inaugurates intelligence. Here, more locally, taste institutes sapience.
>
> (Serres, 2009: 154)

'Taste institutes sapience', Serres reminds, and two are the truths it discloses. On the one hand, the post-human truth of ecology: taste as the gateway where sensoriality overcomes phenomenology unfolding the immanent, ecological continuum (in) which we are. On the other, the inhuman truth of separation whose knowledge can be savoured.

Meillassoux (2009: 82) proposes that we "transform our perspective on unreason, stop construing it as the form of our deficient grasp of the world and turn it into the veridical content of the world as such – we must project unreason into things themselves". In this sense, what we

> took to be a negative characteristic of our relation to things – viz., that we cannot know whether the principles of cognition are necessary or contingent – is

> in fact a positive characteristic of things-in-themselves . . . What is absolute is the fact that everything is necessarily contingent or 'without-reason'.
>
> (Brassier, 2007: 67)

What could be a more explicit evidence of the senseless stubbornness of the real than the indigestibility of its materiality to the all-ingesting human mind? Not a deficiency of our digestive apparatus, not a limit to our capacity to know, but a feature of the real itself, an ontological indigestibility signalling the absence of (human) sense from the real, its radical indifference, neutrality and impassibility to our inescapable placed-ness in it.

If 'transcendental' is employed in reference to a field of enquiry which is 'beyond' the human, the personal, the subject/object distinction, but also, as we saw, beyond 'mere' relations, opening up a dimension of thinking, acting and thus living in a 'world not for us' – then taste appears consistent with a transcendental empiricist enterprise, a praxis whereby the very caesura between knowing and the world is savoured: rather than the sensible being a way out of representation and knowledge, that is, what is 'savoured' here is such a speculative appreciation in itself. In this way overcome are the limits of human knowing (i.e., my incapacity to know) and human sensing (i.e., my incapacity to escape the phenomenological circle), without however abdicating to knowledge, as in the dissolution of post-human sensoriality. Instead, knowledge is opened "to the inhuman and the superhuman durations . . . beyond the human condition", the inhuman becomings that escapes our phenomenological sentimentality and exactly for this reason are the condition of possibility for our becoming (Deleuze, 1991: 28).

Simultaneously intelligible and sensible, knowledge and pleasure, taste may in this sense be reconfigured from a human *je ne sais quoi* to the inhuman knowledge of the veridical content of the real; from a human pleasure dependent on a given 'lack' to be filled, to an inhuman desire that, inscribing such a lack *within* the real itself, is able to truly savour it.[11] Thinking and savouring the indifference of the world and its empty impassibility is what paradoxically allows to unfold the ethico-political potential of aesthetics, as encapsulated in the famous Deleuzian injunction "not to be unworthy of what happens to us", i.e., to be faithful to a world not for us, a world never fully reducible to the relations we trace (2004 [1969]: 149). Accordingly, by deactivating its self-immunising mechanism of exception, we may open law towards a real that remains utterly indigestible to its juridifying machine, a reality that law must face nonetheless, thus forcing it to reorient itself to such an ultimately non-juridifiable reality.

VI

> The law . . . is not justice, but only the gate that leads to it. What opens a passage towards justice is not the erasure of law, but its deactivation and inactivity (*inoperosità*) – that is, another use of law.
>
> (Agamben, 2005: 64)

The mechanism of exception is the digestive mechanism of law. Law deals with the world by *including* it *de jure* as re-presentation, whilst *excluding* it *de facto*, as sensorial materiality. Law's application is always premised on such *a priori* mechanism, a topological machine whereby the "the space in which the juridico-political order can operate" is created and defined (Agamben, 1998: 19). Any legal intervention depends on a prior and violent "foundational ontological gesture" whereby the *where* through which the spatiolegal is to be articulated in the form of a cartographic representation is constituted: a state, or a space, of exception (Minca, 2006: 389). Accordingly, there is no rule – both in the sense of rule and ruling – without a space of exception.

Law's exceptional juridification of the world, i.e., the reduction of the world into legal categories, functions as a process of ingestion. Law ingests its outside (that is, what law presupposes as its outside) by *tasting* it, and emitting moral judgements accordingly. It is exactly by reducing the world to speech, text and language that law manages to ingest it whilst 'anaesthetising its mouth' (Serres, 2009: 153). Yet, as already argued, whilst law is a *project* seeking to transcend and control the sensorial, it is also a *process*, a diffuse normativity emerging out of the intermingling of bodies and senses. This process is to be dissimulated: law's ingestion of the world must not betray any pleasure, compromise, indulgence or indeed, remainder. Distance, immunity, sterility: law's experience of taste must be anaesthetised and abstracted from its materiality.

This is particularly relevant with respect to senses. In fact, law appears to construct the sociocultural parameters of 'good taste', common sense and sensibility out of which law's dealing with senses supposedly emerges. At the same time, law in this way manages to dissimulate the fact that senses are blended or anaesthetised by something other than the individual. In other words, law maintains an illusion of phenomenological immediate perception and evaluation of senses, while on another level it builds sociopolitical and cultural repositories of sensorial construction that dissimulate the fact that the law is behind all this, orchestrating both senses and its very own apparent absence of involvement (Mandic et al. 2013). The phenomenology of senses is thus elevated to a quintessential corollary of personal freedom, as the freedom to taste, smell, hear. . . . In this way law allows us to think that we own our senses in full phenomenological immersion, whilst hiding the fact that it is within the socio-legal structuration of the very socio-cultural-legal atmosphere in which we are immersed, that senses come to be perceived as individually owned (Philippopoulos-Mihalopoulos, 2013).

A complex configuration which can be perfectly observed in the way taste is normatively constructed, through a split between a merely personal, relativistic and subjective immediacy which *non disputandum est*, and a supposedly objective field of experts emitting normative judgements – the realm of wine-tasting offers a perfect example, as we are to see soon.

VII

> The goodness of the law thus lies precisely in creatively displacing the selfhood that was bringing life down.
>
> (Masciandaro, 2013: 55 n56)

That law's appropriation of the world is performed through senses (that law is a process that emerges from the materiality of senses) is evidently problematic for an institution whose *raison d'être* is the capacity to transcend the contingent, the subjective, the elemental, the affective and indeed the inhuman materiality to which the sensorial exposes it. Yet, merely deconstructing law's mechanism of exception is an insufficient, often merely self-satisfying exercise in critique. Same goes for any anarchic intention to get rid of law that, besides the contradictions in which it gets entangled, forgets that the absence of law *is* the hidden presupposition of its logic of exception (Severino, 1980).

According to this logic, a given sameness is posited, the norm, to which legal subjects must constantly approximate. They *ought* to respect the law, a compliance enforced by surveillance and control, judgement and punishment. Qualitatively different from the norm is the *model*. As de Sutter explains, "every rule requires, in absolute terms, its observance (or the penalty of sanction for inobservance); while each model demands, in its own way, its betrayal (or the penalty of ridicule for imitation)" (2012). As an example, de Sutter mentions the *kare-sansui*, the sand and rock garden in Kyoto's Ryoan-ji temple. This "simple assemblage of gravels and rocks, not representing anything other than itself", provides a minimal set of elements, whose potentially infinite variation will always betray and yet never deny the open structure of the garden itself (ibid.). The highly normative Western art of gardening is based on the constant judgement between a here-and-now and an ideal sameness to which the garden ought to approximate, according to a logic of obligation, control and sanction. The Japanese art of gardening instead relies on a differential model that, rather than an always incomplete (and thus guilty) reiteration, implies an always-new repetition, not a matter of abstract (exceptional) compliance but of embodied, stylistic variation.

Unsurprisingly, the composer John Cage was extremely interested in the *kare-sansui*, and more generally in the potential of the model as an open structure able to make the normative logic of rhythm tilt, so as to unleash the contingency of sound. Hence the famous notion of de-familiarisation, according to which the composer

> neither resists the unrest of this sensorial chasm nor asserts himself with the hegemony of an outside agent . . . but rather assumes the status of a trigger, a catalyst, that which clears space for the infiltration of sound's unruly wilting.
>
> (Mohaghegh and Golestaneh, 2011: 490)

The refusal to impose control on sound, in other words, does not imply abandonment to non-control. Instead, it entails the construction of an apparatus (the model) *through* which the normativity of sound could be unlearned so that, once sounds are no longer possessed or produced, they can be *used*.

Richard Grusin (2015: 131) terms the fallacy of 'transparent immediacy', the perspective that "holds that the subject's contact with the real depends upon the erasure of the medium, which correlates and thereby obscures the relationship between subject and the world".[12] It is likewise fallacious to pretend to simply get rid of law, in order to attain a more original, innocent and a-legal relation with the world. In this contradiction falls the naivety of phenomenology, with its prioritisation of 'natural' perception, as well as, we may say, the iconoclastic urge of non-representational approaches. After all, as Meillassoux (2009) reminds, is not the simple critique of representation merely the critique of one correlation (representation), in the name of a more original (e.g., non-representational, post-human etc.) one? This is a negative strategy, that "to withdraw the pure sensible from representation and to determine it as that which remains once representation is removed (a contradictory flux, for example, or a rhapsody of sensations)", which Deleuze already warned against (1994 [1968]: 56).

Different is a strategy which, rather than simply dismissing law, or representation, challenges their mechanism of exception: that is, the literally pr*event*ive mechanism whereby they function by *taking in* the chaotic, ever-escaping outside (life, world, space. . .) and domesticating it, simultaneously *including* space by *excluding* its conflictual, eventful and contingent materiality. This is what both the minimalist composer and the Japanese gardener do: they do not simply oppose or dismiss a normative mechanism of exception, they seek instead to dismantle it or, so to speak, to *profanate* it.

Agamben defines profanation as the strategy according to which 'something – a power, a function, a human operation – is made inoperose without being simply destroyed, but rather freeing the potentialities that there remained non-actualised, in this way allowing a different use of them' (2014: 245, my translation). The possibility to simply *using* things beyond possession was also at the core of the Franciscan notion of life in 'absolute poverty' (*altissima povertà*): not simply an injunction to live a life in poverty, but in *non-proprietary* relation with the world and its objects (Agamben, 2011).[13] Significantly, this concept does not point to a praxis *exterior* vis-à-vis law, but rather one able to make the very relation on which law's mechanism of exception rests, tilt.[14] Key dispositif in this strategy is a peculiar and eminently 'legal' apparatus, the Franciscan '*regola*' (i.e., rule). The *regola*, centred on St. Francis's dictum: *vivere secudum formam sancti Vangeli* (to live according to the form of the Holy Gospel), functions according to a logic that is analogous to that of the model. It is not meant to be a set of rules to be followed, that is, but a paradigmatic model – here, the life of Jesus – to be differentially repeated, i.e., embodied, into a style of living: not a matter of 'applying a norm to a life, but of *living* according to that form' (ibid.: 124, my translation).[15]

A juridical dispositif, the *regola*, in this case becomes an instrument to open a paradoxical space of non-law within law, by means of deactivating its exceptional mechanism of appropriation (ibid.: 142). To dig a void within law means re-orienting law towards a world *not for law*, that is, towards the very event of its encounter with a non-juridifiable world from which law is inextricable nonetheless. To profanate law, that is, or, following Alexandre Lefebvre (2008: 235–236), to de-familiarise it by "experimentally allowing the law to be affected by an encounter" or again, in Thanos Zartaloudis's words, to open law to "the experience of encountering the limit of the law, where one encounters the possibilities *of* the law (its own juridical potentiality) and all other non-juridical possibilities *to* law" (2010: 279). This is what to 'have done with judgement' means: not a call to 'have done with law', but rather, a call to have done with its normative ingestion of the world. Beyond the dogmatic observance of law, its revelatory critique or anarchic dismissal, thus lies the possibility of its profanation, whereby the unactualised potentialities of law are released, to be 'commonly' and constructively *used*.[16]

By looking at an example that brings together law, taste and wine, in the following, concluding sections, I explore the potential of this profanating strategy vis-à-vis the two converging ways in which taste is normatively entrapped: on the one hand, the transcendent set of legal protocols and normative judgement whereby it is defined and controlled; on the other, the implicit normativity that aliments the assumption of taste as belonging to the realm of subjective judgement and phenomenological immediacy.

VIII

> Never one has the right to let the fermentation of the living escape in a purposeless *dérive*.
>
> (Sloterdijk, 2015: 683–684, my translation)[17]

Wine is wine insofar as the law says so.[18] Wine is a fermented grape juice whose taste-olfactory sensations are the result of the coming-together of grapes, technique, technology, soil, geography, climate . . . a contingent assemblage of human and non-human, tangible and intangible elements, known as *terroir*, crystallised by legal regulations. Winemaking is accordingly a necessarily 'constrained' praxis, differently for instance from perfume-making, or even brewing.[19] The translation of *terroir* into law is normally provided by the regime of *appellation*, or Protected Designation of Origin (PDO), which defines, controls and protects the typicity and typology of a wine through precise qualitative and quantitative requirements regarding grapes, terrain, techniques and technologies (Barham, 2003). First legally defined in France (most notably through the 1919 law on the *Appellation d'Origine* and the 1935 legislative decree instituting the AOC) and then developed by each wine-producing country worldwide, PDO regulations are a normative device aimed to maintain desirable standards of quality associated with given geographical indications while preventing adulteration and frauds. They are enforced through a system of rules (fittingly termed *disciplinare* in Italy), surveillance through controls at wineries and judgement via tasting commissions.

If on the one hand the PDO system provides both the *making* and the *tasting* of wine with a solid normative territorialisation, on the other hand the globalisation of wine market engenders a parallel process of deterritorialisation, according to an approach that is seemingly antithetical to that of *terroir*: the logic of the *brand* (Monin and Croidieu, 2006). This eminently customer-oriented approach relies on detecting the consumer demand and tailoring wine accordingly, altering its characteristics as required, through invasive chemical intervention (Colman, 2010). What counts is no longer the capacity of wine (its taste) to express a *terroir*, but its adaptability to a given consumer taste, which is in turn determined by the evaluations provided by few influential wine-critics and magazines, whose normative power to shape global wine taste, and thus market, is immense. Within this logic, wine's *consistency* and *appeal* to consumer taste is paramount, in a self-referential circularity connecting famous wine critics (the definers of taste) and skilled 'flying winemakers' (the crafters of taste), i.e., wine-consultants working for multiple wineries, whose skills are employed to override any excessive influence and contingency of singular *terroirs*, so as to tailor wines according to wine-critics taste and, through them, consumer expectations.[20]

The mythical figure is the American critic Robert Parker, inventor of the 100-point scale system of wine-rating and trigger to the worldwide *Parkerisation* of wine: namely, the global tendency to shape wines according to his taste.[21] Since 'Parkerising' a wine would be guarantee of high score, and thus high sales, from the end of the 90s wine has been globally standardised according to the 'American taste'.[22] The consequent risk for "wine to become simply another manufactured beverage whose flavours are manipulated to match perceived consumer preferences" (Goode and Harrop, 2011: 248) is perfectly encapsulated by the philosophy of the gigantic Australian wine-producer Yellow Tail, according which "to maintain the consistency of the brand, the winery also had to intervene in the winemaking process to override the influence of *terroir*" (Colman, 2010: 105). What better example of the immanent surfacing of a normative standard by means of the systematic erasure of wine's materiality, as well as of the implicit complicity between capitalism and de-materialisation?

Yet, there is also a precise normative ideology of taste underlying this logic, best summarised by a Barolo wine producer's common-sense: "the proof of the wine, after all, is in the drinking. If you've got a great wine, it doesn't really matter how you made it" (Roberto Voerzio, quoted in Negro et al. 2007). This ideology elevates taste as the only discriminant for evaluating wine, whilst reducing taste itself to the phenomenological sensation of the taster: a whole ontology of socio-historical-legal relations and their role in striating and channelling taste is thus removed.[23] Furthermore, within this framework the intrinsic agency of the wine-object is removed from the picture. As John Cochran argues referring to a different field (molecular gastronomy), and yet with absolute relevance to our discourse,

> by taking human sense as its end goal [this approach] takes the basic structural features of entities to be expressed in immediate events *for us* ... disavows chance and shapes ontology into a series of targets that must be hit in order to maintain the normative goals of the field in which the professional participates.
>
> (2011: 317, emphasis in original)

Reduced to an inert object to be shaped by socio-technical interventions, the wine is made vulnerable to uncontrolled commodification, and the whole process is drastically excised from social, political and environmental concerns: all that counts is whether the wine tastes good whilst, of course, the extent to which such a definition of *good* is normatively shaped is conveniently overlooked.

One may say that the PDO system allows for countering this outcome, by providing small growers with 'collective property rights' against the "homogenizing fetish of 'the brand'" (Andrew Jefford, quoted in Legeron, 2013). However, as many note, the PDO system often becomes a cumbersome, over-bureaucratic device that systematically invisibilises *terroir* into a rigid techno-legal normativity, maintains power relations in place by naturalising their historical, politico-legal constitution and prevents the emergence of different singularities, ultimately becoming yet another facilitator or wine's uncontrolled commodification.[24] This is because, I believe, the ideology of taste underlying the PDO system remains the same as the brand logic. The latter prioritises the phenomenological domain of the consumer's hedonistic sensoriality, emphasising one's freedom to taste – necessary corollary to the liberal freedom of choice. Here, the normative role played by wine-critics' judgement in shaping the phenomenology of wine-tasting itself remains untold. In the PDO system instead, the normative role of judgement (via tasting commissions) in shaping taste is explicit. Here, the sensorial experience of the final consumer is subordinated to wine's capacity to comply with the written norm.

The opposition between PDO system and brand logic is merely apparent; however, both split taste into a wrenching dualism, only differentiating in the way such dualism is internally articulated. Both logics are shaped – explicitly in the former, implicitly in the latter – by the ideology of professional wine-tasting, grounded on the distinction between immediate 'naked' pleasure and analytical evaluation, phenomenological sensation and disembodied judgement. According to this implicit *hylomorphism*, the *expert* (the sommelier as wine-critic or member of a tasting commission) is able to differentiate between the subjective, merely sensorial experience of tasting and the objective, truth-revealing judgement, whereby wine is assumed as an inert object whose properties are made visible, measurable and assessable (Brighenti, 2013). This represents a Kantian tribunal of oenological reason that allows for control to be guaranteed, taste to be standardised, winemaking to be normalised. Wine is not inert, however, but an "expressive material that fundamentally exists in the dimension of becoming" (ibid.: 39). It is a dimension that taste encounters in the form of an event irreducible to phenomenological immediacy. Taste is simultaneously a relation (mediation) and the event of this relation, both non-phenomenological (virtual), as well as "felt, embodied, near": "the embodied immediacy of the event of mediation . . . the immediate affective experience of mediation itself" (Grusin, 2015: 132–133).

How to overcome the wrenching duality into which it remains split (normative evaluation vis-à-vis a general idea, subjective and groundless judgement), so as to unfold this dimension? Perhaps we may mobilise Deleuze's formula here: to *have done with judgement*, since it is only by dismantling its judgemental apparatus that taste is released as a contingent and non-presentational taking place, an impersonal and inhuman event. An event for which we may translate Deleuze's enigmatic injunction, to be worthy of the event by *understanding*, *willing* and *representing* it (2004 [1969]).

Understanding, as being open to "the irreducible heterogeneity of a real event" taste expresses, which Antoine Hennion (2007: 106) sees as resonating in the impersonal *it* that, in Italian as in French, indicates the act of drinking a wine (*se boit, si beve*). *Willing*, that is, the sensorial embodiment of the impersonal event of tasting, by the being open and vulnerable to its pleasure and pain, ready to be *surprised* by taste without entrapping it within a merely subjective sensation: "if there is indeed bitterness, let it not be *my* bitterness" (Masciandaro, 2013: 49).[25] *Representing*, i.e., the *use* of representation as an aesthetic strategy to 'free' the event from its state of affair, to free taste from its capture into the dichotomy of normative knowledge and subjective pleasure.

A recipe to carve a notion of taste able to bridge the split between knowledge and sensible, without however dissolving one into the other: at the same time a speculative predisposition to the taking place of the event and a phenomenological embodiment of the event of tasting thus freed from its reduction into a mere state of affairs. A strategic move that requires the dismantling of the exceptional dispositif of judgement without succumbing to the naïve belief on the transparent immediacy of sensation. This can be paradoxically done, as hinted above, not with or against but rather *through* law. A law, however, that has been appropriately profanated, its mechanism of exception tilted, so as to be reoriented and constructively *used*. This is the strategy that the so-called Natural Wine Movement allows to explore.

IX

> May I disappear in order that those things that I see may become perfect in their beauty from the very fact that they are no longer things that I see.
>
> (Weil, 2002[1947]: 42)

The Natural Wine Movement (NWM) is not really a movement but more precisely an umbrella term including different winemakers, gathering around various associations and international festivals, who share a common reaction against the normativity of wine that is instantiated within both logics of *brand* and PDO.[26] This movement implicitly challenges the dualism that subtends both logics and their reduction of wine to an inert matter to be objectified via the mysterious capacity of a sommelier – either sitting in a tasting commissions, or writing for a world-renown magazine – to surgically split subjective pleasure and objective analysis according to precise socio-legal regulations, and to articulate a judgement that would bring into (commercial) life the given wine.

Inspired by visionary gurus of agriculture like Rudolph Steiner and Masanobu Fukuoka, and informed by the work of its putative father, Jules Chauvet, natural winemaking may be defined as a *minimalist* approach to winemaking, aimed to limit human intervention in both the vineyard and the cellar. *Too bad humankind is here*, Chauvet once exclaimed. Hence his wish for winemaking to 'return to natural things': not a naïve attempt to unfold a pristine nature, to be sure, but an explicitly constructivist enterprise, depending on the development of advanced skills and 'robust technologies' in order to protect and preserve the micro-organisms (e.g., yeasts, bacteria) involved in the whole winemaking process (Cohen, 2013: 276). These non-human bodies Chauvet saw as crucial in providing wines with their so-called flavour and typicity, and thus as the veritable builders of the much-coveted link between *terroir* and taste: the key to the geo-oenological personality of a wine. The 'naturalness' Chauvet sought did not entail any technophobic regression to primitive practices, but a sort of techno-animism in which what was to be minimised, or banned, were all those invasive practices threatening the life of the non-human winemakers.

Chauvet's minimalistic suggestions constitute the bulk of today NWM's principles.[27] Besides the technical details, what is interesting here is how the posthuman ontology of NWM is articulated with a normative approach that potentially dismantles the exceptional logic of law: both the written law of PDO and what I referred to as the implicit normativity of taste, which ruptures taste between (objective) standards and (subjective) pleasure. Incidentally, at times this strategic potential is diluted by the rhetorics of 'naturalness' that some within the NWM employ instrumentally to exploit the positive association with those ideas of 'good', 'authentic', 'genuine', 'natural' and 'pure' that form the basis of contemporary society's symptomatic *orthorexia*.[28] The implicit suggestion of 'natural wines' as being somehow qualitatively and morally superior is clearly problematic and exposes NWM to easy and in this case deserved critiques, as for the case of Slow Food's 'good, clean and fair' rhetoric (Schneider, 2008).

A more interesting critique of the NWM is the one emphasising the supposed absence of written rules, certification bodies and shared definitions. In the absence of manifest, legally-sanctioned standards, the critique goes, the term 'natural' is meaningless, and moreover suggestes unfair divisions in the winemaking community. This critique stigmatises NWM's theoretical underpinning and practical approach as, at best, a vague and 'nonsensical' ideology and, at worst, a dishonest marketing plot, both redundant and unfair vis-à-vis the commonsensical fact that, ultimately, what counts is whether a wine does or does not 'taste good' (e.g., Teague, 2013; Wark, 2013).

Although often inaccurate and unfair (especially when coming from those who are defending their traditional market position), such critiques cannot be lightly dismissed, since they allow to capture the contradictions in which at times NWM rhetorics end up entangled. What particularly concerns me here is the way in which, by addressing some of these points, we may be able to show the peculiar normative strategy informing the NWM and the way it is able to challenge the relation between law and taste both externally (the legislation of taste) and internally (the implicit normativity of taste). This may allow to unfold a deeper significance of the NMW approach, lying beneath and indeed often against the very rhetorics their proponents often endorse.

Fundamentally, the NWM challenges two assumptions of mainstream winemaking. First, the exceptional 'logic of the norm' that articulates its legal apparatus. Second, the dualism that underlines the understanding of taste as exposed above, i.e., the separation between the 'freedom' of a phenomenological sensation that *non disputandum est*, and its implicit determination by the normative standards sets up by the experts. Let us see these two points in details.

First, *law*. With at times vehement attacks to the PDO framework and somewhat anarchic rhetorics, the NWM may appear to endorse an anti-normative, libertarian stance vis-à-vis winemaking. "We don't need rules for *vin naturel* – NW-maker René Mosse exclaims – it's not about an administration giving us rules, tasting the wines, and saying whether they are good or not" (in Signer, 2016). This seems to be indeed the impression of the French *Commission National 'Vin Biologique'*, that recently argued that the definition of 'natural' represents a 'space of non-law' (*espace de non droit*), as such requiring to be addressed.[29] A more careful look, however, shows that the NWM is far from being a nomophobic movement. If anything, its extensive web of restrictions vis-à-vis winemaking suggests the contrary. The NWM does not simply refuse, but more precisely profanates the PDO framework, dismantling its exceptional logic, not in the name of an anarchic freedom to make and taste wine, but rather in the direction of an *alternative* normativity altogether. It is instructive to read the guidelines (monastically named: *regola*) of the Italian consortium *Vini Veri* (true wines):

> the movement does not aim to fixate into a "rule" the criteria of selection of the producers that identify themselves with it, but rather to encounter who shares ideologically and philosophically a culture of transparency, naturalness and search for the expression of the land.[30]

Here it is not only the PDO framework, but more generally the logic behind any official 'designation' (with its certifying bodies and enforcing procedures) to be challenged, to the point of dismissing also other certifications (e.g., 'organic' or 'biodynamic'), even though the majority of *Vini Veri* members would fit within them. "Rules can be rode by fashions – the *regola* continues – and nothing is easier than to impose a rule to then violate it".[31] Statutes like this one are legally binding, in the form of an associative pact among the members, yet do not include forms of control such as surveillance and tasting commissions but trust the winemakers on following the shared regulations they agreed upon.

Instead of crystallising winemaking into a *disciplinare*, the *regola* proposes a set of guidelines that is simultaneously too *wide* (since, differently from the PDO, it does not regulate the use of specific grapes in specific locations and rather concerns winemaking in general, whatever the grape, soil or terrain used), and too *narrow* (since it places extremely strict limits to winemaking), for either the PDO or the brand logics to be compatible with. In a seemingly paradoxical move, the highest degree of generality allows for the maximum of expression of the singularity of a given *terroir*.[32]

The *regola* does not concern a simplistic refusal of regulations, as in the 'refusal to accept responsibility' that Elizabeth Povinelli laments vis-à-vis the anti-normative bend of various instances of contemporary 'radical' thought (2014; Colebrook, 2014). Moreover, the *regola* avoids reasserting a classic dichotomy, that of law vs. non-law, which in fact is what sustains the logic of exception itself, that on the presupposition of a non-legal outside grounds its all-ingesting legitimation. Instead, it sets up to dismantle law's exceptional normativity: regulations remain in place, yet they are of another kind. No longer shaped by a transcendent norm enacted via surveillance, checks and tasting commissions, such regulations emerge constructively out of the coming-together of bodies that is the *terroir*. The *regola* works more as an open structure (a model) than as a norm: it is no longer a way for the winemakers themselves to gain higher control on the whole process, but rather a tool to carve a space of limited control, in which the role of the winemaker becomes that of a trigger, a catalyst, aimed to detect or invite 'nonhuman contingencies' within the process itself (Negarestani and Mackay, 2011).

Second, *taste*. The tasting commissions, argues NWM's pioneer Nicolas Joly of *Coulée of Serrant*, "don't say that your wine is not good, but that it is too different from the AC's [i.e., PDO's] 'defined taste' for you to be included".[33] Opposing this logic for the NWM does not mean endorsing subjective relativism, but rather to open taste to the contingency of its singular event, with all its asperities, harshness and apparent faults. 'Natural wines' are in fact often characterised by an array of visual, taste and olfactory qualities that were so far ostracised as 'faults' by tasting manuals, commissions, experts and consumers alike: e.g., smell of manure, orange colour, unexpected fizziness, extreme acidity, cloudy appearance, etc. Such 'errors' are now reclaimed as necessary by NW-makers, since the expression of a *terroir* is deemed far more important than either the attempt to please the consumer in advance or the necessity to comply with legally binding tasting standards. "I make wines that please me, wine of my own local area, wines of Sennori. They are what they have to be and not what you want them to be," thus read the defiant label of Tenute Dettori wines.[34] 'What is fundamental', argues Dario Tiraboschi of *Fattoria Mondo Antico*, 'is that the wine be expression of the *terroir*, even if I know that, for what concerns the common taste, our territory does not express the best, but it is better like this, because this is what our territory can give'.[35] As Carlo Tabarrini of Margò winery summarises, 'the taste is the sum of the year, of the factors that sanctioned the evolution of certain yeasts, acidity, aromas. It is not so much taste to be important, it is the truth'.[36]

Or, we may say, to be important is the truth of taste, one that has not to do with subjective pleasure or objective norms, but with the event of the encounter between a tongue and a terroir. This event, the *regola* and other similar sets of guidelines, implicitly aim to 'liberate' taste from crystallisation into the official normativity and its frozen configuration of expert judgements and customer-oriented standardisation. Let us be clear: obviously, that wine tastes good remains crucial. Yet, the dispositif of the *regola* allows to release this *good* from its frozen normativity, thus letting a novel normativity to emerge, one which may include other colours, textures and smells, no longer pre-judged against in advance. It is such a profanation, following Agamben's definition, that allows for taste itself to be reoriented: no longer as sensation in and for itself, but a sense *through which* the 'truth' of the terroir may be expressed. To use Roger Haden's term, thus taste becomes a gateway to the tangible and intangible, sensible and intelligible materiality of a *tastescape* (2011).

§

Of course nothing guarantees that normative crystallisation and rampant commodification will not entrap NWM as well. In fact, for some of its components, this already occurred. After all, this chapter is certainly not meant as an uncritical endorsement of the movement. What I found particularly compelling in it is the strategy it sets up, a strategy that *uses* law, by profanating its exceptional operations, in order to open a praxis of winemaking and tasting that is attuned to the coming-together of human and nonhuman bodies that a *terroir* is, and therefore to the contingency of this encounter and the materiality of its 'living law' (Brighenti, 2010). Thus emancipated from normative judgement, taste is no longer split into a phenomenological sensation and a given norm according to which it is to be assessed, but is projected back into wine as the singularity of a *terroir* that only through an 'inhuman' apparatus – the *regola* – can be sensed.

Notes

1 'It is not so much taste to be important, it is the truth.' Carlo Tabarrini, *Margò Winery*, Italy, interviewed by the author.
2 This impossibility to provide a reason for the visible, for the beautiful, in ancient times was solved by accompanying science (which *explained* phenomena but could not save their appearance, could not provide the reason for their beauty) with divination, e.g., astrology, providing a knowledge that is not known – this is then the *saving* role of Plato's ideas (in Agamben, 2015).
3 'The event is not what occurs (occurrence), it is within what occurs, the pure expressed, which signals and awaits us.'
4 Accordingly we should strive to avoid "any dogmatic confusion of the event with the essence, but also any empiricist confusion of the event with the accident" (ibid.: 54).
5 "By 'correlation' – Meillassoux explains – we mean the idea according to which we only have access to the correlation between thinking and being, and never to either term considered apart from the other" (2009: 5–6).
6 In this way a "superior empiricism" is disclosed, "capable of stating problems and of going beyond experience towards concrete conditions" (Deleuze, 1991 [1966]: 30).
7 Sartre (1970: 4–5) defined Descartes's a *digestive philosophy*, according to which "the spidery mind trapped things in its web, covered them with a white spit and slowly swallowed them, reducing them to its own substance". Yet, it seems that it is from Kant's institution of correlation that philosophy becomes a truly digestive enterprise.
8 On the notion of inhuman apparatus, see Wark, 2015.
9 The quote is taken from the anonymous 13th-century tractatus *Summa de Saporibus*, of which three copies still remain, in the Bodleian Library (Oxford), British Library (London) and Biblioteca Laurenziana (Florence). In an engaging study on this text, Burnett (1991: 230) translated the quoted passage as follows: 'only taste is ordained above all the other senses as properly and principally the investigator of the natures of things'.
10 On these themes, Emmanuel Levinas, Jacques Derrida and Jean Paul Sartre of course come to mind.
11 Criticising the Lacanian approach, Deleuze proposes an understanding of desire which is emancipated from a reactive relation to *lack* – as in the classical psychoanalytical view – and is rather understood as dynamic, generative, *pure process* constituting the multiplicity of space: "desire includes not lack; it is also not a natural given. Desire is wholly a part of a functioning heterogeneous assemblage". Instead, 'pleasure' is understood as interruption of the flow of desire, its entrapment within the cage of the person, the individual, the subject. . . (2006: 130).
12 Mediation, accordingly, is not "an intermediary to the understanding of the nonhuman world" but "a property of the nonhuman world itself" (ibid.: 137).
13 According to St. Francis, the possessive conception of man as *dominus sui actus* i.e., proprietor of his own actions, was an original sin (Agamben, 2011: 171).

14 Instead, when facing the mounting pressure of the Church, Franciscan theologians reformulated the notion of *usus pauper* into that of *usus facti* (factual use), which indicated a series of acts (e.g., minimum amount of eating, drinking, wearing clothes) supposedly without juridical implications. Any quest for exhuming a dimension of life or praxis 'outside' of law, however, implicitly confirms its mechanism of exception, which exactly on the presupposition of a dimension 'beyond law' rests. The Franciscans' nemesis, Pope John XXII, did lucidly address the source of this contradiction by arguing that the condition of possibility for *using* a thing is to possess it: in other words, any use *necessarily* implies a 'proprietary subject', and thus any non-proprietary use is, simply, impossible (ibid.).

15 On the notion of paradigm as not the *de jure* condition of possibilities of a science, but its *de facto* existence, see Agamben, 2009.

16 Likewise, Deleuze speaks of a 'living usage' of representation, whereby representation is not simply dismissed but rather put in communication with something 'extra-representational', as a sort of vehicle for the event to be expressed, to avert its entrapment and 'sclerosis' into a mere state of affairs (2004 [1969]: 146).

17 '*Non si ha mai il diritto di lasciare fuggire la fermentazione del vivente in una deriva senza scopo*'.

18 The definition of wine has been today crystallised by the French *Loi Griffe* (14 August 1889), the first of a series of legislative initiatives stating that: 'no one shall expedite, sell or cause to be sold under the name of wine any product other than that deriving from the fermentation of fresh grapes'.

19 As Luca Turin (2007) reminds, whilst the perfume-maker can assemble whatever chemical components in order to produce a given 'smell', winemakers are required to respect a territory.

20 Obviously, consistency and consumer appeal are crucial aspects of winemaking in general. What is peculiar here is the direction of the global circuit of taste, flowing from the indisputable taste of the wine-critic. Also peculiar, vis-à-vis the more general significance played by critics and reviews in every ambit of aesthetics, is the global impact that a tiny number of critics/magazines is able to achieve.

21 Agostini and Guichard (2007) single out, as precursors of Parkerisation, the influence of the French oenologist Émile Peynaud.

22 Note that, although global norms of taste and leading wine-critics are changing, as the next section shows, Parkerisation is still a dominant logic, especially in the vast new wine-markets of Russia or China. As a rough indication, a standard 'Parker-style' wine would be smooth, fruity, full-bodied and powerful, characteristics that may be provided by intense wood-ageing (preferably in new-wood *barriques* which allows for maximising the impact of wood on the wine), overripe grapes, high extraction through longer maceration, filtration, micro-oxygenation (to soften the wine), reverse osmosis (to increase concentration), artificial colorants, industrial yeasts etc. (see McCoy, 2006).

23 On the dependence of taste on socio-cultural as well as economical relations, see Negro et al. (2007) on the controversy between 'traditionalists' and 'modernists' on the use of small or big barrels in the Barolo region; see also Goldberg (2011) for an intriguing account of the battle for the use of *Gallisierung* (a technique to reduce the acidity of wine by adding a sugar-water solution to the pre-fermented grape must) in the Mosel River Valley.

24 On how the PDO system risks freezing *terroir* into space vulnerable to uncontrolled capitalisation, see Banks and Sharpe (2006) and Murray and Overton (2011); on the significant example of Bordeaux wines, see Jacquet and Laferté (2005).

25 On the notion of taste as surprise, in the etymological sense of being-taken from above (*super-prehensus*), see Hennion and Teil (2004).

26 Among the most important associations: L'Association des Vins Naturels, La Renaissance des Appellations, Vini Veri, Vinnatur etc. Among the most important festivals: RAW, Real Wine Fair, Villa Favorita etc.

27 Briefly: use of insecticides, herbicides and artificial fertilizers, but also other added chemicals (e.g., artificial products modifying colour, flavour and texture of the wine); no addition of

sugar (*chaptalisation*), little or no addition of sulphur dioxide; no filtration, de-alcoholization, micro-oxygenation, reverse osmosis and other similarly interventionist processes; no use of standardised industrial yeast, since only autochthonous yeasts, already present in the grapes, would guarantee a properly *terroir*-ised fermentation; little use of wood-ageing, given its potential, if abused, to conceal terroir and uniform wine; etc. Obviously this is not the place to discuss technical details, moreover also depending on the specific typology of wine (e.g., sweet, sparkling etc.). There are numerous recent books introducing NW in technical, social and philosophical terms. See for instance Feiring (2011) and Legeron (2014).

28 The term, literally meaning 'correct appetite', is used to indicate the contemporary obsession with righteous eating and healthy diet.

29 Retrieved from www.inao.gouv.fr/content/download/1628/16397/version/1/file/Lettre%20d'informations%20P%C3%B4le%20Vins%20n17%20-%201er%20avril%20 2016.pdf. Proposals to provide 'natural wines' with a dedicated designation have been recently made both in Italy and France.

30 Retrieved from www.viniveri.net/en/consortium/guidelines/

31 "'[W]e are not organic, even though our 'rule' imposes conditions within the vineyard and the cellar that are far more severe than those of the various 'certifications'" (ibid.).

32 They could be said to function as a sort of Spinoza's common notion, neither abstractly global nor specifically local, but rather general, and insofar as general permitting to be employed contextually and practically, while preventing freezing territorialisation or absolute deterritorialisation.

33 Quoted in Legeron (2013).

34 Retrieved from www.tenutedettori.it/en/.

35 Interviewed and translated by the author.

36 Interviewed and translated by the author.

Bibliography

Agamben, Giorgio, *Homo Sacer: Sovereign Power and Bare Life*, Stanford: Stanford University Press, 1998.

Agamben, Giorgio, *Remnants of Auschwitz: The Witness and the Archive*, New York: Zone Books, 1999.

Agamben, Giorgio, *State of Exception*, Chicago, University of Chicago Press, 2005.

Agamben, Giorgio, *The Signature of All Things: On Method*, New York: Zone Books, 2009.

Agamben, Giorgio, *Altissima povertà. Regole monastiche e forme di vita*, Milano: Neri Pozza, 2011.

Agamben, Giorgio, *L'Uso dei Corpi*, Milano: Neri Pozza, 2014.

Agamben, Giorgio, *Gusto*, Macerata: Quodlibet, 2015.

Agostini, Hanna and Guichard, Marie-Françoise, *Robert Parker, Anatomie d'un Mythe*, Scali, 2007.

Banks, Glenn and Sharpe, Scott, 'Wine, Regions and Geographic Imperative: The Coonawarra Example', *New Zealand Geographer*, 62(3), 173–184, 2006.

Barham, Elizabeth, 'Translating Terroir: The Global Challenge of French AOC Labeling', *Journal of Rural Studies*, 19(1), 127–138, 2003.

Bently, Lionel and Flynn, Leo (eds), *Law and the Senses: Sensational Jurisprudence*, London, Chicago: Pluto Press, 1996.

Bergson, Henri, *Matter and Memory*, New York: Zone Books, 1988 [1896].

Brassier, Ray, *Nihil Unbound. Enlightenment and Extinction*, Basingstoke: Palgrave, 2007.

Brassier, Ray, 'Reason Is Inconsolable and Non-Conciliatory. Ray Brassier in Conversation with Suhail Malik', in Malik, Suhail, Cox, Christoph and Jaskey, Jenny (eds), *Realism Materialism Art*, New York, Berlin: Sternberg Press, 2015.

Brighenti, Andrea Mubi, 'On Territoriology', *Theory, Culture & Society*, 27(1), 2010.

Brighenti, Andrea Mubi, 'Remarks for a Territoriology of Wine Tasting', in Danilo Mandic, Caterina Nirta, Pavoni Andrea and Andrea Philippopoulos-Mihalopoulos (eds), *Law and the*

Senses Series: The Taste Issue. Non Liquet: The Westminster Online Working Papers Series, 2013, https://nonliquetlaw.wordpress.com/2013/05/28/law-and-the-senses-series-taste/.

Burnett, Charles, 'The Superiority of Taste', *Journal of the Warburg and Courtauld Institutes*, 54, 230–38, 1991.

Caillois, Roger, 'Mimicry and Legendary Psychaestenia', *October*, 31, 17–32, 1984 [1935].

Calvino, Italo, *Sotto il sole giaguaro*, Milano: Garzanti, 1986.

Cochran, John, 'Object Oriented Cookery', in Reza Negarestani and Robin Mackay (eds), *Collapse VII: Culinary Materialism*, Falmouth: Urbanomic, 2011.

Cohen, Paul, 'The Artifice of Natural Wine: Jules Chauvet and the Reinvention of Vinification in Postwar France', in Rachel E. Black and Robert C. Ulin (eds), *Wine and Culture. Vineyard to Glass*, London, New York: Bloomsbury Academic, 2013.

Colebrook, Claire, *Sex After Life: Essays on Extinction, Vol. 2*, Michigan: Open Humanities Press, 2014.

Colman, Tyler, *Wine Politics: How Governments, Environmentalists, Mobsters, and Critics Influence the Wines We Drink*, Berkeley: University of California Press, 2010

Deleuze, Gilles, *La Logique du Sens*, Paris: Les Éditions de Minuit, 1969.

Deleuze, Gilles, *Bergsonism*, New York: Zone Books, 1991 [1966].

Deleuze, Gilles, *Difference and Repetition*, New York: Columbia University Press, 1994 [1968].

Deleuze, Gilles, *Fuori dai cardini del tempo: Lezioni su Kant*, edited by Sandro Palazzo, Milano: Mimesis, 2004.

Deleuze, Gilles, 'Desire and Pleasure', in David Lapoujade (ed.), *Two Regimes of Madness*, Los Angeles: Semiotext(e), 2006.

Deleuze, Gilles, *Cinema 1: The Movement-Image*, London: Continuum, 2013 [1983].

de Sutter, Laurent, 'Gardening the Law: Rules and Models in the Japanese Art of Gardening', paper presented during Gardens of Justice: The Critical Legal Conference 2012, Kungligla Teknikska Högskolan, Stockholm (Sweden), 14–16 September 2012.

Feiring, Alice, *Naked Wine: Letting Grapes Do What Comes Naturally*, Boston: Da Capo Press, 2011.

Goldberg, Kevin D., 'Acidity and Power: The Politics of Natural Wine in Nineteenth-Century Germany', *Food and Foodways: Explorations in the History and Culture of Human Nourishment*, 19(4), 294–313, 2011.

Goode, Jamie and Harrop, Sam, *Authentic Wine: Toward Natural and Sustainable Winemaking*, Berkeley: University of California Press, 2011.

Grusin, Richard, 'Radical Mediation,' *Critical Inquiry*, 42(1), 124–148, 2015.

Guha, Manabrata, 'Vague Weaponizations, or the Chemistry of Para-Tactical Engagements', in Reza Negarestani and Robin Mackay (eds), *Collapse VII: Culinary Materialism*, Falmouth: Urbanomic, 2011.

Haden, Roger, 'Lionizing Taste: Toward an Ecology of Contemporary Connoisseurship', in Jeremy Strong (ed.), *Educated Tastes: Food, Drink and Connoisseur Culture*, Lincoln: University of Nebraska Press, 2011.

Hamilton, Sheryl, Majury, Diana, Moore, Dawn, Sargent, Neil and Wilke, Christiane, *Sensing Law*, Abingdon: Routledge, 2017.

Hennion, Antoine, 'Those Things that Hold Us Together: Taste and Sociology,' *Cultural Sociology*, 1, 97–114, 2007.

Hennion, Antoine and Teil, Geneviève. 'Le goût du vin. Pour une sociologie de l'attention', in Véronique Nahoum Grappe and Odile Vincent (eds), *Le Goût des Belles Choses. Ethnologie de la relation esthétique*. Paris: Maison des Sciences, 2004.

Jacquet, Olivier and Laferté, Gilles, 'Appropriation et identification des territoires du vin: la lutte entre grands et petits propriétaires du "Corton"', *Cahiers d'Économie et Sociologie Rurales*, 76, 10–27, 2005.

Kant, Immanuel, *Critique of Judgement*, Cambridge, MA: Hackett Publishing, 1987 [1790].

Kant, Immanuel, *Critique of Pure Reason*, Cambridge, MA: Hackett Publishing, 1996 [1781].

Kristeva, Julia, *Powers of Horror: An Essay on Abjection*, New York: Columbia University Press, 1982.

Lefebvre, Alexandre, *The Image of Law*, Stanford: Stanford University Press, 2008.

Legeron, Isabelle, 'Can We Still Trust the AC System?', 14 February 2013. www.rawwine.com/blog/can-we-still-trust-ac-system.

Legeron, Isabelle, *Natural Wine: An Introduction to Organic and Biodynamic Wines Made Naturally*, London, New York: CICO Books, 2014.

Mandic, Danilo, Nirta, Caterina, Pavoni, Andrea and Philippopoulos-Mihalopoulos, Andreas (eds), *Law and the Senses Series: The Taste Issue. Non Liquet: The Westminster Online Working Papers Series*, 2013. https://nonliquetlaw.wordpress.com/2013/05/28/law-and-the-senses-series-taste/.

Masciandaro, Nicola, 'The Sweetness (of the Law)', in Danilo Mandic, Caterina Nirta, Andrea Pavoni and Andreas Philippopoulos-Mihalopoulos (eds), *Law and the Senses Series: The Taste Issue. Non Liquet: The Westminster Online Working Papers Series*, 2013. https://nonliquetlaw.wordpress.com/2013/05/28/law-and-the-senses-series-taste/.

McCormack, Derek, 'Geography and Abstraction: Towards an Affirmative Critique', *Progress in Human Geography*, 36(6), 715–734, 2012.

McCoy, Elin, *The Emperor of Wine: The Rise of Robert M. Parker, JR., and the Reign of American Taste*, New York: Harper, 2006.

Meillassoux, Quentin, *After Finitude an Essay on the Necessity of Contingency*, London: Continuum, 2009.

Minca, Claudio, 'Giorgio Agamben and the New Biopolitical Nomos', *Geografiska Annaler: Series B, Human Geography* 88(4), 387–403, 2006.

Mohaghegh, Jason B. and Golestaneh, Seema, 'Haunted Sound: Nothingness, Movement, and the Minimalist Imagination', *Environment and Planning D: Society and Space* 29(3), 485–498, 2011.

Murray, Warwick E. and Overton, John, 'Defining regions: The Making of Places in the New Zealand Wine Industry', *Australian Geographer*, 42(4), 419–433, 2011.

Negarestani, R. and Mackay, R. 'Introduction', in Reza Negarestani and Robin Mackay (eds), *Collapse VII: Culinary Materialism*, Falmouth: Urbanomic, 2011.

Negro, Giacomo, Hannan, Michael T., Rao, Hayagreeva and Leung, Ming. 'No Barrique, No Berlusconi: Collective Identity, Contention, and Authenticity in the Making of Barolo and Barbaresco Wines', *Working Paper* no. 1972, Stanford University, 2007.

Philippe, Monin and Croidieu, Grégoire. 'Competing "Terroir" and "Brand" logics, and violating genetic codes in the wine industry', *The European Institute for Life-long Learning*, Working Papers 6, 2006. https://learninghub.em-lyon.com/exploitation/detailstatic.aspx?RSC_BASE=SYRACUSE&RSC_DOCID=104388&TITLE=&_lg=en-GB.

Philippopoulos-Mihalopoulos, Andreas, 'Atmospheres of Law: Senses, Affects, Lawscapes,' *Emotion, Space and Society*, 7, 35–44, 2013.

Plato, *The Dialogues of Plato*, trans. B. Jowett, New York: Random House, 1920 [4th C. BCE].

Povinelli, Elizabeth, 'On Biopolitics and the Anthropocene. Interviewed by Mat Coleman and Kathrin Yusoff', *Society and Space*, 6 March 2014. http://societyandspace.org/2014/03/06/on-biopolitics-the-anthropocene-and-neoliberalism/.

Ronchi, Rocco, 'Introduzione a Jean Paul Sartre' introduction to Jean-Paul Sartre, *La trascendenza dell'ego: una descrizione fenomenologica*, Milano: Marinotti, 2011.

Ronchi, Rocco, *Gilles Deleuze*, Milano: Feltrinelli, 2015.

Sartre, Jean-Paul, *The Transcendence of the Ego: An Existentialist Theory of Consciousness*, Now York: Noonday Press, 1957.

Sartre, Jean-Paul, 'Intentionality: A Fundamental Idea of Husserl's Phenomenology,' trans. Joseph Fell, *The Journal of the British Society for Phenomenology*, 1(2), 1970.

Sartre, Jean-Paul, *Nausea*, London: Penguin, 2000 [1938].

Schneider, Stephen, 'Good, Clean, Fair: The Rhetoric of the Slow Food Movement', *College English*, 70(4), 384–402, 2008.

Serres, Michel, *The Five Senses: A Philosophy of Mingled Bodies*, trans. M. Sankey and P. Cowley, London: Bloomsbury Academic, 2009.

Severino, Emanuele, *Destino Della Necessità*, Milano: Adelphi Edizioni, 1980.

Shaviro, Steven, 'The "Wrenching" Duality of Aesthetics: Kant, Deleuze and the "Theory of the Sensible"', 2007. www.shaviro.com/Othertexts/SPEP.pdf.

Signer, Rachel, 'Does "Natural Wine" Deserve Its Own Classification?', *Eater*, 8 March 2016. www.eater.com/drinks/2016/3/8/11175218/natural-wine-category.

Sloterdijk, Peter, *Sfere III. Schiume*, Milano: Raffaello Cortina Editore, 2015.

Teague, Lettie, 'The Actual Facts Behind the Rise of Natural Wine', *The Wall Street Journal*, 11 July 2013. www.wsj.com/articles/SB100014241278873244361045785796502088839 68#articleTabs%3Darticle.

Thacker, Eugene, 'Spiritual Meat: Resurrection and Religious Horror in Bataille', in Reza Negarestani and Robin Mackay (eds), *Collapse VII: Culinary Materialism*, Falmouth: Urbanomic, 2011.

Turin, Luca, *The Secret of Scent: Adventures in Perfume and the Science of Smell*, New York: Faber & Faber, 2007.

Wark, McKenzie, 'Absolute Spectacle', in Suhail Malik, Christoph Cox and Jenny Jaskey (eds), *Realism Materialism Art*, New York, Berlin: Sternberg Press, 2015.

Wark, Tom, 'Impressions of the Natural Wine Movement', *Fermentation: The Daily Wine Blog*, 8 July 2013. http://fermentationwineblog.com/2013/07/impressions-of-the-natural-wine-movement/.

Weil, Simone, *Gravity and Grace*, Abingdon: Routledge, 2002 [1947].

Woodward, Keith, 'Events, Spontaneity and Abrupt Conditions', in Ben Anderson and Paul Harrison (eds), *Taking-Place: Non-Representational Theories and Geography*, Farnham: Ashgate, 2010.

Zartaloudis, Thanos, *Giorgio Agamben: Power, Law and the Uses of Criticism: Power, Law and the Uses of Criticism*, Abingdon: Routledge, 2010.

8

Synaesthesia

The mystical sense of law

Nicola Masciandaro

Figure 8.1 Wheel of the Senses, Longthorpe Tower, Peterborough, Cambridgeshire, UK, ca. 1320–1340.

For to everyone who senses something there comes about, in addition to the apprehension of the thing that he is sensing, also a certain self-awareness [*sunaisthēsis*] of [the fact] that he is sensing.

– Alexander of Aphrodisias

"Synaesthetic perception is the rule [*la règle*]" (Merleau-Ponty, 2002: 237). The question of the relation between law and the senses necessarily touches upon the synaesthetic nature of all perception. As law itself is not something properly observable, but is rather a principle operative through a non-circumscribable matrix of material, imaginal, and intellectual forms, so the sensing of law is unintelligible without reference to the principle of synthesis which governs sensation, that is, the common sense and sensing of sense first named by Aristotle's commentators as *synaesthesia*. "Formed by the addition of the prefix 'with' (*sun-*) to the verb 'to sense' or 'to perceive' (*aisthanesthai*), the expression in all likelihood designated a 'feeling in common,' a perception shared by more than one" (Heller-Roazen, 2007: 81). That it is the glossators and not the philosopher who coined the term reveals the proportion between the with-sensing of perception and the with-thinking of commentary (from *com-minisci*, to invent) as a reflective act of searching out "the animating element in . . . textual objects that bears no name," of "find[ing] the secret source of incompletion sealed in every work of thought" (Heller-Roazen, 2007: 80). Like the formal inseparability of law and commentary, this synaesthesia of 'synaesthesia' indexes the broader perceptual sphere wherein our sensing of law's being (*what* law is and *that* law is) is an activity that takes place within the traditionary *margin* of the given, "the gap between the thing to be transmitted and the act of transmission" (Agamben, 1999: 107). The essential unboundedness of this margin, and with it the uncircumscribable nature of law itself, is captured in Nietzsche's definition of consciousness as commentary: "All our so-called consciousness is a more or less fantastic commentary on an unknown, perhaps unknowable, but felt text" (Nietzsche, 1997: 78). So synaesthesia touches upon the mystical sense of things, that mysterious sense, a we-know-not-what *that*: "Not how the world is, is the mystical, but that it is" (Wittgenstein, 1998: 6.44). In sum, both the origin of the concept of synaesthesia and the commentarial nature of awareness point to the need for understanding synaesthesia as not only an aspect of law's relation to the senses but as the very interface between the sense of law and the law of sense. Synaesthesia is the law because synaesthesia senses, without sensing it as such, law per se.

Accordingly, it is necessary to understand the synaesthetic sense of law within a universal scope, as applicable to all objects of consciousness. The law of synaesthesia reflects the universality of law as the unlimited binding of all things to the unknown and perhaps unknowable reality or truth which is beyond law. Synaesthesia's inescapable necessity, the fact that nothing is ever sensed without something else being sensed *with* it, is of a piece with law's summit, the "law of liberty" (Augustine, 1955: 47) or "law beyond law" (Badiou, 2003: 88) traditionally identified with love as the principle of unity and absolute force of attraction governing all life and being.[1] As Hegel observes,

> The unification of all laws in universal attraction expresses no further content than just the bare concept of the law itself . . . In contrast, then, with determinate law stands universal attraction, or the bare conception of law . . . the pure conception of law transcends not merely the law . . . but also transcends law as such. (Hegel, 2003: 86)

Transcendent and immanent, abstract and literal, this law of law is found no less in the midst of the process of defining law. For the determination or 'laying down' of law (from the PIE root *legh-* 'to lie, lay'), which of necessity must communicate its own act, cannot be made except through the gravitation of perception itself, specifically, the identification of conformity or similarity in dissimilarity. The inscription of law, the binding of its principle to the letter, is a reflection or reverberation of the synthetic appearance of law in the first place. As objects are perceived through forms that synthesise their properties, so law, like a 'line' of force, is literally the little form (*formula*) perceived to pertain among the more-than-one cases or events to which it applies. Thus law is properly not indicated but referred to – *it*'s the law.[2]

> What is a law, then? It is a formula to which real events truly conform. By 'conform,' I mean that, taking the formula as a general principle, if experience shows that the formula applies to a given event, then the result will be confirmed by experience.
>
> (Peirce, 1998: 314)

Such conformity constitutes the matter of law, whether projected onto things as that to which they should conform, or perceived from them as that to which they will conform – keeping in mind of course the universal specularity of all vision (intellectual, imaginal, sensory), whereby projection and perception, extramission and intromission, are always co-implicated in the field of experience. It is this inescapable simultaneity of action and passion which is the medium of law's autopoietic and tautologous force, whose atmosphere is marked by the limitless circularity of the mirror. Thus, Philippopoulos-Mihalopoulos speaks of the social 'lawscape' as "the epistemological and ontological tautology" and "the interfolding of law and the city in both a material and an immaterial sense" (Philippopoulos-Mihalopoulos, 2013: 36, 35).

As there is no inherent limit to what experience can confirm, so is there no limit to the order of laws. The universality of law lies not in fixity but in flexibility, in the openness by which one law may always rule over or be ruled by another law without diminishment of either's essence. Just as the judicial fulfilment of law ideally takes place in the synderetic space of reflection, wherein seemingly irreconcilable intellectual and affective perceptions are found to touch in a non-contradictory moment of mutual suspension – "Mercy and truth have met each other: justice and peace have kissed" (Psalms 85:10) – in the same way, the order of law is one of coexistent supervening orders that contact each other without incoherence. Matter, life, and thought all proceed according to their own immanent laws, operating and impinging upon each other without diminishing the integrity and legal autonomy of their spheres. Each is irreducible to yet capable of seamless interaction with the other. Laws of atoms and laws of logic have everything and nothing to do with each other, just as the ultimate will of Reality or God does everything and nothing, effortlessly governing as pure act the world through itself.[3] Paradoxically bound to its own free play, the universality of law rules everything synaesthetically, by means of an open superimposition of laws upon laws all working together in a mysterious manner.[4] Synaesthesia is phenomenally on par with the spontaneity of the absolute as the purposelessness governing all purposes and may itself be considered as a direct intimation of the paradoxically 'endless plan' of reality which "never make[s] plans, never change[s] plans" (Baba, 1964: 49).[5] Or as Meillassoux, exploding facticity into the absolute itself, affirms in *After Finitude*,

> Everything could actually collapse: from trees to stars, from stars to laws, from physical laws to logical laws; and this not by virtue of some superior law whereby everything is destined to perish, but by virtue of the absence of any superior law capable of preserving anything, no matter what, from perishing.
>
> (Meillassoux, 2008: 53)

As an ineradicable superfluity or inexplicable surplus presence in the 'natural courtroom' of experience, synaesthesia testifies to the incontrovertible truth that, as Einstein said, "There is something essential about the Now which is just outside the realm of science" (Davies, 1995: 77). The inescapability of synaesthesia is on par with an ever-new permanent trace of the unstoppable present, a light-speed glow of "the hysterical ubiquity of the law" (Philippopoulos-Mihalopoulos, 2013: 35).

Non c'è due senza tre – no two without three. The withness of synaesthesia, a spark leaping between senses,[6] gives witness to how law is discerned in the space of the third, in the between-and-beyond zone of (un)likeness whose navigation is the hallmark of intelligence:

> the greatest thing by far is to be master of metaphor. It is the one thing that cannot be learnt from others; and it is also a sign of genius, since a good metaphor implies an intuitive perception of the similarity in dissimilars.
>
> (Aristotle, 1941: 1479)

The question of law's connection to synaesthesia thus impinges upon the interface of law and poetry, exposing the ontological depth of metaphor as a medium of law and life.[7] Like a subtle ruling of the blank page of awareness, synaesthesia orders the relation between the possibility and the actuality of perception. So Marks argues that "in synaesthesia, perception lays the groundwork for language" (Marks, 1990: 28) and Weber speaks of "the synaesthetic and ecstatic space of aliveness" as "an inner relationship of space that makes possible the real spaces of the world . . . and that lays a metaphorical and synaesthetic basic grid on the world" (Weber, 2016: 122).[8] The unitive doubling inherent to synaesthesia, such that even our simplest perceptions are perceptions of things synaesthetically *like* themselves, is a variant of the paradoxical essence of nature as governed through itself, as ever producing out of itself things which are at once other than and more of itself. As Ricoeur explains in *The Rule of Metaphor*, "If *mimêsis* involves an initial reference to reality, this reference signifies nothing other than the very rule [*règne*] of nature over all production. But the creative dimension is inseparable from this referential movement. *Mimêsis* is *poiêsis*, and *poiêsis* is *mimesis*" (Ricoeur, 1977: 44).

In these terms, understanding the synaesthesia of law carries the potential to reanimate awareness of the poetic agency of our acts of perception vis-à-vis law's various domains, restoring our senses (corporeal, imaginative, intellectual) to their commentarial role as interpreters and shapers of the being of law in all of its forms.[9] The law is *made* for the human, not the human for the law.[10] The synaesthetic rule of sense is an imperative to realise more and more the hidden unity of law's polysemy, the secret link between law (*lex*) as the truth that binds (*ligare*) and the truth that is read (*legere*).[11] Reading the sense of law synaesthetically holds open the book of boundless intelligence, "*legato con amore in un volume*" (*Paradiso* 33.86), that binds and reads us from within: "Understanding implies an intimate knowledge, for *intelligere* (to understand) is the same as *intus legere* (to read inwardly)" (Aquinas, 1947–8: 1204). The little spark of synaesthesia, touching both the sense of law and the law of sense, leaps the void between positive and natural law wherein it seems "now completely impossible to form a new uniform concept [of law]" (Schröder, 2008: 71). It may thus serve as a light in the dark

Table 8.1 Arthur Rimbaud, "Voyelles"

Voyelles	*Vowels*
A noir, E blanc, I rouge, U vert, O bleu: voyelles,	A black, E white, I red, U green, O blue: vowels,
Je dirai quelque jour vos naissances latentes:	One day I will tell your latent birth:
A, noir corset velu des mouches éclatantes	A, black hairy corset of shining flies
Qui bombinent autour des puanteurs cruelles,	Which buzz around cruel stench,
Golfes d'ombre; E, candeurs des vapeurs et des tentes,	Gulfs of darkness; E, whiteness of vapors and tents,
Lances des glaciers fiers, rois blancs, frissons d'ombelles;	Lances of proud glaciers, white kings, quivering of flowers;
I, pourpres, sang craché, rire des lèvres belles	I, purples, spit blood, laughter of beautiful lips
Dans la colère ou les ivresses pénitentes;	In anger or penitent drunkenness;
U, cycles, vibrements divins des mers virides,	U, cycles, divine vibrations of green seas,
Paix des patis semes d'animaux, paix des rides	Peace of pastures scattered with animals, peace of the wrinkles
Que l'alchimie imprime aux grands fronts studieux;	Which alchemy prints on heavy studious brows;
O, Suprême Clairon plein des strideurs étranges,	O, Supreme Clarion full of strange stridor,
Silences traversés des Mondes et des Anges:	Silences crossed by Worlds and Angels:
– Ô l'Oméga, rayon violet de Ses Yeux!	– O, the Omega, violet beam from His Eyes!
	(Rimbaud, 2005: 140–141)

night of juridical nihilism, the willful "forgetfulness of natural law and justice... [that] is ultimately rooted in the negation of the occurrence of synderesis" (Stepien, 2014: 397).

Toward this end, this chapter will now proceed in the form of commentary on a classic and authoritative poetic articulation of the principle of synaesthesia: "Voyelles" by Arthur Rimbaud. The aim of the commentary is less to do critical justice to the poem than to perceive it exegetically to be *a pronunciation of the mystical sense of law*. While the poem speaks about synaesthesia, there takes place within it another hidden word: the call of the poet as the one who utters law and the call of law as poetry. Law is the 'secret source of incompletion' sealed in the poem's thought. "Voyelles" is an openly secret demonstration of the fact that the poetic word of synaesthesia pronounces law.

Littera vocalis – "Voyelles"

The title of the poem is the name for the letters of voice.

> The vowel is, etymologically speaking, a sign of voice (in Latin, *littera vocalis*), an audible *vox* breathing life into the inert *notae* of writing . . . vowels are letters that represent pure sound, occupying that dimension of speech closest to a cry, or to music.
>
> (Bergeron, 1998: 106)

The poet's topic is, emblematically, the place of poetry as the scripting of spirit, the marking of voice which bears an original connection to law as a linking or authoritative marking of the sacred threshold between spirit and letter, the inscription of the voice and command of truth. "And he gave to Moses, when he made an end of speaking with him upon Mount Sinai, the two tables of the testimony, tables of stone, written with the finger of God" (Exodus 31:18). Proportionally, the poem sets down a law of correspondence between vowels and colours by virtue of a divinatory act of inscription, resonating with the ancient practice of invoking and/or naming the divine through the vowels as an imitation of the universal order.[12] Indeed the autograph shows the poet's hand conspicuously linking the first consonant and vowel of the title with a surplus loop – a spontaneous image of the synaesthetic bond of spirit and matter that is incidentally legible as the first letter of *loy* or 'law':

Figure 8.2 Arthur Rimbaud, autograph manuscript of "Voyelles" (detail).

In these terms, the title intimates the interface between poetry and law, the writing of sound and sense whose originary gesture, uniting inscription and indication, effects a mutual translation between the one and the many, just as the five fingers of the hand (many of one) synthesise into the movement of the digit-index as the 'hand' of the fingers (one of many).[13] Out of the double nature of the first letter (the divine trace of writing-as-pointing and pointing-as-writing) is produced the doubleness of law's fabled tablets whose essence, reflected between the Decalogue and the charity's 'double law', is guarded by the manicule, namely, within the haptic margin of commentary as what holds and preserves the originary gesture and command.[14] So the poem's singular first word, which is doubled at the end of its first line and is at once a saying and a showing of its topic, both signifies a many that cannot be pronounced as one and announces the poem as a poem about itself, as an autopoietic event. Furthermore, the title manifests the differential generation of the name or sign of a thing as no less the mark of the originary fault/failure/wound of expression, the institution of the gap between saying and said. Just as "we cannot make an indication without drawing a distinction" (Spencer-Brown, 1969: 1), spirit cannot be scripted without that severance of itself into inside and outside which reverberates in the doubled boundaries of title/poem and text/commentary. Here the fundamental relation between autopoiesis and fiction (fr. *fingere*), or the poetic threshold between fact and fiction, also comes into view. The vowels cannot be spoken without the fiction of "vowels," the inscription of a finger, just as the world, "in any attempt to see itself as an object . . . must . . . act so as to make itself distinct from, and therefore false to, itself" (Spencer-Brown, 1969: 105).

The doubling made manifest in the poem's title both mirrors and is the double nature of synaesthesia, namely, the inseparability of sensing and the sense of sensing that is also the ground of polysemy. Scripting *avant la lettre* the inscription of the vowels that will follow in the first line, the title registers the continuity between synaesthesia and presence, and thus the mystery of the image as an appearance of something *before* itself, the experience of which poetry in a special way provides, as "the work of art does not simply refer to something, because what it refers to is actually there" (Gadamer, 1986: 35). In these terms, the title anticipates law by analogy: vowels are to the concept of spirit as "Voyelles" is to the sense of law. As spirit lays down the law of itself as vowels, "Voyelles" lays down the poetry of itself as law. Already, before being given as such, the issue of the plurality and count and togetherness of the vowels is at stake, the question of the necessity and contingency of their system or togetherstanding (from *syn* + *histanai*, 'cause to stand'). Who names the vowels? Do they name themselves? What is the order between their name (*voyelles*) and determination (*A E I U O*)? Is the system open or closed? The questionality of the poem's title stands on the threshold of the question of law's poetry, and more properly, its autopoiesis or self-generation. In the poet's utterance of the vowels around a circle drawn from the title to the end of the first line – "'Voyelles' . . . *voyelles*" – is heard "law's unutterable paradox," namely, "whether law is lawful or unlawful" (Philippopoulos-Mihalopoulos, 2010: 82). More specifically, the ambivalently necessary/contingent colouring of the vowels, the circular cut of their undecidable decision, manifests the correlative paradox of law as "a normatively closed but cognitively open system" (Luhmann, 1988: 20). As law is paradigmatically what both binds and attracts (see note 1), so does the synaesthetic circuit of the poet's vowel system, the law of its spirit, open the world through its own closure.

While this analogical anticipation of law as theme of "Voyelles" is semantically tenuous, there is contextual support that Rimbaud's inspiration was inherently informed by the question of law. First, there is the influence, via Baudelaire's "Correspondances," of the Swedenborgian universal 'law of correspondences,' with which Rimbaud's poem becomes associated in the developing "mystique of synaesthesia as a form of supreme perception" (Dann, 1998: 39). Second, there is the anarchic legalism of Rimbaud's visionary project of "reaching the unknown by a derangement [*dérèglement*] of all the senses" (Rimbaud, 2005: 371) – a 'deregulation' of sense which in "Voyelles" takes the complementary form of a ruling of synaesthesia, as expressed in Rimbaud's subsequent self-correcting comment on the poem in which the poetic and commentarial senses of *invention* become indistinguishable: "I invented [*inventai*] the colour of the vowels! – A black, E white, I red, O blue, U green. – I regulated [*réglai*] the form and movement of each consonant, and, with instinctive rhythms, I prided myself on inventing a poetic language accessible, some day, to all the senses. I reserved translation rights" (Rimbaud, 2005: 285).[15] Lastly, the poem itself, seeding its own "intellectual gold rush" (Robb 200: 136) is composed in the form of commentary or gloss, genres whose "loss . . . as creative forms" corresponds with the a-traditional nature of modernity as a situation in which the margin between the letter and the spirit of law is at once lost and exploded into omnipresence, where "there is a truth, without the possibility of transmitting it; there are modes of transmission, without anything being either transmitted or taught" (Agamben, 1993: 160). It is precisely this margin, in the formula of a synaesthesia whose "flavor of omniscience is almost tangible" (Robb 200: 136), that "Voyelles," in the sublime indifference of its own spontaneity, works to actualise and renew, wielding with perfect impotence and power the "irreparable fracture" in Western culture between "Law in its literalness and [in] its spiritual sense . . . between subject matter and truth content" (Agamben, 1993: 159–160).[16] When all is said and done – as if commentary ever finishes – what the poem sensibly produces is the actuality or pure fact of law, in other words, the truth of its own writing as an uncircumscribable source of real significance, no less a revelation "rising over a vast pilgrim city of critical commentary" (Robb, 2000: 137) than "an arbitrary and inchoate" (Cohn, 1973: 126) vision whose validity is its own whyless fact. As Verlaine observed, "*Moi qui ai connu Rimbaud, je sais qu'il se foutait pas mal si A était rouge ou vert. Il le voyait comme ça, mais c'est tout*" (Rimbaud 1960: 405) [I who knew Rimbaud know that he did not care at all whether A was red or green. He saw it that way, that's all].

Lex – A noir, E blanc, I rouge, U vert, O bleu

The first line gives the text of which the poem will become the first commentary, setting the vowels in order via a series of parallel appositions to colours. Crucially, the accordant juxtaposition equates vowel and colour without equating them, establishing a rule of correspondences which is of the nature of law itself as the principle of accord between disparate things. As the being of law is perforce occluded in the phenomenon of which it is the law, so the logic of apposition both is and is not an elision of the verb 'to be.' Between "A" and "noir," *is* is present by being absent and absent by being present. The beauty of apposition – a disclosure of the intersection between poetry and law – is that it expresses relation in a manner that encompasses all the modes of predication (univocity, equivocity, analogy). By means of apposition, the colours 'of' the vowels are thus given in the form of synaesthesia itself, in the pure withness of being side by side, next to each other in a space that embraces a continuum between identity and difference. On the one hand, the relation between each vowel and colour is fixed, determined as set down in a series without space for the terms to be otherwise. On the other hand, the relation between each vowel and colour is open, free to be otherwise precisely because the series has no immutability other than its own givenness, the fact of its being set down as such. This is expressible by saying that "*A noir*" translates simultaneously to 'A is black' and 'a black A,' that it signifies both as a definitive statement of the colour of the vowel and as simple picturing of a black letter A (which, befitting the firstness of the first letter, it also 'ironically' actually is, provided the ink is black). In other words, the verbal form of the line produces the paradox of perceptual binding which is conspicuously found in grapheme-colour synaesthesia, where the "synesthete . . . experience[s] print and synesthetic colour simultaneously, appearing in the same place without the two colours blending together" (Alvarez and Roberton, 2013: 317). Between the pre-established matrix of the five vowels and the innumerable spectrum of colour, between the alphabetical fixity of the letters and their writability in any pigment, there is thus a profound and essential play concerning the nature of law as the mutual binding of unity and multiplicity, a shimmering of the threshold between necessity and freedom. This shimmering may be understood as the interplay between the vertical and horizontal dimensions of the appositive series. As each vowel is bound into an order of horizontal succession (AEIUO), so each is also liberated vertically by free association with a colour. Law is equally the stricture of necessity and the condition of freedom, the synaesthetic inscription of a truth that is free of law.[17] The letters of the spirit that "blows [*pnei*, *spirat*] where it will" (John 3:8) resound with flying colours, fluttering spontaneously in the indefinable yet still systematic space of being, in the unbounded gap between the abstract concreteness of *what* is sensed and the concrete abstraction *that* it is. The unspoken first rule of "Voyelles" is that the sense of law is synaesthetic, just as, correlatively, "a broad spectrum of people share a set of underlying rules which systematically support cross-modal correspondences, felt either explicitly in synesthetes, or implicitly by everyone else" (Simner, 2013: 161).

Synaesthesia is the mystical or hidden sense of law in the sense that what law itself senses is freedom, just as synaesthesia manifests the inescapable freedom of sensation, the ecstatic capacity of the sense of sense to be otherwise than sense, whether in the form of a sensation of one sense by/as another or in the form of the 'suprasensory' sense *that* one is sensing (or that there is anything for that matter). Rimbaud's ruling of the vowels via the relative freedom of colour – a freedom mysteriously conditioned by the hidden rules of synaesthesia – partakes of the antinomian essence of law as a fact ruled by that which is beyond law, as an index of the hidden reality of the eternal individual or soul which, as Porete says, "is above the law/Not contrary to the law" (Porete, 1993: 196).[18] As Meister Eckhart affirms, "It is a certain and necessary truth that he who resigns his will wholly to God will catch God and bind God, so that God can do nothing but what that man wills" (Eckhart, 2009: 92). Like a pure literalisation of this ultimate, mystical double-bind of the individual and the infinite, self and reality, the line traces an open path of rectitude, walking from Alpha to Omega in the paradox of a straight circle. Each step of the line, namelessly naming vowel with colour, marks the threshold of law and freedom in two ways simultaneously, both by holding open the truth of the letter and by determining it, as I will now explain.

First, each colour functions as a simple or arbitrary marker of the pure fact or *that* of the vowels, a sign of the vowel before the vowel that is phenomenally occluded in the corporealisation of its becoming-letter. Here the synaesthesia of vowel and colour reflects the unseen first image of all seeing, the pure ground of perception to which perception is paradoxically blind. This is the non-imaginal image which for Bonaventure is no different from the purest being (*purissimum esse*) of divinity:

> How remarkable, then, is the blindness of the intellect which does not take note of that which it sees first, and without which it can know nothing. But just as the eye, when it is concerned with the variety of colours, does not see the light through which it sees other things . . . so the eye of our mind, intent as it is on particular and universal beings, pays no attention to that being which is beyond every genus even though it is that which first comes to the mind, and it is through this that all other things are known.
>
> (Bonaventure, 2002: 115)

Correlatively, the obscurity of the relation between colour and vowel indexes the immanent, invisible *seen* that passes unseen in perception, the dark light of seeing itself of which we see only the fact that we must be seeing it. Similarly, Eriugena defines the divine image within human nature, through which the "created world . . . is the vision of God – in both senses of the word" (Carlson, 2008: 94), as the mind's darkness to itself: "the Divine likeness in the human mind is most clearly discerned when it is only known that it is, and not known what it is . . . what it is denied in it [*negatur in ea quid esse*], and only that it is affirmed" (Eriugena, 1999–2000: IV.73). Being quite simply the presence or trace of unmasterable reality in the most familiar midst of sensible things, this ineradicable darkness wherein which all things are seen is at once a delight and a terror: "The horror is that we know that we see God in life itself" (Lispector, 1964: 154).[19] So in the sensing of all law there remains the sense, precisely through the very fact that law is being sensed, of something beyond law that will never be grasped as law, something like the first impossible unbound link in the chain of being which must be there in first place for there to be any binding of things at all. The senselessness of *A noir, E blanc, I rouge, U vert, O bleu* carries the weight of the dark, infinite gravity of finitude, the burden of the brute factical law of all things being as they are that is no less a sensing of the absolute freedom of reality. Such is the sublime profanity of law, the paradox that it is surpassable only in submission, that the realization of freedom "take[s] place only in the midst of life, for it is only in the midst of life that limitation can be experienced and transcended, and that subsequent freedom from limitation can be enjoyed" (Baba, 1967: III.13). Or as Agamben says, "The world – insofar as it is absolutely, irreparably profane – is God ... The root of all pure joy and sadness is that the world is as it is" (Agamben, 1993: 90).

Second, each colour functions no less as a determination and definition of the specific nature of the vowel, its *what*. For however arbitrary the association may appear, the fact remains that there is truth in it, whether because "everything resembles everything else up to a point" (Plato, 1961: 326) or because in some profound way, as Anaxagoras said, "everything is in everything" (Anaxagoras, 2007: 48). There is always, on one level or another, some actual relation between the vowel and the colour, a coincidence in their characters which cannot be disregarded as unreal because – sensibly, imaginally, or intellectually – it is actually there, manifest in the world inside and/or outside us. Whether we will or no, *A noir, E blanc, I rouge, U vert, O bleu* impresses us and makes its own immediate and palpable sense, striking the eyes of body and mind in certain way. Here the synaesthesia of vowel and colour reflects, not the general and ungraspable ground of sense, but its piercing specificity, the fact that in sensing things one cannot escape perceiving something in preference to all else. As per the concept of the "photograph's *punctum*" as "that accident which pricks me" (Barthes, 1980: 27), there is in sensation always some aspect of excessive intensity and proximity, the unaccountable focus of what causes an impression. In contrast to the first image which one always must be sensing but seemingly is not, the specificity or point of perception has the character of something one seemingly need not, but cannot help, sensing. This is the reverse paradox of the previous, that of limitation-in-freedom, of the fixity of seeing which, being free to see whatever is there, nevertheless binds itself to the rule of a specific and individual vision. And this too is a principle of mystical becoming. As Angela of Foligno says,

> true love ... does not say 'I am not held to any law,' but always subjects itself ever more to the law; and when there is no law, it makes its own law. For the love of God is never idle.
>
> (Angela, 1993: 229)

Likewise our perception of the world is saccadic, pulling itself in profound restlessness between impressional points of awareness, ruling the space of vision with the traces of the eye's own freedom.

In these two ways, the vowel-colour couplings of the first line, at once saying nothing and saying too much, signify as doubly reversible images of the freedom of law and the law of freedom, just as we may imagine the marginal space of appositional relation as functioning like an invisible mirror. More succinctly, synaesthesia has the *look* of law as the specular threshold of freedom. It is the face of the receptive-projective or intro-extromissive form of the binding of our senses to the world which, as the spiral path of experience shows, is forever and indistinguishably at once curving around necessity and swerving toward freedom. What matters here, as in all poetry, is *that* the line matters, that it bears authority in a manner which authorises its recognition as no less authoritative over *what* is recognised in it. Synaesthesia mirrors law as mirror of our senses, reflecting the element of freedom in our perception of laws, both in the sense that the form of law is necessarily regulated by our depth of vision and in the sense that freedom lies in governance of our perceptions, in observing – in both senses – their laws. As Dann recognises, "the meaning of synaesthesia is meaning" (Dann, 1998: 65). Just as "it is impossible for our intellect to understand anything actually, except by turning to the phantasms" (Aquinas, 1947–8: 429), which "are to the intellectual soul what colour is to the sight [*De Anima*, III.7]" (Aquinas, 1947–8: 431), so is there no law without poetry, and no rights, as Vico understood, without the masks of persons, the fictions of identity through which the voice of authority sounds (*per-sonare*).[20] In these terms, the five vowels, in accord with the synaestheic wheel or five-fold "mirror of sensible things [*speculum sensibilium*]" (Bonaventure, 2002: 62) through which one may realise the truth or "pass to God, the highest creative Artist" (Bonaventure, 2002: 53),[21] form the mirror wherein the voice of the poet – and the one who speaks by hearing it – sees reality, not only as what is mutely evident, but as what will be when it is more truly seen, as if for the first time. Synaesthesia and the law coincide in the blinding and binding specular nature of things, just as the poem ends with an ocular image of reality, of the eternal abyss that "gazes back into you" (Nietzsche, 1998: 68) – *rayon violet de Ses Yeux!* For, "whoever looks at himself in this mirror can have no help or remedy against seeing something which promptly causes him to fall in love" (de Meun, 1994: 25).

I will – *Je dirai quelque jour vos naissances latentes*

Rimbaud's poetically authoritative binding of the vowels to colours recapitulates – intentionally or not – Dante's etymological derivation in the *Convivio* of the concept of poetic authority from an obscure Latin verb, *auieo*:

> It should be known, then, that "authority" is nothing but "the pronouncement of an author [*atto d'autore*]." This word, namely "auctor" without the third letter c, has two possible sources of derivation. One is a verb that has very much fallen out of use in Latin and which signifies more or less "to tie words together," that is, "auieo." Anyone who studies it carefully in its first form [*ne la sua prima voce*] will observe that it displays its own meaning, for it is made up only of the ties of words, that is, of the five vowels alone, which are the soul and tie [*anima e legame*] of every word, and is composed of them in a different order, so as to portray the image of a tie. For beginning with A it turns back to U, goes straight through to I and E, then turns back and comes to O, so that it truly portrays this image: A, E, I, O, U, which is the figure of a tie. Insofar as "author" is derived and comes from this verb, it is used only to refer to poets who have tied their words together

> with the art of poetry [*arte musaica*]; but at present we are not concerned with this meaning [*al presente non s'intende*]. The other source from which "author" derives, as Uguccione attests in the beginning of his book *Derivations*, is a Greek word pronounced "autentin" which in Latin means "worthy of faith and obedience." Thus "author," in this derivation, is used for any person deserving of being believed and obeyed. From this comes the word which we are presently treating [*al presente si tratta*], namely "authority"; hence we can see that authority means "pronouncement [*atto*] worthy of faith and obedience."
>
> (Alighieri, 1990: IV.6)

The verb *auieo* does not in fact exist and appears – underscoring the binding force of the poetic word – to have been the invention of Uguccione da Pisa. The subtle manner in which the poet here handles his source, citing the canon lawyer for the official meaning of his discourse and not for the 'non-intended' or marginal point that clearly interests him more, makes the poetic interface of law and invention, the power of the word to "make it new" as Pound said, all the more conspicuous.[22] As critics have noted, this self-marginalizing and auto-commentarial gesture, like Dante's anonymous naming of himself as the notary of Love – "'*I' mi son un che, quando/Amor mi spira, noto, e a quell modo/ch'e' ditta dentro vo significando*'" (*Purgatorio* 24.52–4) [I in myself am one who, when Love breathes within me, take note, and to that measure which he dictates within, I go signifying] – only intensifies and magnifies the potent actuality of the poetic word, the depth of its gerundive power that, in living analogy with the divine, bears an authority higher than philosophical and imperial authority by virtue of being their very ground.[23] Dante's paraliptic pronouncement of *auieo* is on par with his response to Evangelist's request to "tell where your soul is focused [*s'appunta*]" (*Paradiso* 26.7–8): "The Good that satisfies this court [*corte*] is Alpha and O of all the writing [*scrittura*] that Love reads [*legge*] to me, whether soft or loud" (*Paradiso* 26.16–8). Similarly, "Voyelles" pronounces itself as something the poet will one day say, promising to say the reading that it is already and yet becoming. Like the self-doubling poet-pilgrim who makes his otherworldly journey "*per tornar altra volta/là dov' io son*" (*Purgatorio* 2.88–9) [to return another time there where I am], Rimbaud turns the synaesthetic wheel of his verse with the motion of a spirit that will speak for the first time what it already has. "We shall not cease from exploration/And the end of all our exploring/Will be. . . " (Eliot, 1943: 59).

Given the matrix of possible correspondences between the two poets' works, which has inspired the interpretation of one as the "code" of the other,[24] "Voyelles" may indeed be a manner of silent recitation and creative rebinding of Dante's spiritual concept of the vowels, a *rilettura* of his law of poetic authority, one whose authenticity per force lies in not tying itself to its historical source. Rimbaud's conspicuous reordering of the letters to preserve the symbolism of beginning and end around the axis of the I – "Ego sum Alpha et Omega" (Revelation 1:8) – does look to be a mirroring of Dante's verb of authority, in which the E and U are imaginally reversed: A-U-I-E-O -> A-E-I-U-O. But to explore the significance of such enchanting details is both outside our present intention and risks missing the point of their truth. For the force of poetic authority lies precisely in the invention of words whose significance at once precedes and exceeds their interpretation, in the production of senses and meanings so striking that they *exhaust* interpretation, in both senses. The truth of the poetic image lies in the power of its activity, in its being energetically more than itself, not restricted to its own binding. Its meaning is evental, found firstly in its actuality, the self-pronouncing fact *that* it goes signifying. In other words, just as Dante's *auieo* imaginally "displays its own meaning," as if delighting in the amplification of its own being which is the aim of all action,[25] the sense of the poetic word is synaesthetic in the sense of being a sensation impossibly at once distinguishable and indistinguishable from the fact that one is sensing it. Such is the too-palpable mystical dimension of the poetry, which realises at the level of sound and letters and breath the mind's highest visions, hiding in plain sight "things which do not have any images that are like them without actually being what they are" (Augustine, 2002: 470). And such is the word of law, whose authority, because it touches the hiddenness of first and last things, compels in a mystical manner, beyond affirmation and denial, so that to affirm and follow its truth one must also – and more importantly – deny it. As Pseudo-Dionysius writes in *The Mystical Theology*:

> Since it is the Cause of all beings, we should posit and ascribe to it all the affirmations we make in regard to beings, and, more appropriately, we should negate all these affirmations, since it surpasses all being. Now we should not conclude that the negations are simply the opposites of the affirmations, but rather that the cause of all is considerably prior to this, beyond privations, beyond every denial, beyond every assertion.
>
> (Pseudo-Dionysius, 1987: 136)

So in synaesthesia, one discerns the negative essence of freedom as the spontaneous capacity of things to be other than what they are, to as it were give birth to themselves beyond themselves, like Rimbaud's inspired vowels, in unforeseeable ways. In the dialetheic incoherence of synaesthetic awareness is reflected the immanent rule of the transcendent reality beyond being, the "law of the lawless Infinite. . . [which] is eternally real and at the same time illusory. . . [the] law that governs the universe – all its ups and downs" (Baba, 1973: 257–258). As Clarice Lispector's most "self-consciously fictional" (Moser, 2009: 357) and transparent avatar Angela Pralini says, "Coherence is mutilation . . . I only sense through a vehement incoherence" (Lispector, 1974: 98). Similarly, Rimbaud's phantasmagoric glossing of the vowels ultimately signifies less in the positivity of description than in the negativity of its distortion, in the fictive twist of the "dissimilar shape" through which, as the self-fabricating author of the *Celestial Hierarchy* testifies, the "mind. . . [is] provoked to get behind the material show, to get accustomed to the idea of going beyond appearances to those upliftings which are not of this world" (Pseudo-Dionysius, 1987: 153).

In the mysteriously generative and paradoxically superior definitiveness of negation is heard the secret intimacy of poetry and law, which in antiquity "are both *carmen* and both concerned with reading" (Lowrie, 2009: 327). For if on the one hand the word of law is haunted by its lack of power to govern the excessive sense and metaphoricity of its own text,[26] and on the other it is threatened – under its own imperative to control – with restriction to a meaning so coherent that it ceases to communicate the truth of its own command or show it as worthy of faith and obedience, then the invention of law is exactly a matter of a musicality that can rule sense beyond the letter from within it, the art of a formula whose performance preserves the essence and synaesthetic spirit of its perception in the first place. The authority of poetry and law intersect at the crossroads of definition, between the delight (and consolation) that music alone provides – "Only music gives definite answers" (Cioran, 1995: 80) – and the desperation (and conviction) out of which law is fashioned in the first place: "We define only out of despair. We must have a formula, we must even have many, if only to give justification to the mind and a façade to the void" (Cioran, 1975: 48). And so the hidden voice of poetry, grounded in the insight that "matter . . . owes its subsistence to absolute beauty" (Pseudo-Dionysius, 1987: 151), must continually return to turn the mind forward into the mystery its own present, towards the synaesthetic today that is missed by misreading the truths of physical nature as so many *thou-shalt-nots* or prohibitions of experience:

> Synesthetic perception the rule [*la règle*], and we are unaware of it only because scientific knowledge shifts the centre of gravity of experience, so that we have unlearned how to see, hear, and generally speaking, feel, in order to deduce, from our bodily organization and the world as the physicist conceives it, what we are [*que nous devons*] to see and hear and feel.
>
> (Merleau-Ponty, 2002: 237–238)

Correlatively, the synaesthetic work of the poetic word, vis-à-vis the sense of law, is to translate truth into will, to deregulate authority from the strictures of formulation and rebind law to the freedom of its own being. As Eckhart says, "The just man serves neither God nor creatures, for he is free, and the closer he is to freedom, the more he is freedom itself" (Eckhart, 2009: 130). This also means that the rule of synaesthesia, as universal law, makes the restriction of art to aesthetics illegal. For the light of synaesthesia exposes, no less subjectively than objectively, that the "distinction of beauty from utility is logical, not real (*in re*)" (Coomaraswamy, 1977: 25). As the very medium of sense, the principle whereby sensation can never be separated out from other orders of awareness, synaesthesia witnesses the inescapably rhetorical force of perception, how one is, whatever one's putative intentions, substantially moving and shaping oneself and others by how and what one chooses to sense, above all, by using or abusing the freedom of sensation itself. This is exemplified in a famous hadith, traditionally interpreted as a proscription of backbiting, which forms a perfect complement to Aristotle's classic example of the common sense as what discerns sweet from white (Gregoric, 2007: 165): "Jesus and his disciples passed by a dog's carcass. The disciples said, 'How foul is his stench!' Jesus said, 'How white are his teeth!" (Khalidi, 2001: 122). The sign of the poetically truer law is that, like Dante's *auieo*, it shows in itself the actuality of its truth, reflecting as in a mirror the immediate difficulty of following its path.

What, then, does Rimbaud's synaesthetic pronouncement give birth to? What is the latency of the vowels that it will one day speak? In a letter to a friend, the poet's vision stretches itself forth anagogically towards an impossible and inevitable future that is somehow already given, that *must* and *will* be:

> A language must be found . . . This language will be of the soul for the soul, containing everything, smells, sounds, colors, thought holding on to thought and pulling. The poet would define the amount of the unknown awakening in his time in the universal soul . . . Poetry will not lend its rhythm to action, it *will be in advance* [*en avant*]. These poets will exist.
>
> (Rimbaud, 2005: 379)

More recently, the philosopher Meillassoux has envisioned the immanent beyond of a 'fourth world,' a new order of beauty and justice that will without reason or cause emerge from the "three orders that mark the essential ruptures of becoming: matter, life, and thought" (quoted in Harman, 2011: 99). For Rimbaud, the future lies in the invention of a language that properly directs life, leads it in advance of itself, not by governance, but through universal mediation of the synaesthetic word. Likewise, "Voyelles" places its reader in the *midst* of its truth, as a third one who appears between the law and its commentary, at the interface and synthetic threshold of its significance.[27] And for Meillassoux, the advent of the fourth world – one whose formal correspondences to the traditional idea of the soul as the eternal life of three orders of sense and being (gross, subtle, mental) is clear[28] – lies in the self-invention of a "vectorial subject . . . a living passage between the thinking of this world and the justice of the ultimate world" (Meillassoux, 2010: 478). Like the visionary poet who writes between this world and the next, at the threshold of the known and the unknown, and like the mystic who becomes "neither oneself nor someone else" (Pseudo-Dionysius, 1987: 137), this subject is someone "turn[ing] oneself into a human being who is neither only 'here' (world 3) nor already 'there' (world 4) but who is *already between here and there*" (Meillassoux, 2010: 478). For both poet and philosopher, the pole of spiritual and material revolution is thus an individual who is also a synaesthete of law in the universal sense, one who, standing within-without the spokes of his own centre (see Figure 8.1), freely revolves with both hands the wheel of the order of things, turning the spin of time which has "the capacity to bring forth situations which were not at all contained in precedent situations" (Meillassoux, 2011: 232). This – as I see it – is the essential shape of the "pronouncement [*atto*] worthy of faith and obedience" to be seen in Rimbaud's vowels: that the violet beam from His or Her Eyes [*Ses Yeux*] is forever regulated, like the specular measure [*modo*] of Dante's amorous inspiration, according to the force and depth of one's own. However, the sense of this rule, and thus access to the universality of its realm, calls for a very different angle of vision than our passing world routinely demands, one that simultaneously "lives askance" (Lispector, 2012: 131) and yet refuses absolutely to see the individual as an epiphenomenon or mere secondary appearance in the margin of reality.

Notes

1 Classic expressions of this complex idea include the double law of charity on which "depend all the law and the prophets" (Matthew 22:40), also conceived as the "royal law" (James 2:8) and letter of the Spirit written "not on tablets of stone but on tablets of human hearts" (2 Corinthians 3:3); Boethius's metrum on love as "What binds [*ligat*] all things to order, / Governing earth and sea and sky" (Boethius, 1973: 227); and Dante's cosmic vision of "*l'amor che move il sole e l'altre stelle*" [Love that moves the sun and the other stars] (*Paradiso* 33.145). So law is generally definable as the inciting–restraining regulator of action – "Law is a rule and measure of acts, whereby man is induced to act or is restrained from acting: for *lex* (law) is derived from *ligare* (to bind), because it binds one to act" (Aquinas, 1947–8: 993 [*Summa Theologica*, I-II.90.1]) – or more universally as simply the ground of influence, the enclosure where cause and effect are bound to each other: "Where there is a law, one thing is able to influence another, whether it be a planet drawing apples towards its center, or a fire melting artworks, windows, and toys. A law means that one entity or field influences another in a specific way whenever these make the appropriate sort of contact" (Harman, 2011: 39–40). Together, the two sides of the equation of law and binding/attraction – law as love and love as law – reflect the inherent unity of reality: "Life and love are inseparable from each other. Where there is life, there is love. Even the most rudimentary consciousness is always trying to burst out of its limitations and experience some kind of unity with other forms. Though each form is separate from other forms, in reality they are all forms of the same unity of life. The latent sense for this hidden inner reality indirectly makes itself felt even in the world of illusion through the attraction which one form has for another form. The law of gravitation, to which all the planets and the stars are subject, is in its own way a dim reflection of the love which pervades every part of the universe" (Baba, 1967: I.156). On the sensorial logic of law as binding, see Nicola Masciandaro, "The Sweetness (of the Law)," *Non Liquet* (2013): 40–60.

2 As Derrida observes, "one cannot speak *directly* about justice, thematise or objectivise justice, say 'this is just' or even less 'I am just,' without immediately betraying justice, if not law (*droit*)" (Derrida, 1992: 10).

3 "God does everything and at the same time He does nothing. He leaves everything to the natural and supernatural forces prevalent in the spiritual panorama of the universe" (Baba, 1958: 38). Cf. Jane Clark, "'He Governs the World through Itself' – Ibn 'Arabi on Spiritual Causation" (www.ibnarabisociety.org.uk/podcasts/archives/1008/clark.mp3).

4 Aquinas defines eternal law as the *plan* of all laws, immanently operative through time's inescapable participation in eternity: "law denotes a kind of plan directing acts towards an end. Now wherever there are movers ordained to one another, the power of the second mover must needs be derived from the power of the first mover; since the second mover does not move except in so far as it is moved by the first . . . Since then the eternal law is the plan of government in the Chief Governor, all the plans of government in the inferior governors must be derived from the eternal law. But these plans of inferior governors are all other laws besides the eternal law. Therefore all laws, in so far as they partake of right reason, are derived from the eternal law. Hence Augustine says (*De Lib. Arb.* i, 6) that 'in temporal law there is nothing just and lawful, but what man has drawn from the eternal law'" (Aquinas, 1947–8: 996 [*Summa Theologica*, I-II.91.1]). Cf. "The mystery of the universe is hierarchic in structure. There are graded orders, one supervening upon the other. The spiritual panorama of the universe reveals itself as a gradient with laws upon laws. Superimposition of one type of law over the other implies elasticity and resilience of lower laws for the working out of higher superseding laws" (Baba, 1958: 33).

5 "Reality is Existence infinite and eternal. Existence has no purpose by virtue of its being real, infinite and eternal. Existence exists. Being Existence it has to exist. Hence Existence, the Reality, cannot have any purpose. It just is. It is self-existing. Everything – the things and the beings – in Existence has a purpose. All things and beings have a purpose and must have

a purpose, or else they cannot be in existence as what they are. Their very being in existence proves their purpose; and their sole purpose in existing is to become shed of purpose, i.e., to become purposeless" (Baba, 1963: 62).

6 The figure of the *spark* pertains in a special way to both synderesis and synaesthesia. "Just as the spark is that part of fire which is purer and hovers above the whole fire, so synderesis is that which is supreme in the judgment of conscience. And it is according to this metaphor that synderesis is called a spark of conscience" (Aquinas, 1994: 325 [*De veritate*, 17.2.3]). Similarly, synaesthetic experience, in the sense of sensing one kind sense as another, is associated with scintillation, as in Théophile Gautier's classic account of *audition colorée* – "the sounds gushed forth blue and red in a shower of electric sparks" (qtd. in Riccò, 2014: 167) – and the more specific phenomenon of the sound phosphene, "a type of synaesthesia characterised by a transient flash or spark of light . . . which is triggered by a sudden sound" (Blom, 2009: 480).

7 See Milner S. Ball, *Lying Down Together: Law, Metaphor, and Theology*, Madison, WI: University of Wisconsin Press, 1985; Dennis R. Klinck, "Metaphor," chapter 10 of *The Word of the Law: Approaches to Legal Discourse*, Ottawa: Carleton University Press, 1992; and Wendy Wheeler, "Delectable Creatures and the Fundamental Reality of Metaphor: Biosemiotics and Animal Mind," *Biosemiotics* 3 (2010): 277–287. William Wordsworth, in his *Preface to the Lyrical Ballads*, considering "the various causes upon which the pleasure received from metrical language depends," communicates the depth and breadth of the synaesthetic dimension and provides a sense of its operation as a power within all experience: "Among the chief of these causes is to be reckoned a principle which must be well known to those who have made any of the Arts the object of accurate reflection; namely, the pleasure which the mind derives from the perception of similitude in dissimilitude. This principle is the great spring of the activity of our minds, and their chief feeder. From this principle, the direction of the sexual appetite, and all the passions connected with it, take their origin: it is the life of our ordinary conversation; and upon the accuracy with which similitude in dissimilitude, and dissimilitude in similitude are perceived, depend our taste and moral feelings" (Wordsworth, 1876: II.95–96).

8 On synaesthesia and metaphor, see Lawrence E. Marks, *The Unity of the Senses: Interrelations among the Modalities* (New York: Academic Press, 1978), 181–255.

9 As the photographer Ansel Adams noted concerning a collaborative work, "the pictures do not illustrate the text, nor does the text describe the pictures. I prefer the term 'synaesthetic,' as two creative elements join to produce a third form of communication" (qtd. in Root-Bernstein, 1999: 303).

10 The maxim, reprising Jesus's statement that "The Sabbath was made [ἐγένετο, *factum est*] for man, not man for the Sabbath" (Mark 2:27), is founded on the produced or generated nature of law.

11 The etymological ambivalence – "*lex uno modo dicitur a legendo, alio modo a ligando*" (Alexander of Hales) – is fundamental to the Western concept of law and through the 17th century the "theological and philosophical currents divide themselves in many ways according to the two possible etymologies: on the one hand, a juridical law, that which is written and read (*lex<legere*) and, on the other hand, an eternal law, a law of nature (given and imposed by nature) which has particular characteristics and which is a rule for all of creation (*lex-<ligare*)" (Armogathe, 2008: 277).

12 As recorded in the *Greek Magical Papyri*, "Lord, I imitate you by [saying] the seven vowels, enter and hear me" (Betz, 1992: 189). The Neopythagorean mathematician Nicomachus of Gerasa defines the spiritual nature of the vowels in connection to the cosmic order as follows: "the tones of the seven sphere, each of which by nature produces a particular sound, are the sources of the nomenclature of the vowels . . . when they are combined with the materiality of the consonants, just as soul is combined with body . . . they have potencies which are efficacious and perfective of divine things" (translated in Shaw, 1995: 184). On

the vowels as divine name, see Naomi Janowitz, Naomi, *Icons of Power: Ritual Practices in Late Antiquity* (University Park, PA: Pennsylvania State University Press, 2002), 59–61.

13 Simplicius, in his commentary on Aristotle's *De Anima*, draws a proportional analogy between the fiveness of the hand's fingers and common sense in order to explain the perception of common perceptibles, attributes of objects (e.g., shape, magnitude, number) which are perceivable by more than one sense (Gregoric, 2007: 81).

14 See Nicola Masciandaro, "The Severed Hand: Commentary and Ecstasy," *English Language Notes* 50.2 (2013): 89–98. On the doubleness of the law of charity, see Jordan Kirk, "What Separates the Birth of Twins," *Glossator* 5 (2011): 1–18.

15 As Carruthers explains with respect to the classical and medieval concept of poetic and rhetorical *invenio*, "Having 'inventory' is a requirement for invention. Not only does this statement assume that one cannot create ('invent') without a memory store ('inventory') to invent from and with, but it also assumes that one's memory-store is effectively 'inventoried,' that its matters are readily-recovered 'locations'" (Carruthers, 1998: 12). Likewise, Rimbaud also simply creates the vowels' colours by listing them, by mnemonically counting them into a commentarial order of correspondence. Interestingly, the vowels play an important role as sites of recollection in premodern memory-craft. In the memory wheel of Giordano Bruno, invention and the vowels literally meet in the outermost ring, where the names of inventors are placed within radiating columns "all marked with the lettering of the thirty divisions of the wheels and subdivided into fives, marked with the vowels" (Yates, 1966: 214). Similarly, the jurist Peter of Ravenna's *Phoenix* outlines an "exacting technique for attaching images to individual syllables based on vowel location" (Engel et al., 2016: 50). The wheel is also an important medieval symbol of the unity of the senses, as figured in the "synaesthetic wheel" painting in Longthorpe Tower (Casagrande, 1985, 2004). Consciously or not, symbolist synaesthesia reprises associational forms invented in the mnemonic arts of premodern rhetoric and jurisprudence. As we may imagine Rimbaud's poem reimagined in the form of a memory wheel, so does the memory-theatre of Nature in Baudelaire's "Correspondances," a temple of "living columns [*vivant piliers*]" and "forest of symbols [*forêts de symbols*]" (Baudelaire, 1993: 19), provide the traditionally proper architectural form of "the *intercolumnia* often recommend as background for memory work" (Carruthers, 1998: 177).

16 Translation modified.

17 As Dante observes in the *Convivio*, the invention of written law is on par with the practice of the good whose essence has no need of law: "There are also activities which our reason contemplates as an act of the will, as for instance giving offense or assistance, standing ground or fleeing in battle, and remaining chaste or yielding to lust. These are completely subject to our will, and therefore we are considered good or evil, because they are completely of our own making; for as far as our will can reach, so far do our activities extend. Since in all of these voluntary activities justice must be preserved and injustice avoided, and this justice may be lost in two ways (either through not knowing what it is, or through not willing to follow it), written Law was invented [*trovata fu*] in order both to establish it and to administer it. So Augustine says, 'If men had known it (namely justice) and, when known, had observed it, there would have been no need of written Law.' Therefore it is written in the beginning of the Old Digest that 'Written law is the art of well-doing and justice'" (Alighieri, 1990: IV.9).

18 Cf. "When one escapes 'law', and merges in God who is beyond law, he becomes God. There is no binding . . . Law cannot touch him, but he touches law, grasps law, acts like an ordinary human being and uses power to make others free from law" (Baba, 1955: ch 33).

19 Cf. "The world – insofar as it is absolutely, irreparably profane – is God" (Agamben, 1993: 89).

20 "[A]ncient jurisprudence was throughout poetic. By its fictions what had happened was taken as not having happened, and what had not happened as having happened . . . It introduced so many empty masks without subjects, *iura imaginaria*, rights invented by imagination. It rested its entire reputation on inventing such fables as might preserve the gravity of

the laws and do justice to the facts . . . all the fictions of ancient jurisprudence were truths under masks . . . a severe poetry" (Vico, 1976: 390).

21 As Sikka explains, "for Bonaventure, the senses . . . provide the most basic information by means of which the God within the world is known. Through their mediation, the elements that make up the greater world, the *macrocosmos*, are reconstituted within its reflection in the lesser world, the *minor mundus* of the soul" (Sikka, 1997: 15).

22 Correlatively, Ezra Pound did not invent this dictum, but took it from an ancient Confucian text (North, 2013: 169–171).

23 "[E]ven as it apparently sets off poetry as a separate, and inferior, field of discourse, this definition makes poetry into the ground of all verbal discourse, and attributes to it the power to generate the totality of meanings through language. From this perspective, far from being inferior to the authority of the Philosopher and the Emperor, the poet's, rooted in language itself, is the constitutive ground out of which theirs arises . . . Dante's focus on vowels is ultimately related to their deliberate omission from the Tetragrammaton . . . to make the poet 'master of the vowels' is to make him a theologian, indeed more than Aquinas's theologian, and certainly more than any classical philosopher limited to the resources of human reason alone, since he is uniquely capable of 'filing in the blanks' in our knowledge and representation of God" (Ascoli, 2011: 118–119).

24 "*Cette these se propose de démontrer que le code . . . pour déchiffrer les image cryptiques de Rimbaud se trouve en dépôt dans l'oeuvre d'un autre poète – un poète qui . . . avait lui aussi . . . visé à atteindre la perception de l'inconnu*" (Frankel, 1975: 16). Frankel, without drawing a connection to Dante's *auieo*, interprets Rimbaud's later comments on "Voyelles," in his 'retraction' *Alchimie du Verbe*, as part of his confession of having been enchanted – "*je croyais à tous les enchantements. J'inventai la couleur des voyelles!*" (Rimbaud, 2005: 284) – by Dante's vision (Frankel, 1975: 204).

25 "For in all action what is principally intended by the agent, whether he acts by natural necessity or voluntarily, is the disclosure or manifestation of his own image. Whence it happens that every agent, insofar as he is such, takes delight. For, because everything that is desires its own being and in acting the being of an agent is in a certain way amplified, delight necessarily follows" (Alighieri, 1965: I.13.2–3).

26 "The problem of textuality is not nonsense, but too much sense. One might say that control of meaning is the first meaning, the origin or arche of law: *logos* . . . . But what of the weakness of the logos? The weakness of the logos, or of the law, is just that, starting with itself, it cannot bring everything under control" (Bruns, 1992: 29).

27 On the relation between mediation and rule, see Alexander R. Galloway, "Love of the Middle," in *Three Inquiries in Media and Mediation* (Chicago: University of Chicago Press, 2014).

28 For example, Augustine understands eternal life as a perfection of vision that synthesises, at once transcending and remaining within, the three levels of perception we now experience and utilise more darkly: "Then, you see, all things will be crystal clear and out in the open without any false impressions, distributed without any ignorance in their respective orders, the bodily, the spiritual and the intellectual, in perfect bliss with their natures entire and undiminished" (Augustine, 2002: 506). Similarly, in the four-fold medieval scheme of scriptural exegesis, the mystical or anagogical sense, termed the "foretaste of paradise," is the "locus of intellectual synaesthesia" (McLuhan, 2015: 10) wherein the other senses (literal, moral, allegorical), which also correspond to the physical, spiritual, and intellectual levels of being, are synthesised and led beyond themselves into the real presence of what they signify.

Bibliography

Agamben, Giorgio, *The Coming Community*, trans. Michael Hardt, Minneapolis: University of Minnesota Press, 1993.

Agamben, Giorgio, *The Man Without Content*, trans. Georgia Albert, Stanford: Stanford University Press, 1999.

Agamben, Giorgio, *Infancy and History: On the Destruction of Experience*, trans. Liz Heron, London:Verso, 1993.
Alighieri, Dante, *De monarchia*, ed. Pier Giorgio Ricci,Verona: Mondadori, 1965.
Alighieri, Dante, *Il convivio (The banquet)*, trans. Richard H. Lansing, New York: Garland, 1990.
Alighieri, Dante, *Divine Comedy*, ed. and trans. Robert M. Durling, 3 vols., Oxford: Oxford University Press, 2011.
Alvarez, Bryan D. and Roberton, Lynn C., "Synesthesia and Binding," in *The Oxford Handbook of Synesthesia*, eds. Julia Simner and Edward M. Hubbard, Oxford: Oxford University Press, 2013.
Anaxagoras of Clazomenae, *Fragments and Testimonia*, trans. Patricia Curd, Toronto: University of Toronto Press, 2007.
Angela of Foligno, *Complete Works*, trans. Paul Lachance, New York: Paulist Press, 1993.
Aquinas, Thomas, *Summa Theologica*, trans. Fathers of the English Dominican Province, New York: Benzinger Brothers, 1947–48.
Aquinas, Thomas, *Truth, Volume II: Questions X-XX*, trans. James V. McGlynn, S.J. Indianapolis: Hackett, 1994.
Aristotle, *Basic Works*, ed. Richard McKeon, New York: Random House, 1941.
Armogathe, Jean-Robert, "Deus Legislator," in *Natural Law and Laws of Nature in Early Modern Europe : Jurisprudence, Theology, Moral and Natural Philosophy*, eds. Lorraine Daston and Michael Stolleis, Burlington, VT: Ashgate, 2008.
Ascoli, Albert Russell, *Dante and the Making of a Modern Author*, Cambridge: Cambridge University Press, 2011.
Augustine, *Letters, Volume 4 (165–203)*, trans. Sister Wildrid Parsons, Washington, DC: Catholic University of America Press, 1955.
Augustine, *On Genesis*, trans. Edmund Hill, O. P., Hyde Park, NY: New City Press, 2002.
Baba, Meher, *God to Man and Man to God: The Discourses of Meher Baba*, ed. C. B. Purdom, London: Gollancz, 1955.
Baba, Meher, *Beams from Meher Baba on the Spiritual Panorama*, San Francisco: Sufism Reoriented, 1958.
Baba, Meher, *The Everything and the Nothing*, Beacon Hill, Australia: Meher House Publications, 1963.
Baba, Meher, *Meher Baba Calling*, eds. Jamshed B. Mistry and J. Flagg Kris, Woombye, Australia: Meher Baba Foundation, 1964.
Baba, Meher, *Discourses*, 6th ed., 3 vols., San Francisco: Sufism Reoriented, 1967.
Baba, Meher, *God Speaks: The Theme of Creation and Its Purpose*, 2nd ed., New York: Dodd, Mead & Co., 1973.
Badiou, Alain, *St. Paul: The Foundation of Universalism*, trans. Ray Brassier, Stanford: Stanford University Press, 2003.
Barthes, Roland, *Camera Lucida: Reflections on Photography*, trans. Richard Howard, New York: Hill and Wang, 1980.
Bergeron, Katherine, *Decadent Enchantments: The Revival of Gregorian Chant at Solesmes*, Berkeley: University of California Press, 1998.
Betz, Hans Dieter, *The Greek Magical Papyri in Translation, Including the Demotic Spells, Volume 1: Texts*, Chicago: University of Chicago Press, 1992.
Blom, Jan Dirk, *A Dictionary of Hallucinations*, New York: Springer, 2009.
Boethius, *Consolation of Philosophy*, trans. S. J. Tester, Cambridge, MA: Harvard University Press, 1973.
Bonaventure, *Itinerarium Mentis in Deum*, trans. Zachary Hayes, Saint Bonaventure, NY: Franciscan Institute, 2002).
Bruns, Gerald L., "Law and Language: A Hermeneutics of the Legal Text," in *Legal Hermeneutics: History, Theory, and Practice*, ed. Gregory Leyh, Berkeley: University of California Press, 1992.
Carlson, Thomas A., *The Indiscrete Image: Infinitude and Creation of the Human*, Chicago: University of Chicago Press, 2008.

Carruthers, Mary, *The Craft of Thought: Meditation, Rhetoric, and the Making of Images, 400–1200*, Cambridge: Cambridge University Press, 1998.
Casagrande, Gino, "The Wheel of the Five Senses in Longthorpe Tower," 2004, http://www.gicas.net/wheel.html.
Casagrande, Gino and Kleinhenz, Christopher, "Literary and Philosophical Perspectives on the Wheel of the Five Senses in Longthorpe Tower," *Traditio* 41 (1985): 311–27.
Cioran, E. M., *A Short History of Decay*, trans. Richard Howard, New York: Arcade, 1975.
Cioran, E. M., *Tears and Saints*, trans. Ilinca Zarifopol-Johnston, Chicago: University of Chicago Press, 1995.
Coomaraswamy, A. K., *Traditional Art and Symbolism*, ed. Roger Lipsey, Princeton: Princeton University Press, 1977.
Dann, Kevin T., *Bright Colours Falsely Seen: Synaesthesia and the Search for Transcendental Knowledge*, New Haven: Yale University Press, 1998.
Davies, Paul, *About Time: Einstein's Unfinished Revolution*, New York: Simon & Schuster, 1995.
Derrida, Jacques, "Force of Law," tr., Mary Quaintance, in *Deconstruction and the Possibility of Justice*, eds. Drucilla Cornell, Michael Rosenfeld, and David Gray Carlson, New York: Routledge, 1992.
Pseudo-Dionysius, *The Complete Works*, trans. Colm Luibheid, New York: Paulist Press, 1987.
Eckhart, Meister, *The Complete Mystical Works*, trans. Maurice O' C Walshe, New York: Herder & Herder, 2009.
Eliot, T. S., *The Four Quartets*, New York: Harcourt, 1943.
Engel, William E., Rory Loughnane, and Grant Williams, ed. *The Memory Arts in Renaissance England: A Critical Anthology*, Cambridge: Cambridge University Press, 2016.
Eriugena, John Scotus, *Periphyseon (De Divisione Naturae)*, eds. I. P. Sheldon-Williams and Édouard A. Jeauneau, trans. John. J. O'Meara, 4 vols., Dublin: Dublin Institute for Advanced Studies, 1999–2009.
Frankel, Margherita, *Le code Dantesque dans l'oeuvre de Rimbaud*, Paris: Nizet, 1975.
Gadamer, Hans-Georg, *The Relevance of the Beautiful and Other Essays*, trans. by Nicholas Walker, ed. by Robert Bernasconi, Cambridge: Cambridge University Press, 1986.
Gregoric, Pavel, *Aristotle on the Common Sense*, Oxford: Oxford University Press, 2007.
Harman, Graham, *Quentin Meillassoux: Philosophy in the Making*, Edinburgh: Edinburgh University Press, 2011.
Hegel, G. W. F., *The Phenomenology of Mind*, trans. J. B. Baillie, New York: Dover, 2003.
Heller-Roazen, *The Inner Touch: Archaeology of a Sensation*, New York: Zone Books, 2007.
Khalidi, Tarif, The Muslim Jesus: Sayings and Stories in Islamic Literature, Cambridge, MA: Harvard University Press, 2001.
Lispector, Clarice, *The Passion According to G. H.*, trans. Idra Novey, New York: New Directions, 1964.
Lispector, Clarice, *Soulstorm*, trans. Alexis Levitin, New York: New Directions, 1974.
Lispector, Clarice, *A Breath of Life*, trans. Johnny Lorenz, New York: New Directions, 2012.
Lowrie, Michèle, *Writing, Performance, and Authority in Augustan Rome*, Oxford: Oxford University Press, 2009.
Luhmann, Niklas, "The Unity of the Legal System," in *Autopoietic Law: A New Approach to Law and Society*, ed. Gunther Teubner, Berlin: de Gruyter, 1988.
Marks, Lawrence E., "Synaesthesia: Perception and Metaphor," in *Aesthetic Illusion: Theoretical and Historical Approaches*, eds. Frederick Burwick and Walter Pape, Berlin: de Gruyter, 1990.
McLuhan, Eric, *The Sensus Communis, Synesthesia, and the Soul: An Odyssey*, Toronto: BPS, 2015.
Meillassoux, Quentin, *After Finitude: An Essay on the Necessity of Contingency*, trans. Ray Brassier, London: Continuum, 2008.
Meillassoux, Quentin, "The Immanence of the World Beyond," in *The Grandeur of Reason: Religion, Tradition, and Universalism*, eds. Conor Cunningham and Peter Candler, London: SCM Press, 2010.

Meillassoux, Quentin, "Potentiality and Virtuality," in *The Speculative Turn: Continental Materialism and Realism*, eds. Levi Bryant, Nick Srnicek and Graham Harman, Melbourne: re.press, 2011.
Merleau-Ponty, Maurice, Phenomenology of Perception, trans. Colin Smith, London: Routledge, 2002.
de Meun, Jean and de Lorris, Guillaume, *Romance of the Rose*, trans. Francis Horgan, Oxford: Oxford University Press, 1994.
Moser, Benjamin, *Why This World: A Biography of Clarice Lispector*, Oxford: Oxford University Press, 2009.
Nietzsche, Friedrich, *Daybreak: Thoughts on the Prejudices of Morality*, ed. Maudemarie Clark and Brian Leiter, Cambridge: Cambridge University Press, 1997.
Nietzsche, Friedrich, *Beyond Good and Evil: Prelude to a Philosophy of the Future*, trans. Marion Faber, Oxford: Oxford University Press, 1998.
North, Michael, *Novelty: A History of the New*, Chicago: University of Chicago Press, 2013.
Peirce, Charles Sanders, *The Essential Peirce: Selected Philosophical Writings, Volume 2 (1893–1913*, ed. Peirce Edition Project, Bloomington: Indiana University Press, 1998.
Philippopoulos-Mihalopoulos, Andreas, *Niklas Luhmann: Law, Justice, Society*, New York: Routledge, 2010.
Philippopoulos-Mihalopoulos, Andreas, "Atmospheres of Law: Senses, Affects, Lawscapes," *Emotion, Space and Society* 7 (2013): 35–44.
Plato, *The Collected Dialogues of Plato*, eds. Edith Hamilton and Huntington Cairns, Princeton: Princeton University Press, 1961.
Porete, Marguerite, *The Mirror of Simple Souls*, trans. Ellen L. Babinsky, New York: Paulist, 1993.
Robb, Graham, *Rimbaud*, New York: Norton, 2000.
Riccò, Dina, "Scientific Production on Synaesthesia," in *Synaesthesia: Theoretical, Artistic and Scientific Foundations*, eds. María José de Córdoba, Dina Riccò, Sean A Day, Grenada: International Foundation Artecittà, 2014.
Ricoeur, Paul, *The Rule of Metaphor: The Creation of Meaning in Language*, trans. Robert Czerny, Kathleen McLaughlin, and John Costello, London: Routledge, 1977.
Rimbaud, Arthur, *OEuvres*, ed. S. Bernard. Paris: Garnier, 1960.
Rimbaud, Arthur, *Rimbaud: Complete Works, Selected Letters*, trans. Wallace Fowlie, Chicago: University of Chicago Press, 2005.
Root-Bernstein, Robert and Michèle, *Sparks of Genius*, Boston: Houghton Mifflin, 1999.
Schröder, Jan, "The Concept of (Natural) Law in the Doctrine of Law and Natural Law of the Early Modern Era," in *Natural Law and Laws of Nature in Early Modern Europe: Jurisprudence, Theology, Moral and Natural Philosophy*, eds. Lorraine Daston and Michael Stolleis, Burlington, VT: Ashgate, 2008.
Shaw, Gregory, *Theurgy and the Soul: The Neoplatonism of Iamblichus*, University Park, PA: Pennsylvania State University Press, 1995.
Sikka, Sonya, *Forms of Transcendence: Heidegger and Medieval Mystical Theology*, Albany, NY: State University of New York Press, 1997.
Spencer-Brown, George, *Laws of Form*, London, Allen & Unwin, 1969.
Simner, Julia, "The 'Rules' of Synesthesia," in *The Oxford Handbook of Synesthesia*, eds. Julia Simner and Edward M. Hubbard, Oxford: Oxford University Press, 2013.
Stepien, Katarzyna, "Synderesis and the Natural Law," *Studia Gilsoniana* 3 (2014): 377–398.
Vico, Giambattista, *The New Science*, trans. Thomas Goddard Bergin and Max Harold Fisch, Ithaca, NY: Cornell University Press, 1976.
Weber, Andreas, *Biopoetics: Towards an Existential Ecology*, Dordrecht: Springer, 2016.
Wittgenstein, Ludwig, *Tractatus Logico-Philosophicus*, tr. C.K. Ogden [Mineola, NY: Dover Publications, 1998], 6.44.
Wordsworth, William, *The Prose Works of William Wordsworth*, ed. Alexander B. Grosart, 3 vols., London: Edward Moxon, 1876.

9

Touching you, touching me in law and justice

Toward a quantum holographic process-informational understanding

Dragan Milovanovic

Introduction

What does it mean to be in touch when doing law? This chapter concerns the metaphysics of touching in law and new directions in understanding its physicality, as well as potentially new directions to centre positive emotions and holistic thought. We advocate a critical confrontation with Newtonian-based ontologies and their replacement by a quantum holography orientation. Can we develop alternative vistas cultivating a socius based on positive emotions? How can touch be seen more in terms of being in tune, that is, in resonance? What vistas are opened for a transformative justice?

Formal rationality has enabled liberation from the dark ages and some of the injustices that characterised those eras. However, without further development and adaptation to new data, formal rationality can become an impediment in terms of the law, and it risks outgrowing its usefulness. The post-Enlightenment privileging of a Newtonian ontology is being challenged by quantum holographic theory. Through this theory, the sensorial, so far repressed as contrary to the principles of logic, rationality, and utilitarianism, is finding a new basis in the reconceptualisation of consciousness, social constructions, and becoming. This chapter concerns the contributions of quantum holography to law, with particular focus on touch, and the recently discovered role of the heart as a sense organ.

Karen Barad (2015: 153) asks, in the act of touch, "what is the measure of closeness?" and "which disciplinary knowledge formations . . . do not have a stake in, if not a measured answer to, this question?" The traditional legal answer is operationalised in assault and battery prohibitions. Whereas battery generally entails some illegal contact, assault does not necessitate it, but does require some act. Battery entails some contact that is intentional, harmful, or offensive, where no consent by the victim exists.[1] We shall extend this notion of touch to investigate biosocioemotional forms of contact based on a quantum holographic ontology, insomuch as all entities are fundamentally wave-emitting and wave-absorbing complexities as well as intra-actively interconnected becomings.

In section II we will highlight the relation of the sensorial to law by way of a holographic lens, particularly looking at the mechanism for accessing and decoding information (PCAR, phase conjugate adaptive resonance) and how perception images ("logons") are created; the role of the heart as a generator of bioemotional waves and their effects; and a model of an inter- and intra-subjectively constituted subject in Schema QD and relation to bioemotionally constituted perception images in law. We then (section III) move to Karan Barad's insightful work on touch and revise her work on emotionality along with applying key concepts drawn from Deleuze and Guattari and by incorporating our Schema QD and other concepts from the previous section. An emergent justice is suggested by way of Levinas and Barad, but is revised with a quantum holographic orientation. Our final section (IV) looks at touch and resonance as a basis for a transformative justice.

Sensorial and law: quantum holographic view

Law practice regularly restricts expressions of the sensorial that are usually found at dynamic play in the constitution of "reality." Juridical disciplinary mechanisms render the multiple possibilities inhering in being human a uni-accentuation, normalised within a universality. The task before us is to bring back the multiple sensorial dimensions that are constitutive of agency in a dynamic societal order, a "socioemotional field." The quantum holographic mechanism of phase conjugate adaptive resonance offers key insights for the understanding of the role of senses in agency. Marcer et al. (1998, 2011) have already suggested that PCAR is applicable to all the sense organs. Let us first briefly indicate the relationship of PCAR to Schema QD and the generation of logons or "space time constrained quanta of information." We will then move onto the work of Bradley and Barad before we turn to law, touch, and the potentials for transformative justice.

i. PCAR and logons

PCAR is the mechanism by which holographically encoded information embedded in the bioemotional field[2] is accessed, decoded, and the latter projected "out there" as "reality." It is a two-way process. All entities are vibratory, emitting distinct frequency patterns reflective of their states.[3] Absorbers of these wave-forms decode the patterns, match them with memory stores, collapse the possibilities to one, and send this information back "out there" via a "conjugate wave" along the same pathway ("standing wave") as the incoming wave-form. "Reality" is constituted "out there" in the process. Schema QD (section iii) suggests that there is an inter- and intra-subjectively constituted entity that takes up residence in various discursive regions and contexts, from where an "I" as a particle-form and an object are instantiated. A distinct signature wave is constantly being emitted by each person encoding information about themselves, which is equivalent to a "reference beam" that accesses holographically encoded information in the ambient field, an "in-formation" field[4] (Laszlo, 2007). As Bradley (2007, 2016b) has demonstrated, contrary to classical holography where there is one-to-one correspondence between the reconstructed virtual image and the entity or phenomenon, quantum holography, following the work of Dennis Gabor (1946) and relying on Heisenberg's (1949)[5] uncertainty principle, states that perception images constructed are better conceived as "logons," "spacetime constrained quanta of information." Bradley's (2016a) recent work also shows that these logons embed bioemotional wave-forms emanating from the heart.

Briefly, logons, termed by the Nobel Prize recipient Dennis Gabor (1946),[6] are particular "cuts" of otherwise flows, fluxes, and intensities encoded as interference patterns[7] in the ambient (holographic) field. These "cuts" are depicted as sinusoids (sine waves). The mathematical construction entails positing two interacting but orthogonal dimensions: the everyday spacetime domain in which we navigate, and the spectral domain where interference patterns ("Fourier coefficients") are created that reflect the evolving configural relations found in the spacetime domain. These interference patterns are also dynamic holograms.[8] At the intersections of the two dimensions a sinusoid is generated, reflecting changing configural relations and their encoding as spectra. It is on this developing wave-form that we can make distinct cuts representing snapshots of reality. There are minimal limits to cuts by which information is recognisable. They represent, again, changing configural patterns in the spacetime domain, which in their turn can be represented by spectra. In other words, oscillation patterns can be encoded based on frequency, amplitude, and phase. Since configural patterns are constantly changing, so too must spectra reflect their intersecting wave-forms. Thus, employing Heisenberg's uncertainty principle, we can with some precision capture *either* the movement as a whole *or* particular moments, but not both simultaneously. Moreover, the eye has been found to operate according to the Fourier transforms, a procedure by which the "out there," everyday activity in the spacetime domain, along with its constantly changing configural patterns, is transformed into frequency patterns in the spectral domain.[9] A reverse Fourier transform converts interference patterns (Fourier coefficients) in the spectral domain into images projected back to the spacetime domain.

The additional process of PCAR produces standing waves between the vibratory emissions "out there" and a backward time referral wave due to the inner working processes of the brain along which information is channelled.[10] It is the inter- and intra-subjective dynamics of Schema QD, to which we shall turn in section iii, that shapes these spectral patterns producing logons that are then projected out there, constituting reality.

Bradley's (2007, 2016a, 2016b) insights add a bioemotional wave representing emotionality originating in the heart, pre-dating brain and conscious development, that infuses all logons with degrees of emotionality, as we shall see below. The question of consciousness and agency in law is often a question reduced to calculation, categorical definitions, formal rationality, and disembodied subjects. In order to provide a model that is quantum holographically informed, we follow Barad's (2010: 8, emphasis in original) observation:

> [A]gency . . . is not something that someone or something *has* to varying degrees . . . agency is not held, it is not a property of persons or things: rather, agency is an enactment, a matter of possibilities for reconfiguring entanglements. So agency is not about choice in any liberal humanist sense; rather, it is about the possibilities and accountability entailed in reconfiguring material-discursive apparatuses of bodily production, including the boundary articulations and exclusions that are marked by those practices.

In an interview (2012), Barad acknowledges shying away from the "*how* of agency." To this we turn and build. In addressing this question, namely the "how of agency," the work of Bradley and that of developers of the notion of PCAR is most relevant as contributing to our conceptualisation of agency in Schema QD. We first turn to Bradley's work.

ii. Bioemotional field and the role of the heart

Raymond Bradley's (2007, 2016a, 2016b) innovative theorising in quantum holography and its application to the social has suggested the functionality of the heart in shaping brain and mind. The HeartMath Institute, with which Bradley is affiliated, has produced some convincing empirical research (see McCraty et al., 2009) which demonstrates that the heart is more than an organ pumping blood; it is also the largest generator of electromagnetic waves, 5,000 times more powerful than those of the brain, that can be registered up to 6 feet away.[11] This wave-form holographically encodes bioemotional information.[12] That is, a variety of emotional states have associated particular measurable patterns of heart rhythms which radiate in every direction (Bradley, 2016a: 45; McCraty et al., 2009).[13] Bradley demonstrates that the wave-forms emitted by the heart register incoming perturbations *prior* to the brain. The brain then responds, and consciousness follows.

The heart wave-forms differ in the form of emotional display. The two identified by the HeartMath Institute are positive and negative emotions. Positive emotions, such as appreciation and love, produce heartbeat patterns that are "smooth, ordered, coherent." They produce an organised emitting (electromagnetic) wave measureable by spectral analysis.[14] Negative emotions, such as frustration, anxiety, or anger, on the other hand, produce heartbeats that are "erratic, disordered, incoherent patterns" registered by a correspondingly erratic electromagnetic field.

Bradley and his colleagues have suggested that positive emotions are connected to a highly efficient state called "psychophysiological coherence." In this state, one is highly attuned to the socioemotional in-formation field of the group.[15] That is, a greater sensitivity to and awareness of others prevails. "When the movement of energy is intentionally regulated to form a coherent, harmonious order," McCraty et al.

(2009) argue, "information integrity and flow are optimized. This, in turn, produces a stable, effective system function, which enhances health, psychosocial well-being, and intentional action in the individual or social group." Bradley (2016a, and forthcoming: 134) argues heart-to-heart information flows optimally in states of entrainment and coherence, such as in close friendship and love.[16]

Bradley (2007) has shown how greater possibilities of intuitive practices result. "Passionate attention," as a form of love, can be conceptualised as a reference beam that provides a pathway to nonlocal information and intuitive practices. This wave-form[17] intersects with incoming wave-forms to produce interference patterns. Continued practice, in turn, produces a phase transition to even a higher "positive emotional hyper-state" referred to as "emotional quiescence" (Bradley, 2016c, 2016a, 127, 261) which has a distinctly different form to that of psychophysiological coherence. During this state, contrary to Freud's (2010) rejection of an "oceanic feeling," one witnesses a "deep sense of inner peace," a deeper sense of harmony, and a pathway to accessing universal consciousness. We will return to this shortly. First, let's visit Bradley's notion of a socio-affectional field and how it relates to touch and law.

Bradley applies his analysis to group formations and solidarity. Ongoing interactions (we prefer, following Barad, "intra-actions")[18] generate continuous patterns of interference patterns which capture the configural relations of the group. These are encoded within the group's socioaffective field, and also within members' brains as holograms. Members continuously engage in matching incoming wave-forms of the group with their internalised holograms, creating the sense of a distinct group. Where resonance, a sense of being in tune (touch), exists, a collective consciousness of the group is prevalent. Members remain continuously in touch, attuned to this socioaffective field.

In a group with high positive emotions, we would surmise that more heart-to-heart intra-actions take form; that is, following Bradley and McCraty et al. (2009), emotionality associated with the heart precedes brain recognition, that in turn precedes consciousness. A field marked by negative emotions would reduce mutually responsive intra-actions (touching the Other, being touched by the Other). Heart wave-forms that then trigger brain activity would be more erratic, disorganised, unfocused. Brain activity would work less efficiently and be greatly denied intuitive forms of thought as well as pathways toward community solidarity. Lacking in bonds of solidarity, mutual respect, and support, it would seem, then, that in this state there would be a greater demand for social control, à la Leviathan, with due process safeguards rooted in formal rational forms of logic and abstractions (such as the juridical subject in the form of the reasonable man in law). It would also seem more likely that in conditions of overly competitive utilitarian capitalism, increased state capture and axiomatisation (Deleuze and Guattari, 1987) would find justification and support. In this process, the "law machine" as one form of abstract machines (Deleuze and Guattari, 1987, 2006) would have full hold; indeed, not only self-justifying and hegemonic, but also creating the subjects it needs – the "criminal justice system" producing deviants (Milovanovic, 2014b).

Bradley (2016a, forthcoming) conceives a group as a distinct bounded field or "sphere of operation." However, boundaries are better identified by incorporating the cosmologist's understanding of the holographic principle[19] as encoding all information of the internal bulk, as well as providing the basis of optic arrays[20] that flood the interior. Group members access and decode this information (now knowledge) and project it back "out there" into the bulk sphere as the reality of the group via PCAR. This accessing is a form of touching. Schema QD tells us about the role of the inter- and intra-subjective ethical and moral agent shaping logons by her/his powers of "response-ability" (Barad, 2015). There remains both choice in the nuanced form of reality construction and the influence of configural patterns of the group contributory to the final shape of logons.

iii. Schema QD, PCAR and bioemotionally constituted perception images and subjects in law

Diagrammatically, Schema QD[21] is composed of four relationally constituted entities in dynamic evolution that produce a distinct signature wave.[22] It is an intra- and intersubjectively constituted ethical/moral subject, modelled, following modifications of Jacques Lacan's (1977) Schema R, as Schema QD. Four core components[23] of the subject (ego, ego-ideal, Other, and community generalised other) are situated on each corner of a Möbius band. This band, in turn, is the fundamental cell of the topological construct called a cross-cap. For Lacan, as well as for this author, it depicts the dynamic states of instantiated subjectivity. That is, each figure-eight "cut," a tracing of the outlines of a Möbius band, executed on the cross-cap[24] produces the dynamics for the momentary appearance of a particular perception (Lacan's *realité*), more a logon, a trace of which remains encoded within the socioaffective in-formation field.[25] This is accommodative of Barad's notion of an "agential cut" – not a Cartesian cut, but rather a cut connected by ongoing intra-actions. Perceptions arise with the ongoing inter- (intra-) relations of these four components and their combined shaping effects. A particular "I" of discursive production as well as a particular object appears in process. Prior to an instantiation, we have wave-forms in existence reflecting potential states of the subject. Each person's unique Schema QD signature wave is constantly emitted outward in wave-form, holographically encoding all information about the person. The signature wave[26] is a "reference beam" that accesses the in-formation field and, with the dynamics of Schema QD informed by bioemotional heart wave-forms, decodes the embedded information via PCAR constituting knowledge. A co-constitutive intra-active performative discursive practice culminates the constitution of particle-forms (objects with bounded identities and properties) and the momentary appearance of a distinct self-determining individual, an "I" that takes up residence in discursive production.

At rest, an attractor state prevails. With perturbation by some externally emitting source, signature waves are modulated and encoded information retains a trace at the quantum level with that which it intra-acts. The bioemotional heart wave-form first responds to incoming waves, whose registration of the information is modulated and then spreads in all directions, including the brain.[27] Consciousness of the event has not yet been registered. The relational dynamics of the four primary components of Schema QD produce distinctive matrices, each matrix with a distinct modulated signature wave. With incoming wave-forms from an emitter, these interact producing a conjugate wave backward in time to the emitter, a channel ("standing wave") for information flow. A number of images/perceptions become momentarily constituted in a state of coherence in a superposition state. It is with the ever-present primordial heart wave that this superposed state is hypercathected,[28] instantiating[29] one of the images, now a particle-form, which is information sent back to the emitting source.

With a perception image (along with an "I") now instantiated in particle-form, societal or subcultural "templates for action" (scripts, action schemas, sensorimotor schemas) are activated for action. These, too, initially appear in superposition form from which one is instantiated as a particle-form; that is, the particle-form becomes the basis of actual activity. In law, the world of fiction and mass media increasingly provide the material from which action patterns are created (see Sherwin, 2011). Fact and fiction become indistinguishable, a Baudrillardian hyperreal. In our schema, logons.

But how precisely is this encoded information accessed and decoded? To update the argument, the key is the notion of phase conjugate adaptive resonance developed by Marcer and Schempp (1998) and Mitchell and Staretz (2011). All entities emit vibratory waves that holographically encode all information about that entity at quantum level. A receiver of these waves decodes the information by way of a Fourier transformation. Through a reverse Fourier transform, this information is sent back (conjugate wave), along the same pathway to the emitter, by way of an established "standing wave" between the two. It is along this standing wave (channel) that information is returned to the source without any time delay (atemporal). The image is projected and constructed, then, "out there," at the source. A much-rehearsed example is snapping one's fingers. One senses its taking place out there, where the snapping is taking place, and not in the brain. For some, such as John Cramer (2016) and his "handshake model," this is also equivalent to the collapse of the wave function.

It is established that perceptions are dynamically constructed, are more logon in form and always reflect an inherent indeterminacy, are rendered more stable object/particle-form by "abstract machines"[30] (measuring/observing apparatus or "operator" according to quantum mechanics), and tend, in political economy, to exclude information of marginalised members.

Our view, building on Bradley's insights, is that some notion of agency must also be included, such as Schema QD. Each of the four core components of its constitution remain in relation, in dynamic states. For example, take the ego–Other relation. Each component exists in potentiality, meaning it has degrees of probability of being expressed in a certain form. The Other, following Jacques Lacan (1977) and Emmanuel Levinas (1988), is always present, and it is through this Other that one's ego is constructed. We become attuned to the Other in our very construction of ego. We must touch and be touched by the Other to establish resonance, opening an information channel by the standing wave created for an optimal flow of information. Consider the dyad ego-community generalized other. Each component in the dyad is co-constituted in performative actions, in everyday discursive practices. The latter conjures up Levinas's analysis of "the third," representing an external standard.

The ethical subject is thus constituted by various relations, such as ego–Other, ego–generalised other, ego–ego-ideal, etc. Together, as noted earlier, these form a matrix which takes on more stable form in context, in "intra-action." A distinct signature wave is instantiated, reflecting the matrix developed, which is transmitted outward in wave-form, encoding all information about the person and the distinct matrix. Simultaneously, an "I" and "object" emerge in instantiated form. Bradley alerts us to how various states lead to possible intra-actions with others. Jock Young (2011), for example, distinguishes between two forms of "othering" that are historically specific. One form, "conservative othering" is categorical, rigid, exclusionary, stigmatising, and diminishing; another form is "liberal othering" which still continues diminishing and distancing the other due to the other seen as lacking in control, education, civility, rationality, etc., but in more hidden and pervasive forms. Levinas's work points to an alternative form of othering, more in line with Martin Buber's (1971) classic call for an "I-thou" based on reciprocity, openness, and attunement (touch) with/to the Other.

Against this backdrop, we want to show how Karen Barad's work on touch can be enriched with an additional useful component of holography. We extend traditional legal understandings of touch to include degrees of attuning to and attunement with the Other.

Quantum holography and the sensorial in law

An abstract machine, such as disciplinary mechanisms, converts agents into a circumscribed particularity in context. The wave function (Ψ)[31] – representing a person superposed in potentials states[32] in movement (wave-form) – collapses to an instantiated particle-form in context, such as the legal arena. This process is in accord with Deleuze and Guattari's (1987) notion of subjectification, or better, objectification. Consider, for example, the primal identity changes from citizen to a "person of interest," a suspect, accused, convicted, and the master status is created in turn.[33] Rather than various possible expressions of identity that remain in a superposition state and captured by the wave function, one identity becomes the dominant objective form. Holography offers us additional understandings of the indeterminacy inherent in the process, as well as the freer space within which agency is creatively constituted. Our concern here is to relate the former introduction to quantum holography and Schema QD to the sense of touch in law, particularly building on Karan Barad's insightful quantum approach. This is opposed to conventional law with its linear logic, formal rationality devoid of an emotionally based active agent, and its inherent determinacy traced to a "clockwork universe" that follows the ontology of Newtonian physics, even if free will, ironically, is often considered an integral part of this paradigm.

The usual legal understanding of touch, in terms of bodily assault and battery,[34] fails to sensitise us to the multi-level nature of touching, or being in touch. Quantum holography does not stop at the traditional legal emphasis on corporeal externality defined by the boundaries of the skin. The notion of nonlocality already makes clear that being in touch can occur instantaneously over vast distances, even defying the supposed speed limit of light itself, to Einstein's chagrin. Since every "thing," every person, emits distinct wave-forms, and since absorbers are fully capable of registering at some level their intensity,[35] then touch becomes a central concept in understanding being human. Karan Barad's work is suggestive, especially in the way it applies Bohrian quantum mechanics to such theorists as Derrida, Levinas, Foucault, and Butler. Consider Barad's statement (2015: 153): "all touching entails an infinite alterity, so that touching the other is touching all others. Including the 'self,' and touching the 'self' entails touching the strangers within." Let us examine this further.

Barad, a physicist by formal training turned philosopher, informed by Niels Bohr (2010) and postmodern social philosophers Jacques Derrida, Michel Foucault, Donna Haraway, and Judith Butler, is a key developer for a quantum understanding of touch. Most relevant are her two essays, "On Touching – The Inhuman That Therefore I Am" (2015) and "Quantum Entanglements and Hauntological Relations" (2010).[36] Barad's (2007) opus *Meeting the Universe Halfway* lays out her quantum approach in social philosophy. We want to extend her argument in incorporating a holography dimension, a quantum holographic approach which furthers her agenda of a justice-to-come.

Briefly, Barad's quantum approach distances itself from a focus on individual agency and notions of intentionality. Her "agential realism" suggests that "agency is 'doing' or 'being' in its intra-activity" (Barad, 2007: 178). Rather than employing *interaction* with its presumption of pre-existing subjects, her neologism "intra-action" suggests that agents and objects only come into being in engagement, in action, in relation. "Mattering" happens during the engagement of some measuring/observing apparatus (including a conscious agent, some audience, a scientific instrument, etc.) and phenomenon. Neither objects nor agents with clearly defined boundaries and distinct properties pre-date intra-action. They are mutually constituted in their relational becomings. In her essay on touching, she argues "all material 'entities' are entangled relations of becoming, there is also the fact that materiality 'itself' is always already touched by and touching infinite configurings of other beings and other times" (2015: 7). And further, "Touching is a matter of response. Each of 'us' is constituted in response-ability. Each of 'us' is constituted as responsible for the other, as being in touch with the other" (ibid.).

Barad suggests that "justice-to-come" can be further developed by extension of Emmanuel Levinas's concern for the Other. Echoing Levinas,

> living compassionately requires recognizing and facing our responsibility to the infinitude of the other, welcoming the stranger whose very existence is the possibility of touching and being touched, who gifts us with both the ability to respond and the longing for justice-to-come.
>
> (ibid.: 10)

Barad's focus, then, is in "response-ability to the entangled other" (Barad, 2010: 265). Response-ability, moreover, is not of one's choosing; rather, it is part of being human, an integral element of becoming in the world where self and other are mutually constitutive, not unilaterally predefined. Of course, we could qualify this notion of response-ability by citing processes that objectify, that separate us from the Other, traced to the nature of abstract machines in capitalist political economy.

Barad's quantum approach can be furthered by the addition of holography. Derrida's (2005) critique of Jean-Luc Nancy's (2008) essay rests on key principles of undecidability and unpredictability, fitting with Heisenberg's (1949) uncertainty principle and with Bohr's (2010) indeterminacy principles in quantum mechanics. Indeed, in our view, the subject cannot be reducible to a corresponding identity with the Other. A space always exists between self and Other within which emergents play themselves out. Self is constituted through the Other but is not reducible to it. Further insights are generated by Bradley's (2016b) development of quantum holography by integrating the work of Gabor's (1946) notion of the logon. That is, the spacetime (everyday world of activity) and spectral domains (frequency domain) can be orthogonally framed where their intersections produce a sine wave that can incur "cuts" in its dynamic state of movement. A logon is a particular "cut" or slice of this wave; it is a snapshot of an otherwise dynamic state in movement, in transformation. Of course, everything is in relational movement. Uncertainty, therefore, exists in any snapshot of this dynamic flux. Fixing an event in time and space at any instance and thereby gaining a static understanding of the snapshot comes at the cost of its temporal developmental process, its constantly changing nature.[37] Law practice, for example, attempts to capture "intent," "will," "bad faith," and "responsibility" at a particular time and space, whereas these clearly vary along with their spatiotemporal contexts in relation to the dynamics of Schema QD.[38]

Touch, to return to Bradley's model, could be conceptualised as a form of established resonance; that is, being in tune with the Other and groups whose characteristic signature waves interact. Where they coincide, we have an interference pattern and resonance. The bioemotional field of a group, or one established between humans in intra-action, provides a common in-formation field which is subject to accessing, decoding, and projecting out there to the emitting source a virtual image of the entity or phenomena. In this sense, the logon can be a refinement of Barad's Bohrian-derived notion of "phenomena." They are not primordially objects but relational entities: only in specific intra-action does one witness particle-form expression. As Barad (2010: 261, emphasis in original) tells us, "phenomena are not located in space and time; rather, *phenomena are material entanglements enfolded and threaded through the spacetimemattering of the universe*." And "memory – the pattern of sedimented enfoldings of iterative intra-activity – is written in to the fabric of the world."

Reconceptualised, memory exist as spectra, interference patterns, or holograms, encoded in a holographic/in-formation field. The notion of an in-formation field, a socioemotional field, of course, is suggestive of the continuous development of relational entities in spacetime within which degrees of touching are instantiated. Again, a particular slice, as we have developed by our Schema QD, is a logon, but infused by an ethically and morally becoming, relational subject. PCAR, as we have seen, is the process by which this holographically encoded information is being accessed, decoded, and projected back to the emitting source as "reality."[39]

Schema QD indicates that an ego/self experiences touch at various levels, frequencies, intensities, and duration: with the ego-ideal, Other, community generalised other, discursive subject positions, abstract generalised other, and potentially a universal consciousness. The modes are not locatable in time and space as objects, but rather are, following Barad, enactments, reconstituted by way of repetition and ongoing intra-action. They are not marked by distinct boundaries and properties but appear in more "objective" form in use, in every day intra-action. Within each level we find entanglements, ego with the Other, ego with the community generalised other, etc. An "I" and a particular object (perception image, or logon)[40] are simultaneous emergents in this ongoing intra-action; they do not precede volitional action. We are always already in entangled probabilistic states with varying capacities of response-ability (ability to respond). These can vary due to harms of reduction and harms of repression (Milovanovic and Henry, 2001), forms of objectification, capture and diminishment. Our responses leave a trace (Barad, 2010: 265) in any instantiation: in our view, holographically encoded information in the information field. The speaking subject, a momentary objectification in the form of an "I", now finds a place to speak within a particular discourse.

Our ethical duty to the Other always already pre-exists action in the form of our ability to respond; it is not something chosen by the agent, nor is it a product of calculation (Barad: 265). The ethical, then, already exists in our ongoing intra-actions, in our "response-ability." With an ethical response-ability we posit a moral response-ability, the latter responding to some contrary interpretations of Libet's (2004) and McCraty et al.'s (2009) work as relegating the conscious agent an illusion (since our brain is set in motion prior to consciousness, so it is said, we are merely automatons). The following sequence has been established by very precise research: the heart begins to respond (touched), as measured by electromagnetic changes, 4–5 seconds prior to incoming wave-forms of an event not yet realized (McCraty et al: 209);[41] the brain becomes activated (EEG patterns) 1.5 seconds after the heart registers an impending event. Brain activation follows generation of heart wave-forms (encoding emotionality). For Libet (2004: 134, 137), not factoring in the heart wave-form, an external sensory signal produces electric activities in the brain at least one second prior to movement (motor action). It takes at about 400 milliseconds (msec, or 0.4 seconds) to 500 msec for a "readiness potential" to develop, whereby potential motor responses (Pribram's "plans of action," 1991) are being formulated unconsciously. It takes another 350–400 msec for conscious awareness to develop ("an awareness of the wish to move," ibid.: 137b).[42] Ergo, for the illusionists, we are automatons. However, recent research has pointed out the play of a "conscious veto" (Libet, 137–156; Schultze-Kraft et al., 2015). Approximately 150 msec (or 200 msec according to Schultze-Kraft et al., 2015) prior to some motor response, a window for a conscious veto develops (i.e., a batter checking his swing); after this, the sensorimotor schemas begun in the brain unconsciously work to completion (a point of no return, i.e., a batter swinging and feeling dejected after doing so). Libet leaves open the question of the precise mechanism of the veto, and if more than one possible motor action, which one? We trace its source to the dynamics of the four interacting components of Schema QD, that is the ego's relations to the Other in constituting self, to one's ego-ideal as a desirable person, and to the community generalised other representing group norms, all in conjunction with ongoing contextual intra-actions, the collapse of superpositioned possibilities to one, and its shaping in the form of a logon and its often implicitly suggested action patterns – together constituting an agent of moral response-ability. Of course, we are left with further contextual analysis in determining when the conscious veto is clearest at play, or compromised and pacified. Telling indicators are revealed early in positive emotions (smooth wave-forms) and correlative greater attunement (resonance, touch) with others and access to nonlocal intuitive possibilities particularly in the state of "psychophysiological coherence" (see Bradley, section ii); or negative emotions (erratic wave-forms) displayed by the heart organ and greater difficulty for attunement/touch, nonlocal access, and intuitive practices. In sum, with an ethical response-ability one finds a moral response-ability.

All this suggests an embodied, active, emotional, and creative agent, and that entangled relations of positivity provide the milieu within which maximal variability, diversity, and nonlocal intuitive practices flourish. In accordance with this development, dissipative structures, following dynamics systems theory, provide both temporary stability and the basis of yet further iterative intra-action toward new dissipative structural forms.

Law, beginning with the indoctrination in law school to formal rationality, deductive logic, and syllogistic reasoning (as an abstract machine), constitutes subjects (a process of subjectification due to the shaping influence of the prevalent iterative form of intra-actions). The socioaffective legal milieu restrictively encodes information. Being fully human is denied under the name of logic, rationality, order, finality. Touching, by which we mean being in tune with the Other, is diminished as legal realities are being constituted. We await justice-to-come, but like for Godot, we are in for the long wait.

The newly "minted" graduates of law schools now find themselves in legal practice. Drawing from Henri Bergson and Gilles Deleuze, Lefebvre (2008) has shown how a complex event is converted into a legal case: an otherwise nuanced, dynamic event is reduced to a (legal) characterisation of "what happened." Reconceptualised, we witness how objectification, or collapsing the wave function to a narrow particle-form, produces order, stability, and linear coherent story-telling, and in the process, diminishes the Other to a category, devoid of the mutually constitutive, relational dynamic of being and becoming. Emotionality, touching, and being touched by the Other is also greatly reduced; however, holographic encoding is holistic and thus the unsaid remains a subversive undercurrent as non-instantiated superposed possibilities remain active.

Critical race theory's strategy of "counter-story telling"[43] is a start to remedying this objectification and repression. It is a way of reviving the Other and relational contributions to the bioemotional in-formation field. In other words, alternative logons constructed will also find new encodings of information that become embedded in the in-formation field. Critical feminist and queer theorists have offered multiple forms of identity as well as alternative reality constructions (logons, "cuts"), brought into sharp relief by those identifying with LGBTQ+, perhaps most revealing in the "Q" (questioning) form (Puar, 2007). The duality of bodies and mind, the former often associated with the irrationality of the senses, the latter with rationality and logic, can find a new reconciliation in the notion of the emergent "nomadic subject," or "multiplicities" articulated in the form of a Möbius strip where inside and outside are interconnected in forming an ongoing synthesis, a becoming. The subject, an "I" that emerges in the context of intra-action, does so simultaneously with the object it creates; neither of them pre-exist the intra-action. This is shown in Schema QD, and particularly the dynamic form portrayed by the topological structure of the cross-cap constituted by an infinite number of Möbius bands, each framing a slice, a cut of the subject, and "reality."[44] A unique "I" emerges, represented by a distinct signature wave that undergoes continuous variation (modulation) as it engages in intra-action in the in-formation field, both informing and being informed in the process.

Law is constrained by its conceptual logic that insists on distancing, categorising, and systematising into dominant ideological forms; on the other hand, corporeal logic,[45] an informed logic of the heart, persists and is a constant basis of disruption of repetition and dominant forms. Both of these are encountered on the twist of the Möbius band.

Touching, resonance, and transformative justice

Bradley's most recent work[46] on a higher state of attunement (love), built on positive emotions and continuous emissions of bioemotional attentional waves, suggests that the potential for a universal consciousness may be attained by increased intuitive nonlocal practices. This provides insights into conceptualising components of a transformative justice and law and the promotion of becoming over being. Barad's work, reconceptualised along quantum holography and an integration of agency with Schema QD, are further suggestive for a "justice-to-come."[47] We are suggesting that touching is attuned to Levinas's call for an infinite duty of care to and for the other, perhaps best incorporated in critical feminist thought as the ethics of care. We have conceptualised various modes of being in touch: with self, with ego-ideal, with the Other, with the community generalised other, and with a higher state of consciousness perhaps most suggestive in Bradley's development of a universal consciousness.[48]

We follow recent empirical research demonstrating dynamic forms of quantum holograms which are characterised by quantum superposition. Each dynamic hologram,[49] in other words, represents various potential states in quantum superposition and only by way of PCAR, the shaping effects of Schema QD, and the bioemotional impact of the heart wave-form are these accessed, decoded, and a single version projected back "out there" as being reality.[50] Real-time dynamic holograms are continuously updated as opposed to static holograms which, once created, cannot be updated. It is in ongoing repetition in intra-actions that relatively stable forms are produced of the configural features present, yet always subject to change by disruptions of the conventional.[51] The key operators are abstract machines that are embedded in a specific socius and often appear in nuanced forms in context. However, latent subversive variants (e.g., superposed possibilities not activated) always threaten to be instantiated.

Justice-to-come is connected to disruptions of conventional repetition.[52] This occurs when intra-actions begin to reflect greater positive emotions whereby attunement is associated with appreciation, love, compassion, and a sense of connectedness with the Other and all entities in the cosmos.[53] In this state of "psychophysiological coherence" the heart emits a continuous smooth wave toward the brain which registers this in its everyday functioning and of subsequent consciousness that is infused with positive emotions. Here also exists a continuous reformulation of attractor states associated with each of the four key components of Schema QD, which inform more orderly-disorderly butterfly attractors whereby small additional inputs produce disproportional effects that are the occasion for creativity, growth, and transformative justice practices to come.

Touch in this development is associated with being in tune, resonance, and creating standing waves by which understanding of self and Other(s) is more openly explored. Here, connectedness[54] reaches all levels of the psychic functioning, producing Freud's "oceanic feeling." Perhaps, too, the heart field is the basis of the development of Freud's hypercathexis, which is contributory to the collapse of the wave function; that is, superposed recollected images during contemplation collapse to one.

Psychophysiological coherence provides the impetus for Levinas's infinite duty of care for the Other (e.g., the ego–Other relation in Schema QD). In this view, Deleuze and Guattari's notion of *desire* as production, an ongoing search for differentiation, temporary stable dissipative structures (assemblages), followed by deterritorialisation and reterritorialisation due to disruptive practices, is most efficacious.[55] Agency, in this view, is brought back in, but not as a static phenomenon that is possessed by a localisable entity with objectively defined distinct boundaries and properties.[56] We are in accord with Barad's (2010: 25) point that response-ability is about "our active engagement of sedimenting out the world in certain kinds of ways and not others. Being attentive to ways in which we are re-doing, with each intra-action materially re-doing the material configurings of spacetimemattering." An ethical principle must counter harms of reduction and harms of repression (and its investors/investment in harm, Milovanovic and Henry, 2001) – often adjustments to various abstract machines and disciplinary mechanisms in political economy – by allowing genuine response-ability, an ability to respond. It must advocate the expansion of positive emotions, continuous differentiation, multiple possibilities, and ever-new plateaus (dissipative structures) that are both orderly (territorialised) and disorderly (deterritorialised).

Justice-to-come, law-to-come, justice, and ethics demand principles of justice based on normative theory. Elsewhere (Milovanovic, 2014a: 198–199), we have provided two first approximations.[57] This addresses more egalitarian law practices (distributive and retributive principles) and also recognises and responds to theorists, such as Feigenson (1997), who strongly critique open-ended use of sympathy in justice-rendering practices. No, sympathy is not connected with "anything goes," but can be defined by ethical evaluative measures. Derrida's (1990) distinction between law and justice, the former more connected with formal rationality and calculation, the latter more with a gift without measurement or calculation, in line with Levinas's call for an infinite duty of care for the other, must give way to reconnecting law *and* justice. In this reconnection, touch becomes a key component in formulating an agent such as in our inter- and intra-subjectively constituted ethical and moral subject, contributing to a socius that intra-actively generates greater positive emotions and joyful relations in socioaffective in-formational fields and in the development of a transformative justice.

Conclusion

We have embarked on developing a new paradigm rooted in ontological principles derived from quantum mechanics and holography. The notion of touch, resonance, or being in tune has many levels of exploration. The direction has been set: the development of a more positive form of law bringing back in the agent and cognizant of her/his response-ability, co-constitutively contributory in the social construction of reality. There are many intriguing and productive lines of inquiry that remain for further thought. This begins the new journey.

Notes

1 See online, *Find Law*, "Assault and Battery Overview." Downloaded, 10/1/16, http://criminal.findlaw.com/criminal-charges/assault-and-battery-overview.html. Non consenting touch at the workplace could include hugging, kissing, stroking, massaging, back-patting, hair-ruffling, handshakes held too long, linking arms, light slapping of the buttocks, hip bumping, putting an arm around someone's shoulders or a hand on their arms, holding someone's hand, poking, or pointing with a finger.

2 This field is intimately immersed in the quantum field, a vibratory flux of energy and emergents, termed the "zero point field" (ZPF), or as in Laszlo (2007), the "in-formation" field, a repository of dynamic holograms.

3 An entity, or "phenomenon" according to Barad (2007), is constantly interacting with other frequency waves forming interference patterns (basis of dynamic holograms) reflecting their attributes. Constellations, or larger patterns, can often be carried forth in optic arrays (Gibson, 1979) and accessed and decoded via PCAR. In more active forms of an attentional gaze, each unique Schema QD signature wave initiates the PCAR process, producing perceptions in the form of logons, object-forms, and "reality."

4 Laszlo (2007) offers the idea that we are all immersed not in empty space, but in an "in-formation" field where holographical information is encoded. Memory images and one's quantum holographic lexicon does not reside within the brain, but is encoded "out there" in the information field. The brain is a transducer that accesses and decodes the field. This insight was already suggested by Bergson in 1896 with his *Matter and Memory*.

5 A key contribution is that both momentum and location cannot simultaneously be defined. Define one with precision and the other becomes imprecise. Consider snapshots of reality by a camera. The shot, while conveying much information of the moment, comes at the cost of understanding reality as actually being constantly created.

6 See also Pribram's application to brain processing (1991: 28–43, 70–73; 2013: 215–225).

7 Consider throwing two stones into a calm pond. Each makes ripples and where these waves meet, an interference pattern is created which retains all information about the stone – weight, velocity, direction, etc.
8 Long-term memory, in this view contrary to conventional neuroscience literature, is not stored in the brain but "out there" in the in-formation field (Laszlo, 1995). Arguably, short-term memory is momentarily stored in the holographically based brain as Fourier inscriptors (Pribram, 1991). In this model, the brain is a transducer, accessing and decoding holographic information stored in the in-formation field.
9 Without the work of the eye and its capacity to do forward and reverse Fourier transforms, what would be seen "out there" is a blur much like a fuzzy screen before adjusting the focus (Pribram, 2013).
10 Cramer (2016) has offered the "handshake model," on which Marcer, Schempp, and Mitchell build, indicating the forward and backward movement that implicates backward time referral, where in the reverse direction, no time lapses. In quantum mechanics time does not flow just in the forward direction, particularly demonstrated in "quantum erasure experiment" versions of the double-slit experiment.
11 By the use of magnetometers.
12 This comports with more everyday conventional wisdom that intuitively we conceive the heart as the basis of emotionality, and the brain, on the other hand, of rationality.
13 Bradley (2016a: 102) shows how socioaffective dialog has its beginnings in infant-parent early development. "The socioaffective transmissions between mother and child not only contain encoded information on their internal psychological states as individuals, but also contain information on their feelings and emotions, mediated through the interconnection of their respective heart fields."
14 McCraty et al., 2009.
15 This field includes the spectral domain or interference patterns that encode information holographically.
16 "individuals in a psychophysiologically coherent state gain a heightened sensitivity to non-local information encoded in the heart fields of those around them" (ibid., 134).
17 Quantum mechanics relies on the "double-slit" experiments that have been continuously validated indicating that objects are not ontologically primal; rather, all begin with a wave-form, all are vibrational, with a distinct frequency pattern. (For accessible YouTube presentations, see www.youtube.com/watch?v=M4_0obIwQ_U ; for an animated version, see www.youtube.com/watch?v=DfPeprQ7oGc.) It is when two wave-forms meet that interference patterns are created, recording all information of contributing wave-forms. Laszlo's (2007) provides the example of two ships at sea. Where their wakes intersect we find interference patterns which, on decoding, portray speed, tonnage, direction, etc. of the respective ships. The double-slit experiments establish that the wave-form undergoes a transformation when observed or measured into a particle-form, what we see as objects.
18 Barad (2007: 33), building on Neils Bohr, a founding figure of quantum mechanics, insightfully uses intra-action instead of interaction, since the latter already assumes what is in need of explanation, that is the appearance of distinct separate objects and determining subjects rather than just wave-forms ("phenomena"). It is in the intra-action of the measuring/observing apparatus (consciousness) and "phenomena" that object forms appear with clear boundaries, properties, meanings, and identities. Double-slit experiments suggest this. This is a co-constitutive, intra-active, performative discursive practice.
19 Mathematical research on black holes has led cosmologists to draw implications for our normal everyday three-dimension reality in identifying a bulk region surrounded by a boundary on which all information of happenings in the bulk are encoded in holographic form (see for example, Susskind, 2009). In the strong version, the interior bulk is but a projection from the boundaries, existing as holograms and what we see as "reality."
20 Gibson (1979) has argued that optic arrays encode information, including "affordances," what the system more readily allows as possibilities.

21 For a visual and accessible online depiction, see my earlier version in "Quantum Holographic Criminology," 5 *Journal of Theoretical and Philosophical Criminology* 2:1–29 (2013), particularly pp. 17, 19.
22 An earlier version was developed in my *Quantum Holographic Criminology* (2014).
23 Two other contributory constructs are discursive subject positions (structurally defined roles that are discursively constituted) and abstract generalized other (macro-level normative order).
24 For the construction of the cross-cap and viewing the Möbius band within it, see http://web1.kcn.jp/hp28ah77/us27g_cros.htm
25 Each person's unique signature wave leaves a trace of itself with all that it engages. In this sense we are fundamentally interconnected with all others.
26 Bradley (2016b, 48) has identified as a "passionate attentional wave" or a bioemotional attentional wave.
27 Studies continuously show that the heart reacts to perturbations prior to the brain and prior to consciousness (Radin, 2006). Of course, this does not mean that the person is a determined entity, an automaton, for, as Radin demonstrates, a "veto" can be exercised on earlier developments, and, too, the Heisenberg principle undermines precision and thus allow small inputs having disproportional effects as dynamics systems theory suggests. The shaping effect of Schema QD is also efficacious.
28 Borrowing a term used by Sigmund Freud in *The Interpretation of Dreams* (2010).
29 Equivalent to the collapse of the wave function.
30 Concept developed by Deleuze and Guattari (1987).
31 Schrödinger has provided a definitive equation referred to as the Schrödinger equation that portrays how a wave function evolves over time. $|\Psi|^2$ depicts the probability of any of the possible states in superposition to appear. See www.physlink.com/education/askexperts/ae329.cfm and also https://plus.maths.org/content/schrodinger-1
32 Each with a probability of instantiation.
33 Elsewhere (Milovanovic, 2014b) I have revisited labeling theory to indicate how the identity process culminating in the "secondary deviant" can be explained by quantum holography dynamics.
34 This is a negative form of law; a positive form of law is found in incipient form in restorative justice practices and more genuinely developed in transformative justice. The form of law itself, as Deleuze argues (see Lefebvre, 2008), is questionable for its static nature unlike the form theorized by legal realists and supported, for example, by the works of pragmatist Richard Rorty (1989) with his notion of the "good prophet" and "intuitive leaps" accounting for change.
35 Intensity is related to frequency patterns with distinct phases, amplitudes, and frequencies. See the accessible YouTube video www.schoolphysics.co.uk/age16-19/Wave%20properties/Wave%20properties/text/Intensity_and_amplitude/index.html
36 The former comments on Derrida's (2005) critique of Jean-Luc Nancy's (2008) *Deconstruction of Christianity*.
37 Each entity ("phenomenon") is a complex of emerging interference patterns (dynamic holograms).
38 Each might correlate with Gibson's (1979) "affordances," the latter varying in intensity, frequency, and duration.
39 An intriguing possibility well worth further exploration is posed with Maldacena and Susskind's (2013) recent paper that quantum entanglement can be explained by wormholes. These are a form of tunneling connecting two or more spacetime regions, captured in their formula ER = EPR following the Einstein, Podolsky, and Rosen "EPR" paper (1935a), and particularly the ER paper (1935b) establishing the so-called Einstein-Rosen bridges. Suggestive is that at the center of Schema QD is a singularity as witnessed in the topological cross-cap, and this may be conceived as one form of the Einstein-Rosen bridges. Perhaps this is an internal source of intuitive practices that works along with Bradley's external

source in the form of resonance. For a philosophical view of the EPR and ER papers, see https://plato.stanford.edu/entries/qt-epr/ and https://arxiv.org/pdf/1704.04648.pdf

40 Unlike a Cartesian "cut," a quantum holographic "cut" is a logon. This is accommodative to Barad's notion of an "agential cut," a continuous separating and putting together, a "joining and disjoining."

41 See also Bradley (2016a). Typical experiments provide subjects with randomly viewing peaceful or violent events on a computer screen where subjects press a button acknowledging one rather than the other. Studies show that the subject's heart wave-form is already responding before an event appears on the screen.

42 In many habitual activities, motor action follows within 100–200 msec of sensory input and only after the response, if asked, does one linearily reconstruct what happened (Libet, 109). This notion of "antedating" (ibid.: 91, 113, 121) is backward time referral and can change what seemingly already has already happened in the past. Quantum erasure experiments, derivatives of double-slit experiments suggesting that the wave-form is collapsed to a particle form by observation or measurement, have offered numerous experiments to substantiate this counterintuitive possibility.

43 See, for example, Delgado and Stefancic (2017).

44 Lorraine (1999: 137) has explained the formation of identity: "personal identity could entail a kind of continual transformation in a corporeal dance with others in which we acknowledged and celebrated the interdependent activity of self-making. That is, personal identity could be refigured as a continual shaping and reshaping of self in concert with others."

45 On corporeal and conceptual logic see Lorraine (1999: 7–8, 113–117, 227).

46 See Bradley (2016a, 2016c).

47 This expression is borrowed and further developed by Barad (2015) and draws from Derrida.

48 We could also highlight and build on a touching of self, developed by Karan Barad. That is, with critical and engaged response-ability with one's co-constituted intra-active performative constructions of the ego-ideal we could unravel various "layers" of relevancies that are the basis of assessment of personal ethics, from the most superficial connected with mass media and dominant ideology, to an intermediate layer brought about by popular cultures for self-examination, to the deeper levels of the meaning of it all.

49 Laszlo (1995: 31) has referred to dynamic holograms as "Schrödinger-wave holograms."

50 The heart wave-form, perhaps, could be connected to an élan vital, libido, vitalism as in Deleuze's definition of desire as production, or what Schrödinger (2012) referred to as "free energy" (sometimes, negative entropy or negentropy).

51 They are more dissipative structures, to borrow from dynamic systems theory.

52 Deleuze and Guattari's (1987) "war machine" comes to mind, a form of disruption, a deterritorialization and a reterritorialization along new lines of flight. For them, all is in continuous variation which we read as wave functions, with superposed possibilities. "Minor" forms emerge when suppressed and repressed possibilities are instantiated, giving disenfranchised subaltern an alternative basis of creating reality.

53 Perhaps, too, this is the seed for the development of new assemblages and dissipative structures as is suggested by Deleuze and Guattari (1987) by way of an initial "refrain," a tune or melody.

54 Barad (2015) tells us, "so much happens in a touch: an infinity of others – other beings, other spaces, other times – are aroused."

55 Recently, a leading figure developing a quantum model of the brain, Stuart Hameroff, often co-authoring with the highly respected mathematician, Roger Penrose, has developed a "quantum pleasure principle" (see www.huffingtonpost.com/stuart-hameroff/darwin-versus-deepak-whic_b_7481048.html). It remains open as to the possibility of this being integrated in the model here developed.

56 The "Q" in LGBTQ becomes the dominant moving force toward new configurations of identity.

57 One principle concerns distributive justice, the other retributive justice. Each advocates both an ongoing becoming-minoritarian (Deleuze and Guattari, 1987) and an affirmative nomadology (Holland, 2011) based on a quantum holography ontology and epistemology.

Bibliography

Barad, Karen, *Meeting the Universe Halfway*, Durham: Duke University Press, 2007.

Barad, Karen, 'Quantum Entanglements and Hauntological Relations of Inheritance,' *Derrida Today*, 3(2), 240–268, 2010.

Barad, Karen, 'Matter Feels, Converses, Suffers, Desires, Yearns and Remembers,' in Rick Dolphijn and Iris Van De Tuin (eds), *New Materialism*, Michigan: Open Humanities Press, 2012. http://quod.lib.umich.edu/o/ohp/11515701.0001.001/1:4.3/–new-materialism-interviews-cartographies?rgn=div2;view=fulltext.

Barad, Karen, 'On Touching – The Inhuman That Therefore I am,' in Kirsten Stakemeier and Susanne Witzgall (eds), *Power of Material/Politics of Materiality*, Zurzch: Diaphaes, 2015.

Bohm, David. *Wholeness and the Implicate Order*, New York: Routledge, 1983.

Bohr, Niels, *Atomic Physics and Human Knowledge*, New York: Dover Books, 2010.

Bradley, Raymond T., 'A Psychophysiology of Intuition,' *World Futures*, 63(2), 61–97, 2007.

Bradley, Raymond T., 'The Lens of Love,' 2016a.

Bradley, Raymond, T., 'Bonds and Quanta,' *Journal of Theoretical and Philosophical Criminology*, 7(2), 95–136, 2016b.

Bradley, Raymond T., The Lens of Love: Holographic Eye of Universal Consciousness, 2016c.

Buber, Martin, *I and Thou*, New York: Touchstone Publishers, 1971.

Busemeyer, Jerome and Bruza, Peter *Quantum Models of Cognition*. Cambridge: Cambridge University Press, 2014.

Cramer, John, *The Quantum Handshake*, Berlin and Heidelberg: Springer, 2016.

Deleuze, Gilles and Guattari, Felix, *A Thousand Plateaus*, Minneapolis: University of Minnesota Press, 1987.

Deleuze, Gilles and Guattari, Felix, *Kafka: Toward a Minor Literature*, Minneapolis: University of Minnesota Press, 2006.

Delgado, Richard and Stefancic, Jean, *Critical Race Theory*, New York: New York Press, 2017.

Derrida, Jacques, 'The Force of Law,' *Cardozo Law Review*, 11, 920–1045, 1990.

Derrida, Jacques, *On Touching – Jean-Luc Nancy*, Stanford: Stanford University Press, 2005.

Einstein, Albert, Podolsky, Boris and Rosen, Nathan, 'Can Quantum Mechanical Designation of Physical Reality be Considered Complete?' *Physical Review* 47, 777–780, 1935a.

Einstein, Albert and Rosen, Nathan, 'The Particle Problem in the General Theory of Relativity,' *Physical Review* 48(1), 73–77, 1935b.

Fiegenson, Neal, 'Sympathy and Legal Judgement,' *Tennessee Law Review* 65(1), 1–79, 1997.

Freud, Sigmund, *The Interpretation of Dreams*, New York: Basic Books, 2010.

Gabor, Dennis, 'Theory of Communication,' *Journal of the Institute of Electrical Engineering*, 93, 429–441, 1946.

Gibson, James, *The Ecological Approach to Perception*, Mahwah, NJ: Lawrence Erlbaum, 1979.

Heisenberg, Werner, *The Physical Principles of Quantum Theory*, New York: Dover Publishers, 1949.

Holland, Eugene, *Nomad Citizenship*, Minneapolis: University of Minnesota Press, 2011.

Lacan, Jacques, *Ecrit*, New York: Norton, 1977.

Laszlo, Ervin, *The Interconnected Universe*, Hackensack, NJ: World Scientific Publishing, 1995.

Laszlo, Ervin, *Science and the Akashic Field*, Rochester: Inner Traditions, 2007.

Lefebvre, Alexander, *The Image of Law*, Stanford: Stanford University Press, 2008.

Levinas, Emmanuel, *Entre Nous: Thinking of the Other*, New York: Columbia University Press, 1988.

Lewin, Kurt, *Principles of Psychology*, New York: Munshi Press, 2007.
Libert, Benjamin, *Mind Time*, Cambridge: Cambridge University Press, 2004.
Lorraine, Tamsin, *Irigaray and Deleuze*, Ithaca: Cornell University Press, 1999.
Maldacena, Juan and Susskind, Leonard, 'Cool Horizons for Black Holes,' 2013. https://arxiv.org/pdf/1306.0533v2.pdf.
Marcer, Peter and Schempp, Walter, 'The Brain as a Conscious System,' *International Journal of General Systems* 27(1), 231–248, 1998.
McCraty, Rollin, Atkinson, Mike, Tomasina, Dana and Bradley, Raymond T., 'The Coherent Heart,' *Integral Review* 5(2), 10–115, 2009. www.heartmath.org/assets/uploads/2016/04/coherent-heart-integral-review-2009.pdf.
Milovanovic, Dragan, *Quantum Holographic Criminology*, Durham: Carolina Academic Press, 2014a.
Milovanovic, Dragan, 'Revisiting Societal Reaction,' *Crimen* 5(2), 123–135, 2014b.
Milovanovic, Dragan and Henry, Stuart, 'Constitutive Definitions of Harm,' in Stuart Henry and Mark Lanier (eds), *What Is Crime?* Boulder: Rowman and Littlefield, 2001.
Mitchell, Edgar and Staretz, Robert, 'The Quantum Hologram and the Nature of Consciousness,' *Journal of Cosmology*, 14, 1–19, 2011.
Murdoch, Dugald, *Niels Bohr's Philosophy of Physics*, Cambridge: Cambridge University Press, 1990.
Nancy, Jean-Luc, *Deconstruction of Christianity*, New York: Fordham University Press, 2008.
Pribram, Karl, *Brain and Perception*, Mahwah, NJ: Lawrence Erlbaum, 1991.
Pribram, Karl, *The Form Within*, Westport: Prospectas Press, 2013.
Puar, Jasbir, *Terrorist Assemblages*, Durham: Duke University Press, 2007.
Radin, Dean, *Entangled Minds*, New York: Paraview Pocket Books, 2006.
Robbins, Stephen, 'Bergson, Perception and Gibson,' *Journal of Consciousness Studies*, 7(5), 23–45, 2006.
Rorty, Richard, *Contingency, Irony and Solidarity*, Cambridge: Cambridge University Press, 1989.
Schultze-Kraft, Matthias, Birman, Daniel Rusconi, Marco, Allefeld, Carsen, Gorgen, Kai, Dahne, Sven, Blankertz, Benjamin and Haynes, John-Dylan, 'The Point of No Return in Vetoing Self-Initiated Movements,' *PNAS*, 113(4), 1080–1085, 2015.
Schrödinger, Erwin, *What Is Life?* Cambridge: Cambridge University Press, 2012.
Sherwin, Richard, *Visualizing Law in the Age of the Baroque*, London: Routledge, 2011.
Susskind, Leonard, *The Black Hole War*, New York: Little, Brown and Company, 2009.
Young, Jock, *The Criminological Imagination*, New York: Polity Press, 2011.
Wendt, Alexander, *Quantum Mind and Social Science*, Cambridge: Cambridge University Press, 2015.

10

Turbulent legality

Sovereignty, security and the police

Illan rua Wall

A heuristic device

What would it mean to think about law in the moment of popular political crisis, in the moment where it is contested by 'the people' or a multitude? In order to understand the difficulty of such a venture, let us for a moment heuristically imagine a miscellany of something that we might call 'conventional legal theory and jurisprudence', featuring names like Raz, Dworkin, Hart, Austin, Rawls, Fuller, Finnis, Kelsen or Posner. While it is obviously difficult to identify commonality between such diverse thinkers, we can, at the very least, say of this pastiche that it tends to start from a stable Western legal order, with an obedient and at times empowered populace. This obedience is motivated by a sense of justice, self-interest, reason, morality, contract, maximisation of utilities, some variety of habit, or perhaps a combination of these elements. However, the stability of this order is of the utmost importance. It takes on the character of the unsaid and the unquestioned. Indeed the reflections on the character of law become nonsensical and impossible without the calm stability.

Some of the most popular of these theories begin by posing a moment that stills the complexity that surrounds us. Imagine yourself in Rawls's 'original position', behind the veil of ignorance, or in the chambers of Dworkin's Judge Hercules as he relaxes after his best possible decision: listen to the sounds; feel the texture of the moment; absorb the atmosphere. . . . The cloud where you sit in disembodied form behind the veil of ignorance (do you 'sit' when disembodied?) does not rattle with thunder and flash with lightning. In Judge Hercules's chambers, you will not hear the people protesting the outcome of the decision on the steps of the court, or the sobs of the loser from inside the courtroom. Both the imagined ideal judge and the original position get us to place our thoughts in a space of stillness. The calmness of the surroundings, of the scenario, allows us to make a decision, to identify and to understand. But it is not just that the theoretical moves exude stability: the theories themselves maintain a fundamentally *peaceable* nature of legal order. Stability allows processes such as the different heads of government to articulate rationally, it means that the force that is brought to bear on the wrong-doer is not fundamentally unjust because it is regular and unbiased, or the calm juridical balancing acts which allow for 'proportionate' measures and the unperturbed identification of the means that are absolutely necessary in any given circumstances. In short, it is the stable, orderly nature of'the Law' upon which the debates and theories are built.

This chapter suggests that such a sense of the calm upon which law is based is a result of a legal anaesthetic. One is numbed to the (quasi-)legal forms which precede one's thinking about law. That is, an atmosphere of docility and obedience must first be produced, and only then can the theorists above worry about the nature and definition of law. This chapter will focus on the orders of the police and sovereignty. These are introduced not as two interesting and particular ways in which 'the Law' deals with 'disorder' or 'turbulence', but to insist upon a reimagining of the starting points for thinking about law in itself. It is not just that these different starting points give us a different (univocal) sense of law, but that from them it becomes impossible to think about 'law in itself'. The question that motivates many of the above theorists – What, or How is Law? – itself becomes impossible. Instead, the sense of law that emerges from disorder and turbulence is always partial, in the sense of being incomplete and partisan; it is always fuzzy and impermanent.

Turbulence, disorder, atmosphere

In his work on migration flows, Nikos Papastergiadis develops two senses of turbulence. Firstly, he says it is a 'noun for describing the unsettling effects of an unexpected force' (2000: 4): Imagine, if you would, a smooth linear flow of air – a laminar flow as it is in technical language. As this flow encounters an object it is forced to change direction, and in the wake of this object the flow is disturbed, disordered. Thus, the classical definition of turbulence is a series of successive instabilities in the smooth flow (of a gas or fluid). In the social sciences we might use this sense of turbulence to describe an unexpected event and its aftermath – the Tunisian revolt of 2011 or the Brexit referendum of 2016 were both turbulent in the sense that they were unsettling and unexpected. But Papastergiadis adds, we can also use it on a different level, it can be 'a metaphor for the broader levels of interconnection and interdependency between various forms that are in play in the modern world' (2000: 4). Here he is relying upon a certain consonance between work done in the last forty years in mathematics, physics and the philosophy of science on one hand, and social and political phenomena that appear disordered and chaotic on the other. In the philosophy of science, Prigogine and Stengers explain:

> For a long time turbulence was identified with disorder or noise. Today we know that this is not the case. Indeed, while turbulent motion appears as irregular or chaotic on the macroscopic scale, it is, on the contrary, highly organised on the

> microscopic scale. The multiple space and time scales involved in turbulence correspond to the coherent behaviour of millions and millions of molecules. Viewed in this way, the transition from laminar flow to turbulence is a process of self-organisation.
>
> (1984: 141–142)

Or as Papastergiadis puts it: turbulence is a formulation for 'movements [that] may appear chaotic' but which have a 'logic and order within them' (2000: 4). Papastergiadis uses turbulence to describe the apparent disorder of global flows of migration and displacement. In that context he finds a seemingly infinite complexity, which troubles the way that traditional political analyses employ more simple linear ideas of cause and effect. Within a turbulent system, as William Connolly explains, causality is 'emergent' (2011: 171).

Emergent causality is to be distinguished from traditional linear causality, with its distinct and independent cause and effect. Rather, in emergent causality, causes become effects, and effects suddenly become new causes. Paul Carter explains: 'Turbulence is associated with open systems, with networks; it is not simply a complex and unpredictable cultural or physical environment. It is the *phenomenon of feedback*' (Carter, 2014: 1, emphasis added). A multitude of happenings leads to accelerating and cascading events beyond the cause of any one person or thing. Instead of someone causing some event in a moral, political or legal sense (an agent-oriented linear causality), turbulent events spiral. They rapidly accelerate and decelerate in ways that appear chaotic because of their complexity. There are multiple (and competing) causal reasons for events.

> The emergent condition [here we could think of a state in economic crisis, or a crowd in protest] is affected by external forces that infect, invade, or infuse it and by activation within itself of previously untapped capacities or self-organisation. The emergent grows out of spiralling movements . . . back and forth between these elements. Sometimes an accumulation of internal stresses and fractures assumes priority, eventually reaching a tipping point at which an abrupt change occurs. Sometimes the initial trigger comes from outside, spurring a new response of self-organisation inside that succeeds or fails. Often the two processes interact in an intimate way.
>
> (Connolly, 2011: 171)

As Connolly notes, emergent causality often frustrates attempts to predict outcomes because the factors involved are just too complex. This lack of control then becomes precisely the site of political danger.

Borrowing Papastergiadis's distinction and putting it into the context of popular disorder (which is the only disorder and turbulence that this chapter will address), I want to suggest that we can identify his two senses of turbulence with two different scales. The first sense of turbulence is dis-ordering, the interruption or negation of an order. *Disorder* in this context is a moment where a crowd or crowds contest, protest, declare or otherwise disrupt the everyday relations and activities.[1] Obviously not all protests will constitute a disorder, and not all disorder necessarily entails violence (the Hong Kong Umbrella Movement is a good example of this, see Ng, 2016; Matthews, 2016). *Turbulence*, on the other hand, requires that we see logics and orders at play before and after, as well as within, the spectacle of disorder. It requires that we think about the situatedness of the disorder and the relations beyond its spatial and temporal confines. Turbulence, as Papastergiadis suggests, is the 'broader levels of interconnection and interdependency'. It sometimes give rise to a moment, or further moments of disorder, but often populations are managed so that docility is ensured. Crucially then, to understand turbulence you have to simultaneously 'zoom out' to see the myriad ways an event relates across time and space, and at the same time 'zoom in' to the minute level upon which the events become more than a chaotic disorder. Disorder is dis-ordered only on certain temporal and spatial scales, it is dis-ordered only from certain perspectives.

Before we begin, let me introduce one more idea: atmosphere. Atmospheres are all around us, some palpable and significant for us, but most merely passing and unnoticed. They are a sharing-out of affect, at once produced and shared by (human and non-human) bodies in space. Teresa Brennan asks us to think about what happens in intense atmospheres. She says: 'If I walk . . . into the atmospheric room . . . and it is rank with the smell of anxiety, I breathe this in' (2004: 68). Sara Ahmed insists that affects stick to us, but they are never simply prior to the mood that we are in (2010). Thus, for instance, the atmosphere of anxiety in an exam hall will stick differently to a candidate about to sit the exam and an examiner about to invigilate. The people in the exam hall generate waves of atmosphere, which affect the people therein. As Andreas Philippopoulos-Mihalopoulos explains: 'An atmosphere spreads through and in-between a multiplicity of bodies like a sticky substance' (2015: 122). For Brennan and many of the so-called affect theorists, atmosphere is a material and not simply a subjective event. It cannot be explained simply as a discursive relation between subject positions (their hopes, expectations, desires, needs and self-interests) and 'objective conditions' (the exam hall, or the city in crisis).

In the intensity of a turbulent atmosphere, instability occurs as people are affected (perhaps) more intensely, more unpredictably or more deeply by particular events. A good instantiation of this is to be found in the Kerner Report of the US Presidential Commission on the 1967 long, hot summer of riots. The Commission described how disorder emerged from an increasingly 'disturbed social atmosphere'. In this atmosphere,

> tension-heightening incidents . . . became linked . . . with a reservoir of underlying grievances. At some point in the mounting tension, a further incident – in itself often routine or trivial – became the breaking point and the tension spilled over into violence.
>
> (Kerner Report, 1967)

What is interesting in this is not simply the manner in which massive historic injustices become connected to recent injuries, insults and indignities. These connections had been made many times before and after, but rather the manner in which the shared affects that gathered around such indignities ignited 'civil disorder'. The *atmosphere* brought people out onto the streets. What we find in moments of turbulence, and particularly in moments of generalised disorder, is an intensely palpable atmosphere. When a city is brought to crisis by popular disorder, particularly where such unrest continues for an extended span of time, there is a sort of tension, excitement, expectation, fear, dread, a general quickening in the pulse of a city. And this atmosphere changes people; it affects conceptions of the possible, the probable and the necessary. But let us begin.

Security and the police

In politics, disorder is often understood as a threat. It is instability which produces dangers to economic growth and development; it is understood as opening the possibility of the violence of all versus all, the breaking of social bonds; it is at once a cause and effect of states becoming categorised as 'fragile'. And in all of this, disorder is rendered as a question of deepening or intensifying *security*. But security is not something static; it is not simply the 'absence' of insecurity or the 'presence' of social peace. Security is a way of discursively framing an event or object. Once placed within a logic of security, the object or event changes in significance. Critical security studies, at least as the subject was conceived by the Copenhagen school, insists that we must think about *securitisation* rather than security (Buzan et al., 1998). Securitisation is the process of rendering an object or question in relation to a threat to its existence. If a problem presents an existential threat, then extraordinary responses are not just possible but necessary (cf. Honig, 2011). Securitisation becomes a way of rendering the most extra-ordinary policies as ordinary. In the realm of emergency politics, any issue 'can be dealt with swiftly and without the normal (democratic) rules and regulations of policy-making' (Taureck, 2006: 3). Any political issue might be securitised, but some are more readily securitised than others.

Popular disturbances will often interrupt the everyday functioning of the state, circulation of people and things will be disrupted, the economy will suffer even before shop windows are broken or banks are occupied. In this sense, protests are readily securitised – they are apparently a threat to the everyday order and smooth functioning of democracy and capitalism. The response to popular disturbance across Western Europe and North America has been to establish a paramilitary 'third force', between the police and the military. In France, for instance, the *Compagnies Républicaines de Sécurité* and the *Gendarmerie Mobile* have long been established (see Fowler, 1979; Fassin, 2013). Likewise in post-colonial states where the technologies of colonisation almost universally took the form of intense public order policing in the name of subjugation and pacification, militarised police forces with responsibility for public order are the norm. But in the UK the 'third force' is a very recent event, occurring in the period between the mid-70s and the early 90s (Northam, 1988). In response to the 1976 Notting Hill Carnival, the police began to wear armour while on public order duty. Initially this consisted of shin-guards, cork-lined helmets with chin straps and large heavy Perspex shields. Following a briefing to the Association of Chief Police Officers in 1981 from colonial police forces in Hong Kong and Northern Ireland, British police forces introduced significant new technology (new armour, shields, gas, weapons and vehicles) and new tactics (Northam, 1988: Cashmore and McLaughlin, 1991; Brogden and Ellison, 2012).

It is important to note that in the colonial context, the question was not how to restore order after a momentary lapse, but rather how to re-establish docility of populations which might collectively withhold consent (see Northam, 1988). In this context, public order police would often rely on 'show of force'. Former Commissioner of the Royal Hong Kong Police, Roy Henry, explains that public order policing was conceived as 'the projection of police units in an efficient, effective and *formidable* manner which creates an atmosphere in the riotous mobs of apprehension and awe which could be close to *fear*'. If this atmospheric projection is successful, then 'the crowd will scatter: "They run like the dickens!"' (quoted in Northam, 1988: 136, emphasis in original). In the UK from the late 90s and particularly in the mid-2000s, the police began to employ other (more peaceable) first-line tactics in order to better control and discipline protest, but elsewhere the tendency to employ the 'show of force' tactics has intensified. Perhaps few more so than in certain states in the US. Since 9/11, federal programs have supported local police forces in purchasing tanks, armoured personnel carriers, sniper equipment and other heavy armoury (Balko, 2013). This was most visible in the response to the Ferguson protests in 2014, where curfews were enforced with stun grenades, tear gas, rubber bullets and wooden baton rounds. But what really shocked people at the time was the extreme force that was threatened by heavily armed officers in combat armour, supported by snipers atop armoured vehicles (see Taylor, 2016).

This is a first sense of security: a process of securitisation where riots and strikes are portrayed as an existential threat to the public order, legitimating increasingly nuanced and at times violent police tactics. Crucially, this understands a protest as an object which requires a response; the nature of the response is framed by the discourse in which it is situated. Securitisation then is one among many discursive situations, and as the Copenhagen school suggested, it was capable of being 'desecuritised'. However, with Vaughan-Williams (2015 and 2012) or Aradau and van Munster (2011), we might understand a different, broader sense of security, where the question is not *simply* of the moment of disorder which might be securitised or desecuritised. We might typify this as the difference between the management of disorder and the management of turbulence. But what would it look like to address turbulence more generally rather than the narrower sense of disorder? Let us follow this different line of reasoning.

The rule of law is understood to provide the conditions under which society can be governed with regularity and neutrality between individuals. A state that accords to the rule of law is thus entitled to defend itself from those who seek systemic change outside of the conventional political system. In this sense, the rule of law is the key signifier of a 'just' order. It is posed against the instability of popular disorder. The police play a key role as the upholders of this value. The police power is apparently circumscribed by the legal order that transcends it. This model of police power emerges at the end of the eighteenth century when the old idea of the *polizeistaat* was reconceived by a succession of liberal thinkers. The *polizeistaat* and the concept of 'police' as it emerged in the sixteenth century in Europe was a way of controlling populations increasingly freed of feudal dependence and control (Dean, 1991: 59). The *polizeistaat* was 'dedicated to three purposes: the protection of the population, the welfare of the state and its citizens and the improvement of society in all its aspects' (Chapman, 1971: 15–16). 'The object of the police is to keep a community thriving so that its subjects may prosper, and prevent anything hindering the common good' (Dean, 2010: 109). Its regulations covered the

> minutiae of social life, including the means of comfort, public health, food and wine adulteration, expenses at christenings, weddings and funerals, the wearing of extravagant clothing, the behaviour of citizens at church or during festivities, the maintenance of roads, bridges and town buildings, public security, the regulation of the provision of goods and services, the performance of trades and occupations, religion, morals and manners, the behaviour of servants towards their masters.
>
> (Neocleous, 2000: 3)

This intense regulation of the social and economic order was not about the enforcement of criminal law, as we now conceive of the police function. Rather, it was about undermining the activities that were perceived as 'damaging to communal good order' (Neocleous, 2000: 4).

Neocleous suggests that the early liberalism of the eighteenth and nineteenth centuries pushed back against the *polizeistaat* (the rule of good order) opposing it to the *rechtstaat* (the rule of law). In England this would be conceived of as the distinction between the 'criminal' and 'municipal' police (Colquhoun, 1797). Law was reconceived as the freedom from regulation. '[O]rder became law's empire', with the criminal police function being gradually redefined in the early nineteenth century: 'no longer an almost universal force with unlimited powers to pursue the common happiness, police was reconceptualised as a more limited force with clearly specified powers and focused on the prevention of crime and internal security' (Neocleous, 2000: 32). Police power in liberalism was reconceived within, and subject to, the legal order. It was thought of as bound by law and bound to protect law. Walter Benjamin famously challenges this image of the police in the 'Critique of Violence'.

> The assertion that the ends of police . . . are always identical or even connected to those of general law is entirely untrue. Rather, the 'law' of the police really marks the point at which the state . . . can no longer guarantee through the legal system the empirical ends that it desires at any price to attain.
>
> (Benjamin, 1978: 287)

Agamben glosses this: 'The rationales of "public order" and "security" on which the police have to decide on a case-by-case basis define an area of indistinction between violence and right' (2000: 104).

Neocleous concurs with Benjamin and insists that the idea of law as generative of police power should be inverted: the police perform the powers they feel that they need and subsequently rationalise their actions in terms of law, he argues. When these rationalisations become too unrealistic or blatant, the legal order, he insists, changes to accommodate the apparent needs of the police through either judicial development or legislation: 'rather than police carrying out law as made by Parliament, Parliament has made laws which have legitimized existing police practice. "Law reform" is often little more than a product and legitimation of police operational practices' (Neocleous, 2000: 98). He cites a number of examples for this, but overstates the case, evacuating law of function independent of police. Benjamin puts this differently, suggesting that police violence (that is state-legitimised violence) is law-preserving (*rechtsetzend*). But more controversially, he suggests that it is also a law-making violence (*rechtserhaltend gewalt*).

> [T]he police intervene 'for security reasons' in countless cases where no clear legal situation exists, when they are not merely, without the slightest relation to legal ends, accompanying the citizen as a brutal encumbrance through a life regulated by ordinances, or simply supervising him.
>
> (Benjamin, 1978: 287)

The police is a force that goes beyond law in a myriad of invisible and difficult to identify manners (cf. Bataille, 1985), but this is not simply the subjection of law to the police, as in Neocleous. Robinson explains Benjamin's insight:

> Police violence is especially insidious since it lacks the limits of both kinds of violence: the requirement of victory in law-making violence, and the prohibition on inventing ends in law-preserving violence. It is a means for the state to achieve the ends it desires 'at any price', when it does not feel law is sufficient to obtain them. In contrast to law, which has a place and time of decision, policing operates as a ghostly, diffuse, amorphous presence.
>
> (Robinson, 2013)

However, it is not just that the liberal picture of the police (as both protector of and subjected to law) is flawed. Benjamin's idea of the police connects up with the broad sense of police as social ordering. As we have seen, he says that the police 'accompany the citizen as a brutal encumbrance'. In a different context, Foucault would later say that police, in the full and broad sense of the term, 'govern not by law, but by a specific, *a permanent and a positive intervention in the behaviour of individuals*' (Foucault, 2000: 415, emphasis added; cf. Rancière, 1998: 1–42). The novelty of police power, particularly from the late eighteenth century, was that it became more subtle and flexible. For Foucault, police is the discourse in which the 'techniques of discipline, surveillance and bureaucracy needed to foster [the] welfare of the population' could be linked in a fundamental way to 'the security, external strength and power of the state' (Dean, 2010: 115). In this way, 'police science' (*polizeiwissenschaft*) opened the possibilities of the biopolitics that marks our time.

If we understand police as a broad term for the immanent fabrication and maintenance of social order (Neocleous, 2000: x), we can see that the idea of the recent securitisation of disorder that I began with is flawed. It is not a matter of simply securitising certain objects – like a protest or even revolt, but of security as a *dispositif* which structures the very milieu in which we live. As the most direct challenge to order, popular disorder is one key object that security seeks to prevent, but not simply through force of arms. This is the mistake of those who talk about the recent securitisation of the police, referring to post-9/11 militarisation, the rise of SWAT teams and the growing arsenal of the police (for instance Swaine and Holpuch, 2014; Balko, 2013). This is just one (admittedly spectacular) way that the police power seeks to prevent disorder. The police force also employs a myriad of other responses: from negotiation and 'consent-based policing' of protest, to the employment of crowd psychologists to train police in public order tactics, or the raising of the stakes of protest by randomly selecting past protestors for prosecution. This demonstrates just some of the *police force's* approach to disorder. But much more interesting are the myriad of ways that crowded popular political action is 'designed out' of modern democracy: from Foucault's description of governmentality and biopolitics which governs populations and discipline which generates docile bodies to Rancière's 'distribution of the sensible' which creates a regime of visibility and invisibility (1998), there have been many significant theorisations of this management. And so to conclude this first part, it is important to distinguish between the securitisation of disorder and the much broader phenomenon of the management of turbulence. Once we move beyond simply observing the role of the police force, who securitise protest to militarise or develop further powers, and understand the broader frame of the production of docility, then we have begun to understand the question of popular *turbulence*. It is a matter of the immanent government of bodies, a science of managing populations. Disorder is that moment of unrest, protest, riot, but turbulence are those eddies of affect, those atmospheres of dissent that might unfold as disorder, or that might be pacified and calmed. Police names the management of both turbulence and disorder.

Sovereignty

Police is the immanent and profane management of bodies, an ordering that seeks to design out turbulence and disorder by minute intervention in everyday life. But there is a second and deeply entwined order of pacification: sovereignty. This is an order that is understood historically in relation to the sacred, and which today still claims a certain transcendence. Thus, the way we can talk about it must shift from the gritty debates about police, control and social order to the apparently abstract and rarified confines of theologies, constitutions and sovereigns. The basic point is that practices of sovereignty are aimed at the maintenance of majesty. Majesty is understood in relation to the 'dignity' of the office, the regalia, the symbols and the ceremonies. However, sovereign glory is *not* a property of the office, as we will see, but rather it is something that is practiced (Agamben, 2011). Glory is a relation, a certain elevation from which the one-above towers over those-below. But as a relation it must constantly be performed, it does not adhere *naturally* to the one-above but must instead be maintained. For the glory and dignity of the sovereign to remain, there must continue to be glorification. The performativity of glory and majesty in general is too large an issue for this chapter; however, there is one key element of it that I will address. In democratic constitutionalism, we find glory as an aura that surrounds the people. But as Loughlin and Walker explain: 'The people, in Maistre's words, "are a sovereign that cannot exercise sovereignty"; the power they possess, it would appear, can only be exercised through constitutional forms already established or in the process of being established' (Loughlin and Walker, 2007: 1). The people are a sovereign that *must not* govern, because they are unruly and disordered, unless directed through government. This characterisation establishes democratic sovereignty as a span of time, a suspension in which past and future turbulence and disorder is held off. In this, we can begin to see the relation between the police and the sovereign. The former are agents, the latter is the object of this suspension. In this section I will propose an idea of sovereignty as an appropriation of a past turbulence. This appropriation is an act of glorification of the sovereign, which appropriates the aura of the people while differs and defers its turbulence.

The first move of the constitutional order is appropriation. The most obvious reason for wanting to associate a constitutional order with the revolution that perhaps preceded it is that the revolution established the political grounds upon which the new order is based. In this sense, there appears a historical tie between the violence of the revolution and the constitutional order that draws the revolution to an end. Thus, for instance, the American constitution and the institutions that it gives birth to is understood as the culmination of the revolutionary process (for a full discussion of the complexity of this see Frank, 2010). However, in many states, perhaps despite a revolutionary history, there is only a tenuous tie between the current order and a moment of constituent power; in England because of the civil war history and 'glorious revolution'; or indeed even in France where the revolutionary history is succeeded by counter-revolution and successive republics. Even in the absence of any historical tie to a revolutionary moment, the significant symbolic power of a people tearing down a constituted order is often projected through 'agents'. Think for instance of the many images of US troops the tearing down of the statue of Saddam Hussein and 'liberating' Iraq. These moments are often spectacular and excessive and give the turgid text of the constitution a hint of excitement by conveying the majesty of the new state by association with the spectacular violence of the change of constitutional order.

The process of appropriation is not straight-forward, however, because it is important for a liberal constitutional order to also separate the revolutionary violence from the new political order. In *Democracy and the Foreigner* Bonnie Honig gives us a beautiful reading of this moment of constitutional foundation (2003). She begins with Rousseau's paradox of politics: the people under the *ancien regime* is marked by the impurity and injustice of the old monarchy. Given this imprint of the old order, Rousseau is stuck wondering how the people could found a just polity? Instead it is likely to reproduce the defects of the old order, the only system with which it is familiar. Rousseau resolves this through the *deus ex machina* of a foreign founder who generates a just republic by putting some to the sword, before withdrawing to allow the people to take on their sovereign mantle. Thus, for Rousseau there is a purifying violence (of the constituent moment) which does not infect the new constitutional order. Honig insists that this script is all too neat. Instead she reads Rousseau's story alongside Rene Girard's analysis of the scapegoat, asking whether the foreignness of the founder in Rousseau is as simple as it initially seems. From Girard, she finds that the scapegoat is often designated foreign, but that this foreignness may be constructed in the process of scapegoating. The scapegoat need not be an outsider, rather he may be, or may become, 'a foreigner because he is a scapegoat' (Honig, 2003: 34). In other words, the entire foreign-ness of founding moments becomes a projection of the founding polity. The founding violence is projected outward as a way of sealing off the real violence of foundation. The founding moment is appropriated *and* made foreign as the constitution and its people celebrate and acclaim it. 'Thus', Honig explains, 'we tell ourselves, the violence that touches our regime is contained and final rather than boundless and cyclical' (Honig, 2003: 38).

The new constitution gives the people a final unity that was only ever partial in the constituent moment. However, it does so by producing the myth that the 'people spoke' (as a unity) in the moment of giving the constitution. What the constitution glorifies in the constituent moment is a substantive unity in action: the glorious people standing forth against the unjust order and proclaiming the new just order. But this substantive unity is something that could *only* emerge in the new sovereign order, where the subject reflects back on the constituent moment and attributes to it an 'originating' status (Lindahl, 2007). In the disorder of a revolutionary moment, what is necessarily absent is any sense of a substantive unity in action. As Frank makes clear, it must be constantly imagined and produced in the identification of the people with unitary figures (2015). This partiality of the people in the moment of its action, however, does not mean that it is somehow illegitimate, just that it remains 'incomplete' (cf. Honig, 1991; Wall, 2015). Put otherwise, every revolutionary group is simply seditious (because it is incomplete) until they win, when they become glorified as 'founding fathers' (rarely, it seems, do we come across glorification of 'founding mothers' in this context). Every attempt to claim constituent power in the present can already be delegitimised because the crowd that gathers in the squares and streets is *not* the people (qua total unity in action). The people then become the impossible pristine fetish object of the constitution, never to return to disrupt the sovereign order. It takes up a symbolic role as the absolute legitimation of the constitution and its established order.

The constituent moment must differ from the constitutional order, and it cannot be altogether banished. Constitutional orders seek to render it always past by setting conditions that forever defer it. Locke's rendering of a right to revolution is a good example of this deferral. This would seem to be a high point for a real constituent power that finds its place within the constitution. He makes this sense of constituent power explicit: the people retain a latent right to revolt against the constitutional order if it transgresses their rights. They may 'resume their original liberty, and, by the establishment of a new legislative . . . provide for their own safety and security, which is the end for which they are in society' (Locke, 1690: §222). The sovereign will not become a tyrant, Locke says, as he stands in a precarious position. He is always fearful of the return of the people. Locke's constituent power of the right to revolution is a 'final right', in that it is the right that guarantees all other rights. It must always be put off until the trust between the sovereign and the people is entirely sundered. In this, Locke proposes constituent power at the beginning and end of the body politic. The constituted order is thus the suspension of constituent power, from which it draws its authorising quality. Constituent power allows the sovereign order to be seen as spectacularly at risk and vulnerable: But of course, today, there is an everyday invulnerability produced by the broad sense of police, as we have seen in the preceding section. However, while Locke is glorifying sovereignty by celebrating the process of its future reconstitution, he also attempts to guard against its exercise. He sets preconditions upon the right to revolt which often go unremarked. Foremost among these are the determination of the subjects of revolt and the end that the revolt might achieve.

Locke gives us a glimpse of the limitation of the subject of revolt in one of his little known essays on money (1997). He explains that labourers rarely think above their bare subsistence, arguing that they do not have mind for matters of state and the higher calling of government.[2] Kain notes that

> [i]t never occurs to Locke that in the normal course of events the poor concern themselves with anything but bare subsistence. When they do, it does not occur to. . . [him] that it may be for some legitimate reason. It is a problem of mismanagement.
>
> (Kain, 1993: 56)

For Locke, the poor do not think beyond subsistence. Politics and revolution are a matter for the likes of his patron, the Earl of Shaftsbury. Ultimately, this fits with Locke's basic ontology of the political, where civil society is created through the demarcation of private property. Rationality, in this scheme, is generated through taking, holding and administering private property. The poor, as those who were without property, were excluded from this rationality (cf. Tully, 1993, on the similar state of American indigenous claims to territory and rationality). Locke's conception of the right to revolt, as the acme of political subjectivity, is fundamentally pre-figured by the question of property. This precondition establishes that the poor or the indigenous may not revolt. Theirs is a life below politics.

Let us be clear, I am suggesting that sovereignty is an appropriation of the turbulence of the constituent moment, where the violence of the disorder is differed, and the possibility of its return is deferred. In this way sovereignty is constituted as suspension. The past and future revolt 'belongs' to the democratic state, becoming the protector of the people and the bearer of the revolution. The majesty passes to the state, which then manages its population to hold off turbulence. This then is the key element of glorification that I set out to describe in this section. Crucially, the connection that I am making between sovereignty as suspension and glorification is not just passing. The Christian theological sense of glorification comes from a Latin translation of the Greek *doxa*, which here could be rendered as 'expectation', that is the act of projecting a future that has yet not arrived. Glorification is the action undertaken in expectation of a future event. Further, glorification is intimately linked to power. But as Agamben suggests, this raises a perplexing question:

> If power is essentially force and efficacious action, why does it need to receive ritual acclamations and hymns of praise, to wear cumbersome crowns and tiaras, to submit itself to an inaccessible ceremony and an immutable protocol . . . why does [it] . . . need to become solemnly immobilized in glory?
>
> (Agamben, 2011: 195)

Majesty must constantly be created through rituals, from the more 'ancient' occasions with crown, robe, orb and sceptre to the more 'modern' US presidential inauguration, pledge of allegiance and state of the nation address, or French tricolour and Marseillaise. As Kertzer mentions briefly in his major work *Ritual, Politics and Power*, the more insecure the sovereign, the more seriously the ritual must be performed (Kertzer, 1988: 176). While we must be careful with this generalisation, it does underline the purpose of glorification to *sustain* the sovereign order, holding off the 'return' of the constituent moment.

In a fairly standard post-Foucaultian vein, thus far we have seen police and government as distinct from sovereignty. Police-government signifies the process of technological management of life through immanent and particular mechanisms of governing. Sovereignty, then, becomes the celebration and glorification of the constituent power of the people (through the constitution's institutions) in order to hold off its return. In this sense, we can see the overlap between the two. The sovereign and police are knitted together. As Agamben makes clear in *The Kingdom and the Glory*, the practice of glorification, so central to sovereignty, is an *economic* practice. He poses the distinct theological poles in Christianity of the transcendent God the father who is the uncreated creator, but who cannot intervene in the world; and God the son that is begotten of the father although still created outside of time, but who intervenes on earth to open heaven by way of an economy of salvation (through the 'providential machine'). Agamben explains that this theological sense of an economy (of salvation) is fundamentally connected with the Foucaultian sense of government-police. This is not the time to explore this thesis in any depth (see Minca, 2009; Watkin, 2012; Whyte, 2013), I adduce it merely to underline that the practice of glorification which creates the transcendence (as transcendent) is already of the government-police order. If glorification, which is the process of creating and maintaining transcendence of the God-sovereign, is already an economic practice, then the simple bifurcation between immanent police-government-economy and transcendent sovereignty breaks down. And this is precisely the point. The 'different orders' of police and sovereign that I held apart throughout this chapter must be understood as an articulation, a mobile and flexible joint. More than that, they represent practices that are always already immanent to one another.

Atmospheres of turbulent legality

I want to suggest by way of closing that a key way of understanding this collapsing of one order into the other is to understand the doctrine of the sovereign peace. In the UK this is known as the Queen's peace, but it will be familiar to other jurisdictions as the 'public peace' or 'peace, order and good government' (Yusuf, 2014), and other similar formulations. I turn to this in conclusion to underline the immanence of police and sovereign orders to one another. This interspersal is at the heart of what I am calling 'turbulent legality'.

On the 29th of April 2011, the day of the royal wedding between 'Wills and Kate', a small number of zombies began gathering in Soho Square. Or, at least, that had been the plan of the Royal Zombie Wedding Flash Mob. They wanted a party and picnic. But the police closed three of the four entrances to the square and few if any zombies got through. Those already there realised that the zombie apocalypse was not going to happen that day and decided to leave the square. In their own words, 'we were fairly inoffensive members of the undead, who ate some homemade "brainssss" cake earlier in the day, and travelled on to Starbucks' (Farnell, 2011). It was a great surprise to the innocuous undead to be escorted from Starbucks by the police and detained pursuant to the prevention of a breach of the peace. The zombies – all of good character as the appeal later makes clear – were brought to various police stations and detained until after the wedding had taken place. They were then released and no charges were pressed. While they challenged their preventative detention, the Court of Appeal ultimately upheld the centuries-old police power. In the 1994 *Liberty and Order*, P.A.J. Waddington had noted the intensity with which such ceremonial events were policed. He explained the intense planning process where the police were encouraged to 'take control of the area . . . for weeks prior to its occurrence' (45). This included sealing manholes, closing roads, inch-by-inch searches of the route, the deployment of anti-sniper sharpshooters, the patrol of possible mortar sites, and the screening and intensive surveillance of the crowds. But this control did not just extend to excluding terrorist attack:

> acts of protest that would diminish the *dignity of the occasion* are rigorously prevented. A person carrying a tin-whistle that might have been blown during the two minute silence at the Cenotaph on Remembrance Sunday was ejected from the crowd. People thought to be preparing pacifist protests during Trooping the Colour were stopped and searched, and then escorted from the area.
>
> (Waddington, 1994: 45)

It is in this context that we must understand the fate of the zombies in 2011. Their flash mob was not to take place in *any* public space, but in the vicinity of a royal ceremonial event. In this space the ordinarily innocuous zombie picnic, that would go unmolested by the police in any other setting, took on an especial significance. Their presence ran the risk of lessening the *dignity* of the event – of the calm and orderly atmosphere of sovereign glorification. This then is the point where the management of turbulence and sovereign glorification cross-over in the most obvious of ways. The zombies threatened no violence, but their bloody costumes of wedding dresses seemed to re-perform the symbolism of the state's ritual. The police's greatest fear was that the zombies would operationalise their metaphor by throwing worms and maggots at the wedding party outside Westminster Abbey (*R (Hicks) v. Commissioner of the Police of the Metropolis*, para 13), underlining that the royal institution perhaps was an order that had lived beyond its time. The zombies were playing through metaphor on the *splendour* and the *stateliness* of the day.

It is at moments like this that the Queen's peace is at its most intense. But the doctrine is at play everywhere in public and stately space. Sir Carelton Kemp Allen explained the doctrine in terms that I think are important:

> The 'peace of our Sovereign Lady the Queen' has been described by . . . Maitland, as an 'all-embracing atmosphere' in our law, and, we may add, in our whole social life. We could not breathe in any other atmosphere, and we take it for granted as if it were part of the order of nature.
>
> (Allen, 1953: 3)

This rather tantalising suggestion that the Queen's peace might be thought of as an atmosphere rather than a willed or commanded order is not developed by Allen. Academic analyses of public order tend to focus on sovereign and police power, rule of law and rights. This type of analysis misses the very real, but often imperceptible sense in which the Queen's peace (or 'public order') is an affective state, a collective sense of order and calm regularity. Crucially, as Allen underlines, this is precisely not 'natural' or unfashioned. It is *produced* in and by law, that is in sovereign glorification and police ordering.

Although he refuses to identify it simply with public order, this is the process that Andreas Philippopoulos-Mihalopoulos calls the dissimulation of law in atmosphere (2015: 73). When law as an 'extensive institutional affect' (2015: 69) shifts from a visible spatiolegal process to become invisible, then Philippopoulos-Mihalopoulos suggests it has become atmospheric. Atmospheres are the perfect hiding place, he tells us: 'We are all inside atmospheres. . . . Yet we are not aware of the atmosphere. [As such a]n atmosphere is the perfect enclosure' (2015: 6). As law becomes atmospheric we become inured to its structuring presence, we acclimatise. In this sense, the Queen's peace as a calm atmosphere of normality signifies a withdrawal or a diffusing of law. Put into his terms, the public peace is one way that the law spatialises (and space legalises) itself. Law and space exist in a tautological relation – what he calls the lawscape. Whether human or non-human, whether animal, vegetable or mineral, 'Every body lawscapes. The law in the lawscape emanates from every body, without discernible origin' (2015: 69). For Philippopoulos-Mihalopoulos, the key ontological element of law/lawscape is its tendency to invisibilise. '[I]n/visibilisation is not just a game on the side, but the lawscape's only mechanism of ontological continuation: its ultimate purpose. This is all the lawscape is' (2015: 75). Thus invisibilisation becomes the key aspect of law, and atmosphere, which is the way law invisibilises itself, becomes the core of this beautiful legal theory.

This should not be read as a wholesale adoption of Philippopoulos-Mihalopoulos's theorisation of the lawscape, however. At the heart of his work is a commitment to absolute immanence that we do not share. For him there is nothing outside this plane of immanence. My work has drawn on Jean-Luc Nancy's idea of 'trans-immanence', an awkward neologism that attempts to express an immanent reaching beyond (see Wall, 2012: 130). For Nancy, 'sense' is an immanent transcendence, something which is shared, in the sense of being both held together and separated out. There is no space of full transcendence, a God-space from which a unitary sense could be made of the world. Instead, the sense of the world is the process of world-ing (*mondialisation*) (for further discussion and explanation see Nancy, 1997; Kujndžic, 2005; or Wall, 2012: ch 8). From this disagreement, which is too significant to draw out fully here, the theories must travel in radically different directions. In essence, it could be summed up by saying that for me, there is an outside to law. Instead of Philippopoulos-Mihalopoulos's claim that law is everywhere in all things (albeit differentially), I contend that there are more productive ways of conceptualising legal atmospheres. Without the need to find law in all things, the function of atmosphere changes. No longer is it simply a play in dissimulation. There are moments of 'stateliness' and 'dignity', where law's public order is manifested as an intense atmosphere. Courtrooms are often a good example of this, or occasions of state. These manifest an intense atmosphere which is not invisibilised. Law becomes atmospheric, but not invisible or imperceptible. Equally, in so-called public order situations (i.e., protests, strikes, riots, etc.), we find intense atmospheres that belong neither to law nor the protestors/strikers/rioters (cf. Philippopoulos-Mihalopoulos, 2015: 108–109).

Therefore, we must return to the question with which I began: what would it mean to think about law in the moment of popular political crisis, in the moment where it is contested by 'the people' or a multitude? What would it be to think a turbulent legality? Placed against the miscellany of conventional jurisprudes and legal theorists, I hope the answer is clear: law is not simply rational legal decision; it is not simply an exercise of decision and order. In moments of turbulence the very conditions of such theorisation disappear. By starting from stable order to theorise law, these theories end up being incapable of responding to popular dissatisfaction with anything other than an intra-systemic direction. Movements are told that they must either conform to the straight-jacket of rights, or be subject to repression through police violence and prosecution. Beyond this simple blindspot, I have begun to identify the modalities of law as it iterates through the distinct rationalities of police and sovereignty. Between these poles, the question is of the dignity of the realm, the majesty of the sovereign's peace, the various techniques of individual subjectivation and population management, and the ways in which security is manifested to defeat any possibility of popular mobilisation. In between the past and future revolt, dissent and contestation are symbolically celebrated as the essence of democracy, but in terms of a praxis, they are left to the police function. The point of this chapter is ultimately that the thrust of an ugly profane police management, and the appropriation of a people's after-glow for the transcendent glory of sovereign, although radically different in tenor, are two sides of the one coin. They are the janus-face of law's order, neither simply within law nor beyond, but constitutive. This is where the question of a 'turbulent legality' take us. It starts from the practices of ordering, rather than taking order as the start.

Notes

1 There are of course myriad other disorders and turbulences, but this is a chapter about popular disorder.

2 'For the laborers share, being seldom more than a bare subsistence, never allows that body of men time or opportunity to raise their thoughts above [subsistence], or struggle with the richer for their [share], . . . unless when some common and great distress, uniting them in one universal ferment, makes them forget respect, and emboldens them to carve to their wants with armed force; and then sometimes they break in upon the rich, and sweep all like a deluge. But this rarely happens but in the mal-administration of neglected, or mismanaged government' (Locke (1997) and discussed in Kain, 1993: 55–56).

Bibliography

Agamben, Giorgio, *Homo Sacer: Sovereign Power and Bare Life,* Stanford: Stanford University Press, 1998.

Agamben, Giorgio, *Means without End: Notes on Politics*, Minneapolis: University of Minnesota Press, 2000.

Agamben, Giorgio, *State of Exception*, Chicago: Chicago University Press, 2005.

Agamben, Giorgio, *The Kingdom and the Glory*, Stanford: University of Stanford Press, 2011.

Ahmed, Sara, 'Happy Objects', in M. Gregg and G. Seigworth (eds), *The Affect Theory Reader*, Durham, NC: Duke University Press, 2010.

Allen, Carleton Kemp, *The Queens Peace*, Oxford: Stevens and Sons Ltd, 1953.

Aradau, Claudia and Van Munster, Rens, *Politics of Catastrophe: Genealogies of the Unknown*, London: Routledge, 2011.

Arendt, Hannah, 'What is Authority?' in H. Arendt (ed.), *Between Past and Future*, New York: Penguin Classics, 91–141, 2006.

Benjamin, Walter, 'Critique of Violence,' *Reflections,* New York: Schocken Books, 1978.

Balko, Radley, *Rise of the Warrior Cop: The Militarization of America's Police Forces*, New York: Public Affairs, 2013.

Bataille, Georges, 'The Psychological Structure of Fascism,' in Alain Stoekl (ed.), *Visions of Excess*, Minneapolis: Minnesota University Press, 1985, 139.

Brennan, Teresa, *The Transmission of Affect*, Ithaca, NY: Cornell University Press, 2004.

Brogden, Mike and Ellison, Graham, *Policing in an Age of Austerity, A Postcolonial Perspective*, London: Routledge, 2012.

Buzan, Barry, Waever, Ole and de Wilde, Jaap, *Security, A New Framework for Analysis*, London: Lynne Rienner Publishers, 1998.

Carter, Paul, '*Touchez* – The Poetics of Turbulence', *Performance Review*, 19(5), 1, 2014.

Cashmore, Ellis and McLaughlin, Eugene, *Out of Order: Policing Black People*, London: Routledge, 1991.

Chapman, Brian, *Police State*, London: Macmillan, 1971.

Colquhoun, Patrick, *A Treatise on the Police of the Metropolis*, 1797. http://archive.org/stream/atreatiseonthepo35650gut/pg35650.txt (accessed 25 April 2016).

Connolly, William, *A World of Becoming*, Durham, NC: Duke University Press, 2011.

Dean, Mitchell, *The Constitution of Poverty*, London: Routledge, 1991.

Dean, Mitchell, *Governmentality: Power and Rule in Modern Society*, 2nd edition, Thousand Oaks, CA: Sage, 2010.

Douzinas, Costas, *Philosophy and Resistance in the Crisis: Greece and the Future of Europe*, London: Polity Press, 2013.

Farnell, Chris, '#17: The Royal Wedding Zombie Flash Mob: Breach of the Peace (of the Dead),' http://chriswritesapocalypses.blogspot.co.uk/2011/05/17-royal-wedding-zombie-flash-mob.html 01/05/2011 (accessed 09 January 2017).

Fassin, Didier, *Enforcing Order*, London: Polity, 2013.

Foucault, Michel, *Power: Essential Works Vol 3*, New York: New Press, 2000.

Fowler, Norman, *After the Riots*, London: Davis Poynter, 1979.

Frank, Jason, *Constituent Moments*, Durham: Duke University Press, 2010.

Frank, Jason, 'The Living Image of the People,' *Theory & Event*, 18(1), 2015.

Hardt, Michael and Negri, Antonio, *Declarations,* New York: Argo Navis, 2012.

Honig, Bonnie, 'Declarations of Independence: Arendt and Derrida on the Problem of Founding a Republic,' *The American Political Science Review*, 85(1), 1991, 97.

Honig, Bonnie, *Democracy and the Foreigner*, New Jersey: Princeton University Press, 2003.

Honig, Bonnie, *Emergency Politics: Paradox, Law, Democracy*, New Jersey: Princeton University Press, 2011.

Jefferson, Tony, *The Case against Paramilitary Policing*, Maidenhead: Open University Press, 1990.

Kain, Phillip J., *Marx and Modern Political Theory*, Maryland, Rowman and Littlefield Publishers, 1993.

Kerner Report: 'Report of the National Advisory Commission on Civil Disorders,' 1967. http://faculty.washington.edu/qtaylor/documents_us/Kerner%20Report.htm (accessed 10 January 2017).

Kertzer, David, *Ritual, Politics and Power*, New Haven, CT: Yale University Press, 1988.

Kujundžic, Dragan, 'Empire, Glocalisation, and the Melancholia of the Sovereign,' *The Comparatist,* 29, 86, 2005.

Lindahl, Hans, 'Constituent Power and Reflexive Identity: Towards an Ontology of Collective Selfhood,' in Martin Loughlin and Neil Walker (eds), *The Paradox of Constitutionalism*, Oxford: Oxford University Press, 2007.

Locke, John, 'Considerations of the Consequences of Lowering of the Interest and Raising the Value of Money,' in John Locke (ed.), *Locke: Political Essays,* Cambridge: Cambridge University Press, 1997.

Locke, John, *Second Treatise of Government*, (1690) "http://www.earlymoderntexts.com/assets/pdfs/locke1689a" www.earlymoderntexts.com/assets/pdfs/locke1689a.pdf (accessed 25 April 2016).

Loughlin, Martin and Walker, Neil, *The Paradox of Constitutionalism*, Oxford: Oxford University Press, 2007.

Matthews, Daniel, 'Narrative, Space and Atmosphere a Nomospheric Inquiry into Hong Kong's Pro-Democracy "Umbrella Movement",' *Social & Legal Studies*, 2016.

Minca, Claudio, 'The Reign and the Glory: Or, Reflections on the Theological Foundations of the Credit Crunch,' *Environment and Planning D: Society and Space*, 27, 177.

Neocleous, Mark, *The Fabrication of Social Order*, London: Routledge, 2000.

Neocleous, Mark, *War Power Police Power*, Edinburgh: Edinburgh University Press, 2014.

Ng, Jason, *Umbrellas in Bloom: Hong Kong's Occupy Movement*, Hong Kong: Blacksmith Books, 2016.

Northam, Gerry, *Shooting in the Dark*, London: Faber & Faber, 1988.

Papastergiadis, Nikos, *The Turbulence of Migration: Globalization, Deterritorialization and Hybridity*, London: Polity Press, 2000.

Philippopoulos-Mihalopoulos, Andreas, *Spatial Justice: Body, Lawscape, Atmosphere,* Oxford, London: Routledge, 2015.

Prigogine, Ilya and Stengers, Isabelle, *Order Out of Chaos*, London: Heinmann, 1984.

Rancière, Jacques, *Disagreement: Politics and Philosophy*, Minneapolis: University of Minnesota Press, 1998.

Robinson, Andrew, 'Walter Benjamin: Critique of the State,' *Ceasefire Magazine*, 31 December 2013. https://ceasefiremagazine.co.uk/walter-benjamin-critique-state/ (accessed 05 April 2016).

Swaine, Jon and Holpuch, Amanda, 'Ferguson Police: A Stark Illustration of Newly Militarised US Law Enforcement,' *The Guardian*, 14 August 2014. www.theguardian.com/world/2014/aug/14/ferguson-police-military-restraints-violence-weaponry-missouri.

Taureck, Rita, 'Securitization Theory and Securitization Studies,' *Journal of International Relations and Development*, 9, 53, 2006.

Taylor, Keenanga-Yamahtta, *From #BlackLivesMatter to Black Liberation*, Chicago: Haymarket Books, 2016.

Tully, James, *An Approach to Political Philosophy,* Cambridge: Cambridge University Press, 1993.

Vaughan-Williams, Nick, *Border Politics: The Limits of Sovereign Power*, London: Routledge, 2012.

Vaughan-Williams, Nick, *Europe's Border Crisis: Biopolitical Security and Beyond,* Oxford: Oxford University Press, 2015.

Waddington, P.A.J., *Liberty and Order: Public Order Policing in a Capital City*, London: UCL Press, 1994.

Wall, Illan rua, *Human Rights and Constituent Power: Without Model or Warranty*, London: Routledge, 2012.

Wall, Illan rua, 'Notes on an "Open" Constituent Power,' *Law, Culture and the Humanities*, 11(3), 378–392, 2015.

Watkin, William, '*The Kingdom and the Glory:* The Articulated Inoperativity of Power', *Res Publica: Revista de Filosofia Politica*, 28, 235, 2012.

Whyte, Jessica, *Catastrophe and Redemption: The Political Thought of Giorgio Agamben,* New York: SUNY Press, 2013.

Yusuf, Hakeem O, *Colonial and Post-Colonial Constitutionalism in the Commonwealth: Peace, Order and Good Government*, London: Routledge, 2014.

Zartaloudis, Thanos, 'Government/*Oikonomia*', in A. Murray and J. Whyte (eds), *The Agamben Dictionary*, Edinburgh: Edinburgh University Press, 2011.

Cases

R (Hicks) v. Commissioner of the Police of the Metropolis [2014] WLR(D) 30.

Part III
Body

11

Sequences on law and the body

Elena Loizidou

Introduction

I begin with an apology. Being asked to contribute to the *Routledge Handbook of Law and Theory* is both an honour and a daunting prospect. The contributor has to make decisions on the organisation of the chapter, decisions over which work would be cited and even propose possible future-oriented directions on the specific topic asked to contribute. An apology means a statement in defence of something said but also an account of something. So when I say that I begin with an apology, I use apology here in the second sense of the word, in terms of giving an account, and in this instance an account of how the body has been taken up in critical legal discourse.

This chapter sketches an account of discursive and material critical legal writings on law and the body. It begins with the discursive and proceeds to the material sequence. This ordering is not meant to designate a hierarchy of accounts in the sense of x sequence being more radical or valuable than the other.[1] Nor does this ordering intend to propose a historical progressive narrative. Such a suggestion would have been preposterous and untrue, as research in both sequences is still ongoing. Instead what you witness is an attempt to delineate in a meaningful manner the abundance of work within this field of legal research. Andreas Philippopoulos-Mihalopoulos has recently (2016) argued that the discursive and the material bleed into each other. He does so by alerting us to the existence of material metaphors in law. These metaphors 'are more than mere figures of speech' (Philippopoulos-Mihalopoulos, 2016: 46) which, if attention is given to the way they occupy and affect our spatial and physical legal worlds, could potentially open us to a 'new conceptualisation of justice' (Philippopoulos-Mihalopoulos, 2016: 46). If, as he suggests, these metaphors bridge the gap between the linguistic and the material, then we can argue that they even challenge the very formulation of an account on law and the body that I am offering here. What is the point, we may ask, of talking about discursive and material sequences, if language and metaphors are material? Whilst Philippopoulos-Mihalopoulos's invitation to see the bleeding of the material into the discursive is an exciting possibility, I find myself nevertheless worried about this invitation. I worry that by collapsing the discursive with the material we may end up having a theoretical hierarchy that privileges material accounts of the body over discursive ones (despite this of course not being Philippopoulos-Mihalopoulos's intention). Instead, as I have suggested in earlier writing (Loizidou, 2008), such a danger may be averted if we understand these sequences of law and the body as being complementary to each other. This complementarity may give us a more multifaceted understanding of the limits of legal justice. I invite you to read these two sequences in this way, in the hope that they will provoke different sequences in the future.

Just a note on the term *sequences*. Roland Barthes (1977), in his essay 'Rhetoric of the Image', suggests that when an audience or a reader is bombarded with a plethora of textual information, the reader will attempt to put some order onto it, to create an absolute meaning. Sequences facilitate this process of meaning creation. While I use here the word *sequence* in Barthes's sense, I am not by any means suggesting that a totalising meaning of how we understand scholarship on law and the body can be achieved through these sequences. We should see these sequences as facilitating the creation of new or indeed the destruction of existing sequences.

Law's body

Critical writings engage with the issue of law and the body from two angles. One angle is critical of positivist accounts of law that depict law as a machine that consistently and fairly applies in order to reach justice. Law, they suggest instead, is like a body (symbolic and physical). The other critical angle focuses on the ways in which law inscribes and affects our bodies. This chapter focuses mainly on the second angle, in which law has been related to the body. Nevertheless, I think it is important to understand how these two angles relate to each other.

Law has *no one* physical body.[2] It has instead multiple physical bodies. The physical body of the law comes in the shape of its judges,[3] clerks, lawyers, claimants, complainants, its accused, its jury, its security officers and its police force,[4] and so on. The multiple bodies of the law work continuously to deliver law's primary good, the good of justice. Justice is not of course always delivered, and most of the times remains an imaginary or utopian goal for law. Most of everyday law practices involve making cost-effective decisions (plea bargaining) and trying to avoid its most important practice, that of the trial. So law ultimately is an institution with rituals, practices and a body of laws. Its body of law, or corpus, is made visible in its dusty case law books (Goodrich, 1990) or in their electronic form. Through its multiple bodies, law endeavours to *order* around, command and regulate our bodies, the bodies of citizens, denizens, animals (see the regulation of pit-bulls in the UK, *Dangerous Dogs Act 1991*)[5] and those who are yet to fall under its jurisdictions (e.g., unborn children). Law commands us to use or enjoy our bodies in particular ways or adjudicates on the way in which we use and enjoy our bodies. Nevertheless, this ordering or commandment, even the adjudication, has not secured our full agreement. In such cases of disagreement, we agonise individually or together to challenge its commands (e.g., women's voting rights). This agonism has produced a series of critical scholarship since the late 1980s in the field of law and the body emanating from legal scholars in feminism, gay and lesbian and queer studies, and race theory, medical law and many other areas.[6] They offered a sustained critique to the ways in which the law ordered and regulated our bodies by introducing the body into legal scholarship, elucidating the ways in which gendered, racialised and sexual minorities, the working class and disabled and aging subjects have been either discriminated against or treated as abject by the law. It is important to note what this scholarship is reacting against. It is reacting not only against the restricting ways in which law addresses the body, but also against the theoretical perspectives that posit law as a mechanical operation that uses reason to deliver judgments and justice bereft of any prejudices. It is a critique on the positivist and analytical accounts of law with which we are accustomed through the writings of Kelsen, Austin, Hart, Nozick and others.[7] The present chapter tracks this critical scholarship that draws from a variety of disciplines (such as philosophy, sociology, cultural studies, literature, psychoanalysis, race theory, post-colonialism and others) and organises it around two sequences, namely discursive and material approaches on law and the body. It will be impossible to cite or engage with all the writings of legal scholars on the body, therefore the work cited here is only indicative of these sequences and non-exhaustive.

As I suggested above, law has been presented for years as having *no* body. Nevertheless, a significant number of works, in their aim to critique positivist accounts of law, end up giving the law a body. Peter Goodrich has systematically demonstrated in legal theory that law represses and detaches itself from the body. As he suggests in *Languages of Law* (1990), this process of repression and detachment paints the institution of law – common law – as a machine. While the mechanistic and rational image of law is meant to give the impression that it delivers justice to all fairly and equally, Goodrich suggests that the opposite takes place. Law instead imposes itself onto life, our lives, while being equally disinterested in engaging with our experiences, needs and desires. The only interest law has is to superimpose itself upon life 'so as to render it homogeneous, a reproduction, an image in the glass' (Goodrich, 1990: viii).

> In attacking the legitimacy of desire and particularly in circumscribing the domains and occasions of bodily pleasure, the common law embarked upon a rigorous and unrelenting attack upon the history of everyday life. The evident aversion of the lawyer, of the moralist, to the sensuality of material existence, to the history of the body, to philosophical hedonism in all its forms – as semantic play, as the pleasure of the text, as the theatre of lived history – is eventually to be understood, can only be understood, as an escape of memory, a flight from the past as it was spoken and lived, and exodus from history if by history we mean the memory of what has lived, recuperated through material structures, through the body and through discourse.
>
> (Goodrich, 1990: 5)

Goodrich sets out to reveal the ways in which the institution of law suppresses desires, memories, imagery and symbols. To some extent we may be able to say that Goodrich's task in *Languages of Law* is twofold: on the one hand, he is telling the story of how law moulds our bodies and life more extensively according to its image; and on the other, he is sketching the body of law which more often is understood as a machine. Recall that most of positivist jurisprudence saw the law and its operations as a mechanical rational operation (Kelsen, 1934), bereft of any morality, passions or politics, for accordingly this would be the way to arrive at justice.

The focus of the critical legal studies movement in the UK was to challenge such presuppositions, by pointing to both their limits and their distortion of the truth about law (Goodrich, Douzinas, Fitzpatrick, Philippopoulos-Mihalopoulos). It is within this movement that Goodrich proposes to take seriously the body and its distortions that it has undertaken in law. In his later writings, such as *Oedipus Lex: Psychoanalysis, History, Law*, Goodrich puts the legal profession on the couch and reveals to us not only how lawyers have forgotten their bodies ('the law consumed them and left them spent, deprived of civility, humor, and emotion' (Goodrich, 1995: 145)) but moreover how it has repressed certain bodies (women, migrants and other aliens) and images. In *Law in the Courts of Love* (1996), Goodrich continues persistently to bring back the body to law, by introducing us to a women's court in Paris and its pronouncements on amorous affairs. In his work on emblems, *Legal Emblems and the Art of Law* (2014), Goodrich reveals how emblems, their interpretation and analysis, are essential in our understanding of the constitution of personhood and citizenship (Haldar, 2014: 304). Goodrich persists once more in his engagement of the law to a body by taking its visual artefacts seriously and demonstrating convincingly how, as Haldar puts it, 'images govern. Images both transmit law and structure personality, relations, things and actions' and '[a] failure to account for the 'visibilities' of law condemns law (as a number of emblems studied by Goodrich make clear) to blind administration' (Haldar, 2014: 308). While the themes and topics in Goodrich's writings may differ from work to work, there is a consistent analysis of how law governs by bringing to the foreground discourses and images that law has repressed from the realm of its study and scholarship.

There are methodological, theoretical, thematic and other differences between the scholarship that engages with the law and the body and Goodrich's account of how law cuts off the body from its practices and how it ends governing repressively. Nevertheless, there are also similarities in the fact that like Goodrich's work, such scholarship provides us with material and discursive accounts of the body and its relation to the law. It is to these sequences that I turn to now.

There are of course a variety of discursive and materialists accounts of the body. The aim here is not to offer a detailed account of these sequences but rather sketch them in a general way. What you find below is a brief description of the meaning of the concepts 'discursive' and 'material' and how they have been utilised within critical legal scholarship.

First, we need to recall that most legal theory, until the emergence of critical legal scholarship first in the US in the late 1970s[8] and in the UK in the early 1980s,[9] attended to the law as a machine that rationally adjudicated contestations, represented social norms and delivered justice at a distance from morality, politics and other cultural phenomena. It was represented as pure, immune from external influences. Again, as indicated earlier, the main representatives of this account of law were the positivists and analytical jurisprudes. What the critical studies movement in general achieved was to break up this fantasy about the law and demonstrate the social, political, philosophical and other dimensions of law as well as to demonstrate the variety of ways in which law operates, as well as the various sources (images, symbols) and practices (rhetorics). We have seen some of these presented in the brief reconstruction of Goodrich's work above.

Overall, the *oeuvre* of critical legal studies made visible the body that was an *invisible presence* in the pre-critical studies literature. There are two main sequences in the scholarship in law and the body in which the body is made visible: discursive and materialist theories. Discursive writings on law and the body take as a basic presupposition that the legal body is constructed through legal language, legal images, legal symbols and signs, as well as culture more generally. Material writings, in turn, focus on the materiality of the body and law's relation to this. What do we mean by the materiality of the body of law? Most critical legal studies work engaged with the material body as fully fleshed, corporeal, affective, different in process, and becoming (for example, the gender is attributed by birth), affective, collective and how it is produced, formed, moved and transformed across different sites and spaces. Both material and discursive accounts on law and the body challenge the way in which the body has been fixed by law and its discourses.[10]

The discursive sequence in law and the body scholarship

In engaging with the discursive turn in the critical legal scholarship around the law and the body, we are engaging in a particular way of representing law's relationship to the body. Moreover, we are putting the body at the centre of legal scholarship. In *The Order of Things* (1966, 2002), *Archaeology of Knowledge* (1969, 1989), and 'The Order of Discourse' (1970; 1987: 48–78), Foucault engages explicitly with discursive practices.[11] In the aforementioned writings, Foucault tries to understand and account for how certain subjects, such as the insane, are excluded from the production of knowledge and constructed as being unable to talk the truth. In *Madness and Civilization* (1961, 1989), we see Foucault analysing how reason is privileged in our 'will to knowledge'. By 'making [madness] . . . an *object* for analysis' (Gordon, 1987: 48), Foucault attempted to erase the distinction between inclusion/exclusion that puts madness outside the realm of knowledge. His drive to give a voice or make visible subjects and objects that have been both made silent and rendered invisible prompted Foucault to turn to 'those rules, systems and procedures which constitute, and are constituted by our "will to knowledge"' (Gordon, 1987: 48). In doing so, he identified that discursive practices determine the boundaries, define and fix objects and subjects, as well as produce sets of norms that become the foundation for concepts and knowledge more general (Foucault, 1970, 1987: 199). If either objects or subjects do not fit within given boundaries or norms, they are denigrated to silence, invisibility or simply rendered unintelligible. Discourse, which travels in the form of linguistic practices, images, signs and symbols, is inextricably linked to power, or put otherwise it exercises power by both constituting and reproducing the system (political and social order) 'through forms of selection, exclusion and domination' (Gordon, 1987: 48). Discourse reproduces a truth through the above forms. Foucault wanted, as he writes in the foreword to the English edition of *The Order of Things*, to reveal through a discursive analysis the 'unconscious of knowledge' (Foucault, 1966, 2002: xi).

Within the critical legal studies field in the UK, one of the first academics to engage with the Foucauldian discursive analysis was Les Moran. Moran's *The Homosexual(ity) of Law* (1996) returns the homosexual body to law. The aim of the book was to investigate the ways in which common law categorises the male homosexual body. Moran sets out to provide a detailed account of the language that law uses to describe male homosexuality, and homosexual acts, since the decriminalisation of homosexuality. Law uses a particular lexicon to describe the male homosexual (homosexual instead of gay or queer, popular in everyday life and activism) and male homosexual acts (buggery). In following the lexicon of law, Moran demonstrates how law 'fashions human relations' (Moran, 1996: 9). As he explains, 'the lexicon of law . . . is . . . a depository of terms through which contemporary human relations are produced, determined and limited' (Moran, 1996: 9). In following a Foucauldian discursive analysis, Moran was able to produce an account of how the homosexual is produced within law, and simultaneously point to the discriminatory aspects of such productions that lead to an unjust criminalisation of homosexual men and their sexual practices in the UK.[12] Sharpe similarly exposes the ways in which the law constructs and produces the transgender body.[13] In *Transgender Jurisprudence: Dysphoric Bodies of Law* (2002), Sharpe focuses on cases where transgender subjects find themselves before the law. Sharpe meticulously shows us the inherent prejudices within law: as litigants in marriage cases we find that law treats transgender subjects with homophobia; as subjects of anti-discrimination law, we find that they are being constructed without consistency on the part of law either through biological determinations (i.e., one is a woman either because anatomy and chromosome designate as such) or through a psychological determination that seeks harmony between the way one feels and appears in the world. Depending on which of these two determinations the law uses, transgender subjects may be found as being eligible or not to bring an anti-discrimination case to the courts. What Sharpe reveals overall is how phobia and arbitrary tests act against transgender subjects and simultaneously disavow the ways in which they identify themselves. Sharpe's analysis of the ways in which transgender bodies are constructed in case law reveals how the so-called 'non-normative' subjects are subjugated by law. Indeed, Sharpe's subsequent book, *Foucault's Monsters and the Challenge of Law* (2010), takes seriously the figure of the monster or the abnormal. It follows the monster through its Foucauldian genealogy as well as its legal manifestations and its normalisation. The transsexual, conjoined twins and human/animal admixed embryos are the legal figurations of the monstrous that Sharpe takes on. In contrasting the Foucauldian genealogy of the monstrous with that of common law jurisprudence, Sharpe brings to our awareness that law 'orders' the normalisation of monstrous bodies by requiring their physical re-shaping. Recall that Foucault in his

Abnormal Lectures at the Collège de France tracks the genealogy of the category by focusing on three figures: 'the human monster, the individual to be corrected and the onanist' (Davidson, 2003; x–vii) and a shift from a regulation of the body to a regulation or correction of the soul (Foucault, 2003: 263–290). The figure of the human monster, Foucault informs us, was a legal category that designated a breach of the laws of nature. Subsequently, this way of thinking has influenced the medical professions and their understanding of the dangerous individual. Sharpe similarly tracks the figure of the transsexual, conjoined twins and inter-species mixings and reveals common law's inability to deal with subjects who challenge either sex binary (transsexual) or who cannot adhere to singular embodiment (conjoined twins) or inter-species mixings (human/animal). Sharpe, perhaps unintentionally, reveals above all that the law cannot allow anybody to have two or multiple bodies. We can say that law still categorises those that do not follow the order of nature – those who precisely challenge that there is such a natural order of life – as abnormal.

In *Femininity in Dissent* (1990), Alison Young engages in the ways in which the media and law work together to produce the female body. Taking as her example the women's peace camp and demonstrations at Greenham Common,[14] Young offers a discursive reading of the way in which the female body is constructed by the media and the criminal justice system. While not following explicitly a Foucauldian method of analysis, she shows how the media and the criminal justice system constructed the women protesters and campers at Greenham Common peace camp as filthy, dirty and feckless (Young, 1990: 56). Focusing on these media and criminal justice constructions and drawing mainly upon the feminist writings of post-structuralist feminists such as Helene Cixous and Julia Kristeva, Young is able to point to the phallocentric character of these two institutions and the ways in which women's difference is disavowed. In showing this through powerful visual and textual analysis, Young was one of the first critical legal scholars to point out how, through images and language, the female body and femininity is constructed but simultaneously works against those constructions.

Following a feminist Foucauldian approach, Julie Wallbank in *Challenging Motherhood(s)* (2001)[15] takes the figure of the lone mother as the focus of her analysis and provides a rich account of her social and legal demonisation. The lone mother, her body and her state of mind is challenged and treated unjustly by law in various instances, such as paternal contact cases and social support issues. In challenging paternal contact, for example, mothers take their cases to courts and present evidence that shows clearly that it would not be in the best interest of the child (because the father may have been violent towards the child and/or her; Wallbank, 2001: 70) to give contact to the fathers. Yet they often find that the courts reject their challenge. Wallbank takes us through a close reading of cases that relate to paternal contact and reveals that the lone mother is constructed in such instances as 'implacable' and somewhat too emotional[16] to be able to care best for their children. In pointing out these constructions of the lone mother's body and the so-called legal 'truth', Wallbank alerts us to the legal failures and injustices that haunt these constructions.

The construction of women in legal texts is also the theme that runs through Maria Aristodemou's[17] *Law and Literature: From Her to Eternity* (2000), where she engages in a textual and discursive analysis of literary texts. Literature, like law, Aristodemou argues, is a law-making machine. As such it produces or constructs bodies. Like Young and Wallbank, she focuses on the feminine body in multiple literary texts (Camus, Borges, etc.) to expose how literature *like* law colonises women. Using psychoanalysis and feminist theory, such as that represented by the work of Helene Cixous, Aristodemou draws our attention to the myriad ways in which women's bodies have been colonised by white male law: when women or more precisely women's acts do not fall within the norm are deemed by law (and in this case literature as law) as being irrational and in need of being punished either through exclusion, denigration or murder. Aristodemou's analysis of Aeschylus's *Eumenides* shows astutely how justice is described as establishing 'law and order' (Aristodemou, 2000: 65), and contrasting it to the way Clytemnistra (the adulterous Queen who killed her husband) in *Agamemnon* is treated, she is described as combative and manly (Aristodemou, 2000: 67). Drawing our attention to Clytemnestra's characterisation, Aristodemou shows precisely how certain norms around order are well embedded in Western literary understandings of legality but moreover how women that deviate from such norms are rendered unintelligible, forceful and in need of being ordered. Literature as a text of law, a text about law and a cultural testament to our understanding of the world, reproduces the same binary hierarchies we witness in legal texts that make any woman not inhabiting these norms monstrous.

We have seen so far how critical legal scholars engaging with discursive analysis of the body has provided us with some understanding of how the body is constructed in law. What is noticeable, whether it is the homosexual body, the woman demonstrator, or the mother or a literary representation of women, is that these authors show how law manages to pass its constructions of the body as truth. The effect of law's legal construction on the bodies of women and homosexual men is undoubtedly unjust and has material effects – women/mothers, for example, as Wallbank shows in *Challenging Motherhood(s)*, may find themselves having to communicate with a violent ex-partner over the best care of their children. Such a situation leaves many women exposed to the possibility of further violence from their ex-partners and fathers of their children. Law surrenders lone mothers to the very precarious and dangerous situations and relations that they were trying to avoid, escape and challenge.

In 1992, Patricia Williams published the outstanding *The Alchemy of Rights and Race: A Diary of a Law Professor* whereby she brings the biographical to bear witness to law's and legal academy's racist practices and rationalities. While writing within the US critical legal studies movement, she is critical of the ease in which human rights are critiqued. Critical legal scholars have described human rights as sheer rhetoric that fails to recognise, represent and protect humanity. Williams instead argues that human rights are productive and shows how they give access to the public realm to disenfranchised peoples, such as Black Americans. *The Alchemy of Rights and Race* renders visible the multiple ways in which racialised, and particularly black, bodies have been excluded and treated prejudicially in law and in everyday encounters. Through everyday racisms, Williams exposes the prejudices and injustices of our social norms. In the UK it was not until 2004, when Williams's namesake, Patricia Tuitt, published *Race, Law, Resistance*,[18] that critical legal studies had its first sustained engagement with racism and the law. In *Race, Law, Resistance*, Tuitt offers in six powerful essays an analysis of how law itself racialises and discriminates against minorities, including Black bodies. Her analysis focuses on the ways in which subjects (the slave, the refugee), legal doctrine (doctrine of causation, reasonable man), the concept of sovereignty and unsanctioned violence are insufficient in addressing racism (for example, the legal doctrines of causation and reasonable man) and moreover law is implicated in continuing discrimination and violence on racialised bodies.[19]

Piyel Haldar in *Law, Orientalism and Postcolonialism* (2007)[20] provides us with a powerful critique of colonial law. At the centre of his discursive analysis, drawing on psychoanalysis, critical theory, literature and classical jurisprudence, we find the legal subject, which, Haldar argues, has been colonised through the permission of pleasure. Law used pleasure in British India (Haldar's area of study) as a way of subjugating the people of India to a Western legality. While pleasure was permitted, any sign of excessive pleasure, such as access to more than one sexual partner in the case of the sultan, became the site for legal intervention. Haldar takes us through instances where the colonised subjects' pleasures are deemed repugnant, excessive and in breach of modern practices of civility. In his chapter 'The Sultan's Enjoyment' (Haldar, 2007: 53–82), Haldar shows how the luxurious attires of kings, the lavish gardens or the invigorating smells of flowers and spices were viewed by the law as depicting excessive pleasures needing to be regulated and controlled; otherwise, such pleasures were thought of being capable of turning colonised subjects into despots. What the various regulations of pleasure and enjoyment in British India show us, Haldar argues, is not that the colonised subject was excessive in indulging an enjoyable life, nor that they were potentially to become despots. This was instead a fantasy concocted and projected by the coloniser and the law onto colonised populations because of their fear of becoming despotic subjects and laws. Ironically, as we know, they have succeeded in becoming precisely despotic colonisers and laws.

What we notice so far in the rich literature around law, discourse and the body is a strong desire on behalf of critical legal scholars to articulate the myriad ways in which law regulates our bodies and consequently organises our lives. The body becomes part of discourse and is the object of analysis. What we do not get at least explicitly[21] from discursive analysis on the body, primarily because all the attention is placed upon how the law constructs the body, is an articulation of what the body wants. We do not get any insights on what these bodies of women, homosexuals, lesbians, colonised people and people of colour and their intersections[22] need or desire. We do not, to put it metaphorically, hear the heart beats and pulsations of these multiple bodes. Theories of materiality, as we shall see, tend to entertain the body, the affective body in particular, and reveal both its desires and needs. The difference between these two sequences on the body is that the discursive accounts focus on analysis of how law accounts on the body, or put otherwise on interpretations of the body (discursive), while the material sequence allows the body to speak (materially) for itself. Nevertheless, discursive accounts on the legal body do manage to break away with the more positivistic traditions of legal theory (described earlier in the chapter) and present us with an embodied legal subject.

Before we move on it is important to note that some discursive accounts on law and the body do not always present embodied subjects as purely recipient of power, norms and laws. Some discursive studies also show how bodies either resist or subvert power, norms and laws.[23] Such work tends to draw on Judith Butler's accounts on gender performativity and the ways in which bodies *subvert* the categorisations that various configurations of power (i.e., law, culture, politics, etc.) try to impose on them. The work of Judith Butler and the ways in which the body operates in law has been the focus of my work. In *Judith Butler: Ethics, Law, Politics* (2007), I show how same-sexed bodies exposed to us the 'fantasmatic character of gender formation and identification (Loizidou, 2007: 37).[24] How then does this differ from a constructionist account of the body? While both theoretical perspectives will adhere to the fact that we are formed by language, power, etc., Butler's theory of gender performativity allows us to see that naming, for example, somebody as a boy is nothing but a citational practice that through a constant recitation makes one be identified as a boy. This identity, however, is not necessarily the truth or, put otherwise, it obscures the fact that our genders are not static but always under construction. By pointing to the fantasmatic 'character' of gender and to the fact that gender is always in a process of becoming, we subvert normative notions of the body. We can see that the body does not want to be 'closeted' in a static category, or rather that bodies overflow such categorisations. Bodies thus are able to subvert the categorisations that law or norms attribute to them. For example, women have been attributed with particular normative characteristics, passive, irrational, feminine, etc., yet gay, lesbian, trans and queer movements subverted these normative characteristics and demonstrated that to be a woman one does not need to be a feminine woman but could also be a butch lesbian.

The philosopher Adriana Cavarero has also been very important in providing us with an account of the body that is not held hostage to power. In her book *For More Than One Voice: Toward a Philosophy of Vocal Expression* (2005), Cavarero argues that the voice, the distinct sound that we emit, is what makes us unique and simultaneously undoes the very norms that are set to form us as subjects. Cavarero sets out to show how Western metaphysics have separated speaker from speech and are invested in the faculty of thinking. In doing so, Western philosophy since its inception made speech into something that we study, for example, within the discipline of linguistics, and consequentially has separated it from the body. Accounts on speech consequentially become generalised and universal rather than focusing on the singular voice of the speaker and their uniqueness. By invoking the voice, Cavarero aims to return speech back to the speaker and in doing so to show the relationship between speech and voice and remind us of the materiality of speech. Elisabetta Bertolino in her writings on human rights and women's bodies draws explicitly on Cavarero's work to show how the body resists through the voice.[25] This is also the theme of some of Patrick Hanafin's work in his analysis of feminism and embodiment.[26] Cavarero, therefore, is not making discursive accounts of the body redundant, but rather seeks to show through her writings the relationship between the discursive and the material.

Nevertheless, accounts that show how the body subverts power, in law and the body literature, remain few and far between.[27] Judith Butler is another philosopher working at the borders of the material and the discursive that enable us to see how the body subverts power. I have situated here Judith Butler's uptake by critical legal scholars within the discursive tradition of law and the body. Alas, it is important to note that her work nevertheless does not seat comfortably within this tradition.. What connects Butler's various writings is a particular concern: how we may create better conditions for life. Such creation for Butler, as I showed elsewhere (Loizidou, 2008: 29–51), entails an agonistic relationship between the various spheres of life, ethical, political, legal. The body is central to her articulation of all these three spheres of life. It is also well known that her understanding of bodies is one that sees them being formed by and through norms (linguistic or otherwise). But, as I explained (Loizidou, 2008: 29–51), her bodies are neither discursive nor material but, rather, both. And as the various spheres of life, if they are to achieve better conditions for life, must retain an agonistic relationship to one another, the same agonistic relationship must be sustained in relation to our knowledge of the body, or between the two competing bodies (discursive and material). This opens an antagonistic relationship between the discursive and material bodies best analysed by Butler in her essay 'How Can I Deny That These Hands and This Body Are Mine?' (Butler, 2001: 254–273). In this essay, Butler exposes how in Descartes's *First Meditation* there is a certain refusal of the discursive body to be reduced to the material and the material to the discursive. In the *First Meditation*, Descartes sets out to demonstrate how the senses or the body are not reliable sources of knowledge. Butler reads in Descartes's mistrust of the body a certain tension. On the one hand, he doubts the body and, on the other,

> the very language through which he calls the body into question ends up reasserting the body as a condition of his own writing. Thus, the body that comes into question as an "object" that may be doubted surfaces in the text as a figural precondition of his writing.
>
> (Butler, 2001: 258)

This, she argues, destabilises the distinction between the material and the figural that the *First Meditation* intends to create. It is important therefore to note that, while most critical legal scholarship may focus on Judith Butler's discursive accounts of gender, her work also draws on both the discursive and the material body.

Scholars working within the material sequence on law and the body as you see in the forthcoming section (unlike Cavarero's and Butler's investment on the *relationship* between the discursive and the material body) articulate the body as purely a material entity and are more interested in the *relationship* of the body to other material entities.

The materiality sequence in scholarship on law and the body

When we talk of materiality and the body, we refer to those works that understand the body 'being processed and . . . assembled and made up from the diverse relays, connections and relationships between artefacts, technologies, practices and matter which temporarily form it as a particular kind of object' (Blackman, 2008: 133). Lisa Blackman, a media and cultural studies scholar, explains how research that takes the materiality of the body as its theoretical spectrum enables us to see that the body is constantly being made and re-made, and is in process, as well as affecting and being affected by the world. Scholars that focus on the materiality of the body primarily draw on the philosophy of Gilles Deleuze and Felix Guattari. Gilles Deleuze in his 'What Can a Body Do?' (1997: 217–234) writes, drawing on Spinoza's *Ethics*, 'What a body can do corresponds to the nature and limits of its capacity to be affected' (1997: 218), making us aware of what is internal and external to a body, whether objects or nature can both affect a body at a given moment and a body can affect anything else also. We can see that this type of philosophical encounter with the body cannot be very easily absorbed by legal philosophical scholarship, as it places all its attention to affect and the body, and none on rules and laws. So when it comes to work within law that engages with affective theory, we find very little.[28] The usefulness of this thereoetical approach on law and the body lies in enabling us to understand the affective side of our bodies and law's inability to account for the affective body..

Critical legal thinkers that have worked with affect theory are very few. We can note the work of Hanafin with the feminist Deleuzian philosophers Rosi Braidotti and Claire Colebrook. These three authors have published in 2009 the edited collection *Deleuze and Law: Forensic Futures* that engages with the affective body and law. Hanafin's essay 'Rights of Passage: The Constitutional BioPolitics of Dying' in the aforementioned edited collection is an example of such work. Hanafin draws on the body of the terminally ill patient who wants to die and Deleuze's concept of 'as already gone' to point out that while for some the body's death does not stand as an obstacle or limit to thinking, in law the wish to die becomes an opportunity to talk about the right to life and consequently limit to thinking about death. It is not though until Philippopoulos-Mihalopoulos book *Spatial Justice, Body, Lawscape, Atmosphere* (2015) that we gain a sustained presentation of how bodies get constituted, not just through rules but also through space.. In *Spatial Justice*, we are told that '*spatial justice is the conflict between bodies that are moved by a desire to occupy the same space at the same time.*' (Philippopoulos-Mihalopoulos, 2015: 3, emphasis in original). The bodies we are told earlier are not just human bodies but an assemblage of bodies, human, non-human, post-human. *Spatial Justice,* therefore, by putting these assemblages of bodies at the centre of the question of justice, 'when bodies claim the same space at the same time' (p. 3), enables us to see that 'dispute', a conflict of desires, may require a different ontological engagement than a mere decision over which side is right or wrong. It may require, as the book suggests, a withdrawal, so bodies in withdrawal enable themselves to continue affecting the world.

Within the materiality sequence in law and body, we also find authors that engage with the philosophical concept of plastic materiality that the philosopher Catherine Malabou brings to the fore. Bhandar and Goldberg-Hiller tells us that 'Malabou's materialism is rooted in an attempt to rethink the relationship between neuroscience and philosophical conceptualization of consciousness and the self' (Bhandar and Goldberg-Hiller, 2015: 8). The term 'plasticity' Malabou has inherited from Hegel. It is a term that designates the ongoing making of the subject, its movement and plastic 'character'. In their wonderful edited collection, *Plastic Materialities: Politics, Legality, and Metamorphosis in the Work of Catherine Malabou* (2015), Bhandar and Goldberg-Hiller introduce us not only to Malabou's concept of plastic materiality but also to a number of scholars, some working within the field of critical legal studies, who engage with this concept and its application on the body, biological or otherwise. As Bhandar and Goldberg-Hiller note, Malabou's work and particularly her concept of plasticity provide us with a different understanding of the relationship between thinking and body. While the Western philosophical tradition of metaphysics has kept an understanding that separated the process of thinking from the body, and whilst the body was seen as a vessel for sensations and, as noted earlier in relation to Descartes, was described as an unreliable source for the production of knowledge, for Malabou this division becomes obsolete when one follows neuroscientific developments. Thinking is not anymore a process that takes place in the mind but instead 'is built into our bodies' (Bhandar and Goldberg-Hiller, 2015: 1). Bhandar and Goldberg-Hiller propose that this new material understanding of the body can open up new ways of seeing how law operates, but also potentially relieve law from producing injustices. Indeed we can say this is made possible by the simple fact that the body is no longer considered a non-viable source for truth. Allan Pottage's essay 'Autoplasticity' in the same edited collection by Bhandar and Goldberg-Hiller (2015: 73–90) engages with the plasticity of reproductive technologies, DNA and epigenetics to show how Malabou's proposition that the symbolic and the biological (discursive and material in our case here, or mind and body) distinctions still hold in Foucault is not necessarily valid. This means, he argues, that we do not need to deconstruct further, as Malabou suggests, the concept of sovereignty which is at the core of Foucault's engagement with the symbolic and the biological. In 'Insects, War, Plastic Life' (2015: 169–185), Renisa Mawani shows how the human/non-human, drones and bees, merge into one another, once more reminding us that perhaps categories such as human, monstrous, etc., that law tries to hold onto, cannot be sustainable. Critical legal research drawing on Malabou's work as we have seen engages with the multiple ways in which the body, invested in thought, now enable us to see the limits of legal discourse. It is less clear though how this research enables us to see how the law can be challenged. While we may argue that despite the fact that the mind/body distinction may collapse in Malabou's work, and that thought becomes materially embodied, allowing what others called subjugated knowledges to emerge to the surface and provide us with new vantage points to see the world, it nevertheless retains the law, not perhaps as a law with two bodies (a symbolic and a biological one) but rather in the figure of the mythical Lernean Hydra. My point here is that it is not the need to collapse the discursive with the material that will undo the sovereign and ensure justice and equality, but rather our ability to create a different way of relating to the problem of the sovereign. It is not, in other words, the constitution of the sovereign that is our problem but our inability to imagine how to create a world without the sovereign.

Research that engages with the material body in law has predominantly bracketed out any discussions on the discursive body. This work takes it for granted that the body is a material entity and proceeds to discuss the various ways in which the material body *alerts* us to the inadequacies of an embodied legal discourse to address the political and economic challenges that are before it. If we take, for example, Philippopoulos-Mihalopoulos's *Spatial Justice*, we may use it to demonstrate that even if rules are applied correctly they will not be a solution to social and economic inequality because of inadequate affordable housing and wealth inequality. Such research, we may say, challenges the very idea of the sovereignty of law itself. Further, work like the one mentioned above which is influenced by Malabou, collapses the discursive and the material body. The significance of this type of work is to open up new ways of relationality and creation, as in Mawani's work that shows relations between the animal and technological that a legal discourse or a discursive analysis on the law on the body would not have otherwise revealed. The material sequence in law and the body enables us to see why we may not need law in forming an understanding of our social and political relations. Whether it does provide us with ways to create a world without law, or whether indeed it proposes that this is possible, is less clear.

Conclusion

I would rather avoid offering a conclusion. Readers will be able to conclude for themselves the various sequences in which studies in law and the body exist. I mentioned two, but I am sure within these we can see already very different flights of inquiry. It is important though to note that despite the fact that the second sequence in law and the body does not hold a large number of authors, I think it is the most exciting one. It is one that shows very clearly that the body is much more vibrant than the taste of sawdust that law often leaves in one's mouth, as Kafka mentions. It is the one that shows precisely that there is a multiplicity of bodies (human, animal, technological) that interact and clash with one another. And if we are to take them seriously, we will need to invest in understanding how they relate to each other as materialities. As Butler has warned us, it may be important to hold in mind that discursive accounts of the body do not necessarily get subverted or undone by material sequences, nor should we embrace them without thinking to what extent the absorption of the discursive to the material may provide us with a totalising knowledge – a knowledge that will exclude any-body (pun intended) that does not fall within its sphere of vision.

Kafka, in his letter to his father, approximated the study of law with the activity of eating sawdust (Kafka, 2015: 91). Here is how he describes the process of learning the law:

> for the few months before the exams, and in a way that told severely on my nerves, I was positively living, in an intellectual sense on sawdust, which had moreover, already been chewed for me in thousands of other people's mouths.

Indeed, we may find ourselves agreeing to this description. The study of law, and law itself, has this very wooden property. Over the last 20–30 years though, as we have seen, by putting the body at the centre of their analysis, critical legal researchers have managed to give some flavour to the otherwise woody law. As research into the material body, its affects and other dimensions is expanding, we may see, although one can never be certain about outcomes, law being slowly phased out from legal theory, while the body, objects and the affect may just become our analytical toys. As this research may expand, we will also see the emergence of new discourses on law and the body. To account for what we sense as new, we may need the assistance of language and words.

Notes

1 It is true that in the fields of political theory, feminism and philosophy these two sequences have been pitted against each other. A prime example is Nancy Fraser's attack on Judith Butler's work. Judith Butler's discursive accounts of the body were criticized by Fraser for not accounting for material accounts on the body, see Fraser, N. (March-April, 1998) "Heterosexism, Misrecognition and Capitalism: A Response to Judith Butler", *New Left Review,* I:228 pp. 140–149; Judith Butler, (January-February, 1998), "Merely Cultural", *New Left Review,* I:227 pp. 33–44.

2 I am fully aware of the argument that law travels or is transmitted through the body of the sovereign, which as we know from Ernst Kantorowicz (1997) has two bodies, a natural body and body political. The king or by extension the crown symbolises also the law, and by extension we may suggest that this dual body is transferred to the institution of law. Goodrich, in *Languages of Law* (1990: 53–110) makes this point. Recently, the philosopher Catherine Malabou pointed out that the image of the split body is also present in philosophy. More precisely she argued that the split between the natural and the political body creates a hierarchy which puts the political body at the top. Her work attempts to bring together or to show that this split can't be sustained given the advances in science that demonstrate that even the biological has its own body political or symbolic body (Malabou, 2015: 35–46). Malabou therefore makes us aware of the multiple bodies that exist in an attempt to break the split between the political and physical body. Following Malabou, I want to suggest that instead of seeing law being divided between two bodies, imagining that there are monolithic legal movements, we can recognise it as having multiple natural and symbolic bodies. I should say that Kantarowitz's political body is a symbolic body.

3 Some research has been done on the judicial body – see, for example, Moran (2013) and Goodrich (2015).

4 Some work has been done on police and their gender, racial constitution; see, for example, Reiner (2010).

5 For an analysis of the regulation of dogs, see Dyan (2015). For more general discussions of law and the animals, see Otomo and Mussawir (2013).

6 For example, for criminal law and public law, see Lacey (1998) and Hunter and Mack (1997). For tax law, see Grbich (1996).

7 For a sustained critical account of these writers, see Douzinas et al. (1991) and Douzinas and Geary (2005).

8 The writings of Duncan Kennedy and Roberto Unger, for example, have been some of the earlier articulations of this type of scholarship. For an account of this movement, see Kennedy and Klare (1984) and Hunt (1986).

9 For an account of the British version of critical legal studies, see Fitzpatrick and Hunt (1987); Goodrich (1992); Murphy (1999).

10 See Loizidou (2008).

11 I mention Foucault here because he is a philosopher who has influenced extensively the critical legal studies movement. Only recently, for example, we have seen the publication

by Ben Golder (2015) and Ben Golder and Peter Fitzpatrick (2009), *Foucault's Law* on the influence of Foucault in critical legal studies.

12 For more critical legal work on law, body and sexuality, that follows a discursive approach, see Gross (2009); Monk (1998); Loizidou (1998); Loizidou (1999); Lamble (2014; 2009); Sabsay, (16 May 2016).

13 See Sharpe (2010; 2002).

14 In September 1981 a group of women, Women for Life on Earth, camped outside an RAF military camp in Berkshire to demonstrate against the UK government's stationing missile cruises in the camp. The camp was on Greenham Common and it came to be known as Greenham Common Peace Camp. The camp was dismantled in 2000. At the high levels of activity of the Peace Camp there were regular calls for demonstrations around the RAF military camp. On 1 April 1983 demonstration, something like 70,000 women protested and hundreds of women were arrested.

15 For more discursive writings on the construction of the figure of the mother and reproductive rights in critical legal scholarship, see Cain (2009); Hanafin (2012; 2007).

16 This is a point that Joanna Conaghan, 2000, explores in her excellent survey of feminist theory.

17 For more theoretical work on the construction of women in law, see Drakopoulou (2014) and Conaghan (2013).

18 Of course we have earlier critical writings on law and race in the UK but they mainly take place outside the law. See, for example, Hall et al. (1978).

19 See also Motha (2010) and Bhandar (2012).

20 See also Motha and Perrin (2002); Bhandar (2011); Rush (1990); Hanafin (2001).

21 While there is an account in Wallbanks (2001) and Young (1990) of women's voices, the analysis that ensues in their work focuses mainly on how law subjugates their voices, demands and aspirations. The protagonist of these analysis is law or more precisely an unjust law. Women's subjectivity then ends up being presented through the legal discourse.

22 Intersectionality is a phrase coined by Krenshaw in 1989 to show that subjects are constituted by a variety of social identities (race, ethnicity, gender, sexuality, etc.). In order to understand oppression and its operations, we have to study how it operates through and at these intersections (see Krenshaw, 1989). For recent examples of intersectional research on law and the body, see Motha (2007) and Cooper et al. (2008).

23 See also McNeilly (2016).

24 For a critique of the linguistic materiality divide in relation to writings on law and the body, see Loizidou (2008).

25 See Bertolino (2008; 2006).

26 See Hanafin (2013; 2008).

27 See Bhandar (16 May 2016).

28 Critical legal scholarship which engages with emotions, law and the body should not be confused with affect. Deleuze states that for Spinoza emotions or passions are not affections: 'An affection is not a passion, except when it cannot be explained by the nature of the affected body: it then of course involves the body, but is explained by the influence of other bodies. Affections that can be completely explained by the nature of the affected body are active affections, and themselves actions' (Deleuze, 1997: 219).

Bibliography

Aristodemou, Maria, *Law and Literature: From Her to Eternity*, Oxford: Oxford University Press, 2000.

Barthes, Roland, 'Rhetoric of the Image', trans. S. Heath in *Image Music Text*, London: Fontana Press, 32–51, 1977.

Bertolino, Elisabetta, 'Beyond Ontology and Sexual Difference: An Interview with the Italian Feminist Philosopher Adriana Cavarero', *differences: A Journal of Feminist Cultural Studies*, 19(1), 128–167, 2008.

Bertolino, Elisabetta, 'The Politics of Subjectivity: In the Women Law and Development Discourse', *Australian Feminist Law Journal*, 25, 119–42, 2006.

Bhandar, Brenna, 'Plasticity and Post-Colonial Recognition: Owning, Knowing and Being,' Law and Critique, 22(3), 227–249, 2011.

Bhandar, Brenna, 'Dis-assembling Legal Form: Ownership and the Racial Body,' in M. Stone, I. Wall and C. Douzinas (eds), *New Critical Legal Thinking: Law and the Political*, London: Routledge, 112–127, 2012.

Bhandar, Bhandar, 'Status as Property: Identity, Land and the Dispossession of First Nations Women in Canada', *DarkMatter*, 16 May 2016. www.darkmatter101.org/site/2016/05/16/status-as-property-identity-land-and-the-dispossession-of-first-nations-women-in-canada/

Bhandar, Bhandar and Goldberg-Hiller, John (eds), *Plastic Materialities: Politics, Legality, and Metamorphosis in the Work of Catherine Malabou*, Durham and London: Duke University Press, 2015.

Blackman, Lisa, *The Body*, Oxford: Berg, 2008.

Braidotti, Rosi, Colebrook, Claire, and Hanafin, Patrick, *Deleuze and Law: Forensic Futures*, London: Palgrave Macmillan, 2009.

Butler, Judith, 'How Can I Deny that these Hands and this Body are Mine?' in T. Cohen, B. Cohen, J. Miller and A. Warminski (eds), *Material Events: Paul De Man and the Afterlife of Theory*, Minneapolis, London: University of Minnesota Press, 20, 254–73, 2001.

Butler, Judith, 'Merely Cultural', *New Left Review*, I(227), 33–44, January–February, 1998.

Cain, Ruth, '"A View You Won't Get Anywhere Else"? Depressed Mothers, Public Regulation and "Private" Narrative', *Feminist Legal Studies*, 17(2), 123–143, 2009.

Cavarero, Adriana, *For More Than One Voice: Toward a Philosophy of Vocal Expression*, trans. A. P. Kottman, Stanford: Stanford University Press, 2005.

Conaghan, Joanna, 'Reassessing the Feminist Theoretical Project in Law', *Journal Law and Society*, 27(3), 351–385, 2000.

Conaghan, Joanna, *Gender and the Law*, Oxford: Oxford University Press, 2013.

Cooper, Davina, Grabham, Emily and Krishnadas, Jane (eds), *Law, Power and the Politics of Subjectivity: Intersectionality and Beyond*, London: Routledge Cavendish, 2008.

Davidson, I. Arnold, 'Introduction' in Arnold I. Davidson (ed), *Michel Foucault: Abnormal Lectures at the Collège de France*, trans. G. Burchell, New York: Picador, 1999, x–xxvi, 2003.

Deleuze, Gilles, 'What Can a Body Do?' trans. M. Joughin, in *Expressionism in Philosophy: Spinoza*, New York: Zone Books, 217–234, 1997.

Douzinas, Costas and Geary, Adam, *Critical Jurisprudence: The Political Philosophy of Justice*, Oxford: Hart Publishing, 2005.

Douzinas, Costas, Warrington, Ronnie and McVeigh, Shaun, *Postmodern Jurisprudence: The Law of Text in the Text of Law*, London: Routledge, 1991.

Drakopoulou, Maria, 'Samuel Pufendorf, Feminism and the Question of "Women and Law",' in M. Drakopoulou (ed.), *Feminist Encounters with Legal Philosophy*, London: Routledge-Cavendish, 66–91, 2014.

Dyan, Colin, *With Dogs at the Edge of Life*, New York: Columbia University Press, 2015.

Fitzpatrick, Peter and Hunt, Allan, *Critical Legal Studies*, London: Blackwell, 1987.

Foucault, Michel, *Abnormal Lectures at the Collège de France*, trans. G. Burchell, New York: Picador, 1999, 2003.

Foucault, Michel, *Madness and Civilization: A History of Insanity in the Age of Reason*, trans. R. Howard, London, New York: Tavistock/Routledge, 1961, 1989.

Foucault, Michel, *The Archaeology of Knowledge*, London: Routledge, 1969, 1989.

Foucault, Michel, *The Order of Things: An Archaeology of the Human Sciences*, London, New York: Routledge, 1966, 2002.

Foucault, Michel, 'The Order of Discourse,' in R. Young (ed.), *Untying the Text: A Post-structuralist Reader*, London, New York: Routledge and Kegan Paul, 48–78, 1970, 1987.
Fraser, Nancy, 'Heterosexism, Misrecognition and Capitalism: A Response to Judith Butler', *New Left Review*, I(228), 140–149 (March–April, 1998).
Golder, Ben, *Foucault and the Politics of Rights*, Stanford: Stanford University Press, 2015.
Golder, Ben and Fitzpatrick, Peter. *Foucault's Law on the Influence of Foucault in Critical Legal Studies*, London: Routledge, 2009.
Goodrich, Peter, *Legal Discourse: Studies in Linguistics, Rhetoric and Legal Analysis*, London: Palgrave Macmillan, 1987.
Goodrich, Peter, *Languages of Law: From Logics of Memory to Nomadic Masks*, London: Weidenfeld and Nicholson, 1990.
Goodrich, Peter, 'Critical Legal Studies in England: Prospective Histories,' *Oxford Journal of Legal Studies*, 12(2), 195–236, 1992.
Goodrich, Peter, *Oedipus Lex: Psychoanalysis, History, Law*, Berkeley, Los Angeles, London: University of California Press, 1995.
Goodrich, Peter, *Law in the Courts of Love: Literature and Other Minor Jurisprudences*, London, New York: Routledge, 1996.
Goodrich, Peter, *Legal Emblems and the Art of Law: Obiter Depicta as the Vision of Governance*, Cambridge: Cambridge University Press, 2014.
Goodrich, Peter, 'The Judge's Two Bodies: The Case of Daniel Paul Schreber', *Law and Critique*, 26(2), 117–133, 2015.
Gordon, Colin, 'Governmental Rationality: An Introduction', in G. Burchell, C. Gordon and P. Miller (eds), *The Foucault Effect: Studies in Governmentality with two lectures By and an Interview by Michel Foucault*, Chicago: The University of Chicago, 1–52, 1987.
Grbich, Jennifer, 'The Taxpayer's Body: Genealogies of Exertion' in P. Cheah, D. Fraser and J. Grbich (eds), *Thinking through the Body of Law*, New South Wales: Allen & Unwin, 136–60, 1996.
Gross, Ayeal, 'Gender Outlaws Before the Law: The Courts of the Borderland', *Harvard Journal of Law & Gender*, 32, 166–231, 2009.
Haldar, Piyel, *Law, Orientalism and Postcolonialism*, London: Routledge, 2007.
Haldar, Piyel, 'A Gesture: A Review of Peter Goodrich, Legal Emblems and the Art of Law: Obiter Debicta as the Vision of Governance (Cambridge University Press, 2014)' *Law and Humanities*, 8(2), 304–318, 2014.
Hall, Stuart, Chas, Critcher, Jefferson, Tony, Clarke, John and Roberts, Brian, *Policing the Crisis: Mugging, the State, and Law and Order*, New York: Palgrave Macmillan, 1978.
Hanafin, Patrick, *Constituting Identity: Political Identity Formation and the Constitution in Post-Independence Ireland*, Aldershot: Ashgate, 2001.
Hanafin, Patrick, *Conceiving Life: Reproductive Politics and the Law in Contemporary Italy*, Aldershot: Ashgate, 2007.
Hanafin, Patrick, 'Voicing Embodiment, Relating Difference: Towards a Relational Legal Subjectivity', *Australian Feminist Law Journal*, 29, 77–90, 2008.
Hanafin, Patrick, 'The Embryonic Sovereign and the Biological Citizen: The Biopolitics of Reproductive Rights,' in C. Gearty and Costas Douzinas (eds), *The Cambridge Companion to Human Rights Law. Cambridge Companions to Law*. Cambridge, UK: Cambridge University Press, 191–213, 2012.
Hanafin, Patrick, 'A Voice Beyond the Law: Reading Cavarero Reading Plato,' in M. Drakopoulou (ed.), *Feminist Encounters with Legal Philosophy*, London: Routledge, 9–19, 2013.
Hunt, Allan, 'The Theory of Critical Legal Studies,' *Oxford Journal of Legal Studies*, 6(1), 1–45, 1986.
Hunter, Rosemary and Mack, Kathy, 'Exclusion and Silence: Procedure and Evidence', in N. Naffine and J. R. Owens (eds), *Sexing the Subject of Law*, London: Sweet and Maxwell, 171–92, 1997.
Kafka, Franz, *Letter to the Father*, New York: Schocken Books, 2015.

Kantorowicz, H. Ernst, *The King's Two Bodies: A Study in Medieval Political Theology*, Princeton, NJ: Princeton University Press, 1997.

Kelsen, Hans, 'The Pure Theory of Law: Its Method and Fundamental Concepts', *Law Quarterly Review*, 50(4), 474–498, 1934.

Kennedy, Duncan and Klare, Karl, 'A Bibliography of Critical Legal Studies [TRS],' *Yale Law Journal*, 94, 461–90, 1984.

Krenshaw, Kimberley, 'Demarginalizing the Intersection of Race and Sex: A Black Feminist Critique of Antidiscrimination Doctrine, Feminist Theory and Antiracist Politics', *University of Chicago Legal Forum*, 140, 139–167, 1989.

Lacey, Nicola, *Unspeakable Subjects: Feminist Essays in Legal and Social Theory*, Oxford: Hart Publishing, 1998.

Lamble, Sarah, 'Unknowable Bodies, Unthinkable Sexualities: Lesbian and Transgender Legal Invisibility in the Toronto Women's Bathhouse Raid', *Social and Legal Studies*, 18(1), 111–130, 2009.

Lamble, Sarah, 'Queer Investments in Punishment: Sexual Citizenship, Social Movements and the Expanding Carceral State', in J. Haritaworn, A. Kuntsman and S. Posocco (eds), *Queer Necropolitics*, London: Routledge, 2014.

Loizidou, Elena, 'Heavenly Creatures, Matricide and Criminal Law's Obsession with Confessions', in L. Moran, D. Monk and S. Beresford (eds), *Legal Queeries*, London: Cassell, Cassell, 1998.

Loizidou, Elena, 'Sex @ the End of the Twentieth Century: Some Re-marks on a Minor Jurisprudence', *Law and Critique*, 10(1), 71–86, 1999.

Loizidou, Elena, *Judith Butler: Ethics, Law Politics,* London: Routledge, 2007.

Loizidou, Elena, 'The Body Figural and Material in the Work of Judith Butler', *Australian Feminist Law Journal*, 28, 29–51, 2008.

Malabou, Catherine, 'Will Sovereignty Ever Be Deconstructed?' in B. Bhandar and J. Goldberg-Hiller (eds), *Plastic Materialities: Politics, Legality, and Metamorphosis in the work of Catherine Malabou*, Durham, London: Duke University Press, 35–46, 2015.

Mawani, Renisa, 'Insects, War, Plastic Life' in B. Bhandar and J. Goldberg-Hiller (eds), *Plastic Materialities: Politics, Legality, and Metamorphosis in the work of Catherine Malabou*, Durham, London: Duke University Press, 169–185, 2015.

McNeilly, Katherine, 'After the Critique of Rights: For a Radical Democratic Theory and Practice of Human Rights', *Law and Critique*, 27(3), 268–289, 2016.

Monk, Daniel, 'Beyond Section 28: Law, Governance and Sex Education' in L. Moran, D. Monk and S. Beresford (eds), *Legal Queeries*, London: Cassell, Cassell, 1998.

Moran, J. Les, *The Homosexual(ity) of Law*, London, New York: Routledge, 1996.

Moran, Les, 'Sexual Diversity in the Judiciary in England and Wales; Research on Barriers to Judicial Careers', *Laws*, 2, 512–538, 2013.

Motha, Stewart and Perrin, Colin, 'Deposing Sovereignty after Mabo', *Law and Critique*, 13(3), 231–338, 2002.

Motha, Stewart, 'Veiled Women and the Affect of Religion in Democracy' *Journal of Law and Society*, 34(1), 139–162, 2007.

Motha, Stewart, '"Begging to be Black": Liminality and Critique in Post-Apartheid South Africa', *Theory, Culture, and Society*, 27(7/8), 285–305, 2010.

Murphy, Tim, 'BritCrits: Subversion and Submission, Past, Present and Future', *Law and Critique*, 10(3), 237–278, 1999.

Otomo, Yoriko and Mussawir, Edward (eds), *Law and the Question of the Animal*, London: Routledge, 2013.

Philippopoulos-Mihalopoulos, Andreas, *Spatial Justice: Body, Lawscape, Atmosphere*, London: Routledge, 2015.

Philippopoulos-Mihalopoulos, Andreas, 'Flesh of the Law: Material Legal Metaphors', *Journal of Law and Society*, 43(1), 45–65, 2016.

Pottage, Alain, 'Autoplasticity' in B. Bhandar and J. Goldberg-Hiller (eds), *Plastic Materialities: Politics, Legality, and Metamorphosis in the work of Catherine Malabou*, Durham and London: Duke University Press, 73–90, 2015.

Reiner, Robert, *The Politics of the Police*, Oxford: Oxford University Press, 2010.

Rush, Peter, 'Killing Me Softly With His Words: Hunting the Law Student', *Law and Critique*, 1(1), 21–37, 1990.

Sabsay, Leticia, 'From Being Sexual to Having Sexual Rights', *DarkMatter*, 14, 16 May 2016. www.darkmatter101.org/site/2016/05/16/from-being-sexual-to-having-sexual-rights/

Sharpe, Andrew, *Transgender Jurisprudence: Dysphoric Bodies of Law*, London: Routledge, 2002.

Sharpe, Andrew, *Foucault's Monsters and the Challenge of Law*, London: Routledge, 2010.

Tuitt, Patricia, *Race, Law, Resistance*, London: Glasshouse, 2004.

Wallbank, Julie, *Challenging Motherhood(s)*, London: Routledge, 2001.

Williams, Patricia, *The Alchemy of Rights and Race: A Diary of a Law Professor*, Massachusetts: Harvard University Press, 1992.

Young, Alison, *Femininity in Dissent*, London, New York: Routledge, 1990.

12
On resisting bodies

Laurent de Sutter

For a few breasts more

On October 15, 2012, in front of the Hôtel Bourvallais, home of the French Ministry of Justice, on Place Vendôme in Paris, some unexpected activity was taking place, involving journalists, police officers and a gang of feisty young women. This was not a big surprise: since the young women were part of the French branch of Femen, the movement created four years before in Kiev by Anna Hutsol, Oksana Chatchko and Alexandra Chevchenko, some fuss (and bare breasts) definitely *was* to be expected. This time, the women were protesting against a decision, taken by the tribunal of Fontenay-sous-Bois, in the western *banlieue* of Paris, to release ten out of the fourteen men accused of having participated in a series of gang rapes in the staircases of their building block. Despite very strong evidence, the judge seemed to have considered that their actions were not heavy enough to deserve punishment – while those found guilty were only condemned to mild sentences, from three years with suspension up to one mandatory year. For the members of Femen, this was another manifestation of patriarchal contempt for the body of women, a way to affirm that, in the end, the latter only are properties which males, whatever their status or actions, should be able to dispose of as they please. As usual, the way of demonstrating exercised by the young woman was spectacular and brutal – running towards the open door of the palace, uttering provocative slogans and displaying slogans painted on their bare chest, the most striking being "Justice Fucks Us". Of course, the guards slammed the door in their face, allowing journalists to witness the inevitable fight that would happen when the police force would try and calm things down – but in such a way that it would only render the situation more hectic. Yet, this time, the women were not prosecuted, unlike one year later, when they decided to upset the peace of Notre-Dame and forced their way into the cathedral to toll the bells – as a celebration of Pope Benedict XVI's resignation. Even though they were found innocent of the charges against them, this trial became the first of a long series, half of which were initiated by infuriated Catholic or extreme right-wing groups and half by Femen militants themselves, protesting against the violence targeted against them. If the bare breasts and noisy slogans of the group members were disturbing people to the point where they would judicially complain, then the women would add insult to injury by using the same means, as absurd, as unjust and as patriarchal as they were.

When justice fucks us

"Justice Fucks Us": by painting this slogan in black letters on their skin, the French Femen were not only making a provocative statement, aimed at attracting the attention of the press and causing some debate among politicians and intellectuals. What they were saying was much more profound than this: it was a description of a certain legal and judicial regime of the body – the regime involved in the way justice was performed in countries such as France, where the so-called rule of law reigns supreme. According to this description, justice was not to be conceived as a moral tool, tentatively reforming bad actions and (sometimes) bad intents when they eventually occurred, but something whose mere existence already meant some sort of an intervention into the physical realm. The "Justice Fucks Us" slogan should not be read as an exaggeration conceived to make the headlines and to be easily repeated, but as a way to state a truth that could not be stated otherwise than in an hyperbolic way – namely, the fact that, in reality, justice *really* fucks us (Ackerman, 2013).[1] Justice infiltrates the body and the mind like a social democrat version of a body-snatcher, progressively taking control of all aspects of our lives, only leaving aside what is of no importance within its system of value – and that isn't much. Every word, every gesture, every move of the body always already belongs to the realm of justice, even if none of them had caused any damage or provoked any harm; justice fucks us because it takes our bodies as a toy for its own enjoyment. What the men did in Fontenay-sous-Bois was nothing compared to what the women who got raped let them do – and, somehow, justice was recognising its own face in the one of the little bastards thinking that fucking girls in their ass against their will was a cool thing to do. This was what the young Femen wanted those who witnessed their flash mob on Place Vendôme to understand: justice was not some higher moral instance "judging" what was happening in the world, but a worldly being itself, with its own urges and desires, exercised upon the body of other beings. By showing their own breasts, what the Femen militants wanted to demonstrate was that, behind the moral posturing of justice, what justice was interested in was precisely this – the signs of a libidinal life of bodies, titillating it too much for its own comfort. If bodies were what justice wanted, then it would be what justice would get; only, it would get them in a way that would force it down its throat, so that it chokes, and finally admits what its façade of respectability was trying to hide.

Anything but thought

Three hundred fifty years before the event on Place Vendôme, in the quiet little village of Rijnsburg near Leiden, in The Netherlands, Baruch Spinoza was slowly putting together the pieces of what would become his masterpiece, *the Ethics*. It was a hard thing to do, since he was already busy with another book dedicated to the work of his French colleague René Descartes, and also was trying to earn a living giving private philosophy lessons and grinding lenses – which gave him less time to devote to his other book.[2] Yet, the most important claims of the work were taking shape, if only because he had already attempted to develop a primitive version of his system of ethics in a previous book, titled *On the Improvement of the Understanding*, at that time just published. Among the numerous arguments developed in the *Ethics*, there was one of which no prefiguration could be found in any of his other publications, namely a singular and compelling theory of the body, understood as "affection". The first definition, opening the second part of the *Ethics*, was defining the body as what manifested, in the realm of extension, the very essence of God; according to Spinoza, anything that would manifest this essence in the extended matter could be said to be a body (Spinoza, 1674: 354). Of course, one had to agree on what "extended matter" would mean before being able to understand the full reach of this definition; if the realm of extension only designates the material world, then a body would only be counted as belonging to this world. But, for Spinoza, things were a little more sophisticated: the world of extended matter could be correctly delineated only through its contrasting with the world of "Thought", being the realm of what the Dutch philosopher called "the spirit", from which every body is to be excluded (Spinoza, 1674: 415). So, following a later development in the *Ethics*, a body is what a spirit is not; it is the extended manifestation of the essence of God, provided that this extension doesn't reach the level of Thought – whose sole reality precisely is that it is not extended matter. For Spinoza, it was then obvious that the world of extension encompassed much more than mere material phenomena; as a matter of fact, it could include *anything but Thought* – anything but the pure idea of what was without any extension at all, that is the pure idea of God himself. If one was to accept this idea, then everything was body; and the only way to know it, since bodies are not limited to material things, is to "feel" them, to experience the fact of being affected by them.

What a body can do

A body is whatever affects – and, conversely, can be affected – there is no body outside the realm of affection, that is, outside the realm of the fact that it is not indifferent, that it is not possible to do as if they were not existing and making a difference. This difference is what Spinoza called "*potentia*", that is the "power" of a body to affect another body in any way, whatever the essence of these two bodies, the nature of their relationship and the determination of the context of their affection. "Nobody so far has succeeded in determining what a body can do", wrote Spinoza in the famous second Proposition of the third part of the *Ethics*; nobody has dared to try and think what the *potentia* of a body is, outside of the realm of Thought (Spinoza, 1674: 416). For the time, this was a harsh critique, since it implied that, until the moment Spinoza decided to elaborate his concept of the body, the history of philosophy actually was the history of the spirit – for which the body was only providing contingent support. What Spinoza said to his fellow philosophers was that the spirit was everything and nothing at the same time, and that it was high time to strike back to the body, since bodies were constituting the quasi-totality of the world, even if it was a totality without Thought. If Thought was what allowed for conceiving how the world of bodies was manifesting the very essence of God, this world should have been considered as being formed of all that existed, since everything but God (or its idea, which was the same) was body. The consequence, of course, was that, according to Spinoza, affection and *potentia* were almost one and the same thing; what a body can do is precisely affecting other bodies, and *potentia* only designates the possible intensity of this affection. What is certain is that this intensity is always superior or inferior to zero; a total absence of affection is what characterises essence, as the idea of God, which only belongs to the realm of Thought – a realm very rarefied indeed, since there is only one being inhabiting it. Succeeding in determining what a body can do, as Spinoza argued, meant succeeding in determining the intensities of affection that this body can cause, or of which it can be the subject; it meant determining the singular *mode* of affection proper to this body. Contrarily to what was commonplace at the time when Spinoza wrote, it is not the nature of a body which dictates its regime of relationship with other bodies, but the intensity of its affection that will allow for its consideration as a body *per se* – or, to put it more simply: affection *is* the body.

Visiting the sex dolls factory

When they were claiming that "Justice Fucks Us", the young Femen women knew what they were doing; if justice was literally fucking them (and everyone else), it was not by way of its hypothetical sexual attributes, but of a certain regime of affection. Justice was producing a "fucked body", so to speak – a body which would tolerate sexual invasion as it would tolerate other forms of coercion if they were exercised in the name of the law; justice was producing a body constituted of sexual affects. Of course, stating that law and justice had something to do with desire and sexuality was not new – Gilles Deleuze and Félix Guattari, reading Franz Kafka's legal theoretical evergreen novel, *The Trial*, has already pointed this out, among many others (Deleuze and Guattari, 1975: 79).[3] But what the young women were doing was different; they were suggesting that, rather than being grounded on some sort of suppression of the sexual, justice was about instilling it into new bodies, in such a way that it would constitute them as sexual bodies. If indeed the system of justice was a system saturated with obscure fetishes and perverse desires, it was not their imposition upon existing bodies that provoked the feeling of being fucked, but the fact that they defined a regime of affection making it impossible to avoid being fucked. The dirty little secret of justice was its enjoyment at fabricating little puppets that wouldn't have any other role than the one of satisfying its urges, as disgusting and as fundamentally unjust as they may seem; justice was but a factory producing sex dolls. The problem was that these sex dolls were not happy; or, at least, *some* of them were not happy, and were not ready to let the system of justice go on without resisting it – which is why the group of Femen militants gathered on Place Vendôme in the first place. To the reality of the fact that justice was fucking them, they wanted to oppose another regime of affection, which would turn their bodies into something different, capable of other things than accepting their doll status, developing another *potential*. As Spinoza as pointed out, a regime of affection is never unilateral; on the contrary, the capacity to affect is always accompanied by a capacity to be affected – and vice versa; to be constituted as a sexual body didn't mean that backfiring was prohibited. On the contrary, deploying a regime of affection was not without odd consequences, since intensities always manifest a sort of freedom, as well as a tendency to contaminate domains that were supposed to remain out of sight or out of reach – and that is exactly what happened.

My body, my rules

It is the judicial attempt at building a fuckable body that led to the sudden irruption of anger from Femen members; and it was in order to answer this attempt that some of the women preferred to write a different slogan than "Justice Fucks Us" on their chest. This slogan read "My Body, My Rules", and was a staple of the Femen guerrilla-style flash mobs catalogue – so much so that it is quite difficult to trace its origin, which obviously extends far beyond the short history of the Ukrainian movement. What is for certain is that the slogan is part of a more general regime of discourse attached to feminism, of which said movement has often been considered being an incarnation of its fourth wave – which the founders of Femen have coined "sextremism". But, besides this, it seems that it is impossible to determine who, when or where it was first uttered: "My Body, My Rules" belongs to the world of abstract wisdom, albeit a very aggressive one, aiming at making clear that any attempt at negating it would not be welcomed with open arms. "My Body, My Rules" meant that the existing link between law (or the system of justice supposed to apply it) and bodies has nothing natural to it, and that the regime of affection under which they are subsumed can be resisted – and even *asks* for such resistance. It could be read like this: "You want to rule my body? You want my body to become a result of your ruling? Then, you'll get what you ask for – but with a rebound in your face you didn't expect. Now, who's ruling what, huh, *fucker*?" As a slogan, "My Body, My Rules" implied the fact that what was described actually didn't exist; it was a way to recognise that even if I somehow inhabit my body, this body is not ruled by me, but by someone (or something) else, turning it into its own thing. But, at the same time, it was also a warning to all those who thought that the situation was under control and that nothing had to change – even more than a warning, it was already a sign that the situation was indeed changing, and would continue changing. Of course, the slogan was based upon an assumption that lawyers might find hard to swallow: the one stating that the rules applying to my body really are my rules – namely, the rules that I have decided to apply to my own case, whatever the more general rules are. What the Femen women were saying is that general rules never apply to a body, because for them to be applicable, a given body could be exchanged for any other body; and the problem was that it was this generality of the body that they were denying to those who wanted to rule their body.

Freedom and its discontents

From the point of view of positive law, the slogan "My Body, My Rules" was an absurdity; as every law student very soon learns when he or she enters law school, we are not the owner of our body; we are not allowed to do whatever we want with it. The civil law system has even devised a concept to explain why this is so: the concept of *indisponibilité du corps humain* – the "unaffordability" of the human body, meaning that our own body actually always stays beyond our legal reach. It is this principle that justifies why, during a long period of history, it was prohibited to commit suicide – and it is still this principle that is behind numerous attempts at banning abortion, prostitution, self-mutilation or drug consumption, for instance. If such a principle does not exist in common law, the way of thinking implied by its existence has never ceased to also flourish in common law countries, as even the most remote examination of the legislation applicable to the human body will prove. For law, the freedom to dispose of one's own body cannot be an unlimited freedom; there must be limits to this freedom, and the definition of these limits should not be left to those who own or possess it (it is a tricky matter to determine which concept applies here) (Wall, 2015). As usual, the reasons justifying the adoption of such a limitation brought to the freedom to do as one pleases displayed lots of paternalistic overtones, based on the argument that people don't really know what they want, and that some know it better than they do themselves. What the Femen wanted to make clear through their use of the "My Body, My Rules" slogan was precisely that they couldn't care less about this paternalistic stance – and that they expected to be taken very seriously when they affirmed their will to be the sole ruler of their body. Not only were they perfectly aware of what they were doing, but also this awareness implied a crystal-clear understanding of the fact that the first target of their action was the type of paternalism implying that they knew not what they were doing. On the contrary, paternalism was the first moment of the long process through which justice was trying to fuck bodies; as in every horror story, the one of the relationship between justice and the body starts by the encounter with someone who wants to do you some good. Well, the Femen women were not interested in people who wanted to do them good; the only person, they claimed, from whom they were sure that there was absolutely no good to be expected, were none others than those claiming the opposite.

Between person and thing

The paradox of the curious regime of interaction between law and the body is the following: the more you try to affect bodies, so that you would make them what you want them to become, the more they will resist and produce counter-affections. For as long as the history of philosophy criticised by Spinoza, the history of legal thought has been in denial towards this curious rule of the physics of affection, as if bodies were only the passive surface of inscription for whatever might pop in the head of the legislator. The Femen women put it openly: you cannot do without bodies – you can definitely try, and act as if "legal subjects" (for what this concept is worth) were only minds on a fleshy vehicle, but, in doing so, you would only reproduce a two-millennia-long prejudice. This prejudice has been thoroughly synthesised by Roberto Esposito when he described the legal history of the body as a perpetual hesitation between "person" and "thing", between making it the headquarters of the subject, or a mere *res* upon which logistical strategies are to be enforced (Esposito, 2015). The origin of this hesitation is very clear: as is made obvious in the opening paragraphs of Gaius's famous textbook, the *Institutes*, the Roman lawyers already considered that the realm of law was to be divided between rights attached to persons, to things or to actions – the legal means to act in justice (Gaius, 1979: 2). When Gaius was writing and teaching, at the end of the 2nd century, this distinction already represented an indisputable *summa divisio*, based on a silent anthropology relegating the body (or bodies) into some kind of oblivion. The fact that the different rights were to be linked to different attributes of the body didn't cross the mind of the Roman lawyers, nor of all those who inherited from them, up to the precursors of the French Civil Code, in the 18th century, such as Jean Domat or Robert-Joseph Pothier. For them, too, it was not necessary to discuss Gaius's distinction, since it had given birth to such a sophisticated legal landscape that even questioning it would lead to reconsider each and every one of its category – starting with the most important one: property (Garnsey, 2007).[4] They were right: introducing the body into this game would be a catastrophe – at least, for those would take for granted that its structure, and the division upon which this structure is grounded, are fundamentally legitimate, or even *natural* (as some continue to claim it to be). What the Femen militants reminded the short-sighted legal scholars who thought so was that it was quite the contrary: nothing was less "natural" than this.

The network of affections

Bodies are constructed through affections – affections and counter-affections, running in sometimes contradictory directions, and making each and every one of them the singular sum of these contradictions: there indeed is nothing natural to this. Whether it is constructed as the vehicle of a "person", or as a "thing" upon which forces can be exercised (such as the force of fucking), the body is never a mere composite of flesh and blood, biologically born out its own cellular development. The idea that the body would be the place of what Giorgio Agamben called "*zoè*", or "bare life", life without mediation, is as absurd as to consider that feelings, objects, dreams, institutions, and so on would not have a body at all – because they are something *else* (Agamben, 1997). As Spinoza said it, it is the affection that creates the body, so much so that body can be anything capable of a level of affection that is not zero; when we speak about bodies, we shouldn't think "flesh and blood", like phenomenologists do, for instance.

This is something the Femen women have understood perfectly well when they picked the "My Body, My Rules" slogan: they were not (or not only) mentioning its carnal dimension, but all the facets without which it wouldn't be a body at all. This included language, manners, posture, accessories, behaviours, values, and so on; what they wanted to be recognised the rulers of was *everything* – every single aspect of how their body was affected and was capable of affecting others in return. None of these various facets was natural, or the expression of a type of life that would precede any form of social being or of social construction – since the only thing that we can know of a society precisely is the network of affections somehow bonding the bodies constituting it. What the Femen "My Body, My Rules" slogan meant was that the body could be the place for an answer opposing itself to the legal attempts at ruling all these aspects of life, and, at the same time, at denying its mere existence behind its rejection as a non-legal category. But such an answer implied the assumption of the necessity to reconstruct the social network of affections in another way – to intervene everywhere where the affective management of bodies was at work, that is way beyond the limits of courts and tribunals. Law and justice were only small players in a bigger game of forces, of which they were the obedient servants, even though, of course, they were also trying to satisfy their own urges, as was rendered manifest at the end of the Fontenay-sous-Bois trial – and its obscene verdict.

Cyborg jurisprudence, a very short introduction

Every body is an augmented body – a body augmented by the gigantic amount of language, history, values, rules, investments, accessories, etc., that manifest the existence of zones of affection beyond, above, under and so on its mere flesh, bones, blood and nerves. We are all cyborgs, even though the cyborg in question has very little to do with the man-meets-machine imaginary born out of the cyberpunk movement in the beginning of the 1980s; rather than mundane versions of Robocop, we are affection-enhanced beings. When she devised her famous "Cyborg Manifesto", from 1983 onwards, Donna Haraway was perfectly aware of this – and this precisely is what she wanted to emphasise: the fact that the idea of the purity of a flesh, animated by conscience, was an enormous mistake (Haraway, 1985). It was precisely because of this mistake that the Western world had suffered such a long tradition of rejection of the body, as being never spiritual enough, pure enough, detached enough from what was considered as the burden of worldly existence. For whatever it was worth, a body was only a dirty mixture of contingent matter, which was excepted from ontological relegation by the miracle of conscience – the moment when unanimated flesh metamorphosed into animated being, even accessed to being as such. According to Haraway, this was not only false, but also stupid and vicious, since the only tangible effect of such an understanding of what a body is was to lead to an ethics and a politics of the body that would always lead to the choice of purification. Whether it was about education, punishment or simply control, the social, ethical and political process of civilisation implied a sort of selection aiming at achieving the least contaminated body possible – civilisation being the purifying agent itself:

to civilise is to purify. The contradiction of such an argument was obvious: the more you claim to purify, the more you affect – the more you add to a given body bodily features corresponding to the very idea of the civilised body that you want to enforce upon existing individuals. In such a process of civilisation, law had obviously played its role, not only dreaming of its own purity (the purity of the legal subject), but also contributing generously to the purification required by those who had the lead on its development and enforcement. Even if its technical plasticity could have allowed law to welcome the becoming-cyborg of bodies, the circumstances surrounding its effectiveness have prohibited this to happen: the human body, seat of the subject's mind, was to remain protected.

A moment of sextremist fury

The scandal caused by the Femen women could be considered as belonging to the stream of thought opened by Haraway: not only were they refusing to satisfy themselves with a definition of the body limited to its flesh, but they were also conscious of the role played by the idea of civilisation in this definition. Among other things, their "sextremism" was an answer to the attempt at civilising the body – including the fact that a civilised body was supposed to appear in a certain way, and to behave in a certain way, in the public space, that is, tautologically, in a civilised way. The Femen women resisted this; they refused to behave like civilised young persons, adopting contained manners and dressing like everyone else, so that their body could only be seen in the way that it was supposed to be seen – say, as a commodity for the male gaze. They were noisy, they were brutal, they publicly showed their breasts – they were the perfect embodiment of a certain type of mythological monster, the furies, the perfect incarnation of the moment when women become too dangerous to be called women anymore. They were spitting on the soft beauties of purity, knowing that purity, like law, always hides safes full of dirty little secrets, perversely enjoyed in private by those who publicly testify of their high moral concerns and generous political goals. They wanted their body to break the consensus about bodies, especially as far as justice and law were concerned; this civilised consensus, and the legal neutrality backing it, was what we should get rid of, if we want to simply reconcile with what bodies really are. They were militant in denouncing the lie of legal neutrality, so that the militant dimension of neutrality might, some day, render possible another type of neutrality, devoid of any hidden agenda – neutrality indeed being the worst form of militant activism. This is the reason for which their weapon of choice was their breasts, and their credo called "sextremism": they knew perfectly well that the dirty little secrets hidden behind the veil of neutrality always concerned sex, lust or desire. The attempt at purifying bodies from their inner cyborg nature was an attempt at avoiding confrontation with desire, through a game of power that would render its fulfilment easier or more gratifying for those pulling its strings or occupying the first seats. To transform oneself into a fury was then a way to say that these attempts were doomed to fail – and that dirt was not theirs to be perversely enjoyed but constituted our basic common condition.

From being to having

When Spinoza was insisting on the fact that what counted the most in a body was not so much the types of affection that it could call for, but the power or intensity of these affections, he was implying that the ontology of the body was a fluctuating ontology. The being of a body is not something that is decided once and for all; it is a being that passes through stages where it more or less is, depending on the intensity of the various affections targeted towards it, or that it targets towards others. Gabriel Tarde, when not busy with his duties as a judge in Sarlat, in the south-west of France, tried to draw the ultimate consequence from this transitory ontology and offered a synthetic description of what was happening when being could not be asserted anymore. According to him, as he stated in his *Monadologie et sociologie* in 1893, a careful observation of the network of affections within which every "being" is involved should lead to the realisation that the world "being" itself should be abandoned (Tarde, 1893) (Alliez, 1999: 86). Rather than an ontology of "being", what affections and intensities force us to take into account is an ontology of "having", that is, an ontology of the qualities that we "possess", and that are the only features of any being: *we are only insofar as we have.* Obviously, to say so was not trying to devise some obscure metaphysical plot in order to save capitalism and consumption from its predictable pitfalls; rather, it was a way to account for the variability of being and also for its collective dimension. If we are only insofar as we have, then our "being" depends exclusively on the regime of affections that we have succeeded to set up for it; it also means that the solidity of this "being" depends on the solidity of the network of affections defining it. The main consequence of this strange shift was, of course, that the difference between "being" and "society" could never be firmly drawn: as the result of a network of affections, every "being" already is some kind of a "society"; we never are one, we are absolutely numerous and plural. This is also why bodies cannot be dealt with as if they were mere merchandise or commodity; being entangled in a network of affections, they still carry the network with them when they are tentatively disposed of – so that they are never alone to resist. The resistance of a body never rests upon the power of the mind animating it; it is the very resistance of the network of affections constituting its being, at the same time that it constitutes the reciprocal being of all those that are affected by it, or that affect it. This, and nothing else, is its *potentia*.

Another hacker manifesto

Bodies are cyborgs in many ways: not only do they exceed the limits of the human flesh, but they also blur the boundaries of identity and the difference separating the individual from the collective; in sum: *bodies are a fucking nuisance.* It is this power of nuisance that the Femen militants wanted to activate in order to disturb the quiet comfort of the Hôtel Bourvallais. They wanted to expose the network of *negative* affections that the judicial power opposed to the possible positive affections of which every body is susceptible. The difference between the two, for Spinoza, was a crucial matter: if we are only insofar as we have, then the direction taken by the affections that we have will determine the quantity of our being – since we can more or less be. Negative affections produce a diminishing of our being, its reduction into a negligible quantity, detached from others, so making it easy for everyone to make us dance the way they like – or to fuck us as they please, if this is what they want. Conversely, positive affections lead to the augmentation of our being – the very same kind of augmentation rightfully allowing Haraway to claim that there are no bodies, physical or else, but augmented bodies. The augmentation of a body does not concern the amount of gadgets or prosthetics with which we surround ourselves (or, at least, not only) but mostly the added affections and added intensities defining the power of our being-into-the-world, to quote a famous Nazi philosopher. The aggressiveness of the Femen women should then be interpreted as a way to agitate people and make them aware of the network of negative affections within which they are trapped, and through which their being is reduced to impotency. It was not a call for revolution, or an attempt at a coup, or whatever else of that kind, but an intervention at the place where the management of affections has become the main task: the media existence of all things, as an echo chamber for affections. The women knew that the press is a fantastic tool for spreading affections, albeit superficial ones, and that this tool would only react under certain conditions – precisely the promise of a certain intensity of affections, whether positive or negative. By playing the game of open physical provocation, they tried to add to their own power of affection the one of the media dispositive which they would tease by such a promise – under the guise of what media can never resist: tits and violence. What the Femen did was to hack the media machine in order to further augment their own being.

The natural life of law

Law is the corseting of the networks of affection; it is what rigidifies the possibilities of affections and regulates their intensities; it is what produces a sort of homeostasis of bodies, and of their mutual affections – or, at least, what tries to. For there is a difference between this programme – which is perfectly compatible, as history has shown, with the most reactionary ideologies – and what happens in practice, when judges, law enforcements agencies and lawyers realise that, indeed, bodies are a nuisance. The corseting, the rigidifying, the regulation and the homeostasis are only ideal goals that legal theorists of a certain kind, in the dusty silence of their cabinet, might dream law to perform; unfortunately for them, the legal life of bodies chooses paths that have nothing to do with those dreams. The fact is that there is a major flaw in the ideological programme of the legal control of bodies: it ignores that bodies can be almost everything (that is: everything but the idea of God), so that law, too, should be considered as a body – and not some overarching power. Corseting, rigidifying, etc., are modes of affection of the law, competing with other modes of affection in a world that never stops witnessing the confrontation between them; it only happens that this modes benefits from *loads* of augmentations. As Bruno Latour said, in his ethnography of the highest administrative jurisdiction in France, the Conseil d'Etat, law is but a fragile fabric, a network of its own, whose only power lies in what it holds together; without it, it would be properly nothing (Latour, 2002: 283).[5] This is because it involves so many people, institutions, files, documents, buildings, vehicles, pens, copy-machines, and so on, that it can affect other bodies with more intensity than these bodies can affect it in return; it certainly is not because of the dreams of legal theorists. So much so that, as a body, law, too, is a nuisance; law, too, resists the affection by other bodies and tries to expand its being by adding always already more bodies to its network of affection – as, again, Tarde had pointed out before anybody took notice. In his *Les transformations du droit*, the same year as *Monadologie et sociologie*, Tarde had insisted on what he called the "perpetual enlargement of legal relationships", the fact that law involved more and more bodies into its network of affections (Tarde, 1893: 76).[6] He was right: the natural life of law makes it a living body – something that never ceases to change, evolve and reframe its own network of affections according to those from which it benefits or suffers, as any other body would do.

In praise of backlashes

When they started shouting at the guards standing in front of the Ministry of Justice, the Femen women wanted to draw attention to this paradox: some bodies are more important than others – but this importance might very well prove to be usurpation. If they decided to hack the media system so that they could annex its *potentia* of affection to their own, it simply was in order to unbalance through fame the opposition of the law, so that they would not be immediately crushed by a much more powerful body than theirs. By doing so, they wanted to show that the homeostatic stabilisation of the networks of affection under the authority of law was a mere delusion – and that there was nothing easier than to disturb that homeostasis, even though, here too, backlashes should be expected. But this was what they wanted to create: a circuit of backlashes causing more backlashes, so that the fragile balance of the state of affairs might be unbalanced to the point where another status for neglected bodies could be formed. They wanted law to backlash, because backlashing is how a homeostatic state of affairs starts to destroy itself, to dissolve by itself its own fragile balance – that is, to stop mimicking death and to start living again, even though it is an uncomfortable life. This is how a body resists: not in directly confronting another body, but in modifying the entire ecology of affections making it what it is, so that its place within the network of affections of another body begins to move a little bit and provides room for change. Contrary to what some might think, the Femen strategy of provocation was neither primitive nor vulgar; it was what was necessary in order to create the self-unbalancing of an institution, even if this self-unbalancing was infinitesimal. Sometimes, too much is what is just necessary – and the Femen militants had understood it all too well; they knew that excess was what was required in order to force the law to answer (or, if not law directly, then the bodies who have the power to decisively affect law). Did they succeed? Of course not – or, at least, not in the eyes of those for whom success means revolution, upheaval or any other majuscule modification of the political and legal landscape of what they persist in calling a "society", or a "nation", or even a "country". But yes, if it is to make us aware of something that the narcotic sleep of contemporary capitalism has made undesirable for us to hear, because the comfort of homeostasis is also our comfort, as citizens as much as, say, legal theorists. Then again, legal theorists are disturbed by almost everything.

Notes

1 See also *Femen: Manifeste*, Paris, Utopia, 2015. For more biographical accounts, see Bouton, Eloïse *Confessions d'une ex-Femen*, Paris, Ed. du Moment, 2015; and Fourest, Caroline *Inna: Les paradoxes d'une Femen*, Paris, LGF, 2015.
2 On Spinoza's biography, see Nadler, Steven, *Spinoza: A Life*, Cambridge, Cambridge University Press, 1999.
3 For a commentary, see De Sutter, Laurent, *Deleuze: La pratique du droit*, Paris, Michalon, 2009.
4 See also Xifaras, Mikhaïl, *La propriété: Etude de philosophie du droit*, Paris, Presses Universitaires de France, 2004.
5 See also Latour, Bruno, *Enquête sur les modes d'existence: Une anthropologie des modernes*, Paris, La Découverte, 2012, p. 357 *sq*. For a commentary, see McGee, Kyle, *Bruno Latour: The Normativity of Networks*, London, Routledge, 2014. Yet, for a critique, see De Sutter, Laurent, "Plasma! Notes on Bruno Latour's Metaphysics of Law", *Latour and the Passage of Law*, McGee, Kyle, (ed.), Edinburgh, Edinburgh University Press, 2015, p. 197 *sq*.
6 For a more detailed account on this point, see De Sutter, Laurent, *Magic: Une métaphysique du lien*, Paris, Presses Universitaires de France, 2015.

Bibliography

Ackerman, Galia, *Femen*, Paris: Calmann-Lévy, 2013.
Agamben, Giorgio, *Homo Sacer I: Le pouvoir souverain et la vie nue*, fr. trans. Marilène Raiola, Paris: Le Seuil, 1997.
Allard, Laurence, Gardey, Delphine and Magnan, Nathalie (eds), *Féminismes*, Paris: Exils, 2007.
Alliez, Eric (ed.), in G. Tarde, *Monadologie et sociologie*, Paris: Les Empêcheurs de penser en rond, 1999.
Bouton, Eloïse, *Confessions d'une ex-Femen*, Paris: Ed. du Moment, 2015.
Deleuze, Gilles and Guattari, Félix, *Kafka: Pour une littérature mineure*, Paris: Minuit, 1975.
De Sutter, Laurent, *Deleuze: La pratique du droit*, Paris: Michalon, 2009.
De Sutter, Laurent, *Magic: Une métaphysique du lien*, Paris: Presses Universitaires de France, 2015.
De Sutter, Laurent, 'Plasma! Notes on Bruno Latour's Metaphysics of Law', in Kyle McGee (ed.), *Latour and the Passage of Law*, Edinburgh: Edinburgh University Press, 2015.
Esposito, Roberto, *Persons and Things: From the Body's Point of View*, London: Polity Press, 2015.
Fourest, Caroline, *Inna: Les paradoxes d'une Femen*, Paris: LGF, 2015.
Gaius, *Institutes*, ed. Julien Reinach, Paris: Les Belles Lettres, 1979.
Garnsey, Peter, *Thinking Property: From Antiquity to the Age of Revolution*, Cambridge: Cambridge University Press, 2007.
Latour, Bruno, *La fabrique du droit: Une ethnographie du Conseil d'Etat*, Paris: La Découverte, 2002.
Latour, Bruno, *Enquête sur les modes d'existence: Une anthropologie des modernes*, Paris: La Découverte, 2012.
McGee, Kyle, *Bruno Latour: The Normativity of Networks*, London: Routledge, 2014.
Millet, Jean (ed.), in G. Tarde, *Les transformations du droit*, Paris: Berg, 1994.
Nadler, Steven, *Spinoza: A Life*, Cambridge: Cambridge University Press, 1999.
Spinoza, Baruch, *L'Ethique*, 1674 in Tarde, Gabriel, *Oeuvres complètes*, Caillois, Roland, Madeleine, Francès and Misrahi, Robert (eds), Paris: Gallimard, 1954.
Tarde, Gabriel, *Oeuvres de Gabriel Tarde*, vol. 1, *Monadologie et sociologie*, 1893.
Tarde, Gabriel, *Les transformations du droit: Etude sociologique*, 1893.
Wall, Jesse, *Being and Owning: The Body, Bodily Material and the Law*, Oxford: Oxford University Press, 2015.
Xifaras, Mikhaïl, *La propriété: Etude de philosophie du droit*, Paris: Presses Universitaires de France, 2004.

13

Insect wars

Bees, bedbugs and biopolitics*

Renisa Mawani

As climate change, global food shortages, and permanent conditions of war have become matters of public debate in the Western contemporary moment, insects have repeatedly made headlines in local, national, and global news. In 2012, the *New York Times* reported "clumps of homeless bees" in New York City that were disrupting outdoor public places, including restaurant patios. The bees were allegedly swarming, a multitude that was frightening patrons and unsettling businesses. This aggregate of homeless bees was highly unusual. Since 2006, entomologists have reported a puzzling decline in bee populations, a phenomenon now known as colony collapse disorder (Johnson et al., 2009). Against the disappearance of bee species in Europe and North America, New York City's spring swarm nearly doubled those of previous years. Although the bees temporarily disturbed city life, beekeepers and enthusiasts were pleased. The "homeless bees" suggested a potential rise in bee populations, in this instance, the likely outcome of an unusually warm spring (Rueb, 2012). Several months later, the *New York Times* reported another infestation also affecting New York City residents. This time, the problem was not bees but bedbugs. "Reading in bed, once considered a relatively safe pastime, is now seen by some as a riskier proposition. That's because bedbugs have discovered a new way to hitchhike in and out of beds: library books" (St. Louis, 2012). Unlike the homeless bees occupying outdoor spaces, New York City's bedbugs were entering and inhabiting the most consecrated sites of intimacy: the bedroom. The city's insect problems continue. Commuters have expressed repeated outrage at the growing numbers of bedbugs on New York City subways. In one month alone, there were at least 21 "bedbug sightings," prompting the removal of infected subway cars from the city's busy transit system and causing delays for impatient commuters (CNBC, 2014).

New York's bee and bedbug problems are not specific to the city or to the U.S., for that matter. The decline of bees and the proliferation of bedbugs represent a growing urgency in many global cities, including London and Sydney. Indeed, many national and local governments have passed legislation to safeguard bees from harm and extinction, and to contain and eventually eliminate the proliferation of bedbugs. In the U.K., for instance, the shorthaired bumblebee, which disappeared in 1988 as a result of declining wildflower meadows, has recently been imported from Sweden and reintroduced into the Kent countryside. Eighty per cent of British plants are reliant on insects for pollination. According to recent estimates, "these creatures contribute more than £400m a year to the UK economy" (Morelle, 2012). The bumblebee is vital to Britain's food supply and therefore in need of legal and environmental protection. Meanwhile, Sydney is fighting its own insect wars. According to ABC News, bedbugs are "staging a comeback." One Sydney pest control company blames overseas travel: "travellers are the main culprits responsible for bringing bedbugs to Australia after they come from countries with high infestation," this source explains (White, 2011). The resilience of bedbugs in New York, Sydney, and in other major cities has encouraged the enactment of new laws aimed primarily at landlords, as I discuss further below.

Read together, what these seemingly disparate reports from New York, the U.K., and Australia suggest is that bees and bedbugs have become critical agents in Western global cities: disruptive, ungovernable, and perhaps most importantly, inseparable from human life and death. The mutability of bees and bedbugs and their divergent responses to changing urban ecologies illustrate what entomologists have termed insect plasticity. As multicellular organisms, insects are the species that have most successfully adapted and diversified to changing planetary conditions. Of the 1.4 million forms of biological life that have been identified by scientists thus far, insects comprise one million (Moczek, 2010: 594). A single genome displays a remarkable capacity to accommodate a wide range of phenotypes that are responsive to environmental conditions, including fluctuations in climate (Moczek, 2010). The result of insect plasticity has been twofold: the production of new forms of insect life, as well as an unprecedented resilience of certain species. Whereas global climate change has held devastating effects for some animal species, it has presented new opportunities for insects to divide, differentiate, and evolve. This is not to suggest that insects are indefinitely plastic or indestructible, for that matter. Plasticity can be adaptive and non-adaptive, generating new possibilities for life and death (Nylin and Gothard, 1998). Bees, as concerns of colony collapse disorder suggest, have been devastated by global ecological transformations, which is why New York City's swarm seemed so exceptional. Bedbugs, on the other hand, have the ability to thrive, mutate, and multiply in densely populated cities. They have successfully adapted to hostile conditions, becoming increasingly resistant to chemical treatments. But it is important to note that the demise of bees and the fecundity of bedbugs in North America, Europe, and Australia are not separate or distinct problems. They are interdependent and even inseparable. The use of certain pesticides, which has been linked to bee deaths, has created more stringent laws in the U.S., Canada, and the U.K. These legal prohibitions – aimed at protecting bees and saving human food supplies – have generated flourishing conditions in which bedbugs have multiplied.[1]

In this chapter, I begin developing a methodological approach to law and social theory that takes the interrelationality of human-nonhuman life and death seriously. Specifically, I consider insects as biopolitical agents that carry important legal and political consequences for the environment and for the longevity of human life. The plasticity of insects, I have suggested elsewhere, has become vital to discussions over life and death in ways that demand an urgent rethinking of prevailing conceptual frames and schemas (Mawani, 2015). The biopolitical, as Michel Foucault (2003) once formulated it, cannot be conceived in terms of human life alone. Rather, his ideas must not only be expanded and elaborated in ways that account for nonhuman life but also for the increasing entanglements between human and nonhuman death. For Foucault (2003), biopolitics was never about life alone. It was about the quality and intensity of life as healthy and pure that necessitated the distribution of racial death.[2] I return to this point in the concluding section. For now, let me say that under current conditions of permanent war, and against persistent efforts to safeguard Western freedoms at home and abroad, bees and bedbugs have extended juridical regimes and modes of surveillance, creating new human-nonhuman entanglements. Just as bees as food pollinators are experiencing greater legal protections, they are also being groomed as agents of war that will supposedly make distant battlefields safer for U.S. soldiers and their allies.[3] Bedbugs, by contrast, have become tenacious enemies and unkillable species. As such, they represent potent allegories for terror threats in many Western cities. Invisible, unpredictable, and uncontainable, they infiltrate the body politic and are in urgent need of extermination. Changing global configurations and the growing significance of insects therein demand new ways of thinking that foreground the metaphoricity and materiality of more-than-human life *and* death.

The explosion of animal studies over the past decade provides one framework from which to develop the kind of analysis I am suggesting here. However, the field's racial and colonial blindspots pose significant barriers to analysing human-nonhuman interdependencies, especially their racial asymmetries.[4] Thus, I turn to colonial and postcolonial studies for direction and inspiration. Insects have a long history in colonial contexts, a racial history that proves useful to the project at hand.[5] Historically, the representational force of the racial otherness of insects enabled and even justified mass violence and death (Cesaire, 2000; Mamdani, 2001; Raffles, 2007). This emphasis on the metaphoricity of insects needs to be further expanded to account for the materiality and ferality of various species. The ungovernability of bees and bedbugs in New York, Sydney, and other major cities is not an inevitable part of nature's fury. The insect as ever-changing and adaptable agent is produced through its responsiveness to social, political, and juridical processes. Insect plasticity enables certain species to modify their physiology and morphology in relation to global environmental shifts (Whitman and Agarwal, 2009). The evolution and adaptability of insects is why they can be vital human companions (bees) and human enemies (bedbugs) at the very same time. It is the remarkable capacity of insects to acclimatise to adverse environmental circumstances that have rendered some to be in need of protection and others in need of annihilation, a dynamic that is deeply resonant with colonial and racial violence.

Focused on the geopolitics and biopolitics of insects, this chapter builds on a recent and growing interest in animality in colonial and postcolonial studies. For some readers, this may be a curious starting point. As critics point out, these fields have not fully engaged with the nonhuman animal (Ahuja, 2009). If animality has featured prominently in colonial and imperial violence, its study may seem misguided and even inappropriate, especially as Indigenous peoples and communities of colour in the global North and South continue to struggle for their humanity.[6] But as others note, animal studies can be instructive and generative in expanding the scope of colonial and postcolonial studies (Armstrong, 2002; Chagni, 2016; Livingston and Puar, 2011). Animal studies and posthumanism have developed concomitantly with postcolonial studies, through commensurable critiques of racial injustice that seek to problematise the singularity and supremacy of the human (Ahuja, 2009: 556). Building on these discussions and returning to key insights in the work of Frantz Fanon (2004) and Aime Cesaire (2000), I begin sketching out a conceptual and methodological orientation that foregrounds human-nonhuman relations and the juridical line that divides them in the first place. Unlike the field of animal studies, which typically focuses on fleshy animals as "companion species" (e.g., dogs), I turn to insects.[7] Specifically, I ask, how bees and bedbugs have been appropriated and absorbed into shifting regimes of global racial power and to what effect? What makes insects so compelling to think with, I suggest, is their unruliness and their physiological distance from human species.

This chapter is both exploratory and speculative. It does not offer a fully formed analysis of the insect as biopolitical agent. Rather, it serves as an invitation for further discussion and deliberation. Drawing on colonial and postcolonial studies, the first section considers how animality has featured representationally in these fields. Specifically, I trace the insect through the anticolonial writings of Fanon (2004) and Cesaire (2000). In section II, I reflect on the changing materiality of bees and bedbugs in contemporary conditions of global war. Specifically, I examine how these and other insect species have been mobilised as juridical figures in struggles over life and death, historically and in the current moment, both in the colonies and in global cities. The life of bees and the death of bedbugs, I contend, are tightly braided through concerns of Western freedom, mobility, and longevity. In the conclusion, I return to Foucault's (2003) lectures on biopolitics. Here, I consider the political and legal stakes in analysing the metaphoricity and materiality of insects as biopolitical agents, and the directions we might push further. Colonial studies teaches us that life and death, whether human or more-than-human, cannot be easily separated. The longevity of European life has always depended on racial death. Changing geopolitics point to the asymmetries of multispecies worlds, the juridical and racial distribution of human-nonhuman life and death, and its relevance for law and theory.[8]

Animals and (post)colonialism

At first glance, it appears that colonial and postcolonial studies have paid very little attention to the nonhuman animal. "In identifying the costs borne by non-European 'others' in the pursuit of Western cultures' sense of privileged entitlement," Phillip Armstrong (2002) argues, "post-colonialists have concentrated on 'other' humans, cultures, and territories but seldom upon animals" (Armstrong, 2002: 413). Even as scholars have questioned the putative distinctiveness of the human (as European man) in Western thought, and as some have problematised the primacy and hegemony ascribed to human agency, many postcolonial thinkers have remained reticent to theorise the role of nonhuman animals in colonial contexts. In his widely read and influential *Provincializing Europe*, Dipesh Chakrabarty (2000) argues that one of the fundamental claims underlying Western thought is the ontological singularity of the human. "One empirically knows of no society in which humans have existed without gods and spirits accompanying them" (Chakrabarty, 2000: 16). Writing of India, Chakrabarty invites his readers into a lively world inhabited by the forces of gods, humans, and spirits. But curiously in his account, this is a domain remarkably absent of nonhuman animals.

More recently, in "The Climate of History," Chakrabarty (2009) reflects on the limits of human knowledge in an age of planetary climate change. In so doing, he usefully ruminates on the interrelationality of human and nature in the contemporary moment. What scientists are saying of climate change, he writes, "challenges not only the ideas about the human that usually sustain the discipline of history" (Chakrabarty, 2009: 198). They call into question "the analytic strategies that postcolonial and postimperial historians have deployed in the last two decades in the postwar scenario of decolonization and globalization" (p. 198). As the threat of climate change has intensified in recent years, Chakrabarty (2009) observes, it has created a crisis of knowledge. All of his own "readings in theories of globalization, Marxist analysis of capital, subaltern studies, and postcolonial criticism over the last twenty-five years, while enormously useful in studying globalization," he admits, have left him unprepared "for making sense of this planetary conjuncture within which humanity finds itself today." Thus, his "Climate of History" seeks to undo "the age-old humanist distinction between natural history and human history," thereby unravelling the nature, culture, and human divide (Chakrabarty, 2009: 199). Chakrabarty (2009) offers a crucial diagnosis as to how the contemporary urgencies confronting the planet demand new conceptual tools. Like much of the scholarship he criticises, however, his "Climate of History" does not engage with necessary questions of nonhuman animality. Rather, his concerns with *anthropogenic climate change* only recast and reinscribe the primacy of human agency. As far as the climate goes, Chakrabarty (2009) explains, the human is no longer a biological agent on the planet but significantly more: "Humans now wield a geological force" (Chakrabarty, 2009: 206).

In many respects, Chakrabarty's (2009) reflections on the limits of postcolonial studies and its inability to sufficiently contend with the challenges of climate change are perceptive and important. The contemporary moment, marked by declining bee populations and a proliferation of bedbugs, as I suggest above, signal just some of the problems with the human-nature divide that has been so tenacious in postcolonial studies and in other fields. The entanglements of human-insect bodies, as the *New York Times* makes clear, signal novel constellations of environmental, political, and juridical power, including new threats to life, as we know it. In some ways, Chakrabarty (2009) is correct. Today's planetary pressures demand new methods and modes of critical inquiry. However, his analysis does not fully explore what these might be. Instead, he reinscribes the exceptionalism of human agency. In his account, humans are forces of nature that are operative on the same scale as other historical and geological processes that have produced "a mass extinction of species" (Chakrabarty, 2009: 207). Like Chakrabarty, I am equally committed to undoing the human-nature divide, which I see to be a Western and colonial construct. But what the global present demands, I argue, are novel analytic and conceptual tools that might *provincialise the human*.[9] By this, I do not mean we should disregard or diminish the human as a political and legal subject. Instead, what I suggest is a repositioning of the human within heterogeneous and interspecies life worlds in which we are dependent, entangled, and inseparable from nonhuman animals, including insects. As I discuss below, there is much at stake in moving from an analytic orientation that foregrounds humans as *the dominant species on the globe* to one that regards humans to be one of many inhabitants in a densely populated and multispecies world.

To date, the nonhuman animal might have received little attention among postcolonial luminaries including Chakrabarty. However, it has a lengthy history in colonial studies.[10] Both Fanon and Cesaire wrote passionately and compellingly on the symbolic influence of animals in colonial contexts. In *The Wretched of the Earth*, Fanon (2004) was well attuned to the interconnections between human and nonhuman life and death. He was particularly aware of how this shifting political line powerfully shaped colonial violence and anticolonial struggles. "The Algerians, the veiled women, the palm trees, and the camels make up the landscape, the *natural* background to the human presence of the French," he wrote. "Hostile nature, obstinate and fundamentally rebellious, is in fact represented in the colonies by the bush, by mosquitos, natives, and fever, and colonization is a success when all this indocile nature has finally been tamed" (Fanon, 2004: 250). For Fanon (2004), the animalisation of the colonised and their "natural" association with the bush, mosquitos, and fever only legitimised colonial violence and racial death. Importantly, French authorities and settlers, in Fanon's (2004) account, did not regard the colonised to be *like* animals; they transformed them into animals: "the terms the settler uses when he mentions the native are zoological terms. He speaks of the yellow man's reptilian motions, of the stink of the native quarter, of breeding swarms." Indeed, whenever "the settler seeks to describe the native fully in exact terms he constantly refers to the bestiary" (Fanon, 2004: 42–43).

Fanon's (2004) reference to mosquitos and swarms provides a critical reminder on the role of insects in colonial contexts. The dehumanisation of colonial populations and the changing intensities of racial violence often gained traction through bodily representations of humans as insects. Mosquitos, cockroaches, and lice appeared with regularity as racial figures that justified the mass murder of Algerians, Tutsis, and Jews, respectively (Mamdani, 2001: 212; Raffles, 2007). These manifestations and expressions of violence were not beyond European or colonial law but part of its animating force.[11] Take the Holocaust for example. "Antisemitism is exactly the same as delousing," Heinrich Himmler pronounced in his speech at the gas chambers.

> Getting rid of lice is not a question of ideology it is a matter of cleanliness. In just the same way, antisemitism for us, has not been a question of ideology, but a matter of cleanliness, which now will soon have been dealt with.
>
> (cited in Raffles, 2011: 141)

For both Fanon (2008: 66–67) and Cesaire (2000: 14), antisemitism was an expression of racial force. Reducing Jews to lice and equating antisemitism with delousing was not a new phenomenon. Rather, it was part of a longer colonial history of racial subjection and dispossession in Europe's colonies.

When the insect is used allegorically in reference to human beings, it becomes much more than metaphor. Euphemisms are embedded throughout Himmler's speech, Hugh Raffles (2007) observes, and are positioned alongside "the most material of histories underlying his parasitic insects" (Raffles, 2007: 558). For Raffles (2007) this "is a history that finally dissolves the distinction between those things that enter from outside (the individual body, the body politic, the foreign body) and those that are always present within (the parasitic animal inside)" (Raffles, 2007: 558). In his reading, it is the "final collapse of distinction between human and insect" that empowered Hitler to justify Germany's extermination campaigns (Raffles, 2007: 558). This shifting juridical line that distinguished human from nonhuman emerged in the colonies, as Fanon (2008) and Cesaire (2000) remind us. Its indeterminacy unleashed changing forms and intensities of colonial-racial violence most evidenced in the expendable body of the slave, the mass murder of colonial populations, and in the ongoing violence directed at racialised and Indigenous populations. But by reading this human-nonhuman line narrowly and in terms of violence alone, we miss important opportunities to expand our repertoires of critique. The collapse of the human-animal divide certainly engenders racial death. However, it invites novel ways to question and challenge the presumed supremacy of the human (as European, white, and male) by rejecting the ontological singularity this figure presupposes.[12]

In *Discourse on Colonialism*, Cesaire (2000) engages briefly with the nonhuman animal and in so doing, gestures to the mutability of the human-nonhuman divide. Pointing to the coevalness of humanism and violence, and departing from Fanon in important ways, Cesaire's (2000) interests include the "boomerang effect of colonization," particularly its devastating effect on European colonists (Cesaire, 2000: 41). Colonisation, in Cesaire's formulation, had the power to dehumanise "even the most civilized man." Those who were part of colonial and imperial projects and who actively animalised the colonised were filled with "contempt for the native." The European coloniser, "who in order to ease his conscience gets into the habit of seeing the other man as an animal, accustoms himself to treating him like an animal, and tends objectively to transform *himself* into an animal," he explains (Cesaire, 2000: 20). The effects of this process were mutually destructive not only to the colonised but also to the coloniser.

What seems especially important to Cesaire (2000) is how the coloniser's disdain for the colonised, and the deployment of violence this necessitated, affected the bodies and minds of Europeans. The "boomerang effect" encouraged the descent of the European self into the very conditions of animality against which he was at war. Importantly, for Cesaire, the European coloniser who self-identified as the ultimate expression of the civilised (hu)man, metamorphosed into insect. The European became "the debauchee, the idler who 'eats the bread of others' and who from time to time is found dead drunk, 'drunk as a bedbug that has swallowed three, barrels of blood during the night'" (Cesaire, 2000: 49). Those colonisers that dehumanised and violated the colonised became insects of the worst kind. They were parasitic bedbugs that lived off the flesh and blood of (colonial) others.

If Cesaire (2000) reflected on Europeans becoming insect, Fanon (2008) remarked on how the colonised as animal could finally become human. The colonised, in Fanon's account, would begin a process of self-realisation through the cultivation of self-consciousness. This process could only be achieved through a struggle against the self and against the colonist. The native "laughs to himself every time he spots an allusion to the animal world in the other's words. For he knows that he is not an animal," Fanon (2004) explains. It is precisely at "the moment he realizes his humanity that he begins to sharpen the weapons with which he will secure its victory" (Fanon, 2004: 42–43). Violence was integral to the process of decolonsiation and to becoming human.[13]

Though the animal may not be a prominent figure in postcolonial studies, Fanon (2004) and Cesaire (2000) offer generative possibilities from which to build and expand further. Each provides a rough sketch of how (in)humanity materialised as the product and outcome of racial and colonial regimes of power. Fanon (2004) and Cesaire (2000) focus, albeit in different ways, on the process of becoming insect/becoming human and the violence that animalisation engendered in the loss of self and the loss of life. As prescient and compelling as their insights are in foregrounding the interconnections of human and animal life and death, their formulations require some recalibration, especially to account for the role of the insect today. Though Fanon (2004: 294) suggestively remarked on forests and swamps as "the natural ally of the native" and vividly described the entanglements of human and nature in colonial violence and anticolonial struggle, both he and Cesaire (2000) remained focused, almost entirely, on the human as the agent of history. For Fanon (2004), the mosquitos, forests, and swamps held no real force in their own right. This is why he viewed the native's reduction to nature and why Cesaire (2000) regarded the colonist's metamorphosis into animality to be so violent and so destructive. Yet, both offer interesting suggestions on ways we might approach the insect through metaphoricity and materiality in contemporary times of war: how the vulnerability of the bee as a biopolitical agent requires new forms of legal protection and the bedbug additional forms of destruction. This more-than-human relationship, as both the bee and the bedbug suggest, is not only about insect-human life but also death. In the following section, I consider how Fanon (2004) and Cesaire (2000) might be elaborated in ways that consider the insect to be a biopolitical and juridical force today.

Insect labour

In his masterful study *Rule of Experts*, Timothy Mitchell (2002) argues that the social sciences, since their inception, have embraced a singular logic in explaining the social and political world. Although this logic has varied, depending on the discipline in question, a guiding assumption is "the existence and power of human beings as social agents" (Mitchell, 2002: 10). Rewriting Egypt's colonial history through the *Anopheles gambiae*, a species of mosquito specific to Sub-Saharan Africa but not previously found in Egypt, Mitchell traces the ways in which the mosquito's introduction to the region was engendered through a series of British colonial interventions, including Britain's occupation and transformation of the landscape most evident in the building of the Aswan Dam. The arrival of the *Anopheles gambiae*, he argues, dramatically altered the region's social, political, and environmental ecologies. The assemblage of new technologies and laws that unleashed violence against the colonised coalesced with this new species of mosquito in ways that produced an unprecedented loss of human life. "What seems remarkable," Mitchell (2002) writes, "is the way the properties of these various elements interacted. They were not just historical events affecting one another at the social level." Rather, the connections between them "were hydraulic, chemical, military, political, etiological, and mechanical" (Mitchell, 2002: 27).

The rise and development of the social sciences, Mitchell (2002) contends, particularly their emphasis on human reason and rationality, has made the nonhuman difficult if not impossible to consider. Yet, the social world – historically and in the contemporary moment, in the colonies and Western cities – suggests that human-nonhuman interactions have engendered many social and political problems. Rather than questioning the overlaps between "human agency" and "nonhuman elements," Mitchell (2002) argues, historical explanations of world events have focused largely on humans as "the agents around whose actions and intentions the story is written" (Mitchell, 2002: 29). Recent discussions of climate change, specifically those that evoke the Anthropocene, tend to recentre the human as the primary force of history. In some ways, this is important. It points to the uneven responsibilities for planetary destruction (Delaney, 2016: 216). But attending to nonhuman elements, Mitchell (2002) urges, invites news questions and approaches that challenge and even undermine prevailing analytic orientations. In the case of the planet, nonhuman animals, and insects in particular, operate as a kind of barometer for colonial and imperial interventions. Ultimately, for Mitchell (2002), repositioning the nonhuman as a force of history "means making the issue of power and agency a question, instead of an answer known in advance" (Mitchell, (2002: 53).

For Mitchell (2002), the one historical thinker that has neither fully followed nor replicated the human-nature divide is Karl Marx. In his descriptions of capitalism, Mitchell contends, Marx did not view capitalists "as agents in their own right, but as those who *personify* the power of capital" (Mitchell, 2002: 30, emphasis added). In this robust and atypical reading of Marx, capital is characterised as an interaction between human and nonhuman elements (Mitchell, 2002: 30). In more conventional approaches, critics have chastised Marx for reproducing and reifying the human-nonhuman divide. For example, in *Capital, Volume I*, Marx (1976) described labour as "a process between man and Nature, a process by which man, through his own actions, mediates, regulates and controls the metabolism between himself and nature" (Marx, 1976: 283). His remarks on labour have been typically interpreted as man's conquest over nature, serving as further evidence of Marx's inability to see and think beyond the human as agent. Marx (1976) writes:

> We presuppose labour in a form in which it is an exclusively human characteristic. A spider conducts operations which resemble those of the weaver, and a bee would put many a human architect to shame by the construction of its honeycomb cells. *But what distinguishes the worst architect from the best of bees is that the architect builds the cell in his mind before he constructs it in wax.*
>
> (p. 283–284, emphasis added)

For geographer and beekeeper Jake Kosek (2010), "Marx famously drew the line between the human and nonhuman on the back of the bee" (Kosek, 2010: 669). In Kosek's (2010) reading of Marx, spiders and bees may perform labour, but "the nonhuman does not engage in planning" beforehand and therefore has little or no willfulness (Kosek, 2010: 669). Marx may not have fully or sufficiently elaborated on the lively force of bees. However, his observations on the labouring insect are especially noteworthy and relevant to geopolitics today. In the contemporary global present, the bee has become an architect, central to U.S. Military tactics, for example (Kosek, 2010).

Insects, and bees in particular, have been mobilised in historical wars of many kinds (Moore and Kosut, 2013: 32–35). In the current moment, what appears novel is how the bee has emerged as a vital technology of sight and surveillance enlisted to remedy and augment the limits of human knowledge. Kosek (2010) links the declining bee population to changing forms of U.S. imperialism. Between 1950 and 2006, he explains, the U.S. has witnessed a 50% decline in the number of honeybee hives. Global environmental changes and the use of pesticides have devastated the world's bee populations. The death of pollinators has imperilled global food sources. What is of particular interest to Kosek (2010) is how these changing conditions have altered the ecology of the honeybee itself. The bee has become an important figure in U.S. concerns over national and global security, surveillance, and militarisation. These interventions "are making bees into sensory prostheses that embody military interests" (Kosek, 2010: 651). In a "planetary frontierland," where the terrains of war are continually shifting, not fully legible, and do not easily map onto existing divides of North/South and East/West, and where distinctions between friends and enemies are constantly in flux, bees have been mobilised as frontline agents that, after training, can seek out chemicals and landmines all in the protection of Western freedoms.[14] No longer merely weapons of war, Kosek (2010) describes honeybees as newly "instrumental in extending the capacity of the human senses," to address what seems beyond human visibility (Kosek, 2010: 656). Bees are believed to be more efficient in detecting landmines and other dangers lurking in the "inscrutable" landscapes of Iraq and Afghanistan. They will eventually replace dogs in zones of war. Yet, there remain many problems. Unlike canines that currently work the frontlines of landmine surveys and are alleged to be suffering from posttraumatic stress disorder, the feral quality of bees, their unpredictability and ungovernability as evidenced in the recent New York City swarm with which I begin this chapter, have rendered them *potential* rather than *actual* forces in war. The honeybee may be "a zoosensor of the future" but for now, it remains an architect, not only of her own cells but also in the planning and production of military knowledges and tactics (Kosek, 2010: 660).

Keeping the geopolitical role of bees in mind, Marx's (1976) insights on labour might be read more generously and in ways that emphasise the materiality of the insect as actor/agent/architect. The growing reliance on bees in war and in the organisation of U.S. military strategies suggests that expanding regimes of surveillance increasingly encompass human *and* nonhuman forces. The changing body of the insect is eroding human-animal divides, in ways that echo Fanon (2004) and Cesaire (2000) in new and interesting ways. Though human-insect entanglements are generating new circuits and circulations of violence, the feral qualities of insects always present the possibility that things may not always go as planned or intended. The dependence of humans on bees for pollination, for military advances, for the expansion of American imperial dominance, and in the pursuit of life (biological, social, political) demonstrates just some of the innumerable connections between human-insect life and death (Moore and Kosut, 2013). Attending to nonhuman elements in conditions of war points to the vicissitudes of global racial power, in which life for some (in the global North) and death for others (in the Middle East and global South), is made possible through insect plasticity (Mawani, 2015).

Bees have received considerable attention due to colony collapse disorder, concerns over pollination and food production, and through their role in the expansion of U.S. warfare. However, they are not the only insects to be mobilised in expanding regimes of surveillance and militarisation. My claim that insects today are biopolitical agents gains additional traction when situated in the context of multiple and overlapping wars: the intended use of insects in wars abroad and the war against insects in urban environments. Insect plasticity has generated many problems for human dominance over battlefields and in global cities. Like New York City's "homeless bees," bedbugs have also mutated, morphed, and transformed in response to environmental pressures. Bedbugs are no longer receptive to pesticides, for example. In New York City, London, Sydney, and elsewhere, they have become geographically uncontainable. Just as bedbugs have acclimatised to the changing flows of city life, the city has also adapted in its own way: creating new forms of expertise, repositories, and sites of knowledge and expanding regimes of law and surveillance. Though examples can be drawn from many major cities, my discussion below centres on New York.

In 2009, New York City adopted Local Law 14, which created a Bedbug Advisory Board to guide and develop the city's prevention and treatment strategies.[15] The Board was asked to make recommendations on how best to address the bedbug problem via treatment and prevention; through tracking and infestation reports; by disposing of bedbug infested items; by training pest management professionals, city workers, and educators; and in public education programs aimed at providing prevention and treatment information and instructions on the rights and responsibilities of landlords, tenants, and homeowners. In their final recommendations, which the Board presented to the mayor and city council the following year, they reported that the current infestation was due to increases in domestic and international travel, population density, the resistance of bedbugs to pesticides, and increased bedbug violations.[16] Between 2006 and 2009, New York City witnessed a 240% increase in bedbug violations, a result of infractions issued to landlords as a result of verified tenant complaints. The Advisory Board described bedbugs to be "a burden on the resources of New York City residents, property owners and health and social service providers in both the public and private sector."[17] Although bedbugs "are not known to transmit disease through their blood-feeding activity," the Board maintained, they "are a pest of public health importance due to the emotional and psychological impact they can have on those affected."[18] After completing their nine-month investigation, the Board concluded that, "Bedbugs are a pest like no other. There is no simple, straightforward, or typical treatment; it requires approaches and resources that are different than most other pests."[19] To be effective, the war against bedbugs has demanded expanding forms of law and surveillance, ones that enlist the participation of new experts, including members of the public, government institutions, and legal institutions, as well as bedbugs themselves. If "strong action is not taken quickly," the Board cautioned, "the impact on residents, business owners, and visitors will continue to increase, thereby increasing economic hardship and *decreasing quality of life*."[20] The death of bedbugs is deemed vital to the quality of human life.

Bedbugs have long been associated with impoverished and racialised neighbourhoods. However, the growing infestation of public areas frequented by the upper middle classes – including hotels, subways, and libraries – has created new and renewed legal and public health concerns. Fears of diminished "quality of life" in New York City have generated a variety of new knowledges and knowledge formats aimed at prevention through education and eradication. The Advisory Board recommended the creation of a Bedbug Portal devoted to providing "bed bug facts," public education, statistics, bedbug cartographies, and information on legal actions. In addition, they recommended the creation of a "Bedbug Academy" aimed at educating the public on treatment and prevention. New York City, like other cities in the U.S., U.K., and Australia, has now become a site of interactive bedbug registries, comprised of maps, statistics, and infestation stories.[21] In addition, there is an iPhone app that provides Apple users travelling to North America from abroad with real-time information that allows them to determine which hotels and neighbourhoods should be avoided. In these changing economies of uncertainty, surveillance, and regulation, entomologists, bedbug breeders, and pest control companies have emerged as vital experts. In 2010, *Forbes* magazine published "America's Worst Bedbug Infested Cities." Their ranking was based on numbers of complaints relative to population and on data collected by leading pest control companies, including Orkin and Terminex. The results are inconsistent. New York City was ranked 7 out of 15 by Orkin and 1 out of

15 by Terminex (Brennan, 2011). What my discussion suggests is that the geopolitics of war and the war on insects cannot be easily separated.

On 20 August 2010, the *New York Times* published an article provocatively titled, "What Spreads Faster Than Bedbugs? Stigma" (Hagar, 2010). The commentary detailed the disruptive effects that bedbugs have had across many New York City neighbourhoods and the ways in which infestation has transformed the city's political economy and its social relations. "Fear and suspicion are creeping into the social fabric wherever bedbugs are turning up, which is almost everywhere," the *New York Times* reported. New Yorkers, we are told, no longer enjoy the freedom of mobility that they once did. Many are reluctant to go to movies and to sit on park benches. Tutors and music teachers are losing their clients, as are upscale Manhattan hotels. Even the Brooklyn District Attorney's Office has been affected. After several reports of bedbugs, "there were attorneys that did not want to come to our building," said one assistant district attorney, who wanted to remain anonymous (Hagar, 2010). These fears of infestation may be new to some but not to others. Bedbugs are "a part of life," explained one Bronx resident. "What am I going to do? Walk around with a fumigation can?" "It's like terrorism," said another woman, "Just cross your fingers and keep going" (Hagar, 2010). The analogy between bedbugs and terrorism is particularly revealing. The changing behaviours of New Yorkers as they respond to bedbugs, especially their presumed loss of freedom, seems strikingly reminiscent of post-9/11 fears.

In New York City and elsewhere, bedbug invasions – like threats of global terrorism – have dramatically altered spatial configurations. Like the figure of the terrorist who is believed to be newly invisible in the global war on terror, bedbug infestations in upscale neighbourhoods and government offices point to the uncertainties of life and the impossibilities of containment. The threats are invisible, unpredictable, and uncontrollable. They demand urgent, exceptional, and coercive measures. Bedbugs have infiltrated prestigious hotels and upscale locales, demonstrating the porosity of borders. As Cesaire so vividly described it, the bedbug infiltrates and occupies, it drinks the blood of the body politic, which is its vital source of life. In the contemporary moment, the corporealities and geographies of infestation are not fully visible or knowable. Like the ungovernable and uncontainable threat of terrorism, in which bees are being trained for some time in the future, bedbugs continue to multiply in ways that resist human control. The war on insects demonstrates the limits of human agency and the interdependence of human-nonhuman life and death. Tracing these interrelations demands new conceptions of biopolitics that take both metaphoricity and materiality seriously.

Biopolitical agents

What kinds of conceptual and methodological tools are available in law and social theory to advance a multispecies critique of the global present? How might colonial and postcolonial studies be expanded beyond its anthropocentric humanism to consider today's geopolitical conditions in which new racial and colonial divides abound? The insect as biopolitical agent, as I have suggested throughout, invites new approaches and innovations to reading philosophies and legalities, imagining ontologies, and practicing politics.

Fanon (2004) and Cesaire (2000) may not have been confronted with the same racial, political, and juridical entanglements of insect life and death as we are today. However, both were attuned, in their own ways, to the interconnections between humans and insects in the changing conditions of colonial life. Each pointed to the mutability of the juridico-political line that distinguished humans from insects. The colonised and the coloniser could become insect, and potentially human, through racial, anticolonial, and violent struggles. But for Fanon (2004) and Cesaire (2000), the mosquito and the bedbug were powerful *metaphors* of dehumanisation. To characterise insects as biopolitical agents demands an expanded view of biopolitics itself.

Animal studies scholars have offered suggestive and interesting ways to expand biopolitical regimes to account for nonhuman life (Braverman, 2016; Mawani, 2015; Shukin, 2009; Wolfe, 2012). Perhaps more than any other thinker, Foucault's (2003) lectures and writings on biopolitics have been especially generative, offering fragments on how we might consider multispecies worlds and the entanglements of human-nonhuman relations. But to focus on "life," the "living," or "liveliness" is to address only part of the problem.[22] The challenge, as I see it, is not only in the lively and the living, but also in the dead and the dying. What gives Foucault's (2003) conception of biopolitics such critical analytic potential is his emphasis on the inseparability of life and death. This is the crux of biopolitics as he sees it: the liveliness of some depends on the death of others. The point that human-nonhuman life is interdependent can only be a starting point. Human-nonhuman life and death, we must remember, remain deeply entangled. To be sure, the nonhuman encompasses animals, insects, and other forms of life. However, it also includes those humans continually reduced to animality, as Fanon (2004) and Cesaire (2000) make clear.

The insect as biopolitical agent is not a passive life force that is integral to human liveliness and longevity. Rather, it is feral and ungovernable, thereby demanding new legalities and means of control. The liveliness of multispecies life and its relation to death, as the case of bees and bedbugs makes clear, is not predicable or symmetrical. Recall that the global decline in bee populations is partly the result of pesticide use. The growing prohibition of pesticides in the U.S., Canada, and the U.K., which is intended to protect and prolong bee life, has produced a fecundity of bedbugs. Humans may be reliant on bees for pollination and thus for global food supplies, but the proliferation of bedbugs has made life unliveable for many living in global cities. "The nonhuman agencies," Mitchell (2002) reminds us, "enter into human partnerships not just as passive elements to be costed and arranged, but as dynamic and mobile forces with their own powers and logics" (Mitchell, 2002: 299). The swarms of homeless bees and proliferating bedbugs, reported in the *New York Times* as disrupting city life, reveal the changing configurations of power that move through human-nonhuman life and death in the troubled global present. However, the ungovernability of insects as agents of war and as enemy species may carry the potential to disrupt racial constellations of law, politics, and violence, revealing the fallibility of the human in a multispecies world.

Notes

* The ideas developed here were first presented at the "Knowledge Brokers and Knowledge Formats" Symposium in honour of the late Professor Richard Ericson and held at Green College, University of British Columbia (2011). I would like to thank the participants for their comments, suggestions, and enthusiasm. Special thanks are due to Andreas Philippopoulos-Mihalopoulos for his patience and persistence and for his insightful comments on an earlier draft.

1 Many have claimed that mid-twentieth-century restrictions on the use of DDT has made it more difficult to eradicate bedbugs. Others argue that governments are more concerned with the use of pesticides in agriculture in order to protect bees and are therefore unwilling to develop effective measures to eradicate bedbugs. See Borel, 2012.

2 The passage I have in mind reads as follows: "The fact that the other dies does not mean simply that I live in the sense that his death guarantees my safety; the death of the other, the death of the bad race, of the inferior race (or the degenerate, or the abnormal) is something that will make life in general healthier: healthier and purer" (Foucault, 2003: 255).

3 For a wonderful analysis of bees and war, see Kosek, 2010.

4 This is a proliferating field and too vast to summarise in a single note. Some significant contributors include Haraway (2008), Wolfe (2003, 2012), and Shukin (2009). In the context of law and legal studies, see Braverman (2016).

5 For discussions of insects in the British and American Empire, respectively, see Esmeir, 2012, Ahuja, 2011, and Kosek, 2010.

6 For a useful discussion of the human-nonhuman in the global racial present, see Da Silva, 2007.

7 On "companion species," see Haraway (2008), especially chapter 1.

8 Some scholars use "multispecies" (see Ahuja, 2009), others use "interspecies" (Livingston and Puar, 2011), I use the two interchangeably.

9 "Provincializing the human" is borrowed and adapted from Chakrabarty's *Provincializing Europe*, in which he argues that Europe is both vital and insufficient to postcolonial critique.

10 Postcolonial studies is often periodised through the publication of Edward Said's (1978) *Orientalism*. Although Fanon and Cesaire have both been key inspirations to the emergence and development of the field, they are seen as its predecessors and not contributors to postcolonial studies. To maintain this distinction, I refer to their work as "colonial studies."

11 One of the most compelling accounts of the Holocaust as state bureaucracy is Bauman's (1989) *Modernity and the Holocaust.*

12 I am drawing here on the potentiality that Deleuze and Guattari (1987) ascribe to "becoming animal" while remaining attentive to racial violence and its realisation. See chapter 10.

13 Fanon's reflections on violence, which is the title of the first chapter, have been very controversial.

14 I am drawing "planetary frontierland" from Bauman (2002).

15 New York Bed Bud Advisory Board, Recommendations for the Management of Bed Bugs in New York City, April 2010. Access full report here http://council.nyc.gov/downloads/pdf/bed_bugs_report_2010.pdf (accessed September 2011).

16 New York Bed Bug Advisory Board, 2010.

17 Ibid., p. 4

18 Ibid.

19 Ibid.

20 Ibid., p. 5 emphasis added.

21 Ibid., Recommendations, p. 9–11.

22 My reference to life and liveliness is in response to Cary Wolfe's characterisation of animal studies and biopolitics. See Wolfe (2016): xx.

Bibliography

Ahuja, Neel, 'Postcolonial Critique in a Multispecies World,' *PMLA*, 124(2), 556–563, 2009.

Ahuja, Neel, 'Abu Zubaydah and the Caterpillar,' *Social Text*, 29(1), 127–149, 2011.

Armstrong, Phillip, 'The Postcolonial Animal,' *Society and Animals*, 10(4), 413–419, 2002.

Bauman, Zygmunt, *Modernity and the Holocaust*, New York: Cornell University Press, 1989.

Bauman, Zygmunt, 'Reconnaissance Wars of the Planetary Frontierland,' *Theory, Culture, and Society*, 19(4), 81–90, 2002.

Borel, Brooke, 'Will We Ever . . . Get Rid of Bedbugs?' *BBC Future*, www.bbc.com/future/story/20121019-will-we-ever-get-rid-of-bed-bugs 19 October 2012 (accessed 1 September 2014).

Braverman, Irus (ed.), *Animals, Biopolitics, Law: Lively Legalities*, New York: Routledge, 2016.

Brennan, Morgan, 'America's Most Bed Bug Infested Cities,' *Forbes*, www.forbes.com/2010/12/22/worst-cities-bed-bugs-real-estate-personal-finance.html 22 December 2010 (accessed 11 September 2011).

Cesaire, Aime, *Discourse on Colonialism*, New York: Monthly Review, 2000.

Chagni, Fayaz, 'Can the Postcolonial Animal Speak?' *Society and Animals*, 24(6), 619–637, 2016.

Chakrabarty, Dipesh, *Provincializing Europe: Postcolonial Thought and Historical Difference*, Princeton: Princeton University Press, 2000.

Chakrabarty, Dipesh, 'The Climate of History: Four Theses,' *Critical Inquiry*, 35, 197–222, 2009.

CNBC.com, 'Bedbugs Spotted 21 Times on New York Subway,' www.cnbc.com/id/101963886# 2 September 2014 (accessed 3 September 2014).

Da Silva, Denise Ferreira, *Toward a Global Idea of Race*, Minneapolis: University of Minnesota Press, 2007.

Delaney, David, 'Lively Ever After: Beyond the Cult of Immateriality,' in Irus Braverman (ed.), *Animals, Biopolitics, Law: Lively Legalities*, New York: Routledge, 2016.

Deleuze, Gilles and Guattari, *A Thousand Plateaus: Capitalism and Schizophrenia*. Trans. Brian Massumi, Minneapolis: University of Minnesota Press, 1987.

Esmeir, Samera, *Juridical Humanity: A Colonial History*, Stanford: Stanford University Press, 2012.

Fanon, Frantz, 'Racism and Culture,' in Fred Lee Hord (Mzee Lasana Okpara) and Jonathan Scott Lee (eds), *I am Because We Are: Readings in Black Philosophy*, Boston: University of Massachusetts Press, 1995.

Fanon, Frantz, *Black Skin, White Masks*, New York: Grove Press, 2008.

Fanon, Frantz, *Wretched of the Earth*, trans. Richard Philcox, New York: Grove Press, 2004.

Foucault, Michel, *'Society Must be Defended': Lectures at the College de France, 1975–1976*, New York: Picador, 2003.

Hagar, Emily B., 'What Spreads Faster Than Bed Bugs? Stigma,' *New York Times*, www.nytimes.com/2010/08/21/nyregion/21bedbugs.html?pagewanted=all&_r=0 20 August 2010 (accessed 11 September 2011).

Haraway, Donna, *When Species Meet*, Minneapolis: University of Minnesota Press, 2008.

Johnson, Reed M., Jay D. Evans, Gene E. Robinson, May R. Berenbaum, 'Changes in Transcript Abundance Relating to Colony Collapse Disorder in Honey Bees (Apis Millifera),' *PNAS*, 106(35), 14790–14795, 2009.

Kosek, Jake, 'Ecologies of Empire: On the New Uses of the Honeybee,' *Cultural Anthropology*, 25(4), 650–678, 2010.

Livingston, Julie and Puar, Jasbir, 'Interspecies,' *Social Text*, 29(1), 106, 3–14, 2011.

Mamdani, Mahmood, *When Victims Become Killers: Colonialism, Nativism, and the Genocide in Rwanda*, Princeton: Princeton University Press, 2001.

Mawani, Renisa, 'Insects, War, Plastic Life,' in Brenna Bhandar and Jonathan Goldberg-Hiller (eds), *Plastic Materialities: Politics, Legality, and Metamorphosis in the Work of Catherine Malabou*, Durham: Duke University Press, 2015.

Marx, Karl, *Capital Volume I: A Critique of Political Economy*, trans. Ben Fowkes, New York: Penguin Books, 1976.
Mitchell, Timothy, *Rule of Experts: Egypt, Techno-Politics, Modernity*, Berkeley: University of California Press, 2002.
Moczek, Armin, P., 'Phenotypical Plasticity and Diversity in Insects,' *Philosophical Transactions of the Royal Society of Biological Sciences*, 365, 593–603, 2010.
Moore, Lisa Jean and Kosut, Mary, 'Bees, Borders, and Bombs: A Social Account of Theorizing and Weaponizing Bees,' in Ryan Hediger (ed.), *Animals and War: Studies of Europe and North America*, Leiden: Brill, 2013.
Morelle, Rebecca, '"Extinct" Short-haired Bumblebee Returns to UK,' *BBC News*, 28 May 2012. www.bbc.com/news/science-environment-18194778 (accessed 5 January 2016).
New York Bed Bug Advisory Board, *Recommendations for the Management of Bed Bugs in New York City*, New York, April 2010.
Nylin, Soren and Gothard, Katalin, 'Plasticity in Life-History Traits,' *Annual Review of Entomology*, 43, 63–83, 1998.
Raffles, Hugh, 'Jews, Lice, and History,' *Social Text*, 19(3), 521–566, 2007.
Raffles, Hugh, *Insectopedia*, New York: Vintage, 2011.
Rueb, Emily, 'As Swarms Startle New York, Officer on Beat Stays Busy,' *New York Times*, www.nytimes.com/2012/06/19/nyregion/honeybee-swarms-increase-in-nyc-after-mild-spring.html?pagewanted=all&_r=0 18 June 2012 (accessed 3 September 2013).
Said, Edward W., *Orientalism*, New York: Vintage, 1978.
Shukin, Nicole, *Animal Capital: Rendering Life in Biopolitical Times*, Minneapolis: University of Minnesota Press, 2009.
St. Louis, Catherine, 'A Dark and Itchy Night,' *New York Times*, www.nytimes.com/2012/12/06/garden/bedbugs-hitch-a-ride-on-library-books.html?pagewanted=all&_r=0 5 December 2012 (accessed 30 December 2012).
White, Cassie, 'Australia Facing Bedbug Invasion,' *ABC News*, 11 February 2011. www.abc.net.au/news/2011-02-10/australia-facing-bedbug-invasion/1938492 (accessed 25 January 2017).
Whitman, Douglas W. and Agarwal, Anurag A. 'What is Phenotypic Plasticity and Why is it Important?' in D.W. Whitman and T.N. Ananthakrishnan (eds), *Phenotypic Plasticity of Insects: Mechanisms and Consequences*, Enfield: Science Publishers, 2009.
Wolfe, Cary (ed.), *Zoontologies: The Question of the Animal*, Minneapolis: University of Minnesota Press, 2003.
Wolfe, Cary, *Before the Law: Humans and Other Animals in a Biopolitical Frame*, Chicago: University of Chicago Press, 2012.
Wolfe, Cary, 'Introduction: Lively Legalities,' in Irus Braverman (ed.), *Animals, Biopolitics, Law Lively Legalities*, New York: Routledge, 2016.

14

'Anthropocene "Time"?' – A reflection on temporalities in the 'New Age of the Human'*

Anna Grear

Introduction

In this chapter I explore relationships between geological time, the human, the non-human – and law. I offer ways of thinking about time by reflecting on the bodies of law and of humans/non-humans entangled in the material and semiotic conditions of 'the Anthropocene' – before pointing towards the promise of a 'tentacular' epistemology responsive to complexities and dynamic relationalities.

The following reflection deploys Donna Haraway's threefold characterisation of the contemporary era as 'Anthropocene, Capitalocene, Chthulucene' (Haraway, 2014) as a lens through which to reflect upon the nature of the time assumed by mainstream Anthropocene discourse. I argue here that the mainstream account of the Anthropocene emergence reflects the imposition of an underlying Eurocentric colonial conception of time, and that this can be directly related to a fundamentally linear, market-based notion of civilisational 'progress' foundational to core injustices of the contemporary international legal order. The Eurocentric and market-based temporalities visible in the Anthropocene global present, combined with the selective nature of the *Anthropos* assumed by mainstream Anthropocene discourse, fully support Haraway's argument that the Anthropocene could also aptly be named the 'Capitalocene'. The Capitalocene present will be read here as an order of power in which neoliberal eco-governmentality disrupts a plurality of corporeal temporalities in the service of an increasingly dematerialised and temporally compressed financial-juridical order – with increasingly violent material implications. Finally, I reflect on the liveliness of Chthulucene temporalities in order to explore their relevance for onto-epistemic in/justice and legal epistemology in an age of Anthropocene crisis.

Haraway's framing: three stories

Haraway suggests that 'Anthropocene, Capitalocene and Chthulucene' are 'three stories that are too big, and also not big enough' (Haraway, 2014: 00.18). She offers these three stories as simultaneous alternative ways of characterising the current epoch. The current geological epoch, recently named the 'Anthropocene', (Crutzen, 2002) can, she suggests, also be named the 'Capitalocene' and the 'Chthulucene'. The present reflection uses this threefold lens to shape an analysis suggesting that all three ways of naming 'the epoch' (whose very temporal identification is, of course, indeterminate and controversial) have overlapping and distinctive relationships with time and temporalities. The question animating the present reflection is how, in each naming/framing of 'the epoch', certain patterned relationships concerning the construction and deployment of 'time' reflect constructions of agency and the operation of power – including through law. My initial suspicion in relation to this question is that both the Anthropocene and Capitalocene tropes reflect oppressive deployments of abstract time as a technical horizon for linear 'human progress' conforming to historical and contemporary trajectories of Eurocentrism: In this context, the Chthulucene (Haraway's third and countervailing 'story') offers a multiplicity of temporalities – an actuality reflecting processes of materialisation. As Haraway's thought reveals, such processes radically de-centre human agency and enfold it within a multiverse of material agencies. Within the Chthulucene field of attention, temporalities operating at various scales and speeds and expressing multiple modes of lively entanglement challenge, I suggest, the monological chrono-diction that forces 'time' onto the energies of the world. In this light, it is possible that the Chthulucene also invites the development of an onto-epistemic humility radically open to multiple materio-temporalities – and that such attentiveness may even generate a life-world, 'just maybe' (to borrow Haraway's words) '*more liveable*' (Haraway, 2014: 1.05). Might the tentacularity of the Chthulucene inspire and inform legal epistemology? Is there a chance that the temporalities of the Chthulucene might direct attention towards the world's 'independent sense of humor' (Haraway, 1998: 593) as a potential way of re-encountering new dynamics of justice-making?

Time and temporalities – an initial clarification of 'clock time' as a critical target

Before beginning our threefold journey through Haraway's stories, it seems important to trace for the purposes of the present argument the distinction between 'time' and 'temporalities' as the terms will be deployed here. Hoy draws 'a conceptual distinction' between the terms:

> The term 'time' can be used to refer to universal time, clock time, or objective time. In contrast, 'temporality' is time insofar as it manifests itself in human existence. . . . 'lived time,' or 'human temporality' – hence, 'the time of our lives'.
>
> (Hoy, 2009: xiii)

For present purposes, clock time will be accepted as a reference to a time thought to be universal, or objective – and the notion of temporality will be pluralised in order to refer to the multiplicity of lived times and speeds of living materiality. This pluralisation, moreover, is emphatically not limited to 'human lived time' as a referent, but seeks to entangle human lived times in living assemblages of more-than-human temporalities and agencies. It is clear also that temporalities cannot be separated from spatialities, such that temporalities are always intrinsically spatio-temporal.[1] Finally, it is also accepted that the spatio-temporal is always and everywhere simultaneously and inseparably both semiotic *and* material: matter and meaning are inter-permeated (*everything* is materio-semiotic)[2] – and that the materio-semiotic is thus always intrinsic to spatio-temporal assemblages.

Clock time, as Hoy's conceptual definition implies, is often thought of as being objective or abstract time, operating as a stable referent that facilitates the interchangeable uniformity of time as measure (Fuchs, 2014: 101, citing Postone, 1993: 200ff, on the distinction between abstract and concrete time). This notion of time, though, cannot entirely escape its political relations with a particular temporality: For all its conceptual distinguishability from 'lived time', 'clock time' inescapably takes on flesh in human experience, is materially expressed and phenomenologically present. 'Clock time', in other words, can be read critically.

For the purposes of this chapter, clock time will be deployed as a metaphor for the way in which the historical domination exercised by Eurocentric linear 'progress narratives' was facilitated precisely through the expansion of technologies, particularly steam technologies (rail and boat), *requiring* the imposition of clock time upon multiple pre-existing temporalities. Clock time, in other words, will be read here as a kind of disciplinary practice – as a kind of chrono-politics: *Time-discipline* was a powerful tool (May and Thrift, 2001: 33) in the spatio-temporal spread (and violence) of the rationalist European ontological and epistemological 'mastery' expressed through colonial law and praxis. Clock time – much like the Eurocentric figure of 'the human' (and law's archetypal person) whose very specificity is cloaked beneath the surface neutrality of the universal – can be read as a specific form of particularity promoted through a trope of objectivity. As May and Thrift note, 'Western time and space, at least in a Euclidean form, has been seen as a norm which simply does not require investigation' (ibid.). Yet, until the arrival of clock time – even in Europe – time was a variable measure, responsive to the ebbs and flows of living materiality, such that 'in Europe, it was common until the 14th century that an hour had a different length depending on the season' (Fuchs, 2014: 101).

Homogenised clock time appears to have been imposed in the cause of the routinised control of bodies in capitalist production practices – and in the context of colonialism, clock time functioned as an intrinsic aspect of the European imposition of orders of time, space, knowledge and being on indigenous communities and their varied pre-existing temporalities and life-worlds: Clock time operated as a material practice of colonial expansion and of mastery and control (Nanni, 2012; Smith, 1997) and lies, therefore, in the foundations of the current international legal order, which was built upon those self-same colonialist foundations (see the work of TWAIL (Third World Approaches to International Law) scholars, particularly Anghie, 2005).

It is against these opening observations that we turn to the reflections upon time and temporalities in the Anthropocene.

Anthropocene

Haraway opens her reflection by arguing that the contemporary revolution in the natural sciences forces two major shifts in understanding: first, that 'individualism, methodological individualism and human exceptionalism' (themselves intrinsically Eurocentric and foundational, it should be noted, to the colonial encounter) are now 'literally unthinkable' for the most pioneering work conducted across the disciplines; and second, that the 'tissues of being anything at all' demand a long overdue recognition 'that those who *are* have been in relationality all the way down' (Haraway, 2014: 02.20). Against these two important assertions, Haraway sets out both to 'justify' and to 'trouble' the human centrality figured by the terminology of the Anthropocene (ibid., 03.23).

'The Anthropocene' (a term popularised by Crutzen (2002: 415)) is an intrinsically spatio-temporal term, referencing, as it does, a collective reference to 'humankind' as a geological agent operating at the planetary scale – and simultaneously presenting the temporal shift from one epoch to another. The etymology of the term 'Anthropocene' explicitly refers to *Anthropos* ('man') and *kainos* or the 'new'. The term is designed to reflect the claim that the earth system has left the Holocene geological era by entering a new one in which the entire future temporal horizon is dominated by the 'impact of current human activities . . . projected to last over very long periods' (ibid.). Past, present and future are thus necessarily folded into the Anthropocene trope in thoroughly material ways. The terminology simultaneously implicates the impact of the past, the looming pressures of the present and the long temporal arc of the imaginable future. Crutzen's formulation (though he does not characterise it in such terms) is, moreover, inherently spatio-temporal-material. Addressing the impact of past human activities, for example, he writes:

> Considering these and many other major and still growing impacts of human activities on earth and atmosphere, and at all, including global scales, it is thus more than appropriate to emphasise the central role of mankind in geology and ecology by using the term 'Anthropocene' for the current geological epoch.
>
> (Crutzen, 2006: 16)

Scale (including the global), spread through space and atmosphere, action upon the materiality of the earth system, and intricate temporalities are inseparable in this formulation: the Anthropocene, collapsing multiple traditional spatial and temporal boundaries as it does, is intrinsically a spatio-temporal-material phenomenon.

Yet, if any single exigency dominates the Anthropocene horizon, it is surely the threat of the looming climate crisis: 'the most salient and perilous transgression of

Holocene parameters' (Malm and Hornborg, 2014: 63). The threat of terminus lurking in the Anthropocene climate crisis is all-encompassing in scale and scope: Haraway points out that the Anthropocene is intrinsically connected to the scale of the 'global', including in the policy imagination of bodies such as the Intergovernmental Panel on Climate Change. Yet the global – as Haraway also rightly adds – is *highly specific* in its historical and material origins and development (Haraway, 2014: 14.02). The 'global' can be read as a spatio-temporal order of power for which the ideological tilt of the international legal order is pivotal, and likewise, the Anthropocene itself scarcely emerges as a neutral process. The 'history' in Crutzen's account, for example, is far from universal, despite his implicit formulation of it as a species-wide story. Folded into the production of the Anthropocene crisis is the colonial past – and a neocolonial present – expressing a distinctively Eurocentric epistemology largely based on the dematerialised Cartesian rationality that has led, in Merchant's words, to 'the death of nature' (Merchant, 1980). The 'global' is indeed highly specific in its origins and development and the foundations of the current global order rest on colonial industrial foundations expressing Eurocentric assumptions concerning civilisational hierarchy and the objectification of 'nature' (Anghie, 2005; Gonzalez, 2015). As Chakrabarty has argued,

> The phenomenon of 'political modernity', namely the rule by modern institutions of the state, bureaucracy, and capitalist enterprise – is impossible to *think* of anywhere in the world without invoking certain categories and concepts, the genealogies of which go deep into the intellectual and even theological traditions of Europe.
>
> (Chakrabarty, 2007: 4)

It is thus impossible, as Chakrabarty insists, to escape 'Europe' as 'an imaginary figure that remains deeply embedded in *clichéd and shorthand forms* in some everyday habits of thought' (ibid., emphasis in original). And while the mainstream account of the Anthropocene's emergence has been criticised by Morrison for representing 'an effort to expand (rather homogenized) European historical experiences, frameworks and chronologies onto the rest of the world . . . and [for hiding] a disturbing extension of colonial discourse into a postcolonial world' (Morrison, 2015: 75–76), there are nonetheless important critical gains from reading the Anthropocene crisis – particularly climate crisis – as the result of *precisely* such colonial practices. There is related a sense, moreover, in which the international legal order never really became *post*colonial at all.

Indeed, the *Anthropos* of the Anthropocene can be read as being an intrinsically Eurocentric figuration reflecting the historical dominance of a highly particular sexed and racially specific trope of the 'human' (Grear, 2015), and the Anthropocene climate crisis itself as a crisis of hierarchies of being emerging from fundamentally European subject-object relations (Grear, 2014). Crutzen's elevation of steam technology and, in particular, his elevation of the invention of the steam engine, as the origin point of the Anthropocene presents an apt critical target in so far as this reflects, potentially, an element of Eurocentric hubris. However, in a vein sympathetic to critiques concerning the Eurocentricity of Anthropocene discourse, others point out the colonial dark side to steam technology itself.

Eurocentric logics of time and action are implicit in Crutzen's (now mainstream) account. Crutzen traces the Anthropocene's emergence to markers in data 'retrieved from glacial ice cores' revealing the intensification of greenhouse gases (especially CO_2, CH_4, and N_2O) dated from the eighteenth century. 'Such a starting date', he observes, 'coincides with James Watt's invention of the steam engine in 1782' (Crutzen, 2006: 16). Crutzen thus installs an icon of European industrial and technical mastery at the heart of the 'standard Anthropocene narrative' (Malm and Hornborg, 2014: 63). And he is not alone in this: The steam engine is 'often referred to as the *one artifact* that unlocked the potentials of fossil fuel energy and thereby catapulted the human species to full spectrum dominance' (ibid., emphasis added). Accordingly, Morrison's critique of the terminology and concept of the Anthropocene, noted above, readily makes a critical mark.

The Anthropocene climate crisis, however, also reflects the imposition of European frameworks and chronologies on the rest of the world through colonial praxis. The climate crisis richly suggests the centrality of the industrial capitalist fossil fuel economy to the genesis of Anthropocene crisis – an economy that reflected, from its early days, the racist colonial hierarchies imposed and legitimated under cover of law. Malm and Hornborg, for example, argue that the deployment of steam-power was a power exercised by 'an infinitesimal fraction of the population of *Homo sapiens* in the early 19th century' and was fundamentally colonial in motivation:

> A scrutiny of the transition to fossil fuels in 19th-century Britain . . . reveals the extent to which the historical origins of anthropogenic climate change were predicated on highly inequitable global processes from the start. The rationale for investing in steam technology at this time was geared to the opportunities provided by the constellation of a largely depopulated New World, Afro-American slavery, the exploitation of British labour in factories and mines, and the global demand for inexpensive cotton cloth. Steam-engines were not adopted by some natural-born deputies of the human species: by the nature of the social order of things, they could only be installed by the owners of the means of production. A tiny minority even in Britain, this class of people comprised an infinitesimal fraction of the population of *Homo sapiens* in the early 19th century. Indeed, a clique of white British men literally pointed steam-power as a weapon – on sea and land, boats and rails – against the best part of humankind, from the Niger delta to the Yangzi delta, the Levant to Latin America. Capitalists in a small corner of the Western world invested in steam, laying the foundation stone for the fossil economy.
>
> (Malm and Hornborg, 2014: 63–64)

The Anthropocene climate crisis is, in a significant sense, precisely the material outcome of imposing 'European historical experiences, frameworks and chronologies' onto the rest of the world, and in the process, constructing and dominating the 'global'. And the 'time' of the 'global' is a spatio-temporal expansion of European dominance. Indeed, the very ideology of 'progress' in the nineteenth century 'made modernity or capitalism look not simply global but rather . . . something that became global *over* time, by originating in one place (Europe) and then spreading outside it' (Chakrabarty, 2007: 7). The spatio-temporality of Europe, one might say, was made global along a linear conception of time as progress for which historical time itself takes on a '"first in Europe, then elsewhere" structure' (ibid.). And there has been a complex internalisation and replication of this temporal linearity as 'different non-Western nationalisms would later produce local versions of the same narrative, replacing "Europe" by some locally constructed center' (ibid.). Indeed, *so specific* is the global in terms of its historical and material origins and development (Haraway, 2014: 14.02) that, as Haraway notes, there is a sense in which the 'Anthropocene' would better be named the 'Capitalocene'.

Capitalocene

Perhaps in the light of the analysis above, it is unsurprising that at the heart of the standard Anthropocene account, masked by terminology addressing the collective impact of humanity on the earth's climate, there lurks a particularly Eurocentric subject: *Anthropos*. Haraway names *Anthropos* as 'fossil-making man burning fossils' (Haraway, 2014: 10.02) – a term aptly reflecting the centrality of the fossil fuel economy not only to the climate crisis, but to the spatio-temporal 'development' so freighted with Eurocentric hierarchies of being – and dominated by the linear 'time' of civilisational 'progress'. As Huggan and Tiffin point out, 'Western history, in both its Marxist and capitalist incarnations, worked "to assimilate diverse cultures and spiritual traditions into a homogeneous code", at the same time as it naturalised "uneven economic development according to a linear narrative of civilization"' (Huggan and Tiffin, 2007: 2). This narrative of civilisation, intimately imbricated with the expansion of European colonial law, assumed 'European development as the natural goal' and naturalised 'uneven development' to lock 'colonized peoples to a stage in the European past' (ibid.). Critically, a linear conception of historical time was a tool of power for the establishment of Eurocentric capitalist 'progress', such that

> [d]ifferent cultures, with very different notions of time, all found themselves on the lower rungs of the ladder of progress, wrenched out of a time of land and ancestry and subjected to the exigencies of Greenwich mean time or, in its modern form, 'corporate time'.
>
> (ibid.)

Haraway's suggestion is that the Anthropocene is more aptly named the Capitalocene (Haraway, 2014: 16.35). A 'capitalocene' dynamic is implicated in Malm and Hornborg's critique of the Eurocentric and uneven processes involved in the genesis of the Anthropocene climate crisis. Such critique, moreover, converges with powerful critical legal accounts pointing to the foundations of international law as a colonialist-imperialist project (Anghie, 2005). Anghie argues that the ambition of Northern states for 'natural resources' to feed their increasingly industrialised social order and the colonial suppression of 'Third World' peoples lies at the heart of nineteenth-century global expansionism (ibid.: 211). The international legal foundations laid in the colonial era shape the postcolonial global order to such an extent now that it is questionable whether the global order, as noted above, ever became truly *post*colonial at all. The persistence of the colonial dynamic, its capitalistic impulse and its juridical facilitation by law is clear in Simons's statement that

> [t]he underlying purpose of international law that was developed in the context of the colonial and post-colonial eras was precisely the promotion and protection of economic interests of the North. Thus, as newly independent states emerged from colonial rule as sovereign entities and attempted to assert their sovereignty and establish control over their natural resources, Northern states responded using legal doctrines such as state succession, acquired rights, contracts and consent to protect *the interests of their corporate nationals* in these states and to resist the attempts by these new sovereign actors to establish a new international economic order which included their own sovereignty over their natural resources.
>
> (Simons, 2013: 2001)

The locking-in of the future in capitalist terms achieved by the international legal order thus aptly corresponds with Haraway's descriptions of the Capitalocene as a set of processes characterised by 'primitive accumulations and extractions, organizations of labour and productions of technology of particular kinds for the extraction and maldistribution of profit' (Haraway, 2014: 16.51). Both implicitly and explicitly, the Eurocentric concept of a linear 'time' and 'progress over time' was imposed upon pre-existing varied life-worlds and indigenous ontologies, epistemologies and chronologies. The European construct of time as objective measure amounts, I suggest, to a chrono-politics. Colonial 'time' emerges from such a reflection as a spatio-temporal-material assemblage characterised by the primacy of steam technology. Steam technology – and '*the* time' it essentialised – disrupted spatio-temporal relationships, unsettled geographies, disturbed positionalities. Stein argues that in Europe and North America, the 'introduction of railway, telegraph and steamship services radically reoriented geographical and temporal relationships' – developments that were reflected in the phrase 'the annihilation of space and time' (Stein, 2003: 109). Such developments were crucial, of course, to the circulation of capital through global markets, and steam technology played a fundamental role, as was noted above, both in the building of colonial capitalist markets and in the service of a small elite that 'aimed steam power' at the rest of the world (Malm and Hornborg, 2014). The impact of the railway was to shrink space by the speed of movement between places, and Stein suggests that

> the metaphor of 'annihilation' evoked the sudden impact and violence of the railway as it overturned existing notions of time and distance. On the one hand,

> the railway opened up new spaces and made them much more accessible. On the other, the railway seemingly destroyed space and diminished the uniqueness of individual places.
>
> (Stein, 2003: 109)

The imposition of European 'clock time' based around uniform railroad time further undermined distinctive senses of place: the need for scheduling 'gradually made the existence of multiple local times untenable' (ibid.). Significantly, the railway as the expression of European steam technology and market relations was also intimately linked to technological developments in communications. These facilitated simultaneous communication that allowed rail companies to ensure uniform operations across their network of nodes, operations and staff. The social implications of this were profound. Carey, as Stein notes, has argued that such instantaneous communication brought 'changes in language, knowledge and awareness, leading, for example to "scientific" newspaper reporting, with news stripped of its local and regional context' (ibid.). Communication itself was transformed in this process:

> Politically, it made the idea of 'empire' practically possible by allowing distant colonies to be controlled from the centre. Economically, it evened out commodity markets, diminished the significance of local conditions of supply and demand, made geography seemingly irrelevant, and shifted speculation from space to time, making possible the emergence of a futures market.
>
> (ibid.: 110)

Steam technology and the demand of railway systems for a unifying sense of time and communication are thus inaugural to the colonial disciplining of time and space in the foundations of the global order (and implicated – necessarily – in a related eradication of the uniqueness of indigenous place and of multiple indigenous temporalities). The imposition of 'clock time'/'the time'/'corporate time' was operatively fundamental to the colonial (capitalist) foundations of the Anthropocene crisis. The mid-nineteenth-century development of a network of rail, steam-ship and communications technologies produced and imposed temporal disciplinarity and ensured greater global interconnectivity, but 'in widening the gap between the places accessible to the new technology and the rest, . . . intensified the relative backwardness of those parts of the world where horse, ox, mule, human bearer or boat still set the speed of transport' (Hobsbawm, 1975: 60, cited by Stein, 2003: 110). This gap between European and indigenous temporalities, in turn, reflexively fed the myth of European superiority and bolstered the 'emerging nineteenth century ideologies of Western dominance' (Stein, ibid., citing Headrick, 1981 and Adas, 1989).

Such colonising dynamics are central to understanding the climate crisis itself as a *crisis of human hierarchy* (Grear, 2014) and to appreciating the salience of Haraway's claim that the epoch is usefully characterised as the Capitalocene. The Capitalocene remains marked by the 'Europe' without which we cannot even *think* global political modernity (Chakrabarty, 2007). The Capitalocene is the outcome of the savage force of instrumentalist European rationalism, with its linear temporality and the ecocidal material practices that enact its reductive construct of 'nature' (Geisinger, 1999: 52–58) as raw material for the capitalist machine – and the legal subject-object relations that gave these juridical force. The Capitalocene remains an epoch intransigently marked by patterns of eco-violation with which law is thoroughly complicit. These patterns, indeed, reflect and deepen entirely predictable, familiar and well-rehearsed (and to varying degrees, legally mediated) distributions of intra-species and inter-species injustice (see, e.g., Collard and Contrucci, 1988; Nibert, 2002; Dekha, 2008; Nibert, 2013). These patterns are so fundamental to the present epoch that 'the Anthropocene' cannot be properly understood without them.[3] And, central to the spatio-temporal violence enacted in the Capitalocene is the history of a fossil fuel economy inseparably related to the Anthropocene climate horizon (Newell and Paterson, 2010; Koch, 2012), and *locked-in*, by capitalist priorities and juridical structures (including the international legal order itself), to the path-dependencies of the contemporary global fossil fuel regime (Dangerman and Schellnhuber, 2013).

While Haraway argues that the Capitalocene pre-dates the height of European colonial expansionism (in earlier trade relations), there can be no doubt that the Capitalocene reaches its apotheosis in the drives, fractures and regime structures of capitalism as an *imperialistic* ideology (Wood, 2005). The figuration of the Capitalocene thus drives directly at the radical unevenness characterising the contemporary neoliberal legal order and its antecedent periods of primitive capitalist accumulation and enclosure (Ricketts-Curtler, 1920; Westra, 2004).

What of time and temporalities in the Capitalocene? We have already adverted to the space-time compression produced by capitalist industrial demands and the genesis of regularising technologies demanding the deployment of clock time as a mode of chrono-politics expressed as 'corporate time'. We have also seen that such spatio-temporal practices were intrinsic to the juridical expansion of European capitalist ambition across the globe. In these more eco-conscious times, however – in the light of an Anthropocene awakening to the dark side of capitalism's 'progress' – is there hope that patterns of domination might shift? Perhaps. There are certainly signs of extensive social movement resistance to capitalist priorities – for example in the food sovereignty movements in the Global South and elsewhere against the injustices of the neoliberal food regime (McMichael, 2012), in commons-based initiatives and the like,[4] but, notwithstanding such counter-movements and forms of resistance, the hegemonic structures of contemporary order seem to remain firmly in place. Neoliberal power remains adaptive, predatory and in the ascendance. Indeed, counter-movements are all too often placed in a highly ambivalent relation to neoliberalism – frequently re-captured by its re-colonisation of liberatory counter-discourses (Caffentzis, 2010). The general picture at this historical juncture remains troubling, notwithstanding emergent signs of hope: millions of marginalised, colonialised 'others' are still subjected to forms of domination serving Global North imperatives (Gonzalez, 2015), assumptions of a Eurocentric epistemological mastery and ontological priority enacted from 'the centre' (Code, 2006), and the imperialistic residues of 'first in Europe, then elsewhere' time (Chakrabarty, 2007).

If anything, a kind of Global North juridical managerialism in the name of the 'global' grows ever more pernicious in its implications. Intensifying forms of eco-governmentality are legitimated by the concern of 'the centre' with the 'global' management of the planet in the name of various forms of 'security' (Global North security). Such practices are widely (and rightly) accused of being intensifying spasms of neo-colonial domination (Geisinger, 1999).

Environmental law and governance provides a particularly significant example in the Anthropocene context. It is easy to assume that environmentalism would be a progressive counter-movement to market ideology, but environmental law and governance have increasingly turned to 'green economy' thought. Luke, drawing on Foucault's analysis of biopolitics, suggests that the edifice of environmental governance now dominating the realm of the global expresses a distinctively neoliberal market 'environmentality' (Luke, 1995). 'The environment' is fully rendered as a set of 'sites of supervision' through which 'environments can be disassembled, recombined and subjected to the disciplinary designs of expert management . . . redirected to fulfil the ends of other . . . scripts': 'Environmentality . . . embeds instrumental rationalities in the policing of ecological spaces' (ibid.: 65). The policing of such spaces (all over the world) amounts to the striation of the living order into eco-enclosures (spatio-temporally-materially) for practices of financial accumulation. Such practices privilege and enact suspect logics of (capitalistic, Global North-favouring) development discourse (the 'progress narrative' re-presented), precisely as a *rationalisation* for neoliberal governmentality itself (McMichael, 2012; Corson and MacDonald, 2012). As Luke puts it, as 'new mediations of development and growth were constructed after 1945, the geo-power/eco-knowledge nexus of environmentalization came to comfortably supplement the high technology, capital intensive development strategies that have since been implemented' (Luke, 1995 at 67). A 'progress/development'-legitimated chrono-politics is still operative within neoliberal global scripts – scripts profoundly continuous with the early colonising juridical impulses and the linear 'time' of 'progress' lying at the dark heart of the Anthropocene-Capitalocene. The implications of this trajectory remain violent and radically Eurocentric: the resource managerialism intrinsic to such strategies is operationalised by dense networks of corporate-managerial-administrative regulatory regimes facilitating a spectacular range of corporate 'land grabs' and dispossessions in the name of 'environmental protection' – in short, an extensive, planetary land grab driven by the 'rational planning of the planet for Northern security' (McMichael, 2012: 685, citing Sachs, 1993: 20).

The linear temporality implied by 'development' as the later proxy for 'progress' is, of course, not the only temporality at play in the Capitalocene. The contemporary Capitalocene has a linear trajectory, but this trajectory plays itself out in highly varied temporal disruptions and multiple temporalities: disjunctures between the temporalities of capital and of bodily rhythms and seasons; tensions between the wider rhythms and variegated beats of the living order and the striated times of technological systems – and the sense in which, in some developments, temporalities are forced together in the materiality of crops themselves (think of Monsanto's 'terminator' seeds (see below), for example). Then there is the overall sense of velocity, intensification, of temporalities folding in on each other unpredictably, even as the linearity of the 'time' of progress/development retains its overall place as an ideological trope taking us far into an unknown techno-future. Sutherland argues, for example, that

> the network society is characterized by an almost-universal belief in a linear progression of technological development in which incremental and seemingly unremarkable developments in digital technology exhibit an increasingly rapid pace of introduction, presenting a continually shifting, seemingly irreversible telos of speed, mobility and productivity.
>
> (Sutherland, 2014: 57)

He adds later that

> the teleology of speed is more than just a metanarrative of progress; it is a telos of indeterminacy or contingency – the utopian future that drove Enlightenment philosophers is replaced by a distant horizon; one that only retreats further the faster we get. Speed becomes an end in itself: it is not a means to a better future, it is a final cause that infects almost every element of our mediative environment, built upon a narrative of technological development that has long forgotten the rationale – that is, the terminus – of its own existence. This is a teleological nihilism, in which the violence of speed cannot any longer even promise a better world, all it can do is offer itself as a means of acceleration towards a future about which we know little, and hope even less.
>
> (ibid.: 59)

The Capitalocene thus hurls itself towards an unreachable horizon, driven by its compulsion towards limitless growth and intensifying managerialism, while the Anthropocene horizon looms, insisting on ecological limits – full of threat. The sense of temporal dislocation manufactured by the instantaneity of data transmission induces a sense – or perhaps for some even a fantasy – of escaping spatio-temporal limitations – with potentially destructive results. Temporalities collide, inter-penetrate – like reactive elements. Reisch argues that 'the ecological crisis can be read as a clash of different timescales. The timescale of modernity – with the acceleration of technological innovations – collides with the timescales that govern life and the earth ('biological time')' (Reisch, 2001: 371). He points out that nonrenewable resources are consumed at a rate 'infinitely faster that the process of sedimentation' – and that in the case of that most Anthropocene of phenomena, global warming, 'we find that the speed of industrial emissions outstrips the speed of assimilation and that vegetation does not have enough time to adapt to shifting temperature zones caused by the greenhouse effect' (ibid.). The spatio-temporal, here, emphatically, cannot be seen as anything but material. Timescale clashes are, inevitably, spatio-temporal-material collisions. Meanwhile, the financialisation of nature, in which speculation increases on virtual futures (in species extinction, water shortage and the like, traded on markets driven by instantaneous global algorithmic flows) continues apace even as corporate responses to the climate crisis rationalise the impregnation of biological temporalities with altogether different temporalities inscribed into the materiality of crops: Monsanto's terminator seeds, for example, prevent germination, abruptly truncating the biological temporalities of crops with corporate segments of commodified time.

Chthulucene – materiality's spatio-temporal semiosis

Haraway's third framing of the Anthropocene epoch is 'the Chthulucene'. Haraway emphasises two main thoughts in relation to this. First, she points to the way in which biology is shattering the myth of human exceptionalism and individualism, arguing that '[w]e are all lichens now. We have never been individuals. From anatomical, physiological, evolutionary, developmental, philosophic, economic, I don't care what perspective, we are all lichens now' (Haraway, 2014: 22.33). Secondly, Haraway emphasises the 'tentacularity' associated with the Chthulucene.

Haraway's claim that 'we are all lichens now' refers to a phrase from Scott Gilbert, who (with Sapp and Tauber) proposes the necessity for a symbiotic view of life, insisting that 'we have never been individuals' (Gilbert et al., 2012). Gilbert et al. begin by noting the way in which individualism – which emerged 'with the appearance of the independent citizen' (and, we must note here again, this citizen is a quintessentially Eurocentric construct reflecting the ontology of *Anthropos* (Grear, 2015)) – shaped biological assumptions concerning the existence of individual animals, plants and the like. In the second half of the nineteenth century with the emergence of ecology, systems were seen as complements to individuals (Gilbert et al., at 326). With the emergence of ecology, the rigidly binary Cartesian separation between (disembodied, rational) humanity and *the rest* began to fray, but new technologies now emphatically problematise the status of individuality (and thus individualism). New technologies in existence at the present time

> dramatically transform our conceptions. . . [and] have not only revealed a microbial world of complex and intermingled relationships – not only among microbes, but also between microscopic and macroscopic life. These discoveries have profoundly challenged the generally accepted view of 'individuals'.
>
> (Gilbert et al., 2012: 326)

Haraway likewise insists that 'we are all lichens now'. Lichens have been defined as 'symbiotic associations between two (or sometimes more) entirely different types of microorganism' (Deacon, 2013). Importantly, though, 'lichens are unique because they look and behave quite differently from their component organisms. So lichens are regarded as organisms in their own right' (ibid.). Gilbert, Sapp and Tauber argue that *all* 'animals are symbiotic complexes of many species living together' (Gilbert et al., 2012: 326–327).

Haraway's Chthulucene is a world relational 'all the way down' – an entangled world of hybrids and critters: a world of lichens. Framing the Chthulucene as an epoch in the way that Haraway does presents an overt invitation to celebrate the porous movements, drifts and vectors of a world alive and moving at multiple scales and tempos. And just as the biological sciences incontrovertibly reveal complex lively relationalities at all scales, from the microscopic to the macroscopic, so other broadly New Materialist accounts (responding to such science)[5] point to assemblages operating at multiple scales and look explicitly towards the lively meaning-making capacities of materiality itself – to materiality's semiosis. Materialities and meanings co-emerge as materio-semiotic entanglements – and this necessarily means that the world is a multiplicity of overlapping, porously open spatio-temporalities. Chthulucene temporalities are thus also a lively entanglement, and if, as Coole and Frost argue in *New Materialisms: Ontology, Agency and Politics* (2010), 'foregrounding material factors and reconfiguring our very understanding of matter are prerequisites for any plausible account of co-existence and its conditions in the 21st century' (ibid.: 2), so too is humble attentiveness to the materiality of lively time-spaces and spatio-temporal movements.[6]

Indeed, respect for variegated spatio-temporalities is fundamental to countering the violent chrono-politics of neoliberal capitalism. The stakes could hardly be higher in the Anthropocene epoch. Foregrounding material factors and reconfiguring our very understanding of materiality and its multiple temporalities will *necessarily* present

> nothing less than a challenge to some of the most basic assumptions that have underpinned the modern world, including its normative sense of the human and its beliefs about human agency, but also regarding its material practices such as the ways we labor on, exploit and interact with nature.
>
> (Coole and Frost, 2010: 4)

In short, Eurocentric ontological and epistemological assumptions (including chronological constructions) are pervasively challenged by an understanding of matter as 'materialization[,] a complex, pluralistic, relatively open process' in which 'humans [are] thoroughly immersed within materiality's productive contingencies' (ibid.: 7). Such insights cut at the very heart of the idea that 'agents are exclusively humans who possess cognitive abilities, intentionality and freedom to make autonomous decisions and the corollary presumption that humans have the right or ability to master nature' (ibid.: 10).

The epistemic implications of such an understanding are profound. Haraway's insistence that 'we are all lichens now' folds human flesh into a much wider field of materio-semiotic energies. The de-centred human is re-positioned as just one partner in a 'spatial and temporal web of interspecies dependencies' (Haraway, 2008: 11). Politically, such a position has the potential to disturb the chrono-politics of Eurocentric 'progress' so implicit in the Capitalocene trope. Indeed, the managerialism at the heart of the meta-narrative of linear progress/development is thoroughly laid bare to the critical gaze. New Materialist frames of analysis draw together the effects of macro-structural projects such as the international economy, neoliberalism's 'well-honed micro-powers of governmentality' and the sheer materiality of existence as corporeal beings inhabiting 'a world of natural and artificial objects' and having biological needs

(Coole and Frost, 2010: 27). New Materialist framings place all these and more in relations where capitalist agency – and its accumulative market and individuated legal subject – is no longer inevitably prioritised. Indeed, the focus of attention moves away from 'individual bodies, subjects, experiences or sensations' towards 'assemblages of human and non-human, animate and inanimate, material and abstract, and the affective flows within these assemblages' (ibid.: 406). The frame of analysis fully embraces materiality and the affective energies of multiple spatio-temporalities.

For Haraway, embracing the Chthulucene as a way of thinking the Anthropocene epoch holds out hope of 'something – just maybe – *more liveable*' (Haraway, 2014: 01/05). I suggest that central to the search for this 'something more liveable' is fresh attention to what Code has called the *politics of epistemic location* (Code, 2006). Such a politics necessarily involves confrontation with the neoliberal panopticon at the heart of intensifying levels of eco-governmentality. The Chthulucene is, as noted above, an age of 'tentacularity' – and this can easily be read as an invitation to epistemic tentacularity: What if human epistemic engagements were to 'begin in the middle' (Philippopoulos-Mihalopoulos, 2011) rather than at the assumed 'centre'? What if control and commodification fantasies were abandoned in favour of a respectful, tentacular exploration of materiality in all its variegated spatio-temporal expressions? What if such an approach were to yield what Code calls for in the shape of a fully 'ecological epistemology'?[7] And what might this mean for law's epistemic practices?

In Code's words, such an epistemology 'emerges from and addresses so many interwoven and sometimes contradictory issues . . . that its implications require multifaceted chartings' (Code, 2006: 4). This, then, is an epistemology characterised by epistemic practices particularly sensitive to local, situated diversities and

> proposes a way of engaging – if not all at once – with the implications of patterns, places and the interconnections of lives and events in and across the human and nonhuman world . . . in projects of inquiry . . . where epistemic and ethical-political concerns are reciprocally informative.
>
> (ibid.)

A tentacular epistemology would, I suggest, necessarily feel its way along the particular in its unrepeatable singularity and invites a mode of knowing that is knowingly incomplete. This, in turn, invites epistemic relationalities of all kinds, including interspecies engagements – which would necessarily involve attentiveness to relationalities within variegated spatio-temporalities. Might such thinking not inspire new partnerships of knowing? Even for law? Might not such tentacularity invite the thinking of 'the human' into a lichen-like 'mutual and dynamic crafting of people and environments' (Pieraccini, 2012). That this tentacularity is a live possibility for legal systems is already richly implied by Critical Environmental Law's insistence upon the importance of attending to singularity (Philippopoulos-Mihalopoulos, 2011),[8] and by existing modes of epistemic legal praxis that draw upon the mutual crafting of environments by animals and people (Philippopoulos-Mihalopoulos, 2012; Pieraccini, 2012), such that property relations – for example – become the 'contingent product of [both] humans and non-human animals' (Pieraccini, 2012: 273). Such tentacularity could also develop further the rich implications of ecological thought for legal judgment (Pallonity, 2015). Fundamentally, such a world-sensing, situated epistemology would question the 'eye from nowhere' suppositions typical of Western epistemology in favour of a braille-like, gentle and responsive attentiveness to materialisation and its patterns, allowing materiality itself renewing agential significance for law and legal outcomes. Minimally, thinking the Chthulucene positions the human in a de-centred position within an entangled ontology, and in the process, re-constitutes epistemology as an ecologically responsibilised tentacularity: a sensing form of 'onto-epistemology'. This implies practices of radical openness to multiple scales, tempos, movements, flows and relationalities, to ambiguities and puzzles, to incomplete knowing and to a profound and mutually informing intimacy between the epistemic and the ethical. From such thinking, yes, 'something – just maybe – *more liveable*' might emerge.

Ultimately, thinking through the Chthulucene could move beyond the brute Eurocentric deployment of 'time' as power, and in turn, hold out hope for appreciation of the lively flow of spatio-temporalities intrinsic to the world – and to the multiple forms of relationality (human and non-human alike) shaping law as a powerful spatio-temporal-material assemblage.

Notes

* This chapter draws on recent work by the author, in particular, A. Grear, 'Anthropocene, Capitalocene, Chthulucene': Re-encountering Environmental Law and its "Subject" with Haraway and New Materialism' in L. Kotze (ed.) *Re-Imagining Environmental Law and Governance for the Anthropocene*, Hart/Routledge/Elgar Publishing, 2017; and A. Grear, 'Deconstructing *Anthropos*: A Critical Legal Reflection on "Anthropocentric" Law and Anthropocene "Humanity",' *Law and Critique*, 26(3), 225–249, 2015.

1 This is an important implication of Valverde's recent work on the relations between time and space: See Valverde, 2015. See also Philippopoulos-Mihalopoulos, 2015 for an important review of (and corrective to) Valverde's argument.

2 This is a central insistence in Haraway's work.

3 This is a central concern for Malm and Hornborg (2014). See also the work of Bookchin, for whose social ecology account *intra*-species practices of domination were causally decisive for practices of ecological destruction: Bookchin, 2005).

4 See, for a range of essays on the variety of commons and commons-based approaches emerging, Bollier and Helfrich, 2015.

5 An excellent general introduction to New Materialism and its links with emergent science is provided by Coole and Frost, 2010.

6 Some gestures towards such an attentiveness are made by, for example, Critical Environmental Law. See Philippopoulos-Mihalopoulos, 2011.

7 This is the essence of Code's project (Code, 2006).

8 See Philippopoulos-Mihalopoulos, 2012 – and more generally Haraway, 2008.

Bibliography

Adas, Michael, *Machines as the Measure of Men: Science, Technology and Ideologies of Western Dominance*, Ithaca: Cornell University Press, 1989.

Anghie, Anthony, *Imperialism, Sovereignty and the Making of International Law*, Cambridge: Cambridge University Press, 2005.

Bookchin, Murray, *The Ecology of Freedom: The Emergence and Dissolution of Hierarchy*, Oakland: AK Press, 2005.

Bollier, David and Silke, Helfrich, *Patterns of Commoning*, Amherst: Commons Strategies Group, 2015.

Caffentzis, George, 'The Future of the "Commons": Neoliberalism's "Plan B" or the Original Disaccumulation of Capital?' *New Formations* 69, 23–41, 2010.

Chakrabarty, Dipesh, *Provincialising Europe*, Princeton: Princeton University Press, 2007.

Code, Lorraine, *Ecological Thinking: The Politics of Epistemic Location*, Oxford: Oxford University Press, 2006.

Collard, Andree and Contrucci, Joyce, *The Rape of the Wild: Man's Violence against Animals and the Earth*, Bloomington: Indiana University Press, 1988.

Coole, Diana H. and Frost, Samantha, *New Materialisms: Ontology, Agency and Politics*, Durham: Duke University Press, 2010.

Corson, C. and MacDonald, K. I., 'Enclosing the Global Commons: The Convention on Biological Diversity and Green Grabbing,' *The Journal of Peasant Studies*, 39(2), 263–283, 2012.

Crutzen, Paul J., 'Geology of Mankind,' *Nature*, 23, 415, 2002.

Crutzen, Paul J., 'The Anthropocene,' in E. Ehlers and T. Krafft (eds), *Earth System Science in the Anthropocene*, Berlin and Heidelberg: Springer, 13–18, 2006.

Dangerman, Jerome and Schellnhuber, Hans Joachim, 'Energy Systems Transformation,' *PNAS* E549-E558, 2013. www.pnas.org/cgi/doi/10.1073/pnas.1219791110 (accessed 18 February 2016).

Deacon, J., 'The Microbial World: Lichens', Institute of Cell and Molecular Biology, The University of Edinburgh. http://archive.bio.ed.ac.uk/jdeacon/microbes/lichen.htm 2013 (accessed 15 February 2016).

Dekha, Maneesha, 'Intersectionality and Post-humanist Visions of Equality', *Wisconsin Journal of Law, Gender and Society*, 23, 249–267, 2008.

Fuchs, Christian, 'Digital Presumption Labour on Social Media in the Context of the Capitalist Regime of Time', *Time and Society*, 23(1), 97–123, 2014.

Geisinger, A., 'Sustainable Development and the Domination of Nature: Spreading the Seed of the Western Ideology of Nature', *Boston College Environmental Affairs Law Review*, 7(43), 52–8, 1999.

Gilbert, S., Sapp, J. and Tauber, A. I., 'A Symbiotic View of Life: We Have Never Been Individuals,' *The Quarterly Review of Biology*, 87(4), 326–341, 2012.

Gonzalez, Carmen, 'Bridging the North-South Divide: International Environmental Law in the Anthropocene,' *Pace Environmental Law Review*, 32, 407–434, 2015.

Grear, Anna, '"Towards Climate Justice"? A Critical Reflection on Legal Subjectivity and Climate Injustice: Warning Signals, Patterned Hierarchies, Directions for Future Law and Policy', Special Edition *Journal of Human Rights and the Environment*, 103–133, 2014.

Grear, Anna, 'Deconstructing *Anthropos*: A Critical Legal Reflection on "Anthropocentric" Law and Anthropocene "Humanity"', *Law and Critique* 26(3), 225–249, 2015.

Haraway, Donna, 'Situated Knowledges: The Science Question in Feminism and the Privilege of Partial Perspective,' *Feminist Studies*, 3, 575–599, 1998.

Haraway, Donna, *When Species Meet,* Minnesota: University of Minnesota Press, 2008.

Haraway, Donna, 'Anthropocene, Capitalocene, Chthulucene: Staying with the Trouble', A lecture given by Donna Haraway at University of California, Santa Cruz, 5 September 2014. https://vimeo.com/97663518 (accessed 18 September 2015).

Headrick, Daniel R., *The Tools of Empire: Technology and European Imperialism in the Nineteenth Century*, New York, Oxford University Press, 1981.

Hobsbawm, Eric, *The Age of Capital 1848–75*, London: Weidenfeld and Nicholson, 1975.

Hoy, David Couzens, *The Time of Our Lives: A Critical History of Temporality*, Cambridge, MA: MIT Press, 2009.

Huggan, Graham and Tiffin, Helen, 'Green Postcolonialism', *Interventions: International Journal of Postcolonial Studies*, 9(1), 1–11, 2007.

Koch, Max, *Capitalism and Climate Change: Theoretical Discussion, Historical Development and Policy Responses*, Basingstoke: Palgrave Macmillan, 2012.

Luke, Timothy W, 'On Environmentality: Geo-Power and Eco-Knowledge in the Discourses of Contemporary Environmentalism' *Cultural Critique*, 31, 57–81, 1995.

Malm, Andreas and Hornborg, Alf, 'The Geology of Mankind? A Critique of the Anthropocene Narrative', *The Anthropocene Review*, 1(1), 62–69, 2014.

May, Jon and Thrift, Nigel, *TimeSpace: Geographies of Temporality*, London and New York: Routledge, 2001.

McMichael, Phillip, 'The Land Grab and Corporate Food Regime Restructuring', *The Journal of Peasant Studies*, 39(3–4), 681–701, 2012.

Merchant, Carolyn, *The Death of Nature: Women, Ecology and the Scientific Revolution*, New York: Harper Collins, 1980.

Morrison, Kathleen D., 'Provincializing the Anthropocene,' *Seminar*, 673, 75–80, 2015.

Nanni, Geordano, *The Colonization of Time: Ritual, Routine and Resistance in the British Empire*, New York: Manchester University Press, 2012.

Newell, Peter and Paterson, Matthew, *Climate Capitalism: Global Warming and the Transformation of the Global Economy*, Cambridge: Cambridge University Press, 2010.

Nibert, David A., *Animal Rights, Human Rights: Entanglements of Oppression and Liberation*, Oxford: Rowman and Littlefield, 2002.

Nibert, David A., *Animal Oppression and Human Violence: Domesecration, Capitalism, and Global Conflict*, New York: Columbia University Press, 2013.

Pallonity, Tiina, 'Taking Aims Seriously – How Legal Ecology Affects Judicial Decision-Making,' *Journal of Human Rights and the Environment*, 6(1), 55–74, 2015.

Philippopoulos-Mihalopoulos, Andreas, 'Towards a Critical Environmental Law', in Andreas Philippopoulos-Mihalopoulos (ed.), *Law and Ecology: New Environmental Foundations*, Abingdon: Routledge, 2011, 18–38.

Philippopoulos-Mihalopoulos, Andreas, 'The Triveneto Transhumance: Law, Land, Movement,' *Politica and Societa*, 3, 447–468, 2012.

Philippopoulos-Mihalopoulos, Andreas, 'Mariana Valverde: Chronotypes of Law: Jurisdiction, Scale and Governance,' *Journal of Law and Society*, 42(4), 668–673, 2015.

Pieraccini, Margherita, 'Property Pluralism and the Partial Reflexivity of Conservation Law: The Case of Upland Commons in England and Wales,' *Journal of Human Rights and the Environment*, 3(2), 273–287, 2012.

Postone, Moishe, *Time, Labor, and Social Domination: A Reinterpretation of Marx's Critical Theory*, Cambridge: Cambridge University Press, 1993.

Ricketts Curtler, William H, *The Enclosure and Redistribution of our Land*, Clarendon: Oxford, 1920.

Reisch, Lucia A., 'Time and Wealth: The Role of Time and Temporalities for Sustainable Patterns of Consumption,' *Time and Society*, 10(2), 367–385, 2001.

Sachs, Wolfgang, *Global Ecology*, London: Zed Press, 1993.

Simons, Penelope, 'International Law's Invisible Hand and the Future of Corporate Accountability for Violations of Human Rights' *Journal of Human Rights and the Environment*, 3(1), 5–43, 2013.

Smith, Mark M, *Mastered by the Clock: Time, Slavery and Freedom in the American South*, Chapel Hill and London: University of North Carolina Press, 1997.

Stein, Jeremy, 'Time-Space Compression' in J. May and N. Thrift (eds), *Timespace: Geographies of Temporality*, London and New York: Routledge, 2003, 106–119.

Sutherland, Thomas, 'Getting Nowhere Fast: A Teleological Conception of Techno-Social Acceleration,' *Time and Society*, 23(1), 49–68, 2014.
Valverde, Mariana, *Chronotypes of Law: Jurisdiction, Scale and Governance*, Abingdon: Routledge Glasshouse, 2015.
Westra, Laura, 'Environmental Rights and Human Rights: The Final Enclosure Movement,' in R. Brownsword (ed.), *Global Governance and the Quest for Justice: Volume IV: Human Rights*, Oxford: Hart Publishing, 2004, 107–19.
Woods, Ellen M., *Empire of Capital*, London: Verso, 2005.

15

Making lawful animals

Yoriko Otomo

'Animal law' has become a popular phrase, a widely available university course, and a recognised field of legal practice. But what does it mean? There are two possible simple interpretations: first, that the field refers to laws that specifically name non-human animals (welfare laws, food safety laws and endangered species laws),[1] and second, that it concerns laws (all laws, across legal branches) which impact on animals. Let us consider the first interpretation, namely that 'animal laws' refer to legislation that specifies animals by kind. A cursory glance at any animal protection law, domestic or international, reveals Borgesian categories used to include and exclude animals from its remit, so much so that it quickly becomes clear that what is really at stake is not protection as such, but the *naming* of animals.[2] Animal welfare laws by country, for example, generally exclude key commodity sub-species from their broad categories of protected species. These differ from state to state, depending on industrial and cultural practices. Some are very cursory; others simply replicated from 'model laws' imported from a former imperial state. Others still may be quite detailed, listing specific threatened and endangered species, but failing to note that the process of nomination for these lists is both political and circumstantial.

The imperialism of the act of naming aside, there is the very practical difficulty of identifying the billions of species on this earth, with approximately 90% of those species currently unidentified (named and catalogued), and many of those species rapidly becoming extinct.[3] Most animals, therefore, are and were always unknown by modern science. Moreover, this is only taking into account those animals that are 'real': their probable existence is calculated by statistical method. To this we could add beings that are imaginary or *entirely* incalculable yet important to living human cultures around the world. Griffins; Kraken; elves, fauns and fairies; Minotaurs and Medusas; ghosts, mermaids and djinns come to mind.[4] Of the 'real' animals, both known and unknown, the matter of scale, capacity and visibility is conveniently overlooked in laws that impact on animals.[5] Take tardigrades, for example. These are a microscopic animal (also known as a 'water bear', or 'moss piglet') that has been around from 520 million years, with a phylum of 1,250 different species. Some of these species can survive temperatures from one degree warmer than absolute zero to minus 272 Celsius. Other tardigrades can endure powerful radiation. In 2007 the European Space Agency sent 3,000 of these animals into low earth orbit and space and they survived for 12 days on the *outside* of the space capsule (Courtland, 2008). They can live in water and on land and survive crushing pressures. Without water, they use a protein to create a rigid internal skeleton, freezing their own cells. They can be rehydrated back to life after 30 years in this state. Physicists postulate that tardigrades could survive the 4.37-light-year trip to Alpha Centauri (Guarino, 2017). Such animals do not come close to being acknowledged in animal laws, as they are neither food nor pest, disease nor trophy.

The handful of animal species that are actually named in laws, then, have a certain symbolic import for the humans who name them. Indeed, for us to make animals *lawful* – to give them legal status and place them into relation with other things in the world – requires us first to imagine them. This process of imagining such animals is perhaps best described by John Berger as 'an ideal internalized as a feeling surrounding a repressed desire' (Berger, 2009: 27), or rather, a vast field of desires: to have the capacities and sensitivities of worms and wolves and cats and whales; to soar and pounce and swim and dig and love in ways that we cannot articulate. There are desires of consumption, control, extermination, and reproduction. We feel these and give to them the forms of the regal elephant, the gliding eagle, the killing lion, the patted dog, all of whom become our protective totems (Otomo and Prost, 2016). A distance grows between these ideals and the individual animals themselves, who are almost never noted in the legal sphere. Once the named kinds of animals are selected, heated arguments break out at international gatherings on which to include in hierarchies of animal-ness, and on the grades, modes and circumstances of 'protection'.[6] At such meetings, the names and images themselves remain key fetishes.[7]

There is another reason for which we produce these ideals, and that is to buffer our own anxieties surrounding the uncertainty of what it means to be human.[8] Does the fact that we share a surprisingly large part of our DNA with worms, with rats, and almost all of it with chimpanzees, have a flattening, posthuman effect on what it means to be human? Or do we assume that our 1% of genetic difference performs a magic that transforms us into a kind of being entirely distinct from the 99%? If so, the stakes of imagining and naming are very high. Indeed, the creation of a story and lexicon that insists upon our exclusivity is central to the justification of the modern state.[9] While secular political life is based on the Enlightenment tradition that calls transcendence into question, it nonetheless insists on the primacy and uniqueness of human matter. As such, law that regulates this matter, that flesh – the flesh of the earth and of living beings – becomes a necessary means of creating a distinction between a human and non-human world. And so it is in order to maintain this contradiction (of human-as-rational matter and human-as-supra-matter), we have created 'legal regimes': 'international environmental law' is there for 'protecting nature'; 'animal welfare laws' are there for 'protecting animals'. This creates a rhetorical universe that carves out 'the animal' and 'the environment' as entities that somehow exist as universal norms. To have such rules that distinguish humanity from *that* kind of life is reassuring, particularly if those rules can be superimposed globally.

The function of this framework of 'regimes' is to sever whatever pre-existing relations there might have been between human and non-human worlds.[10] Safe in the knowledge that the question of *matter* has been cordoned off, the modern/global human operates in an exclusive domain, dealt with by the glorious laws of international trade, of war, of cyber security, and of crime and insurance. And yet, we are lonely. The fact is that our rate of human consumption – enabled by centuries of global resource extraction and transfer – has led to the planet's sixth mass extinction crisis (Ceballos et al., 2017). Every indicator for the flourishing of non-human life has plummeted. While post-imperial visions of human mastery (technology that allows the human to be all-seeing, creating, fast-moving) are being realised, we are at the same time untethering ourselves from the material conditions of biological life.[11] Not only are we alone as a species, but our psycho-social lives are suffering for the lack of an affective connection to the earth. This is exacerbated by the tremendous amount of energy required to turn our faces away from the suffering that we *know* is caused by our insistence on our ontological exclusivity.

At first glance it may seem impossible to change this story, which has proliferated along the shipping routes and dinner tables of empire. But let us remember that our current framework of global law has only emerged in the blink of an evolutionary eye, and there are many other long-standing stories which we can turn to. Alternative ways of being and thinking – about home, community, responsibility, responsiveness – can be found in the fairy tales of pre-modern Europe, just as much as in Aboriginal communities in Australia and native communities elsewhere. Hidden under the bedsheets of each monolithic national culture there lies a panoply of folk tales, subcultures, religions, and communities who nurture their own lessons for regulating the human relationship to the world.[12] For lawyers thinking about how to draw a line under the current political economy, a greater insistence on sentiment and on sensibility might be required, as well as an openness to different ways of thinking about time, place, and kinship.[13] Above all, such a change requires a movement away from the *global*, the monolithic and the universal, and towards 'regimes' that are particular and varied. The embrace of difference calls for a broader skill set too, to the one we lawyers possess: skills better developed, perhaps, through anthropology, history, music, languages, and cultural geography.

Let me give a brief example of someone who has thought about this kind of difference in the specific context of the question of the human/animal. Lafcadio Hearn, a writer who settled in the town of Kumamoto in southern Japan, became known for noting local folktales and ghost stories. In the following extract, he writes about a dog who sleeps at the gate of his house, reflecting on her howl:

> [T]he night-howl of the white creature in my close forces me to wonder whether she does not mentally see something really terrible, – something which we vainly

> try to keep out of moral consciousness: the ghoulish law of life. Nay, there are times when her cry seems to me not the mere cry of a dog, but the voice of the law itself . . . Only by eating each other do beings exist! Beautiful to the poet's vision our world may seem, with its loves, its hopes, its memories, its aspirations; but there is nothing beautiful in the fact that life is fed by continual murder, – that the tenderest affection, the noblest enthusiasm, the purest idealism, must be nourished by the eating of flesh and the drinking of blood. All life, to sustain itself, must devour life.
>
> You may imagine yourself divine if you please, but you have to obey that law. Be, if you will, a vegetarian: nonetheless you must eat forms that have feeling and desire. Sterilize your food; and digestion stops. You cannot even drink without swallowing life. Loathe the name as we may, we are cannibals; all being essentially is One; and whether we eat the flesh of a plant, a fish, a reptile, a bird, a mammal, or a man, the ultimate fact is the same. And for all life the end is the same: every creature, whether buried or burnt, is devoured, and not only once or twice, nor a hundred, nor a thousand, nor a myriad times! Consider the ground upon which we move, the soil out of which we came; – think of the vanished billions that have risen from it and crumbled back into its latency to feed what becomes our food!
>
> Perpetually we eat the dust of our race, the substance of our ancient selves. But even so-called inanimate matter is self-devouring . . . Stars give being to worlds and devour them; planets assimilate their own moons. All is a ravening that never ends but to recommence. And unto whomsoever thinks about these matters, the story of a divine universe, made and ruled by paternal love, sounds less persuasive than the Polynesian tale that the souls of the dead are devoured by the gods. Monstrous the law seems, because we have developed ideas and sentiments which are opposed to this demoniac Nature.
>
> (Hearn, 1899: 32–33)

Hearn's suggestion that the howl of the dog who lives with him is 'the voice of the law itself' is based on a feeling that the dog speaks a kind of truth, or at least expresses an originary regulatory force. Indeed, Hearn calls this truth 'the ghoulish law of life': 'only by eating each other do beings exist!' He goes on to talk about this necessary consumption in a register that modern law would be hard-placed to operate: consumption can be understood (in Hearn's terms) both on a planetary scale (stars devouring worlds) and as taking place between the living and the dead, the material and the divine. 'Perpetually we eat the dust of our race, the substance of our ancient selves', says Hearn, in a sobering reminder of geological time. While Victorian England at the turn of the century was at the zenith of her empire with her global law-making machine working at full capacity, Lafcadio Hearn sat in his Kumamoto cottage, arguing that 'the story of a divine universe, made and ruled by paternal love, sounds less persuasive than the Polynesian tale that the souls of the dead are devoured by the gods.' This universe he describes sounds very much like the image of the modern state, even as it is a critique of Judeo-Christian ontology. These models mirror one another insofar as secular authority (of states, of international law) is based on a valorisation of 'masculine' virtues. One of these virtues is the capacity to produce 'human life' – or at least guarantee human*ness* – by symbolic means, i.e., through legal narrative and a tight control over the terms of public discourse.

We could transform these terms by claiming the vocabulary of 'law', as Hearn does, and reinstating it to a 'natural law'; or by unveiling the cultural specificity of the Judeo-Christian worldview by placing it, in the same register and sentence, alongside a Polynesian one. What I offer below is a different intervention: the familiar (for a Western audience) story of the Last Supper, from the perspective of the food that was once alive. Unlike Hearn, who is able to take a large-scale and long-distance view of consumption, my primary concern in this reflection is with the minutiae of the astonishingly inconsequential suffering caused by the ideology that drives the story of modern law:

Eating strangers for supper

I'm getting dressed for dinner as
You said we'd eat at half past eight
The fire's lit, the table's laid
Friends are waiting at the gate

In they trickle, two by two
They laugh and bare enamelled teeth
I learned I was to be your feast
You're embarrassed at my fate

You know I loved the wind like you
You know I warmed from sun like you
You know I felt the grass like you
Damp beneath our feet

As you break my bones, my breast
As you tear my skin, my legs
As you take my final breath
You'll deny you knew me

They sit on thrones and gnaw my bones
They swallow to forget
The welfare they have given me
Is a life sentence in debt

I know you love the wind like me
I know you're warmed by sun like me
I know you feel the grass like me
Damp beneath your feet

The bloody maws of jurisdiction
Leave my kin bereft
This rite of human fiction
That hides a world of shame

Drink from the cup of judgement
And tomorrow we'll be free
Unnecessary grief can wait
Until the break of day

You know I loved the wind with you
You know I yearned for sun with you
You know I felt the grass with you
Damp beneath our feet

Here I am also thinking about the denunciation that takes place with every act of consumption; an act of forgetting that takes place simultaneously – to invoke Berger – with the internalization, through flesh-eating, of an ideal that is a feeling surrounding a *lack*. This lack is caused by the detachment, not of a piece of our body, but of our body from an original body – the original body – whomever or wherever that may be. Religious and patriarchal rituals of eating flesh and drinking blood (or its substitute) hold out the promise of making good that lack.[14] The cure, then, is surely not another 'animal' law which reassures us that the body which remains is nonetheless a whole, hermetic, ontological miracle. Rather, this body should be returned to those traditions of thought that have richer modes of expression and explanation.

The opening question of this intervention was: what is animal law? I explained at the beginning of this chapter that it could either be referring to laws that specifically name animals, or to laws that involve/impact on animals. This slippage creates a dangerous soporific effect: it allows us to pretend that the violence we enact on other beings as well as on ourselves is being moderated. This very pretence facilitates – even accelerates – our alienation from the earth. In this chapter I explained how the regimentation of our relationship to the world at large is the result of a dominating culture that, through naming, shapes the way in which we see ourselves (as a transcendent species), while also justifying the political form of the modern state. If we are to remain useful to our kin, we lawyers and legal scholars need to think far more broadly about the scale of our world, both in terms of time and in terms of space. Who inhabits the (lawful) world? To 'humans' we could add non-human animals, of course, as well as imaginary beings, monsters, ghosts, god(s), the dead, geological features (woods, seas), and forces (tides, the sun, the fates). While this may at first glance seem unfamiliar, messy, and impossible, these inhabitants of law have never been far beneath the surface. Indeed, they are right here, if we would look at them.

Notes

1 I have written critiques of these elsewhere: 'Law and the Question of the (Non-Human) Animal' (2011); 'Species, Scarcity and the Secular State' (2013); 'Law' (2017).

2 Jorge Luis Borges's well-known fictional taxonomy of animals described in his essay *The Analytical Language of John Wilkins*, trans. Lilia Graciela Vázquez, Buenos Aires: Argentina, 1942, include animals: "That belong to the emperor; embalmed ones; those that are trained; suckling pigs; mermaids; fabulous ones; stray dogs; those that are included in this classification; those that tremble as if they were mad; innumerable ones; those drawn with a very fine camel hair brush; those that have just broken the flower vase; those that, at a distance, resemble flies." An example of this type of taxonomical exercise can be seen in the Victorian (Australian) *Prevention of Cruelty to Animals Act, 1986,* which defines 'animal' as:
   (a) a live member of a vertebrate species including any –
      (i) fish or amphibian; or
      (ii) reptile, bird or mammal, other than any human being or any reptile, bird or other mammal that is below the normal mid-point of gestation or incubation for the particular class of reptile, bird or mammal; or
   (b) a live adult decapod crustacean, that is –
      (i) a lobster; or
      (ii) a crab; or
      (iii) a crayfish.

3 It is important to note that there are currently over 66 thousand vertebrate and over 1.3 million invertebrate species of animals that have been taxonomised (with vertebrates, such as those noted in this Act, constituting approximately only 5% of animals). A recent study states that 86% of all species on land and 91% of species in the sea are yet to be discovered, described and catalogued. The IUCN Red List – the most comprehensive endangered species monitoring system we have – accounts for less than 1% of world species: Camilo Mora et al. (2011).

4 There are many excellent treatises on each of these topics, but one in particular stands out for its title and for the length of time between writing and publication: *The Secret Commonwealth (of Elves, Fauns and Fairies).* This book was written by Robert Kirk (a Scottish clergyman) in 1691 as a serious study, but was not printed until 1893 by the renowned folklorist Andrew Lang. This text is noted in another (more fictional) book by Jorge Luis Borges, *Book of Imaginary Beings* (1969).

5 Incidentally, these are all laws - zoning laws, for instance, create geographic boundaries that determine the conditions of life for non-human animals; trade laws influence which animals will and will not be consumed on an industrial scale;.

6 At every Conference of the Parties of the Convention on International Trade in Species of Fauna and Flora 993 UNTS 443, 1975, for example, there are extended debates as to the listed status of many of the threatened and endangered species.

7 There is a fascinating visual economy in the images of non-human animals that is a discussion for another time. Put briefly, I think that the beautification of 'nature' in the 'wildlife' photograph trade (this trade includes those who publish and view them) is not a simple commodification of life, but rather, a violent process of reducing ideas of 'nature' into pictures of still life.

8 An excellent text that strips this anxiety down to its essence is Clarice Lispector's *The Passion According to G.H.*, 2012 (originally published in 1964).

9 I have written about this at length elsewhere: Otomo, 2016.

10 My thanks go to Simon Archer for our enriching conversations on this topic and his helpful suggestions.

11 A great number of scholars have tracked this movement, most evidently from the 1970s onward in environmental/human geography studies, women's/gender studies, peace/war

studies, art, critical theory, cultural studies, anthropology, history, literature, politics – indeed, there are few disciplines that have remained unaffected by this observation.

12 The politics of collecting, recording, and recounting these lessons is the subject of lengthy debate in anthropology, literature, music, and religious studies. I cannot do justice to these scholars by citing a handful here (particularly given that my research is primarily in English), and merely note that the work I have been turning to most often on this topic are those books by the fairy tale specialists Marina Warner and Jack Zipes, as well as Lafcadio Hearn, discussed below.

13 As above, there is powerful indigenous scholarship to be found around the world, much of it touching on the disjunct between colonial and indigenous ideas of 'subjectivity' and 'nature'. Scholars publishing in English on indigenous laws tend to be based in Canada, Australia, New Zealand, India, and the U.S., while many scholars working on indigeneity and law in Spanish are based in Latin America. Anthropologists based in the North, such as Marilyn Strathern, Michael Taussig, Arjun Appadurai, and Luis Eslava, are my academic guides, alongside the teachings of my grandmother, Buddhist nuns and monks, and indigenous elders in Australia.

14 For an excellent explanation of the relationship between patriarchal ideology and meat-eating, see Carol Adams's classic text *The Sexual Politics of Meat* (Continuum, 1990, with an anniversary edition published by Bloomsbury in 2015).

Bibliography

Berger, John, *Why Look at Animals?* London: Penguin, 2009.

Borges, Jorge Luis, *The Analytical Language of John Wilkins*, trans. Lilia Graciela Vázquez, Buenos Aires: Argentina, 1942.

Borges, Jorge Luis, *Book of Imaginary Beings*, trans. Norman Thomas di Giovanni, Buenos Aires: Argentina, 1969.

Ceballos, Gerardo, Ehrlich, Paul R. and Dirzo, Rodolfo, 'Biological Annihilation via the Ongoing Sixth Mass Extinction Signaled by Vertebrate Population Losses and Declines' *PNAS*, 114(30): E6089–E6096, 2017.

Courtland, Rachel, 'Water Bears are First Animal to Survive Space Vacuum', *New Scientist*, 8 September 2008.

Guarino, Ben, 'These Animals Can Survive Until the End of the Earth, Astrophysicists Say' *Washington Post,* 14 July 2017. www.washingtonpost.com/news/speaking-of-science/wp/2017/07/14/these-animals-can-survive-until-the-end-of-the-earth-astrophysicists-say/?utm_term=.db4a86e1010d.

Hearn, Lafcadio, *Ghostly Japan*, New York: Little, Brown & Company, 1899.

Kirk, Robert, *The Secret Commonwealth (of Elves, Fauns and Fairies)*, London: David Nutt, 1893.

Lispector, Clarice, *The Passion According to G.H.*, trans. Idra Novey, New York: New Directions, 2012.

Mora, Camilo, Tittensor, Derek P., Adl, Sina, Simpson, Alastair G.B., Worm, Boris, 'How Many Species Are There on Earth and in the Ocean,' *PLoS Biology*, 9(8), 2011.

Otomo, Yoriko, 'Law and the Question of the (Non-Human) Animal', *Society and Animals*, 19(4), 383–391, 2011.

Otomo, Yoriko, 'Species, Scarcity and the Secular State,' in Yoriko Otomo and Edward Mussawir (eds), *Law and the Question of the Animal: A Critical Jurisprudence*, London: Routledge, 2013.

Otomo, Yoriko, *Unconditional Life: The Postwar International Law Settlement*, Oxford: Oxford University Press, 2016.

Otomo, Yoriko, 'Law,' in Ron Broglio, Lynn Turner and Undine Sellbach (eds), *The Edinburgh Companion to Critical Animal Studies*. Edinburgh: Edinburgh University Press, 2017.

power immediately – a change that is based, significantly, on moral considerations. Justice is expressed as an articulation of power and morality: "if one had the *power* to put it to rights, it was one's *duty* to do so" (emphasis added). The judgment that follows is immediate and violent. It is based not only on what Grace perceives as justice to herself – a kind of vengeful justice – but also on what Grace sees to be justice for "humanity."

Grace gives orders for the inhabitants of Dogville to be executed. She orders Vera's children to be shot while Vera watches, calling up the parallel situation of Vera smashing Grace's figurines while Grace was made to watch. The children hold some moral culpability for Grace's suffering, independent to their mother's actions. The film carefully establishes the collective culpability of almost everyone in the community, so that there is reason in their being punished so thoroughly: the sexual violence of the men, the social violence of the women, even the humiliation inflicted by the children – their cheerful cruelty in ringing the bell each time Grace is raped. The open set establishes the visibility of the crimes committed against Grace, and the community's complicity in these crimes: everyone in the community sees what Grace is experiencing, but nobody takes any steps to assist her. The viewer experiences a sense of justice when Grace retaliates. Even though her orders carry implications of revenge, it does not seem altogether disproportionate to the cruelty and abuse the townspeople had inflicted on her. It seems appropriate, too, that Grace shoots Tom in the head herself – as he betrayed her on so many levels.

But when the baby – who is incapable of responsible action – is shot, the viewer realises that a logic beyond individual or collective responsibility is at work. Grace argues that this annihilation of the baby is necessary to prevent further acts of victimisation: "it could happen again. Somebody happening by, revealing their frailty." The futurity of the community, symbolised by the baby, must be therefore be annihilated "for the sake of other towns, for the sake of humanity." For Grace, the particularity of Dogville must be destroyed. Dogville is the aberrant exception that needs to be removed for the protection of universal humankind. This view changes the interpretation of the town of Dogville as an allegory of humanity ("But dogs only obey their own nature, so why shouldn't we forgive them?") to an aberrant exception. Dogville is a deviant community, which needs to be removed for the protection of humanity: "If there is any town this world would be better without, this is it."

In this last sequence of Grace's violent revenge, 'justice' is disarticulated from sovereignty: it is not the will of the people but Grace's will, instrumentalised through the mafia, that brings about Dogville's demise. The mafia authority here is thematised as unlawful, backed by neither morality nor the will of the people. Von Trier explained in an interview with Stig Björkman, the idea for *Dogville* came from Pirate Jenny's song in Brecht's *Threepenny Opera*: "I listened to that a lot and was really seduced by the great revenge motif in the song: 'And they asked me which heads should fall, and the harbour fell quiet as I answered "All"' (2003: 243–244). This is 'justice', or violence, based only on arbitrary will; as arbitrary as the "change of light" Grace witnesses towards the end of the film. Grace's humility has also been a ruse: it is revealed that by arriving in Dogville, she set out to prove that there is an alternative to her father's mafia-logic of power/violence. Dogville, however, proves not to be the exception to her father's law. The traumatised victim becomes the violent oppressor, representing a logic of justice that has justified the wars and laws of modernity.

Democratic consensus is the means by which Grace is accepted into the community and offered conditional hospitality. It is also the means by which she was excluded and exposed to the community's law, revealing this law to be a form of naked power. Grace can only take her revenge – "for the sake of the future, humanity," her "own dignity," as she says – by assuming the corrupted power offered to her by her father, and then having assumed this socio-symbolic mandate, by proceeding to order the destruction of Dogville and its woeful inhabitants.

i. Aesthetic and affective argument

Von Trier adopts Brechtian techniques to suspend affective identification through dramatic estrangement: the use of chalk lines, John Hurt's ironic and intrusive narration and the lack of props thematising the film's status as representation. In addition to borrowing part of the plot from Brecht and Weil's *Pirate Jenny* (Lübecker, 2011: 162), von Trier also recalls the American realism and melodrama of Thornton Wilder's *Our Town* (1938). This combination of affective alienation and affective excess means that the viewer is both drawn in and critically distanced from the affect of the film. As viewers of *Dogville*, we can never lose sight of the fact that we are watching a film, or of the film's status *as* representation. The film has an explicitly narrative form – a prologue and nine chapters – and is framed by the commentary of an intrusive and ironic narrator. Storytelling is further thematised by Tom, the town philosopher, who describes Grace's arrival in Dogville as offering an "illustration" to its inhabitants. This is paralleled by what Grace describes as her own "illustration" (of violence towards the town) at the end of the film. We also witness the accretion of meaning throughout the film: the dog's barking comes to stand in for the cruelty of humanity; the gooseberry bushes come to signify Grace's arduous but socially unrecognised labour; and the clanging bell refers to Grace's torture and humiliation. We see the ways in which the community comes to define its own meanings, and also the ways in which these definitions do not match Grace's 'reality'.

The play of genre in the telling of Grace's story complicates this reading, and opens Grace's story to a wider interpretation of gender violence. Genre is not merely a 'stylistic device,' but constitutes ways of being (Frow, 2006: 2; see also Derrida, 1980: 55). Different genres can reveal something of how worlds are created and maintained. Certain genres and modes have the capacity to introduce a critical framework or sensibility, foregrounding and making visible certain narratives *as* narratives, which would otherwise be experienced as true and real (Antaki, 2013: 977). Law is aggressive in its assertion of an exclusive jurisdiction over the subject matter it judges. It is also aggressive in excluding other authorities in making its judgments. For Derrida, this tactic of singularity is at the core of any archive's violence:

> The one guards against the other, it protects itself from the other. . . . It keeps and erases the archive of this injustice that it is, of this violence that it does. . . . The determination of the self as one is violence.
>
> (1996: 78)

The 'power' of consignation within the archive lies in the act of "gathering together signs" in the coordination of "a single corpus", which refuses heterogeneity (Derrida, 1996: 8). The insistence on singularity is crucial to the vesting of authority. Derrida provides the metaphor of the exterior and interior of the archive, and explains that the boundary between them is guarded to preserve this singularity (1996: 10). State law speaks with one voice and authority, and guards its archive against others: there is "no archive without outside" (Derrida, 1996: 11); its archive is a "place of election where law and singularity intersect in *privilege*" (Derrida, 1996: 8, emphasis in original).

The cultural domain provides a space in which to engage with the time and space of violence outside law's frameworks – to refuse to accept the terms of dominant legal, political and social imaginaries in representing and adjudicating events. Engaging exemplary counter-texts in this mode provides a way to challenge law's forms, not least through experiences of "affective dissonance" (Antaki, 2013: 977).

Dogville references both a universal 'humanity' and a contingent historically specific subject, which provides a way to draw out and complicate theorisations of the moral, legal or 'natural' human. Moreover, *Dogville* uses a number of different genres in its exegesis of the human condition – realism, allegory, minimalism – to call attention to the politics of different practices of representation, and the relation of these to concepts including justice, fairness and equality. Formally, the film negotiates allegory and historical specificity: Tom is the 'everyman' character, but one who is particularised as a citizen of a town that comes to be seen as aberrant. Although there is an allegorical aesthetic to the film – produced by its narrative structure, the ironic, intrusive narrator and the representation of characters as types – this is complicated by the manner in which it is routed through the Great Depression, and evokes the specific historical events of slavery and genocide. At times, the film appears to be making assertions about bare human nature – that when put under pressure, people will act 'like dogs.' At the same time, however, it seems to refuse the possibility of doing so without referencing a specific, historic moment: "by infusing sentimentalism with irony, turning standard documentary tropes into a means for representing the paradoxical condition of radical universalism *and* incommensurability" (Quinn, 2001: 340, emphasis in original). Similarly, *Dogville* uses both identification and disidentification – invoking the aberration of the town in its judgment of liberal logics, but then appealing to its status as 'human' – in order to invoke our judgment of Grace's actions. Although it makes use of a Depression-era working class aesthetic, the film's concern is not so much with a reading of a particular historical moment but with the production of sets of modernist logics that produce material effects. The inhabitants of Dogville are both particularly aberrant and universally 'human.' The 'every town' status of Dogville is disrupted at the beginning of the film by the ironic description of the town and its inhabitants by the English-accented narrator, as well as by the way in which it is marked as working class and historically specific. The effect is to disrupt logics that have historically been used to justify violence, logics that instrumentalise ideas of community, romance, justice, small white American towns, self-reliance, charity, mercy and 'grace.'

ii. Affective complicity in Dogville

Complicity attends the very idea of exchange. The characters reproduce our own status as audience and here, von Trier questions the very act of being a spectator. The camera captures the rape scene in the context of the political condition of the town's collective guilt, shifting from Dogville's collective subject to the projected audience watching. Although Dogville takes up some of Brecht's political aesthetics, the viewer is not interpellated as a positive force for change, as she is for Brecht. Indeed, focalisation in the film is ambivalent: the viewer identifies with Grace for most of the film, and yet we are also given an omniscient point of view of the community and presented with Grace's suffering as though it were a moral and political problem.[2] When the camera captures the actors watching Grace's rape, we share the community's point of view – not Grace's – but then we return to Grace's point of view. So, as viewers, we are encouraged to intellectualise Grace's suffering at the same time that we anticipate it. At the point of final reversal and judgment, when Grace enacts revenge, we realise that we have been identifying with a problematic subject. We are likely to maintain our identification with her, however, and feel some relief at her apocalypse, while at the same time judging the excess of Grace's violence and feeling the discomfort of that passive position of judgment. The film exposes our own complicity as honorary liberal thinkers with Dogville and with Grace, as well as our own sado-masochistic satisfaction with the destructive conclusion. Here, the jurist is a voyeur, someone who takes ambivalent pleasure in pain.

The film plays with a poetics of exceptionalism, and is ambivalent about the relationship between violence and law. The inhabitants of Dogville argue that they are upholding the rule of law when they are clearly exploiting Grace's labour, as the unlawful figure, both a stranger and seeking asylum. The townspeople argue that this is justified by the exceptional circumstances of their poverty and historically hard times, in addition to their justification under the principle of exchange/contract. These arguments are thematised throughout the film and are continually shifting. When the townspeople violate Grace, through slavery and rape, they present their violence as a necessary evil. When Grace argues for the execution of Dogville, she argues that her violence is a necessary good – evoking the figure of the victim whose unique call to an exceptional justice may transcend laws.

The film mobilises different categories of 'vulnerability' and 'victim,' demonstrating and critiquing the ways in which victimhood is instrumentalised. The town uses its status as economic victim to subjugate Grace; and in turn, Grace uses her status as wronged victim to justify her annihilation of the town's inhabitants. The film thereby provides a critique of the kinds of stories in which the 'other' is a threat, as a perpetrator to the subject with whom we are supposed to identify, in turn justifying revenge, retaliation and pre-emptive justice. The film invokes subjection in order to prove its point about the use of particular logics in modernity – the ways in which subjectivity is articulated with subjection, and the ways in which subjection becomes instrumentalised. This is the logic of genocidal violence – a claimed frailty or vulnerability used to justify violent actions against a particular group of people. For Walter Benjamin, modern law comes from this kind of genocidal exclusion, and such violence is required for the continuing formation of the state: "All violence as a means is either lawmaking or law-preserving", and is "implicated in the problematic nature of law itself" (1968: 115). Law asserts an exclusive role in the adjudication of violence, thereby establishing its own jurisdiction, and thereby either 'making' or 'preserving' itself. Law's claim to an exclusive role in adjudicating violence has been central to the production of law's authority in modernity, and central, too, to modernist politico-philosophical analyses of law's authority. As well as the norm-producing nature of these representations, violence here is operating in the context of the law, in ways that shore up the law's logics and authority. In 'Critique of Violence,' (1968) Walter Benjamin provides one account of the ways in which violence is taken up in the domain of law (not violence "as such"), arguing that violence operates in the legal domain as a concept produced by and one that organises particular logics in which the law is invested. In this essay Benjamin provides an exposition of the logics of natural and positivist law, which are organised by "means" and "ends," and produce violence that is sanctioned and unsanctioned by the law (1968: 279). The critique of violence as it operates in this domain requires a "historico-philosophical view of law" in order to properly historicise and contextualise the production of these logics. This is why "the critique of violence is the philosophy of its history" (Benjamin, 1968: 299) – violence is a concept haunted by different logics. If tracked as a figure produced across Western legal philosophy, 'violence' emerges as destabilised, a concept that shores up or organises different logics at different historical moments, naturalising different world-views. Benjamin argues that the law represents itself as mediating and adjudicating violence, and this is power-making (1968: 293). The law's adjudication of violence cannot be trusted for many reasons, but Benjamin's account demonstrates how violence becomes instrumental in shoring up the law's processes. Jacques Derrida continues Benjamin's argument by arguing that the adjudication of violence in the law becomes instrumental in supporting the law's claim to authority: its adjudication is "said to found the law or state" (1968: 31).

Derrida and Benjamin are helpful in thinking about the ways in which the law's adjudication of violence acts to support both the legal state, as well as its effects in producing norms which carry their own violence. Derrida considers "law," "justice" and "morality" within the schema of violence: violence is an operating idea that organises these concepts, and naturalises a particular world-view. The paradox is that law claims it is adjudicating violence but rather violence becomes the occasion for it to justify its own infliction of power/violence. The key, for Derrida, is that the concept of "origins" is abstract, not historical – the moment of origins "always takes place and never takes place" (1992: 31). These are not Rousseauian origins but rather a continuing, animating concept: for Derrida, origins are about moments of "emergence," "foundation," "iterability" (1992: 43). While these moments are neither inherently "just nor unjust," they are represented as just through a "discourse of self-legitimation" (Derrida, 1992: 36). Such moments are "*said* to found law" (emphasis added) (Derrida, 1992: 35). It is the control over the means of representation that is crucial, both to the "emergence of justice" (Derrida, 1992: 35) and the violence that is inherent in this representation. Legal origins are suspect: we should sense that they are really assertions of power, and accompanied by violence.

Dogville not only illustrates the deadlocks of liberal reasoning, but the aesthetics of it, and the way it feels to be a complicit player within it – not only the moral position of this point of view, but the pleasure and pain of it. Aesthetics and affect are not epiphenomenal to questions of justice; when we go beyond the analysis of the social contract as a logic or concept, and explore it instead as an aesthetic, we see how contract animates violence in democracy beyond reason, no longer marking exchange but instead figuring violent exploitation. Ultimately, *Dogville* rejects the possibility that liberalism's promises (of equality, justice, etc.) can be achieved by participating in the conditions of abstraction – that is, intervention cannot succeed where it is based on debates about the quality of abstract values of fairness or equality. In liberal traditions, reason is naturalised as the key mode of constituting and critiquing legal and political forms. *Dogville* points to what opens up, in terms of both critique and possibility, when aesthetics or affect become the mode of enquiry. Despite the logical deadlock of the film's denouement, there is the possibility of moving between aesthetic and empathic positions – for example, empathy, disgust, pleasure and horror; between the abstract and the particular positions of Grace and the villagers, even the dog. Inhabiting these different positions perhaps opens up new critical modes – for example, re-thinking the nature of contract from Grace's position.

The figure of the contract 'haunts' the legal imaginary in Avery Gordon's sense: "haunting is one way in which abusive systems of power make themselves known and their impacts felt in everyday life, especially when they are supposedly over and done with" (2008: xxi). Above, I have shown how to provide a reading in which materiality and textuality are imbricated, indicating new, interdisciplinary ways of knowing – knowing that goes beyond categories of law and even of gender, and that takes account of the role of the relation between representation and materiality.

Notes

1 For examples of this turn, see Desmond Manderson, *Kangaroo Courts and the Rule of Law: The Legacy of Modernism* (Routledge, 2012); *Genres of Critique*, eds. Karin Van Marle and Stewart Motha (Stellenbosch: 2013, Sun Press); Mark Antaki, "Genre, Critique and Human Rights," *University of Toronto Quarterly*, Volume 82, Number 4, Fall 2013, pp. 974–996.

2 As Abella and Zilkha explain, the mise-en-scene "lures the spectators into believing they occupy an almost transcendental position in relation to the events" (2004: 159).

Bibliography

Abella, Adela and Zilkha, Nathalie, '*Dogville*: A Parable on Perversion', *International Journal of Psychoanalysis*, 85, 1519–1526, 2004.

Antaki, Mark, 'Genre, Critique and Human Rights', *University of Toronto Quarterly*, 82(3), 974–996, 2013.

Artaud, Antonin, *To Have Done With the Judgment of God*, New York: Viking, 1933.

Artaud, Antonin, *Oeuvres Completes*, Paris: Gallimard, 1978.

Atkinson, Adam, 'On the Nature of Dogs, the Right of Grace, Forgiveness, and Hospitality: Derrida, Kant, and Lars von Trier's *Dogville*', *Senses of Cinema*, 36, 2005.

Bainbridge, Caroline, 'The Trauma Debate: Just Looking? Traumatic Affect, Film Form and Spectatorship in the Work of Lars von Trier', *Screen*, 45(4), 391–400, 2004.

Begam, Richard and Moses, Michael (eds), *Modernism and Colonialism: British and Irish Literature, 1899–1939*, Durham: Duke University Press, 2007.

Benjamin, Walter, 'Critique of Violence', in H. Arendt (ed.), *Illuminations*, trans. H. Zohn, New York: Schocken Books, 1968.

Best, Stephen, *The Fugitive's Properties: Law and the Poetics of Possession*, Chicago: University of Chicago Press, 2004.

Björkman, Stig (ed.), '*Dogville*', in *Trier on von Trier*, trans. N. Smith, London: Faber and Faber, 2003.

Brandt, Per Aage, 'The Political Philosophy of a Dogville: On Dogville by Lars von Trier', *P.O. V. Film and Politics*, 16, 2003.

Brighenti, Andrea, '*Dogville*, Or, The Dirty Birth of Law', *Thesis Eleven*, 87, 96–111, 2006.

Buchanan, Ruth and Johnson, Rebecca, 'Strange Encounters: Exploring Law and Film in the Affective Register', *Studies in Law, Politics and Society*, 33–60, 2009.

Bush, George, 'President Bush Addresses the Nation', 19 March 2003, https://georgewbush-whitehouse.archives.gov/news/releases/2003/03/20030319-17.html.

Chakrabarty, Dipesh, *Provincialising Europe* Princeton: Princeton University Press, 2007.

Connolly, W. E. *Neuropolitics: Thinking, Culture, Speed*, Minneapolis: University of Minnesota Press, 2002.

Cooppan, Vilashini, *Worlds Within: National Narratives and Global Connections in Postcolonial Writing*, Stanford: Stanford University Press, 2009.

Deleuze, Gilles, *Essays Critical and Clinical*, trans. Daniel W. Smith and Michael A. Greco, London and New York: Verso, 1998.

Derrida, Jacques, 'The Law of Genre', *Critical Inquiry*, 7, 55, 1980.

Derrida, Jacques, 'Force of Law: The "Mystical Foundation of Authority"', in D. Cornell, M. Rosenfield and D. Gray Carlson (eds), *Deconstruction and the Possibility of Justice*, London: Routledge, 1992.

Derrida, Jacques, *Archive Fever: A Freudian Impression*, trans. E. Prenowitz, Chicago: University of Chicago Press, 1996.

Dimock, Wai Chee, 'Planetary Time and Global Translation: "Context" in Literary Studies', *Common Knowledge*, 9(3), 488–507, 2003.

Ebert, Roger, '*Dogville*', 9 April 2004, www.rogerebert.com/reviews/dogville-2004.

Fibiger, Bo, 'A Dog Not Yet Buried – Or Dogville as a Political Manifesto', *P.O. V. Film and Politics*, 16, 2003.

Frow, John, *Genre (The New Critical Idiom)*, London: Routledge, 2006.

Gordon, Avery F., *Haunting and the Sociological Imagination*, Minneapolis: University of Minnesota Press, 2008.

Hartman, Saidiya, *Scenes of Subjection: Terror, Slavery, and Self-Making in Nineteenth-Century America*, New York: Oxford University Press, 1997.

Honig, Bonnie and Marso, Lori J., 'Lars von Trier and the "Cliches of Our Times"', *Theory and Event*, 18(2), 2015.

Horeck, Tanya, *Public Rape: Representing Violation in Fiction and Film*, London/New York: Routledge, 2004.

Kendall, Tanya and Kendall, Tina (eds), 'Lars von Trier's *Dogville*, A Contemporary Feel-Bad Film', in *The New Extremism in Cinema: From France to Europe*, Edinburgh: Edinburgh University Press, 2011.
Lübecker, Nikolaj, 'Lars von Trier's *Dogville*, A Contemporary Feel-Bad Film', in T. Kendall and T. Horeck (eds), *The New Extremism in Cinema: From France to Europe*, Edinburgh: Edinburgh University Press, 2011.
Manderson, Desmond, *Kangaroo Courts and the Rule of Law: The Legacy of Modernism*, London: Routledge, 2012.
Nietzsche, Friedrich W., Walter Kaufmann, R. J. Hollingdale, and Friedrich W. Nietzsche, *On the Genealogy of Morals*, New York: Vintage Books, 1989.
Quinn, Jeanne Follansbee, 'The Work of Art: Irony and Identification in *Let Us Now Praise Famous Men*', *Novel: A Forum on Fiction*, 34(3), 338–368, 2001.
Rancière, Jacques, 'The Ethical Turn of Aesthetics and Politics', trans. J-P. Deranty, *Critical Horizons*, 7(1), 1–20, 2006.
Reichmann, Ravit, *The Affective Life of Law: Legal Modernism and the Literary Imagination*, Stanford: Stanford University Press, 2009.
Rigby, Nigel and Booth, Howard J. (eds), *Modernism and Empire: Writing and British Coloniality 1890–1940*, Manchester: Manchester University Press, 2000.
Scarry, Elaine, 'The Made Up and the Made Real', *Yale Journal of Culture and Humanities*, 5, 239–264, 1992.
Sielke, Sabine, *Reading Rape: The Rhetoric of Sexual Violence in American Literature and Culture, 1790–1990*, Princeton: Princeton University Press, 2002.
Sinnerbrink, Robert, 'Grace and Violence: Questioning Politics and Desire in "Lars von Trier's *Dogville*"', *Scan: Journal of Media Arts Culture*, 4, 2, 2007.
Wilder, Thornton, *Our Town: A Play in Three Acts*. New York: Coward McCann Inc, 1938.

Cultural texts

Antichrist, film, directed by Lars von Trier. Germany: Zentropa Entertainments, 2009.
Breaking the Waves, film, directed by Lars von Trier. USA: Argus Film Produktie, 1996.
Dancer in the Dark, film, directed by Lars von Trier. Denmark: Zentropa Entertainments, 2000.
Dogville, film, directed by Lars von Trier. Sweden: Zentropa Entertainments, 2003.
Manderlay, film, directed by Lars von Trier. Germany: Zentropa Entertainment, 2005.
Wilder, Thornton, *Our Town: A Play in Three Acts*, New York: Coward McCann Inc., 1938.

17

From decaffeinated democracy to democracy in the real in ten (Lacanian) sessions

Maria Aristodemou

Transference

At a protest in London in April 2016 demanding the resignation of Prime Minister David Cameron, protesters held one minute of silence in memory of Democracy. The irony of exercising the democratic right to mark the passing of democracy is worth noting. Democracy, it seems, is all the more spectacular and loaded with symbolism when it's working the least. That is, democracy is full of momentous and powerful meaning when it is an empty signifier: the right to democracy can be exercised, and spectacularly exhibited, as long as it is empty. Should, god forbid, that right come with a loaded signified, a demand or a message that needs more than staging (the ousting of a prime minister, for example) the limits of democracy become apparent. This chapter will take the paradox of contemporary stagings of democracy as its starting point and suggest that one way we can move beyond the democratic right to be ignored is by drawing a distinction between what I call decaffeinated democracy and Democracy in the Real.

While much has been written (and continues to be written) on the meaning of democracy in political, legal, as well as popular and social media, this chapter takes a different approach: it addresses it through the lens of psychoanalysis by laying the patient, Democracy, on the couch; the Lacanian couch in particular. In a series of ten sessions, of varied length but more or less short and expensive, it will guide the sick patient from the cosy state of what I term 'decaffeinated democracy' to democracy in the real, a democracy, as I argue, that is properly ethical; one where the subject of the saying and the subject of the said, the subject of enunciation and the subject of the enunciated, are not divorced and hopelessly alienated as subjects of empty speech, but are one with their desire. As we will see, this is a rare event, whether the subject is in analysis or in politics, and the reason it is rare is that full speech, in analysis or in politics, *hurts*.

Symptom

So Democracy had a breakdown at its place of birth (as we are forever reminded), the gulf between the saying and the heard became so unbearable that the only option is to put the patient on the couch. Any patient in analysis can only experience a metamorphosis if the analysis addresses and penetrates not only her symbolic and imaginary registers but what Lacan calls the Real. In particular, she must come to terms with desires which may be perverse and not as laudable as she may think they are. In our case, it would involve acknowledging not only the virtues but the obscene core at the heart of democracy. To excavate these desires it is not enough to address legal, political and economic structures (which dwell in the realm of the symbolic) or even practices and ideologies (which dwell in the realm of the imaginary); we must instead penetrate the Real and in particular that part of the Real that terrifies us so much that we have hidden even from ourselves: the extimate.

What is wrong with meeting the patient at the level of the imaginary? From his paper on the mirror stage on, Lacan never stopped reminding us that a patient's own image of herself is fundamentally distorted: a mis-recognition (2006a, 80). Our precious identity is constructed from mis-identifications and copies of other people. So when the patient is busy describing herself, the last thing the analyst should do is take her at her word: to do that the analyst would be reinforcing the patient's mis-recognitions. How do we resist the temptation of meeting the patient at the level of her imaginary (and no doubt imaginative) narratives and instead meet her at the level of the Real, where an intervention will make a difference? The problem, as analysts find out daily when listening to their patients' ramblings, is that most of our speech about ourselves is idle chitchat; what Lacan called 'empty speech'. For the analyst to respond to the patient's empty speech is to perpetuate her delusions. The challenge is to listen to Democracy's protests about herself, her constant complaints about other systems, nod wisely and ignore them. The analyst must bear in mind that the demands Democracy makes, her constant protests, may well be false demands, hiding her real desires.

Rather than taking the patient at her word, the analyst will look *beyond* the patient's empty speech to hear her 'full speech'. In contrast to empty speech which maintains the distance between the *I* as speaker and *I* as subject of the message, full speech implicates the subject's desire. For Lacan that place is not far from the place where the subject's enjoyment resides: truth, he says, is 'the sister of that forbidden jouissance' (1991: 61). Full speech emerges when the subject comes to articulate her secret, shameful and indeed hitherto unconscious enjoyment. A true analysis will try to penetrate beyond Democracy's monotonous retellings of her own story and pierce through to her real yet repressed desires. It is at this doubtless painful but real level that we can hope to encounter the patient's secret and disavowed kernel.

Crisis of belief, and of disbelief

As the analyst is Lacanian, and one can't take the lack out of Lacan, we can take for granted that our political and economic arrangements are not only lacking but will always be more or less lacking. What we are witnessing, I suggest, is not only a political or economic crisis, but a crisis of ideas and of beliefs: in short, a crisis of fantasy, of Belief in a Big Other of Government and all that it represents (or does not). Gone are the days, if they ever existed, of blind faith in a Big Other, whether local or global. In the West, belief in democracy became ideological, that is, as Althusser pointed out concerning every ideology, profoundly unconscious (2005: 233); repeated protests that we believe in democracy served first and foremost to create a community of believers, presuming to differentiate a 'civilised' West from non-democratic 'savages'.

Belief in democracy, like all beliefs, needs the believers' investment, their fantasy, to sustain it. How does such a fantasy function? The practice and rituals of democracy, and in particular the media frenzy during election time, foster a belief in the system, a belief which, like all beliefs, functions vicariously and from a distance – we believe because we believe someone else believes – and functions as the guarantor of our faith (Žižek, 2001). Democracy is one such object presupposed by its faithful believers; it is, as Badiou argued, an 'untouchable emblem', beyond discussion and beyond question (2010). Democracy as an object of desire, writes Badiou, is a given: we are given no choice not to desire it, as if it is a crime not to be a democrat (Badiou, 2005: 78). What is it that rendered democracy such a given? One suggestion is that the 'people's will' took the place of God's will in modernity; if that is so, to paraphrase Lacan, the belief in democracy, like the belief in God, once it is stripped of its logical consistency, indeed, *especially* when it is stripped of its logical consistency, becomes stronger than ever: it becomes unconscious (1979: 59).

Yet in the last few decades, increasing sabotage of the claims of democracy on the one hand by neoliberalism in the West and on the other by aggressive interventions in its name abroad, belief in democracy has begun to wane. We are witnessing increasing symptoms of what I call decaffeinated democracy: apathy, passivity, withdrawal, depression. Witness for example the case of Joan Edwards in August 2013, a story that strained the British public's credibility: a deceased retired nurse called Joan Edwards had apparently left in her will the sum of half a million pounds, her lifetime savings, to 'whichever government is in office.' The ruling coalition of Conservatives and Liberal Democrats promptly pocketed the bequest, before a public outcry forced them to surrender it to the coffers of the public purse. As Joan's will had stated 'whichever government is in office', and the Con-Lib coalition were indeed the government of the day, what was the outcry about? My suggestion is that the people of Britain found it hard to believe that anyone could still believe in the government. Joan Edwards was one of those rare remnants of a bygone era when people still believed in a Big Other of government. Most of us are more likely to distrust, ridicule, curse and berate the government than shower it with praise, let alone money. When people appeal to democracy today, we need to check that they are not being ironic.

Death by representation

Why the suspicion of irony? Because another symptom of decaffeinated democracy, I suggest, is a particularly severe if not terminal case of the sickness of representation.

What is the sickness of representation? In our all-too-human and relentless obsession with representing the world around us, whether in writing, images or sounds, we forget that something always gets lost every time a signified is dragged into the registers of signifiers. The minute we represent something, the 'thing' itself dies, and we are left with the empty shell of its representation; or, as Lacan kept repeating, the word is the murder of the thing (2006: 262). Representation is always a lie because there is always a distance between the representation and the thing represented: representation is never a perfect fit. It is no surprise, therefore, that politicians (those who supposedly 'represent' us) are known first and foremost for their capacity to lie.

If language alienates us from the thing itself, what are we to make of our 'civilisation', built after all on a Babel of languages? Freud, famously, had little hope for the promises made by so-called civilisation (1930); indeed, as Jacques-Alain Miller adds 150 years later, perhaps we are now past civilisation and its discontents, and are at the point of civilisation and its horrors (1991). The point can be pushed further: not only is our civilisation, in its insistence on representation at the expense of the thing itself flawed, but representational democracy is an extreme version of this sickness. Representational democracy, the argument can go, is the apotheosis of our culture's fetishism, where our voices are taken over by others so only the fact of enunciation but not the substance of the enunciated remains to be heard. In our case, I suggest democracy has become the arch-signifier at the cost of emptying itself: like the phallus, it has become a signifier without a signified. Representation functions to clothe the Real but when the clothes are badly fitting, they rip and the nakedness shows through: every child can see that the Emperor is wearing no clothes.

Homo democraticus

If representation is a lie, why do we persist with it? The short answer is that Democracy, like Law or God, functions as a limit: something that is structurally necessary to close the system: since no system is complete without an arch signifier, every system ends up inventing a fictional arch-signifier whose role is to effect this closure. This arbitrary limit is not true or false, just or unjust, but simply necessary just like a circumference is necessary to close a circle. Yet democracy, like theocracy and nomocracy, needs belief to sustain it, a fantasy which, as we just saw, is wearing thin. The secular religion of democracy was supposed to supplant God by deifying man: not just any man, but the Cartesian thinking being whom Kant went on to celebrate as the autonomous self-legislating individual. Democracy, in contrast to many gods and many religions, prides itself not on issuing prohibitions from above, but on enabling the subject to partake of the machinery of governance and of law-making.

Do we have faith in this so-called sovereign, autonomous, self-legislating individual? What does psychoanalysis make of him or her? Badiou does not think much of this subject: the crucial traits of homo democraticus, he says, are egoism and pleasure-seeking: 'Homo democraticus is an avaricious old fellow, grafted onto a craving adolescent' (2010: 11). For psychoanalysis, this is a trait not only of homo democraticus but of all speaking beings. Freud appreciated the deluded and deluding nature of the ego, reminding us that our precious ego is no more than the leftovers of those we loved as well as those who rejected us (1921: 107). For Lacan the ego, our precious 'identity,' is a fallacy, that is, imaginary, arising from our captivation by the image: rather than the seat of knowledge or psychic health, the ego is a sickness we suffer from, 'the human symptom par excellence, the mental illness of man' (1991: 62). Its job is not to tell us the truth about ourselves, but to continue in self-perpetuating delusions, deceiving others, but most of all deceiving the subject herself.

In the run-up to the Greek referendum, one group, concerned that a No vote might precipitate Greece's exit from the EU, campaigned under the banner #menoumeevropi (#stayineurope). The sad irony of this, as of all identifications, is that on realising that the Other (in this case, Europe) we want to be part of does not want us as we are, rather than giving up we try to become like her so that we'll be loved by her. Perhaps there was no sadder indication of the desperate nature of this call to the Other than the same group holding a banner with a pro-Europe message outside Downing Street: the message, as with all letters, did arrive, complete with spelling mistakes. So keen are we to be loved by and recognised by the Other that the subject keeps sacrificing herself to bring the Other into existence. Yet as Lacan reminds us, all the sacrifice proves is that we are trying 'to find evidence for the presence of the desire of this Other' (1973: 275). Even when the outcome is catastrophic, the subject still sees it as a sign: it confirms that the Big Other does exist and is running the show, that her suffering is not the result of blind chance. Unfortunately, even the subject's suffering and sacrifice at the altar of the Other is, ultimately, meaningless; all it confirms is the subject's belief in an Other who would supposedly be the beneficiary of the sacrifice. The subject is no more fulfilled or enlightened after her self-destruction; her death does not redeem or sanctify her. Instead, like Kafka's heroes, she dies uncomprehending 'like a dog' (251).

For the fantasy of sacrifice to be traversed, the subject would have to come to accept that her sacrifice is meaningless: that there is no Big Other who demands or benefits from her sacrifice. The subject, that is, must sacrifice her enjoyment of sacrificing herself: to sacrifice the sacrifice, as Žižek puts it (1999). In a cruel twist that might have shuttered precisely the fantasy of sacrifice, the very Europe the #menoumeevropi group were keen to remain part of thought very little of Greek people's credentials for being 'European': in June 2015 the German newspaper *Die Welt* ran a story suggesting that contemporary Greeks are not 'real' Greeks, since they are not the descendants of Pericles or Socrates but a 'Turkish-moulded mixture of Slavs, Byzantines and Albanians.'[4] Given their bastard origins, it concluded, the only appropriate response was to expel them from this haloed union of 'real' Europeans.

The empty god of form: democratic fundamentalism

Is it *this* sad and insecure subject that Kant put his trust in when advocating the virtues of self-legislation? In his seminar on *The Ethics of Psychoanalysis*, Lacan credits *The Critique of Practical Reason* for divorcing ethics from religion and from any notion of the Good: Kant's maxim, he says, 'takes us a step further in the direction of an even greater, if not the greatest, detachment from what is known as a Sovereign Good'

(1992: 77). With Kant, what determines the morality of our action is not its *content*, but its *form*: formal law is the only 'Good', Kant acknowledges, and that form does not prescribe any particular content. As Deleuze describes it, with Kant 'the Law is no longer dependent on the Good, on the contrary, the Good is made to depend on the Law' (1989: 80–81). Applying this maxim to democracy, we can say that what determines democracy is not its *content* but its *form*, and form does not prescribe any particular content. So democracy doesn't depend on the Good, on the contrary, the Good depends on democracy: since the *form* is enough, whatever the outcome of the ballot, it is Good; the UK referendum on EU membership in June 2016 and the US elections in November 2016 are two painful examples in point: however much we may dislike the substantive result, provided the *form* was followed, we are obliged to view the outcome as 'good'. If we are obliged to see form, devoid of content, as Good, we are left, as Žižek might say (paraphrasing and extending here) with 'cold, rational imperative for democracy within the limits of reason alone' (2002: xci).

Psychoanalysis is not as confident that pure form can solve all problems; for psychoanalysis, when form is all there is, and no specific content is prescribed, form functions like a taboo: like the superego that Freud compared it to, the categorical imperative operates in a 'compulsive fashion and rejects any conscious motives' (1913: xiv). The danger, I suggest, is that the Empty God of Democracy can end up functioning as a categorical imperative, binding the subject more effectively than any concrete demand. This is because when the form is empty and the substantive content is unknown, we become even more tied to it. As Žižek points out, the lack of a specific demand imprisons the subject more effectively: paraphrasing we can suggest, Democracy doesn't want anything from you *except your very soul* (2003: 170). Or, as Lacan points out, 'the more a discourse is deprived of intention, the more it can be confused with truth, with *the* truth, with the very presence of truth in the real, in an impenetrable form' (2005: 16).

Lacan has more bad news for Kant: the core of Kantian ethics' demand for the impossible, he suggests, is a recipe for a pervert's enjoyment, because adherence to pure form generates its own enjoyment: Alenka Župancic explains this paradoxical alliance between obscene pleasure and duty: it's as if 'the pathological', she writes, 'takes revenge and imposes its law by planting a certain kind of pleasure on the path along which we follow the categorical imperative' (1996: 120). Even when we follow the categorical imperative, our motives for following it cannot escape pathological self-interest. The same, I suggest, can be the fate of the demand for democracy 'warts and all' as a recent slogan proclaimed. When the injunction to democracy becomes a categorical imperative, it becomes what I call democratic fundamentalism: if democracy is sacred, everything can be done in its name, including killing. Witness a US ex-president who put himself in the position of the instrument of democracy. Democracy was not only US's gift to other people but God's gift to people, so George Bush had no choice but to act as God's agent and bestow democracy to all and sundry, whether they wanted it or not.[5] If, as Lacan insisted, without God everything is prohibited, the inverse becomes *with* God (in our case, *with* democracy) everything is permitted (2007: 119–120).

To extrapolate Jacques Rancière's analysis of human rights, it may be that democracy was never intended to be universally available to free and equal beings. While some subjects benefitted from it, other subjects' encounter with democracy is through the so-called right of 'democratic intervention'. As Rancière suggests in a poignant parallel, what do rich people do with clothes they no longer want? They give them to charity (2004). The same seems to be the fate of democracy: once it served its purpose amongst people who are 'like us', it becomes the doctrine of imposed democratic intervention for people who do not look like us and who may, or may not, want to look like us.

In short, empty form, even in the form of democracy, does not absolve us from the task of *politics*. It is the political decision, the subject's 'Act', as Lacan calls it, not the supposedly neutral form, that holds the promise of genuine transformation: of the subject, as well as of the system.

Hole in the Big Other

We noted already the public's bemused disbelief in the case of a subject who continued to believe in the Big Other of government. In the case of the EU, this disbelief is even more pronounced. For a large section of the public, as the British referendum in June 2016 sadly showed, when it comes to the Big Other of the EU, it seems to resemble more Kafka's inscrutable Court than a benign divinity: as Žižek reminds us apropos Kafka's *The Castle*, what looks sublime and powerful when seen from afar is nothing but 'a pile of shit' when you get close (2001). What indeed do we see, when we look at EU institutions close up? The first thing that strikes constitutional lawyers is that the EU suffers from major blindspots when it comes to democracy.

From its beginnings, the EU's claim to legitimacy was plagued because of its emphasis on executive decision-making rather than legislative politics. Although it promised to inaugurate a new era of democratic transformation, a third way between direct democracy and representative democracy, the outcome was far from both ideals (Dahl, 1989; Crum, 2005). As Philip Allott noted as early as 1991, in Brussels 'what started out as a game of American football ended up as a game of soccer' (2487). In its early years the European Court of Justice, as it was then called, presided over an unprecedented and shockingly fast extension of Community powers, never failing to endorse each and every request for addition to its competences. As Joseph Weiler describes the 'jurisdictional mutation' in his seminal piece 'The Transformation of Europe', 'the principal actor instigating extension was the Court itself, although, of course, at the behest of some plaintiff' (1991: 2403). By the second stage of this transformation in Weiler's account, not only was no state activity immune from Community encroachment, it also became impossible to find an activity which was *not*, in the Court's view, within the objectives of the Treaty. As Weiler chronicles, in the 1970s and 1980s limits to the Community's competences were eroded to the extent that there *were* no limits:

> the de facto usage of Article 235, from 1973 until the Single European Act, implied a construction, shared by all principal interpretive communities, that opened up practically any realm of state activity to the Community, provided

> the governments of the Member States found accord among themselves . . . the principal feature of the period lasting from the mid-1970's into the 1980's is that precisely in this period, one of political stagnation and decisional malaise, another important, if less visible, constitutional mutation – the erosion of the limits to Community competences – took place.
>
> (1991: 2403, 2453)

Despite the erosion of limits to Community competences, the Community's increased powers did not go hand in hand with its structures: states, as Allott describes it, behaved as if the concept of democracy were a minor eccentricity if not folly, so in their dealings in Brussels they behaved like 'feudal barons' in charge of their respective national territories (1991: 2490).

With the Court instigating a continuous extension of Community powers, national law was absorbed and subsumed by Community law to the extent that, as Weiler put it, 'There simply is no nucleus of sovereignty that the member states can invoke against the community' (1991: 2435). In a meticulous analysis of the pivotal case of *Casagrande*, which sought clarification on the ambit of European Council regulations and their precedence, if any, over domestic law, the Court, Weiler suggests, 'acted as if it were an empty jurisdictional space with no limitations on the reach of Community law' (1991: 2403). In the long run, as Weiler notes in a later piece, the much-lauded appeals to democracy and representation were reduced to 'fast-track' versions of their imaginary ideals: the Commission would make decisions which were then presented to the European Parliament on a take-it-or-leave-it basis (Weiler, 2002: 564). Crucially, what Weiler accurately described as the 'seismic' event setting up the single European currency in the Treaty of Maastricht, was never approved by democratic means: not one European government sought their people's approval before handing over monetary sovereignty to the European Central Bank.

Since Weiler's seminal piece, there have been no shortage of constitutional lawyers both within and without the EU to point out the institutions' continuing democratic deficit (Crum, 2005; Davies, 2006; Follesdal and Hix, 2006; Abels, 2009; Bartl, 2015). It is not only the fact that the opportunities for EU citizens to participate in the decision-making process are limited: 'If citizens' participation is the "lifeblood" of democracy', Abel warns, 'the European Union suffers from anaemia and is in desperate need for a remedy' (2009: 2). The deficit is also substantive because at the very point where we would expect the political to come in, we encounter goals that are deemed to be beyond discussion: 'the institutional design of the EU "government" (the European Commission)', Bartl summarises, 'is premised on the possibility of uncontroversial common goals . . . goals and objectives are considered fixed, and the only possible realm of disagreement concerns the choice of the most efficient level for accomplishing predetermined tasks' (2015: 24ft1, 26). More specifically, the common market and the liberalisation of goods and services are taken as Goods in and of themselves and therefore immune to debate. As community goals are set in stone, the only question is how best to implement them, a task for which no citizens are needed, only experts (Davies, 2006): ministers, that is, to administer to spreading and implementing of the sacred gospel.

The god of the market and bureaucracy

We see here the contrast between Democracy's protest, that it is nothing but an empty vessel for receiving the will of the people through the ballot, and its contemporary manifestations. Although democracy is supposed to be content-less, not all and any content is allowed: only democracies that promote neoliberalism are allowed; and if they do not espouse neoliberalism willingly, they will be 'encouraged', if not compelled, to espouse it. As we saw earlier, the mandate from 61% of the Greek electorate to reject austerity was no match for the absolute injunction that only liberal economic policies could be imposed for a new bailout to be renewed.

Contemporary political theorists like Wendy Brown berate and bemoan the fact that capitalism undermines, compromises and erodes democracy of so-called equals: 'the construal of *homo oeconomicus* as human capital leaves behind not only *homo politicus*, but humanism itself' (2015: 42). This again is no news to European lawyers who for five decades have been witnessing a promotion of the market at the expense of democracy of Hayekian proportions. For Hayek, neoliberalism not only doesn't need democracy but also is more important than democracy; the market, he insisted in a letter to *The Times*, is indispensable to personal freedom while the ballot box is not (1978). It is no coincidence that in other letters to *The Times*, Hayek praised not only Mrs Thatcher's policies but also the policies of her friend Pinochet.[6] If Hayek worried that the beast of democracy might erode the free market, the path taken by the European Union exceeded his wildest dreams; indeed, what Pinochet's dictatorship achieved in Chile was achieved 'legally' in the EU through the European Court.

The relentless pro-market caselaw of the European Court of Justice (ECJ) treated public utilities as it treated private profit-making companies and proceeded to 'liberate' them, in other words, privatise them. As Marija Bartl summarises, 'Relying on the competition provisions of the EU Treaties, the Court interpreted EU primary law in a manner that paved the way for the liberalisation of services of general economic interest' (2015: 28). Meanwhile the Commission developed a singularly monotheistic view of the European subject as a powerful and insatiable consumer: her right to shop for the best deal at all hours of the day and night across every European country was the Commission's primary concern: the gospel according to the Commission, is that 'empowered and confident consumers' will drive Europe into the future (2015).[7]

Wendy Brown, following Foucault, also bemoans the replacement in domestic sphere of government by governance (2015: 115); again, this was already the case in the EU from its inception. When nearly two centuries ago Karl Marx observed that 'The bureaucracy is the imaginary state alongside the real state; it is the spiritualism of the state' (1970: 55), he didn't foresee that a super-apparatus would emerge where the real state would be hard to detect, but its spiritualism, its bureaucracy, would be clearly visible, perhaps even all there was. Why is bureaucracy so essential to a modern state, and to the EU in particular? Bureaucratic rules and hierarchies try to give the appearance of an automatic ordering system, of a self-founding law, a law without a lawmaker, a command without a commander, an 'act' without an actor. In Lacanese, we can say bureaucrats obsessively try to fill the void with rules, forms and unending procedures, so the Big Other's lack doesn't show.

Of course bureaucrats themselves are loath to reveal the process of law-making: 'To make public the mind and the disposition of the state', Marx continues, is 'to the bureaucracy a betrayal of its mystery'. There is always an actor, though, and an act, often a violent one, even if it remains hidden. Sooner or later, the cracks, as with any system, show through. In the case of the EU, increasing protest at the secrecy of its meetings in inverse proportion to their impact led to increasing leaks, including from ex-insiders keen to expose the political decisions behind so-called neutral administration. The 'revelations', if we can call them that, revealed what we all suspected all along: that the supposedly insignificant administrator wields untold and unaccounted-for power.[8] So despite the fact that Eurogroup finance ministers meet as if they are civil servants, to give the appearance of non-political proceedings, in 2012, as Habermas describes, the head of the European Central Bank Mario Draghi 'simulated a fiscal sovereignty he didn't possess' and subsequently the ECJ signed off his unconstitutional move.[9] The bureaucrat who leaked information to BBC journalist Robert Peston that caused a bank run in the run up to Greece's referendum is another case in point: the anonymous bureaucrat behaved not only against the rules, but made new rules: since the ECB mandate is to ensure currency stability, provoking a bank run was an overtly political move. All state actors, however, feigned ignorance: 'Don't blame *us*', they implied, 'it was all the fault of a careless bureaucrat'.[10] As Alenka Župancic puts it, 'what is most dangerous is not an insignificant bureaucrat who thinks he is God but, rather, the God who pretends to be an insignificant bureaucrat' (2000: 97). Perhaps the EU is replete with so-called insignificant bureaucrats who act, and in a sense, *are* Gods.

Bureaucratic systems invariably generate an excessive enjoyment, which, as Kafka's fiction and films like Terry Gillian's *Brazil* depicted, is hard to give up: bureaucracy's ultimate prohibition, in effect, is to make the system efficient. Since the system thrives on reproducing itself, for an outsider to come in and attempt to remedy its problems (whether that is Greece's short-lived Finance Minister Yanis Varoufakis or Robert De Niro's plumber) is anathema. Why is such a powerful system so nervous? Could it be that, as is the case with all so-called Big Others, it is at its heart pathetically impotent? After all, the arch-creed of any bureaucracy is that *quod non est in actis, non est in mundo*: what is not on file is not in the world (Vismann, 2008). If reality, as the bureaucrat insists, is what is found in files and if only what is on file is in the world, then destroying the files erases any unwanted reality. In the same way that in Chile an artist recently set on fire the records of student debts, other debts can also metaphorically, if not literally, go up in smoke.[11] In our digital age, a computer virus, as the group Anonymous lets us know all too frequently, is all it would take to bring mighty bureaucracy's power tumbling down, with cataclysmic effects for those it administers.

Original crime

What is, after all, this 'community' (European or any other) that we supposedly belong to and that, in our example, the Greek government was loath to disturb? It is not just small children, Freud reminds us, that fear being alone: 'The individual feels incomplete if he is alone' (1922: 118). The divided speaking being longs to connect with similarly divided others and be admitted to the group. To avoid being alone, she will accede to the rules, including the abuses of the group. Unfortunately, what holds a community together is not (only) shared values but often shared crimes: that is, not a noble belief in shared values but a shared dirty secret is, as Žižek has argued, more likely to bind the members of the community together (1994). Community cohesion, moreover, is usually at the expense of an excluded other. There is nothing like a threat, real or imaginary, of a dangerous 'other' to rally people into solidarity and form a so-called 'community'. The community's shared guilt at excluding, and often worse, this other further affords members of the community a specific form of enjoyment which is hard to give up but also to acknowledge. As Freud pointed out, 'It is always possible to bind together a considerable number of people in love, so long as there are other people left over to receive the manifestation of their aggressiveness' (1930: 114).

This is also the case for the constitution of a legal community. As Freud hypothesised with his myth of the primal father in *Totem and Taboo*, the founding gesture of the legal system is the murder of the father. The sons' shared guilt for this crime and collective disavowal of this guilt is responsible for creating and maintaining a community of legal subjects: 'The totem meal, which is perhaps mankind's earliest festival, would thus be a repetition and a commemoration of this memorable and criminal deed, which was the beginning of so many things – of social organization, of moral restrictions and of religion' (1913: 142). Once the new system gains supremacy, the last thing any of its members will mention is the crime at its origin. No wonder ideology distracts us daily by drawing attention to individual transgressions of the law, forgetting the absolute transgression that set up the Law itself. Like Brecht's 'what is the robbery of a bank compared to the founding of a new bank', the founding of a new legal system was preceded by a crime so great it overthrew the existing system and set up a new one. Once the crime is universalized, as Žižek explains, it no longer appears as a crime but it turns transgression into a new order (2002: 208–209). It is therefore arguable that, compared to the transgression that is the creation of the EU itself, ordinary debtors such as the members of PIIGS[12], appear amateurs. We could add, what is a few billion euros' debt in comparison to the crime that set up the ECB in the first place?

The crime at the heart of the EU was from the start the exclusion of the refugee: European integration since its inception has gone hand in hand with exclusion, an exclusion which kept and continues to keep its members bound to each other. The rhetoric of the migrant as threatening the homogeneity of European identity was present even before the current refugee crisis, with immigration and asylum-seeking being regularly and deliberately confused: as Jef Huysmans showed as early as 2000, 'Immigration has been increasingly politicised through the question of asylum, or more precisely through the (con)fusion of immigration and asylum . . . Europeanisation of migration policy indirectly sustains nationalist, racist and xenophobic reactions to immigrants' (755, 766). Weiler presciently pointed out the same fear four decades ago:

> It would be more than ironic if a polity with its political process set up to counter the excess of statism ended up coming round full circle and transforming itself into a (super) state. It would be equally ironic that an ethos that rejected the nationalism of the Member States gave birth to a new European nation and European nationalism. The problem with the unity vision is that its very realization entails its negation.
>
> (1991: 2481)

This grim prediction is the position we find ourselves in forty-five years later: Europe's loosening of statehood has turned it into a super-state, European identity has turned into euro-racism, and the elimination of internal borders has led to the strengthening and outright closure of external borders: no one can come into Fortress Europe, except, of course, to shop.

Fear of democracy

Given the Big Other is revealed regularly to be dangerously impotent, given what holds us together are not shared values but shared crimes, why the continuing clinging to an empty shell? Has democracy died but we are refusing to bury it, rendering it into a ghost that haunts contemporary debates? On this tenth session, I venture a suggestion as to Democracy's extimate core: are we attached to Democracy precisely because it's empty? The sobering news could be that we do not repress our desires because of democracy; instead, we have democracy *because* we have repressed our desires. We may need to consider that at the root of calls for democracy lies our preference to believe that our problems are not the result of our antagonisms and limitations, but the natural and inevitable outcome of the ballot. Such an explanation is infinitely more digestible to the subject than blaming others, or herself. So contrary to our noble insistence that democracy is based on universal reason or autonomy, we have to contemplate that it may be animated by repression of our desire.

For decades, parliamentary democracy did a good job of pacifying the masses, leaving the decision-making to the state apparatus so the appearance of choice was maintained even though the people never participated directly in the decision-making process. And when they did voice their opinion, through public protests and demonstrations, the form of them having spoken was taken to be sufficient to demonstrate democracy while the content of what they said was declared irrelevant. The global public protests against embarking on the war against Iraq, for instance, were used by both Bush and Blair as examples of functioning democracies, even while the substantive message of those protests was ignored. This scenario was echoed during the global 'Refugees Are Welcome' protests.[13] Massive demonstrations took place throughout Europe yet this did not encourage governments to open their borders; instead, the

German government that had initially welcomed refugees announced it was rethinking its policy.[14] As a fictional minister put it, 'demonstrations never achieve anything, if they did we wouldn't allow them' (Saramago, 2007: 120). In other words, modern democracies function and can pose as democratic as long as the citizens are passive; when citizens become active, the limits of democracy become all too apparent.

Since fantasies, however, including the fantasy of democracy, are notoriously difficult to dislodge, it takes a major trauma to let them go. The last few years have delivered trauma after trauma for would-be believers whose belief has been shaken out of its complacency. From Greek voters whose No was ignored in the summer of 2015 to the Brits staging a requiem for democracy at Westminster in April 2016, people have not only abandoned but are traversing the fundamental fantasy that Truth and the Good reside in contemporary 'decaffeinated', as I have called it, democracy.

Yet it is not enough for the subject to *see* that democracy has become decaffeinated; this newly found sight has to be accompanied with the desire to *act* on one's seeing. 'This is where', Lacan suggests,

> the political impact takes place. It concerns this question in act: Out of what knowledge is the law made? Once one has uncovered this knowledge, it may happen that that changes. Knowledge falls to the rank of symptom, seen from another perspective. And this is where truth comes in.
>
> (2007: 186)

The 'act' is the psychoanalytic equivalent of an explosion, in the subject and in turn, in her relationship to the Big Other. What is the nature of this Act? First, as Alenka Župancic argues, the ethical act cannot look for guarantees within ethics itself: ethics by definition cannot define what is ethical because what is ethical is what breaks and remakes the parameters of ethics (2000). Rather than presupposing any notion of the Good, the ethical Act *determines* what is good. For the same reason, the ethical act is not legal or illegal but *beyond* legality: the Act *redefines* the law and the boundaries of what is forbidden and what is permitted, changing the parameters of what is possible in a political system: "the ethical cannot be situated within the framework of the law and violations of the law. In relation to legality, the ethical presents a surplus or excess' (Župancic, 12).

The opening following such an Act is far from benign; the subject cuts off her existing links and takes a leap into the unknown, without guarantees: at that point, as Lacan warns, the subject encounters 'absolute disarray' and she 'can expect help from no one' (1986: 304). Like a subject at the end of analysis, the subject encounters the truth in the form of the non-existence of the Big Other; the EU that she was so keen on joining and remaining part of is as divided and lacking as she is. This terrifying leap is what is required of the subject: to return to, and extend, Mladen Dolar's discussion of psychoanalysis and the political, politics is not an affair of the government but of the individual; the political appears when the relationship between the individual and the Big Other not only shifts, but when the individual takes the plunge and *acts* on this shift. In short, the political subject is an ethical subject in Lacan's sense: one who has untied herself from the fictions, ideologies and imaginary identifications which stood in for her desire, and legislates for herself, not for the Other. The political subject is the subject that has dethroned the subject supposed to know and has taken on the task of self-legislation *in the real.*

It is not a surprise therefore that coming back to my example of Greece, my sad conclusion is that the Syriza government abandoned the analysis just when they came face to face with democracy in the real. When they faced the abyss of cutting ties with the Big Other of the European Union, rather than take the plunge into the unknown, they ran back to Mrs Merkel's bosom, reckoning that that, painful as it was, was better than cutting the umbilical cord with the EU. For psychoanalysis, that is the real tragedy: choosing a decaffeinated lie rather the truth of the Real.

Is there anything we can rescue from the tragedy? Every signifying system contains within it an excessive element, a real that eludes it: from democracy in the real to decaffeinated democracy something gets lost, an excess that continues to resist. Even when instances of decaffeinated democracy shake our belief in Democracy with a capital D, we may lose our capacity to believe but we do not lose our capacity *not* to believe: our doubt remains doubtful. My suggestion is that the symbolically dead but nevertheless undead vampire of democracy in the real continues to haunt contemporary politics. As the staging of a requiem for democracy at Westminster in April 2016 showed, we can say, a la Galileo, that, despite all the traumas, the ghost of democracy in the real, *eppur si muove*

Notes

1 www.syriza.gr/article/SYRIZA—-THE-THESSALONIKI-PROGRAMME.html#.WG_7zrGcY0Q Its '40-point programme' included increased taxation for incomes over €500,000, increased minimum wage and free health benefits to the unemployed, homeless and those with low salaries. http://links.org.au/node/2888 (accessed 23 October 2017).

2 The referendum and its outcome were closely watched and reported throughout the world: a sample of the running commentary from major news outlets: www.theguardian.com/business/live/2015/jul/05/greeces-eurozone-future-in-the-balance-as-referendum-gets-under-way—eu-euro-bailout-live
http://europe.newsweek.com/greeks-vote-reject-aid-package-referendum-official-projection-329816?rm=eu
www.reuters.com/article/us-eurozone-greece-idUSKBN0P40EO20150705
www.newyorker.com/news/john-cassidy/oxi-a-historic-greek-vote-against-austerity
(accessed 23 October 2017).

3 www.theguardian.com/business/live/2015/jul/12/greek-debt-crisis-eu-leaders-meeting-cancelled-no-deal-live (accessed 23 October 2017).

4 *Die Welt,* 11 June 2015, www.welt.de/geschichte/article142305296/Griechenland-zerstoerte-schon-einmal-Europas-Ordnung.html. For an English translation see www.zerohedge.com/news/2015-06-14/merkel-mouthpiece-die-welt-suggests-dna-based-eu-membership-greeks-are-not-real-gree (accessed 23 October 2017).

5 For a recent analysis of the role of democracy in the 'Bush Doctrine', see Maria Helena de Castro Santos and Ulysses Tavares Teixeira, 'The essential role of democracy in the Bush Doctrine: the invasions of Iraq and Afghanistan, Rev. bras. polít. int. vol.56 no.2 Brasília July/Dec. 2013.

6 For a detailed discussion of Hayek's 'Chile connection' see Robin, C. (2013) 'Nietzsche, Hayek, and the Meaning of Conservatism' www.jacobinmag.com/2013/06/nietzsche-hayek-and-the-meaning-of-conservatism/ (accessed 23 October 2017).
7 European Commission, A European Consumer Agenda, 2012; http://ec.europa.eu/consumers/archive/strategy/docs/consumer_agenda_2012_en.pdf (accessed 23 October 2017).
8 'Varoufakis Unplugged: The London Call Transcript' http://blogs.ft.com/brusselsblog/2015/07/27/varoufakis-unplugged-the-london-call-transcript/ (accessed 23 October 2017).
9 Habermas, J (2015), 'Why Angela Merkel Is Wrong on Greece' www.socialeurope.eu/2015/06/why-angela-merkels-is-wrong-on-greece/ (accessed 23 October 2017).
10 Robert Peston, 5 July 2015, 'Greek Banks "Days Away from Running Out of Cash"' www.bbc.co.uk/news/business-33403008 (accessed 23 October 2017).
11 'Chile Students' Debts Go Up in Smoke', The Guardian, 23 May 2014 www.theguardian.com/world/2014/may/23/chile-student-loan-debts-fried-potatoes (accessed 23 October 2017).
12 PIIGS is the acronym used to describe several debtor European nations: Portugal, Italy, Ireland, Greece and Spain.
13 www.theguardian.com/world/2016/sep/17/thousands-march-in-refugees-welcome-rally-in-london (accessed 23 October 2017).
14 www.independent.co.uk/news/world/europe/angela-merkel-refugees-germany-lost-control-crisis-would-turn-back-time-a7320726.html (accessed 23 October 2017).

Bibliography

Abels, Gabriele, 'Citizens' Deliberations and the EU Democratic Deficit', 2009, https://papers.ssrn.com/sol3/papers.cfm?abstract_id=2131362 (accessed 23 October 2017).

Allott, Philip, 'The European Community Is Not the True European Community', *Yale Law Journal*, 100, 2484–2500, 1991.

Althusser, Louis, *For Marx*, London: Verso, 2005.

Badiou, Alain, *Metapolitics*, London: Verso, 2005.

Badiou, Alain, 'The Democratic Emblem', in Giorgio Agamben et al. (eds), *Democracy in What State?*, New York: Columbia University Press, 2010.

Bartl, Marija, 'The Way We Do Europe: Subsidiarity and the Substantive Democratic Deficit', *European Law Journal*, 21(1), 23–43, 2015.

Brown, Wendy, *Undoing the Demos: Neoliberalism's Stealth Revolution*, London: Zone Books, 2015.

Crum, Ben, 'Tailoring Representative Democracy to the European Union: Does the European Constitution Reduce the Democratic Deficit?', *European Law Journal*, 11, (4), 452–467, 2005.

Dahl, Robert, *Democracy and Its Critics*, New Haven: Yale University Press, 1989.

Davies, Gareth, 'Subsidiarity: The Wrong Idea, in the Wrong Place, at the Wrong Time', *Common Market Law Review*, 43(1), 63–84, 2006.

Deleuze, Gilles and Leopold von Sacher-Masoch, *Coldness and Cruelty & Venus in Furs*, London: Zone Books, 1989.

Dolar, Mladen, 'Freud and the Political' *Unbound*, 4(15), 15–29, 2008.

Follesdal, Andreas and Hix, Simon, 'Why There Is a Democratic Deficit in the EU: A Response to Majone and Moravcsik', *Journal of Common Market Studies*, 44, (3), 533–562, 2006.

Freud, Sigmund, *Civilization and Its Discontents, The Standard Edition Volume XXI, (1927–1931)* London: Hogarth Press, 1930, 1955.

Freud, Sigmund, *The Future of an Illusion, The Standard Edition Volume XXI (1927–1931)* London: Hogarth Press, 1927, 1955.

Freud, Sigmund, *Group Psychology and the Analysis of the Ego, Standard Edition Volume XVIII (1920–1922)*, London: Hogarth Press, 1921, 1955.

Freud, Sigmund, *Totem and Taboo, the Standard Edition, Volume XIII (1913–1914)*, London: Hogarth Press, 1913, 1955.
Gandrud, Christofer and Hallerberg, Mark, 'Does Banking Union Worsen the EU's Democratic Deficit? The Need for Greater Supervisory Data Transparency', *Journal of Common Market Studies*, 53(4), 769–785, 2015.
Hayek, Friedrich, 'The Principles of a Liberal Social Order', *Il Politico*, 31(4), 601–618, 1966.
Hayek, Friedrich, *Letters to the Editor*, 'Dangers to Personal Liberty', *The Times*, 11 July 1978, 15.
Huysmans, Jef, 'The European Union and the Securitization of Migration', *Journal of Common Market Studies*, 38(5), 751–777, 2000.
Kafka, Franz, *The Trial*, London: Penguin, 1953.
Lacan, Jacques, *The Four Fundamental Concepts of Psychoanalysis*, London: Penguin, 1973, 1979.
Lacan, Jacques, *Freud's Papers on Technique, Book I (1953–1954)*, New York: W.W. Norton, 1975, 1991.
Lacan, Jacques, *The Ethics of Psychoanalysis, Book VII (1959–1960)*, London: Routledge, 1986, 1992.
Lacan, Jacques, *The Other Side of Psychoanalysis, 1968–1969 Book XVII*, New York: W.W. Norton, 1991, 2007.
Lacan, Jacques, *The Triumph of Religion*, London: Polity, 2005, 2013.
Lacan, Jacques, 'The Mirror Stage as Formative of the *I* Function', in *Écrits*, New York: W.W. Norton, 2006a.
Lacan, Jacques, 'Function and Field of Speech and Language in Psychoanalysis', in *Écrits*, New York: W.W. Norton, 2006b.
Lacan, Jacques, *Anxiety: The Seminar of Jacques Lacan Book X*, Cambridge: Polity, 2014.
Leeson, R. *Hayek: A Collaborative Biography: Part V, Hayek's Great Society of Free Men*, London: Palgrave MacMillan, 2014.
Marx, Karl, *Critique of Hegel's Philosophy of Right*, Oxford: Oxford University Press, 1970.
Miller, Jacques-Alain, 'Ethics in Psychoanalysis', 1991, www.lacan.com/frameV1.htm (accessed 23 October 2017).
Rancière, Jacques, 'Who Is the Subject of the Rights of Man?', *The South Atlantic Quarterly*, 297–310, 2004.
Robin, C., 'Nietzsche, Hayek, and the Meaning of Conservatism', 2013, www.jacobinmag.com/2013/06/nietzsche-hayek-and-the-meaning-of-conservatism/ (accessed 23 October 2017).
Saramago, Jose, *Seeing*, London: Vintage, 2007.
Vismann, Cornelia, *Files: Law and Media Technology*, Stanford: Stanford University Press, 2008.
Weiler, Joseph, 'The Transformation of Europe', *Yale Law Journal*, 100, 2403–2483, 1991.
Weiler, Joseph, 'A Constitution for Europe? Some Hard Choices', *Journal of Common Market Studies*, 40(2), 563–580, 2002.
Žižek, Slavoj, 'Superego By Default', *Cardozo Law Review*, 16, 925, 1994.
Žižek, Slavoj, 'The Thing from Inner Space,' 1999, www.lacan.com/zizekthing.htm (accessed 23 October 2017).
Žižek, Slavoj, *On Belief*, London: Routledge, 2001.
Žižek, Slavoj, 'From Western Marxism to Western Buddhism', 2001, www.cabinetmagazine.org/issues/2/western.php (accessed 23 October 2017).
Žižek, Slavoj, *For They Know Not What They Do: Enjoyment as a Political Factor*, London: Verso, 2002.
Žižek, Slavoj, *The Puppet and the Dwarf: The Perverse Core of Christianity*, Cambridge, MA: MIT, 2003.
Žižek, Slavoj, 'From Democracy to Divine Violence', in Giorgio Agamben et al. (eds), *Democracy In What State?*, New York: Columbia University Press, 2010.
Župancic, Alenka, 'Kant With Don Juan and Sade', in Joan Copjec (ed.), *Radical Evil*, London: Verso, 1996.
Župancic, Alenka, *Ethics of the Real*, London: Verso, 2000.

18

Why law's objects do not disappear

On history as remainder

*Christopher Tomlins**

One of law's more supple conceits is its ontology of equivalence. Law's equivalents stand for, they purport to take the place of, all that exists in life's discordant realm in a state of spatial, temporal, material, corporeal, sensorial *difference*. Equivalence commensurates the inhabitants of that realm (people, things, relations) as completely as may be necessary for their transduction into another immanent reality – the transactional universe of legal recognitions and nonrecognitions. In that universe, once restated as legal persons, physical persons become – for civic or commercial or criminal purposes – correspondent. Their differences evaporate. They are "bodies."[1] Once restated as property, physical objects, however unlike in kind, begin to manifest essential commonalities, become components of a category, homologized by the application of a legal ontology. Law's fiction – its "as if" – stands ready to corral the utterly unassimilable, but this is a fiction living within an already fictive domain, an exception for exceptions. Discourses of contract render relationships as diverse in their intimacies as marriage and employment transactionally congruent. Law routinely transubstantiates difference, produces sameness. In the service of managing life, law annihilates liveliness.

Law drains difference from the actuality of all these inhabitants by containing them within an imaginary dimension of perfect exchange. The containment is temporal, predicated on the proposition that at the moment of its apprehension, which is necessarily the present, that which differentiates the particular object of attention from law's equivalent has simply ceased to be. The object is created anew, in law, "like a number without any awkward fraction left over" (Nietzsche, 1983: 61). But the transubstantiation can never quite be complete. There is always an uncontained remnant, the *agio* or excess, the "awkward fraction left over," the obstinate remainder that defies the perfection of equivalence, the symmetry of its exchange. We know it is there because it expresses itself to us as the object's past – its revenant once-was.

"[I]t is a matter for wonder: a moment, now here and then gone . . . returns as a ghost and disturbs the peace of a later moment" (61). Let us call this surviving remnant the object's soul; not just its once-was, that is, but its living-on. And let us think of history as the means by which the soul communicates its living-on.

In this chapter I explore three propositions, or ways of thinking: of law as a dimension of not-quite-perfect exchange; of objects' surviving traces as souls; and of history as the means by which those surviving traces live on either with or against (but always separate from) law's transactional transubstantiations. In a fourth part, which spills over into a concluding fifth, I offer a gloss on what may happen when the three propositions combine.

In the beginning was the word: equivalence and exchange

Elizabeth Mertz has observed that "legal epistemology," by which she means the "distinctively legal ways of approaching knowledge" taught in law's classrooms and employed in law's texts, "has an interestingly double quality" (Mertz, 2007: 3, 213). Law's double epistemological character inheres in its simultaneous existence in two dimensions, the concrete and the abstract, between which it constantly shuttles. In the concrete, law encounters life's quotidian ephemera – a transaction, an agreement, a swindled consumer, a grieving mother, "a defective coffee urn, mislabeled poison, a loaded gun . . . a defective carriage . . . a bursting lamp" (Mertz, 2007: 64) – to which it must perforce respond. In order to respond, law shuttles to the abstract, where life's vibrant details can be assigned to doctrinal categories in order to reach legal conclusions – dangerous/not dangerous, for instance; or liable/not liable. Law's shuttle is a labor of translation, of "events and actors into their corresponding legal categories and roles" (Mertz, 2007: 131–132).

In the process, Mertz says, something is lost. Law's categories are founded on a "quest for commensurability." To restate "relatively concrete facts" at the levels of abstraction entailed by commensuration requires erasure of "the 'detailed particulars of a socially situated narrative'" of no importance to legal doctrine but of indubitable social relevance (214). "Vast differences in the cultural meaning of particular kinds of actions or items are elided and translated into a common legal language." Translation "collapses historical time and social context in the service of a new legal framework whose organizing principle is a genealogy of texts" (64). Immersion in law's language schools neophytes to distance themselves from the cleavages that, in an idealist's world, law would address. But not all forms of social experience evaporate. In Mertz's account, law's genealogy of texts perpetuates social inequality (213). Under its cloak of impersonality and abstraction, law's apparent step away from social context "conceal[s] the ways that law participates in and supports unjust aspects of capitalist societies" (134). Law's double epistemological character is actually a double political character. *Traduttore traditore.*

As is not uncommon in contemporary socio-legal studies, Mertz takes for granted the priority of the social in ontological explanation (see Constable, 2008; Tomlins, 2007, 2016). Law's apparent relation to social experience – rejecting "details and contexts that many would deem important for making just moral assessments" while slyly accommodating those that perpetuate "injustices and power inequalities" (Mertz, 2007: 134, 213) – is thus determinative of its being. Law is not just translating at arm's length; it is up to its neck, doing social work in disguise.

What, though, of the very difficulties in tutoring translation that Mertz's study illustrates? Is law so superficial a language that we should deny it a way of meaning of its own, distinct from sociality, treat it as nothing more than "a false illusion . . . to lull those in its sway" (Mertz, 2007: 213)?

Walter Benjamin identifies the translator's task to be "finding the particular intention toward the target language which produces in that language the echo of the original" (1996: 258). Both the words "intention" and "echo" signify the problematic distance between original and target, between languages. As to intention, "we must draw a distinction in the concept of 'intention' between what is meant and the way of meaning it" (257). Languages all mean the same; what is meant in each is identical. Their ways of meaning, however, are entirely distinct. The task of the translator consists, then, "in relating the distinctive ways of meaning in different languages to one another, and secondly and correlatively, in bringing out what is ultimately 'meant' – signified – by these different but related ways of meaning" (Weber, 2008: 71). Society and law, we may argue, are identical in what they mean, but the *relation* between what each means is in no sense straightforward, because their ways of meaning, their syntaxes, are quite different (see, e.g., Teubner, 1993). In that the ultimate task of the translator is the integration of all languages into one "tensionless" language, society and law may each, finally, be expressed as "pure language"; but pure language "no longer means or expresses anything" (Benjamin, 1996: 259, 261). Pure language relates to nothing external to itself. It is purely syntactical, "in-significant" as Samuel Weber so acutely puts it (2008: 78). The creation of relationships among "sentences, works of literature, and critical judgments" (Benjamin, 1996: 259) remains dependent on translation.

Translation between original and target produces only the "echo" of the original, for two reasons. First, the "essential quality" of the original "is not communication or the imparting of information" – at least not with the idea of being translated in mind. Hence translation is itself neither a subordinate nor a dependent activity, focused on the transmission of pre-existing content, but a form of composition in itself, focused on the original's "translatability," its potential not to endure as such, but to be realized anew (Benjamin, 1996: 253, 254, 262; see, generally, Weber, 2008: 53–94). Translation "shift[s] the emphasis from the ostensibly self-contained work to a relational dynamic that is precisely not self-identical but perpetually in the process of alteration, transformation, becoming-other" (Weber, 2008: 59). Second, and as this suggests, translation does not signify the original but something different, the afterlife of the original. That is, translatability signifies a historical relationship in which the life of the original takes its leave, and the original is transformed in translation.

> The reason, in short, why works are translatable, is that they have an afterlife. And they have an afterlife because in the process of living, they are also dying, or at least

> departing, taking-leave from themselves, and this from their birth. Translation does not alter this leave-taking; it does not overcome it or 'signify' anything that would nullify the departure of the original. Rather, it confirms that departure by creating a move elsewhere, a transformation, in which "the original 'undergoes a change'"
>
> (Weber, 2008: 66, 67).

By introducing a Benjaminian conception of translation, we can underline the fallacy in representing the relationship between sociality and law as no more than a translative shuttle in which essential elements of the former are illegitimately erased by the latter. First, law has its own way of meaning; second, translation does not erase originals but transforms them. Finally, in its transformations, translation confirms the original has an afterlife. And more as well. "Benjamin introduces another German word to describe it: not just *Nachleben* [afterlife] but *Fortleben*: living on, but also living away. *Fortleben* is a life that is already moving elsewhere" (Weber, 2008: 67). Here is the soul of the original that is its past (its once-was), its afterlife that survives in translation, and its living-on that moves elsewhere, lost in translation. If we understand law's translations in these terms, rather than as erasures of originals, we will see that even despite itself its exchanges – between life and language, even between its own languages – can never be perfect.

"He had known me only by sight," Joseph Conrad writes of the Harbour-Master in his novella *The Shadow-Line*,

> and he was well aware he would never see me again; I was, in common with the other seamen of the port, merely a subject for official writing, filling up of forms with all the artificial superiority of a man of pen and ink to the men who grapple with realities outside the consecrated walls of official buildings. What ghosts we must have been to him! Mere symbols to juggle with in books and heavy registers, without brains and muscles and perplexities; something hardly useful and decidedly inferior.
>
> (Conrad, 2001: 44; and see Benjamin, 2002a: 227)

Ghosts and symbols, perhaps, but not, even to the Harbour-Master, absences. Instead awkward fractions that are always left over. Residues.

In the beginning was the corpse: object lessons

The corpse is the first human residue, the first original to be translated and endowed with an afterlife. "The presence of the dead enchants our purportedly disenchanted world," writes Thomas Laqueur. The dead "dwell in us." They "haunt the living even when it is quite clear they do not and cannot exist" (Laqueur, 2015: 1, 14, 17, 79). In part, the insistence of the dead inheres in their materiality. Laqueur writes of the "aura" of physical remains (43, 48, 53, 80); the corpse is not simply the sign of an absence, but is itself a presence, or rather the presence of a difference, a body unlike other bodies, "*unliving*" (83, emphasis in original), signifying a departure but itself remaining as "remains," another awkward fraction left over. In part, the dead's insistence is of that which has absented itself. And although the replacement of an ancient by a modern regime of death – of resurrection and redemption by sanitary disposal and crematoria – has meant that the signified departure is no longer perceived by modernity as the flight of an immortal soul, death's enchantment remains, its index now "history [which] came to challenge, if not replace, metaphysics in creating 'a living solidarity with what is gone'" (186).

The living – the pre-dead, one might say – are bodies individuated by names. There is no guarantee: in law the living named body may still lose its individuation. Commoners with names – Henry Norris, William Brereton, Francis Weston, Mark Smeaton – become no more than "bodies" to be "brought up" for trial and execution in Hilary Mantel's sequel to *Wolf Hall* (Mantel, 2012: 432–433). Others, more common still, are never named at all.[2] But in modernity's slaughterhouse far too many corpses have gone missing for the body ever to serve as a reliable signifying remainder by itself. If these honored dead are not to remain "unknown," names become ever more important (Laqueur, 2015: 364–488). Thus what history indexes is not the corpse, as such, but the name. Names "make absent lives present in the here and now." They are metonymic. "A name is a cenotaph for the person who once bore it, an abyss in which we may gaze into the fullness of a life that is no more. In the names of the dead . . . we glimpse the numinosity of history" (Runia, 2014: 91).[3]

Numinosity? Roland Barthes argues the name has a purely "economic nature." The name

> is an instrument of exchange: it allows the substitution of a nominal unit for a collection of characteristics by establishing an equivalent relationship between sign and sum: it is a book-keeping method in which, the price being equal, condensed merchandise is preferable to voluminous merchandise.
>
> (Barthes, 1974: 95)

Once more, seemingly, we encounter a shuttle between concrete (a collection of characteristics) and abstract (nominal unit), another quest for commensurability that renders name meaningless, or meaningful only through exchange. But Barthes deliberately undercuts his own claim of equivalence. For "the economic function (substitutive, semantic) of the Name is stated with varying degrees of frankness." The "variety of patronymic codes" means a variety of signifieds, those that "accept the currency of the Name as pure convention" – arbitrary, depersonalized – and those that do not, that "maintain the patronymic substitute is *filled* with a person," and that insist the "appellative currency be in gold" (95, emphasis in original). If modernity has substituted the name for the soul, modernity's names exhibit *Nachleben* and *Fortleben* no less than its other translations.

Laqueur demonstrates just how badly the modern regime of death needs the living on and living away of the dead in the name. The names of the dead are "shadows of shadows," reinscriptions of loss that are "a trace of a trace" (2015: 366). But their evanescence is nailed down in endless lists, remainders "inscribed securely on a memorial wall as the unmoving shadows of men, as stand-ins for the dead whose bodies are nowhere yet everywhere close by" (417). History and memory may have replaced the metaphysics of the old regime of death, but the dead enchant "again and again" by their very persistence (550). They cannot bury themselves – hence the work of the dead is in fact and always the work of the living, who are "endlessly inventive in finding new work for the dead" to do (550) – but through history and memory the dead make their own clamorous demands that it would be idle to ignore. For safety, for example, or for vengeance.

Or for power. Here law's equivalencies take on a considerable significance; "shadows of shadows" thicken in substance. "The law plays a critical role in enabling people to live on following death" because it enforces certain of their living wishes, whether these concern "their body, property, or reputation" (Madoff, 2010: 152). Though at common law the corpse is the property of the state, state statutes in the United States grant the pre-deceased considerable discretion over the disposition of their post-mortem remains. US law also grants the pre-dead post-mortem control of property in perpetuity, ever more generous protections of copyright, and ever more stringent restraints on infringement of reputation. If the dead – at least the wealthy dead – now live on in name rather than merely in slumber awaiting resurrection, it is because law has granted the gold of their appellative currency a lasting luster. "The rising power of the American dead" (Madoff, 2010) is such that it challenges again (as in the era of entail) Thomas Jefferson's contention "*that the earth belongs in usufruct to the living*; that the dead have neither powers nor rights over it" (Jefferson, 1789, emphasis in original, and see Brewer, 1997). In the desire to transmit wealth on condition, the awkward fraction left over – the one per cent of the one per cent, as it were – has assumed a monstrous capacity.

We may find the human agency enabled by this intergenerational "living-on" comprehensible, even if it is dead human agency. What of extra-human agency? Power in things? "In the pre-modern world," writes Charles Taylor, "meanings are not only in minds, but can reside in things, or in various kinds of extra-human but intra-cosmic subjects" (2007: 33). Taylor's most potent example is holy relics, but also "other objects . . . endowed with sacramental power, like the Host, or candles which had been blessed at Candlemas" – all empowered things, embedded in the cosmos, capable of imposing meanings (32, 33, 150). "In the enchanted world, the meaning exists already outside of us, prior to contact; it can take us over, we can fall into its field of force. It comes on us from the outside" (34; and see Honig, 2015).

Taylor's "porous boundary" between human subjects and "charged things" with incorporated meanings and causal capacities (35, 36–39) is hardened by Cartesian dualism: meanings can exist only in minds that think; matter is mechanism; from the firm boundary between mind and matter the self emerges. "Science and virtue require that we disenchant the world, that we make the rigorous distinction between mind and body, and relegate all thought and meaning to the realm of the intra-mental" (131). But objects are not so easily conquered (Bennett, 2010). What of the auratic art work, which "sees us," and "in its classic plenitude, seems to return our gaze" (Eiland and Jennings, 2014: 59, 515)?[4] What of the non-auratic work, the epitome of which, for Benjamin, was the intensely allegorical baroque *Trauerspiel* (mourning play)? In the *Trauerspiel*, "props, emblems, and . . . depersonalized, cipherlike human figures" wander the stage, "things and thinglike humans" with "no intrinsic relation to a meaningful present or to a history of salvation" but "instead invested by the allegorist with a hidden and wholly fallen significance" (Eiland and Jennings, 2014: 228). Plots turn on "some trivial stage-property" which "bears down on the victim." What Benjamin describes as "apparently dead objects" secure power over human life. They "take on a life of their own, avoiding or denying the messages and meanings that the playwrights themselves may be seeking to represent" (Benjamin, 1998: 132; Martel, 2012: 58). In the fallen world of the mourning play, "chance, in the sense of the breaking down of the action into fragmented elements or things, corresponds entirely to the meaning of the stage property" (Benjamin, 1998: 133). Humans and things occupy the same level of existence. "Humans are treated as things, and things as human" (Weber, 2008: 152). Emblems replace names. Objects rebel. The revenant dead haunt the action from the spirit-world (Benjamin, 1998: 136; Weber, 2008: 152; Martel, 2012: 58). These are not legality's post-mortem projections of living wishes; these are animated remainders.

Lewis Hyde's classic account of gift exchange reveals another porous boundary, between thing and "life." Whether in itself naturally alive or inert, the gift bestows life and increase – "the core of the gift, the kernel," its "spirit [*hau*]" – on both recipient and, through the circle of reciprocation, giver (1983: 36). Hyde argues the distinction alive/inert actually lacks meaning "because even when a gift is not alive it is treated as if it were, and whatever we treat as living begins to take on life." As a result, gifts "are *felt* to increase – in worth or in liveliness – as they move from hand to hand" (25, emphasis in original). The increase that is bestowed, moreover, "stays in motion and follows the object," creating both spiritual facts "when gifts are the agents of a spirit that survives the consumption of its individual embodiments," and social facts in that the circulation of gifts "creates community" (37).[5] Gifts that cease to be gifts, that are converted to commodities and sold out of the circle of gift exchange, are "used up" – wasted. "In a group that derives its cohesion from a circulation of gifts the conversion of gifts to commodities will have the effect of fragmenting the group, or even destroying it," for the gift's increase no longer follows the object. Instead it remains with the seller, "stays behind as profit" (21, 23, 37, 75).

Citing Marcel Mauss (1967), Hyde's account treats property removed from the gift circle and commodified as a literal loss of life and identity, for the gift economy blurs the distinction between persons and things. "Things had a personality and a virtue of their own," Mauss writes of ancient Roman law. "Things are not the inert objects which the laws of Justinian and ourselves imply. They are a part of the family [*familia*]." Justinian law, however, divided the *familia* into *res* and *personae*. It "passed beyond that antiquated and dated gift economy, encumbered by personal considerations, incompatible with the development of the market, trade, and productivity," heralding modernity's "system of property, alienation and exchange" (Mauss, 1967: 46, 48, 52; and see Hyde, 1983: 86).

Yet even the object at the core of modernity's system, the commodity, is endowed with a form of "life," for although, as Marx observed, it is "at first sight, a very trivial thing, and easily understood," in fact, on closer examination, it is "a very queer thing, abounding in metaphysical subtleties and theological niceties" (Marx, 1967: 71). True, Lukács could claim that "beneath *the cloak of the thing* lay a relation between men . . . beneath the quantifying crust there was a qualitative living core" (1971: 169, emphasis added) that, once revealed, made possible a recognition "of the fetish character *of every commodity* based on the commodity character of labor power," such that Marx's commentary on commodity fetishism "contains within itself the whole of historical materialism and the whole self-knowledge of the proletariat seen as the knowledge of capitalist society" (169, 170, emphasis in original). But Marx himself was in less of a hurry. "A commodity is . . . a mysterious thing" – in other words something other than a cloaked relation (Marx, 1967: 72). Commodity production was the most general and embryonic form of bourgeois production; it made an early appearance and its fetish character was hence "comparatively easy" to understand.

> But when we come to more concrete forms, even this appearance of simplicity vanishes. Whence arose the illusions of the monetary system? To it, gold and silver, when serving as money, did not represent a social relation between producers, but were natural objects with strange social properties. And modern economy, which looks down with such disdain on the monetary system, does not its superstition come out as clear as noon-day, whenever it treats of capital?
>
> (Marx, 1967: 82–83)

Under such circumstances it was all too understandable that "a definite social relation between men" should assume "in their eyes, the fantastic form of a relation between things" (72). This was what Benjamin would call *phantasmagoria*, the idolatrous effect of the fetishized commodity writ large as an entire social apparatus of human actors and the objects that acted upon them, demanding representation (Martel, 2012: 47–48), and knowable only from its remainders, "the rags, the refuse" (Benjamin, 2002a:460).

The enlivened thing is no stranger to legal history. We have already encountered it in Mauss's observations on early Roman law. In medieval and early modern law, "the Christian can feel the spirit move inside all property. Everything on earth is a gift and God is the vessel" (Hyde, 1983: 139). Unsurprisingly, then, property – whether thing or animal – that "moved to the death" of a person was held responsible (considered possessed of an evil will and required to make recompense as such) and given back to God as a *deodand* (Dayan, 2011: 128). The common law rule was eventually abolished in 1846, but we still destroy animals that injure or kill humans, though now our reasoning is hygienically scientific; behavioral rather than retributive (209–252). The law of slavery was in largest part a law not of persons but of animate objects. To hire a slave from the slave's owner, for example, was considered a contract of bailment, and, said Joseph Henry Lumpkin, Chief Justice of the Georgia Supreme Court, "the hirer is bound to exercise ordinary diligence in taking care of the property." Not just "a proper regard for the interest of the owner" demanded it, but "humanity to the slave," for they were "incapable of self-preservation, either in danger or in disease" (*Gorman v. Campbell* 14 Ga. 137, 143 (1853); see, generally, Dayan, 2011: 113–176).

Science and technology studies (STS) and actor network theory (ANT) have alerted us to the continued porosity of the boundary between people and things, the capacity for all actants within a relational network, human and non-human, to become mediators, to exhibit forms of agentive capacity. Hyde argues that law has shed "the emotional and spiritual content of a total social phenomenon" (1983: 88) – in other words that its dessicated translations create perfect equivalents that leave no remainders. But Bruno Latour has applied STS/ANT's mode of thinking to the analysis of law (although not without some difficulty, see, e.g., Tomlins, 2012: 48–50), in a fashion that is of considerable significance for the history of law.[6] What are the larger implications of this? Latour argues they are both epistemological and ontological. They are epistemological because "*all* questions of epistemology are questions of social order. In other words, there are no true transcendences. Either you have the two – that is, social realism and natural realism, or you get rid of the two" (Crawford, 1993: 261, emphasis added; see, generally, Latour, 1993, Davies, 2017). To continue:

> What do you get when you put the two together and begin to trace in addition to the horizontal axis – from realism to socialism – another vertical axis? You get a grasp on the sort of objects science and technology are interested in – the quasi-objects, which are collective because they circulate . . . They are "real," but real quasi-objects do not have the characteristic of being things out there, passive and boring, waiting to be unveiled. Things become active, and the collective becomes made of things – circulating things – which do not have the characteristics they have in the realist argument. So these hybrids (quasi-objects) start resembling what our world is made of. It is not that there are a few hybrids; it is that there are *only* hybrids. And the endpoints – the purely social relation, which will be used for the social constructivist argument, and the purely natural construction, which will be used for the naturalist argument – don't exist. They might exist, but only as belated end products. They appear or are called upon once all the arguments have already been settled.
>
> (Crawford, 1993: 261, emphasis in original)

From this epistemology it is but a short step to ontology.

> What I am doing is a crossing of ontology and social theory with actor theory. Actor theory is more ontological because it talks about the things and not the meaning of the things. It also talks about the social, but not the Durkheimian social . . . You can't alternate between social realism and naturalism, and then throw in some semiotics or discourse analysis. You must do the three together; then immediately you realize that in science studies we have, all along, been studying phenomena that have the characteristics of being narrative, collective, and outside. They are quasi-objects; they are not of our own making. We build them collectively, and they are narrated. That is it: real, narrated, social. It

> is perfectly simple. Now if these characteristics are put together, you have the trace – the trajectory in a network.
>
> (Crawford, 1993: 264)

The quasi-object is more than an object. It is an object plus (or *plus*). It has no exact equivalent and so it leaves a trace; a fraction is left over.

In the beginning was the deed: committing history

I have argued that whereas law creates (and functions through) equivalents, history is the register of the trace, the living-on, of the object. Hence, unlike law's content, history's content is remainders, whether of people, things, or events. An event, Slavoj Žižek tells us, is an "effect that seems to exceed its causes" (Žižek, 2014a: 5). In other words, whether an event exists depends on the creation of an excess, something that previously did not exist. Were there no excess, or residue, there would be nothing (whether person, thing or event) for history to register (Foucault, 2014: 81).

Excesses come in many forms. If, as Goethe's Faust declares, in the beginning was not the word but the deed (Goethe, 1834: 46), for there to be history at all the deed cannot be complete. For if the deed is complete nothing will have been left undone, and if everything is done there can be no remainder. In which case there is no history: no time, no past. Completion dispatches both. This is why if history is to begin, Creation must be undone by the Fall.[7] And this is why, whether considered as a historical category (origination) or as an event, origin involves repetition as well as singularity.

> An 'origin' is historical in that it seeks to repeat, restore, reinstate something anterior to it. In so doing, however, it never succeeds and therefore remains 'incomplete, unfinished.' Yet it is precisely such incompleteness that renders origin historical. Its historicality resides not in its ability to give rise to a progressive, teleological movement, but rather in its power to return incessantly to the past (the repetitious cycle of coming-to-be and passing-away) and, through the rhythm of its ever-changing repetitions, set the pace for the future.
>
> (Weber, 2008: 89)

Both singularity and repetition are forms of excess: singularity in Žižek's sense of exceeding cause; repetition in the sense of the incompletion of the deed, the remainder. Each leaves a trace. Totalitarianism, one may say, is the attempt of the profane to eliminate every remainder, every trace; to complete, and thus to end history. This is why "*even the dead* will not be safe from [this] enemy if he is victorious" (Benjamin, 2003: 391, emphasis in original).

To write of history as a register of traces alone, however, is insufficient. The act of registration is not passive. History is a constant struggle of making and being made, a struggle over what trace will register – what will count, what will be ignored and forgotten. Gottfried Keller notwithstanding, the truth *will* run away from us. For "the true image of the past flits by," to be seized only "at the moment of its recognizability" or "never seen again" (Benjamin, 2003: 390–391). The practice of history, whether in the form of classic historicism (Tomlins, 2012: 37) or its more modern legatees, such as the *longue durée* of the Annales school (e.g., Braudel, 1995), exhibits powerful explanatory biases to accumulation and continuity, so much so that the Dutch philosopher of history, Eelco Runia, has pronounced professional history hosophobic – allergic to mess (matter "out of place" as Mary Douglas observed).[8] For Runia, history moves in "unforeseeable leaps and bounds . . . neither implied nor determined by what the actors – that is, ultimately, we ourselves – bring to the diving board" (Runia, 2014: xiii). When confronted by "the new – the exhilarating, frightening, sinful, sublimely new" (effects that exceed their causes), however, historians overwhelmingly approach it linearly and contextually, as the product of what has been (xiii). Effects cease to exceed their causes, calm returns, remainders that persist are diminished to wholly manageable proportions and, filed within the historian's taxonomy of what has been, fulfill expectations. The present is produced from the past by the necessary effect of concatenation; the past is derived from the present by the present's narratives of fact. One is reminded of James Franklin Jameson more than a century ago, likening himself to an artisan patiently fashioning the mounds of knowledge-bricks that would form history's walls, trusting "that the best architect that ever was cannot get along without bricks, and therefore trying to make good ones" (see Higham, 1965: 25).

Continuity fashions history as temporal linearity, a problematic characterization that historians overcome with (but in doing so, perpetuate) strategies of representation: "Pasts – understood as the non-present, the absent – are literally re-presented in the present through historical narratives and/or imaging. The past thus seems accessible only as representation, which is then made to produce meaning through hermeneutic reading" (Banerjee, 2015: 963). Representationalism allows the past to have meaning only in its relationship to "history" considered as the present's science of representing. "[W]e make meaning of the past by referring it to the present, and of the present by referring it to the past, producing a circularity in which the ontological status of the past becomes irrelevant" (963). This is why "every age must strive anew to wrest tradition away from the conformism that is working to overpower it" (Benjamin, 2003: 391; see also 391–392).

Representationalism, says Runia, is "a histrionic defeatism about the ability to know the world, coupled to a dissimulated determination to turn the medium into the message" (2014: 146). For in fact we exist in a condition of temporal simultaneity, in which "'presence' wells up from the past into the present" through metonymic "fistulae" or "'leaks'" in time, in which "the past is, in a very real sense, *bigger* than us, an attribute of the field we are in . . . a part of the reality in which we operate" (67, 105, emphasis in original); an excess. Linearity and taxonomy are our own organizational impositions on time, the creation of order. But fashioning continuity is simply a denial of "man's inordinate ability to spring surprises on himself" (xi, 55, 59). History is not "a foreign country, something of the past" but "something of the present, something operative in the here and now . . . in us" (108). To grapple with both the operative presence of the past and the reality of discontinuity (the deed that precedes its comprehension, the sublime historical event, "monsters of our own making," wars and revolutions) requires of historians a willingness "to come forward with questionable hypotheses about how we actually *make* history, how the new erupts from the old, how we mutate and evolve by acting in ways that somehow we recognize as historical" (145, emphasis in original).

Mutation and evolution have nothing to do with "progress" (116). The deed is pure action, what Runia calls "flight forwards," the vertiginous leap away from quotidian contingencies that makes history. "Sublime historical events are cascades of fleeing forward brought about by people who sensed or thought that they could thrive in ever more uncertain, unpleasant, or downright dangerous circumstances" (166). Only in the wake of the event comes complexity, "the clutter of accomplished facts with which we find ourselves when our fleeing forward has come to an end" (168). And with complexity come the scholars, whose task is to harmonize the event with what went before, reduce its dissonance, tame its excess, cabin its remainder, subordinate the deed to word (8–9, 125–127). But the event itself – contingency become necessity – "cannot be reduced to simple change" (Žižek, 2014a:159–160).

The hatch and brood of time?[9] Alchemy and abstraction

Let us now attempt our gloss.

In 1539, in Staufen – a small town in the Black Forest region of Germany lying below the castle of Baron Anton von Staufen – there occurred the "miserable death" of one Doctor Faustus, "an extraordinary nigromancer"; that is, practitioner of black magic, alias necromancer (Binswanger, 1994: 1–2). Faustus had been summoned to Staufen by the Baron who, fallen on hard times, was in need of alchemical gold. Whether or not Faustus succeeded is unrecorded, but his fame caught the eye of Christopher Marlowe and, rather later, of Goethe. In Marlowe's late sixteenth-century text, theological themes are uppermost, unleashed by Faustus's fabled pact with Mephistopheles. Two centuries later, however, Goethe makes the legend an allegory for commodification – the destruction of the commons and its gift economy, and the monetization of all values. Alchemy's "artificial gold" is re-presented as a scheme to create paper money, backed by imaginary mineral resources and made material by state authority. "No one will actually demand that the state redeem the notes with gold," writes Hans Christoph Binswanger. "The idea that one *could* – the mere sense of security – is enough." Legible paper emissions magically raise "the 'buried treasure'"; an immediate increase of wealth occurs "without labor or actual effort" (14, emphasis in original).

As Adam Smith noted, the consequences are profound. Though labor was "the real measure of the exchangeable value of all commodities," once money had become "the common instrument of commerce," the exchangeable value of a commodity came to be estimated not by the quantity of labor that could be had in exchange for it, but by the quantity of money. And once paper took the place of gold and silver money,

> the quantity of the materials, tools, and maintenance which the whole circulating capital can supply, may be increased by the whole value of gold and silver

> which used to be employed in purchasing them. The whole value of the great wheel of circulation and distribution is added to the goods which are circulated and distributed by means of it,

moved by "The judicious operations of banking" along "a sort of wagon-way through the air" (Smith, 1976: 48–49, 296, 321).[10] Smith readily admitted that nothing could be secure once "suspended upon the Daedalian wings of paper money" (321). Marx and Engels would use the same metaphor to the same end. "All fixed, fast-frozen relations, with their train of ancient and venerable prejudices and opinions, are swept away, all new-formed ones become antiquated before they can ossify. All that is solid melts into air" (Marx and Engels, 1955: 58).

Alchemy's transmutations are dependent on an additive, "a qualityless, mysterious – and therefore black – primal substance" (Binswanger, 1994: 7). What, we may ask, is the additive that transforms paper into money? In Goethe's *Faust* it is the imperial signature – or more precisely the legality it bestows. And what is it that turns the latent, prospective wealth of paper money into value? "Faust's answer," says Binswanger, "is unequivocal: 'property and dominion I want to gain'" (1994: 18). Nature is appropriated and converted into money values through a particular kind of property right that revolutionizes prior conceptions of the relationship between nature and property. "By *property* Faust does not simply mean landed property in the sense of a *patrimonium*" – inherited property that brings with it a duty to tend nature, human reciprocity with thing.

> What he has in mind is rather the *dominium* or property right of Roman law, which grants the owner the right to treat his property exactly as he wishes – as master [*dominus*]. This right is the *ius utendi et abutendi re sua*: 'the right to make use of and consume what is yours.'
>
> (Binswanger, 1994: 19, emphasis in original)

In Runia's terms, Faust has committed history; he has fled forwards in a "horrendous, sublime" act (Runia, 2014: 13). And with his flight the economy we encountered in section II, the gift economy "in which nature and labor dominate" falls to "the alchemical economy, in which money and money capital play the decisive role" (Binswanger, 1994: 89).[11]

For Binswanger, money capital is the alchemical economy's mysterious additive that enables Faust's revolution (28), the philosopher's stone (3) that creates ever more of itself from itself, as in Marx's famous theogeny of capital (1967: 154). But (as Binswanger notes) Goethe's *Faust* is at least as much a citation of transmutational law – of the Bank of England's legally authorized paper money issues, of the *Code Napoleon*'s recreation of ownership as "the right to enjoy and use things in the most absolute manner" (1994: 31–32). The alchemical economy's additive, its qualityless primal substance, one may argue, is not money capital but law.

What law creates for this economy is imaginative abstraction – "man's ability to distance himself from nature through his intellect *and to construct a world with its own laws and goals*" (1994: 53, emphasis added). Examining that world, Brenna Bhandar (2014: 206) finds it constituted by a "conflation of self with property" that reproduces the "blurring of boundaries between thing and person" with which we have already become familiar, but on decisively altered terms, those of human mental ascendancy. Blurred boundaries produce both the slave as commodity, the person that is simultaneously a commoditized thing, and the slave's master, the person for whom ownership is not merely a consequence of prior possession but an extension of self. We are familiar with Locke's derivation of title from the self's original mixture of labor with resources (Locke, 2001: 12–22). But Locke is still a fixture of the pre-alchemic economy. Faust's flight forwards puts him instead squarely in the company of Jeremy Bentham, whose notion of ownership, "an *expectation* of being able to use the property as one wishes" (Bhandar, 2014: 209, emphasis in original), is far more of an abstraction than Locke's, an emanation not of labor but of the owner's very self, "not material" but "a mere conception of the mind," its desires and fears (Bhandar, 2014: 210; Bentham, 1871: 112, 115):

> *Pain of Losing*. Every thing which I possess, or to which I have a title, I consider in my own mind, as destined always to belong to me. I make it the basis of my expectations, and of the hopes of those dependent upon me; and I form my plan of life accordingly. Every part of my property may have in my estimation, besides its intrinsic value, a value of affection, as an inheritance from my ancestors, as the reward of my own labor, or as the future dependence of my children. Every thing about it, represents to my eye that part of myself which I have put into it – those cares, that industry, that economy, which denied itself present pleasures to make provision for the future. Thus our property becomes a part of our being, and cannot be torn from us, without rending us to the quick.

It hardly needs emphasizing that Bentham's "expectation" theory of property, "the persuasion of being able to draw such or such an advantage from the thing possessed, according to the nature of the case" (1871: 112), is no different from Faust's *dominium* – "the right to make use of and consume what is yours." Faust resembles Bentham, too, in his desire to build "a look-out tower" on the literal ruins of the gift economy "whence I can view the boundless space" that is his domain (Binswanger, 1994: 38, 89–90, 94). Noting Faust's triumphant exclamation, "The traces of mine earthly being cannot in aeons perish," Binswanger comments that "Faust has, in his imagination, overcome mortality" (38). One might consider Bentham guilty of the same conceit – the man who considered property grounded on a relation "not material" but "metaphysical . . . a mere conception of the mind" (Bentham, 1871: 112); the man "who had himself dissected by his favorite student and asked that his eviscerated body be stuffed so that it could preside over the governing body of University College London" (Laqueur, 2015: 65). But neither can overcome their dependence upon "the work of law" to affirm, enact, complete their metaphysics. "Property and law are born together, and die together. Before laws were made there was no property; take away laws, and property ceases" (Bentham, 1871: 113).

Neither Faust nor Bentham could avoid law, but that hardly mattered. Law's work of abstraction, after all, was done on their behalf. In any case, both had other things to worry about.

Bentham was afraid of ghosts.

> In no man's judgement can a stronger persuasion of the non-existence of those sources of terror have place than in mine; yet no sooner do I lay myself down to sleep in a dark room, and my eyes keep open, these instruments of terror obtrude themselves.
>
> (Bentham, 1962: 84)

Who were they, these ghosts? They were the remainders that Bentham's laws, his system of legislated social disciplines, had failed to snuff out: unobserved convicts, unmanaged paupers, uncivilized savages who would tear at the heartstring of his property. They were, in a word, history – living on beyond, or despite, his "machine of legally maintained social relations" (Annette, 1979: 75).

Faust, too, is history's hostage. In the legend, Faustus pledges his soul in return for Mephistopheles's services. But not in Goethe's *Faust*.

> What does the soul matter to Faust, or to modern man, who sees his whole happiness in technological progress and the *infinite* growth of prosperity? It would be easy for Faust or modern man to pledge his soul: it would be pledging a nonvalue

something never to be realized (Binswanger, 1994: 49, emphasis in original). Mephistopheles is no fool. Faust must pledge something important – time. If he loses, "*time* will be *finished* for him" (49, emphasis in original).[12] What does this mean? Binswanger explains (50, emphasis in original):

> What really matters to Faust is time itself, since he wishes to eternalize it in the sense of the alchemical process, *while still in this life*. He pledges the asset that is far more important to himself and to contemporary man than a soul: time's infinity in the sense of unlimited progress and the unlimited growth of the economy.

What is the wager? It is that Faust will experience a "supreme moment" in time that he will not willingly surrender to the eternalized passage (the *nunc stans*) of time (Binswanger, 1994: 48; Goethe, 1834: 66):

> If ever to the passing hour I say,
> "Yet stay awhile, thou art so beautiful!"
> Then bind me in thy fetters hand and foot;
> Then willingly I'll perish; then be tolled
> My passing bell; then be thy service ended.
> The clock may stand – the hand drop off – time be
> For me no more.

Faust's conceit is that his eternalized alchemical economy will conquer history. He wagers that he cannot be overcome by time, that no metonymic "spot of time" can pierce him through (Runia, 2014: 100–105). "He pledges humanity's *time*. And *this* wager Faust loses." The loss, says Binswanger, is inevitable. "He loses *time* the very moment he imagines he can hold onto it with his vision of eternal progress" (Binswanger, 1994: 50, emphasis in original). In a moment that bears every possible resemblance to what Alain Badiou would term "an event" – namely the realization of a positive value of existence at a site of maximal intensity (Badiou, 2011: 286) – Faust smashes into the remainder that contradicts "eternal progress." Like Bentham, his mental ascendancy proves vulnerable to history. "By blindly raising his existence to such a moment, Faust loses the bet; and in this sense," Binswanger concludes, "the play *Faust* has a bad ending" (48).[13]

Conclusion: the mad dance of the opposites

It is well known that some years ago, Patricia Williams also wrote of alchemy, specifically *The Alchemy of Race and Rights*. She did so, one might say, to plead against another bad ending. In its zeal to unmask law's instabilities and indeterminacies, Critical Legal Studies (the US variant) had concluded that "rights" were meaningless, nothing more than "talk" that masked the reality of powerlessness, the "universalism of need and oppression" (Williams, 1991: 164, and generally 146–165). Williams's own relationship to law was fraught – "Some part of me knows that it is intelligent for me to be schizophrenic" (207). So she well understood why CLS might find law's rights talk vacuous. "Law" was hypostatized schemata of categorization and definitional polarity; it was "transcendent, acontextual, universal legal truths" on one hand, "pure procedures" on the other, articulated in either case by "objective 'unmediated' voices" – the bench, the bar, the academy. Law was an avoidance of the real, a language that spoke hypnotically of rights and precepts, accompanied by a spirit that was "utterly meaningless or empty" (8–10, 16).

Nevertheless, Williams resisted CLS's dismissal of rights. She resisted not because, critical theory notwithstanding, she clung to an inherent value in the reified concept – "right" – itself. She did not. She resisted for the entirely different reason that an "immense alchemical fire" (163) had created something out of law's vacuous nothing.

The fire of which Williams wrote was the fire of race. Race was the alchemic additive that forged rights out of law's emptiness.

> To say that blacks never fully believed in rights is true. Yet it is also true that blacks believed in them so much and so hard that we gave them life where there was none before; we held onto them, put the hope of them into our wombs, mothered them and not the notion of them. And this was not the dry process of reification, from which life is drained and reality fades as the cement of conceptual determinism hardens around – but its opposite. This was the resurrection of life from ashes four hundred years old.
>
> (Williams, 1991: 163)

If the additive of race showed that "rights" could be given substance, the objective should not be to discard rights as "empty" but to generalize upon the discovery by spreading them across all of abstraction's blurred boundaries.

> In discarding rights altogether, one discards a symbol too deeply enmeshed in the psyche of the oppressed to lose without trauma and much resistance. Instead, society must *give* them away. Unlock them from reification by giving them to slaves. Give them to trees. Give them to cows. Give them to history. Give them to rivers and rocks . . . Flood [all of society's objects and untouchables] with the animating spirit that rights mythology fires.
>
> (Williams, 1991: 165, emphasis in original)

It does no violence to Patricia Williams's alchemy of race and rights, or to its lessons, if it is amended in one particular. Her alchemic additive is less the concept, race, than African American life experience in contest with white supremacy; or in other words, history – the remainders of bodies written in pain and blood, of rags and refuse. The amendment does no violence because it is already present in Williams's account: it is clear that her understanding of the meaning of "race" is experiential and historical. Williams's own self-understanding is soaked in her family's history (for example, 154–155). Her alchemical fire conjures "the resurrection of life from ashes four hundred years old." It fuses a nation from "the kindling of several generations" (163). But this is a particular kind of history. It is not the anodyne "change over time" of professional self-description, it is Eelco Runia's "flight forwards," the vertiginous leap that is precisely *away* from "the clutter of accomplished facts" into the abyss of *making* history. For "the individual unifying cultural memory of black people is the helplessness of living under slavery or in its shadow" (154). In that shadow what choice is there but "flight forwards"?

Runia (2014: 116) has told us flight forwards has nothing to do with "progress" and everything to do with what Žižek calls "the mad dance of the opposites" (Žižek, 2014b:26). Dialectics, in other words. The terrain is crowded. Capital, too, "is ultimately engaged in nothing but a desperate flight forwards in an attempt to escape its own debilitating inherent contradiction" (166). Even as Patricia Williams's fire painfully refines rights from four hundred years of debt-slavery, capital is busily recreating rights as indebtedness (Žižek, 2014b: 48–57).

We are human, so we have no choice but to remember. But remembrance brings with it the power to judge and find worthy, or to reject and destroy. The critical theory that Williams would enlist in her work is knowledge formed in judgment of the past; it represents opportunity for a new knowledge of right (and rights) formed in the present that overcomes, or at least combats, what are presented to us as life's accomplished facts. *This* is the real service that history can perform in the mad dance of the opposites, history as remainder. For even slaves leave traces: inky scratches in ledgers (Johnson, 2013: 244–279); Conradian ghosts that can haunt Benthams.

> [S]ince we are the outcome of earlier generations, we are also the outcome of their aberrations, passions and errors, and indeed of their crimes. It is not possible wholly to free oneself from this chain. If we condemn these aberrations and regard ourselves as free of them, this does not alter the fact that we originate in them. The best we can do is to confront our inherited and hereditary nature with our knowledge of it, and through a new stern discipline combat our inborn heritage and implant in ourselves a new habit, a new instinct, a second nature, so that our first nature withers away.
>
> (Nietzsche, 1983: 76–77)

By definition, a mad dance of opposites can have no certain outcome. "But here and there a victory is nonetheless achieved" (77).

Notes

* I wish to thank Genevieve Renard Painter for her acute reading of an earlier draft of this chapter and her multiple suggestions for revision.

1 Just as, say, for an astronomer, a "celestial body" is any natural body outside the Earth's atmosphere.

2 For example:

Enter Clown.

Tamora:	How now, good fellow! wouldst thou speak with us?
Clown:	Yea, forsooth, an your mistress-ship be emperial.
Tamora:	Empress I am, but yonder sits the emperor.
Clown:	'Tis he. God and Saint Stephen give you god-den: I have brought you a letter and a couple of pigeons here.
Saturninus:	(reads the letter) Go, take him away, and hang him presently.
Clown:	How much money must I have?
Tamora:	Come, sirrah, you must be hanged.
Clown:	Hanged! By' lady, then I have brought up a neck to a fair end.

Exit.

This brief encounter occurs in IV.4 of *Titus Andronicus* (Shakespeare, 2000), line 39–50. Francis Barker (1993: 167–168) comments as follows: "This moment is stunning . . . strange, unheimlich, and, I have found, haunting. It pointed me to some historical research." Barker finds (178–179) that during the 65 complete years (1559–1624) comprising the reigns of Elizabeth I and James I – in effect Shakespeare's era – 24,664 men and women were executed in England and Wales, and 11,441 died in gaol. Expressed in terms of the modern (1989) English and Welsh population, these figures equate to annual totals of 4,697 executed, and 2,179 dead in gaol. For the United States (1988) they equate to annual totals of 22,862 executed, and 10,604 dead in gaol. For UK estimates for a later period (1770–1868) see Gatrell, 1994.

3 However, see Honig (2013: 61–66) for queer critique of the AIDS Names Project quilt and its staging of death as post-political.

4 Benjamin defines aura as "a strange tissue of space and time: the unique apparition of a distance" resting on "uniqueness and permanence" (2002c: 104–105); resting, too, not on creation but on the distance from creation that transmission and reception create.

5 In creating/sustaining community, gift circulation should be read as a central element of the "customs in common" that characterize economies of the commons (common pasturage, common fields, gleaning rights, and so forth). See, generally, Neeson, 1983, Thompson, 1991, and section IV of this chapter.

6 Examining the broad trend in the humanities toward (a) dissolution of "the dichotomy between subject (human, social, representational) and object (thing, material, real)" and (b) realization "that characteristics we traditionally associate with people, such as agency and activity, are not the sole preserve of humankind," Tom Johnson (2015: 408–411) argues for a particular impact on how law is to be understood. "First, law is commonly seen as a discourse, something that is distinct from, yet gives meaning to, things in the 'real world.' This severance is in fact highly suspect: law does not stop at the end of legislation or the pronouncement of a verdict, but goes on to have important effects in the world. Thus, the very idea of 'the law' as a discourse separate from 'real life' is itself 'a crucial boundary-making event' (citing Delaney, 2002: 79). This is not simply to claim, as many historians now recognize, that law cannot be studied apart from its social and political context. It is, rather, to conceive 'law' as a quality that can inhabit physical stuff, as well as legal treatises and social practices." Second, "past legal systems attributed certain characteristics to humans and non-humans." The objective for legal history should be to study how and why they did so, how "legal processes formed one of the means by which "objects" were created and policed . . . Law projected a certain kind of materiality, and these projections manifested in material things."

7 We should note that having begun by linking Creation to deed, not word, Faust will later link himself to Creation and claim its completion: "the deed is all" (Goethe, 2003: line 10187). But as we shall see (in section IV), he is mistaken. "Only the Messiah himself completes all history," writes Benjamin, as if in admonition, "in the sense that he alone redeems, completes, creates its relation to the messianic" (Benjamin, 2002b: 305).

8 "Uncleanness is matter out of place," Douglas wrote in 1966. "Uncleanness or dirt is that which must not be included if a pattern is to be maintained" (Douglas, 2002: 50). As she indicated (202–203) here she was following William James (1920, 133), who had offered for consideration "the interesting notion . . . of there being elements of the universe which may make no rational whole in conjunction with the other elements, and which, from the point of view of any system which those elements make up, can only be considered so much irrelevance and accident – so much 'dirt' as it were, matter out of place." James, of course, found this phenomenon of interest. Quantitative scholars prefer to "clean" their data – eliminate its "noise."

9 There is a history in all men's lives,
Figuring the natures of the times deceas'd;
The which observ'd, a man may prophesy,
With a near aim, of the main chance of things
As yet not come to life, who in their seeds
And weak beginning lie intreasured.
Such things become the hatch and brood of time...
Henry IV, Part II, III.1, line 1785–1791.

10 Smith's "great wheel of circulation" irresistibly recalls William Hogarth's intensely allegorical "Emblematical Print on the South Sea Scheme" (1721) a commentary on financial speculation and greed. See "Who'll Ride?" at https://en.wikipedia.org/wiki/Emblematical_Print_on_the_South_Sea_Scheme#/media/File:William_Hogarth_-_The_South_Sea_Scheme.png

11 Note for comparison what Goethe has to say about the meaning of the words "property and common ownership" in his later *Wilhelm Meisters Wanderjahre* (published 1821): "nobody should touch the capital, whereas the interest will belong to everybody in the

normal course of things. The owner of a country estate who manages his affairs according to this rule but is therefore reproached because his estate is not yielding the profit it should, replies: 'I regard the deficiency in income as an expenditure which gives me pleasure, as I am thereby making the lives of others less difficult; I do not even have the trouble of this gift having to go through my hands, and so everything adjusts itself once more'" (Binswanger, 1994: 104–105).

12 See Goethe, 1834: 64–66.

13 On the terms I have advanced in my section IV gloss, Faust's downfall (like Bentham's fear) signifies not simply ruination at the hands of time, but also exposure of what Andreas Philippopoulos-Mihalopoulos calls "The subterfuge of abstraction, law's greatest weapon of epistemological distance." Abstraction is "the way in which law has tricked us" into looking past its materiality. Just as the history I am advancing is a materialist history of remainders, for the law, too, the implication is "not only that it is material through and through but that, significantly, the law has always been material" (Philippopoulos-Mihalopoulos, 2014: 415).

Bibliography

Annette, John, 'Bentham's Fear of Hobgoblins: Law, Political Economy, and Social Discipline', in B. Fine, R. Kinsey, J. Lea, S. Picciotto and J. Young (eds), *Capitalism and the Rule of Law: From Deviancy Theory to Marxism*, London: Hutchinson & Co., 1979.

Badiou, Alain, *Polemics*, trans. S. Corcoran, London and New York: Verso, 2011.

Banerjee, Prathama, 'Eelco Runia. *Moved By the Past: Discontinuity and Historical Mutation*', (Review), *American Historical Review*, 120(3), 963–964, 2015.

Barker, Francis, *The Culture of Violence: Essays on Tragedy and History*, Chicago: University of Chicago Press, 1993.

Barthes, Roland, *S/Z: An Essay*, trans. R. Miller, New York: Hill & Wang, 1974.

Benjamin, Walter, 'The Task of the Translator', trans. H. Zohn, in M. Bullock and M.W. Jennings (eds), *Walter Benjamin, Selected Writings, Volume 1, 1913–1926*, Cambridge, MA: Harvard University Press, 1996.

Benjamin, Walter, *The Origin of German Tragic Drama*, trans. J. Osborne, London, New York: Verso, 1998.

Benjamin, Walter, *The Arcades Project*, trans. H. Eiland and K. McLaughlin, Cambridge, MA: Harvard University Press, 2002a.

Benjamin, Walter, 'Theological-Political Fragment', trans. E. Jephcott, in H. Eiland and M.W. Jennings (eds), *Walter Benjamin, Selected Writings, Volume 3, 1935–38*, Cambridge, MA: Harvard University Press, 2002b.

Benjamin, Walter, 'The Work of Art in the Age of Its Technological Reproducibility', trans. E. Jephcott and H. Zohn, in H. Eiland and M.W. Jennings (eds), *Walter Benjamin, Selected Writings, Volume 3, 1935–38*, Cambridge, MA: Harvard University Press, 2002c.

Benjamin, Walter, 'On the Concept of History', trans. H. Zohn, in H. Eiland and M.W. Jennings (eds), *Walter Benjamin, Selected Writings, Volume 3, 1935–38*, Cambridge, MA: Harvard University Press, 2003.

Bennett, Jane, *Vibrant Matter: A Political Ecology of Things*, Durham, NC: Duke University Press, 2010.

Bentham, Jeremy, *Theory of Legislation*, trans. R. Hildreth (from the French of Etienne Dumont), London: Trübner & Co., 1871.

Bentham, Jeremy, *The Works of Jeremy Bentham, Volume Nine*, New York: Russell & Russell, 1962.

Bhandar, Brenna, 'Property, Law, and Race: Modes of Abstraction', *UC Irvine Law Review*, 4(1), 203–218, 2014.

Binswanger, Hans Christoph, *Money and Magic: A Critique of the Modern Economy in the Light of Goethe's Faust*, Chicago, London: University of Chicago Press, 1994.

Braudel, Fernand, *The Mediterranean and the Mediterranean World in the Age of Phillip II* (2v.), Berkeley: University of California Press, 1995.

Brewer, Holly, 'Entailing Aristocracy in Colonial Virginia: "Ancient Feudal Restraints" and Revolutionary Reform', *William and Mary Quarterly*, 54(2), 307–346, 1997.

Conrad, Joseph, *The Shadow-Line: A Confession*, London: Electric Book Company, 2001.

Constable, Marianne, 'Elizabeth Mertz. *The Language of Law School: Learning to "Think Like a Lawyer"*', *Law & Society Review*, 42(2), 433–435, 2008.

Crawford, T. Hugh, 'An Interview With Bruno Latour', *Configurations*, 1(2), 247–268, 1993.

Davies, Margaret, *Law Unlimited: Materialism, Pluralism, and Legal Theory*, Abingdon, OX: Routledge, 2017.

Dayan, Colin, *The Law Is a White Dog: How Legal Rituals Make and Unmake Persons*, Princeton: Princeton University Press, 2011.

Delaney, David, 'Beyond the Word: Law as a Thing of This World', in J. Holder and C. Harrison (eds), *Law and Geography*, Oxford: Oxford University Press, 2002.

Douglas, Mary, *Purity and Danger: An Analysis of Concepts of Pollution and Taboo*, London, New York: Routledge, 2002.

Eiland, Howard and Jennings, Michael, *Walter Benjamin: A Critical Life*, Cambridge, MA: Harvard University Press, 2014.

Foucault, Michel, *Wrong-Doing, Truth-Telling: The Function of Avowal in Justice*, trans. S.W. Sawyer, Brin F. and Harcourt B.E. (eds), Chicago: University of Chicago Press, 2014.

Gatrell, V.A.C., *The Hanging Tree: Execution and the English People, 1770–1868*, Oxford: Oxford University Press, 1994.

Goethe, Johann Wolfgang von, *Faust, Part I*, trans. Warburton Davies, London: Simpkin and Marshall, 1834.

Goethe, Johann Wolfgang von, *Faust, Parts I & II*, trans. A.S. Kline, Poetry in Translation, 2003. www.poetryintranslation.com.

Higham, John, *History: Professional Scholarship in America*, New York: Harper & Row, 1965.

Honig, Bonnie, *Antigone, Interrupted*, Cambridge and New York: Cambridge University Press, 2013.

Honig, Bonnie, 'The Laws of the Sabbath (Poetry): Arendt, Heine, and the Politics of Debt', *UC Irvine Law Review*, 5(2), 463–482, 2015.

Hyde, Lewis, *The Gift: Imagination and the Erotic Life of Property*, New York: Random House, 1983.

James, William, *The Varieties of Religious Experience: A Study in Human Nature* (Being the Gifford Lectures on Natural Religion Delivered at Edinburgh in 1901–1902), New York: Longmans, Green, and Co., 1920.

Jefferson, Thomas, 'Thomas Jefferson to James Madison, 6 September 1789', in P.B. Kurland and R. Lerner (eds), *The Founders' Constitution* (Chapter 2 'Popular Basis of Political Authority' Document 23). http://press-pubs.uchicago.edu/founders/documents/v1ch2s23.html.

Johnson, Tom, 'Medieval Law and Materiality: Shipwrecks, Finders, and Property on the Suffolk Coast, ca. 1380–1410', *American Historical Review*, 120(2), 407–432, 2015.

Johnson, Walter, *River of Dark Dreams: Slavery and Empire in the Cotton Kingdom*, Cambridge, MA: Harvard University Press, 2013.

Laqueur, Thomas W., *The Work of the Dead: A Cultural History of Mortal Remains*, Princeton: Princeton University Press, 2015.

Latour, Bruno, *We Have Never Been Modern*, trans. C. Porter, Cambridge, MA: Harvard University Press, 1993.

Locke, John, *Second Treatise of Government*, South Bend, IN: Infomotions Inc., 2001.

Lukács, Georg, *History and Class Consciousness: Studies in Marxist Dialectics*, trans. R. Livingstone, Cambridge, MA: MIT Press, 1971.

Madoff, Ray D., *Immortality and the Law: The Rising Power of the American Dead*, New Haven, London: Yale University Press, 2010.

Mantel, Hilary, *Bring Up the Bodies*, London: Fourth Estate, 2012.
Martel, James R., *Divine Violence: Walter Benjamin and the Eschatology of Sovereignty*, Abingdon, OX, New York: Routledge, 2012.
Marx, Karl, *Capital, A Critique of Political Economy: Volume 1, The Process of Capitalist Production*, trans. S. Moore and ed. E. Aveling, Engels F., New York: International Publishers, 1967.
Marx, Karl and Engels, Frederick, *Manifesto of the Communist Party*, Moscow: Foreign Languages Publishing House, 1955.
Mauss, Marcel, *The Gift: Forms and Functions of Exchange in Archaic Societies*, trans. I. Cunnison, New York and London: W.W. Norton, 1967.
Mertz, Elizabeth, *The Language of Law School: Learning to 'Think Like a Lawyer'*, New York: Oxford University Press, 2007.
Neeson, J.M., *Commoners: Common Right, Enclosure, and Social Change in England, 1700–1820*, Cambridge, New York: Cambridge University Press, 1983.
Nietzsche, Friedrich, 'On the Uses and Disadvantages of History for Life', in *Untimely Meditations*, trans. R.J. Hollingdale, Cambridge and New York: Cambridge University Press, 1983.
Philippopoulos-Mihalopoulos, Andreas, 'Critical Autopoiesis and the Materiality of Law', *International Journal for the Semiotics of Law*, 27(2), 389–418, 2014.
Runia, Eelco, *Moved by the Past: Discontinuity and Historical Mutation*, New York: Columbia University Press, 2014.
Shakespeare, William, *Titus Andronicus*, R. McDonald (ed.), New York: Penguin Books, 2000.
Smith, Adam, *An Inquiry Into the Nature and Causes of the Wealth of Nations*, R.H. Campbell and A.S. Skinner (eds), Oxford: Oxford University Press, 1976.
Taylor, Charles, *A Secular Age*, Cambridge, MA: Harvard University Press, 2007.
Teubner, Gunther, *Law as an Autopoietic System*, Oxford: Blackwell Publishers, 1993.
Thompson, Edward P., *Customs in Common*, New York: The New Press, 1991.
Tomlins, Christopher, 'How Autonomous Is Law?', *Annual Review of Law and Social Science*, 3, 45–68, 2007.
Tomlins, Christopher, 'After Critical Legal History: Scope, Scale, Structure', *Annual Review of Law and Social Science*, 8, 31–68, 2012.
Tomlins, Christopher, 'Debt, Death, and Redemption: Toward a Soterial-Legal History of the Turner Rebellion', in D. Cowan and D. Wincott (eds), *Exploring the Legal in Socio-Legal Studies*, London: Palgrave Macmillan, 2016.
Weber, Samuel, *Benjamin's-abilities*, Cambridge, MA: Harvard University Press, 2008.
Williams, Patricia J., *The Alchemy of Race and Rights: Diary of a Law Professor*, Cambridge, MA: Harvard University Press, 1991.
Žižek, Slavoj, *Event: A Philosophical Journey Through a Concept*, Brooklyn, London: Melville House Publishing, 2014a.
Žižek, Slavoj, *Trouble in Paradise: From the End of History to the End of Capitalism*, Brooklyn, London: Melville House Publishing, 2014b.

19

Must the law be a liar? Walter Benjamin on the possibility of an anarchist form of law

*James R. Martel**

Introduction

For all of his radicalism and critiques of the false forms of law that are currently practiced, Walter Benjamin offers us precious little in the way of actual formulations for how an alternative form of law might work. Part of this stems from the fact that this author is unusually allergic to asserting his authority in the text; much of his work serves to undermine his role as author, leaving the reader to her own devices, and hence modeling the kind of decentralized and, I would say, anarchist legal and political practices that Benjamin supports.[1] Another part of his reluctance to speculate on alternative practices comes from Benjamin's notion, akin to Marx's own, that attempting to speak for the future merely colonizes it with the phantasms and projections of the present. Rather than rendering the future into "homogenous, empty time" as liberalism and fascism do, Benjamin seeks to leave the future to those who live in it, focusing instead on the present and the past.[2]

In turning his back on phantasms of futurity, Benjamin is not abandoning those who live after him to their fate but rather demonstrating a way to live in time where one is not bound by the teleologies that normally are determinant. This may be particularly true for matters of law. The law is perhaps most susceptible to teleologism and thereby to what Benjamin calls "mythic violence," because it is a creation of almost pure projection; the power of the law for Benjamin (and from him Derrida and many other contemporary thinkers) lies in the way it mystifies its own origins, the way it demands to be obeyed even as it has no true basis for such authority. The law resorts to teleologies of time, of ancient pasts and eschatological futures, to assert itself into human temporality. It is violent, not only physically but also in terms of the force of its own self-assertion, precisely because it remains eternally anxious about its own nebulous origins.

In my view, this quality of law makes it supremely "archist," that is, the opposite of anarchist. The demand for an end, for teleology and violence, are symptomatic of the way that archist law must endlessly repeat its own origins, violently imposing itself onto it subjects. In this chapter, I will counterpoise this depiction of archist law with the possibility of an anarchist law, that is a law that is not based on projection and the need for assertion and ends (hence something that corresponds more to what Benjamin calls "pure means.") Taking up small hints that Benjamin offers that it is possible to practice a form of law which is both anarchist and nonviolent (that is, anti-mythic), I will think further about what such a law might look like, focusing especially on the convergence of law and materialism (and more particularly, the way that materiality can be a counterforce to projection and phantasm). What does law become, in other words, when it is divorced from its own ends, from what passes for truth and justice? Is there anything that remains of such law and, if so, what effect does it still have on the human community that is connected with it?

To look at these sorts of questions, I will look closely at Benjamin's writing on law, concentrating on one central section of his "Critique of Violence," which I think is particularly helpful in terms of suggesting the kinds of political and legal practices Benjamin favors. The section in question lies in the middle of the essay after Benjamin considers the way that the law seems to be inherently archist, mythic and violent. Contesting the way the law seems hopelessly teleological, Benjamin asks, "Is any nonviolent resolution of conflict possible?" his answer is "Without doubt" (Benjamin, 1996a: 244).

In this section of the text, as part of his contention that law can be nonviolent, and hence, potentially anarchist, Benjamin makes three central claims: first, that contrary to what might be expected, the practice of anti-mythic nonviolence is already an everyday occurrence even under conditions of liberalism; second, that material objects and materially based techniques of resistance are critical for any nonviolent practice; and third, and perhaps most surprising, that one of the markers of a nonviolent practice is that it has no sanction on lying. I would like to treat these claims in reverse order, focusing first and especially on Benjamin's refusal to forbid lying when it comes to matters of law.

This last may seem extremely unexpected since it seems that Benjamin's entire life's work is set against lying; his condemnation of mythic violence seems to be, on the face of it anyway, a call against the very kinds of false assertions and baseless teleologies that are the hallmark of capitalism and what Benjamin calls "the phantasmagoria." Why then would he argue that a nonviolent practice of law and politics would not permit any sanction on lying? In what follows, I will explain why I believe that Benjamin is not being inconsistent in this claim and furthermore how an important set of nonviolent and anarchic political and legal practices stem from this one insight. I will follow that discussion with a more general discussion of the techniques and modes that Benjamin advises in order to transform a set of anarchist and everyday forms of resistance into a larger and more sustainable set of legal and political practices that are based on nonviolence.

Above all, in laying out these arguments, I seek to take what amounts to a set of hints and suggestions by Benjamin and think further about how they apply to an anarchist practice of law. I mean anarchist law not only in the sense that this is the kind of law that anarchist communities might already practice or have already been practicing, but also a form of law that is anarchist in its very form, that is, a law which decapitates its own basis for authority and which must learn to function and remain meaningful without such guarantees. As I will show, the idea of a law whose authority comes only from the way it is practiced, that has no recourse to ancient precedent or a future justice, and which eschews the violence of projection and phantasm, is not easy to describe, much less put into effect.

In seeking to discuss this possibility, Benjamin reinforces the anarchist methods he is espousing with a practice of textual anarchism as well. Rather than direct the reader, he speaks of these anarchist practices in ways that are piecemeal and rather opaque. In doing so, he refuses to set down this alternative notion of law in the same "black letter" form that the archist variants of law employ. This other form of law is to be created, altered, lost and recreated over time; any discussion of it must remain speculative, be made in snatches and provide just a glimpse of whatever anarchist law is and does.

Even if he does convey some idea of what might constitute an anarchist legal practice, I don't think Benjamin's response that nonviolence can be practiced "without a doubt" means that we can readily or unproblematically walk into such a form of law. Indeed, the anarchist practice of law, as I hope to show, is a difficult path precisely because it always risks falling back into its archist opposite, because law as such seems to demand that it be something besides pure means.

In this way, Benjamin warns us as much as he inspires us to pursue the possibility of a form of law that is not archist, mythic and violent. In a text that both explains and subverts the formations of law and authority, he engages with a language that is normally captured by phantasm in order to describe the very thing that it is designed to exclude. By looking at the negative spaces, the hints and aporias that he leads us to, we can begin to think more carefully about what an anarchist practice of law might entail with all of the caveats and possibilities that Benjamin sends our way.

Before moving into the essay proper, let me offer two caveats of my own. The first, one that often needs to be stressed when discussing Benjamin on violence, is that when I speak of violence and nonviolence, I am not referring to physical violence per se. In the "Critique of Violence," Benjamin uses the German term "*gewalt*" which means something more like force. As already noted, he uses the term to refer to the way the law projects or forces itself upon its subject population, the violence of its own self-assertion. Sometimes this assertion manifests itself as physical violence (as when Benjamin tells us that the law uses capital punishment to "jut manifestly and fearsomely into existence"), but that is only symptomatic of a deeper, mythic violence (Benjamin, 1996a: 242). Accordingly, Benjamin's condemnation of violence as projection does not mean that he is against the use of physical violence in all cases (he tells us for example that even the commandment "thou shalt not kill" cannot be taken literally), just as the absence of physical violence does not mean that we are in a condition of nonviolence. To put this into a contemporary lexicon, I think that Benjamin would have no problem with "punching fascists," but his greater concern is the deeper violence of projection that underlies both fascism and liberalism.

The second caveat is that in this chapter I will be speaking both of nonviolent and anarchist practices of law, using these terms fairly interchangeably, but they do not mean exactly the same thing. Nonviolence here describes an approach to law, while anarchism describes a particular set of practices that may or may not employ nonviolence. It is unfortunately very possible for anarchism to be violent – that is to say, to engage in projection and myth – and there are forms of nonviolence that are not necessarily anarchist. Yet I do not mean to suggest that these terms are wholly unrelated; where anarchism and nonviolence touch, there I think we find our most radical challenge to archism.[3]

The sanction on lying

In the "Critique of Violence," Benjamin discusses several modes of organization and practice that achieve nonviolence (specific examples of which will be discussed slightly later in the chapter). He writes that:

> For in [such practices] not only is nonviolent agreement possible, but also the exclusion of violence in principle is quite explicitly demonstrable by one significant factor: there is no sanction for lying. Probably no legislation on earth originally stipulated such a sanction. This makes clear that there is a sphere of human agreement that is nonviolent to the extent that it is wholly inaccessible to violence: the proper sphere of "understanding," language.
>
> (Benjamin, 1996a: 245)

Before turning specifically to the question of the sanction against lying, which he references here, let me first note something more general about the quality of language and speech for Benjamin. When Benjamin writes that there is one "sphere of human agreement that is nonviolent . . . the proper sphere of 'understanding,' language," he is referring to one area (others will be discussed later in this essay but this is the prime example) where the state and its phantasms have no power or reach. "Understanding" language refers to the idea that in order to make themselves mutually intelligible, there must be widespread agreement between speakers on the rough meaning of words. Such a view is very akin to what Hobbes has to say on the subject. For Hobbes, as for Benjamin, language is an inherently anarchic and self-organizing system. The sovereign, in Hobbes's view, may be the last and final reader, the ultimate determiner of meaning, but he or she is not the best or only such judge.[4] In fact, the sovereign sits atop an enormously complex network of language users where, by the time his or her decision is called for, an infinite number of prior and irrevocable decisions have already been "made," not by a committee or by any sovereign authority but by the infinite and myriad (and, I would once again add, anarchic) conversations and decisions that are made on a daily basis and without violence or projection each and every day.[5]

These decisions about language are not "true" in the sense that whatever term they project onto language corresponds with some actual and divinely offered notion of that term – Benjamin very much militates against thinking that way. To think that language is in fact true is to enter into a discourse that the law considers its own territory, the territory of determining what is true and what is a lie. Language itself is not therefore a "lie" but it isn't truth either.[6] It is a moving target, a mutual and contingent marker of agreement and hence nonviolent, neither quite rivalling nor supporting the law's imagined source of its authority and power. Yet the fact that language has this character does not mean that it poses no threat to legal authority; the fact that the law must express itself in this very same language as that formed by these anarchic speech networks is an indication of the crisis that law is always faced with. The law is always asserting its own interpretations of words and phrases as if they were definitive, as if it didn't, like the sovereign itself, make those "decisions" in the context of a much larger speech community wherein meanings are made and remade everyday and by everyone without regard to rank or authority.[7]

This picture of the law's condition, then, helps explain the law's sanction on lying. If the chaotic and decentralized process of linguistic decision-making that the law is always located within can be characterized as a zone of threat and danger to "the truth," then the law positions itself as being the savior and bolster against this danger. The conceit that the law, which is in a sense the biggest liar that there is (along with the state), determines and punishes "lying" is a projection – as is always the case with law – of its own anxieties onto those formulations that it sees as rivals to its authority and power. Thus, to put it in a nutshell, for Benjamin it is not that nonviolent practices condone lying but rather that the very question of truth is absent when nonviolent practices (like language itself) are in play. As I will explain further in this chapter, when decisions and choices are made in the decentralized and anarchist mode that Benjamin favors (that is, when they are practiced in accordance with nonviolence), there is no question of lying one way or the other. No one is expected to be able to speak the truth, and every statement is not an assertion but rather a contribution to an ongoing and fluid alternative form of legal and political discourse. There is no sanction on lying in these cases, not because everyone is speaking the truth but rather because every utterance is assumed to be the subject's own and must be assessed and engaged with as part of a much larger conversation, wherein notions of lying and fraud are not involved or germane.

This is not to say that under conditions without this sanction someone who is self-interested might not say things for their own selfish purposes, or that people can never make things up which they know are not the case. It is rather that, without the pose of an external authority to judge the validity of such statements, no statement would be treated as valid on its face; everything would be subject to the legal and political decisions and judgments of the larger community, much as language itself functions (I could choose, for example, to suddenly start calling a tomato a "rabbit," but chances are no one else would go along with me, or if they did, they'd come up with a different term for rabbit so as to distinguish between the two things).

In a sense, the very concepts of lying and fraud are themselves only reflections of the law's conceit that it determines truth. To impose a sanction on lying is to claim (falsely) that language *can* speak truth and that it is the law's "duty" – but really the law does this not for the sake of truth but for the sake of its own self-assertion – to impose a regime of truth on what it claims would otherwise be a passel of lies. The law is thus projecting its own lying outwardly onto others, and this entire charade would be meaningless and empty in a nonviolent and anarchist context. In this way, the law turns its anxiety about its own basis for authority into a means to stamp out the living evidence that it in fact has no authority (that is, the fact that we, the subject of law, speak without recourse to truth every time we open our mouths to communicate).

i. Lying and contracts

One of the most critical upshots of this understanding of the law's relationship to lying has to do with the question of contracts. For Benjamin, contracts are themselves an integral part of the violence of law. In the "Critique," Benjamin writes:

> We are above all obligated to note that a totally nonviolent resolution of conflicts can never lead to a legal contract. For the latter, however peacefully it may have been entered into by the parties, leads finally to possible violence. It confers on each party the right to resort to violence in some form against the other, should he break the agreement. Not only that; like the outcome, the origin of every contract also points toward violence. It need not be directly present in it as law-making violence, but is represented in it insofar as the power that guarantees a legal contract is, in turn, of violent origin even if violence is not introduced in the contract itself.
>
> (Benjamin, 1996a: 243–244)

In this way, the prohibition on contracts is directly related to the prohibition on lying. The law sets itself up as the arbiter of promises and, once again, arbitrates the standards for falseness and truth. In this way, the violence that is inherent in the law is transmitted, via the contract, to the contracting parties involved. Insofar as the contract is the fundamental basis for liberal capitalism, this amounts to a mechanism by which state – and mythic – violence is transmitted to every individual in society (insofar as virtually all of us are bound by one contract or another and the social contract – as least as a theoretical model – binds us one and all).

The contract is also problematic for a second reason for Benjamin insofar as it not only seeks to bind the parties involved into a false projection of its authority but also to the future when the contract is supposed to come into effect. For Benjamin, the future, as already noted, is meant to be held in abeyance, not filled with "empty homogenous time." The contract is perhaps the epitome of such an enforced form of temporality, because it seeks to order and rationalize (hence homogenize) a future that it fills with its own falseness (hence empty).

This connection between the sanction on lying and state violence thus has huge implications for liberal theory and even some left of liberal forms of politics and law that do not entirely repudiate the contract. The very idea of a binding contract, one that has to be enforced by some third and external force is, in Benjamin's telling, inherently violent. It is a reflection and consequence of a deeper violence of which physical violence (what we usually mean by violence in English) is once again only the symptom.

ii. Blackmailing the state

Another quite paradoxical consequence of the law's ban on lying for Benjamin comes in the way that the law, on behalf of the state, sometimes makes agreements that are against the state's explicit interests. Benjamin writes that "in prohibiting fraud, law restricts the use of wholly nonviolent means because they could produce reactive violence" (Benjamin, 1996a: 245). For Benjamin, the response to state violence can certainly be – and often is – violent too. He goes on write,

> This tendency of law has also played a part in the concession of the right to strike, which contradicts the interests of the state. It grants this right because it forestalls violent actions the state is afraid to oppose. Did not workers previously resort at once to sabotage and set fire to factories?
>
> (Benjamin, 1996a: 245)

Here, the law in effect "saves" the state from its own tendency to an absolute violence, via a projection of a more subtle but highly effective form of violence of its own. The law "allows" the workers to strike but it does so only to assert, once again, its own basis for authority as well as to sell its own brand of violence as something altruistic and beneficial. In fact, both the violence of the state and the violence of the law amount to extending their own violence to the workers so that they too are caught up in the performance of a violence that seems to have no recourse.

At this point in his text, Benjamin cites Sorel's critical – and well-known – distinction between the political strike and the proletarian general strike. The former is itself a violent response to state violence; it is an attempt to extort concessions from the state while remaining very much within the capitalist system. In this way, the political strike doesn't merely extend violence from the law onto the population but acts back on the state itself. Although this might seem like it would be a good thing for Benjamin, in fact engaging with violence as such merely condemns the workers to a yet greater complicity with capitalism and phantasm (so in this way, the fact that the law "allows" this worker's violence in a way that contradicts the state's direct interest does not free them from violence but seduces them into a form of violence that is less legible as such). Once the workers engage in this kind of violence (thanks to the law's interference), the workers cannot beat the state at its own game; when they enter into a contest with the state on such violent terms, the state will always win (even if a change in leadership is the result, in the end the state itself will survive any particular gang of leaders so long as they are committed to violence and projection as such).

In contrast to such a compromising form of resistance, Benjamin tells us that the general strike:

> Sets itself the sole task of destroying state power . . . The general strike clearly announces its indifference towards material gain through conquest by declaring its intention to abolish the state . . . Whereas the first form of interruption of work is violent, since it causes only an external modification of labor conditions, the second, as a pure mean, is nonviolent. For it takes place not in readiness to resume work following external concessions and this or that modification to working conditions, but in the determination to resume only a wholly transformed work, no longer enforced by the state. . . . For this reason, the first of these undertakings is lawmaking but the second anarchistic.
>
> (Benjamin, 1996a: 246)

Here we see that nonviolence is always possible and it involves a refusal to negotiate, to act or speak according to legal dictates and above all a refusal to project a violence of its own back onto the law or the state (for, once again, in such a contest, the state will almost always be the winner since it is a creature of mythic violence in a way that ordinary subjects are not). We also see that this kind of refusal of violence leads to the political practices that Benjamin calls "anarchistic," hence connecting nonviolence and anarchism quite explicitly.

iii. Pure means

The general strike is one example (but a key one) of Benjamin's assertion that nonviolent action is possible "without doubt." There are many other forms that nonviolence can take. One of the unifying concepts that is common to all of these forms is the idea of "pure means," previously referred to, which Benjamin evokes in the passage cited above (and a term which is repeated quite a few times in the "Critique.") The notion of pure means refers to what happens when mythic – and therefore inherently violent – ends are broken off. The means that were once merely intended to serve such ends find themselves without a purpose and, as such, are returned, as it were, to themselves. In the case of the general strike, by refusing to acknowledge the state's power over them (in a way that is distinctly anarchist), the strikers turn a means (a strike) into something other than an inherently violent interaction (because for Benjamin ends are inherently violent; they partake in – or even constitute – the false projection that is the hallmark of mythic violence). Rather than being a strike "for" some purpose, the general strike is a strike as such.

Perhaps most critically, by upending the violent and illicit claims for authority made by law and the state, the general strike, among other techniques, allows these pure means to be connected to the larger and anarchist patterns of behavior that are usually eclipsed by or submerged in the shadow of mythic violence and the phantasmagoria. Those myriad local and public decisions, an entire symbolic and decisional economy that has nothing to do with violence or capitalism (and which go well beyond human language, as I'll show further), constitutes the very alternative that the law most deeply fears. Not authorized by any projection or recourse to externalities, this alternative set of legal and political practices is based only on itself, a "pure means" indeed, unconnected to any ends (that is, to any set of false and fetishistic practices).

In this way, we can speak of a law of pure means (that is, to ascribe the term "law" to these sets of practices) that rivals and even threatens a law that is based on mythic and violent practices. Whereas normally we cannot conceive of the term law without recourse to all the phantasm and projection of archist practice, Benjamin invites us to recognize both the fact that an alternative practice is already occurring every day and the fact that this practice is not empty but serves to contain and form the community that engages in it. These nonviolent practices work as a bond within a community even without recourse to sanctions about truth, contracts and the other violent apparatus of mythic law. There are both risks and advantages to ascribing the term law to such practices (a question that I will revisit in the conclusion), but to do so challenges the monopoly that mythic law has on our sense of the possible, including what is possible in terms of law.

Divine violence and material techniques

For all of this, Benjamin cautions us that we must not falsely believe that just because we practice forms of nonviolent law all the time that it is easy to do this on a larger scale, or that we can readily step away from mythic practices in general (it may be precisely this belief that helps explain how even anarchists can engage in mythic violence when they think they are "free" of all forms of determination). For Benjamin, the seduction of myth and projection goes deep; it connects to our most fundamental yearnings for truth and justice. Accordingly, we cannot simply resolve on our own to cast off ends but require some help from the material world around us. In the "Critique," Benjamin writes:

> [The objective manifestation of nonviolent forms of practice] is determined by the law (whose enormous scope cannot be discussed here) that says that unalloyed means are never those of direct solutions but always of indirect solutions. They therefore never apply to the resolution of conflict between man and man, but apply only to matters concerning objects. The sphere of nonviolent means opens in the realm of human conflicts relating to goods.
>
> (Benjamin, 1996a: 248)

The first thing to note here is that Benjamin's reference to law does not seem to be entirely negative. This anticipates a move that Benjamin makes later in the essay where he distinguishes between mythic and divine violence. Where mythic violence is, as already noted, a form of projection, a false assertion using screens as varied as God (or the gods but false in any case), or law, nature, reason or the state, divine violence represents God[that is the actual deity]'s own efforts to unmake and disrupt such myths. In prior writing, I have discussed Benjamin's main example of divine violence, the story of Korah, who led a rebellion against the authority of Moses and who was, therefore, swallowed into the earth, along with his followers, leaving no sign behind of his previous existence.[8] As Benjamin writes there, "God's judgment strikes privileged Levites, strikes them without warning, without threat, and does not stop short of annihilation. But in annihilating it also expiates" (Benjamin, 1996a: 250). Here, both the crime and the guilt it produced are erased by God's action. In this way, as opposed to mythic violence, divine violence does not introduce new truths in the world but operates only to disrupt the false truths that have been fomented in God's name. Beyond this effect, divine violence otherwise leaves us very much to our own devices (hence both creating a space for nonviolence as well as enabling the anarchist networks and decisions that we form at all times, even under conditions of phantasmagoria).

Critically, divine violence is undertaken by God alone.[9] Were Benjamin to concede that divine violence (and the access to higher forms of law that it suggests) were available to human actors, it would mean that the whole question of lying and truth would be reintroduced to human actors; we would be repeating the crimes of the (mythic) law in the guise of overcoming them. It is only because divine violence stands distinctly apart from human actors that we can actually give up on the question of truth and lies altogether and, in that way, access the sphere of nonviolent action.

This still leaves a puzzle, however. If human agents are given the possibility of their own nonviolence via acts of divine violence, why does Benjamin state that we always need to have our conflicts and decisions mediated by material objects which seem to have nothing to do with the divine (at least on the surface of things)? What role do goods and material techniques in general play in retaining the possibility of nonviolent relations between human actors? Part of the way towards a possible answer to this question lies beyond the scope of the "Critique." In other writings, especially those that focus on Benjamin's theology, we see an argument on his part that the objects of the world resist the projections – that is, the mythic violence – that human agents pitch onto them. Thus, for example, in his essay "On Language as Such and the Language of Man," Benjamin describes the "deep sadness" the objects of the world express at Adam's expulsion from the Garden of Eden (Benjamin, 1996b: 72). While in Eden, Adam had given a spoken name to correspond to the mute name that God had already given to the objects found there. After the fall, this concordance falls away but the objects of the world remain in a pure state (i.e., as pure means), failing to be commodities and failing to serve as mere means to the phantasmic ends that human beings project onto them. Put more assertively, the objects of the world – including the objects that are our own bodies – can be seen as engaging in a full-on revolt against the false ends that humans see them as serving. By aligning ourselves with this revolt, human beings can further their own resistance to mythic violence.

This material form of resistance may be what Benjamin is drawing upon or referring to when he tells us, "[nonviolent practices] therefore never apply to the resolution of conflict between man and man, but apply only to matters concerning objects." Mediated by objects, human beings have a better chance to defy and resist the projections that are placed onto each and every one of us. When we try to address our conflicts directly between persons, we risk losing the ongoing presence of divine violence, the way it inheres in the very objects of the world that we would seek to fetishize. Put another way, the failure of objects to be what we pretend them to be enables our own failure to be what we are interpellated (that is to say commanded) by law to be as well.

i. Politicizing art

Immediately after the passage cited above in which Benjamin speaks about the requirement for material mediation between human actors, Benjamin gets more specific (albeit also more opaque) when he writes,

> For this reason, technique in the broadest sense of the word is the . . . most particular area [in which nonviolent practices can be engaged with]. Its profoundest example is perhaps the conference, considered as a technique of civil agreement.
>
> (Benjamin, 1996a: 248)

Technique is Benjamin's term for forms of resistance that involve material practices.[10] The term technique derives from *techne*, a Greek word for the arts and engagements with the material world. Elsewhere, Benjamin speaks of "politicizing art," a notion that suggests a way to engage with material objects directly as a way to disable them as sites for state and legal projection and, in this way, lessen the power of that projection more generally.[11] Accordingly, for Benjamin, technique as such (i.e., the mode of "politicizing art") serves to scramble and disenchant the material objects that we normally use as means towards (phantasmic) ends. To give some examples of technique, I must once again briefly leave the "Critique" itself behind, looking towards some other texts of his that were written somewhat later (in this way reading Benjamin in constellation with himself).

As I see it, the entirety of *The Origin of German Tragic Drama* can be read as an exercise in – or an exposition of – technique. Arguing that the German baroque dramatists – the objects of study of that text – lived in a time when the gathering phantasmagoria of modern secularism was yet weak (and the previous regime of strong Christian-based modes of political order was ebbing), Benjamin found this time to be relatively undetermined by phantasmic regimes. In this way, the baroque period offered more possibilities for subversion and resistance than later times would. Although the playwrights in question may have consciously sought to engage in orthodox portrayals of sovereign authority in their plays (the power and glory of kingship being one of the chief preoccupations of plays from the period), Benjamin looks to the materiality of their texts, the forms of letters and symbols that they featured in their scripts, even the costumes and stage props that they employed, as a way to undermine the playwrights' own desires. For Benjamin, the contrast between the divine and political truths (often this was considered to amount to the same thing) meant to be conveyed in these plays and the humble and physical mediums by which these were expressed created a conflict, in that

> the desire to guarantee the sacred character of any script – there will always be a conflict between sacred standing and profane comprehensibility – leads to complexes, to hieroglyphics.
>
> (Benjamin, 2003c: 175)

Benjamin, who also refers to "allegorical script," shows how in such cases the form interferes with the content. Here, the physicality of the sign undermines the truth that the sign is intended to convey (and that is a very good thing, in his view) (Benjamin, 2003c: 176).

All of this seems very accidental; we are fortunate indeed that the objects of the world resist the projections we would place on them, but doesn't that leave human actors entirely passive? If the German baroque dramatists were subversive despite their own intentions to the contrary, is there a way to be subversive in a more sustained and deliberate way? If the concept of technique as "politicizing art" means anything (if the connection that I make between these terms is persuasive), it suggests that there are specific steps that we can take to enhance the degree to which we are able to take advantage of the way material objects interfere with our projections. But what are those steps and how do we approach them?

ii. The conference and the law

Benjamin offers precious little guidance about this possibility, and what follows is largely speculative. For example, in the "Critique," when he writes that "[the] profoundest example [of technique] is perhaps the conference, considered as a technique of civil agreement," Benjamin does not give us much to go on. What might he mean by a conference and how would it (therefore) be informed by this discussion of the technique and the mediation of material objects? To begin with, the German word Benjamin uses for (what is translated as) conference is "*Unterredung*." This term has connotations of mutuality and discussion that has no necessary hierarchical ordering. It is interesting to note that the word serves as a kind of opposite in German for *Überredung*, which has the connotation of persuasion or cajolery, hence a kind of compulsion (or indeed force or violence). True to his radically decentralized understanding of language then, we can say that the conference for Benjamin is the site in which those anarchic forms of language can occur without being eclipsed either by sovereign orderings (wherein modes of hierarchical organization dominate the content of speech) or even by sovereign decisionism about language and its meaning (including the sanction on lying).

But what does it mean that Benjamin calls the conference "a *technique* of civil agreement" [emphasis added]? Insofar as, as already noted, technique always involves material objects, how does this relate to or support the mutuality of the conference and how does this contribute to the notion of "politicizing art"? I can once again only speculate at this point but I would argue that, by analogy with his description of the German baroque dramatists, the very framing of the conference – the symbols displayed, the texts produced, even the physical mechanics of the space and the bodies of those present – would not be seen as "mere means" to a (false) end but rather active parts of a collective endeavor to dispel violence and projection. Only here, rather than relying on the way these objects are always interfering with the myths that we project onto them (and obey in response), there would be a more conscious and consistent desire for the kinds of disruptions that material objects can afford, especially those objects that are normally used to promote and extend mythic projections. A flag, for example, can be seen as a fetish, a stand-in and replacement for the community that it purportedly only represents, but if the failure of the flag to be what it claims to be can be somehow demonstrated (with some connivance by the flag itself, which is only ever a piece of colored cloth), then it serves the opposite function; it remains a site that organizes and calls a community into being but in a way that resists and subverts the "truths" that such symbols normally serve to project.[12] Rather than competing with the community, supplying a false marker that eclipses the community's own anarchic judgments and discussions (conferences), the flag in this sense can merely serve as an empty or failed sign that allows the community its own legal and political expression.[13]

In this way, perhaps we can say that the conference, as Benjamin envisions it, is a discursive space in which technique as such is more visible than it normally is allowed to be. Benjamin gives us no hints about how this might work, but if we think of the conference itself – the discussions, the talking, the representational gestures it entails – as being itself technique, we can see that language that has not been captured and purposed by mythic violence becomes itself a kind of material object, a set of sounds or texts or images, that both resists the meaning that human actors would project onto it and, at the same time, offers a mechanism by which speech can be nondetermining, nonviolent and open to contingent and mutual forms of discourse.

It is here that I would like to focus especially on the question of the law and what the "conference" and technique can do for or to the law per se. At the end of this chapter, I will return to the question of divine law, but for the time being, I'd like to focus on what legal practices human beings can exercise as themselves in ways that are nonviolent. Specifically, what kind of law would emerge from the conference? What kind of law do we have when law becomes open to its own status as technique, when it becomes the basis, that is to say, for the possibility of greater and deeper anarchist practices of law?

Clearly, the legal practices that stem from the conference would require the unmaking of the very grounds of authority that the law (in its mythic form) normally would insist upon. Can the law point to the absence, rather than the presence, of truth? Must – to cite this essay's title – the law be a liar? Can the law itself express or produce nonviolence? I think Benjamin offers some hints (but here again only hints) in terms of how the law can be used as being itself a form of "pure means," how it can be cut off from its own false sources of authorization and in that way serve the opposite agenda that it normally does.

The anarchism of law: "peaceful intercourse between private persons"

When it comes to questions of the law and its instruments, it seems even harder to imagine how the material aspects of the law could help subvert or upend the projections that they normally help to produce. The judge's robe, to take just one instance, is intended to *distance* us from the law, to create a sense of awe and majesty in a person who has been invested with its (mythic and hence violent) authority. Aren't such symbols perpetually caught up in and redolent of the very authority that law illicitly connects itself to? Is there a way for the law as a practice to counter its own projection, it's "jutting" into existence? And, if so, what would replace it?

To think more clearly about such questions, it is first worth returning to that section of the "Critique" where Benjamin describes the anarchist practices that law normally usurps. He does this in several places, all in one dense set of sentences. In one instance (immediately following his question that I cited earlier of whether "any nonviolent resolution of conflict is possible"), Benjamin writes,

> The relationships among private persons are full of examples of this. Nonviolent agreement is possible whenever a civilized outlook allows the use of means of agreement. Legal and illegal means that are all the same violent may be confronted with nonviolent ones as unalloyed means. Courtesy, sympathy, peaceableness, trust, and whatever else might here be mentioned are their subjective preconditions.
>
> (Benjamin, 1996a: 244)

By "unalloyed" means, Benjamin seems, once again, to be referring to "pure means." And he reinforces this when he says a bit later on in the text,

> To induce men to reconcile their interests peacefully without involving the legal system, there is, in the end, apart from all virtues, one effective motive that often enough puts into the most reluctant hands pure instead of violent means: it is the fear of mutual disadvantages that threaten to arrive from violent confrontations, whatever the outcome might be ... We can therefore point only to pure means in politics as analogous to those which govern peaceful intercourse between private persons.
>
> (Benjamin, 1996a: 245)

Here, we have the clearest statement yet of the kind of anarchist ferment that law usually eclipses and seeks to control. But as we see in these two quotes, the functions of law, to adjudicate in conflicts, to judge and to decide, are not the exclusive province of the legal professions but happen every day in the most ordinary and unnoted forms possible. Every time two people figure something out for themselves, or every time a group makes a decision without resorting to lawyers or courts, a nonviolent form of law has in fact been practiced.

Normally this kind of practice, as already noted, comes and goes without comment. As subjects of the law (the mythic law, that is) we tend to ignore any possibility that the law (taken in its normal, archist form) is not itself the only possible mediator of human conflict. This returns us back to the original point, that the law cannot tolerate competition, that it sanctions lying and fraud as a way to make itself seem indispensable to us (but by that very act to ensnare us in a trap of mythic violence). We see in the above quote that the motivations that people have for entering into such peaceful agreements often starts out from the same violent set of premises that law produces in general. As subjects of the law, we all understand "the fear of mutual disadvantages that threaten to arrive from violent confrontations" all too well. Our motivations may be violent (ends oriented), but along the way, we (sometimes inadvertently, sometimes not) leave the sphere of mythic law altogether, but critically not perhaps the sphere of law itself altogether.

Like Marx's portrayal in the *Economic and Philosophical Manuscripts* of workers who initially engage in communist activism for purely selfish (and capitalist) reasons only to discover in one another "human needs" of which they had up until then never been aware, so too for Benjamin does the violence of the (mythic) law tend to drive us towards legal practices that are not violent at all (but of course not recognized, therefore, as being part of law in any way).[14]

To reclaim such practices, to discover the unalloyed or pure means of law that we practice all the time without realizing them as such, it is necessary to avoid, once again, a rush to declare ourselves "free" of mythic violence. We see various examples of "popular justice" that have been practiced in revolutionary periods, when the symbols of the law have been appropriated for radical purposes only to reproduce the same chicaneries and violence of mythic law more generally. Here again, for Benjamin, we are merely substituting one form of illicit rule with another. The actual physical violence that often accompanies such moments may be a testament to how quickly mythic violence can reassert itself.

The belief that the symbols of law, however they are practiced, however altered by revolutionaries, contain in themselves some magic leaven is part of how mythic violence reasserts itself in law, as elsewhere. The risk of that reassertion never goes away (it never can, for Benjamin, because we will always be tempted by fetishism and political idolatry). Yet when those same symbols are understood as failing to convey the power of law, as empty and broken signs (or better still as what they are – pieces of paper, wood, and cloth, sounds and letters), they help to hold open a space where mythic violence is rendered unworkable (if only temporarily). In this way, it becomes possible for the vast anarchist practices of law that we've always been practicing (but which the mythic law has taken all credit for) to assert themselves in the *aporia* opened up by that failure. As such, anarchism itself can be freed of the mythic assertions that it is otherwise not immune to; it can assert its own roots in nonviolent practices in a more systematic, and systemic, way.

i. Diplomacy

This is just one suggestion (and one that Benjamin doesn't really make himself – it is merely an inference from what he does tell us) of how a nonviolent legal practice of anarchism is possible. In another example that Benjamin does supply us with, he tells us that

> fundamentally [diplomats] must, entirely on the analogy of agreement between private persons, resolve conflicts case by case, in the name of their states, peacefully and without contracts.
>
> (Benjamin, 1996a: 247)

Diplomacy, a sphere in which there is no one overriding legal or political authority (although that space has perhaps been diminished since the time of Benjamin's writing), offers another way to see nonviolent practices in action. Note that once again there is no recourse to contracts, no sanction on lying since, it could be argued, diplomats are always assumed to be speaking their interests and not some kind of truth. It is true that diplomacy has led to a great deal of actual violence and it *is* ordinarily based on a projection of a state's authority. Diplomacy often leads to treaties that are, after all, contracts and so forth. But this is not the focus of what Benjamin is talking about. He means that amongst and between themselves, there is no overarching law or authority that binds diplomats. While they speak for their individual states, they are in effect in a state of indetermination vis-à-vis one another and, in this way, they have access to a nonviolent space that most people do not. Diplomacy is therefore similar to the "peaceful intercourse between private persons" in that it reflects the possibility of nonviolent interaction in resolving even some of the thorniest of conflicts, but it may occur in an even greater vacuum of (mythic) law. Here, the absence of overriding forms of authority – a space that is effectively free of sovereignty – does tend to reduce the seductive power of the symbols of each nation's authority.[15] Benjamin goes on to write about this that

> Accordingly, like the intercourse of private persons, that of diplomats has engendered its own forms and virtues, which were not always mere formalities, even though they have become so.
>
> (Benjamin, 1996a: 247)

Here we see that in the space afforded to diplomacy other "forms" and "virtues" can arise that are not merely formulaic recitations of some kind of ghostly authority but are in their own right material practices, "pure means" that resist and subvert legal and sovereign authority (Benjamin, 1996a: 246).

Conclusion: divine violence and the anarchist practice of law

We see then that by avoiding the sanction on lying, allowing for alternative practices to thrive beyond the reach of state violence, there can still be some kind of law and there can still be some kind of politics, but these take on forms that are normally discounted or rendered invisible by "authorized" practices that are sanctioned by long legal and political traditions. Sometimes the anarchic practices are ignored; sometimes they are explained away or distorted (as in the example above as being "mere formalities"). Sometimes, when they rise to the level of a visible competitor to mythic law, they are stamped out altogether, but even with the active interference and hostility of the law, these forms persist and, even as formalities, they point in another direction. The avoidance of the sanction for lying, along with other nonviolent practices, gives a chance – but only a chance – to better access the anarchist networks, the "peaceful intercourse between private persons," that represents unalloyed or pure means.

Here we come to the real challenge that Benjamin's writing in the "Critique" poses to us insofar as the casual decisions we make every day are rendered into "pure means" precisely by the fact that they are not recognized as having any bearing on law or politics, that is, on any ends; their very ordinariness immunizes them from such teleologies. Can they retain this immunity when they challenge the mythic forms of law more openly and forcefully?

For Benjamin, the answer is an assured yes ("without doubt"). We see that even under conditions of phantasmagoria, there are nonviolent actions that people can take that also achieve pure means in ways that do not simply involve flying under the radar. The general strike is the clearest and best example of this. What I take from Benjamin on this point is that fortunately we will always have this anarchist network to draw upon. Under the nose of the law and the state – systems which are congenitally jealous of competition for its power and authority – we will always practice nonviolent forms of agreement (the system could not sustain itself if mythic law had to concern itself with every single decision and agreement). This way of accessing pure means is never going to go away.

But if that is all we have, Benjamin seems to argue, it is not enough. The very fact that he puts this conversation about private agreements and diplomacy in the context of a much more radical text that is devoted to undermining and overcoming the law in all of its mythic practices is evidence of that desire on his part. Benjamin is not content (and I am not either) to say, in effect, "well, we already have nonviolent legal practices so let's leave it at that." The "Critique" is written in response to the perceived horrors of mythic violence and so resting at the level of private agreement is not sufficient.

Even so, Benjamin does not demand one particular response and he does not tell us "what is to be done." Returning to the first point made in this essay, Benjamin avoids using his own authority in the text to determine the direction and nature of the kinds of resistance that he is calling for, lest he trump the ferment of anarchist politics he evokes with his own decisions and desires (if that were to occur, things would quickly become just as mythic as ever). Benjamin's calling our attention to the way that we are all, to some extent or other, already practicing legal and political forms of anarchism, is not so much to see this practice as being good in itself (although I think he believes that) but as a sign that it is within our power to expand such practices. His attention to the anarchist forms of law that we already practice also implies that to push this power further and more openly would not mean to radically innovate or enter some brave new or utopian world but simply to extend what we are already doing, to more actively and directly subvert and upend the legal forms of authority that we otherwise submit to. In other words, to do this would mean to turn our already anarchist practices into a form of anarchism that was nonviolent to the core and hence unavailable – if not permanently, then for a time – for archist usurpations.

In Benjamin's view, this ability is only possible due to the ongoing presence of divine violence in the world. If divine violence is never something that we can practice ourselves (although Benjamin isn't always so clear on this point), it nonetheless is, for Benjamin, the source of our power to remain (relatively) undetermined by mythic forms of legal and political authority. In the "Critique" itself, Benjamin delays his discussion of mythic and divine violence until the essay is well underway, subverting the ends that we may have thought we were reading (at least those who are not familiar with Benjamin) in favor of "pure means," and offering instead a text that defies expectations.

Ultimately for Benjamin, the great destroyer of ends, that which competes with the competitors and usurps the usurper, is divine violence itself. Thus he writes,

> For it is never reason that decides on the justification of means and the justness of ends; fate-imposed violence decides on the former, and God on the latter.
> (Benjamin, 1996a: 247)

Here we see that only God can really determine ends, and human beings are effectively always cut off from those ends; all we can do is project them and, in that way, consign ourselves to further violence. The fact that something as banal as private agreement can be an example of "pure means" indicates the way our lives are deeply affected by the ongoing practice of divine violence which, as I see it, does not come once in a great while in a spectacular gesture but rather is an everyday and constant thing. It is present, as already noted, in the way that objects resist their phantasmic uses, refusing to merely be the commodities that are supposed to meekly serve human interests. It is present whenever we talk or whenever we work out a problem without recourse to (mythic) law or state. Because the absence of ends is not occasional but a permanent state for human beings – despite the fact that the law desperately wants us to not understand this – the possibility of realizing "pure means" can never be taken away from us, even by the most (falsely) authoritarian of states and the most (falsely) mythic of laws. It is simply not within the power of human beings to deprive the world of the ability to resist being consigned to higher ends (that is, human beings can kill and hurt and enforce their vision of such ends but the one thing that they will never be able to do is to make them true; this inability is a font of revolutionary resistance for Benjamin that is the answer to mythic violence itself).

Is it right to call the nonviolent practices that exist at the margins of mythic violence "law"? Is this part of the larger category of law that Benjamin hints at but does not explain further when he writes, "[The objective manifestation of nonviolent forms of practice] is determined by the law (whose enormous scope cannot be discussed here)"? Does that "enormity" include any space for nonviolent and anarchist human practices of law? I think the answer is a bit ambiguous. On the one hand, as we have seen, Benjamin answers "Without doubt" to his question about nonviolent resolutions to human conflicts. Presumably, this must include law as well as other practices (especially since law is so caught up in the resolution of conflicts in the first place). At the same time, I hesitate to affirm this possibility without reservations, because it seems to me perilously easy for this "other" kind of law to swiftly look like the bad and violent practices of law I have already discussed in this chapter. Witness, once again, the ease by which "people's tribunals" reflect the violence that they are formed in response to (I mean this perhaps more in the sense of violence as projected authority than in terms of physical violence, but in the end these two things are connected for Benjamin). If we say that we can only use the term "law" to refer either to divine law/violence (in which case human actors are clearly excluded and there is nothing more to say) or mythic law/violence (in which case, radical actors are to avoid this at all costs), that leaves nonviolent human action out of law entirely.

Yet, at the same time, it seems to me that we open a bit of minefield if we allow the term "law" to apply to those nonviolent practices that nonetheless duplicate and reflect what the law is "supposed to do." Ultimately, I would argue that this is a risk we should be willing to take, for it is only, once again, by directly usurping and co-opting the symbols and mechanics of law that mythic law can be exposed and ruined (if not once and for all then at least for that moment and in that place). It's true that using the term law to refer to human practices that are nonviolent could entail a return to violence and myth itself (and I would go further and argue that this is probably what will end up happening in many cases). Yet such an outcome ought not to prevent us from trying to take law back from myth and violence, to return it to the anarchic sphere from which it properly arises. When we cease to project outwards to gain the authority and the right to make decisions, that is, when we cease to engage in the violence of myth, we may come to recognize, or at least allow for, the validity of what that authority always disguises: a form of law that requires no justification, no sanction on lying, but only its own persistent existence. Without the grandeur and delusion of mythic law, such a practice might not – indeed must not – have the same glamorous and seductive power as the forms of law that we generally recognize. Calling the adjudication of a private argument a moment of "law" has the appeal to me of decentering and redistributing the power of law as such. It is a disappointed and ruined remnant of all that law promises to be. Such a usage suggests, perhaps, an instance of technique, of using the tools we engage with to pursue mythic ends as a weapon against their own usage and, in that way, to render itself into yet another instance of "pure means," of the law as such.

We see then that an alignment between the practice of anarchism and the techniques of nonviolence remains possible even as it is perpetually under threat. From a legal practice of anarchism, grounded as it is in nonviolence and the avoidance of claims to truth and mythic forms of authority, we can see that a political practice of anarchism is also possible (both in the past, present and future). This is a practice that is not immune to myth (nothing could ever be) but which takes advantage of nonviolence as a basis for its own modes of engagement, letting nonviolence and technique serve as a loose guide – the looser the better – for what such a community would actually be and do.

In this way, the law – even in terms of its human practices – is not fated to falsehood, to lying (in the guise of forbidding lying), nor are the subjects who live under and through such a law similarly fated. It is one thing to say that God never lies. It is another to accept the fallible, all too human actor, one who is either stripped of the ornamentation that the law usually offers or who uses those ornaments for subversive purposes (i.e., for technique, for "politicizing art"), and who would (therefore) not know the truth if it was staring her in the face – and for Benjamin it is, at all times – and say that she too is practicing law.

Notes

* Thanks to Andreas Philippopoulos-Mihalopoulos and Maria Javed for their help in making this chapter possible.

1 I discuss Benjamin's attempts to decenter his own authority in his texts in Martel, 2015.

2 Thus, at the end of "On the Concept of History," which was written towards the end of his life, Benjamin famously writes, "The soothsayers who queried time and learned what it had in store certainly did not experience it as either homogenous or empty. Whoever keeps this in mind will perhaps get an idea of how past times were experienced in remembrance – namely, in just this way. We know the Jews were prohibited from inquiring into the future: the Torah and the prayers instructed them in remembrance. This disenchanted the future, which holds sway over all those who turn to soothsayers for enlightenment. This does not imply however, that for the Jews, the future became homogenous, empty time. For every second was the small gateway in time through which the Messiah might enter" (Benjamin, 2003a, p. 397). For Benjamin, "homogenous, empty time" refers to the way that the future becomes purely phantasmatic. Insofar as the future, in his view, does not exist in any way for human beings—Benjamin is perhaps the most purely anti-teleological of all the thinkers that I know—any determination of it from the present represents an attempt to dominate and control in advance what is ultimately a contingent and open process. Whatever is attributed to this future is "homogenous" because it represents only what is desired in the present and so has no distinct or separate character of its own. It is "empty" because such projections bear no relationship to ontology or eschatology; it is merely an assertion, much like the state and the law (as generally practiced) are also assertions for Benjamin, corresponding to the false projection of authority onto screens like God and nature that he calls "mythic violence."

3 I am very much aware of the view that Benjamin embraced anarchism early on and then seemed to abandon it in favor of communism later in his life. I'm of the opinion that, while he did this formally, his theories remained deeply, even increasingly, anarchist throughout his life, whatever label he used to describe his politics.

4 I talk about this in Martel, 2007. See also Kavka, 1986.

5 For more on Hobbes and language, see Hobbes, 1991, Part I Chapter V and in particular pp. 30–31. For Benjamin, violence and projection are two sides of the same coin. Members of a language community, far from projecting, are negotiating with one another to agree on terms that enable their ability to make sense to one another.

6 On this point, Benjamin and Hobbes part company insofar as for Hobbes language is the only possible source of truth that we have (such as it is).

7 This is perhaps less the case in a nation like France where the Academy seeks to control and determine the "proper" use of French, but even there, the Academy is de facto forced to authorize decisions that have not been made by them but by the usage of millions of French speakers around the world.

8 See Martel, 2011a.

9 Although there is some murkiness on this point for Benjamin.
10 In a new book on public things, Bonnie Honig makes an argument about Arendt's views of work (which is normally considered to be a mere backdrop to action) that, in my view, accords very strongly with Benjamin's notion of technique. See Honig, 2017.
11 In "the Work of Art in the Age of Technical Reproducibility," Benjamin describes the way that fascism (and liberalism as well) promotes the distraction of the masses by falsely including them in mass forms of reproduction that in fact are a vehicle for the leader's or the state's projections. He tells us at the end of that essay, "such is the aestheticization of politics as practiced by fascism. Communism responds by politicizing art" Benjamin, 2003b, p. 122.
12 Many artists (Jasper Johns comes immediately to mind in the U.S. context) have experimented with altering the form of flags to express some dissension from the patriotism and nationalism that a flag is normally meant to provoke. I'm not sure that having such a flag would have much of an effect per se upon a conference, but it is suggestive of one kind of direction that the conference could engage with in order to maximize the disruption of phantasm.
13 I discuss something akin to this in my discussion of Assia Djebar's text *Children of the New World*. In that text, Djebar has a character named Youssef witnessing a huge demonstration against French rule in Algeria. She writes that before Youssef, "the green flags of Islam, of the rediscovered dignity of his people, kept advancing" Djebar, 2005. p. 120. Djebar goes on to write, "Youssef, whose only true love was for this shifting reality, this flood tide of wretchedness, would continue his tale. Then his jaws would tighten and he'd add, 'Of course, they were simple rags, bits of sheets patched and sewn by the women for their luminous songs.' 'Filthy rags!' the police yelled, giving their first warning that they[i.e., the flags]'d have to disappear. The flags kept moving forward" Djebar, 2005: 120. Here, we see that flags are exposed as being "only what they are"; sheets and rags. For the French police, this is read as a failure to congeal as a people, but for Djebar, this represents a way for the Algerians to remain undetermined and contingent, hence capable of resisting in a way that the French cannot understand. In its own way, I see this as an example of the conference. I discuss this in Martel, 2011b.
14 See Marx, 1978.
15 Thus, rather than there being one flag, there are two, or many. The symbol becomes limited (or allegorized, to use Benjamin's own term) in this way.

Bibliography

Benjamin, Walter, 'Critique of Violence', in Marcus Bullock, Michael W. Jennings (eds), *Walter Benjamin: Selected Writings Vol. 1, 1913–1926*, Cambridge, MA: Harvard University Press (Belknap), 1996a.

Benjamin, Walter, 'On Language as Such and the Language of Man', in Marcus Bullock, Michael W. Jennings (eds), *Walter Benjamin: Selected Writings Vol. 1, 1913–1926*, Cambridge, MA: Harvard University Press (Belknap), 1996b.

Benjamin, Walter, 'On the Concept of History', in Howard Eiland and Michael W. Jennings (eds), *Walter Benjamin, Selected Writings, Vol. 4., 1938–1940*, Cambridge, MA: Harvard University Press (Belknap), 2003a.

Benjamin, Walter, 'The Work of Art in the Age of Technical Reproducibility', in Howard Eiland, Michael W. Jennings (eds), *Walter Benjamin: Selected Writings, Vol. 4 1938–1940*, Cambridge, MA: Harvard University Press (Belknap), 2003b.

Benjamin, Walter, *The Origin of German Tragic Drama*, New York: Verso Press, 2003c.

Djebar, Assia, *Children of the New World: A Novel of the Algerian War*. New York: The Feminist Press at the City University of New York, 2005.

Hobbes, Thomas and Richard Tuck (eds), *Leviathan*, Cambridge: Cambridge University Press, 1991.

Honig, Bonnie, *The Fight for Public Things*, Oxford: Oxford University Press, 2017.
Kavka, Gregory S., *Hobbesian Moral and Political Theory*, Princeton, NJ: Princeton University Press, 1986.
Martel, James. *Subverting the Leviathan*, New York: Columbia University Press, 2007.
Martel, James, *Divine Violence: Walter Benjamin and the Eschatology of Sovereignty*, New York: Routledge/GlassHouse, 2011a.
Martel, James *Textual Conspiracies: Walter Benjamin, Idolatry and Political Theory*, Ann Arbor, MI: University of Michigan Press, 2011b.
Martel, James, 'Benjamin's Black Flashlight: Promoting Misreading Over Persuasion to Decenter Textual and Political Authority', *Political Theory,* 43(5), 575–599, 2015.
Marx, Karl, 'Economic and Philosophical Manuscripts of 1844', in Robert Tucker (ed.), *The Marx Engels Reader,* New York: Norton, 66–125, 1978.

20

Literary materiality

Alain Pottage

Handbooks were once law books of a certain kind. In the form of the penitential (*liber poenitentialis*), which fixed the tariff for putative or actually declared sins (see Vogel, 1978), and then in the form of the confessional manual, which guided the administration of public or intimate confession,[1] the genre of the handbook or manual was an essential resource for the government of Christian subjects. *Manuale*, from which the terms 'handbook' and 'manual' were directly derived, originally referred to the case or binding which held the book together and ensured its portability and durability. The contents had to be durable too, in the sense of being a resource to which the confessor could return often, and to productive effect. A useful manual was one that effectively condensed the vast body of accrued precepts and commentaries on penitence and confession into a text that was materially ready to hand. Digital media have changed our sense of what it means for a text to be ready to hand. The genre of the handbook still involves a pretension to 'epitomised' and durable knowledge, but the digitised handbook makes academic knowledge ready to hand in a novel way. In the form of the online handbook, the relation between the binding – *manuale* – and the contents becomes contingent; many readers will want to excise only one free-standing PDF chapter from the collection, perhaps ignoring the remainder entirely. The form of the *codex* (enhanced by the capacity of the printing press to facilitate compilation) allowed the contents of a book to be traversed and retraversed within what one might call a 'repertorial' relation of part to whole: pages or sections are identified in terms of their 'place' in the book as a material-textual composite. By contrast, the digitised handbook works within a relation of severable part to whole; one can retrieve a 'part' without leafing through the 'whole'. Here, this example of materiality prompts reflection on the 'material' premises of the law of literary property. The ambition is modest; it is to distinguish three senses of literary materiality, which are presented almost as though they were diachronic moments in the history of literary artefacts, or as indices to distinct epistemes. But it would not be surprising if they were all to some degree present in our experience of today's paper books or pixelated pages. The book is one of the longest-lived technologies in the world, and its various materialisations are likely to persist for some time to come.

Repetitions

We begin with an age in which there was no such thing as authorship; or, if there was such a thing, it was more likely to be ascribed to rulers rather than to writers. According to Kantorowicz, the emergence of literary or artistic authorship was the outcome of a historical process in which the mediaeval juridical concept of papal authority as a power to create something out of nothing (as distinct from a power simply to imitate nature or to give particular form to the general laws of nature) was transferred to temporal sovereigns and thence to the artist:

> [i]t was a cascading of capacities, beginning from the abilities and prerogatives conceded *ex officio* to the incumbent of the sovereign office of legislator, spiritual or secular, to the individual and purely human abilities and prerogatives which the poet, and eventually the artist at large, enjoyed *ex ingenio*.
>
> (Kantorowicz, 1965: 363)

Indeed, it may be that the 'cascade' passed first from legislators to lawyers before reaching poets and artists: 'the jurist, not the visual artist, best represents the mediaeval creator in the sense that he substitutes for reality a fiction that surrounds and explains it' (Boureau, 2001: 17). Whatever the plausibility of this genealogy of genius, the fact is that scribes in the mediaeval world did not think of themselves as the 'authors' of 'works'.

Before the advent of the printing press, and for some time after, there was a flourishing trade in the reproduction of manuscript books.[2] By the twelfth century it had become common practice for monasteries to copy out the text blocks of a book in the scriptorium and then send the manuscript out for embellishment by lay illuminators, and by the end of that century university towns had become the nodal points of a European trade in the reproduction of manuscripts for use in the new faculties of law, theology, and philosophy. The workshops of parchment makers, scribes, text-copiers (*exemplarii*), illuminators, flourishers, and bookbinders were concentrated in certain localities of these towns. Peripatetic artisans moved between European centres, bringing with them both tendencies towards variation – namely, the distinctive cursive styles of Paris, Oxford, or Bologna – and also, at the same time, the means of fostering a certain kind of standardisation, namely the model books, spacing implements and exemplars which were used to train apprentice artisans. Books themselves might travel in the course of their production, perhaps being copied in one country, illuminated or embellished in a second, and delivered in a third (see Ramsay, 2008: 265–266).[3] The various materials of which manuscripts were made were also widely travelled commodities:[4] parchments of various qualities, carbon or iron-gall ink for the main text and vermillion for initials, headings or highlighting, gold leaf or mosaic gold for the illumination of initials, an array of pigments ranging from azure to verdigris for painted figures, and the oak boards, tawed skins, metal bosses, corner pieces and clasps that made up the bindings of the manuscript book. Because books were bespoke artefacts, it was up to the prospective purchaser to contract with each of the artisans whose work went into the finished product, and also, perhaps, to procure some of the materials used by illuminators and bookbinders. The business of commissioning manuscripts was soon facilitated by the emergence of stationers, who negotiated with artisans on behalf of the patron to commission a work of a quality that suited the patron's taste and means.

From the fourteenth century onwards, it became increasingly common for scribes to sign their handiwork, but they were not claiming authorship in any modern sense of the term. The scribe was either a 'transmitter', one whose task it was to pass on 'the precious material of an ancient treasure, and a source of authority', or a 'combiner', whose task was to 'fracture' a text so as to release its inherent truth.[5] It is true that many late-mediaeval manuscripts were produced by readers who commented, edited, or elaborated their source manuscripts in the course of copying them.[6] For example, reader-scribes who considered that their source manuscript deserved an important author might (designedly or otherwise) transform a lesser Hugh or Bernard into Hugh of Saint-Victor or Bernard of Clairvaux (see Reiter, 1996: 156–157). In other cases, the reader-scribe would go further, by interpolating commentaries or introducing entirely new sections so as to make explicit what was only implicit in the 'original' work, or to shape the work for what the scribe took to be its destined readership. These writers 'saw the text as open, not closed, as something to be improved upon, expanded, and made more relevant' (Reiter, 1996: 160). But for the most part these scribes believed that they were in the business of transmission, and they were writing for readers for whom reading was an exercise in recollection and repetition, as distinct from the more expansive modes of readership that flourished in the age of authorship.

It may be more interesting to notice the sense in which each unique scribal 'edition' articulated semantic or mnemonic 'content' into materiality so as to shape the experience of reading. From a bibliographical[7] perspective, 'materiality' is a cipher for the broader assemblage of factors or dimensions that compose the medium of the book.[8] Recall the archetype of the handbook, and the sense in which its component materialities, from the look and feel of the binding or *manuale* to the style of the script and the illumination, shaped the effects of the text. Law books offer another illustration of the ways in which the materiality of manuscripts conditioned the transmission, interpretation, and transcription of the knowledge held in them. The organisation of law books as text blocks (the Sext, the Clementines, or the Digest) framed by marginal glosses (such as those of Placentinus or Azo) made it difficult and time-consuming to copy each text with precision.[9] If learning the law was a matter of retracing the lines of filiation that connected commentaries to a core text block,[10] then obviously the textual *dispositif* had to be reproduced in toto. So the European universities established systems of regulation that introduced controls on quality, and a 'copy-right' of sorts, into the *pecia*-system, under which the scribes were paid by the quire.[11] The object was to promote redundancy rather than variety. Referring to the effects of scribal publication in the university in general, Goldschmidt suggests that the cost of copying was such as to consolidate the canon:

> the conservative persistence of the recognised standard books through an epoch when the volumes extant in the college libraries had to serve successive generations of undergraduate, and were not so easily replaced by more modern treatises [led to] a stagnation in scientific advance in the fifteenth century.
>
> (Goldschmidt, 1943: 23)

Physics

Roman and mediaeval lawyers did not divide manuscripts into a material 'embodiment' and an immaterial 'work'; they treated books as tangible things. The principles that governed property in manuscript books were those that applied to material or tangible things of all kinds. The subtleties of this mediaeval jurisprudence of literary property are recollected in Marta Madero's *Tabula Picta* (2004), which takes its title from the rubric or heading under which the glossators worked out the principles that should govern cases concerning the ownership of books and paintings. A *tabula picta* was a panel painting, a wooden board onto which the painter would layer a ground of glue and gesso before applying the pigments that were used to compose the finished painting. By extension, the rubric came to include texts and commentaries related to the question of the ownership of manuscript books (*chartae*). For mediaeval lawyers, paintings and books were species of the same genus because 'painting and writing happened when someone applied colour or ink to a surface, to a *tabula* in the case of paintings, to a *charta* or *membrana* in the case of texts' (Madero, 2004: 4–5). So the glossators construed books and paintings as composites of diverse kinds of kinds of material; minimally, the wooden or parchment substrate and the pigment or ink applied to it. The analysis of ownership made no reference to the authorship or *ingenium* of the writer, and focused instead on the question of how property rights were affected by processes of material composition and transformation.

The rubric of *tabula picta* turned on a basic scenario (or *casus*): a dispute between the owners of the two essential components of any painting or manuscript. Should the ownership of a manuscript or painting be attributed to the person who owned the underlying parchment or wooden panel, or to the person who owned the inks or pigments applied to that parchment or panel? To address this question one had to know how property rights were articulated into the materials in which they were inscribed. In the Roman law tradition, property rights were treated as though they were compounded into the material objects of which they were predicated, so that the agency of legal form was conditioned by the mechanical or physical competences of material substances. The material quality of property rights was most clearly expressed in the principle that property (*dominium*) would persist only for so long as the material object into which it was compounded survived or remained identifiable.

Although the glossators paid close attention to the nuances of material fabrication, to the composition and texture of pigments and inks, and to the relative weight, extension, or proportion of material ingredients, the 'physics' that lawyers elicited from the materiality of a manuscript was essentially juridical. Borrowing a phrase from Michael Baxandall, Madero suggests that the language of the glossators was 'a conspiracy against experience in the sense of being a collective attempt to simplify and arrange experience into manageable categories' (2004: 44).[12] The effect of this 'conspiracy' was that materiality in the ordinary or familiar sense was translated into a set of categories and processes that were driven more by the dynamics of legal argument than by any 'natural' properties or propensities. Adverting to Madero's study, Yan Thomas observes that although the glossators 'borrowed eclectically from various philosophical currents' in their exploration of the materiality of paintings and manuscripts, their analyses were always focused on a specific question: 'beyond the identity of the *res*, what was in question was the imputation of a right: to whom should the mutable and transformed thing be imputed?' (Thomas, 2005: 56). Although rights were rooted in material things, and were therefore susceptible to the physical processes that affect material things, the glossators were concerned with the question of how to elicit generalisable modes of appropriation from the flux of these processes.

Where a more empirical kind of physics might have observed the formation of complex kinds of composite or hybrids, held together by the action of covalent elements, the object of the lawyers' analysis was to identify one element in the material composite as the most significant or preeminent element, and to ascribe ownership to the person who supplied that element. This in turn required a juridical theory as to which element should prevail, and why. The logic of property is a logic of priority, so when two material substances are composed, as they were in the typified scenario of *tabula picta*, then the property right of one of the original owners has to give way to the property right of the other. One cannot have two exclusive rights in the same *res*. Even if one person has to compensate the other for what they have lost, the principle of exclusivity requires that one right should trump the other. So the textures and dynamics of materials had to be translated into a legal physics that was based on a set of actions that generated a single or predominant form. The basic grammatical operations were 'to be one, to take root, to unite, to blend, to mix, to prevail' (Madero, 2004, 3).[13]

The characterisation of manuscripts and paintings as property changed in the period between the eleventh and the fourteenth centuries. The earlier glossatorial commentaries suggested that a manuscript belonged to the owner of the parchment, on the basis that the substrate should prevail over what was added to or edified upon it, whereas a painting belonged to the painter because the 'paint' (meaning the skill of the painter) was more precious than the *tabula*. Then, as the work of scribes gained in appreciation, the glossators began to suggest that writing was more precious than the *charta* upon which it was written. According to Madero, Azo of Bologna, who was professor of Roman law at the University of Bologna from 1190 to 1220, was the first of the glossators to elevate the art of writing to this status: 'the scribes [*scriptores*] of our time have become painters, and it is almost always evident that the writing is more precious [*pretiosior*] than the *charta*' (cited in Madero, 2004: 53). For the post-glossator Odofredo, the skill displayed by contemporary scribes was such as to warrant elevating writing above painting; as a rule, writing carried its parchment support with it, precisely because of the artistry expressed in textual inscriptions, whereas a painting would carry its support with it only in certain cases. Bartolus proposed yet another criterion of value (*pretiositas*), which started from the premise that liquid things were more precious than dry things. In the case of a *tabula picta*, the pigments covered the surface of a *tabula* so entirely that the liquid prevailed over the dry and the paints attached the board; in the case of *chartae*, the inscriptions accrued to the substrate. There were further complexities to the analysis. For example: did the *tabula* and the pigments applied to it subsist as two distinct but inseparable material layers, such that the pigments carried the board with them by an effect of prevalence, or, was the theory that although the pigments and the board were unalike in raw substance, they nonetheless formed a single thing that was continuous in 'spirit' according to the principle of *ferruminatio*? (Madero, 2004, 32). But what is significant about this particular sense of literary materiality is simply the point that the book was an artefact and effect of juridical physics.

Forma

According to the usual histories, literary property in the modern sense was founded on the suppression of material agency. Instead of eliciting the ontogenetic principle of the work from the 'physics' of its component materials, or from an analysis of the relative prestige of liquid things and dry things, wholes and parts, or of the modes of fusing, joining, or attaching one thing to another, the origination of the work was ascribed to the extra-material or supra-material agency of the author. The historical premises of this theory of origination are summarised in Walter Ong's observation that the printing press was 'the first assembly line in the history of technology' (2002: 118).[14] The printing press had ideological effects: it made (visible) a difference between the spiritual and material dimensions of the work, and, by implication, the difference between the ontogenetic agency of the author and the matter formed by that agency. Friedrich Kittler observes that 'Gutenberg's moveable type was never intended for mass production as such, but rather was supposed to compete with the calligraphic elegance of manuscript pages' (Kittler, 2001: 39–41), but the stamping out of potentially endless numbers of identical copies of typeset manuscripts, each with the same disposition of text, fonts, page numbers, and typographical errors, effectively transformed the significance of the manuscript, from a unique edition or specific artefact into the embodiment of an original immaterial work.

The printing press brought with it an entirely novel sense of the products of a writer's workmanship. Because manuscripts were now destined for mechanical reproduction, writers were conscious that the sheaf of pages that they held in their hands, almost invariably with a view to selling it to a publisher, was the original in a series of embodiments of an intangible 'work'. In other words, it was the prospective coming into being of a series of copies that allowed the manuscript to be perceived as the 'original' of these copies, and which turned originality into an immaterial quality. The effect was to relegate to history the mode of material invention that was possible with scribal publication:

> The economics of printing discouraged experimentation with type and layout. A printed book entailed a capital commitment. A new typeface, one that offered a peculiar graphical effect, was a major investment in cast metal. A new font had to be used to print many books before it repaid itself. And to design a page was in effect to design hundreds or thousands of pages; a great deal of paper got staked on that design. The printing industry could not afford to treat each new edition as a new case, a new problem in the philosophy of printing.
>
> (Wood, 1998: 86)

All of this has been amply discussed; so what difference does it make if one rehabilitates the material agencies that were suppressed by the theory of authorship as spiritual *ingenium*?

Georges Didi-Huberman suggests that the Renaissance sense of artistic invention or authorship emerged from a contrast between two modes of production. The Renaissance period had seen the expansion of various modes of imprinting, exemplified by Pisanello's portrait medals, new techniques of engraving, the development of sculptural techniques, and (last but not least) the advent of the printing press. The prestige of the artist or author is based on the differentiation of two modes of imprinting or moulding: a merely mechanical mode in which the template was a material form and a creative mode in which the template was (first) a mental form:

> The form obtained by an imprint was inconsistent with the ideal of art because it was too closely derived from matter as it already existed and too remote from the idea that was so dear to the classical theory of art. Being both borrowed and imprinted [*à la fois empruntée (prélevée) et empreintée (physiquement marquée)*], form was transferred directly from matter to matter. In order to come into existence it did not have to be formed in the mind of the artist.
>
> (Didi-Huberman, 2008: 121)

The true artist 'moulded with his mind' (Didi-Huberman, 2008: 129), and the mind thoroughly controlled the means by which a style was made material.

The Renaissance understanding of creativity as a process of material 'moulding' has survived into the age of the digital work. The characterisation of the literary work in European law as 'the author's own intellectual creation' assumes that creativity is an innate force or capacity that manifests itself in a distinctive arrangement or patterning of (quasi-)material elements; 'creativity' is a reflex of the combinatorial potential of the elements that inhere in the medium 'moulded' by the creator. Consider, for example, the proposition that the text of a newspaper article qualifies as a literary work because although words

> are not as such an intellectual creation of the author who employs them, . . . through the choice, sequence and combination of those words . . . the author may express his creativity in an original manner and achieve a result which is an intellectual creation.[15]

So literary creativity or originality is a function of the combinatorial potential of the (quasi-) material medium that is exploited by the author. Kittler observes that in the age of the printing press 'the internal process known as "the ability to write" [was] transferred to the external process known as the "typesetters case"' (2001: 40); one might reverse that proposition and say instead that the 'external' or material process of typesetting becomes the archetype of a psychic process of creation. And the model is sufficiently abstract to encompass the case of photography, where other variables are implicitly analogised to the contents of the typesetter's case.[16] To return to my opening observation about the longevity of the book as a form of technology, the spectral materiality of the digital work merely retrenches the archetype of print.

In the imaginary, the process of creation is articulated into the material-combinatory scheme figured by the typesetter's case. The process of invention or creative speculation is construed as a process of 'moulding', so that the creative process is worked out through and expressed in a medium of spectral materiality. And, not only does materiality already permeate or inhabit the figure of 'spiritual' creativity in this way, but the question of what can be created and expressed through the process of moulding is conditioned by the material *dispositif* of the mould.

Here, the etymology of the word 'form' becomes interesting. In Roman culture *forma* could describe either the finished shape and configuration of an artefact or the process by which the artefact was formed. In this latter sense, *forma* expressed the action of imparting, impressing, or imprinting form (Conso, 1990: 564); more precisely, it characterised particular modes of fabrication, involving 'the hardening or solidification, usually in some kind of casing or mould, of a material substance that is either supple (vegetable fibres) or fluid (molten metal) (ibid., 590). Metals – which could be reduced to a molten state and pressed into almost any desired figure or form – were the common examples of materials that could be moulded in this way, but the same sense of *forma* as moulding was sometimes applied to the conformation of a machine (ibid., 578). The relation of counter-form to form was characterised as a complementarity of shape; counter-form was to form as a concave mould was to its convex products. This image of complementarity or enantiomorphism is crucial because it gets at the sense in which *forma* was neither form nor matter, neither counter-form nor form; rather, it was a name for the relation or specific intersection itself, the relation 'formed' between the terms of these distinctions.

The material:material scheme of *forma* suggests an arrangement in which the terms are unmotivated or reversible, so that the privileging of original over copy, or form over matter, seems less assured. In the doubly material scheme of *forma*, and the eminently material processes of contact and impression, agency and receptivity, creation and reproduction began to seem symmetrical. And this is indeed what one finds if one looks more closely at the logic of creation and reproduction that underpins copyright law. In the jurisprudence of literary property, the logic of moulding articulates the two crucial operations of creation and reproduction: on one side, the expression of an artistic idea in a material medium effects a kind of original moulding, fixing an idea in matter; on the other, reproduction reverses the process, abstracting or 'lifting' the idea by replicating the material form in which it was expressed. Crudely, the copy precedes the original in the sense that what is protected by copyright law is what can be copied, or what can be proved to have been copied. So, the original has to have the kind of form that is conjured up by the logic of material moulding.

Opera

Although late mediaeval glossators and modern copyright lawyers construed the materiality of literary works in radically different ways, both styles of jurisprudence were focused on the question of property. For the glossators, the question was how to elicit the form and definition of property from intrications of material substance; for the modern copyright lawyer, the question is how to fix the specific intersection between materiality and intangibility that defines the copyright work.[17] Both modes of reification (precisely because they are modes of reification) abstract literary artefacts from the broader material or technical networks in which they are implicated. For Madero this is something of a virtue. In her account of *tabula picta*, she underscores the taxonomic divide between property and contract, or between the glossators' analysis of property in paintings or writings and their analysis of contracts made between patrons and scribes. The point is to emphasise the peculiarly abstracted or involuted nature of reflection on the question of property – its character as a 'conspiracy against experience'. Because they so readily unfold legal form into social relations, contracts have long been a privileged object of 'law and society' scholarship.[18] And the effect of Madero's emphasis on the distinction between property and contract would be to forestall this tendency to contextualisation.

Against this background, Kant's philosophical justification of copyright is interesting precisely because it is premised on contract or mandate rather than property. The basic proposition, which has prompted a good deal of commentary, is that literary works are means of communication with the public:

> A book is a writing, which represents a discourse addressed by some one to the public, through visible signs of speech. . . . He who speaks to the public in his own name is called the author (*auctor*); he who addresses the writing to the public in the name of the author is the publisher. . . . The publisher, again, speaks, by the aid of the printer as his workman (*operarius*), yet not in his own name, for otherwise he would be himself the author, but in the name of the author; and he is only entitled to do so in virtue of a mandate (*mandatum*) given him to that effect by the author.
>
> (Kant, 1996)

In this passage, Kant identifies the only form of contract that could articulate communication as ongoing or open-ended process; namely, the form of the mandate.

Whereas the legal bond between the publisher and the printer (as workman or *operarius*) was subject to the ordinary form of the contract as a delimited commercial exchange, an agreement for the use of labour time or for the transfer of a specified object, the bond between the publisher and the author had to be construed as a personal obligation that could not be satisfied by the payment of money or the transfer of an object. For Kant, a mandate was 'a positive right against a person, to require of him that he perform something or render me some service', and the 'performance' or 'service' in question would be as enduring as the discourse of the author.

Kant's recourse to the Roman law form of the mandate[19] was prompted by the practical realities of book publication in the late eighteenth century. His essay 'on the injustice of reprinting works' was a contribution to a sustained debate that ran from 1773 to 1794,[20] and which explored various themes inherent in the old form of the privilege. Jean Paul estimated that there were about 300,000 active German-speaking readers at the end of the eighteenth century, by which reckoning the community of German-speaking readers would have been the largest linguistic community in late eighteenth-century Europe.[21] The problem for authors and publishers of works written in German was that this single linguistic community was politically or jurisdictionally divided into a number of polities.[22] So a privilege that secured the exclusive right of publication for a work in one jurisdiction would not prevent the reprinting of that work in a neighbouring territory and, perhaps, its re-importation onto 'home' ground at a lower price. Precisely because it was a potentially profitable form of industry or commerce, some states tolerated or even encouraged reprinting.[23] The Catholic states had lagged behind Protestant states in terms of literacy and book production, but in the 1750s and 1760s Austria overcame this lag to become the third largest producer of German books. The most notorious of the Viennese reprinters was Trattner, 'who embellished his stolen wares with charming little rococo ornaments called Röslein und Zierater' (Friedenthal, 1963: 267) and who mobilised considerable resources in the reprinting of his 'pirated' works. While states and some publishers could profit from this arbitraging of jurisdictions, authors and most publishers considered that the value of their works was being dissipated. So the objective was to found the rights of publishers (and hence authors) on a legal form that was more fundamental or generalisable than the privilege. Kant's essay ends with just this kind of proposition:

> If the idea of publication of a book as such were firmly grasped and elaborated with the requisite elegance of Roman legal scholarship, complaints against unauthorized publishers could indeed be taken to court without it being necessary first to wait for a new law.
>
> (Kant, 1996: 35, some words omitted)

Kant abstracted the empirical realities of the book trade into the categorical forms of his theory of law by distinguishing property from contract. His justification of copyright turned on a distinction between the work as product (*opus*) or industrial manufacture (*opus mechanicum*) and the work as action (*opera*). In one dimension, a literary work is the material object that is edited, reproduced and marketed by the publisher, and purchased and conserved by its readers (the *opus mechanicum*). The right to control the reproduction of a literary work could not be derived from the author's original property rights in the manuscript from which the *opus* was reproduced. These material rights were transferred in their entirety when the author sold the manuscript to the publisher. So the continuing right of the author could not be founded on property; it had to be founded in an inalienable faculty or competence that could only be 'conceded' to the publisher through a mandate:

> [The] right of the author [is] not a right to the thing, namely to the copy (for the owner can burn it before the author's eyes), but an innate right in his own person, namely, to prevent another from having him speak to the public without his consent, which consent certainly cannot be presumed because he has already given it exclusively to someone else.
>
> (Kant, 1996: 35)

When the author sold the manuscript to the publisher, he also entered into a separate, parallel, contract of mandate under which the publisher was authorised to 'carry on the affair' of the author. Kant's theory was that anyone who reproduced a literary work necessarily represented themselves as the agent of the author – their publisher – and given the nature of the publishing business this right would already have been granted exclusively by the author to the authorised publisher.

The relation between the contract of sale and the mandate, or hence the *opus* and *opera*, was such that the material *opus* was just 'a mute instrument for the diffusion of the author's discourse to the public'. In other words, the material book was a vehicle for the expression of actions 'that can have their existence only in a person' (Kant, 1996: 35). This was not true of all creative works. The relation between the work and the book, or between the creative expression of the author (*opera*) and the industrial manufacture (*opus mechanicum*) in which it was materialised and diffused was very different from the relation between the idea and material form of a sculpture or engraving:

> A drawing that someone has made or has had someone else engrave for him or execute in stone, metal, or plaster, can be moulded or cast and so traded publicly by one who buys this product; as always, what someone can do with his thing in his own name does not require the consent of another. For it is a work (*opus*, not *opera alterius*), which anyone who possesses it can alienate without even having to mention the name of the originator.
>
> (Kant, 1996: 34)

One could reproduce a sculpture without the consent of the sculptor because what was reproduced was an idea made material: the style of the sculptor was realised (or exhausted) in the material form of the work. The same was not true of a literary work.

A work was not just a material arrangement of words and symbols; it was a means for relaying the representations represented by the author.

So what is the vitality or action of the work as *opera*? How does the discourse of the author engage the reader? If the book is just a mute medium, then how does the reader elicit or decode from the book the personal, subjective, original message of the author? How does the *opus* transmit the *opera*?

There are properly philosophical answers to that question, which seek to locate Kant's essays on the nature of the book in his broader critical project. But, if one foregrounds the question of the book's material or medial form, one notices the broader *dispositif* in which the literary *opera*, and the critical philosophy that it communicated to an enlightened public, was implicated. Historically, the manuscript book was the medium of a style of painting that was eclipsed by the emergence of perspectival panel paintings. Roman lawyers would have been familiar with Greek, Roman, and Byzantine examples of panel painting, but the questions which concerned mediaeval glossators had to do with techniques of panel painting which flourished between the twelfth and sixteenth centuries, and which ultimately took in some of the most familiar names in the canon of Western art – Giotto, van Eyck, Lochner, and Cranach. There is an appropriately material illustration of the evolutionary relation between manuscript illumination and panel painting: the ground of gesso and glue that was applied to the wooden board of a panel painting was often reinforced with strips of linen or parchment, and in some cases with fragments of illuminated manuscript (Thompson, 1956: 32). One medium cannibalised the other. Perhaps this corroborates Panofsky's celebrated observation that book illumination was not 'killed by the invention of printing' but that 'it had already begun to commit suicide by converting itself into painting. Even without Gutenberg it would have died of an overdose of perspective' (Panofsky, 1953: 28). But what if 'perspectivism' of painting actually re-entered the book, not in the form of painting but as a technique of textual description.

Perspectivism

According to Friedrich Kittler, when Vasari postdated Gutenberg's invention of the printing press to 1457, the same year as he supposed Alberti to have discovered a technique of 'tracing natural perspectives', he made a connection between print and perspective that is essential to understanding literature as an 'optical media technology' (2001, 40–42). The technique of perspective becomes the premise of a literary 'art of seeing', which was in turn the basis of the improbably intimate relationship between Romantic authors and their readers:

> [W]riter and reader adhere to the extra-linguistic, perspectival actuality of objects as such. This imposes a new form of writing on them, which is called (three centuries after Brunelleschi) perspectival. In the future, texts must be written so that it is possible for readers to reconstruct a view of the object written about in the poem even when they have never viewed the object themselves. Indeed, not only must they be able to reconstruct a view of the absent object, but they must also

> be able to reconstruct the view of perspective taken by the equally absent author with regard to the object.
>
> (Kittler, 2010: 91)

The proposition is that the improbably intimate relationship between Romantic authors and their readers – the nexus formed by the work as *opera* – was based on a literary 'art of seeing'. The geometry of perspective, which was discovered by Alberti, and which could be practised in the *camera obscura*, became the imaginary frame of literary production and consumption.

Once literature ceased to be a rehearsal of prior texts, and the themes and enunciative positions contained in those texts, it became the art of representing things as they existed in the world. More precisely, it became the art of re-representing representation; what is represented in Romantic literature is not 'reality' as such but the perspectival field that brings objects into view, and, also, by implication, the perspectivising locus of the author. The literary work is proto-cinematic – the reader replays the optical narrative uploaded by the author. The *camera obscura* becomes a *lanterna magica*. With reference to the literary strategy of Hoffmann's *Devil's Elixirs*, which purported to be based on transcriptions found in an old manuscript, Kittler observes (citing Hoffmann) that 'the individual novel reader does not actually buy the book formed from those papers' at all; rather, the reader acquires '"the manifold images of the *camera obscura* that are revealed to you" [and, by implication, the perspectival field that gives the images and their author to the reader]' (2010: 112). In this period, 'literature itself trades under the name of a quasi-optical medium' (ibid., 93).

And this implicates philosophy. In a proposal that is calculated to provoke the serious Kantian – is there any other kind of Kantian? – Kittler suggests that the perspectivism that is articulated by the material-medial form of the book actually cued up the philosophical innovations retailed in Kant's own works. Johann Heinrich Lambert, the inventor of 'transcendental optics', abstracted the material-geometrical frame of Alberti's perspective, which required a painter to draw out a ground plan and a side elevation, into a set of mathematical functions. This mathematical recreation of 'the perspective of a seeing subject' became the basis of a science that Lambert, using the term for the first time, called 'phenomenology'. Perception was conditioned by what he called 'transcendental' functions:

> The adjective 'transcendental' is a mathematical term that Lambert takes from his transcendent trigonometrical functions and imports into philosophy All that is left for Kant, Lambert's younger friend and pupil, is to go back and generalize this 'transcendental optics' as something that is now called transcendental philosophy. In other words, which are unfortunately seldom used by philosophers: German idealism also emerged from the history of optical media.
>
> (Kittler, 2010: 96)

Incidentally, to return to Kant's distinction between the book (*opera*) and the painting or sculpture (*opus*), it may be that the difference between the two forms is derived from this sense of the book as a quasi-optical medium: however 'auratic' it might be, a sculpture or painting does not communicate a perspectival field in this way. But, keeping in mind the question of what allows a book to function as *opera*, the interesting point is that this 'optical' *dispositif* is doubled by another; one medial frame is wrapped into another.

There are various histories of readers and reading. For example, was there really a reading revolution in the eighteenth century, in which readers shifted from an 'intensive' mode of reading, based on an involuted process of recitation and reanimation, to an 'extensive' mode of reading, characterised by a preference for variety over redundancy?[24] Whatever one's sense of these questions, it may be that the perspectivism of books had to do with the particular kind of know-how that became generalised in the course of the eighteenth century. 'Know-how' here is an operationalisation of the hermeneutic of second-order observation – the practice of observing oneself in the act of observation, and hence of seeing one's observations or actions against the backdrop of the other possibilities of action or observation that seem 'now' to have been open to one.

Hans Ulrich Gumbrecht suggests that this practice became 'habitual' in the eighteenth and nineteenth centuries, as the assumption that one could access objects in the world, or that there was a common perspectival 'ground', became increasingly problematic:

> A second order observer will quickly realize that her perceptions of the world, and the ways in which she will transform such perceptions into units of knowledge or representations, must depend on her different points of view. As it is also evident to a second order observer that the number of possible perspectives is potentially infinite, this will soon lead to the conclusion that, for each object of reference outside the human mind, there is a potential infinity of representations. Within a brief stretch of time around 1800, this sequence of logical steps produced what I would call an "epistemological horror vacui," that is the fear that reference objects capable of having an infinity of representations might, in the end, not exist at all in the ontological sense.
>
> (Gumbrecht, 2011)

This unease is already evident in Kant's critical philosophy, which equivocates between the two epistemic premises of transcendental optics.[25] Print media played a crucial role in the 'habitualisation' of second-order observation because this particular hermeneutic art responded to a problem generated by modes of communication at a distance. If the meaning of any communicative offering is an effect of the way that the recipient observes the act of enunciation of the speaker or writer, and thence 'recombines' information and utterance, then the historical shift from face-to-face communication to communication by means which do not allow the reader to 'see' the act and context of enunciation directly (or the writer to anticipate or recuperate this 'seeing' and adjust their enunciation accordingly) unhitches the elements of communication. What results is 'an immense, unpredictable, expansion of connectivity potential' (Luhmann, 2012: 155); readers of print media have to (re)connect information to utterance by means of various culturally developed practices of second-order observation.

Kant had little to say about the actual contents of printed works. There was no further specification of the 'speech' that was purveyed to the public through the medium of 'visible characters', and there was no discussion of how authors staged the figurative or conceptual 'objects' that they presented to their readers. We know, however, that there was then no single German-speaking 'public'; Jean Paul counted three:

> In Germany there are three publics: 1) the broad, almost uneducated and unlearned one of the lending libraries – 2) the learned one, made up of professors, [theological] candidates, students and reviewers – 3) the educated one, consisting of men of the world and women of breeding, artists and the upper classes, who are at least cultivated by contacts and travel.
>
> (cited in North, 2008: 25)

The novel was a form that was familiar to all three of these publics, and the eighteenth-century novel inducted its readers into the technique of second-order observation. If one leaves aside examples such as Sterne's *Tristram Shandy*, or for different reasons, Richardson's *Clarissa*,[26] most eighteenth-century novels sought to dissimulate the agency of the author, the better to allow the reader to immerse themselves in the plot without being distracted by the authorship. The reader did not have to communicate with the author through the novel. So, if the novel worked as an education in second-order observation, it did so by inducing the reader to participate in a specific differentiation of fact from fiction.

The novel is a kind of machine or technology in the sense that it 'generates its own plausibility itself':

> [A narrative] generates and transports an uncertainty, which it itself produces and renews again and again, and which depends upon further information. It . . . lives off self-produced surprises, self-constructed tensions, and it is precisely this fictional unity that is the structure which enables real reality to be distinguished from fictional reality and the boundary from one realm to the other to be crossed.
>
> (Luhmann, 2000: 54).[27]

Having learned to distinguish 'real reality' from 'fictional reality', the reader is then invited to play with and within the bracketed reality of a fictional narrative. The reader participates in the narrative, not in the mode of immediate identification with the characters and their predicaments, but through an observation of how the protagonists observe. Readers from the eighteenth century onwards learned how to learn from the way that characters in a novel observed, were deceived, reacted to events, and so on. Martin Klepper quotes Henry James, whom he takes to be the most accomplished diagnostician of this mode of perspectivism: 'the figures in any picture, the agents in any drama, are interesting only in proportion as they feel their respective situations; since the consciousness, on their part, of the complication exhibited forms for us their link of connection with it' (Klepper, 2011: 13).[28] Crudely, immersion in a narrative could not help but bring with it more or less explicit feedback effects on the 'reality' lived by the reader. In the course of this exercise of 'try[ing] out virtual realities on oneself' (Luhmann, 2000: 60), what readers learned above all was to see that characters are always 'situated', and see how this situatedness re-presented their own social predicaments.

★

The central story here is one of the suppression of the vitality of literary materiality. Modern copyright law imagines the literary work as a transcendently intangible form, which retains its 'shape' and meaning even as it is replicated into a diversity of material embodiments. The material form of the book is just a vehicle means for the expression of authorial invention. So, for example, Kant's distinction between *opus* and *opera* is typically reinterpreted as a prototype of the modern distinction between expressive personality and mute materiality,[29] despite the fact that Kant says nothing about the personality, and still less the genius, of authors. Modern interpreters retain only the distinction between person and thing, or between the spiritual and the material. But it is interesting to notice how, as it puts this distinction to work, copyright law articulates literary materialities into itself.

First, precisely because it fabricates a species of property, modern copyright law follows closely in the footsteps of the mediaeval glossators in their reflections on *tabula picta*. The language of material *pretiositas* or dignity is now only of antiquarian interest, and modern copyright law addresses intangible works rather than material artefacts, but the fabrication of the intangible still depends on the elaboration of a juridical physics. In the courtroom, copyright jurisprudence deploys a particular forensic technique; it elicits intangible works from their material 'embodiments' by deciphering material textures or traces as the manifestations of an immanent formative principle (the 'work').[30] This involves moving between materiality and intangibility within a process of discursive 'hybridisation' (see Sherman, 2010). But both poles – the material and the intangible – are artefacts of a juridical physics; and, more important, a physics predicated on the spectral materiality of (metaphorically) the 'typesetter's case'. The figure of a material-combinatory medium is the middle term that articulates the relation between the material and intangible. On one side of that relation, material traces manifest the 'creative choices' made by the author. In other words, observable materiality expresses spectral materiality. On the other side of the relation, the virtual or spectral materiality of the 'typesetter's case' conditions how the 'spiritual' or intangible form of the work appears. 'Real' materiality and intangibility are both a function of virtual materiality. It is true that the forensic reconstruction of literary property is less 'material' than the forensics of artistic property; in the case of books, attention is focused on the semantic and thematic composition of the work, whereas the analysis of a painting or design might scrutinize the textures of brushstrokes, or the relative opacity of motifs. But the intangible work is more indebted to materiality than one might suspect.

Notes

1 The classic work here is Michaud-Quantin (1962).
2 This paragraph draws on: Richard Rouse and Mary Rouse (2000), de Hamel (1992), Filippone Overty (2008), Morgan and Thomson (2008).
3 This remained the case even after the advent of printing; printed books would travel as unfinished commodities: '[Books] were sent all over Europe in loose, rough sheets, packed in barrels. Each barrel would contain a certain number of quires – often of different books – and the assembling of these sheets and the making-up of complete copies was the task of the recipient of the consignment' (Goldschmidt, 1950, 10).
4 '[W]riting and decoration required mineral, vegetable and animal constituents which, in some cases, had to be imported from distant places only dreamed of by those who used them. Thus, an illuminated book often shows evidence of the fullest extent of international trade in the Middle Ages' (Michael, 2008, 178).
5 For this sense of scribal transmission and combination, see Barthes (1970, 185). On mediaeval combination, or 'compilation', cf. Hathaway (1989). This mode of recollection and repetition differs from the mode of 'substitution' that, according to Nagel and Wood, characterised the apprehension of images or buildings: '[M]odern copies of painted icons were understood as effective surrogates for lost originals, and new buildings were understood as reinstantiations, through typological association, of prior structures. The literal circumstances and the historical moment of an artifact's material execution were not routinely taken as components of its meaning and function; such facts about an artifact were seen as accidental rather than as constitutive features. Instead, the artifact functioned by aligning itself with a diachronic chain of replications. It substituted for the absent artifacts that preceded within the chain' (Nagel and Wood, 2005, 405).
6 '[S]ome types of mediaeval texts frequently display such radical rewriting during the copying process that they challenge theoretical notions of authorship and textuality. The mediaeval reader/scribe created the text on the page – not as publisher or even as an editor, whose concern it is to preserve and enhance the author's work, but as an author, rewriting, reorganizing, even renaming a work to suit his (or less frequently her) purposes' (Reiter, 1996, 154).
7 In the sense of the work of Donald F. McKenzie (especially 2002).
8 '[I]f we only take time to look closely enough, we will find very few cases, if any, where meaning will oscillate with just one dimension of materiality. A book, for example, is not meaning and materiality – but meaning and pages, characters, a cover, (very often) pictures, impressions of touch, impressions of smell, and more' (Gumbrecht, 2003: 173–178).
9 'The provision of accurate copies of texts was indispensable for studies in canon and civil law. Some of the key texts – most notably, the Digest – were very long, and the writing of texts with marginal glosses was an undertaking that called for more skill (and time) than the average student or teacher was likely to possess' (Ramsay, 'Law' in Thomson & Morgan, *The Cambridge History of the Book*, 250–290, at p 263.
10 For an account of this, see Thomas (2005, 45–73).
11 'Booksellers (or stationarii) would stock copies of texts that had been approved by the university, which itself would have laid down the number of gatherings (peciae) in each book and the price that was to be charged per pecia. A student could only obtain books from one of these stationers, for they had been given a monopoly within the university town; but the student had the option of either borrowing the peciae one at a time and making his own copy or contracting with a professional scribe to write a copy for him. At Bologna and Paris, a university committee examined and verified texts (both new works and, once a year, old

exemplars), and the university then published a list of books with their numbers of peciae and their price; stationers then displayed this list in their shop, together with the names of authorized scribes' (Ramsay, 'Law', at p 264).

12 *Tabula Picta*, at p 3, citing Baxandall (1971, 44).

13 See also p 32, where Madero identifies three basic 'logics': 'A logic of *praevalentia* which allowed one to determine which of two things would accrue to the other, a criterion which, for the glossators, was based on the relation between whole and part, or on prince. A logic that governed forms of union (the opposition between *ferruminatio* and *adplumbatio*), and, finally, a logic based on the classification of things, which followed Stoic physics in distinguishing between simple, composite, and collective things'.

14 The formulation is anticipated by Goldschmidt, 1950, at p 12: 'By utilizing their advantage of cheaper manufacture to the full and marketing a satisfactory substitute for every current type of handwritten book at a much lower price, the printers ultimately put the scriveners out of business altogether and created one of the first mechanised mass-producing agencies that played an important part in our civilization'.

15 *Infopaq Intenational v. Danske Dagblades Forening* C-5/08 (2009), at para 45.

16 See the discussion of portrait photography in *Painer v. Standards Verlag GmbH* C-145/10 (2012), at para 91–92: 'In the preparation phase, the photographer can choose the background, the subject's pose and the lighting. When taking a portrait photograph, he can choose the framing, the angle of view and the atmosphere created. Finally, when selecting the snapshot, the photographer may choose from a variety of developing techniques the one he wishes to adopt or, where appropriate, use computer software. By making those various choices, the author of a portrait photograph can stamp the work created with his 'personal touch'.

17 See, notably, Sherman (2010).

18 The classic modern example is Macaulay (1963), but the turn to contract as a vehicle for 'law and society' contextualisation dates back to Durkheim.

19 In fact, there was nothing truly Roman about Kant's sense of the mandate, which was more akin to the modern form of direct agency.

20 According to the recapitulation effected by Ernst Martin Gräff's *Toward a Clarification of the Property and Property Rights of Writers and Publishers*, published in 1794 (cited in Woodmansee, 1984: 440).

21 North, 2008, at p 25. North estimates a yearly total of 5000 new titles of book and periodical in the years between 1780 and 1782. Compare Edmund Burke's estimate that England had 80,000 readers in 1790 (reported in Altick, 1998: 49). Altick considers this estimate to be 'interesting' in light of the fact that even the most popular novel of the time would have had a cumulative print run of more than 9000 copies, but observes (at p 71) that in the early part of the century Defoe's *True-Born Englishman* had enjoyed a total print run of some 80,000 copies.

22 '[E]ighteenth-century Germany consisted of three hundred independent states. To safeguard their respective investments against piracy, writers and their publishers would have had to obtain a privilege in every one of them. To make matters worse, mercantilist economic policies caused some states not only to tolerate piracy but actively to encourage it as a legitimate source of revenue' (Woodmansee, 1984: 438–439).

23 There was also the internal example of the issuing new privileges for works that were already under privilege: 'Alteration in such cases could mean a mere change of format from quarto to octavo. What mattered was the lower price of the new edition, which could be managed if one did not have to pay the author and used smaller type and cheaper paper' (Selwyn, 2000:185).

24 See Wittmann (1999), discussing a thesis advanced by Rolf Engelsing.

25 See Gumbrecht, 2011: 'If [Kant] was, on the one hand, the last truly great philosopher who could persuade himself that humans had the necessary equipment to capture the world of

objects; nobody on the other side of the epistemological divide pushed possible doubts against such optimism that early and that far'. The point about the two epistemic premises is made by Jonathan Crary, with respect to a different optical technology: the *camera obscura*: 'In the aftermath of Kant's work there is an irreversible clouding over of the transparency of the subject-as-observer. Vision, rather than a privileged form of knowledge, becomes itself an object of knowledge, of observation' (1990, 70).

26 Monied readers of Richardson sought to thwart or diffuse the author's (seemingly malign) intentions by writing their own concluding parts to the novel (see Judge, 2009).

27 See also p 57: '[F]ictionality presupposes that we can know what the world ought to look like in order for the fiction to be able to count as a correct description of the world'.

28 Klepper discerns two intertwined themes in this history of the novel as a perspectival or observational machine: 'on the one hand, the story of an ever more complex approach to the question of observation, driven by scientific advances, philosophical insights and the need for better adapted methods of observing in modernized and globalized society; and, on the other hand, the story of ever more subtle techniques of narrative perspective, driven by a desire to probe, reflect and criticize the way our societies observe themselves' (2011:12).

29 See, notably, Edelman (2004).

30 See Bellido (2014). For an extended discussion of the parallel case of patent law, see Pottage and Sherman (2010).

Bibliography

Altick, Richard D, *The English Common Reader. A Social History of the Mass Reading Public*, 2nd ed., Columbus: Ohio State University Press, 1998.

Barthes, Roland, 'L'ancienne rhétorique. Aide-mémoire,' *Communications*, 16, 172–223, 1970.

Bellido, Jose, 'Looking Right: The Art of Visual Literacy in British Copyright Litigation', *Law, Culture & the Humanities*, 10, 66–87, 2014.

Boureau, Alain, *Kantorowicz. Stories of a Historian*, Baltimore: Johns Hopkins University Press, 2001.

Baxandall, Michael, *Giotto and the Orators. Humanist Observers of Painting in Italy and the Discovery of Pictorial Composition*, Oxford: Clarendon Press, 1971.

Conso, Danièle, *Forma. Etude Sémantique*, doctoral thesis, University of Paris IV: 1990.

Crary, Jonathan, *Techniques of the Observer: On Vision and Modernity in the Nineteenth Century*, Cambridge MA: MIT Press, 1990.

Christopher de Hamel, *Medieval Craftsmen: Scribes and Illuminators*, Toronto: University of Toronto Press, 1992.

Didi-Huberman, Georges, *La ressemblance par contact*, Paris: Minuit, 2008.

Edelman, Bernard, *Le sacre de l'auteur*, Paris: Seuil, 2004.

Filippone Overty, Joanne, 'The Cost of Doing Scribal Business: Prices of Manuscript Books in England, 1300–1483,' *Book History*, 11, 1–32, 2008.

Friedenthal, Richard, *Goethe. His Life and Times*, New Brunswick: Transaction Publishers, 1963.

Judge, Elizabeth F., 'Kidnapped and Counterfeit Characters' in Reginald McGinnis (ed.), *Originality and Intellectual Property in the French and English Enlightenment*, London: Routledge, 2009.

Kantorowicz, Ernst, 'The Sovereignty of the Artist,' in *Selected Studies*, New York: Augustin, 1965.

Goldschmidt, Ernst Philip, *Mediaeval Texts and Their First Appearance in Print*, New York: Biblo & Tannen, 1943.

Goldschmidt, Ernst Philip, *The Printed Book of the Renaissance. Three Lectures on Type, Illustration and Ornament*, Cambridge: Cambridge University Press, 1950.

Gumbrecht, Hans Ulrich, 'Why Intermediality – If At All?' *Intermedialités*, 2, 2003.

Gumbrecht, Hans Ulrich, 'Second Order Observation Historicized: An Epistemological Frame Narrative,' *Design of the In/Human* (online), 2011.
Hathaway, Neil, 'Compilatio. From Plagiarism to Compiling,' *Viator*, 20, 19–44, 1989.
Kant, Immanuel, 'On the Wrongfulness of Unauthorized Publication of Books' [1785], in Gregor (trans and ed.), *Practical Philosophy*, Cambridge: Cambridge University Press, 1996.
Kittler, Friedrich, 'Perspective and the Book', *Grey Room* 5, 39–53, 2001.
Kittler, Friedrich, *Optical Media*, Cambridge: Polity Press, 2010.
Klepper, Martin, *The Discovery of Point of View: Observation and Narration in the American Novel 1790–1910*, Heidelberg: Winter, 2011.
Luhmann, Niklas, *The Reality of the Mass Media*, Cambridge: Polity Press, 2000.
Luhmann, Niklas, *Theory of Society*, volume 2, Stanford: Stanford University Press, 2012.
Macaulay, Stuart, 'Noncontractual Relations in Business. A Preliminary Study', *American Sociological Review*, 28, 55–67, 1963.
Madero, Marta, *Tabula picta. La peinture et l'écriture dans le droit médiéval*, Paris: Ecole des Hautes Etudes en Sciences Sociales, 2004.
McKenzie, Donald F., *Making Meaning: "Printers of the Mind" and Other Essays*, Amherst: University of Massachusetts Press, 2002.
Michael, M.A., 'Urban Production of Manuscript Books and the Role of the University Towns' in Morgan and Thomson (2008).
Michaud-Quantin, Pierre, *Sommes de casuistique et manuels de confession au moyen âge (XIIe–XVIe siècle)*, Louvain: Nauwelaerts, 1962.
Morgan, Nigel and Thomson, Rodney M (eds), *The Cambridge History of the Book in England, 1100–1400*, Cambridge: Cambridge University Press, 2008.
Nagel, Alexander and Wood, Christopher S., 'Interventions: Towards a New Model of Renaissance Anachronism,' *Art Bulletin*, 87, 403–415, 2005.
North, Michael, *Material Delight and the Joy of Living. Cultural Consumption in the Age of Enlightenment in Germany*, London: Routledge, 2008.
Ong, Walter, *Orality and Literacy. The Technologizing of the Word*, London: Routledge, 2002.
Panofsky, Erwin, *Early Netherlandish Painting*, Cambridge, MA: Harvard University Press, 1953.
Pottage, Alain and Sherman, Brad, *Figures of Invention. A History of Modern Patent Law* Oxford: Oxford University Press, 2010.
Ramsay, Nigel, 'Law' in Morgan and Morgan (eds), *The Cambridge History of the Book in England, 1100–1400*, Cambridge: Cambridge University Press, 2008.
Reiter, Eric H, 'The Reader as Author of the User-produced Manuscript: Reading and Rewriting Popular Latin Theology in the Late Middle Ages,' *Viator*, 27, 151–169, 1996.
Rouse, Richard and Rouse, Mary, *Manuscripts and their Makers: Commercial Book Producers in Medieval Paris, 1200–1500*, Turnhout: Harvey Miller, 2000.
Selwyn, Pamela E, *Everyday Life in the German Book Trade: Friedrich Nicolai as Bookseller and Publisher in the Age of Enlightenment*, Philadelphia: Penn State Press, 2000.
Sherman, Brad, 'What Is a Copyright Work?' *Theoretical Inquiries in Law*, 12(1), 99–121, 2010.
Thomas, Yan, 'Res religiosae', in Alain Pottage and Martha Mundy (eds), *Law, Anthropology and the Constitution of the Social. Making Persons and Things*, Cambridge: Cambridge University Press, 2004.
Thomas, Yan, 'L'extrême et l'ordinaire. Remarques sur le cas médiévale de la communauté disparue,' in Jean-Claude Passeron and Jacques Revel (eds) *Penser par cas*, Paris: Ecole des Hautes Etudes en Sciences Sociales, 2005.
Varney Thompson, Daniel, *The Materials and Techniques of Mediaeval Painting*, New York: Dover, 1956.
Vogel, Cyrille, *Les "libri poenitentiales"*, Turnhout, 1978.
Wittmann, Reinhardt, 'Was there a Reading Revolution at the End of the Eighteenth Century?', in Guglielmo Cavallo and Roger Chartier (eds), *A History of Reading in the West*, Amherst: UMass Press, 1999.

Wood, Christopher S., 'Early Archaeology and the Book Trade: The Case of Peutinger's Romanae Vetustatis Fragmenta,' *Journal of Medieval and Early Modern Studies,* 28, 83–118, 1998.

Woodmansee, Martha, 'The Genius and the Copyright. Economic and Legal Conditions of the Emergence of the "author",' *Eighteenth-Century Studies,* 17(4), 425–448, 1984.

Part V
Matter

21

Legalities and materialities

Emilie Cloatre and Dave Cowan

Introduction

This chapter reflects on what materiality-inflected methodologies[1] can bring to an anthropology of law, and to legal studies more generally. Its starting point is an increasing attention across the social sciences and humanities for objects, and thinking beyond the human. These have often, but not only, emerged from science and technology studies (STS), to which we pay particular attention. However, approaches to materiality have themselves become diversified, and their implications for law can similarly be read in multiple ways. At the same time, legal anthropology has helped to re-characterise the complexity of law as a field of social activity by paying attention to its meanings, for actors within as well as outside its own institutions; to its modes of action in practice, again within its explicitly designated spaces as well as its everyday; to its unexpected forms, patterns and directions; to its multiplicity and uncertainty. Approaches within a broadly defined 'legal anthropology' agenda have provided tools to move away from grand and removed theorisation of the law, or an exclusive attention to its own claims, and towards a subtler understanding of law as a relatively fluid, changing and uncertain set of practices. While doing so, legal anthropology has also reminded us of the significance of empirical research to identify and theorise the complex existences of law, a contribution which echoes some of the implications of materiality-oriented theories.

In this chapter, we seek to move these developments on by making two distinct but related contributions: first, to explore the various trends of 'posthuman' understandings of law, and propose that their key contribution is to enable us to push the boundaries of law as a social phenomenon; second, by putting posthuman approaches to legality in conversation with legal anthropology, we do so to argue that one of the strengths of materiality-inflected approaches to law has been its attention to the micro-details of law's unexpected workings, which will continue to need careful, critical, empirical attention.

On their face, these contributions are not particularly startling. However, the pace at and thoughtfulness with which the developments have occurred have led to some tracks which need jumping (to adopt Sassen's metaphor (2006: 8)) and to a period of cross-disciplinary reflection. Our basic argument is that we need to be clear about some of the core terms and that, once we are, the claims of some contributions need to be modified. The particular core term with which we are concerned, as this chapter develops, is law, not in a basic doctrinal excursus (although, in itself, such work would make for a fascinating study of law-on-law replication: see Blomley, 2014) but as an ontological and epistemological problematic. We no longer adhere to a crude binary of materialism and idealism, for, as Conaghan (2016: 29) suggests,

> Matter *matters* because it plays an active role in processes of meaning and apprehension. In this sense, epistemology, as currently understood, must give ground to ontology, including new investigations of the ontological premises upon which critical thinking, particularly that characterised by the cultural or linguistic turn, has been based.

Materiality and 'the social'

The contributions of materiality-inflected approaches to law can be articulated at two levels, at least. On the one hand, they redirected attention to the significance of 'things' or objects, in social practices, and social analysis. On the other hand, this attention to materiality has facilitated an influential revisiting of 'the social' as relational, fluid and contingent. In this chapter, we are particularly interested in those broader implications of materiality-inflected approaches on social theory, and in turn on conceptualisations of law as a social actor. Of course, those two elements cannot be dissociated, and paying attention to materials was, in itself, an important step. As detailed from the late 1970s by proponents of actor network theory (ANT; Latour and Woolgar, 1986; Callon, 1984), objects are not just essential to the constitution of the social, they are also mutually constitutive. Indeed, drawing firm lines between humans and objects was a wrong turn in social theory because humanity is constantly shaped and mediated by an infinite series of devices, from papers or bricks to computers and microchips. Latour's classic, ironic and pseudonymous study of the "sociology of the door closer" (Johnson, 1988) emphasises this problematic. Zooming out from this discussion of the piston automatic door closer, he argues (1988: 303) that "The label 'inhuman' applied to techniques simply overlooks translation mechanisms and the many choices that exist for figuring or de-figuring, personifying or abstracting, embodying or disembodying actors." The dividing line between people and things is negotiable and negotiated.

Materials themselves are complex, both in their histories and making, as well as in their deployment. Jane Bennett (2010) draws on the vibrancy of matter as a constituent of politics. As she puts it, her "aspiration [was] to articulate a vibrant materiality that runs alongside and inside humans to see how analyses of political events might change if we gave the force of things more due" (2010: viii). Callon (1984) reminds us of the dependency of humans and non-humans by observing the negotiations that take place between fishermen and scallops in Brittany. His was not a study of the exercise of human power, knowledge and achievement, of a straightforward perception of power of one over the other, or even clear boundaries between their roles and actions. Instead, it was a study of translations, as he put it, through problematisations, interessement, enrolment and mobilisation. Although no doubt over-structured and programmatic, in each of these modes of action, the human and non-human agents (or 'actants' to borrow from the ANT vocabulary) produced an unchoreographed dance, through which the biologists were seeking to choreograph the collection of scallops. Anne-Marie Mol (2003) opens up this complexity further, by emphasising the multiplicity of individual agents in social processes, where even an apparently fixed material being is in fact deployed across a variety of ontological choreographies. For Law and Mol (1995: 287):

> Materiality is decentred: so suggest our stories about strategies. Better, materialities are decentered. There are multiple materialities performing themselves in manifold ways.

In their analysis, the apparently shocking conclusion is that matter is a set of relations which at different times becomes durable. Here, they hint at another key assumption of materiality-inflected approaches: the idea that materialities do not pre-exist social relations, but are always produced by them. For Haraway "objects are boundary projects" (2007: 126).

Thinking about materiality, of course, has implications for thinking about being humans, and, as a first step, for thinking about bodies. Haraway's work (1991, 2007) is particularly important here, in thinking about bodies per se, and in turn about some of the politics of being human. As she reimagines humans as 'cyborgs', she makes both an observation and a political statement: humans are all socio-technological hybrids, though maybe more visibly so as technological advancements transform the limits of human bodies; but at the same time thinking about ourselves as hybrid enables us to move away from loaded political categorisations. Revisiting how we think of the relationship between bodies, materials, social relations and their co-production rather than co-existence forms the basis of her critical reflexions on sexual difference and feminism.

Bodies in materiality-inflected theories present a degree of ambivalence as social agents and are a good illustration of the implications of thinking about materiality for thinking about boundary-making. They are particularly complex sites of social and political interactions and have become loaded with meaning in ways that are almost always impossible to disentangle. They are political hybrids. At the same time, materiality-inflected theories remind us of the non-uniqueness of bodies as social objects – characteristics are shared with other organisms, other relations, other sites, while constantly dependent on the complexity of each of these. Rethinking the workings of medicines or space, for example, requires us to re-trace some of the processes at stake in making up these things, in negotiating forms of situated knowledges (and their strategies for broader claim-making); but also to retrace the complexity of organisms both on their own and as parts of the broader techno-scientific machinery. Here, the ins and outs of bodies are constantly negotiated, as is the inherence of medicine or space as a field of knowledge, and of its relationship to plants, cultures, buildings, devices etc. (e.g., Fassin, 2007; Biehl, 2013; Langwick, 2011; Blomley, 2016).

Haraway's attention to bodies also enables her to set an agenda for feminist reflections on the production of situated knowledge. Paying attention to the situatedness of knowledge also suggests a more general move away from universal claims towards attention to the micro and always limited, fractal, movements and interactions – a point, both political and methodological, to which we return below, but that for now can be summarised as follows:

> I would like to insist on the embodied nature of all vision, and so reclaim the sensory system that has been used to signify a leap out of the marked body, and into a conquering gaze from nowhere. This is the gaze that mythically inscribes all the marked bodies, and that makes the unmarked category claim the power to see and not be seen, to represent while escaping representation. This gaze signifies the unmarked positions of Man and White.
>
> (2007: 114)

Law and materialities

How then do such studies translate into thinking about law? At one level, such a translation should be smooth, as the workings of law are heavily dependent on materials of all kinds – from the spaces of courtrooms and their peculiar furnishing, to the multiple documents and forms that circulate to 'make law happen', to the very objects that law conditions (from houses to medicines). This attention to the 'things' of law has opened up fresh insights into the everyday workings of legal processes. Artefacts as lively beings of negotiations between actors in legal processes have been at the forefront of this attention. In his analysis of the Conseil d'Etat, Latour (2013) demonstrates the inherent entanglement of materials in the making of decision by judges. Plenty of other studies have opened up new and exciting research in which artefacts are front and centre of the analysis. From consent forms (Jacob and Riles, 2007) to legal files (Van Orschoot and Schinkel, 2015), from leases (Hunter, 2015) to patents (Cloatre, 2013), from international agreements (Riles, 2006) to courtrooms (Mulcahy, 2010), through to the very constitution of bureaucracies (Hull, 2012), researchers have become adept at following the complex roles of artefacts through legal processes. More than neutral intermediaries, these paper-actants have become framed as essential constituents of the orders that law is seen to generate.

But law does not just rely on such materials and artefacts; it also relies on their reproducibility across space and time. A document can be an artefact that functions as "'a technique for interesting'" (Freeman and Maybin, 2011: 160; see also Latour and Woolgar, 1986: 45–50); such documents "anticipate and enable certain actions by others – extensions, amplifications, and modifications of both content and form" (Riles, 2006: 21). Further,

> the document is a translation that also translates. It is intrinsic to those communicative processes in which actors inhabiting different social worlds first enter into relations with each other and then begin to recast or reconstruct themselves, their interests and their worlds. This means simply that the document connects actors and coordinates their actions.
>
> (Freeman and Maybin, 2011: 165)

The production and proliferation in our libraries and on the spaces of the internet of template documents and macros, contractual terms and conditions, which translate law into our everyday lives, are perhaps the clearest illustration of this reproducibility (Radin, 2012). This reproducibility is a key element in the ways in which law achieves its status. The standardisation of things makes an array of new techniques possible. And the standardisation of *legal* documents are crucial technologies in private legal infrastructures as "devices through which particular technical, institutional, political, legal, and economic arrangements fain solidity and durability" (Riles, 2011: 46).

However, we should not rest solely on such physical artefacts but also the apparent truths that they convey. Generations of constitutional lawyers have given us the idea of the rule of law that has been repeatedly inscribed and has become ritualised in public life. We argue that the very idea of the rule of law operates as a "material semiotic" (Law and Mol, 1995: 280–281) through which, as a durable metaphor, it has proudly come to symbolise the essence of Western democratic thought, despite its evident flaws. Attention to materiality as it is translated into law suggests that, in order to get a grip on legal phenomena, we must pay attention to the role of things in shaping, or mediating, interactions. Focusing on materiality in law therefore enables objects to become re-thought as complex blackboxes, that can be opened up to question despite being seemingly uneventful moments of everyday social life.

But as we previously stated, focusing on matter is always about more than simply bringing objects into social analysis: it is about re-questioning networks, relations and events through the opening of what goes as unseen and unquestioned in the constitution of social life. It is this level of analysis which particularly matters to us, notably the conceptual ramifications or implications of materiality scholarship for critical engagements with law. It would be a mistake to understand the import of materiality to law as being only about a renewed attention to things. Focusing critically on materiality also enables the re-thinking of other concepts or processes of significance to, and in, law, layering complexities upon the apparently mundane. Such studies are exemplified by researching processes such as the making and unmaking of time (Grabham, 2016, Valverde, 2014, Blomley, 2003, 2014) or knowledge (Pottage, 2014).

From materiality to the fluidity of law

A key implication of materiality-inflected approaches is the idea that the 'social' is inherently fluid and indeterminate – an idea that is both particularly challenging, and particularly interesting, for thinking about law. Here, the fragility of boundaries and categories, the complexity of processes of ordering, and the entanglement of knowledge, practices, and materiality invite us to rethink the ways in which law should be understood and approached (Cloatre and Pickersgill, 2014). The co-constitution of materiality and practices replaces broader understandings of what we can take as fixed starting points of 'social' analysis. One of the immediate implications for studies of law is the impossibility of the classic distinction between law and society (or, in fact, 'law and' anything); indeed, such a distinction implied by the conjunction collapses entirely. In his introduction to ANT (2005: 7), Latour regards *The Common Place of Law* as the kind of study in which the social question is collapsed by the method.

We suggest that the idea of fluidity has two key implications for materiality-inflected legal scholarship: first, at the conceptual level, these approaches suggest a radical dissolution of the stability of law as a defined social field, whose existence is at any point a given and independent source of norms, seeing in its place a field always in making and deeply entangled in other forms of social making and unmaking or unsettlement. The methodological implications of this insight suggest that a return of ethnographic attention to the day-to-day practices of law and legalities, as well as its localised making, unmaking, settling and challenging, would be more productive than turning legalities in on themselves. A key implication is that the boundaries between the legal and illegal, regulated and unregulated, law and paper and law in action, or indeed of the 'legal' per se, start dissolving once legal processes become analysed in terms of their material making and entanglements. Fleur Johns (2013: 24) has begun this kind of analysis in thinking about how non-legality is made up, in this case international law, challenging those

> international legal studies that seek to apply international law to a world cast in some sense as beyond that law (or vice versa), worry incessantly that international law is not enough for the task of application (or absorption), and hence neglect to scrutinize and tactically engage with those aspects of international legal work that are constitutive of at least some dimensions of that beyond.

Legal processes can be seen as relational and constantly in the making, as practices transform the very objects they seek to engage – from minute artefacts to subjective understandings of law. Through their emphasis on the fluidity of objects and on the relationality of the social, materiality-inflected approaches to law therefore open useful perspectives in interrogating how law is deployed, in apprehending its complex effects and exploring its modes of action. It also raises questions about the very nature of law – and of where the boundaries between legal/non-legal may be drawn. In order to understand these mechanisms and the ontological significance of a move towards materiality, we argue that it is necessary to move beyond the terrain of legal institutions and into the messy spaces of the everyday where these legalities and non-legalities take hold (see, for example, Mezey, 2001). This in turn raises questions about the specificities of both the object of study and the discipline – what is left of the law, and how do we talk about it? As Latour suggested about the weakness of the notion of 'society', is there any sense in which the law is specific or peculiar – or is it always simply ad hoc and fragile? Some of these conversations relate closely to those questions opened up by legal anthropologies, to which we now turn.

Legal anthropologies, from law to legalities

Following the emphasis of materiality-inflected approaches to law requires a particular type of attention to laws' everyday. In many ways, exploring the law outside of its classic, or official, spaces offers a richer picture of its nuanced contours than focusing exclusively on those explicitly 'legal' sites. Here, our argument meets the extensive work that anthropologies of law have produced over the years to move beyond the most clear-cut instances of legal events. In tune with those anthropological studies of law, we argue that, if one wants to appreciate law's ways of acting and its making though social practice/s, one needs to explore law outside its own explicit spaces. This makes our focus different to some extent from those of Latour and others (Latour, 2013; Pottage, 2014), whose attention to materiality has been framed as an exploration of its modes of enunciation. Instead, we want to reflect on the broader questions that legal anthropologists have been asking about law's nature, practices, boundaries – or, to remain within an ANT vocabulary, 'modes of action'. We also remain convinced that empirical engagement and reflection outside the apparently official contexts of law provides a significant set of opportunities for theorization. In these spaces, law's modes of existence are less certain, as the boundaries of 'law' itself are blurred. Instead, and bringing together early ANT and the work of legal anthropologists, we emphasise the importance of micro-events, and materially situated practices, to theorisation. Indeed, one of the most significant contributions of ANT and other materiality-inflected approaches for legal studies is their ability to poke at the boundaries of law, from its fractal side, and engage with some of its more silent and discreet modes of action.

This broader appreciation of law is most clearly addressed in Ewick and Silbey's classic, *The Common Place of Law* (1998). They critique the 'law first' tradition of scholarship, arguing that it has drastically narrowed our vision; and that, despite the research which shows that law "has no center and little uniformity, it is often implicitly assumed that the law is still recognizably, and usefully distinguishable from that which is not law". If we unhinge law from its institutional setting and think about the cadences of legalities in everyday life, "we must tolerate a kind of conceptual murkiness". The key move for our purposes here is away from 'law' to legality, a term that Ewick and Silbey use "to refer to the meanings, sources of authority, and cultural practices that are commonly recognized as legal, regardless of who employs them or for what ends". They provide a material example of this shift – an old chair left on a public street, where snow has been cleared, to hold a parking spot might be seen in a Lockian sense as a marker of exclusivity, ownership/possession as a result of labour. Silbey and Cavicchi (2005: 561) see this chair as "a visual image of the law from the bottom up and from outside of legal institutions". It signals a type of ownership and "often elicits the same sorts of deference and respect accorded more conventional types of property: Other drivers park elsewhere".

This move away from the 'explicit sites' of legal events, and from law to legalities, mirrors that of STS when looking at science from the laboratory to its outside, and from science in the making to the deployment of constituted scientific objects and artefacts. In law, it suggests a move away from a primary focus on the modes of enunciation of the law (though these are relevant) and toward the more fluid spaces of legal meanings, expression and ambivalence. Indeed, a meeting point between materiality-inflected approaches and the longer tradition of legal anthropology lies in their mutual challenge to the boundaries of classic sociological analysis. Materiality approaches have from the outset differentiated themselves from approaches focusing on contextualization – for actor-network theorists, there is no 'context', only interrelationships. As Lezaun and Woolgar (2013) put it: "'materiality', just as 'context' and its cognate terms, needs to be understood as the contingent upshot of practices, rather than a bedrock reality to be illuminated by an ontological investigation" (p. 326). Such an approach meets arguments long-made in legal anthropology, in which the relationship between 'law' and 'society' has been revisited as a more dynamic and co-constitutive set of processes; in which law is more than a static object expected to impact upon, or originate from, a pre-existing society (Morrill and Mayo, 2015). Arguably, materiality-inflected approaches may be taking this notion of fluidity as opposed to fixity to its furthest by seeking to apply it to each of the objects of law, but it also primarily proposes an intervention into 'law and society' debates that seeks to deny the set existence of either. This is what Rose and Valverde (1998: 545) might have had in mind when they argued that there is no such thing as 'the law'. They argued (ibid.) that

> Law, as a unified phenomenon governed by certain principles, is a fiction. This fiction is the creation of the legal discipline, of legal textbooks, of jurisprudence itself, which is forever seeking for the differentia specifica that will unify and rationalize the empirical diversity of legal sites, legal concepts, legal criteria of judgement, legal personnel, legal discourses, legal objects and objectives.

Materiality-inflected approaches also arguably challenge the imagined boundaries between law and its 'others', or the inside and outside of law, meeting in this effort the proponents of legal consciousness traditions. Ewick and Silbey (1998), in their engagement with law in the everyday consciousness of working-class Americans, provided fresh insights into what law may be or claim to be. At the core of their argument is the idea that legalities are transformed, or enacted, in and through the meaning-making processes of those who experience them. In their study, legalities are multiple, and arguably a determinedly 'different' object for each of those that come to experience them, and in turn rewrite them in their own way as a social actor. They compare the reception of legalities to whale-song, an analogy which has resonance with the kind of ontological choreography through which ANT scholarship twists. Like Anne-Marie Mol's sick bodies, legalities are multiple in their everyday ontology. The field of legal consciousness has grown exponentially, focusing at times on the complex consciousness of legal actors, such as disputants and non-disputants as well as those who are outside the system (e.g., Cowan, 2004). The core questions these studies raise are about the fluidity of legalities as they are experienced in everyday life as well as echoing the fluidity of the social. While some have felt uneasy about the apparent dissolution of a core idea of 'law' in legal consciousness (Mezey, 2001; Levine and Mellema, 2001), especially when focusing on the experiences of those only occasionally encountering its institutions, they demonstrate that, in its modes of action, legality may not retain any more solidity than any other social objects; and it is likely to be similarly open to some degree of rewriting and reinventing in the everyday – within, like any objects, the possibilities that networked forces allow. For us, the key significance of these studies is their disembedding from the initial 'making' of law, as it is produced by legislators or in courtrooms. It is not about seizing an unseizable 'original moment', but about reimagining the law as a process of ongoing production.

Of course, the fluidities inherent in legalities do not, as for any other social object, entail their full malleability; they do not necessarily imply a loss of a core, made up of things, languages, codes, institutions, practices, which although constantly changing, reinvented and stretched in new directions, remain recognizable for particular actors at particular times. For Naomi Mezey (2001: 150),

> Although it generally appears in its reified form as a seemingly external object, at heart the law is the accumulation of the tiny and intimate acts of people as they go about their business and try to make sense of the world; in other words, law is the embodiment of social practices.

Susan Silbey (2005) also reminds us that the reinventing of legalities that everyday encounters generate always operates within limits – themselves the result of a myriad of other social patterns: 'Indeterminacy does not make all things possible; it means only that possibilities are not predetermined or fixed' (ibid.: 330).

It is what 'counts' as law that offers one of the most difficult conceptual dilemmas for both legal consciousness scholars and a materiality-inflected revisiting of the law. In the way ANT authors have emphasised the irreducibility of the social, and the fact that notions such as 'the economy' can only be explained through an unpacking of the practices, objects and relations on which they are based (Callon, 2007), the 'legal' may cease to be a useful descriptive category of a generally understood, and shared, concept. Critiques of legal consciousness point to the dissolution of any essence to 'law', which some may want to continue pursuing for political and analytical purposes. Indeed, the contributions of legal consciousness go beyond demonstrating the effects law may have on an outside world, but seek to revisit the boundaries of legalities. One response to this is to suggest that the boundaries lie in the perceptions, attitudes and approaches not of the researched but the researcher in their interpretation of their data. It is perfectly possible to observe that at least some of the stories of their research participants are read by Ewick and Silbey as providing meanings about legalities, when others might not have done so. Naomi Mezey (2001: 153), in her critique of *The Common Place of* Law, illustrates why a move away from the fixity of law also needs to be complemented by an attempt at defining multiple relationalities:

> By looking for the exercise of power in the mundane extremities of everyday life, by locating legality wherever vaguely legal concepts are embedded in social practices, Ewick and Silbey radically reconceptualize what the law is. Losing law in society is partly their point (p. 35). But it also means losing any meaningful distinction between Rita Michaels's experience in divorce court (p. 60) and Charles Reed's protest to the school board about a teacher's transfer (pp. 115–16), or between being arrested and contesting the water bill. To the extent that they have authoritative power in people's daily lives, all the institutions, rules, and conventions that people defer to or defy are equally part of legality.

That is not to suggest that Ewick and Silbey's readings are not valid; far from it; but it does suggest that the ways in which researchers see legalities reflect their perceptions and biases (just as any researcher). Here, as Haraway would suggest, and as we return to below, we are all tied by our own bodily vision. Reflecting on *The Common Place of Law*, Susan Silbey (2005: 347) re-emphasised that legal consciousness is centrally concerned with the production of legality, rather than its effects as a predetermined (and self-referential) object:

> In this work, legal consciousness is decentered in that the research does not document chiefly what people think and do about the law but rather how what they think and do coalesces into a recognizable, durable phenomena and institution we recognize as the law.

Effacing the boundaries of the 'legal'

In reimagining the law as a fluid set of relationships, studies beyond legal ethnographies have offered ways to revisit law's uncertain boundaries in the everyday. They use other starting points to imagine the ambivalence of relationships with, and around, fluid legalities. Anthropological explorations of 'illegalities', and in particular illegal markets, offer a useful starting point here on how to navigate on the borders of the legal, without necessarily using it as a fixed, or even relevant, categorisation. In her inquiry into the counterfeit drug markets of Nigeria, Kristin Peterson (2014) uses the concept of 'speculative markets' to explore the spaces of informal medicines distribution. This enables her to move beyond more classic legal/illegal dichotomies often used when thinking about such drug markets. Perhaps precisely because her central interest is not the law, she subtly moves beyond notions of criminality, and illegality, to reflect on needs, powers and practices in strategies of survival. She demonstrates in nuanced ways the different processes through which the legitimacy and the necessity of those markets is created not just against but also with and through formal state law. Similarly, Janet Roitman (2006), in her exploration of illegality in the Chad Basin, provides another useful example of why it is necessary to move beyond the illusion of a traceable dichotomy between what is *about* (or indeed, against) or not about the law. In exploring the narratives of the bandits' activities, she renders visible the deployment of other systems of normativity that evolve alongside law (legal pluralism) but also navigate across, in and out of it, so as to render the notion of illegality itself redundant/irrelevant. Focusing on some of these ideas, she explains:

> More than just an instrumentalist calculation, or a strategy to maximize economic gains or personal interests, they explain this exercise in maintaining illegality in terms of licit behavior, or what they see as practices that, while not lawful (hence illegal), are nonetheless not forbidden. Illegal activities are rendered licit practice. Licit practice is in this sense understood to be what is allowed or what has become normal practice. This particular domain of illegality – that is, unregulated economic activities and gang-based highway robbery – thus creates a supplementary sense of "licit." For many people in the Chad Basin, "licit" is not simply equated with what is taken to be legal or lawful; "licit" has come to signify practices that are permissible or, to use the terms of my interlocutors, even "legitimate," given the context in which they live.
>
> (p. 249)

Notions of licit and illicit, legitimate and illegitimate, come to complicate what processes of 'illegality' are about, to a point where law ceases to appear as a central determinant in what shapes the normative landscape. As formally illegal economic activities become normalised, they come to coexist with other forms of economies in a way that make differentiations between apparently distinct spaces of social activities more complicated. Here, Roitman's analysis complicates illegalities in a way that echoes Ewick and Silbey's efforts to complicate the notion of legalities (p. 251): 'Despite the contradiction in terms, the illegal realm is a domain of licit behavior; the practice of illegality is an ethics insofar as it is a practice of truth.'

Cloatre and Enright (2016) also move beyond divisions between legal/illegal/non-legal in their study of the history of the contraceptive movement in Ireland. Relying on everyday narratives of those who were engaged in resisting, avoiding and reimagining the Irish prohibition on the sale of condoms for over 30 years, they argue for the inadequacy of imagining a clear boundary between the law and that which breaks it, or is not about it. Of course, *the* law has particular features and constructs particular patterns of powers: being formally within it offers a different form of security than being outside it does. There is a particular precarity to spaces of formal illegality. At the same time, drawing clear boundaries around the law is neither possible nor desirable for social analysis. Instead, and relying on the work of Povinelli (2011), they propose to revisit the engagement of those they study as being about alternative social visions, that are not graspable through the drawing of an imaginary legal/illegal boundary. Formal states of il/legality continue to matter in some ways but are largely constituted through the subjective beliefs and the everyday practices of those who ignore it, challenge it and in turn redefine its modalities of being (Halliday and Morgan, 2013). They are never just a pre-existing state of events.

Of course, the fluidity of the law also has different forms. Even if focusing on legal institutions themselves, those are always permeated by other forms of normativity and social relations. Here, our understanding of the fluidity of law differs from Latour's exposé of the Conseil d'Etat, and our view of legal relations as being of a 'different nature' from others is maybe not fully aligned. At one level of course, what is produced within legal institutions emerges and is self-defined as legal – legal institutions produce a particular kind of legality. But analytically, the relationships produced (and producing) are inherently part of a broader landscape of connections, and emerge not as unique or particular. Again, this is helped by shifting to maybe less familiar terrains than those that have for long predominated legal scholarship. For example, when Peterson follows her informal medicines in a local courtroom in Nigeria, the evasiveness of law, and its inherent hybridity, comes to the fore: legal texts, materials and settings come to produce a particular kind of encounter, but are also entangled with customary expectations, practices and spatialities. Rather than two separate discourses, however, the modes of enunciation of each, as well as their material ramifications, make them impossible to isolate. In the end, the decision of the court is not the one that those who were relying on written laws were expecting, as the legal judgment becomes transformed by the multiple social processes that shape how the spaces in question are understood in the courtroom.

Cloatre (2018) argues that looking at the boundaries of legitimate medicine provides a vantage point from which to seize the porous and hybrid nature of law *and* its boundaries: what falls in and out of medicine or constitutes a legitimate type of healing practice is determined not only by abstractly defined cultural and historical elements, but by grounded and always shifting material embodiments of those histories and cultures and by everyday practices. Medicines are complex sites of legal events. When approaching the boundaries of medicine (away from biomedicine and towards popular or traditional healing, away from tablets and towards herbs, away from the institutions and towards the spaces of informality), endless opportunities arise to see the boundaries of law as a social object crumble (see also Fisiy, 1998). Others have explored the always-renegotiated nature of the law and its others by looking at the interactions between witchcraft and formal legal systems, where endless shifts between them are such that the boundaries of each order become unclear (Niehaus, 2005).

But if legal events are inherently hybrid, spaces that are apparently 'unregulated' may also be permeated by subtle forms of legality and themselves appear as particular forms of socio-legal hybrids. For example, Cloatre's (2013) analysis of pharmaceutical patents shows the unexpected ways in which those supposedly 'legal' tools continue to act in Djibouti, where they have no formal existence, or how the labelling of certain drugs as 'counterfeit' escapes the legal boundaries of the term. Similarly, Harper and Ecks (2013), in following the formally unregulated drug market of Nepal, demonstrate how law-like mechanisms fall into place to recreate networks of power and influence in drug distribution. Throughout these studies, medicines as objects come to challenge the presumption of where law sits, how it acts, or indeed what type of social space it occupies. Drugs shift between categories that law is formally expected to define, through the practices of their many users. Meanwhile, 'unregulated' markets become shaped by myriad legal influences that are often indirect and bear limited relation to what the law may have intended, but demonstrate its (influential) messiness. At stake in those studies are questions about where and how law matters, and what can be drawn from its formal existence or absence. At one level, these are questions about fluidity within the law: how norms travel across jurisdictions, in and out of materials, through unexpected networks, effects and spaces. At the same time, they also invite us to reflect more carefully on the possibility of a boundary between the legal and 'the rest', and on the uniqueness of law. Andreas Philippopoulos-Mihalopoulos (2014) suggests we pay attention to the discreet ways in which the lawscape operates and to the unexpected ways in which silent legalities affect our everyday. Drawing the lawscape is about acknowledging and retracing fractal legalities. Similarly, acknowledging the fluidity of law is about exploring the boundary-making efforts that go into generating both the formal and visible spaces of legality and the discreet, unexpected and everyday inscriptions of legalities as one set of events in the shaping of complex b/orders.

As an example of these kinds of silent but fractal legalities, Cowan et al. (2018) focus on discourses of property ownership produced by marginal home owners. Legal scholars focus predominantly on two opposing theoretical positions – exclusion and an ideal of progressive property, in which certain legal institutional values provide for a stewardship role of the owner – in which they share a singular rather curious feature: both theses about property have a top-down, law-first orientation. In seeking to state what property is and why it is what it is, as well as what it should be, their starting points are law and rights to, as well as over, property. Of course, their orientations are rather different; the ownership thesis types tend to rest with hard-nosed law and economics thinking; the progressives assign legal values to which conflicts over rights to property should aspire. There is also the related concern among property theorists about the sorting processes inherent in property which are said to produce insiders and outsiders. This work, which seeks to uncover the often hidden politics of legal doctrine by reference to legal values, fits within a set of understandings about legal doctrine which highlight both their power and their problematic. As Fox O'Mahony (2014: 411) puts it, "A view from the marginalised outsider provides a valuable mechanism by which to test whether the frames we use to resolve property problems orient us towards immanent solutions that tend to privilege insiders over outsiders (or vice versa)".

However, as Blomley (2013, 2016) has demonstrated, the exclusionist and progressive theses are problematic in their untested empirical assertions. Reading Cowan et al.'s data demonstrates the porousness and fluidity in everyday understandings of ownership among their marginal owners. These are people at the insider/outsider margins, but they firmly express themselves as private owners and assert their superiority over the social rump. They understand property as a form of control, something which was emphasised by their décor and stuff (a position which chimes with the anthropologists of home: Miller, 2010; Hurdley, 2006). They express themselves as being in control but the stories they tell are of being out of control. Their boundaries are not the front door but expressed through their positionality – that is, property for them is what distinguishes them from the rest and is emphasised through things, like potted plants, sweet wrappers or concerns over the dropping of cigarette butts. In this rendering, property ownership performs understandings of tenure and class.

Those stories are interpreted as contradictory and almost incapable of a monochrome analysis. However, they argue that something rather more significant is going on in these narratives. Miller (2010: 96) plays with the word accommodating, arguing that home is not just a place to live but an ongoing process in which we appropriate where we live: "It may imply our changing of a home to suit ourselves, but it can also imply the need to change ourselves in order to suit our accommodation". And we are constantly engaging with this process, changing things as we go. Cowan et al. suggest that they must embrace their participants' contradictory narratives precisely because their participants were changing themselves, as they sought to establish their place in the world both at the level of idea and relationally. They argue that this was what the narratives were telling them, emphasising the complexity and richness of property's everyday lives.

At the same time, acknowledging the non-uniqueness of law places legal scholars in a dilemma: on the one hand, the importance of a critical agenda that continues to explore the dissolution of legalities in the everyday, the uncertainty of its boundaries and the inherent subjectivity of its definition; on the other hand, the underlying question of what law, as an object of analysis and set of social relations, may be, and if and how we can analyse it as a defined thing. This latter question is not one this chapter can answer – or indeed any single analysis could. Instead, it may be useful to reflect on the strategies we may deploy to pursue both these agendas, taking seriously their challenges and continuing to develop understandings of law as an object, or a series of objects, that is multiple, ambiguous, elusive and constantly reshaped both by its own actions and those of its analysts.

Approaching everyday legalities: some methodological implications

Some of these questions, and in particular that of a return to a clearer sense of the legal, have been explored by others. Attending to the modes of enunciation of law, as proposed by Latour and others, is indeed one way to address the question of what law is from a fresh perspective by reflecting on its material mode of existence. However, as we have expressed above, this strand of inquiry has not sufficiently engaged yet with the rich contributions of legal anthropologies that have challenged the boundaries of an imagined, defined, legal space, to make a fully satisfactory intervention on these questions. Even if remaining focused on the question of the making of law and its enunciations, examples such as the court ruling Kristin Peterson describes demonstrate how the process of creating a legal decision may borrow from a multiplicity of languages and practices, that others may not recognise as law in a universalised way.

Annelise Riles (2005) proposes another useful entry point into rethinking about what is specific or special about law, as she puts forward a new agenda for re-engaging legal technicalities. The agenda is important and indeed a useful counterpoint to studies focused on the dissolution of law rather than its own production or language. At the same time, it encounters limits, once again, when moving away from the spaces where law is technical to where it is engaged by its everyday users (e.g., Sally Engle Merry, 1990), to the travels of medicines, to the travels of the lease. The everyday experiences of legalities, as much as they are a challenge to its definition and labelling, play a part in rendering it powerful. As Susan Silbey reminds us, "The law is a durable and powerful human invention because a good part of legality is just this invisible constraint, suffusing and saturating our everyday life" (2005: 331).

Our premise, as we have explained, is that one of the key ways in which materiality-inflected theories are useful for legal researchers is precisely to focus on these other spaces – those where law is experienced, practice, translated, reappropriated and in turn redefined by its many users. Those spaces where what Callon describes as the 'actor-worlds' of law-makers (the imagined spaces where law would be practiced) are rewritten by the messiness of real-life society. Such explorations, inevitably, depend on detailed empirical descriptions of those spaces, that are also informed sufficiently by critical and conceptual tools to open up broader challenges to preconceived ideas of law. In turn, an effect of this is to render visible the more discrete existences of law, that it would be easy for legal analysts to forget or push aside as irrelevant.

For this purpose, we advocate the kinds of theorising about legalities which enable a reflection on the mundane, the everyday, through multiple sources of data that enable the discreet modes of operation of law to become visible. The simple act of box-ticking (and the production of the box categories themselves) involves a variety of translations of the self. Indeed, in one study, the box-ticking exercise was regarded as a method of performing risk, trust and implementation (Cowan et al., 2009: 297).

The key contributions of legal ethnographies are indeed arguably about both the fluidity and the multiplicities of law (Bibler Coutin and Fortin, 2015). In the way that anthropology has reflected on the relation between ethnography and theory (Biehl and McKay, 2012, Fassin, 2013), one of the contributions of materiality-inflected approaches to law may be to encourage us to reflect on what the messiness of the everyday of law, in its materially embedded practices, may contribute to a broader theorization of law as an object – and indeed suggest some limits to over-generalisations. As those traditions open doors for the critical interrogation of law and its limits, they suggest that legalities may continue to be defined as a fluid set of relationships, rather than as a neatly contained social category. By allowing the fluidity of the social to be brought to the front and categorisations to be opened up, one of the great strengths of these approaches may therefore be to enable a new interrogation of law by avoiding its assumptions and pre-defined characteristics.

There are many reasons that make such recognition of the inherent messiness of law aside of its formal modes of enunciation, or expected modes of action, as both practically and theoretically important. One of them, however, is the ongoing need to improve the ranges of voices and experiences that are included in defining what law is and how it works. A focus on formal law and its institutions can only succeed in reflecting the privilege of the status of law and its actors. It tells us nothing about those affected by its eminence (the pigeons and the farmer in Latour's opening story). Indeed, the modes of enunciation of the law as explored in the Conseil d'Etat should be confronted with, compared to and weighed against the ways in which decisions are made, for example, in the Nigerian courtroom just as much as in the everyday decisions of Rita Michaels. What happens in each of the offices and each of the markets of Djibouti, Ghana, Nigeria or the borders of the Chad basin, or in homes around the world, are in themselves inevitably productive of new, diverse, productive and restrictive legalities. We argue that these legalities of the everyday are not just crucial to the ways in which law works, but also attendant to the silences and hegemonic truths produced by legality. These are the productive spaces where legal anthropology and STS can meet, and where materiality-inflected approaches can help us reinvent how we approach legality/law and its boundaries. Although Latour has been recently critical of his own concept of irreduction, the notion may remain helpful in questioning law and approaching it without preconceived notions of its working or of the imagined movements that shape its action.

This goes some way in acknowledging the inevitable situatedness of our knowledge as researchers. Engaging this issue and navigating through the imagined dichotomy between the universalistic claims of science and pure relativism, Haraway reminds us that

> the alternative to relativism is not totalization and single vision, which is always finally the unmarked category whose power depends on systematic narrowing and obscuring. The alternative to relativism is partial, locatable, critical knowledges sustaining the possibilities of webs of connections called solidarity in politics and shared conversations in epistemology.
>
> (2007: 117)

At the same time, both Haraway and Karen Barad (2007) argue that the process of observation is never just that, and never simply about capturing a pre-existing state of being: the process of observation itself contributes to producing and transforming objects as they are being mobilised, complicating yet further the process of empirical inquiry and the very nature of the task.

While no simple solution to the dilemma of engaging law in its defined yet changing multiplicity can be proposed, these are a few ways in which materiality-inflected theories may be useful. By recognising and embracing this shifting and uncertain nature of legalities as relational, and as part of a broader and messier set of connections, materiality-inflected approaches suggest that it is important to pay attention to micro-moments as well as to big events and to the apparently insignificant rather than to the obvious. They also enable us to never take 'the law' or its feature for granted, but to always seek to unpack its particular ways of working, within a particular set of processes or a particular space. Finally it invites us to reflect critically on the nature of ethnographic knowledge: as a necessary entry point to gather and recount some of those complex and localised features, but as an endeavour that needs to remain critical and modest in its own claims. Ethnographic knowledge is always constitutive of the very order it aims to describe, and always inevitably situated and partial. In our collective efforts to conceptualise and reflect on the law, it nevertheless remains a necessary element of understanding better the contours of fluid legalities.

Conclusions

What is left of law, and is there anything that remains characteristic of, or central to, law?

Once we start acknowledging the unexpected effects of law, account for the hybridity of legal discourses, myths and interpretations, is it more than whatever it becomes in materially-embedded practices – and therefore something that we can only understand by observing these practices?

The movement away from the formalistic starting point of law, and its imaginary as something that impacts society as a separate system, started long ago in socio-legal studies and critical legal studies, and indeed materiality-inflected theories offer tools and questions to push this even further. Legalities can then be understood as being constituted through routines and practices, so that they are little more than what actants make of it, or with it, and little more than what the materials it affects and shapes go on to do. Its origins, including institutional origins or textual forms, may matter in identifying its starting point, but, for us, that offers only a very limited snapshot of its vivacity and truth-claims. And indeed, these forms may not make its modes of actions radically different from other forms of ordering, at least in their practice. Law as the expression of state power remains, of course, an important dimension to acknowledge, but once mixed with fluid jurisdictional boundaries, private interests, routinised practices that may or may not follow what the state expected or imagined when laws were drafted, and material travels, this vision of law as an institutionalised exercise of state power becomes limited.

Instead, rendering visible some of this messiness allows for a broader rethink of the meaning of law, its practical deployments, and therefore enables more encompassing critiques of power through its silent as well as overt expressions. In our work on houses and medicines, we can see the potential that this kind of messiness has for legal method and for our appreciation of the everyday heterogeneous practices of legality. However, with Blomley (2014), we think that there is considerable potential in unwrapping the ways in which legality is sold to us as apparently homogeneous when that is not our experience; and, in so doing, there is scope for radically reorienting our approaches and methods for appreciating difference and the significance of the mundane, the blackboxed. So, for example, as the courts in England and Wales move towards digitisation, while their fabric disintegrates, and as the spaces of legality become fractured and spliced with the everyday (or are recognised as such), a focus on materialities opens up new sites for the engagement of socio-legal scholarship enmeshed with our lived experiences as autoethnographies.

Note

1 We use this expression in this chapter to denote the kinds of methodologies in which matter extends beyond human matter, and which emphasise the processes, practices, discursive trajectories and translations of things across time and space.

Bibliography

Barad, Karen, *Meeting the Universe Halfway*, Durham: Duke University Press, 2007.

Bennett Jane, *Vibrant Matter: A Political Ecology of Things*, Durham: Duke University Press, 2010.

Bibler Coutin, Susan and Veronique Fortin, 'Legal Ethnographies and Ethnographic Law', in *Handbook of Law and Society*, Hoboken, NJ: Wiley, 2015.

Biehl, João, *Vita*, Berkeley: University of California Press, 2013.

Biehl, João and Ramah McKay, 'Ethnography as Political Critique', *Anthropological Quarterly*, 85, 1209–1227, 2012. https://doi.org/10.1353/anq.2012.0057.

BBlomley, Nicholas, *Unsettling the City: Urban Land and the Politics of Property*, London: Routledge, 2003.

Blomley, Nicholas, 'Performing property: Making the world', *Canadian Journal of Law and Jurisprudence*, 26, 23–48, 2013.

Blomley, Nicholas, 'Disentangling Law: The Practice of Bracketing', *Annual Review of Law and Social Science,* 10, 133–148, 2014.

Blomley, Nicholas, 'The boundaries of property: Complexity, relationality, and spatiality', *Law and Society Review*, 50, 224–55, 2016.

Callon, Michel, 'Some Elements of a Sociology of Translation: Domestication of the Scallops and the Fishermen of St Brieuc Bay', *The Sociological Review*, 32, 196–233, 1984.

Callon, Michel, 'What Does It Mean to Say That Economics Is Performative?', in D. MacKenzie, F. Muniesa and L. Siu (eds), *Do Economists Make Markets? On the Performativity of Economics*, Princeton: Princeton University Press, 311–357, 2007.

Cloatre, Emilie, *Pills for the Poorest: An Exploration of TRIPS and Access to Medication in Sub-Saharan Africa*, London: Palgrave Macmillan, 2013.

Cloatre, Emilie and Martyn Pickersgill, 'Introduction', in *Knowledge, Technology and Law*, London: Routledge, 2014.

Cloatre, Emilie, 'Traditional Medicines, Law, and the (Dis)Ordering of Temporalities', in S. Beynon-Jones, and E. Grabham (eds), *Regulating Time*, London: Routledge, 2018.

Conaghan, Joanne, 'Feminism, law and materialism: Reclaiming the "tainted" realm', in M. Davies and V. Munro (eds), *The Ashgate Research Companion to Feminist Legal Theory*, Aldershot: Ashgate, 2016.

Cowan, Dave, 'Legal consciousness: Some observations', *Modern Law Review*, 67, 928-58, 2004.

Cowan, Dave, Carr, Helen and Wallace, Alison, *Ownership, Narrative, Things*, London: Palgrave, 2018.

Cowan, Dave, Morgan, Karen and McDermont, Morag, 'Nominations: An actor-network approach', *Housing Studies*, 24, 281-300, 2009

Engle Merry, Sally, *Getting Justice and Getting Even: Legal Consciousness Among Working-Class Americans*, Chicago: Chicago University Press, 1990.

Enright, Mairead and Cloatre, Emilie 'Commentary on MgGee v. AG', in Aoife O'Donoghue, Mairead Enright and Julie McCandless, *Irish Feminist Judgments: Judges Troubles and the Gendered Politics of Identity*, Oxford: Hart, 2016.

Fassin, Didier, *When Bodies Remember*, Berkeley: University of California Press, 2007.
Fassin, Didier, 'A Case for Critical Ethnography', *Social Science & Medicine*, 99, 119–126, 2013.
Fisiy, Cyprian F., 'Containing Occult Practices: Witchcraft Trials in Cameroon', *African Studies Review*, 41, 143–163, 1998. https://doi.org/10.2307/525357.
Fox O'Mahony, Lorna, 'Property outsiders and the hidden politics of doctrinalism', *Current Legal Problems*, 67, 409-445, 2014.
Freeman, Richard and Maybin, Jo, 'Documents, Practices and Policy', *Evidence and Policy*, 7(2), 155–170, 2011.
Grabham, Emily, *Brewing Legal Times: Things, Form and the Enactment of Law*, Toronto University Press, 2016.
Halliday, Simon and Morgan, Bronwen, 'I Fought the Law and the Law Won? Legal Consciousness and the Critical Imagination', *Current Legal Problems*, 66, 1-33, 2013.
Haraway, Donna, *Simians, Cyborgs and Women: The Reinvention of Nature*, London: Routledge, 1991.
Haraway, Donna, 'Situated Knowledges: The Science Question in Feminism and the Privilege of a Partial Perspective' in K. Asdal, B. Brita and I. Moser (eds), *Technoscience: The Politics of Intervention*, Oslo: Oslo Academic Press, 109–134, 2007.
Harper, Ian and Stefan, Ecks, '"There Is No Regulation, Actually" : The Private Market for Anti-TB Drugs in India', in Joao Biehl and Petryna, *When People Come First : Anthropology and Social Innovation in Global Health*, Durham: Duke University Press, 2013.
Hull, Matthew, *Government of Paper*, Berkeley: University of California Press, 2012.
Hunter, Caroline, 'Solar Panels, Home Owners and Leases: The Lease as a Socio-Legal Object', in Dave Cowan and Dave Wincott (eds), *Exploring the Legal in Socio-Legal Studies*, London: Palgrave Macmillan, 2015.
Hurdley, Rachel, 'Dismantling mantelpieces: Narrating identities and materializing culture in the home', Sociology, 40, 717-33, 2006.
Jacob, Marie Andrée and Riles, Annelise, 'The New Bureaucracies of Virtue: Introduction', *PoLAR: Political and Legal Anthropology Review*, 30, 181–191, 2007. https://doi.org/10.1525/pol.2007.30.2.181.
Johns, Fleur, *Non-Legality in International Law: Unruly Law,* Oxford: OUP, 2013
Johnson, Jim, 'Mixing humans and nonhumans together: The sociology of a door-closer', *Social Problems*, 35, 298-310, 2008.
Langwick, Stacey, *Bodies, Politics and African Healing*, Bloomington: Indiana University Press, 2011.
Latour, Bruno, *Reassembling the Social: An Introduction to Actor-Network-Theory,* Oxford: OUP, 2005.
Latour, Bruno, *The Making of Law: An Ethnography of the Conseil d'Etat*, Cambridge: Polity, 2009.
Latour, Bruno, *An Inquiry Into Modes of Existence: An Anthropology of the Moderns*, Cambridge, MA: Harvard University Press, 2013.
Latour, Bruno and Woolgar, Steve, *Laboratory Life: The Construction of Scientific Facts*, Princeton: Princeton UP, 1979.
Law, John and Mol, Annemarie, 'Notes on Materiality and Sociality', *The Sociological Review*, 143, 274–294, 1995.
Levine, Kay and Mellema, James, 'Strategizing the street: How law matters in the lives of women in the street-level drug economy', *Law and Social Inquiry*, 26, 169-207, 2001.
Mezey, Naomi, 'Out of the Ordinary: Law, Power, Culture, and the Commonplace', *Law & Social Inquiry*, 26, 145–167, 2001.
Miller, Daniel, *Stuff*, Cambridge: Polity, 2010.
Mol, Anne-Marie, *The Body Multiple: Ontology in Medical Practice*, Durham: Duke University Press, 2003.
Morrill, Calvin and Kelsey, Mayo, 'Charting the "Classics" in Law and Society: The Development of the Field Over the Past Half] Century', in *Handbook of Law and Society*, Hoboken, NJ: Wiley, 2015.

Mulcahy, Linda, *Legal Architecture: Justice, Due Process and the Place of Law,* London: Routledge, 2010.

Niehaus, Isak A, 'Beyond Rationalism: Rethinking Magic, Witchcraft and Sorcery (review)', *African Studies Review*, 48, 164–165, 2005. https://doi.org/10.1353/arw.2005.0031.

Peterson, Kristin, *Speculative Markets: Drug Circuits and Derivative Life in Nigeria,* Durham: Duke University Press, 2014.

Philippopoulos-Mihalopoulos, Andreas, *Spatial Justice: Body, Lawscape, Atmosphere*, London: Routledge, 2014.

Pottage, Alain, 'Law After Anthropology: Object and Technique in Roman Law', *Theory, Culture & Society*, 31, 147–166, 2014a.

Pottage, Alain, 'Paper Prototypes', in Emilie Cloatre and Martyn Pickersgill (eds), *Knowledge, Technology and Law*, London: Routledge, 2014b.

Povinelli, Elizabeth, *Economies of Abandonment*, Durham: Duke University Press, 2011.

Radin, Margaret, *Boilerplate: The Fine Print, Vanishing Rights, and the Rule of Law,* Princton: Princeton UP, 2012.

Riles, Annelise, 'A new agenda for the cultural study of law: Taking on the technicalities', *Buffalo Law Review*, 63, 973-1033, 2005.

Riles, Annelise, 'Anthropology, Human Rights, and Legal Knowledge: Culture in the Iron Cage', *American Anthropologist*, 108, 52–65, 2006.

Riles, Annelise, *Collateral Knowledge: Legal Reasoning in the Global Financial Markets*, Chicago: University of Chicago Press, 2011.

Roitman, Janet, John Comaroff and Jean Comaroff, 'The Ethics of Illegality in the Chad Basin', in *Law and Disorder in the Postcolony*, Chicago: University of Chicago Press, 2006.

Rose, Nikolas and Valverde, Mariana, 'Governed by law?', *Social and Legal Studies*, 7, 541-51, 1998.

Scheffer, Thomas, *Adversarial Case-Making: An Ethnography of an English Crown Court Procedure*, Leiden: Brill, 2012.

Sassen, Saskia, *Territory, Authority, Rights: From Medieval to Global Assemblages*, Princeton: Princeton UP, 2006.

Silbey, Susan S., 'After Legal Consciousness', *Annual Review of Law and Social Science*, 1, 323–368, 2005. https://doi.org/10.1146/annurev.lawsocsci.1.041604.115938.

Silbey, Susan. and Cavicchi, Ayn, 'The common place of law: Transforming matters of concern into the objects of everyday life', in B. Latour and P. Weibel (eds), *Making Things Public: Atmospheres of Democracy*, Cambridge, Mass: MIT Press, 2005.

Silbey, Susan S. and Patricia Ewick, *The Common Place of Law: Stories from Everyday Life*, Chicago: University of Chicago Press, 1998.

Valverde, Mariana, *Chronotopes of Law: Jurisdiction, Scale and Governance*, London: Routledge, 2014.

van Oorschot, Irene and Willem Schinkel, 'The Legal Case File as Border Object: On Self-Reference and Other-Reference in Criminal Law', *Journal of Law and Society*, 42, 499–527, 2015.https://doi.org/10.1111/j.1467-6478.2015.00723.x.

Woolgar, S. and J. Lezaun, 'The Wrong Bin Bag: A Turn to Ontology in Science and Technology Studies?', *Social Studies of Science*, 43, 321–340, 2013.

22

Law's materiality

Between concrete matters and abstract forms, or how matter becomes material

Hyo Yoon Kang

Problem

The current fascination with objects or matters of law, which for a lack of better description could be described as a 'new materialist' turn in legal scholarship, may be understood as a desire to let matters of law 'speak for themselves' or 'seeing them as they are'. Although it is appealing to bring into legal scholarship the insights afforded by different kinds of new materialisms as, for instance, advanced by Jane Bennett (2010) and Rosi Braidotti (2013), it is by no means clear what thinking about law in these highly heterogeneous new materialist ways would entail.[1] One strand of legal scholarship's 'new' material turn may be tempted to treat law as a material culture so that the analytical focus falls on 'legal' objects. Following the footsteps of the highly popular book *The History of the World in 100 Objects* by Neil MacGregor (2012) might be an interesting pedagogical exercise for making law seem less abstract and removed from the 'real' tactile world. But it would be helpful to pose the ontological question of what legal objects *are*, how they are associated with legality so to be defined and represented as legal – as some are held to be more legal than others – and what value their analysis would bring to the understanding of law.

The more facile ethical and political axiom, which a legal scholar could draw from the new materialist works informed by philosophy and science and technology studies, is that law ought to be more attuned to the innate potentialities and 'vibrant vitalities' of (non-)human matters and their manifestations. Bennett (2010) advances a vitalist notion of matters, primarily through an engagement with the line of philosophical thought pre-occupied with immanence, from Aristotle, Spinoza and Bergson to Deleuze. Such a reinterpretation of vitalism could be interpreted as an understandable reaction against the increasing normalisation of mechanistic and computational visions of life, which are pervasive in the popular adoption of DNA as the code of life, the conception of human mind as a computer and the increasing normalisation of machine intelligence in everyday life.[2] What is novel in these kinds of new materialisms is a political-ethical appeal for non-human lives and inorganic matters to be recognised, cared for and respected on their own terms. These concerns are voiced in different tropes: as an ecology of matters (Bennett, 2010), inter-species ethics (Haraway, 2007; Kohn, 2013), a parliament of things (Latour, 2005). There is an implicit sense, although not always spelled out, that most social systems, including law, are anthropocentric and do not take into account the specificities of divergent matters.[3]

In the context of legal scholarship, these critiques and appeals are not entirely new, and they have been already raised and discussed in many different contexts, particularly at the intersections of law, science and social theory. Law has been at the frontline of critique for inadequate recognition or misrepresentations of some its subjects, both human and non-human.[4] In a more anthropocentric manner, feminist legal scholars especially had long pointed out that law privileges a certain kind of subject – rational, disembodied or abled-bodied – which neglects the multiplicity of situated embodiments which do not adhere to this normalised vision.[5] Legal scholars who have explored different legal regimes as articulations of biopolitical governmentality have voiced similar but distinct critiques, claiming that certain technologies and their legal framings have disciplining as well as other unforeseen effect on the bodies and subjectivities of populations, as for example in the case of human gene patents or issues of data privacy, because of insufficient or misleading legal representations of a 'gene' or of digital codes.[6] Property law scholars, including concerning intellectual properties, and anthropologists have criticised law's inability to take into account cultural or aesthetic specificities of non-living matters, such as land, art works and software codes, for a long time.[7]

It is moreover not a novel insight that non-human, even non-organic, matters are active. There is not much mention in the new materialist studies of the intricate and increasingly large-scale practices and technologies, which are required in order to move, observe and study these 'vibrant' properties.[8] Bennett mentions metallurgy and embryology in *Vibrant Matters* as examples in which matters have been recognised to have vital force. She takes inspiration in Hans Driesch's work in embryology and his theoretical affinities with Bergson but she does not engage more deeply with Driesch's sets of different experimental practices, which were crucial for obtaining different results than Roux and Weismann, nor does she describe how the 'vibrancy' of non-organic matters, such as metals, are perceived or heard.[9] Hearing itself is not an unmediated sensation (Kursell, 2013). Christoph Hoffmann has pointed out that seeing is also "no longer a self-evident activity; what 'seeing' means is, in each instance, an open question" (2017: 40). Bennett's theoretical claims about innate forces of things would be strengthened if they took into account how scientific things and knowledge arise through observations and experiments within the broader history of observations and experimental system, in which concepts are put to test and the status of objects is constantly changing.[10]

Above all, it is extremely difficult to make the forces which hold and move matters 'appear,' let alone to interpret them. Long-standing endeavours in molecular biology, physics and chemistry are devoted to these tasks.[11] The relatively more recent interdisciplinary discipline of materials science, an amalgamation of physics, chemistry and engineering, is concerned with the understanding and invention of new materials.[12] In molecular biology, 'living' matters are increasingly figured digitally in silico rather than in vitro, and thus there is a profound representational and epistemological jump from the vibrancy of a digital bit into the vibrancy of a living organism.[13] Matters are not affective or vibrant by themselves. Also the level of 'vibrancy' is not constant. They can be alert but also dormant. This raises questions about what matters we are talking about and how they become material: when are the matters active and forceful; when are they less so? What makes them this way? Surely matters are lively. Does this mean they are therefore vital or living? If the matters are vital, are they also destined to death? These are critical questions particularly when natural science insights are transposed without intermediation into politics and law, as matters could be understood in essentialist and objectivist ways.[14] Some historical tendencies and examples are solemn reminders, which Bennett has also acknowledged at several points in her book.[15] In light of the organicist and vitalist notions of 'life' which some of the new materialist works endorse, one needs to be careful of unreconstructed and undifferentiated notions of life as "life itself", or "*blosses Leben*", as Benjamin had noted.[16]

Insights from history and anthropology of sciences complicate the picture of a vibrant or vital matter by studying its articulation in an experimental system or other ways of knowledge-making. These disciplines took a material turn in which it was recognised that matters and elements were not self-evident, 'natural' or 'objective' manifestations of 'nature,' but that they needed to be elicited with sensorial training, apparatus and tools, particularly that of representation, and rules about how that should be done.[17] This is because historians and anthropologists of science have long recognised the unpredictability of both human and non-human matters in their mutual interaction, as John Tresch (2016: 2–3) has described:

> Treating the molecular structures of metals and crystals, we find patterns of latent motion and force, a molten potentiality at the heart of what appeared firm and inert; we slip into the vortices and eddies of the recurring materialism of Epicurus.

Hans-Joerg Rheinberger (1997, 2010) has characterised the phenomena in which the scientific object escapes or exceeds the explanatory frameworks as an 'error', 'excess' or 'recalcitrance' of the research object to the researcher.[18] Scientific truth-claims or claims to objectivity are understood as material-semiotic stabilisations of these surprising research matters through a chain of reference of inscriptions and other representational techniques (Latour, 1999). Similarly in law, matters are temporarily stabilised but prove to be difficult to fully govern and regulate: for example, in debates about nuclear power regulation, the unknown effects of technology are transformed into matters of risk, which law deals with normatively, for example through the precautionary principle (Ladeur, 2003). Or as Javier Lezaun (2012) has shown, law fabricates the attributes of reference materials for measurement standards, but legality is also materially shaped. On top of the ability for matters to resist and escape human control, the material objects of legal regulation are also enmeshed in different national and transnational socio-technical imaginaries (Jasanoff and Kim, 2009; Jacob, 2009). It is then not surprising that law devises ways to deal with complexity and multiple contingencies: it blackboxes human and nonhuman matters into different kinds of legal forms and ignores their incalculable and recalcitrant properties for better bureaucratic handling, until the box needs to be opened up and the properties are contested again in litigation.[19] Different kinds of legal regimes, such as health law, environmental law and intellectual property law, attend to the specific properties of its matters in different ways. This difference is due to their very highly specific representational requirements that are not only politically or ethically, but also historically and structurally, shaped. It would therefore be of critical necessity to complicate the claim of the vitality or relevance of matters with a view towards their embeddedness and various articulations within different social and cultural meanings and practices (Haraway, 1991). Legal matters need to be situated.

In the following sections, I do not focus on the ethical-political implications of the new materialist concerns, which again fall into an instrumentalist vision of law as a means towards a better recognition of various matters. This is because I want to avoid the intentional fallacy that the origins or intentions of law can be authored and authoritatively managed (Barthes, 1977: 142–148). Also, the discussion is careful of some of the new materialist tendency to give innate force to 'life', even if understood affectively as an immanent Deleuzian multiplicity or Spinozan *conatus*, because it wants to avoid a biologicist naturalisation of other worlds of meanings.[20] The next section introduces some of the current legal scholarship which take legal materials as its objects of analyses. Then the discussion addresses the missing perspective in the many new materialist works which do not take into account law's specificities: it considers law's matters in relation to the meaning of legal materiality and argues that these two terms need to be differentiated. The chapter posits a mediated understanding of legal materiality in which law articulates its meaning by selectively enlisting and moulding concrete matters. In this picture, law's materiality is unruly and unstable because it is continuously realised through interpretive and multiple representational practices, such as texts, spatial orderings and ritualised performances. Law proves to be a recalcitrant and surprising matter itself, which escapes full control.

The vitality of legality

It is strange that a plea for law to be attentive to the innate vibrancy or properties of its matters ignores law's own matters and specific instantiations of materiality, which is extremely varied and situated across many different social and cultural realms. Such a perspective seems to privilege one materiality over another. Without wishing to deny the importance of affective and economic alienation which laws can cause and be complicit with, it seems that new materialist concerns for the different human and non-human embodied lives conceive law as an instrument of regulation, or do not give it much thought. In her work about the historical specificity of legal speech as both human and computational, Ruth A. Miller has pointed out that the various new materialist theorists have been negligent to the forms and contents of law (2013: 8). Some think about the role of law more, for example Bruno Latour (2013) in *An Inquiry into Modes of Existence*, or others less. Miller criticises the perilous thinking about matters in terms of agency which results in conceiving matter's agency in similar terms to a human one. She argues that

> it is useful and necessary to sideline embodiment and to marginalize agency. . . . it allows for the possibility that linguistic activity can indeed occur apart from humans and apart from human intentions and desires. More broadly, it allows for the possibility that language might be detached from human and nonhuman speakers – not in a metaphorical or discursive way, but concretely and empirically.[21]

Miller puts these arguments forward in response to Bennett's understanding of vibrant matter. Her point is different from attempts to think about the implications of non-human agencies on legal conceptions of agency.[22] Miller points to the lack of sustained elaboration of the meaning and role of law in new materialist theories and politics. What is absent from new materialist approaches is a regard and feeling for the specificities of legal materiality itself. There is neither an openness towards defining and sensing the matters of law nor an attempt to understand legal materiality as a distinct phenomenon.[23]

Perhaps some of the new materialist theories expect too much and at the same time too little from law and its possibilities. Law is not a straight-forward instrumental matter of socio-political engineering or regulation, although it is often employed with such a hope. Law's matters are not always material, and the latter word is meant in the sense of mattering. They are not inherently meaningful or active.[24] Law is moreover not only a representational practice reflecting socio-cultural practices or values, but it is also a specific cultural technique itself.[25] It constructs its own objects and materials rather than 'lagging behind' society or technology.[26] Not all legal materials rest on legal fictions, but many do: constitutions, contracts, corporations, courts, personae and properties. Taking up questions raised by new materialist theories in legal scholarship could, however, afford an occasion to think about law itself as a vibrant and unpredictable matter, rather than seeing it as a hierarchical system of abstract norms or as an inert policy tool. The new materialist demands for being more attuned to the ways matters are, act or speak for themselves raise productive questions about the mode of inquiry of legal scholarship and its political and ethical propriety towards its own object: law.

Law has traditionally been understood as the system of sovereign expressions of norms, acting ideally as an instrument towards justice, sustained by jurisdiction exercised over a population of the living and things by the application and enforcement of abstract concepts, such as dignity, informed consent, property, originality or inventiveness. Its main outward expression and transmission were textual inscriptions, speech acts and proceduralised force. This understanding of law encompasses fields as diverse as legal philosophy and jurisprudence to socio-legal studies. Legal theorists are often concerned with the origin of law, the relationship between sovereignty and law, and the exercise of legal force through the concept of jurisdiction. Socio-legal scholars often focus on the aftermath of laws, normally the social effect of applied legal norms, and may find that it leads to other effects than the legislators had intended. They are concerned with uncovering or bringing to attention injustice, which typically then is formulated into a critique of power that created the unjust law or of a misapplication of law contrary to its aims. As Marianne Constable (2005) points out, such approaches are premised on the belief that laws are instruments of sovereign power and that legal intentions and effects can be causally linked, identified and described accurately and/or fully (2007).[27] The other side of the coin of these assumptions, which are shared both by positivists and socio-legal scholars alike, is that, if laws were designed, applied, enforced, corrected and tweaked, it could further justice. This belief underlies statements, such as 'The law is unjust'. 'The law ought to be fair'. 'This is not what the law ought to be about'. Criticality in this mode of thinking about law points to an identifiable differential between a fully analysable 'is' and a certain 'ought', and law's role is to fill the gap. The term 'lawfare' embodies this kind of legal instrumentalist understanding by both its proponent and its critics but is unable to capture the full penumbra of uncertainty of legal effects in concrete situations.[28] Arguing against such an instrumentalist legal scholarship, Desmond Manderson (1995) has shown that the reading and interpretation of legal texts also requires seeing and listening, allowing for a more complete perception of the legal text and its contexts. His analysis exposes changes in legal representation being analogous to other developments in cultural expressions, such as musical compositions. Approaching law as an aesthetic artefact in itself allows a deeper understanding of its structure and composition.

The 'new materialist' approach in legal scholarship could be seen to be an addition to the aesthetic approach, extending legal scholarship in a different direction. Although it is difficult to situate it within any definite legal realm or approach, it also appears to be less immediately concerned with the legitimacy of law, its founding narratives and origins, or with the overarching abstract pursuit of justice as being synonymous with or attainable through law. There is no presumption that laws will work as they should, and more often legal materials are shown to have unexpected effects on the formulation and interpretation of a legal abstract norm itself. They also show the several steps of mediation between certain legal forms and matters which render some more or less significant than others, such as the primacy of paper over models in the history of patent law (Pottage and Sherman, 2010). Their analyses yield insights into why law is not the easy solution which, when plugged into the gap between norm and reality, transforms political input into desired normative output. In that sense, the legal new materialist approaches are constructivist towards its own subject matter, law. They do not assume that law has a vital essence, which is either rational or physical. If there is a general trend to be identified under that grouping at all, many of the new legal materialist works consider legality as a fluctuating temporal, situated and cultural effect, which needs better understanding in terms of its material composition and concrete practices. They approach law through an examination of legal techniques and materials rather than through a positivist doctrinal analysis of legal cases and statutes. Precisely because of the acceptance that legality is not a given and varies in its force, studies into the *making* of law are seen as relevant and interesting as law's *post facto* effects, which has been predominantly favoured and practiced in legal education through a focus on cases that provide *post facto* narratives or socio-legal analyses of effects of legal enforcement.

Often the 'new materialist' works are awkward to categorise: the analytical gaze is not quite 'inside' the law; rather it is often a mixture of internal and external perspectives, which complicates the depiction of law as a coherent system of rules and their enforcement. Many of the 'new materialist' scholars are trained in law so to be able to take a Hartian internal point of view, but still somehow are sufficiently distant to the legal object of their study to take a stranger's viewpoint. Perhaps it is not a coincidence that these works are uncomfortably situated between multiple disciplinary backgrounds or interests, embodying the 'law *and*' anthropology, sciences, rhetoric, literature, music, approach rather than 'legal. . .'.

The sensibility for law's internal logic and practice is perhaps the reason why many of the legal 'new' materialists have studied legal media of inscription, their circulation and interpretation.[29] Texts, in various forms and genres, are taken as vital matters through which legality is materialised through inscription and speech and institute law as a system of knowledge.[30] Latour's study of *Conseil d'Etat*, for instance, emphasised the specific nature of textual inscription practice in law, particularly the production and interpretation of 'dossiers' (2009, org. 2002). Although the focus on dossiers and drafting might be obvious to 'trained' lawyers, seen with 'non-lawyer's' eyes, the obsessive writing and drafting activities are what stick out. Examples of legal scholarly works that pay attention to specifically legal textual matters and their orderings span diverse legal areas and forms: the drafting of a human rights agreement (Riles, 2000), the format of victim statements at the International Criminal Court (Kendall, 2015), the textualisation of inventions (Pottage and Sherman, 2010), the epistemological and bureaucratic organisation of files in patent practice (Kang, 2012), the act of 'strike through' which paradoxically preserves the inscription of the struck medical practitioner's name in the register (Jacob, 2016), or the creation of colonial property title through registration (Bhandar, 2015).

The emphasis on textual inscriptions does not however mean that other matters of legal representation, their choreographies and settings, are insignificant. Pierre Legendre has argued that the power of hermeneutics is closely related to the place of representation of which the function is the "fabrication of a symbolic universe of mediating objects" through law (1997, 145–146). There are multiple legal representational practices and matters which have been explored in a diverse array of scholarship. For example, the 'law in action' approach as carried out by Thomas Scheffer (2004) takes representational practices seriously by studying the engagement of multiple matters in the law-making process: the courtroom itself, files and the narrative contained in them. Or, before textual documents became the official embodiments of inventions, patents were validated by working models of machines that were staged in litigation and stored in the model rooms of patent offices as material evidences (te Heesen, 2000; Pottage and Sherman, 2010). The status of a copyright work in music involves the cultivation of expertise, technologies employed in evidence, as well as the performance of the expert in court (Bellido, 2016).

Of particular importance for eliciting legal materiality are law's media. They mediate and realise abstract law in the world, as well as performing the intermediation the other way, that is they open the world to law. Cornelia Vismann's works, which have been informed by legal history and the strand of German cultural studies associated with Friedrich Kittler, have been essential in making legal scholarship more attentive to law's techniques of transmission and self-fabrication through its media (2008, 2011, 2012; Vismann and Krajewski, 2007). Legal media can be both tangible and intangible. For example, Fabian Steinhauer argues that law ought not only be conceived as a system of norms and rights but as a practice of cultural techniques, which include rhetorical techniques and devices.[31] Legal meaning is also shaped by physical media, for example as shown in the context of storage and retrieval of trade marks (Bellido and Kang, 2016). It is also an undeniable but underexplored issue that the digitisation of patent documents and classification has brought changes in the operation of the patent system and in the delineation of intellectual property right itself (Kang, 2018), this only being an example of a broader challenges posed to "law's core concepts of corporeality, finitude and authentication" in "computer juridism" (Vismann and Krajewski, 2007). Lastly, perhaps one of the most biopolitical examples of media's formation of law is the use of algorithmic probability calculation within a software for criminal sentencing.[32]

These 'new materialist' accounts of law tend to be more attentive to the particular than to the general. Rather than seeing law as a coherent sovereign force applied through abstract legal concepts to diverse sets of facts, the new materialist approaches tend to regard the very matters and or practices as shaping law's effects and often law itself. This results in a less clear distinction between the subject and object of law, and also complicates the boundaries drawn between legal and the non-legal. Questions of legal ontology (what is law?) merge with questions of epistemology (how do we come to recognise legality?) rather than understanding them as separate realms, similar to the material turn in the history of sciences as discussed earlier.

The above is by all means not a comprehensive sketch of the various strands of recent legal scholarship that are attentive to law's materials. And it needs to be stressed that there is no unity or agreement in these legal works with regards to vitalist notions of matters or with respect to the place of Latourian actor network theory and the notion of *actants* in legal scholarship. Some may but some may not agree with the symmetrical ontology of human and non-human engagements implicit in Latour's *Dingpolitik*. At the risk of misrepresentation, however, I think that they do differ from the socio-legal descriptive uses of actor network theory as a non-interpretive methodology. Often actor network theory is used as quasi-empirical methodology or as agential concepts in socio-legal studies in order to 'follow a matter around'. The concept of *actants* is conveniently used to explain the influence of a non-human or inorganic matter. They are seen as explanations of the different webs in which the same law may become enacted with different effects. The insights for legal scholarship from such descriptions of 'following a matter', however, will depend on what is taken to be relevant matter of analysis and how a matter's relevance is explained and differentiated. In *Science in Action* by Latour and Woolgar, and also later in *The Making of Law*, Latour paid as much attention to semiotic practices and techniques as to the physical matters, both human and non-human.[33] Paradoxically for an acutely textually influenced institution of knowledge, such as law, it seems that some actor network–influenced legal studies do not pay sufficient attention to legal semiotics, and take matters, utterances or inscriptions to be self-explanatory requiring no interpretation or translation.[34] Law, however, is not equal to its matters. Following a 'thing' or even a legal matter around does not yield a better understanding of its legal significance. For example, land is not law, but it can be associated with different forces of legality. Or following a 'case' will yield insight into the way in which law is articulated and enacted but it does not necessarily lead to a better understanding of the legal arguments discussed in the case. It would resemble watching a cricket match without understanding the rules of the game and feeling bewildered but fascinated by the spectacle and rituals of spectatorship. Moreover, the different nodes within law as a network are not meaningful in themselves, as they cannot explain the relationship – and the relative density, or composition – between the different points within a network. Describing how things are assembled or thrown together can provide little explanation of the different performances, voices, gaps in communication, invisibilities and silences in such a network or assemblage. Simplistic and mechanical applications of actor network theory as a description of legal matters can often be ahistorical because they not take into account the evolution of the network itself. Perhaps applying actor network theory as a descriptive methodology might be better suited to explain legal practices which have to deal with frequent change in order to get a better sense of what is going on in the first place, but even then it is not enough in itself for explaining historically persistent patterns or structural tendencies. Without interpretation, it can offer little differentiation into why things do not tend to change as hoped or which points are more or less variable, such as blockages in a network, or even network blackouts. The identification and description of concrete matters is a start, and to be preferred to abstract theorisations of norms and rights, but it is ultimately unsatisfying in furthering differentiation of various degrees of legality and ultimately a more nuanced understanding of law as a material-semiotic performance and fabrication of realities.

Law's materials are not its matters

The usage and meaning of the different notions of 'materiality' in the context of legal scholarship need careful disentangling, for they encompass different conceptual backgrounds and assumptions. Most of all, I am concerned that there often seems to be a lack of distinction between matter and materiality of law, which leads to facile analogies and assumptions of equivalence without affording a better understanding of legal entanglements with worlds in concrete detail. Not denying the creative insights and events which analogies and parallelisms can bring forth, I believe that an inquiry into legal materiality needs to be accompanied by ontological qualifications. Whereas analogies allow relations to be made where there are no causal connections, it can also fail in productive differentiation. 'Everything is the same' can be understood both as inclusionary ethics or as a cutting denigration. Nonetheless, analogical thinking and criticality need not be mutually exclusive.[35] In relation to the question of law's materiality, the often-made equation of matter and materiality would benefit from an inquiry into law's matters and the degrees of legality they elicit.

Above all, it is not clear what law's matters *are* if legal scholarship takes new materialist approaches as a theoretical orientation or as a framework of analysis. As Ian Hacking has asked, "the social construction of what?" Alain Pottage (2012) has asked, "the materiality of what?" in relation to law. The "what" is presumably the law but as long as there is a profound disagreement about what law *is*, it is necessary to find out what *there is* and how it comes to be perceived as being somehow legal. Then the question could be posed slightly differently: what are law's matters? How do we identify law's constitutive ingredients? Rather than asking what acts, sounds, sights and feelings we perceive as being permeated by law, the question then becomes how these come to be regarded and felt as relevant to law and how they come to be spelled out in legal language. Which of these elements come to matter legally and which don't? What are the devices, instruments and procedures that make legal inscriptions material in the sense of meaningfulness? How are these materialities or meanings then performed?

In this regard, the axiom of 'letting the matters speak' does not make much sense. Matters do not become material, or even perceivable, in isolation but are always implicated in other contexts of meanings and meaning makings (Despret, 2013). Matters may speak but we may not be able to hear them for various reasons: it may be acoustic, physical or incomprehensible. One could perhaps trace this lack of hearing to a missing metaethics of mutual listening: we are not listening to matters, both human and non-human, and are unable to make sense of the sounds. The other way around, it is also not clear how matters can be held to be bound to an ethical standard of listening to us. At the same time, we may not really grasp matters fully because it is too difficult to perceive and interpret their sounds, appearances or even touch. This may be so because there are no adequate representational techniques that would enable better interpretation. As Hans-Jörg Rheinberger has noted, matter itself and its representation hover around both the inside and outside of each other: matter becomes material only through representation, and representation itself is an act of interpretation, or coming into a meaning (1997: 182–183). In this view, materials are the matters which are active because they have attained meaning. Piyel Haldar discussed how legal exclusion of hearsay as evidence can be thought about with Heidegger's concept of idle chatter (*Gerede*) as opposed to speech (*Rede*): "Where discourse is sovereign, it is precisely because the subject is subordinated to its language, and such a language aims at revealing the reality of what the discourse is about" (1996: 127).[36] The distinction between law's matters and materiality could be perhaps conceived in the following way: law's materials are the constitutive matters which can have varying degrees of semiotic significance.[37] If there is a specificity to legal materiality in comparison to other materialities, such as a scientific one or economic one, it is that law is already always mediated through the legal form and language games and that it is backed by a normative claim (Constable, 2014). Materiality could be then better grasped as the temporary and unstable articulation of a matter through interpretative practices rather than as a naturalist or essentialist stasis of a physical matter. In this sense it is a truly abstract-material system of signification, nonetheless one which necessarily evolves together with different worlds of beings. What is legally material then? Law's materials are not objects over which law wields its power but its own constitutive ingredients of revealing itself.

In history of sciences, it has long been recognised that matters are not predetermined but arise in material practices and techniques of representation in which the matter exceeds or escapes control. Combining a deep sensibility for Bachelard's and Canguilhem's historical epistemologies and for Derrida's feeling for language, Rheinberger writes:

> It is in the nature of these means, material, graphematic entities, that they are in the capacity of and excess. They contain more and other possibilities than those to which they actually are held to be bound. The excess embodies the historical movement of the trace: the trace transgresses the boundaries within which the game appears to be confined. As an excess, it escapes the definition of the system.
> (1997: 182)

It is precisely through the material practices of experimental systems that the 'excess' and instability of scientific matter are contained. Similarly, law has to cope with indeterminacy of language with which it makes sense of its matters. In studying law's enactments in speech, Marianne Constable's argument of the centrality of language in modern law reflects the above observation about replacement and deplacements of matters, materiality and meaning through linguistic representation and interpretation: "Modern law is bound to language: It uses language, and language is not completely within its control" (2014: 18). As Don Ihde pointed out, "speech is sounded, and sound neither neutral nor reducible to a single layer of meaning" and meaning arises in the "speech event" its normative embodiment is as a phenomenon of silence, listening and sounds. There is always more than information in spoken word" (1977: 24).

Law itself cannot speak as such; it needs to be sounded out, inscribed or depicted by something or someone. It is a value-knowledge which is embodied in different generalising forms with reference to an ideal of justice. It perceives through general abstract categories, which are then applied and also modified in relation to particulars. Legal forms are abstract, but are shaped in particular expressions applied to concrete circumstances. In patent law, for example, an invention has to be novel, but novelty is established as the negative of prior existence as state of art. Novelty has to be represented through specific wording in the patent application document in relation to the concrete inventive matter. Legal materiality is enacted through techniques of inscription, visualisation and their interpretation, such as texts, documents, courtrooms, speech acts, images, architectures and ritualised performances.

Although legality is materialised through different media and the latter shapes the scope and meaning of law, law is predominantly a hermeneutic practice operating in a textual mode, which is implicated with many other representational practices. The courtroom is 'only' a room without the legal significance imbued to it. An offensive publication turns into a legal matter if associated with a legal dispute. A stone becomes a legal object if it is implicated in prescriptive regulation, such as a boundary marker. If there is no adequate legal form to acknowledge a matter, the matter does not exist in and for law. Rules regarding legal standing are good examples of the close relationship between legal form, representation and materiality. The acknowledgment of law's hermeneutic character does not mean that legal materiality is determined only by humans. Legal text is interpreted mostly by human readers but expressed by both humans and non-humans. Increasingly, non-human recipients process legal text as data. The legal matters proper are hence law's text, what it says and omits, and its media, embodiments and techniques. The media are, for example, the analogue and digital inscriptions in codes, commentaries, documents, textbooks, papers, computers, buildings, fences, still and moving images and model organisms. Its techniques are rhetoric, codification, exemplification through cases, classification, interpretation, statistical probability and ritualised performances. Law's materials are hermeneutic elements of arguments which refer to a matter but are not identical to it. Barthes characterised them as "*argumentum*: 'exposition, account, summary, plot outline, invented narrative,' . . . 'instrument of distancing, signboard à la Brecht' not to the object or matter itself, but to 'what he says'" (2002: 5). Law's materials which allow law to be expressed in turn condition what can be said as law and how it is relayed to the world.[38] They are hence arguments, techniques and their media, or what is 'said' to be material, but not the matters or objects themselves. Law's materials are, to quote Barthes again, not "the object or matter itself, but. . . 'what [it] says'". Then the relevant questions become, what is possible to say in law and how did it become so; how is something said, and what is withheld from legal speech?[39]

Law's materiality is both abstract and concrete

Katherine N. Hayles has noted that it is possible to think of "materiality as distinct from physicality" for "re-envisioning the material basis for hybrid texts and subjectivities" (2005: 2). Although law's materiality is not identical to its matters, it is intimately connected to them. That applies to both kinds of law's matters. There are two kinds of physical matters relevant to law: one is its own physical materials, its language, forms of transmission, physical contexts and institutional set-ups; in short, its media and cultural techniques. They are not completely controllable. The others are the physical matters of the world which it deals with: the status of organic and nonorganic matters, as well as their relationship to each other. These are not fully within law's power either. Law's specific materiality can then be understood as a particular and concrete effect of interaction between nonorganic and organic matters and social events in legal language, which is expressed in abstract form and various formats – textual, visual, aural, theatrical and numerical. The very ways in which law is or is not spoken, written, depicted, organised, performed and recorded matter perhaps equally, if not more, as the abstract legal norms and their inscribed existence (Constable, 2007), as well as the physical embodiment of its subject matters. Ideas and things are inseparable from one another (Riskin, 2012: 229). Law in this sense could be characterised as a 'soft abstraction' (Toscano, 2008): law is not completely shut off from the particular, concrete properties of the animate and inanimate matters by which it is surrounded, but it makes them material through relating them to legal arguments.[40] Legal materiality can be understood as a mode by which the concrete matters come to be enlisted to define a matter of law; for example, how an invented scientific object comes to be signified as a patentable invention, or how recording formats and an expert's performance in court interweave to determine the legality of a copy. Therefore, materiality in the legal context is an argumentative, hermeneutic process involving several steps of representation and interpretation, rather than denoting an innate property or a physical thing.

Take plants as an example of legal materiality. Depending on the vantage point from which one observes, the matters of analysis will differ: the matter in the first level of observation is the plant, in the second one the legal text, in the third level other competing legal frameworks or different interpretations from the perspective of other value systems, such as biology. Legal materiality connotes the relations of the plant to the patent. It involves the relationship between the patent document to the legal idea of invention. It also signifies the awkward place of plant intellectual property rights in international conventions or its *sui generis* status outside the conventional categories of intellectual property law (Sherman, 2008: 60–84).

The distinction between matter and materiality and the definition of materiality as the relation between the concrete and the abstract are important because they imply that the relations between matter and legal forms are not unidirectional: the concrete matter can exert significance influence on the way in which the legal form is perceived (for example, the shaping of trade marks through specific media and techniques of search, Bellido and Kang, 2016); but also law "informs the materials" in the sense that law is already "folded into and becomes part of the objects in question" (Sherman, 2008: 565).[41]

The recognition of legal materiality as a relation between the abstract and the concrete produces a level of complexity, which cannot be adequately accounted for by an ethical call to 'let the material things speak' or for an ethics of interspecies encounter (Haraway, 2007) or parliament of things (Latour, 2005). The engagement with matters and material practices in the history and philosophy of sciences suggests that such a balancing act between the abstract forms and regard for concrete matters is productive but needs to be carefully anchored in a reflexive epistemic history in order to escape analytical obviousness and various kinds of naturalist and essentialist reductionism.[42] From the vantage point of the legal scholar, there are at least three levels of observation which would need careful differentiation and further thought. To continue with the plant example,

- the first level of analysis would relate to the concrete particularities of the 'raw' matter as interpreted by law in relation to its abstract form (e.g.

interpreting plants in relation to the legal forms of invention in patent law, or signs in trade mark laws);

- the second level of observation would examine the legal representation of the first relationship (between the plant and its legal status) through particular constellation and mis-en-scène through law's techniques and media (classification, papers, specimens, deposits);
- the third level of analysis would involve the interpretation of the effects of legal materiality from various other interpretive viewpoints (from 'meta'-legal viewpoint: TRIPS, UPOV, other *sui generis* systems of regulation; historical viewpoints: how did the notion of property in plants develop historically?; from the viewpoint of the farmer: what kind of property regime, if at all, makes most sense to her/him depending on location, the kinds of crops cultivated and market pricings?; from the perspective of plant lovers and consumers: how can I find particular crosses or old breeds?; from the perspective of botanists: are the legal classifications similar to other scientific classifications, Linnaean or phylogenetic ones? Are we really talking about the same plant?).

The effect of distinguishing these realms is that it becomes clear that matters and materialities will vary depending on the level of analysis.

Giving attention to law's matters (inscriptions, physical forces and matters, behaviours, relations), their representation (formats, settings, media) and their legal meaning (elicited through interpretation of the relation between abstract legal form and concrete matters) requires a layered way of finding out about the relative degrees of legality, and thus about varying degrees of significance. A 'forensic' gaze on law's concrete matters coupled with a sensibility for the abstract legal form can identify and problematise the nuances and variables in law's materiality.[43] Such an analysis engaging various haphazard, vibrant, living, dead, silent and speaking matters and their legal interpretation results in a complex picture of law and its aleatory effects. This is a different position from the reductionist perspective of equating law's materiality with its matters and of mistaking descriptions as law's ontology. This proposed understanding of legal materiality acknowledges that it is impossible to grasp things 'as they are' and to do full justice by an identical representation of the matters. This insight also implies that law may be a disappointing instrument for recognising the innate vitalities of matters. The mediation between the indeterminacy of language and the sheer 'excess' of meaning inherent in matters occurs through legal materials, its techniques of representation and media. Law can only enlist the concrete matters brought to it and make them meaningful by reading, inscribing, arguing and interpreting them in relation to its abstract forms. In doing so, it also transposes them into other social worlds. The power of legal interpretation is as concrete and as unstable as seemingly solid matters themselves.

Notes

1 The following references do not form a complete list: Barad (2007); Bennett (2010); Braidotti (2013). For new materialist anthologies, see Coole and Frost (2010); Dolphijn and

van der Tuin (2012). Curiously these theoretical works do not seem to be in conversation with long-standing discussions about matter and materiality in anthropology and studies of material culture: see, for example, Miller (1998), (2005); Ingold (2007), (2012); Drazin and Kuechler (2015). The lack of engagement may be perhaps due to the latter's focus on the use and effects of materials in culture and the former being more interested in formulating a political and normative theory of innate affectivity of non-human matters informed by philosophy and some strands of science studies. Although not necessarily mutually exclusive, the philosophies of 'new materialism' are more concerned with matters and their innate, physical and biological agencies, whereas anthropologists of material culture take the manifestations of matters as the starting points into an inquiry of their social and cultural effects.

2 Kay (2000); Helmreich (2000); socialisation of machine intelligence, see IBM (2005). On computation's effect on human subjectivity, see Rotman (2008).

3 In legal scholarship, see, for example, Philippopoulos-Mihalopoulos (2008) (pointing to and moving away from what is perceived as an anthropocentric legal frame). For a critical discussion for jurisprudence of animals, see Otomo and Musawir (2013).

4 Especially in matters of cultural property and colonial dispossession, the question of recognition, particularly from the perspective of critical race studies, has been a long-standing issue: see, for example, Bhandar (2007) and Bhandar and Goldberg-Hiller (2015).

5 Davies and Naffine (2001); Kang (2011).

6 Rouvroy and Bern (2013).

7 For example, on the legal difficulty of recognising different modes of knowledge, see Verran (1998); Anker (2005), Godden (2007); Graham (2010); on the legal propertisation of cultural goods, see Coombes (1998); on copyright's awkward fit and its instrumentalisation for open source software, see Kelty (2008).

8 On what counts as observation, how to do it and its instrumentation, see, for example, Hacking (1982); Crary (1992); Hoffmann (2006); Daston and Lunbeck (2011).

9 For the difference between Driesch and Roux's experiments leading to different outcomes, see Gilbert and Barresi, Developmental Biology (2000); also see chapter 2 in Harrington (1999). Jane Maienschein has argued that the dispute between vitalism and mechanism in developmental biology stems from disagreement about the degree and point of differentiation of the embryo and has thus an epistemological dimension, see (2000: 122–137). The philosopher of science, John Dupré, has argued that ontological questions in sciences are influenced by epistemological tools and choices (1993).

10 See Daston (1999); also Rheinberger on Canguilhem's understanding of history of sciences (2010, 40).

11 On the development of molecular biology as a large-scale endeavour, see Kay (1996); in physical sciences, see Galison and Hevly (1992); in bioinformatics, see Steven (2015) and Leonelli (2016).

12 Gordon (1991, 1st. ed. 1968).

13 Helmreich (2000); Mitchelll and Thurtle (2003).

14 Peter Galison, a historian of science, observes in physical sciences "a focus on novel effects, materials, and objects, but constructed in an engineering of being that values the making and linking of structures with little regard for the older fascination with existence for its own sake" (2017).

15 For a differentiated analysis of the influence of Driesch's holistic vitalism and Uexkuell's biological concept of Umwelt on Heidegger, see Malpas (2011). On the intertwining of heredity, race and eugenics, see Mueller-Wille and Rheinberger (2012, chapter 5). On how the Human Genome Diversity Project became a controversial site of convergence of knowledge, democracy and racism, see Reardon (2004). On the concept of the gene as an epistemic concept, see Beurton, Falk and Rheinberger (2000).

16 I am grateful to Stuart J. Murray for this intervention.

17 Schaffer and Shapin (1986); Klein and Lefebvre (2007); Daston and Galison (2007).

18 See discussion of Canguilhem in chapter 3 in Rheinberger (2010). Rheinberger in *Towards a History of Epistemic Things: Synthesizing Proteins in the Test Tube* developed the notion of excess in discussion of Derrida's notion of *différance* in relation to the experimental research and object, (1997: 183). Latour stresses the importance of eliciting recalcitrance as understood by Stengers and Despret in physics and psychology, also in the context of social science: "devise your inquiries so that they maximize the recalcitrance of those you interrogate" (2004: 217).

19 Classifications are epistemological techniques of ordering things par excellence. On legal classification of plants, see Sherman (2008); on the legal classification of a new kind of invention, see Kang (2012). On scientific matters in legal disputes, see Cambrosio et al. (1990).

20 For an analysis of Spinoza in relation to law, see Slavoj Zizek Philosophy: Spinoza, Kant, Hegel and . . . Badiou! Available at: <www.lacan.com/zizphilosophy1.htm>.

21 In *Seven Stories of Threatening Speech*, Miller (2012: 30) argues that "[i]gnoring bodies and agency . . . makes it possible to recognize far more of the physical and material things that speech or language might do." She proposes an "alternative history of speech. . . – away from Latour's conclusion that speech may no longer be a purely human property, and toward an alternative conclusion that speech in fact never was a human property."

22 There have been attempts by legal scholars to think about the meaning of non-human legal subjects and their agential standings in law, particularly in the context of autonomous machines and artificial intelligence (Teubner, 2007; Rouvroy and Hildebrandt, 2011; Kang, 2014).

23 The edited volume by Bently and Flynn (eds) *Law and the Senses* (1996) was an early attempt to thematise law's relationship to the senses. Most chapters, however, are concerned with legal reception and interpretation of senses, law's sense-making, rather than how law is sensed or felt by whom or what.

24 For example, intellectual properties can be useless; they literally do not always matter. The force of law is not always 'switched on': it can be literally buried in the archive of rules or it can be (re-)activated. Good example of re-activation of a law's materiality is the discussion on the applicability of the Henry VIII clause in relation to 1972 EU Act in *R (on the application of Miller and another) v. Secretary of State for Exiting the European Union* [2017] UKSC 5. Law can be material as a Foucauldian external or internalised disciplinary power, but it is not the only kind of power. Legitimated physical violence and restriction on space are some of the most material ways in which law 'matters'.

25 "Law-making is an operation – or, to put it differently, a cultural technique – executed by a popular assembly" Vismann (2013: 85), discussing Walter Schadewaldt (1978) *Die Anfänge der Philosophie bei den Griechen*. Frankfurt am Main: Suhrkamp.

26 In the context of regulation of plant varieties and breeders' rights, it could be argued that the *sui generis* regime of UPOV is another attempt to take into account the specificities of plants' innate agencies, but Sherman (2008) shows that thereby law also forms biology.

27 Constable (2005), p. 33. For a critique of treating language as an instrument of social power, see p. 51.

28 Dunlap Jr. (3 August 2007), "Lawfare amid warfare", *The Washington Times*. In the context of intellectual property, TRIPs has been often criticized as an instrument of economic and cultural lawfare but the effects of domestic jurisdictions have been more hybrid and materially determined depending on the specificity of the regulatory object and concrete, local conditions, see, e.g., Hayden (2013) or Petersen (2014).

29 On the centrality of files and documents as law's material media, see for example Vismann (2008 (org. 2000), 2011, 2012); Riles (2006).

30 Reflecting Legendre's argument of society as a linguistic organisation involving the scene and the staging of textual representations, see Legendre (2012). For fragments in English translation, see 'Of texts', in Peter Goodrich et al. (2006).

31 In the context of legal acts of separation, for instances, he identifies three legal techniques: "(1.) words which isolate, (2.) speeches that cut and (3.) tables that move." Steinhauer (2014: 130). For an overview, see Steinhauer (2017).

32 *Wisconsin v. Loomis*, 2016 WI 68, case number 2015AP157-CR, available at www.wicourts.gov/sc/opinion/DisplayDocument.pdf?content=pdf&seqNo=171690

33 For a discussion of distinct interpretations and uses of ANT see John Law, 'Actor Network Theory and Material Semiotics.' Version of 25 April 2007, available at www.heterogeneities.net/publications/Law2007ANTandMaterialSemiotics.pdf

34 For a discussion of the various influences of Latour in law, see McGee (2017). For a comprehensive review of actor network theory, its limitations and misuses, see Lezaun (2017).

35 On the combination of identity and difference in images, see Stafford (1999). On law as material metaphor itself, see Philippopoulos-Mihalopoulos (2016).

36 Haldar argues that *Gerede*, idle chat or gossip is "[T]his absent non-identity of voice . . . what we share" and recouping this unreliable voice would be able to "transform the relations between law and justice" (1996: 132).

37 However, non-material writing procedure can also become legally material, involving both specific paper format, forms, writing sequence, desk location, filing system, classification, office architecture etc. See, for example, Hoffmann (2013).

38 I am thinking about Paul Rekret's criticism of new materialisms (2016) which argues that the latter are not attentive to the social forces which shape the epistemological conditions of thought. This critique equally applies to simplistic applications of new materialist approaches to the study of law.

39 "It is precisely what the text does not elucidate that becomes an invitation to our imaginations. . . . Is that we imagine the most, or the most vividly, when an author is at his most elliptical or withholding? (In music, notes and chords define ideas, but so do rests.)" Mendelsund (2014).

40 Alberto Toscano (2008) had suggested the term 'warm abstraction' for the tendency to desire 'the concrete, the form of matter' and criticised it as missing the 'real abstraction' cutting through matter through commodification and value.

41 The co-constitution of law with matters is something which some new materialists do not pay much attention to, as Ruth A. Miller's (2011) historical studies of suffragette movement and constitutional law have pointed out.

42 For examples of work in history of sciences which straddle the ideational and materialist divides, see Kohler (1994); Rheinberger (1997); Daston (2007).

43 "Forensics from the Latin source, means in front of the forum: it is the art and skill of speaking on behalf of objects – narrating convincing histories from objects, convincing enough to become what we can evidence – to a forum of citizens or judges. Forensics is one of the methods that allows objects (or things) to speak or a way of listening to them" Weizman (2010: 258–259).

Bibliography

Anker, Kirsten, 'The Truth in Painting: Cultural Artefacts as Proof of Native Title', *Law Text Culture*, 9, 91–124, 2005.

Barad, Karen, *Meeting the Universe Halfway: Quantum Physics and the Entanglement of Matter and Meaning*, Durham, NC and London: Duke University Press, 2007.

Barthes, Roland, 'The Death of the Author', in *Image-Music-Text*, London: Fontana Press, London, 1977.

Barthes, Roland, *A Lover's Discourse*, London: Vintage, 2002.

Bellido, Jose, 'Forensic Technologies in Music Copyright', *Social and Legal Studies*, 25(4), 441–459, 2016.

Bellido, Jose and Kang, Hyo Yoon, 'In Search of a Trade Mark: Search Practices and Bureaucratic Poetics', *Griffiths Law Review*, 25(2), 147–171, 2016.

Bennett, Jane, *Vibrant Matters: A Political Ecology of Things*, Durham, NC and London: Duke University Press, 2010.
Bently, Lionel and Flynn, Leo (eds), *Law and the Senses: Sensational Jurisprudence*, London and Chicago: Pluto Press, 1996.
Beurton, Peter, Falk, Raphael, Rheinberger, Hans Joerg (eds), *The Concept of the Gene in Development and Evolution: Historical and Epistemological Perspectives*, Cambridge: Cambridge University Press, 2000.
Bhandar, Brenna, 'Recovering the Limits of Recognition: The Politics of Difference and Decolonisation in John Burrow's Recovering Canada: The Resurgence of Indigenous Law', *Australian Feminist Law Journal*, 27, 125–151, 2007.
Bhandar, Brenna, 'Title by Registration: Instituting Modern Property Law and Creating Racial Value in the Settler Colony', *Journal of Law and Society*, 253–282, 2015.
Bhandar, Brenna and Goldberg-Hiller, Jon, 'Law, Sovereignty and Recognition', in *Plastic Materialities: Politics, Legality and Metamorphosis in the Work of Catherine Malabou*. Durham, NC and London: Duke University Press, 2015.
Braidotti, Rosi, *The Posthuman*, Cambridge: Polity Press, 2013.
Cambrosio, Alberto, Keating, Peter and MacKenzie, Michael, 'Scientific Practice in the Courtroom: The Construction of Sociotechnical Identities in a Biotechnology Patent Dispute', *Social Problems*, 37(3), 275–293, 1990.
Coole, Diana and Frost, Samantha (eds), *New Materialisms: Ontology, Agency, and Politic*, Durham, NC, London: Duke University Press, 2010.
Coombes, Rosemary, *The Cultural Life of Intellectual Properties: Authorship, Appropriation and the Law*, Durham, NC, London: Duke University Press, 1998.
Constable, Marianne, *Just Silences. The Limits and Possibilities of Modern Law*, Princeton: Princeton University Press, 2007.
Constable, Marianne, *Our Word Is Our Bond: How Legal Speech Acts*, Stanford: Stanford University Press, 2014.
Crary, Jonathan, *Techniques of the Observer: On Vision and Modernity in the Nineteenth Century*. Cambridge, MA: MIT Press, 1992.
Daston, Lorraine, 'Coming Into Being of Scientific Objects', in Daston (ed.), *Biographies of Scientific Objects*, Chicago: University of Chicago Press, 1999.
Daston, Lorraine, 'Glass Flower', in Daston (ed.), *Things That Talk. Object Lessons from Art and Science*, Cambridge, MA: Zone Books, 2007.
Daston, Lorraine and Galison, Peter, *Objectivity*, Cambridge, MA: Zone Books, 2007.
Daston, Lorraine and Lunbeck, Elizabeth (eds), *Histories of Scientific Observation*, Chicago: University of Chicago Press, 2011.
Davies, Margaret and Naffine, Ngaire, *Are Persons Property? Legal Debates About Property and Personality*, Burlington, VA: Ashgate, 2001.
Despret, Vinciane, 'From Secret Agents to Interagency', *History and Theory*, 52, 29–44, 2013.
Dolphijn, Rick and Tuin, Iris van der (eds), *New Materialism: Interview & Cartographies*, London: One Humanities Press, 2012.
Drazin, Adam and Kuechler, Susanne (eds), *The Social Life of Materials*, London: Bloomsbury, 2015.
Dupré, John, *The Disorder of Things: Metaphysical Foundations of the Disunity of Science*. Cambridge, MA: Harvard University Press, 1993.
Galison, Peter, 'The Pyramid and the Ring: A Physics Indifferent to Ontology', *Research Objects in Their Technological Setting*, 10, 15–26, London, New York: Routledge, 2017.
Galison, Peter and Hevly, B. (eds), *Big Science: The Growth of Large-Scale Research*, Stanford: Stanford University Press, 1992.
Gilbert, Scott and Barresi, Michael, *Developmental Biology* (6th edition), Sunderland, MA: Sinauer Associates; section: 'The Developmental Mechanics of Cell Specification', 2000. www.ncbi.nlm.nih.gov/books/NBK9968/.

Godden, Lee, 'The Invention of Tradition: Property Law as a Knowledge Space for the Appropriation of the South', *Griffith Law Review*, 16(2), 375–410, 2007.
Goodrich, Peter, Barshack, Lior and Schütz, Anton (eds), *Law, Text, Terror*, London: Glasshouse Press, 2006.
Gordon, J.E., *The New Science of Strong Materials: Or Why You Don't Fall Through the Floor*, London: Penguin, 1991(1968).
Graham, Nicole, *Lawscape: Property, Environment, Law*, London: Routledge, 2010.
Hacking, Ian, *Representing and Intervening*, Cambridge: Cambridge University Press, 1982.
Haldar, Piyel, 'Acoustic Justice', in Lionel Bently and Leo Flynn (eds), *Law and the Senses*, London: Pluto Press, 1996.
Haraway, Donna, 'Situated Knowledges: The Science Question in Feminism and the Privilege of Partial Perspective', in Donna Haraway (ed.), *Simians, Cyborgs and Women: the Reinvention of Nature*, London: Free Association Books, 1991.
Haraway, Donna, *When Species Meet*, Minneapolis: University of Minnesota Press, 2007.
Harrington, Anne, *Reenchanted Science: Holism in German Culture from Wilhelm II to Hitler*, Princeton: Princeton University Press, 1999.
Hayden, Cori, *When Nature Goes Public*, Princeton: Princeton University Press, 2013.
Hayles, N. Katherine, *My Mother Was a Computer*, Chicago: University of Chicago Press, 2005.
Helmreich, Stefan, *Silicon Second Nature: Culturing Artificial Life in a Digital World*, Berkeley: University of California Press, 2000.
Hoffmann, Christoph, *Unter Beobachtung: Naturforschung in der Zeit der Sinnesapparate* (trans. Under Observation: Researching Nature in the Time of Sensing Apparatus), Goettingen: Wallstein, 2006.
Hoffmann, Christoph, 'Processes on Paper: Writing Procedures as Non-Material Research Devices', *Science in Context*, 26, 279–303, 2013.
Hoffmann, Christoph, 'Does a Glowworm See? Sigmund Exner's Study of the Compound Eye', *Representations*, 138, 37–58, 2017.
IBM, 'Automatic Computing. White Paper. An Architectural Blueprint for Autonomic Computing', June 2005. http://www-03.ibm.com/autonomic/pdfs/AC%20Blueprint%20White%20Paper%20V7.pdf.
Ihde, Don, *Expanding Hermeneutics: Visualism in Science*, Evanston, IL: Northwestern University Press, 1977.
Ingold, Tim, 'Materials Against Materiality', *Archaeological Dialogues*, 14(1), 1–16, 2007.
Ingold, Tim, 'Toward an Ecology of Materials', *Annual Review of Anthropology*, 14, 427–442, 2012.
Jacob, Marie-Andrée, 'The Shared History: Unknotting Fictive Kinship and Legal Process', *Law and Society Review*, 43(1), 95–126, 2009.
Jacob, Marie-Andrée, 'The Strikethrough: An Approach to Regulatory Writing and Professional Discipline', *Legal Studies*, 37(1), 137–161, 2016.
Jasanoff, Sheila and Kim, Sang-Hyun, 'Containing the Atom: Sociotechnical Imaginaries and Nuclear Power in the United States and South Korea', *Minerva*, 27(2), 119–146, 2009.
Kang, Hyo Yoon, 'Autonomic Computing, Genomic Data and Human Agency: The Case for Embodiment', in Antoinette Rouvroy and Mireille Hildebrandt (eds), *Law, Human Agency, and Autonomic Computing: The Philosophy of Law Meets the Philosophy of Technology*, London: Routledge, 2011.
Kang, Hyo Yoon, 'Science Inside Law: The Making of a New Patent Class in the International Patent Classification', *Science in Context*, 25(4), 551–194, 2012.
Kang, Hyo Yoon, 'Autonomie/Code: Überlegungen zu Software-Rhetorik in Postgenomik und künstlicher Intelligenz', in Jochen Bung und Malte Gruber (eds), *Autonome Automaten. Künstliche Körper und Artifizielle Agenten in der technisierten Gesellschaft*, Berlin: Kritische Reihe, trafo Verlag, 2014.
Kang, Hyo Yoon, 'Ghosts of Inventions: Patent Law's Digital Mediations', *History of Science*, DOI: 10.1177/0073275318770773, 2018.

Kay, Lily E., *The Molecular Vision of Life: Caltech, the Rockefeller Foundation, and the Rise of New Biology*, Oxford: Oxford University Press, 1996.

Kay, Lily E., *Who Wrote the Book of Life?* A History of the Genetic Code. Stanford: Stanford University Press, 2000.

Kelty, Chris, *Two Bits. The Cultural Significance of Free Software*, Durham, NC and London: Duke University Press, 2008.

Kendall, Sara, 'Archiving Victimhood: Practices of Inscription in International Criminal Law', in S. Motha and H. van Rijswijk (eds), *Law, Violence, Memory: Uncovering the Counter-Archive*, London: Routledge, 2015.

Klein, Ursula and Lefebvre, Wolfgang, *Materials in Eighteenth Century Science: A Historical Ontology*, Cambridge, MA: MIT Press, 2007.

Kohler, Robert, *Lords of the Fly and the Experimental Life*, Chicago: University of Chicago Press, 1994.

Kohn, Eduardo, *How Forests Think. Toward an Anthropology Beyond the Human*, Chicago: University of Chicago Press, 2013.

Kursell, Julia, 'Experiments on Sound Color in Music and Acoustics: Helmholtz, Schoenberg, and Klangfarbenmelodie', *Osiris*, 28, 191–211, 2013.

Ladeur, Karl-Heinz, 'Introduction of the Precautionary Principle into EU Law: A Pyrrhic Victory for Environmental and Public Health Law?', *Common Market Law Review*, 40, 1455–1479, 2003.

Latour, Bruno, *Pandora's Hope: Essays on the Reality of Science Studies*, Cambridge, MA: Harvard University Press, 1999.

Latour, Bruno, 'How to Talk About the Body? The Normative Dimensions of Science Studies', *Body & Society*, 10(2–3), 205–229, 2004.

Latour, Bruno, *Making Things Public: Atmospheres of Democracy*, London and Cambridge MA: MIT Press, 2005.

Latour, Bruno, *The Making of Law*, Cambridge: Polity Press, 2009 (2002 org.).

Latour, Bruno, *An Inquiry into Modes of Existence: An Anthropology of the Moderns*, Cambridge, MA: Harvard University Press, 2013.

Law, John, 'Actor Network Theory and Material Semiotics', Version 25 April 2007. www.heterogeneities.net/publications/Law2007ANTandMaterialSemiotics.pdf.

Legendre, Pierre, 'Hermes and Institutional Structures', in Peter Goodrich (ed.), *Law and the Unconscious – A Legendre Reader*, New York: Palgrave Macmillan, 1997.

Legendre, Pierre, 'Of Texts', in Goodrich, Peter, Barshack, Lior, Schütz, Anton (eds), *Law, Text, Terror*, London: Glasshouse Press, 2006.

Legendre, Pierre, *Gesellschaft als Text* (trsl.: Society as Text), Wien, Berlin: Turia + Kant, 2012 (org. 2001).

Leonelli, Sabina, *Data-Centric Biology*, Chicago, University of Chicago Press, 2016.

Lezaun, Javier, 'The Pragmatic Sanction of Materials: Notes for an Ethnography of Legal Substances', *Journal of Law and Society*, 39(1), 20–38, 2012.

Lezaun, Javier, 'Actor Network Theory', in C. Benzecry, M. Krause and I. Reed (eds), *Social Theory Now*, Chicago: University of Chicago Press, 2017.

MacGregor, Neil, *The History of the World in 100 Objects*, London: Allen Lane, 2012.

Maienschein, Jane, 'Competing Epistemologies and Developmental Biology', in R. Creath and J. Maienschein (eds), *Biology and Epistemology*, Cambridge: Cambridge University Press, 122–137, 2000.

Malpas, Jeff (ed.), *The Place of Landscape*, Cambridge MA: MIT Press, 2011.

Manderson, Desmond, 'Statuta v. Acts: Interpretation, Music, and Early English Legislation', *Yale Journal of Law & the Humanities*, 7(2), Article 3, 1995.

McGee, Kyle (ed.), *Latour and the Passage of the Law*, Edinburgh: Edinburgh University Press, 2017.

Mendelsund, Paul, 'What We See When We Read', *The Paris Review*, 14 August 2014. www.theparisreview.org/blog/2014/08/14/what-we-see-when-we-read/.

Miller, Daniel, *Material Cultures. Why Some Things Matter*, Chicago: University of Chicago Press, 1998.

Miller, Daniel (ed.), *Materiality*, Durham, NC and London: Duke University Press, 2005.

Miller, Ruth A., *Seven Stories of Threatening Speech*, Ann Arbor: University of Michigan Press, 2012.

Miller, Ruth A., *Snarl. In Defense of Stalled Traffic and Faulty Networks*, Ann Arbor: University of Michigan Press, 2013.

Mitchelll, Robert and Thurtle, Philip (eds), *Data Made Flesh: Embodying Information*, London: Routledge, 2003.

Mueller-Wille, Staffan and Rheinberger, Hans-Joerg *A Cultural History of Heredity*, Chicago: University of Chicago Press, 2012.

Otomo, Yoriko and Musawir, Ed (eds), *Law and the Question of the Animal*, London: Routledge, 2013.

Petersen, Kris, *Speculative Markets: Drug Circuits and Derivative Life in Nigeria*, Durham, NC and London: Duke University Press, 2014.

Philippopoulos-Mihalopoulos, Andreas, 'In-Environment of Law', in *Cultural Practices, Political Possibilities*, Newcastle: Cambridge Scholars, 218–232, 2008.

Philippopoulos-Mihalopoulos, Andreas, 'Flesh of the Law: Material Legal Metaphors', *Journal of Law and Society*, 43(1), 45–65, 2016.

Pottage, Alain, 'The Materiality of What?', *Journal of Law and Society*, 39(1), 167–183, 2012.

Pottage, Alain and Sherman, Brad, *Figures of Invention*, Oxford: Oxford University Press, 2010.

Reardon, Jenny, *Race to the Finish: Identity and Governance in an Age of Genomics*, Princeton: Princeton University Press, 2004.

Rekret, Paul, 'A Critique of New Materialism: Ethics and Ontology', *Subjectivity*, 2016. doi:10.1057/s41286-016-0001-y

Rheinberger, Hans-Joerg, *An Epistemology of the Concrete: Twentieth – Century Histories of Life*, Durham, NC. London: Duke University Press, 2010.

Rheinberger, Hans-Joerg, *Towards a History of Epistemic Things: Synthesizing Proteins in the Test Tube*, Stanford: Stanford University Press, 1997.

Riles, Annelise (ed.), *Documents*, Ann Arbor: University of Michigan Press, 2006.

Riles, Annelise, *Network Inside Out*, Ann Arbor: University of Michigan Press, 2000.

Riskin, Jessica, 'Machines in the Garden', in Mario Biagioli and Jessica Riskin (eds), *Nature Engaged. Science in Practice from the Renaissance to the Present*, Palgrave Macmillan, 2012.

Rotman, Brian, *Becoming Besides Ourselves: The Alphabets, Ghosts and Distributed Human Being*, Durham, NC, London: Duke University Press, 2008.

Rouvroy, Antoinette and Berns, Thomas, 'Gouvernementalité algorithmique et perspectives d'émancipation', *Réseaux* nd, 1(177), 163–196, 2013.

Rouvroy, Antoinette and Hildebrandt, Mireille (eds), *Law, Human Agency, and Autonomic Computing: The Philosophy of Law Meets the Philosophy of Technology*, London: Routledge, 2011.

Schadewaldt, Walter, *Die Anfänge der Philosophie bei den Griechen*, Frankfurt am Main: Suhrkamp, 1978.

Schaffer, Simon and Shapin, Steven, *Leviathan a the Airpump: Hobbes, Boyle, and the Experiential Life*, Princeton: Princeton University Press, 1986.

Scheffer, Thomas, 'Materialities of Legal Proceedings', *International Journal for the Semiotics of Law*, 17, 365–389, 2004.

Sherman, Brad, 'Taxonomic Properties', *Cambridge Law Review*, 67(3), 560–584, 2008.

Stafford, Barbara, *Visual Analogy: Consciousness as the Art of Connecting*, Cambridge, MA: MIT Press, 1999.

Steinhauer, Fabian, 'Kulturtechniken des Rechts', in Andreas Funke and Konrad Lachmayer (eds), *Formate der Rechtswissenschaft*, Weilerswist-Metternich: Velbrueck Wissenschaft, 2017.

Steinhauer, Fabian, *Vom Scheiden. Geschichte und Theorie einer juristischen Kulturtechnik*, Berlin: Duncker & Humblot, 2014. Partially translated in 'On parting' *Ancilla Iuris*, 2015. anci.ch.

Steven, Hallam, *Life Out of Sequence: A Data-Driven History of Bioinformatics*, Chicago: University of Chicago Press, 2015.

te Heesen, Anke, *patent. eine ausstellung mit 12 objekten*. Catalogue Leaflet for an Exhibition of Patent Models Organized at the Max Planck Institute for the History of Science, Berlin, 2000.

Teubner, Gunther, 'Rights of Non-humans? Electronic Agents and Animals as New Actors in Politics and Law', EUI Max Weber Lecture of 17 January 2007, MWP 2007/04.

Toscano, Alberto, 'The Culture of Abstraction', *Theory Culture Society*, 25(4), 57–75, 2008.

Tresch, John, '"Matter No More": Edgar Allen Poe and the Paradoxes of Materialism', *Critical Inquiry* 42, 865–989, 2016.

Verran, Helen, 'Imagining Land Ownership in Australia', *Postcolonial Studies*, 1(2), 237–254, 1998.

Vismann, Cornelia, *Files: Law and Media Technology*, Stanford: Stanford University Press, 2008 (org. 2000).

Vismann, Cornelia, *Medien der Rechtsprechung*, Frankfurt: Fischer, 2011.

Vismann, Cornelia, *Das Recht und seine Mittel*, ed. Markus Krajewski and Steinhauer Fabian. Frankfurt: Fischer, 2012.

Vismann, Cornelia, 'Cultural Techniques and Sovereignty', *Theory Culture Society*, 30(6), 83–93, 2013.

Vismann, Cornelia and Krajewski, Markus, 'Computer Juridisms', *Grey Room*, 29, 90–109, 2007.

Weizman, Eyal, 'Political Plastics', *Collapse* VI, 257–303, 2010.

Cases

R (on the application of Miller and another) v. Secretary of State for Exiting the European Union [2017] UKSC 5.

Wisconsin v. Loomis, 2016 WI 68, case number 2015AP157-CR. www.wicourts.gov/sc/opinion/DisplayDocument.pdf?content=pdf&seqNo=171690.

Newspaper article

Dunlap Jr., Charles, 'Lawfare Amid Warfare', *The Washington Times*, 3 August 2007.

23

To have to do with the law

An essay

*Andreas Philippopoulos-Mihalopoulos**

1a. **The summons**. It is surprising how little, as a legal academic, I have to do with the law personally. A summons to jury duty, however, is just that: a personal invitation to do with the law, indeed *the* law, the court itself. The summons included its own way out. If I were unable to attend, I should state the reasons on the relentlessly photocopied version of a once probably pristine original form. The provided boxes, faded, vaguely symmetrical, polite, were too small to contain my bourgeois despair. Why despair? On the one hand, the thought of being removed from my life for at least (as the letter emphatically stated) two weeks, and on the other, the idea of enforced enclosure, brought up in me a sort of claustrophobic panic. Yet I tried, substituting emotion with rational argumentation, enumerating in a meticulous list and in tight chronological order (see? no two consecutive weeks free at all, ever) how important my future was (this many trips planned, this many talks to give, that much life to live). My sense of self-importance was of course transparently fragile, attested by the flurried way in which the margins of the application were overflowing with dates, destinations and university names. I stared with a certain melancholy at the lines that should have stayed within the boxes but failed (I was only sent one copy to work with): will anyone manage to decipher those scrawlings? But more seriously, would anyone really care about the veracity or at least the verisimilitude of the list, or is a deferral routinely granted to any semi-convincing application to be excused?

A week later, I received the same much photocopied letter style but with an altogether different affect: I was informed that my cry had been heeded. I was free from the law.

A year to the date, a letter arrives again, this time without a way out. The summons is irrevocable, my future no longer worth listing. I am told that I have a juror number. I am to serve the law. Pack your bags, bid your goodbyes and plunge into the law. The date and place is set. I am not consulted. The tone of the letter is definitive, school-mastery. I fold the letter and put it back into the envelope, mismatching the folding direction with the plastic address window and ending up with the empty part of the letter instead of my address showing through. So much for my singularity. My presence is required because it counts for the justice system, objectivity, impartiality; but really my presence is required because it counts as a number (Badiou, 2008),[1] one of the twelve, holy apostolic randomness, blind impartiality, blank address window.

1b. *The lawscape is every thing*. One of (secular) law's greatest self-dissimulating tricks that keeps some legal positivists happy is to appear as if it only resides in court decisions and statutes. This state of innocence, however, is now irrecoverable. Ever since Eugen Ehrlich's 'living law' (1962), the law has been let out of the courts and freely thrust amongst bodies and things. We now know that everything has to do with the law. After Foucault (2003), our very bodies are shackled with the knowledge that they now carry the law, often oppressively and as perfect instruments of the disciplinary society. Recently, Margaret Davies (2017: 124) has talked about the law

> as a psychosomatic product, as having bodily, psychological, and indeed neurological dimensions. The law subsists at some level in corporeal subjects in their relationship with physical things, not only because law disciplines the body and acts upon it, and not only because it shapes landscapes and space, but because bodies in their temporal and spatial dimensionality enact, create, and perform law.

Law has amply enjoyed its spatial and spatiotemporal turn, with legal geography now part of the accepted norm. The current turn of the law, however, is material: a further coil in the spatial and corporeal turn, not so much different as ampler, more horizontal. Questions of legal agency of things (e.g., Pottage, 2012; Philippopoulos-Mihalopoulos, 2014), law and (more than human) corporeality (e.g., Braverman, 2016b; Grear, 2015), law and technology (e.g., Tranter, 2011, and the whole journal issue), and relatively new methodologies of legal research, such as law and anthropology, law and ethnography and so on, demand new ways of seeing the law.

The law constitutes matter by naming it, forming it, including or excluding it, arranging its physicality and entering its molecular structure: the law determines property lines, permissible chemical compositions, embryonic biological structures. It classifies some humans as citizens and others as illegal migrants, offering rights and slashing lives merely by naming. It distinguishes between pets, animals for clinical testing and animals slaughtered for their meat, determining the fate of these bodies (Braverman, 2012). It allows specific kinds of DNA interventions, and only gingerly considers others. The law is a *fleshy metaphor*[2] for Schmitt's line between friends and enemies, a material verbalisation of the vicissitudes of inclusion and exclusion. It is a semantic edifice of such imposing materiality that, wherever one turns, one is enfolded by the law. In turn, the law is formed by the physicality of these enfolded bodies, whether human, nonhuman or inhuman, material or immaterial, things or ideas. Bodies determine what kind of law is to emerge in given situations, force new kinds of legal thinking, and push the boundaries of legal thought and action according to the needs in hand. In a circular sense then, the law responds to the bodies that regulate. Whether it does so fairly and equitably is often a question of theoretical perspective. The law does transform these bodies in ways that are beneficial to them, but likewise often fails to do so, and its lack of (adequate) response is experienced as failure.

There is a need for a new vocabulary when our minds and bodies are so used to distinctions that we are unable to see beyond them. Delaney's (2010) nomospheres, Sloterdijk's (2006) nomotopes and Valverde's (after Bakhtin's) chronotopes (2015) fall into this category. My contribution to this desire for different conceptualisations has been the lawscape, namely the tautology between law and matter. The lawscape differs from the above in the way it keeps manoeuvring its bodies (which includes our bodies) into regimes of visibilisation and invisibilisation, in the name of the lawscape's self-preservation. This is something that my students, when I ask them to walk the lawscape and come back with their impressions, experience it as claustrophobia and an almost physical sense of asphyxia: if law is everything, there is no way out. And some parts are denser than others.

1c. *Essaying heresy*. Adorno (1984: 171) concludes 'The Essay as Form', his essay on essays, with these words:

> the law of the innermost form of the essay is heresy. By transgressing the orthodoxy of thought, something becomes visible in the object which it is orthodoxy's secret purpose to keep invisible.

Does the law of the essay apply to essays on law? Is what we ('we'?) write essays, trials, experiments? Or just book chapters and journal articles, blogs and extended social media statuses?

But let me start with something even more basic: the writing of our students. Do we encourage, or at least tolerate, heresy? I have worked my way through many first-year student essays, the explicit objective of which is not so much the chosen topic but essay-writing as such, researching and expressing, in short a first soft plunge in the world of academic writing. Year in, year out, they are asked to choose out of a list of topics (role of the judge, law and morality, statutory interpretation and so on), and every year the absolute majority chooses the topic of juries. The majority amongst that majority forms their topic along the lines of a seminar question in their handbook: "What are the advantages and disadvantages of the jury system? Identify 2 or 3 points on each side of the debate." The admittedly well-produced (not by me) handbook provides clear guidance on essay writing. For the introduction, for example, the main requirement is to "set out your approach to answering the question by mentioning briefly the issues you will cover. If you cannot do this then you are not clear on how you are going to approach answering the question. Go back to the question." Following on, "at the beginning of each paragraph state what the issue is." And as for the conclusion, emphatically "do not introduce new ideas!" One of the oral instructions to students, about which I have an extended exchange every year with those responsible for the programme, is not to use the first person personal pronoun. Passive voice, impersonal constructions ("it is submitted") or at the very worst, 'we' is preferable.

Students mostly follow the guidelines, good students at least, whatever this means, and produce balanced, reasonably argued although understandably often hesitant and slightly wooden essays on juries. What is worrying though is that they regularly stop short from taking any position with regards to their chosen 2 or 3 points, and nearly always end up with a conclusion (and a whole text, for that matter) that does not introduce any new ideas (exclamation mark). I imagine that the argument is similar to that other argument that says you have to be able to master figurative painting first in order to move on to abstraction. I am certain that this is no longer considered valid, at least in trendy fine art schools, but there is something not altogether unattractive to it. You must learn the basics first before you fly.[3] And naturally, I am all too aware of the problems of incipient student writing, and I have often found myself imparting the usual essay writing steps as if they were the truth.

But then, what do we sacrifice when we desire an essay to be merely an attempt and not a veritable trial? A trial of error and of bravado perhaps, but also a trial of judgement, of personal exposure and risk-taking? What do we lose when we do not commit any violence to the text, encouraging instead well-formed formlessness?

2a. **En route**. What I objected to was the violence of the law. I was forced to be at a specific place at a specific time, whisked away from my days. But did I object to the object itself; an object that had occupied me ever since I could remember myself? The law has always been for me a question of material boundaries and spatiotemporal temptations. To cross or not to cross, and what happens if I do cross. I had learned (the hard way) to avoid having to do with situations where no option was available. My space of law was fully fleshed out: I would manoeuvre my way through it and try to negotiate my and others' positions. I was a lawyer before I studied law. But I might have stopped being a lawyer during my studies. Law became violent, oppressive, not an option but the only way. Law was displacing me.

In the period between the summons and the jury service day, a different kind of thinking slowly emerged, one that I was no doubt semi-consciously cultivating too: I had been given an opportunity to face my object. I allowed myself to become mildly excited (without however dropping the despair) when listening to other people's jury service stories. I was trying to own the no-option, to submit to the necessity that ultimately determined my freedom (Spinoza, 2000). This was 'the' law after all, the Court, the Old Bailey no less, the great density, the semantic royalty of the highest legal distillation. Prior brushings with the law (visits to a police station for my Greek ID card, my *annus mirabilis* of compulsory military service, dealings with university regulations, buying a flat or even signing my work contract; but also, being a son, a brother, a citizen, a friend, a lover, travelling or walking around or just sitting in a cafe) were mere wisps of the thing looming before me now. To stand before 'the' law, in its blinding visibilisation, is to have to do with the law in a way that makes most lawscapes pale into diluted pleasantries. In the thickness of having to do with the law, a slither of a possibility could just about be seen: the opportunity to, partly, infinitesimally, but perhaps actually, *do* the law.

That first day, I cycled to the Old Bailey in the morning rush hour. I am often worried about arriving late, especially when the time and place are imposed on me. Yet that morning I made a point of choosing the scenic route. The law-in-waiting was oppressing me; I needed to think of spaces of resistance. Urban cycling had made me originally think of the lawscape – both the notion and the term. I remember being impressed (not positively) by the way I obsessively followed the prescribed lanes, and even the often inane London lines and cycling boxes. I was impressed by how well sticking to it would make me feel, and also, disconcertingly, how equally well I felt when disobeying the same things (for justifiable, at least to my mind, reasons). But that morning, I was sliding smoothly, ticking along the various regulations, populating the lanes with an unfamiliar sense of entitlement. I felt co-extensive with the lawscape, being in some sort of control. Perhaps I needed this. I imagined I was heading somewhere where control would be assuredly removed from me. I arrived in good time but wasted about ten minutes trying to park my bicycle where it would not be lifted away by the police. This was not easy. The whole area felt inhospitable.

2b. *The lawscape can be manoeuvred.* The connection between law and matter in the lawscape is not dialectical but interfolded. There is no mutual influence, action-reaction, or synthetic progress towards better law/better society. Rather, there is parallelism at work (Spinoza, 2000: Book III, E2p7). Law and matter co-constitute each other tautologically, indeed simultaneously. Law is matter and matter is law. But law and matter constantly withdraw from each other, forming spheres of contained inaccessibility within the lawscape, while allowing the other side to shine through.

In other words, there are quickenings of law, high densities, spatiotemporal concentrations that throb with authority, il/legality, violence. And there are equally high densities of matter, where law is quietly forgotten, momentarily put to the side. Courts are of the former kind, shopping malls of the latter. Courts of course remain fully material (Valverde, 2015). But their matter vibrates with law, thickens with command, quickens with direction. Likewise, shopping malls remain fully legal, but the law recedes before the consumption drive, the capitalism of the plastic arcade. The law risks dampening the brittle joy of the exchange.

Within that maelstrom of in/visibilisations, bodies are manoeuvred in positions that reinforce the lawscape. The law (of private property) emerges at full force at night when shopping malls gates (themselves also bodies) shut, just as matter (dust, dump, ghosts, rodents) returns when court gates shut. This is less passive than it sounds. Bodies with more power, such as human bodies and amongst them the more privileged or collective or both, employ this manoeuvring to navigate the lawscape. The lawscape is bearable because the law is often manoeuvred into invisibilisation. The lawscape invisibilises the law (we, as lawscaping bodies, invisibilise the law) to enable a façade of normalcy, semblance of freedom, choice as a substitute for free will.

Courts (along with prisons, concentration and refugee camps, nuclear heads, torture instruments, protests and revolutions, and so on) are some of the lawscapes where law is fully visibilised and matter becomes a legal instrument. But for the rest, we have other names (bureaucracy, administration, obligations, ethics, morality, surveillance, health and safety) and we keep on inventing new ones, all in the name of invisibilisation of the law.

2c. *Essaying body*. On the back cover of his book *Essayism* (2017), a book that inspired me to think about writing, Brian Dillon writes,

> Imagine a type of writing so hard to define its very name means a trial, effort or attempt. An ancient form with an eye on the future, a genre poised between tradition and experiment. The essay wants above all to wander, but also to arrive at symmetry and wholeness; it nurses competing urges to integrity and disarray, affection and fragmentation, confession and invention.

What a schizophrenia of desires, what demanding juggling and how un-legal this all sounds. It is as if the essay were an agent itself, having eyes and urges, wandering but also unpredictably arriving. An essay that assembles out of its words a moving and posing body. A material thing, consisting of autonomous and even brazenly strong-headed elements, molecules that manically flit around without however crossing the boundaries of that linguistic mantle. Adorno (1984: 161) again: "In the essay discreet separated elements enter into a readable context; it erects no scaffolding, no edifice. Through their own movement the elements crystallize into a configuration." The configuration, this much-praised internal consistency, also has a shape, an outline, both figuratively and in essayistic terms. A tidiness of sorts that one would think subscribes to the order of wholeness and perhaps symmetry. But it does not stay intact.

Its edges thicken and fade (what is the edge of a forest? Deleuze asks, "the edge of the forest is a limit. Does this mean that the forest is defined by its outline? . . . We can't even specify the precise moment at which there is no more forest", Deleuze, *Cours Vincennes: Sur Spinoza*, 17.02.1981, in Lambert, 2013: 74), spreading next to other edges of other essays, forming a giant effort, not to cover more or to expand or even to convince by conquering, but simply to form a body.

An essay is a body that "would instruct, seduce and mystify in equal measure" (Dillon, 2017: 13). But there is more. Let's think of it as performing its own essayism ("An essay that performs its mode of attention – even better", Dillon, 2017: 121) experimentally yet rigorously, faithful to itself and its organs, immanent in its irony, self-sufficient yet full of holes, focused on its own heresy, as Adorno writes, and the fight it wages towards visibilising something of the orthodoxy against which it is poised. For this, the body of the essay must bring its object (perhaps even itself as object) in sharp spatiotemporal intimacy: "the essay comes so close to the here and now of the object, up to the point where that object, instead of being simply an object, dissociates itself into those elements in which it has its life" (Adorno, 1984: 162). Bring the object to life by pulverising it into zillions of particles of life-affirming materiality. Will life into the body of the essay by bringing its matter forth, even if this entails its disassembly.

How un-legal, therefore, that the text is a body, while for the law every body is at best a text. (And how mendacious to keep on thinking that a text is not a body.)[4]

3a. **Corridors**. The entrance was likewise uncongenial. I would have to brave it every morning for the next two weeks (I expected it would get better but that does not make the first time any easier). Between the first set of doors from the street to the building, and the airport-like security gates inside, a squeezed space made my step feel uncertain (a sort of French Court *Salle des Pas Perdus*). This despite the incontestable direction indicated not only by the arrangement of the space, but also by the staff's curt instructions (for them, it was simply yet another Monday when the new jurors were cattled in). First thing: show your summons. That text, with its stern language and multi-digit juror number, enabled my relevance – another familiar instance where the body is reduced to a text (passport, immigration letter, expulsion notice, military camps, sweatshop stations and so on). I had to empty my pockets, relinquish bags, scarves, jackets and other removable paraphernalia and enter as bare as possible to an affective bubble reminiscent of walking in a new school on the first day of term.

I was moving on a corridor of mild curiosity but mostly dread.

The verticality of the building was immediately displayed ("proceed via these lifts to the jury floor"). Its horizontality, however, will remain a mystery: what would happen if I were to just carry on walking straight, no lifts, just corridors? I would never find out. The jurors' waiting room was high up on the top floor of the building (I was anticipating a basement), in some sort of time-stuck airport-like aesthetics, consisting of endless rows of chairs surrounded by endless posters with endless instructions. Sat next to each other, the summoned ones were waiting for something to happen. A mouthful of London humanity piled up in a building of judgement. No one spoke. Most of us were furiously sending emails to people, telling them that we will be unavailable, or distractedly trying to carry on with work (some on laptops) in a semblance of normality. No one seemed to want to be there. At some point, this unbusiness was interrupted by a member of staff announcing the order of the days to come: wait until you are called. And something about how important the service we were providing was.

3b. *The lawscape is fractal* yet continuous. There is an infinity of lawscapes (all part of the broader lawscape), of various denominations and contexts (personal, local, community, national, planetary and so on), horizontally spread out, "cuttable into many parts without losing coherence" (Morton, 2013: 47). Davina Cooper's work on the *eruv* (1996), the self-delineation of some orthodox Jewish communities, reveals a lawscape layered along the greater London lawscape, but also an *eruv* in Jerusalem or anywhere in the diaspora: an enclosure that is always different, yet always of common characteristics. The culturally and religiously limited lawscape of the *eruv* practiced the same in/visibilisation as any other lawscape (not just *eruv*), visibilising the poles and wire that would delimit the space as either a legal presence that severed space, or a spatial implement that liberated from the law.

While lawscape is horizontal, individual lawscapes can be vertical, employing matter and law variably in order to reinforce power hierarchies. Higher floors in exclusive high-rises are reserved for the (über)rich who can afford to pay for the view and the air, but also for servants whose heads apparently do not require distance from the low ceilings. In some courts, the judge sits higher than anyone else, with the others arranged in various descending layers of visibility (e.g., Mulcahy, 2010). Vertical metaphors are so embedded in language that solidify, often unconsciously and uncritically, the received verticalities, such as colonial and postcolonial oppression of North versus South (Wey Gomez, 2008), capturing happiness ("I'm feeling *up*. That *boosted* my spirits. My spirits *rose*. You're in *high* spirits."), abundance and health ("The numbers keep going *up*." "He's at the *peak* of health. He's in *top* shape.") and even future ("All *up*coming events are listed in the paper. What's coming *up* this week?"), while sadness, illness, poverty and past lie down below, in the South.[5]

The lawscape's temporality is also fractal: the lawscape is based on repetition. It is not taking place until repeated. Lawscaping time requires habit, historicity, links to origin (constructed or actual), dissemination, contagion (lawscaping techniques need to spread in order to become relevant). The repeated lawscape will be part of the broader lawscape, building a lawscaping practice over time. Its geological time is a palimpsest, layered accretions that become incorporated in the planet, embodied within skins, merged with objects, inputted in technology. The second time my neighbour walks across my garden, the third month of waiting to see how bad the current political regime can become, the fourth nuclear threat, the fifth oil accident, the sixth elephant killed by poachers: the one lawscape, Gaia, planet, continuum, Nature or whatever else one wants to call it, fractal yet one, split in infinite temporal shards yet all part of a lawscaping continuum, inescapable except in its invisibilisation.

3c. *Essaying fragments*. "The force and unity of a fragmentary work are precisely the results of struggle and disparities between the parts" (Dillon, 2017: 73). The most productive paradox of an essay is the fragmentation between disparity and unity. An essay that performs this very paradox is a polyvocal body of utterances that surprises, delights and disappoints, all at the same time. Surprise at the choice of topics, the way they have been approached, the new connections with which they have been endowed. Delight at the same, but also at the turn of the phrases, the choice of guiding metaphor or metaphors that will allow the essay to speak in other disciplinary languages and with a bifurcated force, a common front formed by reasoned argumentation and metaphorical completeness. And disappointment because the essay, if it is to be a trial, needs to be the exact opposite of a court trial: it cannot be an enclosure, a theological metaphor or a final testament.[6] It needs to remain incomplete.

> The usual reproach against the essay, that it is fragmentary and random, itself assumes the giveness of totality and thereby the identity of subject and object, and it suggests that man is in control of totality. But the desire of the essay is not to seek and filter the eternal out of the transitory; it wants, rather, to make the transitory eternal.
>
> (Adorno, 1984: 159)

This is the first, formal, step towards building a heresy: follow the desire of the essay. Fragment, open up, refuse to pass judgement! But: take position, thump on the side of the object in order to upturn it, flood it with other voices, break it up – and in the process, break yourself up too.

4a. **Waiting**. Hesitantly, stories started to flit around that room full of strangers: someone who had already been summoned thrice in five years; someone who was trying to get out of jury service altogether because he was a sole business owner; someone who was already sitting in a jury for a particularly complicated case that had already gone on for a month. A sense of solidarity was slowly forming when another announcement interrupted us: practicalities. Do not walk on any other floor except this one; do not use any other lift except for the jurors' lifts; do not use stairs except in an emergency, and then only specific ones; do not use any other toilet except the ones on this floor. You all have a juror number. Please wait till your number is called. Please listen.

There was nothing grand, wood-panelled or gilded on that floor, as you might expect from a place like the Old Bailey. It would seem that the whole floor was economising in grandeur in order to thrust itself up in the gilded bolt of the blind *Iustitia* statue sitting on top of our heads. The chairs were tired and torn. The water at the water fountain was warm. The staff were either behind glass or, when entering the room for announcements, professional but peremptory. The toilets we could use had the same tired look, except that they had a window that opened. The air smelled somewhat different there, less grey. But I had to return to the enclosure in case someone had started calling numbers.

The first two days were spent waiting, in anticipation of some action but also wallowing in a screen-assisted inactivity. The chairs near the scarce plugs were the most popular ones, followed by the ones with natural light. But the room was getting progressively emptier. The waiting was punctuated by the flurry caused by announcements – finally, the Barbarians[7] – of lists of numbers. They would always call more than twelve and often many more, depending on how long the case proceedings were expected to last. My number was called a few times but in the end I always returned to the room because I was surplus. As surplus, we would wait huddled in the back of the courtroom, half-seeing the jurors-to-be and occasionally the judge, waiting for the oath to be taken. There would be those among the twelve asking to be excused, and whose arguments were rejected, at least the ones I witnessed. We, the surplus, would only leave the courtroom once all jurors had taken the oath.

In one case, while waiting in the usual surplus mode, I noticed that all jurors adhered to the religious oath except for the very last one, an apparently Greek woman, who asked to affirm instead.[8] I was impressed. In the context of Greek religious obscurantism, for someone to be brave enough to be different, especially when surrounded by mostly British ethnic nationals who were happy with the religious oath, was remarkable. I could see that we would become friends.

4b. *From lawscape to atmosphere.* Apart from self-perpetuation, the evolutionary potential of the lawscape is to become an atmosphere. An atmosphere emerges when one of the elements of the lawscape (law or matter) becomes so invisibilised that, for all intents and purposes, it disappears. In prisons and courts for example, the potential for a lawscape ceding its ontology to an atmosphere is high, since the invisibilisation of matter is already intense. Likewise in shopping malls, airport duty-free shops, even neighbourhood cafes, where the project (mostly successful) of invisibilisation of law is well under way and a few props help decisively along. Atmosphere is what remains when the lawscape departs, that is to say, when the interplay between in/visibilisation has been replaced by one self-perpetuating, all-containing elemental bubble, one grand dissimulation ("this is not an engineered atmosphere, this is all natural emergence!") that relies on the desire of its own bodies of emergence.

This desire is expressed in affects originating in bodies but always exceeding those bodies, evaporating outwards, becoming suspended dotted lines waiting to be drawn together. Atmosphere consists of these affects, taken together and made into a whole. Atmosphere is the excess of affect that keeps bodies together, through, by and against each other.

An atmosphere is always spatiotemporally specific and can only take place under certain precarious conditions. It requires an enclosure (physical and/or affective) that artificially separates the atmospheric inside from the outside; a hierarchy between inside and outside where inside is always preferable; a demotion of the outside to both a simplistic negative value (you cannot be out there) and to its partial inclusion within (we have all we need here); and a dissimulation of the fact that all these conditions have been attempted at all. Namely: an atmosphere cannot appear to be engineered but merely a spontaneous emergence.

An atmosphere is resilient, its boundaries elastic and its content flexible. The problem with atmospheres is that they ontologically tend towards homeostatic perfection.

They do not often achieve it, but when they do, their effect can be devastating on any desire for questioning, critique, resistance or simply outside. While lawscape opens up spaces of in/visibilisation in which bodies can move differently than prescribed, atmosphere is static. While lawscape allows for options, atmosphere only offers one option, itself. While bodies can navigate the lawscape by allowing the law to become more or less visible, summoning the law when needed and silencing it when not, atmosphere reserves specific places to all bodies included within, without movement. While lawscape dissipates at its edges, fractally moving along other lawscaping configurations and partaking of other layers of in/visibilisations, atmosphere is enclosure, firm perfection, modernist orgasm.

4c. *Essaying the 'I'*. Should I be me when writing an essay? The question is no longer whether research can present objective facts/truths (no), or whether bringing the 'I' in (in terms of pronoun and subject matter) renders the whole thing subjective (and therefore, irrelevant or at best partial) (yes, no, so what). Nor is the question whether the law can be approached from the point of view of the 'I' (yes), or whether the 'I' must sublimate itself to the 'lay person' (what is that?). The question rather is whether the 'I' can bring an understanding of the object of study in a way that allows both full immersion and distance: in other words, whether the 'I' can maintain the role both of an atmospheric object (fully immersed, abandoned to the coercive atmosphere), and a subject (but not necessarily a consciousness) that withdraws from the atmosphere.

One way to achieve this is by progressively dropping the traditional phenomenological method (to which most empirical and some theoretical descriptions subscribe) and allowing the ontology of the description to emerge. In practical terms, this means that while the 'I' initiates the description (of the theory or the empirical work), the focus on the 'I' must be blurred and progressively pass on to the atmosphere. An atmosphere contains the 'I' but also risks flattening it, dissolving it in its illusionary atmospheric community. Writing about it, however, can already be a movement of withdrawal from the atmosphere (withdrawing *in writing*). The writing 'I' fleshes out the affects employed by the atmosphere, and shows them not merely as atmospheric tools (although of course there is writing that simply perpetuates an atmosphere), but rather as something that carries the possibility of resisting and withdrawing from the very atmosphere. The mere act of moving the focus from the 'I' to the atmosphere draws together the various 'I's that partake of the atmosphere, rousing them towards a possible withdrawal from the atmosphere.

The 'I' is multiple. Internally, "the 'I' is both contained and provisional – just as important, it is *dispersed*" (Dillon, 2017: 18). Sure, the 'I' requires a solidity and determination that will carry the desire to go against its own desire (for atmospheric comfort or acceptance) and break away from the atmosphere. Yet, these qualities must also be complemented by the dispersed 'I' and its provisional dipping in various lawscapes at the same time. We are never just one body, operating in a single lawscape, belonging to a single atmosphere. We are always dispersed, multiple. But this dispersion, seemingly a weakness, can be strategically enlisted. Use your dispersion, spread horizontally, take up your minoritarian positions and break free from the atmosphere. And follow the same strategy textually too: think of Bruno Latour's thick description of the Conseil d'Etat (2009), and its gravitational attraction for seemingly un-legal, unimportant details.[9] This deliberate dispersion, this absent-minded focus, those centre-stage curios: often an effective way to flesh out the invisibilised materiality of the law (see, e.g., Carr, 2016).

Is this paradox of the contained yet dispersed 'I' ever contained? Again, only provisionally: the writing 'I' is a manifold and continues to be, however contained it might appear. This means, first, that its various folds are (provisionally) summoned together in order to write in a way that withdraws from an atmosphere (a powerful argument for interdisciplinarity);[10] and second, that the writing 'I' is always collective, externally multiple, in dialogue with others, building its withdrawal on the working and the unworking of its own writing community. A lotus flower writing a polemic.

This is the agency of the writing 'I' as a legal body, namely a body that has to do with the law (the atmospheric law of compliance), but also a body that, partly, infinitesimally, but perhaps actually, *does* the law (the law of withdrawal from the atmosphere).

5a. **Curios.** At the end of the second day, my number was called among the first twelve. What was to be four days of court proceedings had begun. I was relieved to be in a different atmosphere, but also somewhat more apprehensive, as if the limbo room could still hold the possibility of never being called in (and that would be good in some way, or not). Here I was going deeper into an irreversible rut. My fear of and even repulsion for the law kept on being affirmed, but oddly so was my fascination with it. A desire to participate and see what this was all about was taking hold of me. The jury were sat in two rows of uncomfortably stiff and narrow wooden benches, bodies tightly close to each other, with a narrow shelf in a semblance of a desk in front of us.[11] We could not stand or move around, nor of course leave the room. There could be no breaks except when the judge would decide. In case of emergency, we could ask for one. The way to do it would be via written notes, delivered to a clerk who would get up from his seat (slightly lower than us), pick up the note and walk the note to the judge (much higher). We asked for a break twice in the course of the proceedings. The first one was granted. The second was not, and was accompanied by an admonishment on the cost of breaks (toilet breaks, for that matter) to the tax payer. We could take notes in pencil on small pieces of notepad paper, which we could not take with us. We were not to drink water from the bottle because we would be found in contempt of the court. And myriad other norms that we were to discover as the proceedings went along.

The judge, with her amiably avuncular accent and her clarity of goal, commanded the wood-panelled, rather grand bubble. The rest of us, jury, defendant, barristers, witnesses and so on, were placed at various levels along a hierarchical verticality. Over the judge's head, a crest with the British monarchy inscription, that always seemed to me either incomplete or wrong, but in either case, there to impress: *dieu et mon droit* ("god and my right"). The proceedings were tedious, referring to an equally tedious (as I think of it now – at the time, not so) incident. There was a lot about precise movement in space at precise moments, which I, predictably, found somewhat interesting. Yet I would often feel the need to touch the wooden shelf in front of me, perhaps as a grounding gesture. The days carried on, and I was noticing small details: the Mont Blanc fountain pen on one of the barristers' hand; the obsequiousness of behaviours; the sad pride in allocated authority; the cold in the room; the doodles of my fellow jurors; the expressions on the defendant's face; the gender and class imbalances before me; the judge's well-concealed but probably already-formed opinion; and the fact that we as jurors were supposed to exclude all that and focus only on what we were presented with in court.

5b. *Atmosphere is desire.* An atmosphere relies on the desire of the bodies to perpetuate the atmosphere. The atmosphere's greatest coup is its bypassing consciousness (if addressed to humans) and reliance on corporeal desire. This desire is not necessarily to stay in the atmosphere (as might be the case in some material atmospheres, such as a shopping mall) but to perpetuate the ontology of the atmosphere. This is where one needs to be careful about dealing with atmosphere merely phenomenologically, which would lead to an understanding of desire as mood or feel (usually of comfort, belonging etc.). The kind of atmosphere I am referring to here requires an ontological approach that understands desire as the driving force to carry on, an inertia or passive momentum that pushes bodies to carry on moving in the same direction even though the initial push has not been renewed. Atmosphere offers the perfect lab conditions for such a continuous movement: no friction, no outside reality, just a controlled glasshouse.

Desire, in its ontological dimension, does not make ethical choices (not even in the Spinozan sense of what is good for the body and the collectivity in the specific situation). It often just carries on feeding itself. Fear (of authority, of repercussions, of the future, of the outside, of the judgement of the ones inside, and so on) can be an affect that feeds the desire to carry on as usual, clouding over any converse desire to break through and withdraw from the atmosphere.

And so the atmosphere continues ad infinitum or for as long as it does. Inside, however, time stops. Atmosphere captures an infinity of present, static and unchangeable, and freezes it. It can be the future present of an Arian triumph of Nazi Germany (Borch, 2014), the cloying present of a mall candy, the present (solidly founded on a conducive past) of a woman's 'private' domestic sphere, which, as de Beauvoir (2011) had found,[12] muffled desire for difference; or the non-present of a refugee trapped in a camp away from the country she was meant to be in. This is the atmospheric temporality. An all-enclosing bad infinity that silences any possibility of outside.

5c. *Essaying object.* Allowing the ontology of the description to emerge means also eavesdropping into the object and its conditions of emergence. This is textual sculpting: rather than giving a predetermined shape to a piece of wood, a good carver follows the waves of the wood, allowing for the shape to emerge from within its matter. Deleuze and Guattari:

> it is a question of surrendering to the wood, then following where it leads by connecting operations to a materiality, instead of imposing a form upon a matter:

> what one addresses is less a matter submitted to laws than a materiality possessing a *nomos*.
>
> (1988: 451)

Listening to the *nomos* (i.e., the internal, diffused rules of navigating a polyvocal space) of materiality rather than imposing the law on matter means: use matter (the wood, the text), not by submitting it to a law (of predetermined conclusion) but by allowing *through it* the emergence of a diffused, manifold, nomic materiality (Philippopoulos-Mihalopoulos, 2014). Listening to the object and its conditions of emergence is our way, as essayists, to flesh out the strains, marks and wounds of the object itself: its gender oppression, its colonial exploitation, its heteronormative persuasion, its paternalistic force, its racial exclusion, its class slippage, its shaded mirroring of our own little worlds.

Textual hylomorphism (passing from matter to form, and not the other way) seems to be the exact opposite of the way we are taught (and the way we teach) to write essays. Unless you know exactly what you want to say, do not even start. Go back to the question. But how to know where the text will take you before you enter it? How to leave behind the all-consuming atmosphere of the self with its preconceptions, if not by listening to something else, something other?

The next step, however, is the hardest: to reinsert the 'I', after having allowed the text to emerge materially. In reality, the 'I' never leaves the text. The 'I' should nourish and be nourished by the text, discover its continuum with it, and add to the singularity that the 'I' is, but only once it will have lost itself in the text. Losing the 'I' means surrendering to hylomorphism, accepting vulnerability, facing fragility. Losing the 'I' means becoming stronger. This 'I', now fully collective, fully immersed in matter, fully material, needs to return and take up its responsibility.

6a. **Guilty**. The various juries would converge for lunch at the limbo room. Different courts would decide their individual lunch times but on the fourth day I managed to find the Greek juror I had noticed in the other court. Anastasia, as I found out, was an archaeologist who had been living in London for the past decade or so. We formed a small collective of sorts. We shared affects of boredom, impatience, tiredness, cold, bad backs (those benches), irrational (we know now) but genuine fears that our cases could easily go on forever, chocolate biscuits and even interest (I gathered that her case was more engaging than mine, although we were not allowed to talk about it), but not quite fear or anxiety over the law. I was not able to communicate it, and she did not seem affected by it in the same way. But there was something barely disguised behind the daily cycling, the action bits of the proceedings, even the breaks in the toilet with the open window. A melancholy saturated the whole building and everything in it, perhaps a distinctly legal melancholy that I took on like a shawl to protect me against the cold courtroom, a defensive layer of distance, but also an immersion: we are here to judge and judge with serious consequences.[13]

The melancholy had colonised the air we were breathing. On the corridor leading to the courtroom where my case was taking place, torture instruments were exhibited in glass boxes. The barristers were fluttering around, buoyant in what seemed like their very own fish bowl, and the jurors were lining up with a false display of purpose. At one point, probably because I made a mistake but possibly not, I found myself using the urinal (yes, those open male ones) next to one of the barristers in my case. He smiled, winningly I thought, and carried on.[14]

That was a male place, a place for winners, the ones who have nothing to fear, the ones who stand on the right side of the law. So why was I, a juror in full white, male privilege, being made to feel that I was constantly at risk of crossing a line, never to be crossed? That I was not standing on the right side of the law? Why was I feeling guilty?

6b. *Atmosphere is fragility*. Engineering an atmosphere is an unstable affair. It relies for its emergence and perpetuation on the desire of the bodies to perpetuate the atmosphere. If, however, a body desires otherwise, and desires it strongly, it might manage to withdraw from the atmosphere. Then, the atmosphere becomes something different – perhaps a different atmosphere, or a return to a lawscape (same lawscape as before or a reoriented version). This, however, depends on various factors. First, it depends on the strength of the particular body in relation to the strength of the atmospheric matter or law. A collective body (every body is collective, but the specific body needs also to be) organised and with a vision is capable of bringing about the collapse of an atmosphere, even an established one, as we have seen in cases like Cairo's Tahrir Square. Second, it depends on the atmospheric resilience and its ability to have already contained or even instrumentalised occurrences of dissent, conflict, revolt and other affects such as boredom, vulnerability, fear and so on. Third, it depends on the prior lawscape and its ability to be transformed to a lawscape that will serve better the withdrawing body. Fourth, well, it depends on other things too, such as power imbalances, climatological conditions, etc. Just as there is no prescription to engineering an atmosphere, there is no prescription in withdrawing from one. It might work and it might not work, despite best intentions.

This is because, even when perfectly engineered, an atmosphere is a fragile thing, and manifests this in modulations of intensity. It then becomes phenomenologically vibrant, its dissimulation becomes that much more obvious, and the bodies might respond to it by withdrawing from it. But fragility is not unique to an atmosphere. Fragility (Bennett, 2010, or indeed vulnerability in Grear, 2011) is a shared ontological condition. Bodies that partake in it can be as fragile, and, surprisingly, their cracking might take down the atmosphere too.

6c. *Essaying 1. 2. 3.* I used to despise bullet points or lists of any sort when I would come across them in an essay. I certainly would not use them. They would interrupt the flow and would introduce a staccato movement that had usually nothing to do with the way I wanted the rest of the text to be read.

Recently, however, I started to list things, usually characteristics or conditions for the emergence of something or ways to do something. I started appreciating the reading rhythm of the bated breath. I felt a playfulness in the promise for completeness, and indeed for education, instruction even, in terms of 1. 2. 3., sections and paragraphs, this archetypically legal form. But the playfulness I found most attractive could not be, or in any way has not so far been, explicitly incorporated in any of my lists. The playfulness to which I was attracted was not the (subversive even) promise for completeness but the invisible coda at the end of every list, the silent "*etc.*" (Derrida, 2000). It would not have been a sign of rigorous research to admit to an 'etc.' especially when you propose to instruct your readers or to exhaust the law. But it is always there, lurking between the listed items – not necessarily deliberately of course: "The list, if it's doing its job, always leaves something to be invented or recalled, something forgotten in the moment of its making . . . something to be desired" (Dillon, 2017: 27). This implicit "etc.", no longer a private joke, is the space of 'to be desired', of other desires that upset our best laid plans, and a *memento vanitatis* of our supreme delusion that we can list and contain everything neatly.

I felt another playful attraction to lists, that was marking another delusion. Dillon (2017: 24) again: "the appearance of a list in an otherwise narrative or polemic piece of prose introduces – more or less violently – a sudden verticality in the horizontal flow of the text." This verticality, a habitual sign of authorial hierarchy and authoritative announcement (Braverman, 2016a), was playing directly with my own sense of authority as an author, of which I've never had a particularly high opinion ('death of the author' etc.). So I started appreciating the awkwardness with which that vertical pole of 1. 2. 3. protruded in some sort of hypermasculine self-assertion from the horizontal and occasionally even deliberately poetic, whatever that is, flow of some of my texts, reminiscent of a shipwreck's mast sticking out of a calm sea. Lists became my own footnote for the alien authority we are supposed to feel when we write essays on law meant to instruct, educate, transform, help.

I would nearly always reserve the list for the end of the essay, often letting it ramble there instead of a conclusion. By the end of the list, I would have exhausted my will to solidity, and I would try to offer something else instead: a silent "etc.", a space for reader's notes, an ironic, baroque grin at my burdensome authority,[15] or simply just some more horizontality.

7a. **The other room.** The proceedings of the case over, the jury begun its deliberations. A short secret door, which we had never used before, opened up behind us, and we found ourselves in a corridor with a series of identical shut doors. We were led by the clerk through one of them and into a room where we would spend the next three days deliberating. Small room, large round table, wood panelling, *en suite* toilet, agreed knocks on the door, locked in, ready, go. No professions were declared, no background was sought, only what we were presented with was to be discussed. The rut was deepening.

I remember thinking, this is what Derrida meant when he talked about how the whole legal edifice had to collapse before taking a decision. I felt that the judgement we were asked to make should come from a different place. Somewhere less judgemental I suppose. Or less legal and more, what, ethical? affective? and what is the difference? I remember knocks on the door, are we there yet? the judge urges you to reach a decision today. Tomorrow, ok, but you are not allowed to go home, we will provide alternative accommodation. Final day today I hope. Our bodies were aching, etiolated desires that aimed for justice but ended up going in circles. I do not remember much else. I was not taking notes, and even if I were, I was not supposed to have taken them with me. This was almost a decade ago now and at the time I was not planning on writing on it.

We reached a unanimous decision.

7b. *The withdrawing body*. Even if a body withdraws, it remains fragile.

7c. *Essaying justice*. Writing an essay, in the ways I have tried to discuss so far, is a trial. It is not a legal trial, in the sense of enclosure and definitive conclusion, yet it generates the law because it opens up to the trying materiality of the object and its conditions. This opening allows for the hesitant emergence of a law, indeed of a lawscape, that is no longer espoused to forming matter according to its own lawscaping habits, but listens to the hylomorphism of its object (which is the law, but also the text itself).

An essay that listens deeply to a law that in its turn listens deeply to its object. The law of the essay, the essay on the law:[16] convergence that keeps the law turning (textual turn, deconstructive turn, spatial turn, corporeal turn, material turn, future turn) and churning out invisibilities, which, as Adorno says, are in the interest of the orthodoxy to remain invisible. But we withdraw from it.

Still, we must not be fooled. Withdrawing might also end up becoming an atmosphere. No turning, revolt or revolution lasts. And while rendering some things visible, other things necessarily become invisible. The essay constructs its own atmosphere, assembled by the collective desire of the writing 'I's to carry on (critiquing, constructing, transforming, analysing). We forget that atmospheres emerge even in the fight against an existing atmosphere. Heresy can also become orthodoxy. It is hard to withdraw from this new, 'right' atmosphere. It is lamentably comfortable, it is what the REF (the British Universities' Research Assessment Exercise) wants, it is what one's readers expect, and so on. But at those points, when the 'I' begins getting too comfortable in its turning, the 'I' needs to return and strike the 'I'.

This is when the law of the text generates justice: when the text never rests, and the circles (sweaty, claustrophobic, wiggly coils) turn through and against themselves, relentlessly to reveal yet more invisibilities and especially the ones that were generated by our previous, well-meaning heresies. The essay must never rest, the 'I' must never get complacent. This is not a shock strategy, or a marketing scheme to keep your readers reading. This is, simply put, our responsibility: to have to do with the law means to partly, infinitesimally, but perhaps actually, *do* the law; but also to *undo* the law that we have just done, and the law that has done us. All this, in order to carry on, even begrudgingly, having to do with the law. Our work of poetic undoing is never done.

8. **The body**. The limbo room was waiting for my return. My number would have been called in for another case, hopefully not longer than a few days but one could never tell. Relentless justice, the violence of repetition, go through all this

again, different but same perhaps. Anastasia, I assumed, would have already been called on a second case.[17] My body however had other plans. My back had started playing up during the week on the wooden bench and the cold room, and had completely given up by the time we had reached the end of the case. The emotional stress of the case, combined with the fact that I (and I think, most people) had to catch up with our regular job every evening following the intense days in court, was perhaps too much. (I have never been very good at juggling things. Yet, every summer, standing as upright as I can in the shallow sea, with seawater half-way up my body, I try to juggle three juicy peaches. I always fail, and they quickly end up in the water. We eat them up anyway, sweet with an underlining sourness and the saltiness of the seawater on their skin.)

The doctor suggested that I be excused from further service. Odd subjunctive. Perhaps is needed to lend to the subjective, this fragile corporeal subjective, a steady embrace. Letter sent and medical recommendation accepted.

I still felt guilty. Guilty even for my own body that has refused to be the body that the law wanted it to be. There was a failure in me but also a failure around me. The two were intimately although not demonstrably connected.

Notes

* Profound gratitude for the detailed and encouraging reading of this text to Victoria Brooks, Margaret Davies, Davina Cooper, Daniela Gandorfer, Peter Goodrich, Amlan Goswami, Yoriko Otomo, and to my fellow juror Anastasia Sakellariadi.

1 Badiou, 2008, writes about how every being within a situation (not unlike the one described here) remains particular (a particular being that is needed for the perpetuation of the situation) but lacks in singularity. For this reason, every being is exchangeable.

2 Philippopoulos-Mihalopoulos, 2015; see also Bacchi and Beasley, 2004, for the concept of social flesh.

3 "[W]hile standard methods are often extremely good at what they do, they are badly adapted to the study of the ephemeral, the indefinite and the irregular" (Law, 2004: 4).

4 How legal are all those bodies of law, the *corpora juris* that pulsate with "text, territory and terror" (Goodrich, 2006: 33), always channelled through sections and paragraphs. Goodrich has repeatedly shown us how text is body, and how what seems like mere legal textuality is a corporeal explosion. Matter is, after all, inescapable.

5 Examples from Lakoff and Johnson, 2003: 15–17.

6 "Enclosure not only symbolized the independence of law from political, commercial, and social space; it served to restrict access, limit vandalism, minimize the disruption of trial, and, perhaps above all, encourage deference to the administration of justice in a democratic society perpetually anxious about the authority of law and lawyers" (Spaulding, 2012: 316).

7 "Because the barbarians are coming today.
What laws can the senators make now?
Once the barbarians are here, they'll do the legislating." Cavafis, 1992: 47 (from the 1898 poem *Waiting for the Barbarians*)

8 Upon kindly reading this text, Anastasia told me that her choice was made more difficult by the fact that she was the very last in a series of jurors, none of whom had asked to affirm. Yet, as she said, she couldn't start this process on the wrong foot. She had to be true to her own convictions before passing judgment on anyone else.

9 See, however, Pottage 2012, on how Latour's specific focus, despite its potentially resistant and epistemologically revolutionary effect, perpetuates a rather narrow view of what the law is.

10 In Lisa Webley's influential book (2013: 58) on legal writing for students, a precious sentence marks an invitation to heresy: "some students relish the opportunity to break out of the straitjacket of legal sources."

11 "[T]he courtroom contains and twists bodies into its tiny caverns and grand panelled auditoria, with walls built to ensure the painful silencing of already terrorized bodies" (Brooks, 2014).

12 And the subsequent atmosphere that, according to Judith Butler (1986), de Beauvoir forms when she excludes the body's emancipatory role.

13 Peter Goodrich's comment on this part of the text deserves its own, fully unreferenced, footnote: "The atmosphere of melancholia reflects – projects – your clinging to your life, your critical (scholarly/academic) distance, the entering but not entering the space. My sense is that you feel that as well, a different melancholia that attaches to not being able to let go of your sense of identification with those wounded by law."

14 A juicy encounter, Victoria Brooks says. An emblematic encounter, Peter Goodrich says. The court urinals as an inadvertently juicy emblem ("the emblem is a theatrical device, a mode of staging what cannot be said but can be figured, which is to say, shown, enacted, and performed" Goodrich, 2017: 29; "The emblem emblematizes the message of the law" Goodrich, 2006: 24) that animates the textuality of the law of the court.

15 "I would define the baroque as that style that deliberately exhausts (or tries to exhaust) its own possibilities, and that borders on self-caricature" Borges, 2001: 4, from the 1954 preface.

16 Michel de Montaigne, the inventor of the term 'essay' ('essai', usually translated as 'trial') and to some extent its form, was originally a lawyer, who fought against the law with characteristic literary vehemence, and in particular law's ability to generate justice ("there is nothing just in itself, [that] laws and customs shape justice" Montaigne, 1991: 1022) by erecting the law of the essay, the trials of the open form, and a justice of legal fictions ("even our system of law, they say, bases the truth of its justice upon legal fictions" Montaigne, 1991: 603).

17 I later discovered that Anastasia's body had also refused to collaborate. She was found unfit to serve another jury because of the emotional strain that the first case had on her.

Bibliography

Adorno, Theodor, 'The Essay as Form', *New German Critique*, trans. Bob Hullot-Kentor and Frederic Will, No. 32, 151–171, Spring–Summer, 1984.

Bacchi, Carol and Beasley, Chris, 'Moving Beyond Care and/or Trust: An Ethic of Social Flesh', paper presented at the Australian Political Science Association Conference, Adelaide, 29 September–1 October 2004.

Badiou, Alain, *Number and Numbers*, trans. Robin Mackay, Malden, MA: Polity Press, 2008.

Bennett, Jane, *Vibrant Matter: A Political Ecology of Things*, Durham, NC: Duke University Press, 2010.

Borch, Christian, 'The Politics of Atmospheres: Architecture, Power, and the Senses', in C. Borch (ed.), *Architectural Atmospheres: On the Experience and Politics of Architecture*, Basel: Birkhäuser, 2014.

Borges, Jorge Luis, *A Universal History of Iniquity*, trans. Andrew Hurley, London: Penguin, 2001.

Braverman, Irus, *Zooland: The Institution of Captivity*, Stanford, CA: Stanford University Press, 2012.

Braverman, Irus, 'The Legal Life of Threatened Species Lists', in Irus Braverman (ed.), *Lively Legalities: Animals, Biopolitics, Law*, London: Routledge, 2016a.

Braverman, Irus (ed.), *Lively Legalities: Animals, Biopolitics, Law*, London: Routledge, 2016b.

Brooks, Victoria, 'Interrupting the Courtroom Organism: Screaming Bodies, Material Affects and the Theatre of Cruelty', *Law, Culture and the Humanities*, 2014. doi:10.1177/1743872114543767
Butler, Judith, 'Sex and Gender in Simone de Beauvoir's Second Sex', 72 *Yale French Studies*, pp. 35-49, 1986.
Carr, Helen, 'Legal Technology in an Age of Austerity: Documentation, 'functional' Incontinence and the Problem of Dignity', in David Cowan and D. Wincott (eds), *Exploring the 'Legal' in Socio-Legal Studies*, London: Palgrave Macmillan, 2016.
Cavafis, Constantinos, *Collected Poems*, trans. Edmund Keeley and Philip Sherrard, ed. George Savidis, Princeton: Princeton University Press, 1992.
Cooper, Davina, 'Talmudic Territory? Space, Law, and Modernist Discourse', *Journal of Law and Society*, 23(4), 529–548, 1996.
Davies, Margaret, *Law Unlimited: Materialism, Pluralism and Legal Theory*, London: Routledge, 2017.
Delaney, David, *The Spatial, The Legal and the Pragmatics of World-Making*, London: Routledge, 2010.
De Beauvoir, Simone, *The Second Sex*, trans. Constance Borde and Sheila Malovany-Chevallier, London:Vintage, 2011.
Deleuze, Gilles, *Spinoza: Practical Philosophy*, trans. R. Hurley, San Francisco: City Light Books, 1988.
Deleuze, Gilles and Guattari, Felix, *A Thousand Plateaus: Capitalism and Schizophrenia*, trans. Brian Massumi, London: Athlone Press, 1988.
Derrida, Jacques, 'Force of Law: The "Mystical Foundation of Authority"', trans. M. Quaintance, in D. Cornell, M. Rosenfeld and D. Gray Carlson (eds), *Deconstruction and the Possibility of Justice*, New York: Routledge, 1992.
Derrida, Jacques, 'Et Cetera', trans. Geoffrey Bennington, in ed. Nicholas Royle, *Deconstructions: A User's Guide*, New York: Palgrave Macmillan, 2000.
Dillon, Brian, *Essayism*, London: Fitzcarraldo, 2017.
Ehrlich, Eugen, *Fundamental Principles of the Sociology of Law*, trans. Walter Moll, London: Russell and Russell, 1962.
Foucault, Michel, *The Birth of Clinic*, London: Routledge Classics, 2003.
Grear, Anna, 'Deconstructing Anthropos: A Critical Legal Reflection on "Anthropocentric" Law and Anthropocene "humanity"', *Law and Critique*, 26(3), 225–249, 2015.
Goodrich, Peter, 'A Theory of the Nomogram', in Goodrich, Peter, Barshack, Lior and Anton Schütz (eds), *Law, Text, Terror: Essays for Pierre Legendre*, London: Glasshouse, 2006.
Goodrich, Peter, 'Imago Decidendi: Of the Common Law of Images', *Brill Research Perspectives: Art and Law*, 1, 1, 2017.
Grear, Anna, 'The Vulnerable Living Order: Human Rights and the Environment in a Critical and Philosophical Perspective', *Journal of Human Rights and the Environment*, 2(1), 23–44, 2011.
Lambert, Leopold, *The Funambulist Pamphlets 01: Spinoza*, New York: Punctum Books, 2013.
Lakoff, George and Johnson, Mark, *Metaphors We Live By*, Chicago: University of Chicago Press, 2003.
Latour, Bruno, *The Making of Law: An Ethnography of the Conseil D'Etat*, Cambridge: Polity Press, 2009.
Law, John, *After Method: Mess in Social Science Research*, London: Routledge, 2004.
Montaigne, Michel de, *The Complete Essays*, trans. M. A. Screech, London: Penguin, 1991.
Morton, Timothy, *Hyperobjects: Philosophy and Ecology After the End of the World*, Minneapolis: University of Minnesota Press, 2013.
Mulcahy, Linda, *Legal Architecture: Justice, Due Process and the Place of Law*, London: Routledge, 2010.
Philippopoulos-Mihalopoulos, Andreas, 'Critical Autopoiesis and the Materiality of Law', *International Journal of Semiotics of Law*, 27(2), 165–177, 2014.

Philippopoulos-Mihalopoulos, Andreas, *Spatial Justice*, London: Routledge, 2015.
Philippopoulos-Mihalopoulos, Andreas, 'Flesh of the Law: Material Legal Metaphors', *Journal of Law and Society*, 43(1), 45–65, 2016.
Pottage, Alain, 'The Materiality of What?', *Journal of Law and Society*, 39, 167–183, 2012.
Sloterdijk, Peter, 'The Nomotop: on the Emergence of Law in the Island of Humanity', *Law & Literature*, 18(1), 1–14, 2006.
Spaulding, N. W., 'The Enclosure of Justice: Courthouse Architecture, Due Process, and the Dead Metaphor of Trial', *Yale Journal of Law & Humanities*, 24, 311, 2012.
Spinoza, Baruch, *Ethics*, trans. G. H. R. Parkinson, Oxford: Oxford University Press, 2000.
Tranter, Kieran, 'The Laws of Technology and the Technology of Law', *Griffith Law Review*, 20, 4, 2011.
Valverde, Mariana, *Chronotopes of Law: Jurisdiction, Scale and Governance*, London: Routledge, 2015.
Webley, Lisa, *Legal Writing*, London: Routledge, 2013.
Wey Gomez, Nicolas, *The Tropics of Empire: Why Columbus Sailed South to the Indies*, Cambridge, MA: MIT Press, 2008.

24

On new model jurisprudence: The scholar/critic as (cosmic) artisan

Anne Bottomley and Nathan Moore[1]

To have done with judgment

What kind of theory does scholarship of/in/about law need? What can the use of theory make possible? The movement between these two questions, so much more than a slippage, is crucial. In the first, the use of the word 'need' recognises that theory is employed for a reason; the intended use of theory is never innocent, the question is the purpose in turning to seek, claim, create or indeed even presume the necessity of/for theory. This does then, at the least, acknowledge that the use of theory is formed within and through a conjunction of material circumstances which give rise to a perceived 'need' for theory. But then the question is, 'what kind' of theory? Which of course returns to the question: what is it for? or rather, what is the need for it? The problematic is that too often when addressing the use of theory of/in/for law, the issue of (which) 'kind' becomes dominant, and the question of 'need' assumed rather than addressed. It is rather like saying: we all already know theory is important, so let's just get on with it. Posing the question in the second formulation forces a much more active engagement with thinking about the use and practices of theory, and therefore of the material circumstances in which the question is posed. In a more overtly Deleuzean formulation, the question is: what can theory do? Each time that question is addressed and engaged with, it takes form within specific material conditions. However, having said that, it is also, of course, a specific kind of theory, or mode of theorising, which allows for the question to be posed and the materiality of the circumstances in which this occurs to be acknowledged and addressed. This form of (engagement with) theory is pro-active and acutely aware of the material processes of producing/using theory, which includes, of course, the very activity of thinking in theoretical, that is abstract and reasoned, framings. This process of theorising is one of working always in-between the materiality of becoming; becoming abstract, becoming material, taking form from, and within and between, the encounter and the engagement. A process of working through which is one of abstracting from what is being learnt, rather than applying what one already (thinks one) knows. But none of this would have purpose or momentum without a prior impulse: What do we want of theory? What is our desire?

We began with the question of 'need', and have moved to the question of 'desire'. 'Need' can be thought of as a pragmatic recognition of a lack which 'needs' to be met, a space which needs to be filled, an identity which needs to be confirmed. 'Need' can be formulated, coldly, as a purposeful and rational search for a solution to an obvious, even common-sense, problem. Need requires answers, now. Need is needy. Conversely, 'desire' is about a wish for something different, a hope, indeed intention, for something better than we now have. Lack turns back seeking completion through answers; desire reaches forward seeking an openness of potential(ities) which will always address the formulation of questioning rather than the closure of solutions. Theory, in these terms, is a process, not an end. Pursuing this process of theorising is an expression of desire as a kind of ethical ontology, an ethico-ontology. What is then demanded of (the practice of) theory is that it enables patterns of scholarship informed by, if not (yet) committed to, progressive change for a justice which we do not as yet, cannot as yet, know. This is, necessarily, thought and practiced as an inchoate potential within which what is sought (more accurately, forged) are ways, means through and with which, to progress – to move, to develop, to mutate, to become, to create, to make possible.

For Deleuze, such a form of (the practice of) theory is, necessarily, to seek escape from being entrapped by the confines, the (en)closure, of (the practices of) judgment.[2] Deleuze understands the act (and intended consequence) of judgment as a cutting out and off, a setting apart and turning away; a cut (the unkindest cut) which separates, excludes and expels, in the name of (a) transcendent truth:

> No-one develops through judgment . . . judgment presupposes criteria (higher values), criteria that pre-exist for all time (to the infinity of time), so that it can neither apprehend what is new in an existing being, not even sense the creation of a mode of existence . . . such a mode is created vitally . . . Judgment prevents the emergence of any new mode of existence . . . Herein, perhaps, lies the secret: to bring into existence and not to judge. If it is so disgusting to judge, it is not because everything is of equal value, but on the contrary because what has value can be made or distinguished only by defying judgment.
>
> (Deleuze, 1996a: 136)

Judgment may, of course, be the central mark of a particular type of legal system, but it also concerns the practice of judgment by a theorist or critic. For a legal theorist, a critique of judgment will be, most obviously, focused on the practice of judgment in law, but Deleuze reminds us that the process of judgment can also be characteristic of a certain type of theoretical work. To presume to judge, as a theorist, indeed to presume either the need to judge or the inevitability of judgment, is, for Deleuze, not only a failure but a betrayal in that it cannot allow for practices of theory concerned with the potential of 'new modes of existence'. Judgment can only repeat the past; it never learns. It may acquire the shiny gloss of a kind of purity in its continued allegiance to, and persistence in, out-world logic; but it is dead, it lacks vitality, life and future; it is simply that it remains unburied.

We are often reminded that to 'critique', a mode of theory practiced as systematic and close analysis, can be associated, etymologically, with the verb 'to cut'.[3] This association is particularly attractive to critical scholars concerned to 'cut through' false image and ideology in order to reveal truth, especially when this is framed as a cutting-edge enterprise. The Greek verb *krinein*, to separate or divide, leads to *kritikos* that is 'one who is able to make judgments' (the critic as judge). But rather than being limited to the force and violence of cutting as separation and judgment, the etymology of critique is also associated with the root *krei*: 'to sieve, discriminate, distinguish'. It is 'to sieve', rather than to cut or judge, which marks, we will argue here, a practice of theory which is vested in forging a vitalist mode of critique.

To sieve. Earth, wheat, flour: information, ideas, concepts. In Quentin Metsys's 1583 portrait of Elizabeth I,[4] the queen is portrayed carrying an empty sieve, around the rim of which the words *a terra il ben mal dimota insella*[5] are inscribed. It is usually assumed that the use of the iconography of the sieve is no more than an association with virginity,[6] and therefore a sign of the Virgin Queen; however, Ripa[7] uses the symbol of the sieve as also, or alternatively, signalling 'wisdom and discernment' (which can indeed be read as significant in a portrait of Elizabeth as wise, as well as Virgin, Queen). The sieve of 'wisdom and discernment' can replace the cutting sword of judgment as the practice of critique – a very different image of thought, of theory.

To have done with judgment. But to understand how compelling judgment remains, and how much it still curtails the potential of theory in relation to law; we need to trace, to sketch, the material conditions through which theory has been and is formed and practiced in relation to law, or more precisely, scholarship in law schools. Even more precisely, in English[8] law schools:

> what is the habit which constitutes the subject? This is the question posed by pragmatism. English law is a law of custom and convention, as the French is of contract (deductive system) and the German of institution (organic totality). When philosophy is reterritorialised on the State of Law, the philosopher becomes philosophy professor, but for the German this is by institution and foundation, for the French it is by contract, and for the English it is solely by convention.
>
> (Deleuze and Guattari, 1994:106)

Foundational narratives and place making

Fifty years ago, in 1967, an inaugural professorial lecture imaginatively entitled 'Pericles and the Plumber' laid out an argument for the development of legal education and law schools which would draw together the strengths of a liberal academic programme with the technical tradecraft required as preparation for law (legal practice, legislative drafting, decision-making in court etc.).[9] Rather ironically, given the scope of the title framing an argument for creative inter-action, as law faculties in following years debated their role (the provision of legal education and the potential of scholarship in law), the pairing often became reworked into a necessary choice between philosopher prince or technician (and which would you rather be?), rather than a closer critical engagement with Twining's vision of productive collaboration.

Twining's evocation of the figure of Pericles can be situated within a modernist project to (seize and) make 'law' work for the building and delivery of (a better) social justice. Referencing Pericles was a calling forth (speaking out) of a renaissance, a renewal of law and of governance through (the rule of) law: capable of, and legitimated by, a search for social justice as a process of creative discovery.

This modernist project in/for law did not need to presume a necessary potential in law as a progressive force for social justice, let alone that law carried this as inherent promise (the contours of the political ideology of liberalism may seem to shape the modernist project but must be distinguished from it); rather it pushed in and at law to test how far it could be deployed, struggled in and with, as tool and technique, for social justice. Twining's lecture can be historicised as evidencing the culmination of the modernist project in/for law, which still refused to give up on the possibility of potential in law, or indeed in the ideal of social justice itself, and looked forward to the building of an emergent (better) world using, as far as they could be pushed and bent and exploited, the tools of the old world.

The Labour government in the 1960s, still struggling out of the heritage of the restrictions of post-war retrenchment, introduced a second wave of welfare state planning in which law reform was central to the agenda. In 1965, the Law Commission was introduced by a reforming Lord Chancellor (Elwyn-Jones) committed to bringing 'law' into the service of the public as part of a political programme committed to social change. Law needed modernisation, not only in terms of the 'rules', but also in how law was made and applied. Concerns were expressed as to the extent to which the legal profession and judiciary would be prepared for, let alone be prepared to co-operate with, an activist agenda for the development of law and an expanded delivery of legal services. Within this context, Twining's design for pro-active law schools was in accord with Elwyn-Jones's vision for an expansive legal system and the development of a profession working with/for a politics for social change rather than operating (instinctively and institutionally) to protect and maintain the traditions and privileges of the establishment.

In 1967 Elwyn-Jones appointed a committee, chaired by Ormrod LJ, to make recommendations (create designs) for a modern legal education benefiting from a collaboration between profession and academy through the prism of an education for law, rather than limited to a training in law. The committee reported in 1971, by which time the Labour government had lost power and Elwyn-Jones had been replaced by the establishment figure of Hailsham. In retrospect, the report clearly evidences the entrenched power of the legal profession as *the* legal establishment (as well as their ability to defend their interests). A potential role for law schools and academics as active collaborators and partners in law was diminished to a minimum, and the profession successfully asserted the marginal significance of the academy to law.

Ormrod framed legal education, and thereby the work of law schools, through into the 21st century.[10] Whilst recognising a role for an academic stage (education) in legal training, and defending it as properly framed by a liberal arts education, it set the scene for a confrontational struggle between academy and profession played out over the role and purpose of a law degree, and through this vector the issue of the place of law (as scholarship rather than as junior partner to the profession) in the academy. In many faculties it wasn't really much of a struggle at all – the profession exerted control, and the academy (in general) fell into the role of trying to keep them happy. Ormrod confirmed the weak position of law in the English academy; if anything, what had changed was that the profession now confronted and attempted to control the academy, rather than simply ignoring it. The majority of the profession were united in approaching and thinking the law degree purely in terms of a staged approach to 'legal education' as training; and those on the academic side lacked, on the whole, the confidence to assert an academic framing for legal studies which was not hinged onto or validated by reference to professional accreditation.

The weak position of law in the academy was the heritage of a history in England of academic marginalisation from the activity of law. Before the 18th century, the universities of Oxford and Cambridge taught, *inter alia*, the liberal arts and Roman and some Canon Law (an awkward post-reformation fudge), but no common law until Blackstone's lectures in 1753 (Prest, 2012).[11] The Inns of Court provided a process of training for intending barristers in the arts and skills of law (the mysteries of the craft) in an enclosed environment which protected the privileges of the established profession. A more clerk-like set of skills and services (e.g., the design, execution and management of contracts, wills, trusts etc.) was the province of a range of law practitioners, formed into a number of trade guilds, with whom we now associate much of the work undertaken by (the consolidated profession of) solicitors. The delivery of legal services was not associated with benefitting from, let alone requiring, a university education.

Blackstone's project of laying out a systematic account of common law through lectures introducing the principles and rules of common law signalled a move towards making law visible, and thereby accountable, outside of the craft heritage of being trained (with)in common law. Asserting an underlying rationality which could be teased out of common law, and then taught alongside the formal patterns of Roman law, suggested a cohesive, coherent potential which was imminent in the case-material but needed to be brought (in)to light through the labour of scholars/lawyers. The lack of a codified structure and framing could be explained and defended through extrapolating and revealing what was already present without (too much) recourse to importing and attempting to superimpose organisational patterns derived from civilian law – especially as a severe (and foreign, even if Roman) classicism sat awkwardly on the organic, baroque folds and interfolds of common law. Blackstone's pattern of systemisation, through clarification and distillation into an easily digestible form, was one which lent itself to acting as a primer in law.[12] It was, essentially, a conservative and deferential project, and became the template for the beginnings of 'teaching' common law in universities – Blackstone's-letter, rather than simply black-letter.

For Bentham, Blackstone's project of systematisation did not go far enough: Blackstone was too much an apologist and defender (more than simply a describer) of what should be condemned, by scholars as reformers, as the irrational elements of/in common law. To truly address common law systematically was, for Bentham, a chance to deal with what had become visibly in need of change in order to achieve greater, real, systemisation through rationality: his was a project to modernise rather than to defend common law. Bentham's rigorous reformist approach insisted on revealing and expelling common law's excesses; exposing and eliminating confusion, contradiction and lack of clarity in a massive 'clearing up' operation to eliminate the irrational and the discretionary, and thereby limit the power of lawyers to manipulate, rather than simply apply (the rules of) law. This was a form of law designed for the emergent state; delivering, rather than obstructing, state policies designed to promote social stability and economic growth. A centralised system of order and command carried through law, preferably (more efficiently) as rationally codified rules rather than ported through case-based law.[13] Lawyers needed to be legislators for a future, rather than defenders of the past; technocrats applying law with social purpose, rather than craft-workers constructing argument for the benefit of clients.

In 1826, the establishment of University College (London) was the first opportunity to design a 'modern' law school focused on common law. Further, it drew from, intended to combine, two related Benthamite projects. First, the school was designed to train lawyers; a preparation for the practice of law. This was a direct challenge to the traditions of the profession in asserting that intellectual training, rather than merely tradecraft, was the proper foundation for practice.[14] It was also, however, more than preparation for traditional practice; it was a preparation for judgment, for becoming-judges. Inspired by Bentham's ideas, this approach was one which focused on laying a foundation for reforming law through an educated task-force of lawyers. Thus, second, the school was carrying forward the Benthamite project of/for law reform: with lawyers as the conduit for development of common law into a more rational and transparent law-as-rule system.

The ethos of the London development of a university education for law focused on delivering practical (and scientific) courses designed as learning for earning, as well as carrying and propagating a culture of utilitarian commitment to rational reform for a modern world. The law degree programme organised common law into a taxonomy of 'subject' areas, framed through lecture series and textbooks, through which a systematised introduction to the rules (principles and methods) of common law could be promulgated. It was as if in this process of setting down (making visible) the common law, it could become a kind of English version of (modified) codification; a project with which a number of the lawyers who became first-wave academic textbook writers had become familiar when working as civil servants in the India Office.[15] It was also as if the Benthamite project for reform, and training the right kind of lawyers to enable and consolidate reform, could be accomplished by exposing intending practitioners to a more 'academic' (as in 'scientific') approach (revealing, testing, reforming and then protecting the underlying rationality of law), before they entered (the mysteries) of craft training and became vulnerable to the seductive powers of establishment privilege.[16]

The Benthamite design for a modern legal education capable of delivering, rather than impeding, a technocratic design for law's role in carrying reform for state, marginalised, to the point of supressing, a potential for a form of scholarship linking academic law back into civilian traditions[17] and, more importantly, the heritage of humanities and liberal arts. This is underlined in the key lecture series delivered by John Austin, the Benthamite professor of jurisprudence at University College from 1826 until his resignation in 1834. Published as 'The Province of Jurisprudence Determined' in 1832, what became known as a 'positivist' approach to law limited jurisprudence (framed here as 'philosophy of law') to the study of issues arising from (and consolidating the regime of) state law (positive law).[18] Excluded from the study of jurisprudence (and therefore the education of lawyers) were any normative questions concerned with evaluating (judging) law ethically.[19] In such a politically inspired and scholastically limited programme, what was important was to create and maintain a vision of law as no more and no less than a technocratic tool for the delivery of governance – this was skilled plumbing, with Pericles as philosopher off site (and out of sight).

The paradox, of course, was that this challenge to the establishment of the profession could only, at best, allow for uneasy relations between the two whilst the profession remained in control of entry into law and consequently continued to produce a judiciary untrained in, let alone sympathetic to, a Benthamite approach. It did, however, open a potential in a role for academic lawyers as guardians of the more rational approach to law, in which they became monitors of an (at worst) untrained and untrustworthy judiciary. A space, and possibly a place, opened within which academic lawyers moved between describing law as found in judgments, and critiquing those judgments in terms of a schemata for an underlying rationality. However, the principal problem in establishing this as an authentic enterprise for scholarship in law was that it was not only premised on delivering commentary on activities taking place elsewhere, but that these activities were generally pursued without reference to any 'scholarly' commentary developing in their wake.[20]

There were, however, important alliances forged between scholar/lawyers and the emerging political sphere of/for reform developing from close linkages between politicians working for law reform, the establishment of commissions to report on causes of concern and recommend reform, and a new breed of activist civil servants (links often initiated and consolidated through shared clubs and societies, religious practices and kin networks). Links with the profession might be fragile, but links into the politics of law reform were not. The modernist project for law in the academy was carried forward in this alliance, casting scholarship as moving between describing what law 'is', and outlining what law should, or could, be. However, legal scholarship still remained uneasy in establishing an identity which was not dependent upon the professional/practitioner as embodying what was still thought of as the 'true' lawyer; and the banks of undergraduates seated in lecture theatres saw more to attract them in a future of practicing law, rather than choosing scholarship. Pericles did not emerge as a confident figure embodying the full potential of a partnership in/for law, and by 1967, and even more clearly by 1971, the project for delivering social reform through law had reached a point of exhaustion.[21]

The political context to the use of law as a tool of/for governance had become sharply contested. Twining delivered his lecture in Northern Ireland, shortly before 'The Troubles' erupted in a violent challenge to the sectarian politics of privilege and discrimination. The repressive role of the British state was revealed in a willingness to go beyond the rule of law and due process, employing the army to police and introducing internment without trial. This overt exercise of state power, both through and beyond law, forced into the open questions about the power of state, as well as the role of law. The legitimacy of state authority, and the role of law in protecting establishment privileges, was also being challenged in colonies pushing towards independence, and in ex-colonies where privileged minorities acted, through oppressive laws and state violence, to protect the status quo. Twining's background in Africa, and his contribution to the development of legal education (within the context of addressing constitutional planning and designs for post-colonial law) in African states preparing for independence, undoubtedly informed his vision of a law school committed to an activist and engaged emancipatory project. Already a contentious claim in Northern Ireland and many post-independence jurisdictions that law could be used progressively; the potential of law as a challenge (however weak) to coercive state authority remained acknowledged as one mode of defence, and even a possible strategy for challenge.

One significant English development manifested a determination to try to use law for progressive, politically informed, purposes. From the early 1970s, the law centre movement refreshed and reframed a version of the modernist project. 'Radical' lawyers developed a new form of legal service designed to bring legal advice and representation to people with whom the profession had had no interest, and in 'new' areas of law developing, under the auspices of legislative reform, legal protection for disadvantaged sections of society – in social housing, social benefits, employment, discrimination law, etc. Not only did law centres take on individual casework, including test cases, they also campaigned to raise awareness of law and for the need for reform in and through law. The right of access to law, and to be able to use law against power, including the excesses of state power, even when recognising the limits of law (and the power of power), was a pragmatic ideal which fuelled the law centre ethos. Unsurprisingly they found themselves inundated by excessive workloads, dogged by problems with finance, and debilitated by the politics of struggle against establishment (including the profession) and authority (especially when it was authority which provided finance!). But the engaged idealism of the law centre movement, and related projects, inspired a generation of faculty and students to engage with law through law; and it found fertile ground in the new law schools of the 1960s plate-glass universities. The experience of a radical politics of/for law, and the potential for a more progressive education in law, inspired English law schools into forging the beginnings of what became the UK critical legal studies movement.

Two crucial factors pushed forward the development of critique in law at this stage: an increased awareness of the (overtly violent) politics of the English state in Northern Ireland and other colonial settings, and the lack of a practice of consistent theorization to underpin political accounts of the role of law in the rule of law. The critical legal studies movement in the UK was forged out of political engagements and contestations, in the clear and sharp awareness that neither the traditions of legal education nor the limits of jurisprudence provided any useful insights into the condition of law, or the potential for engagement. Thirty years later, Annelise Riles (2006: 16) wrote:

> We are not by any means alone in searching for places of respite from over-determined theoretical paradigms and outworn descriptive tropes.

What are the conditions which led to emergence of this sense, which we recognise so well, of exhaustion?

The territory surveyed: critique emerges

It is central to our argument that we recognise the material conditions within which scholarship (as the potential, use and limits of the practice of theory) arises. To understand the implications and to exploit the full potential of 'theory' we must ground it, briefly but frequently, in order for it (and us) to fly.

'Law' 'and' 'theory'; or perhaps you prefer 'theory' 'and' 'law'. The difference between each formulation might be an innocent process of thinking that one just sounds better than the other, but it can also be used (or read) as a more purposeful decision representing a trajectory in which the first frames the approach to the second. And 'and' is, of course, a problematic linkage. It can be used to suggest 'and as well as', or the very different 'and as a consequence of'. Whilst the first might suggest a bracketing by being brought into an equivalence, even if originating in different registers, the latter denotes a priority in which the first identifies, delineates and explores the second within terms set by the first. Each may have their own (internal) logic,[22] but the question is whether and how one is privileged over the other; because that, quite simply, over-determines how the other is framed and portrayed. It is our contention that, too often, the bringing together of law/theory (or theory/law) has failed to confront, explore and make conscious choices about the *process* of bringing into relation, through distinctive forms of encounter, the material conditions and specific projects which underlie patterns of movement *between* them as well as *through* them. Too much has been simply taken for granted, as if already 'known', in the sense of theorised, but is actually grounded in little more than assertions of common sense and common practice – and the consequence of this has become, we would argue, a blockage on the productive capacity, the activity, of theorising law.

Nowhere is this more visible, and more paradoxical, than in the emergence of 'critical legal theory' out of the critical legal studies movement – the very place where one might reasonably expect (look for) a more nuanced, careful and creative account of patterns of inter-relations between law and theory than in any other area of law school scholarship. To understand how this situational stasis has become such a strangle-hold, we need to ground it back into the material conditions from which it arose. A 'situation' (or 'crisis') in theory is not countered and critiqued simply by more or (an)other theory laid out on an abstract plane unconnected to the materiality of time/place as the grounding from which the processes of theorization emerge. The form of theoretical practice in which we are engaged refuses to treat theory as only, and only ever, operating as an abstraction beyond, and outside of, material conditions.

The practice of theory as an embedded process is, drawing from the traditions of materialist philosophy, the strongest form of critique; a process of critical practice formed through and within a creative and risky, edgy, close engagement with the questions of mess using a compass and a set of diagrams as aids in an adventurous journey, rather than seeking to create a complete map of untrammelled purity which will provide, as long as you can read it correctly and follow it precisely, answers as conclusions and a steady lens through which to view and make visible, at a safe distance, the terrain of law. These are two very different accounts of theory – and we need to understand why one has been perceived as so attractive to contemporary scholars of law, in particular those who think of themselves as critical legal scholars.

As we have outlined, the foundational stories which produced a narrative and rationale for law's place in the English academy have been based not on scholarship, and thereby the potential of theory, but rather in educational training and policy-based research. However, a small thread has always connected legal education with the use of theory, in the teaching (texts and scholarship) of 'jurisprudence' as theory-of-law. *Nota bene*: not theory 'and' law, but theory 'of' law.

The province of jurisprudence has been limited, but not finally determined, by the heritage of Austin's positivism. However, the project of jurisprudence as knowledge-of-law still tends towards a focus on definitions of law, to which either normative or material questions are then added as supplements. For instance, in a recent collection focused on (potential) inter-relations between 'theory' and 'history' of law, the introduction begins with the conundrum that theory is about what law 'is', rather than what law 'does' (the basis of history), and therefore the difficulty of 'theory' being framed together with, or teased out from, materially based practices (rather than being 'applied' to them).[23] Jurisprudence is still wary of being brought to ground: partly because of the heritage of positivism, but also because of the more recent adoption of an abstract mode of philosophy (or rather philosophising) as wisdom-of-law. Philosophy becomes the means through which to move (in)to theory beyond the confines of orthodox jurisprudence. Love of Sophia can replace, or at least open up a space, beyond the worldly figure of Prudence. Theory becomes transcendent – a move out-of-world (away from flesh) in order to seek and be able to discern truth and thereby the truth of law. 'Critical legal studies' became a conduit for the delivery of this form of theorizing into law schools.

Jurisprudence, even in the form of 'internal critique', has not been treated, in practice, as central or foundational to legal studies;[24] but it has (perhaps, in part, because of this) come to provide a space for scholars to identify themselves with the wider enterprise of academic scholarship. In reaching out to theory as abstract philosophy, a means has been found to claim a place in the wider academy through the meritorious and elitist activity of hard abstract thinking. There is then a kind of a virtue in placing theory on the margin in law schools; it allows for a distance from the dominant technocratic project and an escape from the social science frame of policy-based empirical research.[25] Not limited to the boundaries of theory *of* law, these scholastic activities delineate a territory in which law, or at least jurisprudence, can be bought into an encounter with theory by the importation of theory into (or rather 'onto') the terrain of law schools. Scholarship *in* law failed, essentially, to provide sufficient intellectually stimulating material, and isolated scholars from the rest of the academy, particularly the humanities. In a gesture of refusal and reversal, scholars committed to the pursuit of theory flipped identities or rather reference point – no longer law (as practiced in world-out-there) but theory, and therefore the academy, now establishes their credentials, direction and sense of purpose. Theory is then offered as *the* way forward into scholarship, and law becomes simply another terrain for evidencing the importance of theory. The powerful allure of mastering theory is a seductive pull away from law, especially when theory operates to reveal the truth of law hidden by and in law. This from the back cover of a book introducing and delineating 'critical jurisprudence':

> after a long process of decay, legal theory is today characterised by cognitive and moral poverty. Jurisprudence has become restricted and academically peripheral, a guidebook to technocratic legalism and a legitimation of the existent. Critical jurisprudence returns to the classical tradition of a general philosophy of law and adopts a much wider concept of legality. . . . Law's complicity with political oppression, violence and racism has to be faced before it is possible to speak of a new beginning for legal thought, which in turn is the necessary precondition for a theory of justice. *Critical Jurisprudence* offers an ethics of law against the nihilism of power and an aesthetics of existence for the melancholic lawyer.
>
> (Douzinas and Geary, 2005)

Sophia's territorial aspirations: the emergence of critical jurisprudence

A close reading of the argument for (the need for) 'critical jurisprudence' reveals a crucial slippage between framing the project through the limitations of heritage, and then moving quickly into the promise of overcoming, through the assertion, or presumption, that the 'only' route out is to cut through with theory achieved through a 'return to the classical tradition of a general philosophy of law'.[26] To return in order to begin again: a life at last, a rebirth, as philosopher/scholar, a true Pericles.[27] However, whilst we might concur with something of the diagnosis of condition, both the prognosis and the remedy require more careful consideration, especially when framed as something called 'critical jurisprudence'. What are the potentials for practices associated with the terms 'critical' and 'jurisprudence' and then the bracketing of them? What is forged: a sheath or a hinge? Theory becomes jurisprudence; and so jurisprudence becomes theory. Before (the) theory.

The rebirth of jurisprudence as theory is made possible by a doubled movement: the return to an authentic beginning to recast, and thereby find (another) voice, and the practice of critique to reveal, using the old/new voice, the truth (an ethical and aesthetical transcendent 'real') which has been hidden in and by law/jurisprudence. Return, rebirth, reveal. Theoria/Sophia sees all, offers and answers all; however, this is a form of completion which always requires continued proof of need and use(fullness). This form of promise is, so paradoxically, actually a form of entrapment into a continued search for what we have already-been-told is already-there; a completeness just out of reach, even as this formed the ground(ing) which made the beginning of the search possible. This is an ontology of lack; the search for completion through the continual escape of overcoming (made possible through a continual return to find the authentic truth-purity of origins) maintaining momentum through having given allegiance, the commitment of belief, to the knowledge that transcendence is always there in the beyond. Truth and justice can be revealed when we can (through theory) reach them. The question is how this form of theory/theorising became so intimately linked with 'critical' thinking.

The beginning of contemporary critique in law (or rather in the academy of law) was the critical legal studies movement, which then morphed into 'critical legal theory' and from that is now moved into 'critical jurisprudence'; what does this recasting of critique (in/or 'and' law) tell us? How is it made possible? There is, of course, a conjuncture of events and trends which lie behind the emergence of law and critique as critical jurisprudence. We have already outlined the limitations on legal scholarship (including jurisprudence) in English law schools, the domination of a concern with education as training, and the consequent marginalisation of law as an academic subject in universities. Further, we have suggested the significance of a modernist project in law, and its exhaustion, to understanding the present condition of law schools and legal scholarship. The fate of the modernist project is clearly traceable in the changing contours of critique in/of law.[28] The critical legal studies movement of the early 1980s still bore the traces of not only the possibility of radical, emancipatory change through (legal education and) law, but also the continued commitment to a politics of the (or 'a') left. Further into that decade, it became all too clear that neither were, anymore if ever had been, feasible. Critical legal studies began to migrate – from education into (research) scholarship, and from practical politics into the pursuit of theory.

We agree with Douzinas (2005) when he insists on the specificity of the UK critical legal studies movement (rather than the frequently made assumption that the UK movement developed out of, and mimicked, the US critical studies movement). However, he fails to locate the UK movement within the context of the 'critical law' engagement with law, instead focusing, more narrowly, on an account of differences in scholarship and organisation[29] between the UK and the US (with some reference to differences in political conditions and traditions). The focus from which he builds his argument is a characterisation of the UK as marked by an 'impoverished approach to legal study that has been challenged in the last 30 years by legal theory' (2006: 56). The 'last 30 years' is the timeframe of the critical legal studies movement, which now becomes marked as the purveyor (into English law schools) of 'legal theory'. What kind of legal theory can this be? One which delivers, in his terms, a sufficiently theorised jurisprudence to reveal the violence at the root of law (in state), as well as the techniques which law employs (for, and as, state power) to both carry and mask the extent of the truth of that violence. This forecloses, obviously, any potential for a close engagement with law, indeed he argues:

> A distance must always remain, a gap excess or lack must separate normative positions and radical alternatives. To a certain extent, the critic must be a foreigner (to his own tradition), a degree of incomprehension must enter and colour her most accurate description and intimate evaluation.
>
> (Douzinas, 2005: 580)

For Douzinas, to cut away, and maintain the purity of safe distance, is the only way to avoid the deadly, seductive embrace of law. Is Hercules really so powerful? Or might he, in fact, have feet of clay? Are we not capable of discernment? Our concern is that a simplistic reading of the Douzinas model of critical legal studies privileges not only the academy as the only 'way to be critical' (in that sense, this position is too close to Dworkin for comfort), but also draws overly simplistic boundaries between law and state (out there) and critical legal studies (in here). In this he reproduces the common trope of being more concerned with academic credibility than critical merit. It is no surprise that critical studies should be understood as needing, above all, a theoretical grounding in order to move forward. When Dworkin (1986) mockingly challenged the capacity of critical legal studies to contribute to scholarship, it was entirely on the grounds that it was a 'movement' that lacked a unifying theory. Without theory, there can be no critique. With theory, one can build critical jurisprudence. Further, despite Douzinas's insistence that US and UK crits, their methods and their concerns, be distinguished, he does not engage with the context of the common law tradition: it is as if, with the advent of theory, we can all be Europeans now, and reconnect back into the longer, wider history of law and theory (from which we were cut adrift), and so have not need to consider the specifics of our own condition. Law, legal studies and critical theory become globalised into a generalised logic of state/power/law, and neither the operation of the market, nor the specific material conditions of different jurisdictions and juridical histories, are, in the end, relevant. Theory is timeless, and law not bounded by space. Despite his claim to the specifics of the UK critical legal studies movement, allowing the Brits to appear in their own right alongside, rather than behind, the Americans, he moves, all too rapidly, into the wider (but not deeper) framing of a reconnection into 'theory'.

However, this migration does seek to carry forward a political project. Introducing the first 'text-book' for critical legal studies on their publisher's website, the authors, Douzinas and Geary, characterise the critical project in this way:

> (critical jurisprudence) is concerned both with posited law and with the law of the law. All legal aspects of the economic, political, emotional and physical modes of production and reproduction of society are part of critical jurisprudence. This widening of scope allows a radical rethinking of the nature of rights, justice, sovereignty and judgement. A political philosophy of justice today must examine the political economy of law; transitions from Empire to nation; ideological and imaginary constructions through which we understand ourselves and relate to others; ways in which gender, race or sexuality create forms of identity that both discipline bodies and offer sites of resistance. Law's complicity with political oppression, violence and racism has to be faced before it is possible to speak of a new beginning.
>
> (Douzinas and Geary, 2005)

The political agenda has, of course, been widened to encompass all forms of oppression, all plays of power and, at the same time, what is revealed and 'must be faced' is 'law's complicity with political oppression, violence and racism'. Jurisprudence, which for so long suppressed and denied the politics of law, is re-connected (in)to politics in a doubled movement: first, there is the encompassing gesture of recognising *all* forms of oppression as political issues, but, second, at the same time, politics as critique is limited to theory as framed through the orthodox traditions of political philosophy and therefore to politics as state. Law is presented and understood as no more and no less than state power; the role of critique in law is therefore to reveal the perfidious nature of law and the violence of its origin. Law is an institution of state, and the state is the enemy.[30] At a minimum, critique must always be at a sufficient distance in order to resist being sucked back into (seduced back into) law; at best there may be places outside of law in which freedom, true expression, real identity and self-determination can, finally and fully, exist and from which resistance to law can be built. If this heaven is to be achieved it can only be through theory:

> Law's complicity with political oppression, violence and racism has to be faced before it is possible to speak of a new beginning for legal thought, which in turn is the necessary precondition for a theory of justice. *Critical Jurisprudence* offers an ethics of law against the nihilism of power and an aesthetics of existence for the melancholic lawyer.
>
> (Douzinas and Geary, 2005)

This offers, in effect, the complete life-style package of (politically aware) philosopher/scholar to the world-weary lawyer/scholar seeking an identity as 'true' (and at the same time 'progressive') academic, rather than subaltern lawyer. From critical legal studies to critical jurisprudence: the triumph of Theoria as Sophia.

Two trends in particular feed this turn of critique into all-encompassing meta(major)-theory. The first is the adoption of critique as the practice of revelation: an inheritance from The Frankfurt School's practice of cutting away the false in order to reveal the hidden (violent) truth.[31] As law is subjected to critique which (looks for) and exposes both the violence of state power and the suppression of that knowledge of truth through the false idols of democracy and the rule of law, so law can only be reduced to being understood as an agency of state. Ironically, positive law and command theory is rebirthed in critical jurisprudence. 'Law' is no more than an institutional arm of the state which serves to legitimate the exercise of state power, and critical jurisprudence is the revelation of critique carrying the potential of resistance. To evidence the power of this trajectory research case studies tend to be, unsurprisingly, drawn from examples which illustrate the violence of state power carried through law. As if that is all there is to law, or to the politics of critique. And to compound the limitations of this focus on state/law as the central problematic, the politics of either the market or the emergence of societies of control remains marginalised. The practice of critique as critical jurisprudence tends to portray and examine both law and politics through a very limited agenda (reproducing a province of jurisprudence over-determined).[32]

The second trend is towards a specifically transcendental form (or type) of philosophy as if that is the only, or true/best, practice of philosophy. When critical legal scholars challenged the isolationism of English (common) law schools from scholarship in the wider academy, some also realised how isolated they/we had become from scholarship in Europe. It is instructive that at the same time as the critical legal studies movement in England was established in the 1980s, under the auspices of Critical Legal Conference (UK), the network and annual meeting for those interested in critical legal scholarship was the European Conference of Critical Legal Studies (ECCLS) grouping. Whilst early CLC (UK) meetings tended to focus on streams organised around areas of academic law, legal education and radical practice, ECCLS was from the beginning about theory as theory, rather than as an adjunct to scholarship in law. Aware of the paucity of scholarship in law, the attractions of moving, quickly, out of law and towards 'theory' was indicative of a perceived lack, or failure, in legal scholarship *as* scholarship. ECCLS provided a forum through which the formative developments in continental scholarship became available to English scholars. However, this mode of importation into academies unused to the practice of theory (other than the modest theoretical excursions made in jurisprudence) meant that theory tended to be experienced as arriving (from the outside) as fully formed and requiring a great deal of concentration to explore and understand it within its own terms of reference. Rather than emerging from legal scholarship, even as jurisprudence, this engagement with theory was one which became an embrace which required total commitment before turning back to re-encounter (common) law. Was it something in the paucity of previous encounters with theory which led so many critical legal scholars into the arms, the seductive pleasures, of transcendental philosophy? What alchemy mixed from insecurity of lack (as scholar) and desire for fulfilment (as scholar) led to the recovery of the contemplative Platonic mind in turning away from the materiality of flesh/law/world? What aspect of the failure of modernity (or of politics, especially of the left) led back (in)to the search for the purity of transcendent truths (found out-of-time, before or at the beginning of time) and complete ontologies? What was it that led to the embrace of not merely theory, but the fusion of critique with a mode of theorising drawn from a form of political philosophy which looks back and up, rather than forward and down? How is it that the virtuous figure of 'the melancholic lawyer' turned scholar became as much a given as the nihilism of law as power? Material conditions, most especially the perceived need to move on from the failures of modernity and to escape the confines of the legal academy, explain the seductive pull towards the pleasures of mastery of theory and the comforts of knowledge that there is always-truth-out-there (it is just that we cannot quite see it yet, but the outline seems to become visible if we concentrate carefully and are not diverted by distractions).

The strange strength of 'critical jurisprudence' is that it oscillates between the revelation of critique of/in this world, and a promise of understanding founded in an ontology dependent upon a 'beyond', an outside of this world of space/time. Politics becomes, in practice, a continual movement between ethics and resistance, premised on identities and rights born before law and now subjected to the force of law. What is 'critical' is to be outside, and to be outside requires an ontology which is not limited to material conditions but can claim a truth beyond the constraints of time/space (and the dread of relativism). Thus critique is both authenticated by, and at the same time transformed into, a meta-philosophy: a major jurisprudence committed to judgment. Out of the fudge, mess and experimentation of the critical legal studies movement emerges the certainty and authority of critical jurisprudence. Critique arrives as a fully-fledged all-encompassing theory able to claim (through the assertion of bounded identity) its place in the academy.[33] What does this make possible, other than careers and the addition of a chapter to books exploring the patterns of jurisprudence?

Walking with Aspasia: poiesis becomes her

What do we want of the practice of theory? 'We' in this context has a specific reference point: a material immediacy. We are (common) lawyers/scholars concerned with the present conditions of the economics of globalisation, the emergence of control societies[34] and the urgent need for political engagement. We employ theory as a practice through which we seek greater understanding in order to think/imagine a potential for (alternative) futures: a political project. We experience the pleasures of theory, but we want more. We are ethico-pragmatists who seek from the practice of theory a political affect in creating/finding potentiality. It is, we admit, a kind of modern puritanism which finds no attraction in a lifestyle of melancholy, or of dreaming myths of an outside transcendent real; this is a much more messy engagement with the materiality of world, and with ideas as flesh. This is a minor jurisprudence, a modest jurisprudence, which progresses in stutters before it can speak and perseveres in resilience rather than seeking escape in resistance. It draws, through Deleuze, from a philosophical tradition which is not premised in transcendence, but rather in immanence. It looks forwards rather than backwards, and opens itself to desire as opening something new, rather than as a response to the emptiness of lack. This mode of philosophy, this practice of thinking, is not about the purity of definition or completeness of ontological design, but rather the teasing out of potential, motivated by an ethico-ontological imperative. It is premised in a creative process of engagement *with* world rather than as an escape *from* world.[35]

A process of critique should be able to understand that there is choice: we are not limited to only one account of the practice of philosophy, and therefore of jurisprudence, and therefore of law. We are not limited to an emergent orthodoxy that (the best form of) theory is marked by (and limited to) thinking as a form of philosophical practice which insists on abstraction as a process of necessary disengagement from the materiality of circumstance *in order to think, and thereby (in order to) be able to discern truth*. For us, this fetish for distance is problematic: leading to attempts to disengage from the material context and circumstance, and thereby limiting the potential in the question 'what can theory do?' We have to distinguish between practices of philosophy which have become territorialised into following in the footsteps of Plato and his maps; and practices of thinking which free philosophy through (for and out from) engagement with the material world. Not searching in abstraction for truth, but feeling our way into a potential for kinds of truth. Not mastering 'theory' through thought as, and in, mind alone; but through incursions into the world (using all of our senses) which open up and challenge us to think through body and soul as well as, as part of, mind. This is a very different topography, a very different set of contours and a very much more open horizon (more precisely, the opening of a plain of immanence).

Prudence: artisan as (cosmic) critic

Deleuze and Guattari (1994) argue that philosophy is no less and no more than the development and use of concepts which enable us to think. Philosophy, in this sense, employs concepts as techniques, and as long as we are aware of, paying attention to, the technical processes of concept-use we will not get lost (entrapped, territorialised) in the (content of) concepts themselves but rather focus on what is important: what does this make possible? How can we imagine this? By not thinking of concepts as immaterial abstractions but rather as material forms: images of thought, images for thought. Image as diagram: outlines which allow us to, for instance, trace potential in an image of thought which links concepts into patterns for thinking.[36] Imaging, diagramming, creating concepts is a continual movement between abstracting and (re)investing; a de-territorialisation away from and then the oscillating move back into. This is not praxis following after theoria; it is a teasing out, a sifting, from continual use-patterns of (dis)engagement. It is a making, a bringing into existence: it is, it forges, poiesis.

Deleuze and Guattari (1988: 411–412) use the figure of the artisan (not an artist!) to embody, diagram, the practice of creative, engaged thinking. The artisan employs material to craft artefacts; she bends, pulls, hammers and shapes material to give expression to what is carried within/by the artefact. Her hands feel the contours of material and draw shape from it. She works with intensity and closeness, pausing to draw back in order to consider her work and how she might continue it, and then re-engaging. The material, her skill and her imagination explore and shape potential. Deleuze extracts her from metal, Serres (1991: 81) moulds her in bread: *Analysis cuts;*

the baker folds.[37] This is topographical imaging; it feels, as much as sees, the contours and horizons emerging. In crafting artefacts within the materiality of here/now, what is glimpsed and pursued is the cosmic of soon here/maybe now, as always. Concepts allow us to move out of the immediate, but are only useful when we understand how they arose (were crafted) and how we can (as craft) use them. Not the non-world aesthetics of the world-weary; but the well-crafted grounding with which we can reach for the stars.

It is a very different process of engagement with thinking than that espoused by critical jurisprudence, and seems well suited to not only jurisprudence, but especially a jurisprudence of/for contemporary common law:

> When philosophy is reterritorialised on the State of Law, the philosopher becomes philosophy professor, but for the German this is by institution and foundation, for the French by contract, and for the English it is solely by convention.
>
> (Deleuze and Guattari, 1994:106)

Post-Brexit it might seem overly nationalistic to insist on the specificity of time/place as crucial material factors in the crafting of juris-prudence; but the moment of territorial grounding is crucial for theorising to be productive as something other than its own continuation. Common law needs to be engaged with as a specific form of legal reasoning and rationalisation. Unlike the civilian tradition, it is a craft of teasing out from case-decisions principles and concepts which carry law forward (even if only going backward!). It is, as Weber understood and Bentham wished for, not a 'rational' codified system of deductive application, but more fuzzy and pragmatic.[38] If we wish to understand law, to engage with and make (some) sense of law, we must recognise and theorise the different modes of legal reasoning and different processes of rationalisation. Deleuze and Guattari remind us that theory must move through the process of territorialisation: into history/geography as well as, once again, out of immediate space/time. Of course there is a level of abstraction within which we can talk, more generally, of Law as an institution, including as an institution of state, or as a vector for the production and protection of power and privilege; just as there is a further level of abstraction within which we can speak, more generally, of normative concerns and the constant return of questions of legitimacy and authority.[39] But juris-prudence is more than theory of law as generalised and generalising abstraction, in which all is treated as similar or equivalent. Juris-*prudentia* is not limited to or by juris-*sophia* (our apologies for the mixing of Latin/Greek): it is the provenance of Prudence, artisan, and that seems particularly apposite for those of us who work with(in) the common law tradition in insisting that assumptions are not made of law as if it takes only one form, one shape. This opens a potential to become conversant with a multiple of laws (as method and legality) at different times and in different places: teasing out difference and repetition in seeking to understand our heritage(s), and what these legacies have led us towards, as much as recognising what we wish to struggle away from.[40]

Creative, engaged theory is, within our present political conditions, so urgently necessary. What is, or could be, the role of law in countering the excesses of globalised markets or the perfidious strangulation of control societies? Has (common) law become more relevant, or increasingly marginalised? How is (common) law being reshaped? Is there a resilience[41] to be found in, or crafted from, legal concepts and modes of reasoning which may provide us with some tools and techniques (however fragile) for the defence of the most vulnerable, and a challenge to the most powerful? What use might we make of law when we can no longer invest in an exhausted modernist project or the false promise of a 'New Jerusalem'? How do we craft a minor jurisprudence as a modest endeavour which reaches forwards into a new cosmic grounded in becoming-just? How do we avoid the trap of judgement, and have done with it?

Juris-prudence, especially as critique, must be more than the lifestyle of a melancholic scholar[42] or a rationale for a politics of resistance couched as escape to an outside which can never actually be accessed. It must turn away from the seductions of transcendental theory in order to build practices of theory, a new model of/for jurisprudence, which draws from the wisdom of Prudence as an affirmative potential tempered within a sharp understanding[43] of the limitations of the material we work with:

> surely there is no better model for wisdom than . . . Aspasia, held in such high esteem by the much admired (Pericles); her political knowledge and insight, her perceptive skills and penetrating analysis, must be transferred to the canvas in their perfect measure. Aspasia, however, is given to us only in miniature: we must draw her in much greater proportions.

Notes

1 With many thanks, for his support and forbearance, to Andreas.
2 See especially Deleuze (1996a), and also Deleuze (1996b).
3 See, e.g., Douzinas and Geary (2005) and Douzinas (2005).
4 'The Sieve Portrait', Quentin Metsys (The Younger), 1583, Pinacotela Nazionale di Siena.
5 'The good falls to the earth and the bad is caught' (literally 'the bad remains in the saddle'). The grain from the wheat falls through the sieve; what remains is chaff. Attributed to Valerius Maximus by Ripa (1763/1971: 257).
6 Petrach recounts the story of Tullia, a falsely accused Vestal Virgin, who demonstrated proof of her innocence/virgin status by carrying a sieve filled with water through Rome.
7 Ripa (see note 6, above) describes a mature woman holding a sieve in one hand and a rake in the other.
8 The model of the English law school was carried (following the importation of law through conquest) into Wales and Ireland (now divided between the republic and the remaining six counties of Northern Ireland), but not, of course, into Scotland which remains marked by its civilian heritage. Therefore, when 'England' is used in this text, it should be understood that this also includes, by extension, Wales and Northern Ireland.
9 Twining (1967). Revised, in 1997 it became a chapter in Twining's *Law in Context: Enlarging a Discipline*.
10 Until the 2013 Legal Education and Training Review.
11 After a period of trying to establish a career at the bar, and thence into the judiciary, Blackstone returned to Oxford in 1785 as the first holder of the first chair in common law. However, common law was lectured only as an adjunct to the established curriculum, rather

than adapted as a chance to re-think an education in/through common law. The trajectory of Blackstone's career marks a clear preference for the profession, as carrying more social prestige and economic benefit, rather than for scholarship. The presumption that becoming a scholar was a mark of failure rather than a choice remained a strong narrative well into the 20th century. As a further twist in the contortion of English class politics, the majority of 'gentlemen' who attended the 'old' universities had no wish to engage in any profession, including law, any more than they would want to work in trade; gentlemen expected to live on income rather than earn it.

12 Which it indeed became when, published in saddlebag-sized editions, it was carried into America and other colonial incursions; becoming, especially in Anglo-American jurisdictions, a blueprint for law and a template for legal studies. See, e.g., Bilder (2009).

13 This agenda was informed not merely by the political climate 'at home' but also, crucially, by the wish to find a pattern for the efficient governance of India, see, e.g., Wilson (2016). Bentham himself craved the chance to design and impose a complete law system in (onto) a new state: he offered his services (his 'pannomion' design) to the United States, Russia, emergent Balkan and Iberian peninsula states, and Greece: see Bentham (1817), and e.g. Rosen (1992). As with so many of his projects, he was unable to put his design into practice; however, his dream of a complete and rational law system has inspired a large field of academic work presented as not merely dogmatics but as jurisprudence, that is as a 'general theory of law', see, e.g., Tusseau (2014) and Zhai and Quinn (2014).

14 Of course admittance into the profession remained controlled by the professional bodies.

15 The India Office had become something of a training ground for designing a Benthamite programme for governance and law reform through the principles and practices of centralisation, codification and systemization, see Wilson (2016: ch 10).

16 Underlying this history of changes in university education in general, and more specifically the education and training for law, as well as the role and social position of lawyers, is the struggle of the emergent middle classes laying claim to the professions against the traditional privileges of the establishment.

17 Links back into civilian traditions would have been unthinkable for Bentham; he was concerned to emphasise the modernity of his particular approach to codification, one which he could then export to Europe, rather than admit to any pre-code influences on his thinking or designs. He refers disparagingly to 'Rome-law' in his more polemical writing, see, e.g., Bentham, 1817. Further, distinguishing a 'modern' approach to education form the traditions of the establishment (Oxbridge) model was crucial to the reformers.

18 de Champs (2014: 237) quotes Bentham as saying: 'Unless you draw a circle round the whole extent of Jurisprudence you do nothing. While any the least part is left without the circle, the imagination is still distracted and overwhelmed with the idea of immensity. Hide the ends of the fishpond, you fancy it a river.'

19 The continued influence of this approach is found in the 2014 collections curated by Tusseau, and Zhai and Quinn. In the first (at 7) Tusseau argues that: 'Bentham's intellectual tools offer a manageable instrument for jurists to confront the most disturbing aspects of contemporary legal phenomena', even though (as a contributor recognises at 39) this form of jurisprudence is limited to an 'internal examination' of law(s) 'unheeding of their social character'. Indeed, the only contributor, in both volumes, who recognises the significance of the material conditions which gave rise to Bentham's jurisprudence is de Champs, who situates his work, and its influences, within the political context in which it emerged and was received. To be revisited only as an austere academic project, rather than engaged with as a political challenge is, for Bentham, a paradoxical legacy. However, the academic taste for constantly revising underlying rationales through new conceptual (organisational) schemes (without, of course, reference to externalities) remains strong.

20 Reading and referencing academic work has, slowly, been established as an accepted *modus operandi* in the higher courts in the following centuries. However, it remains the case that many of the judges are still not law degree graduates, and many scholars still presume to spend a great deal of their time pointing out where judges have 'gone wrong' (doctrinally) in their reasoning. This raises interesting questions about just how analytically rational common law (as in case law) can or should be, and should begin to engage with the evidence of different modes of reasoning (and how they are manifested in different courts, different areas of law and different periods of time), as well as the extent to which law benefits from (can tolerate) paradox, ambiguity or fiction. However, what is fascinating, in a way, is the extent to which many law scholars still presume the higher ground of rational exegesis when confronted with the often mundane and pragmatic muddle of judgments. Has, one wonders, a kind of *modus vivendi* been established which allows scholars a function rather than an affect? Certainly, the higher courts may refer to scholarship, and even consider it helpful; but it is rarely more than a useful resource which can be cited, if useful to the purpose of the judge, but never as, of itself, determining. The scholar waits in hope for recognition in court, and is praised when it occurs, and meanwhile . . . there is still (and seemingly always) much work to be done pursuing the project for rationalisation, even if it is only, mostly, cited by other scholars. Self-serving and self-referencing, the scholar's academic credentials are built on the continued perfidy of common law. See further on 'legal science and its discontents', Cotterrell (1995: ch 10).

21 This is an English rather than Anglo-American story, and so it is not the time/place to consider the frightening figure of Dworkin's Hercules, the all-knowing god-like philosopher king/judge, a 'bigger and better' Pericles who can find (impose) order in (on) law through recourse to a wider (major) jurisprudence, formed in and through philosophy (and liberalism): 'The courts are the capitals of law's empire, and judges are its princes, but not its seers or prophets. It falls to philosophers, if they are willing, to work out law's ambitions for itself' (Dworkin,1986: 407–409).

22 Here the term 'logic' is deployed following Mol (2002).

23 Del Mar and Lobban (2016). This construction is challenged within the collection (see, e.g., Douglas Scott), but there is a clearly perceived need to struggle out from this beginning, a constraint in itself.

24 Even though most law degrees include a course in jurisprudence or legal philosophy as part of the core of legal studies, it remains on the margin for most law students; something to be got through along with the other (substantive) subjects. It rarely becomes a vector through which students engage with the rest of the curriculum. Law academics tend to cede jurisprudence to colleagues who identify themselves, and their work, as 'theory' in contrast to substantive law. The bridge between theory and substantive law is rarely, even now, crossed with any regularity (from either side). In this account, 'law' becomes, clearly, the academic's account of substantive law, rather than 'law-out-there': that is for 'law in context' or 'socio-legal studies' (which, drawing on social sciences, still tend to focus on 'method' rather than 'theory', and on managerial proposals for reform rather than academic accounts of critique).

25 See, for example, Douzinas (2005).

26 That is, of course, the European traditions of political philosophy from which English jurisprudence had become isolated. The particular conditions of limitation and isolation are presumed – all that is important is to 're-connect', as if that, of itself, will be sufficient.

27 Avoiding, of course, Dworkin's Hercules! Except: what is this text/approach promising? A philosopher to rescue us? But not in court this time! Perhaps, in a book, or a poem, or a gesture of refusal . . . a turning away.

28 As is the wavering fortunes of/in the politics of the left.

29 He rather proudly points to the lack of constitutional status and organisational focus in/for the UK, as if the UK critical conference simply emerged, organically, without need for formal organisational roles. In fact, a serious attempt was made (indeed presumed) for the adoption of a constitution with the usual officers, memberships, voting procedures etc.; and was fought off in a strong critique of conventional modes led by a small group of feminists who persuaded Critical Legal Conference (UK) that it could work without the usual framework (having themselves been used to working with 'open structures' in the women's movement). Douzinas ignores, and thereby obscures, the role of feminism, as well as the heritage of the radical politics of law and legal education, in his focus on the role of theory in the emergence of critical legal studies.

30 And hence the bizarre suggestion by Douzinas (2005: 68) that in order to maintain the momentum and purpose of critique we will need to keep inventing or rather erecting 'a false sovereign', in what he calls the 'New Times' and we call (following Foucault and Deleuze) 'societies of control'. As if somehow a political philosophy born within (and addressed to) state and sovereignty can simply go on being relevant despite utterly changed political conditions.

31 Later augmented, of course, by a faux-Lacanian/Derridean practice of revealing an absence which cannot be filled; a continued process of lack/desire which can never deliver but keeps gesturing forward (or rather further in) towards the promise of a fulfilment just beyond. Hence the melancholy: a draining and at the same time sustaining exhaustion.

32 Contributing to this collapse of law into a one-dimensional image of law is the material factor that an increasing number of post-graduate scholars and faculty in law schools have been trained in disciplines other than (common) law and yet are placed into teaching (common) law subjects at undergraduate level. Ironically this can give rise to a tendency to rely on a reduced form of 'black-letter law' in teaching, at the same time as rejecting it (often through the caricature of black-letter law) in scholarship. Further, presumptions are often made about (common) law which are based on little actual knowledge of (common) law. See, e.g., this comment from a book review by a specialist in law in literature from a civilian jurisdiction: 'the book is concerned with law . . . as a cultural practice. This sounds strange to outsiders of the juridical field that have always considered law as a hard, dreary practice, unimaginative and empirical' (Carpi, 2016: 453).

33 Similar trajectories mark other modes of critique, e.g., feminism, as a movement and political practice into the terrain of (feminist) theory (often as the search for, construction of, an/other ontological framing). See, e.g., Bottomley (2000).

34 See Deleuze (1995 a and b).

35 See, in particular, Deleuze and Guattari (1994).

36 See, e.g., Deleuze (2002), and further Bottomley and Moore (2008 and 2012).

37 See further Bottomley (2016).

38 Which is not to say that we believe (with Weber) that codified systems are more rational, or (with Bentham) that rationality is the norm with which legal systems should be judged; neither are we arguing that one is better than the other: they are simply different.

39 See further Bottomley and Moore (2008).

40 See, e.g., Dorsett and McVeigh (2012) and Barr (2016) as significant contributions to developing a minor jurisprudence which recognises that 'theory' as much as 'law' needs to be part of the practices examined and developed in the office of the (responsible) jurist.

41 Resilience is the key to contemporary political engagement, rather than resistance. We need to endure the office/of the (responsible) jurist/jurisprud. See also the significance of this volume for expanding, shifting and morphing 'theory' in engagements neither limited nor determined by the orthodox province of (critical) jurisprudence.

42 On the dangers of transmuting theory into aesthetic pleasures (and misreading Deleuze!), see Spencer (2016).

43 'Understanding' rather than 'explanation'; this is a teasing out and tracing in outline, rather than a cutting through to reveal an underlying truth.

Bibliography

Barr, Olivia, *A Jurisprudence of Movement: Common Law, Walking, Unsettling Place*, London: Routledge, 2016.

Bentham, Jeremy, *Papers Relating to Codification and Public-Instruction*, London: McCheety, 1817.

Bilder, Mary et al. (eds), *Blackstone in America: Selected Essays of Kathryn Preyer*, Cambridge: Cambridge University Press, 2009.

Bottomley, Anne, 'An Exploration of the Time(s) of Equity, Diagrammed Through Image', *Polemos*, 10(2), 357–388, 2016.

Bottomley, Anne, 'Theory Is a Process Not an End: A Feminist Approach to the Practice of Theory', in J. Richardson and R. Sandland (eds), *Feminist Perspectives on Law and Theory*, London: Glasshouse, 2000.

Bottomley, Anne and Moore, Nathan, 'Blind Stuttering: Diagrammatic City', *Griffith Law Review*, 17(2), 559–576, 2008.

Bottomley, Anne and Moore, Nathan, 'Law, Diagram, Film: Critique Exhausted', *Law and Critique*, 23(2), 163–182, 2012.

Carpi, Daniela, review of Gary Watt, 'Shakespeare's Acts of Will; Law, Testament and Properties of Performance', *Polemos*, 10(2), 453–457, 2016.

Cotterrell, Roger, *Law's Community*, Oxford: Oxford University Press, 1995.

de Champs, Emmanuelle, 'Towards the Pannomion: Limits and Bentham's French Manuscripts', in G. Tusseau (ed.), *The Legal Philosophy and Influence of Jeremy Bentham*, London: Routledge, 2014.

Del Mar, M. and Lobban, M. (eds), *Law in Theory and History: New Essays on a Neglected Dialogue*, London: Bloomsbury, 2016.

Deleuze, Gilles, *Francis Bacon: The Logic of Sensation* New York: Continuum, 2002.

Deleuze, Gilles, 'Control and Becoming', in trans. M. Joughin, *Negotiations*, New York: Columbia University Press, 1995a.

Deleuze, Gilles, 'Postscript on Control Societies', in trans. M. Joughin, *Negotiations*, New York: Columbia University Press, 1995b.

Deleuze, Gilles, 'To Have Done With Judgment', in trans. D. W. Smith and M. A. Grego, *Essays Critical and Clinical*, London and New York: Verso, 1993a.

Deleuze, Gilles, 'Plato, the Greeks', in trans. D. W. Smith and M. A. Grego, *Essays Critical and Clinical*, London and New York: Verso, 1993b.

Deleuze, Gilles and Guattari, Felix, *A Thousand Plateaus*, trans. B. Massumi, London: Athlone Press, 1988.

Deleuze, Gilles and Guattari, Felix, *What Is Philosophy?*, trans. G. Burchell and H. Tomlinson, London: Verso, 1994.

Dorsett, Shaunnagh and McVeigh, Shaun, *Jurisdiction (Critical Approaches to Law)*, London: Routledge, 2012.

Douglas Scott, Sionaidh, 'Legal Theory and Legal History: Which Legal Theory?', in M. Del Mar and M. Lobban (eds), *Law in Theory and History: New Essays on a Neglected Dialogue*, London: Bloomsbury, 2016.

Douzinas, Costas, 'Oubliez Critique', *Law and Critique*, 16, 47–69, 2005.

Douzinas, Costas and Geary, Adam, *Critical Jurisprudence: The Political Philosophy of Justice*, London: Bloomsbury, 2005.

Dworkin, Ronald, *Law's Empire*, Cambridge: Harvard University Press, 1986.

Mol, Annemarie, *The Body Multiple: Ontology in Medical Practice*, Durham and London: Duke University Press, 2002.

Prest, Wilfrid, *William Blackstone Law and Letters in the Eighteenth Century*, Oxford: Oxford University Press, 2012.

Riles, Annelise (ed.), *Documents: Artifacts of Modern Knowledge*, Michigan: UMP, 2006.

Ripa, Cesare, *Iconologia*, Volume 11, 1763, reprinted: E. Maser (ed.), New York: Dover, 1971.

Rosen, Frederick, *Bentham, Byron, and Greece: Constitutionalism, Nationalism, and Early Liberal Political Thought*, Oxford: Clarendon, 1992.
Serres, Michel, *Rome: The Book of Foundations*, trans. F. McCarren, Stanford: CA: Stanford University Press, 1991.
Spencer, Douglas, *The Architecture of Neoliberalism: How Architecture Became an Instrument of Control and Compliance*, London: Bloomsbury, 2016.
Tusseau, G (ed.), *The Legal Philosophy and Influence of Jeremy Bentham*, London: Routledge, 2014.
Twining, William, *Pericles and the Plumber*, Belfast: Belfast University Press, 1967, republished 83 *Law Quarterly Review*, 396–426, 1967.
Twining, William, *Law in Context: Enlarging a Discipline*, Oxford: Oxford University Press, 1997.
Wilson, Jon, *Conquering India*, London: Simon and Schuster, 2016.
Zhai, X. and Quinn, M. (eds), *Utility, Morality and Reform in Bentham's Theory of Law and Public Opinion*, Cambridge: Cambridge University Press, 2014.

Index